D0077052

The End of the Old Regime in Europe, 1776–1789

I: THE GREAT STATES OF THE WEST

——————

FRANCO VENTURI

The End
of the Old Regime
in Europe,
1776–1789

I. The Great States of the West

Translated by
R. Burr Litchfield

PRINCETON UNIVERSITY PRESS

Princeton, New Jersey

Published by Princeton University Press, 41 William Street,
Princeton, New Jersey 08540
In the United Kingdom: Princeton University Press, Oxford

Library of Congress Cataloging-in-Publication Data

Venturi, Franco.
[Caduta dell'Antico Regime, 1776–1789. English]
The end of the Old Regime in Europe, 1776–1789 / Franco Venturi ;
translated by R. Burr Litchfield.
p.   cm.
Translation of La caduta dell'Antico Regime, 1776–1789.
Contents: 1. The great states of the west
ISBN 0-691-03156-8 (v. 1 : alk. paper)
1. Europe—History—1648–1789. I. Title.
D289.V4613   1991   940.2'53—dc20   90-8050

This translation has been made possible (in part) by *The Davide and Irene Sala
Award of the Wheatland Foundation*

This book has been composed in Linotron Baskerville

Princeton University Press books are printed on acid-free paper,
and meet the guidelines for permanence and durability of the
Committee on Production Guidelines for Book Longevity of the
Council on Library Resources

Printed in the United States of America by Princeton University Press,
Princeton, New Jersey

1   3   5   7   9   10   8   6   4   2

Contents

Preface

THE FIRST CRISIS OF THE OLD REGIME, BETWEEN THE SIXTIES AND
the seventies, developed in most unexpected and surprising ways on the
margins of traditional states and empires: in the Corsica of Pasquale
Paoli, in the Greece of the insurrection of 1770, in the revolts of peasants and Cossacks of Pugačev, in the tragic effort of liberty in Denmark,
in the ambiguous Swedish revolution of Gustavus III, and in the rebellions of Bohemian serfs. At the center of Europe, in France, England,
Spain, and the Empire, the need for more energetic and incisive reforms grew, but nothing as yet irreparably shook the foundations of
these great states.

With the beginnings of the American Revolution, and particularly
with the Declaration of Independence in 1776, the decisive crisis began.
The empires of the West—Great Britain, Spain, even Portugal, and
France—were shaken, in different ways but always deeply, by the ideas
of the American insurgents and by the passionate discussion these
aroused everywhere. There was a progression from the problem of independence to the right to determine one's own constitution, from the
will to resist to the proclamation of the rights of man, from the affirmation of freedom of commerce to an effort to combat the mercantile
system in all its manifestations and institutions, which just at that moment was defined and denounced by Adam Smith.

The nation most affected by this enlargement of the general crisis,
at the end of the seventies and in the first years of the eighties, was
England. Defeated by its own rebellious colonists, bent by the Franco-
Spanish coalition, it seemed for a moment to be heading toward a deep
internal change. Popular violence was not lacking in the British crisis;
neither was the emergence of active extra-parliamentary organizations
nor the various efforts to imitate the American Revolution—especially
in Ireland and Scotland—and the rise and affirmation of a current of
an increasingly mature Enlightenment. Paine, Priestley, and Bentham
passed through this from demands for parliamentary reform to a radical restructuring of the nation and advanced, among others, proposals
to introduce universal suffrage. At this time British radicalism constructed its first solid bases. But an immediate political outlet was lacking. The conservative equilibrium reconstituted itself in the eighties, if
with difficulty, thanks partly to the able politics of William Pitt. Great
Britain was on the way to becoming the first industrial nation, but it was

not the first nation to emerge energetically transformed by the final crisis of the old regime.

Elements of conservative resistance were strong and tenacious in the Spain of Charles III, which for a moment seemed to emerge undamaged from the American war. But the fear of a revolt in its own colonies continued to smolder in Madrid, while the rebellion of Tupac Amaru seemed for a moment to give reality to such premonitions. From the most diverse points of the political horizon—economic, religious, literary, artistic—the central and unavoidable question of the nature and function of the Spanish nation appeared more and more threatening. It was no longer a matter, as at the beginning of the century, of understanding the economic and political causes of the peninsula's decline. The very identity of the nation was in question. For this reason the debate about Spaniards and Spain became intense and violent.

Portugal, after Pombal, seemed a fleeting shadow next to the Great Britain of William Pitt, the Spain of Floridablanca, and the France of Necker. But still, even there we encounter the problems that were agitating all of Europe, and the form they took in Portugal is significant and revealing. Mercantile tradition held on tenaciously in Lisbon, cloaked as it was in the maritime glories of the age of discovery. The seeds of Lusitanian liberalism were puny and threatened. The debate on the legacy of the fallen reformer could not help but raise the central problem of political liberty in the country's transformation. If only through a thousand difficulties—typical of the old regime in decay—there was a search even in Portugal for the road toward enlightened politics and economic recovery.

With the beginning of the eighties, the Genevan revolution of 1782, the international peace of the following year, and the rapid increase in revolutionary ferment in the United Provinces, the axis of European politics passed from the great states of the West to the line of the Alps and Rhine. The difficulties of Great Britain and the inability of France to profit from victory and confront its own internal problems turned attention to the ancient republics and to their prospects for surviving and transforming their traditional liberties into more modern and efficient forms. This effort was frustrated both in Geneva and Holland, but the enthusiasms and debates it raised contributed not little to the revival and development of republican ideas.

Meanwhile, political initiative passed into the hands of Joseph II. In his empire the greatest effort was made to resolve from above the problems emerging throughout Europe: from tolerance to the diffusion of the Enlightenment, from the struggle against mercantilism to the new forms economic liberalism took, from freeing the serfs to the relationships among the different components of multinational states. A great and labored effort arose in Vienna, the center of action in this final phase of eighteenth-century reformism, that rightly took the name of Josephism. Revolts in Transylvania, Belgium, and Hungary were the response on the margins of the Empire to this pressure applied from the center. And this gave rise to a new wave of patriotic movements, which contributed to making life in the central European states precarious and insecure at the end of the eighties.

Everything depended on the capacity of Joseph II and Catherine II to defeat the Turks in the valleys of the Danube and on the Black Sea and divide the European territories of the Sublime Porte. Now Greece was no longer a military diversion, as it had been in 1770, but the center of the Russian empress's Hellenic dream. The conquest of Belgrade opened the way to the Balkans for Joseph II. New contacts with the East were established through the Crimea and Georgia. The clash with the Turks proved more difficult than had been anticipated. But the battles on the Black Sea ended by making the creation of Odessa, the city of Odysseus, possible—an extraordinary cosmopolitan fruit of Catherine II's expansion toward the south.

Still, the major obstacles were not in the south, but in the west and north. Poland was rapidly awakening, and Sweden was transforming itself for a moment into the major focus of anti-Russian politics and propaganda that Catherine's expansion had provoked. The eyes of Europe were turned toward the north, toward St. Petersburg, when the first news of the French Revolution arrived from the west. Thus, a return to Paris, to the developing crisis of the Enlightenment there, and to the increasing inability to confront the political problems that France had accumulated for decades, will conclude this effort to observe, from west to east, the final crisis of the old regime.

This, like the other volumes of *Settecento riformatore*, looks at these cosmopolitan realities from the point of view of Italy, through the news, discussions, and adaptations they gave rise to in that land, in Venice as well as in Turin, in Florence as well as in Naples. As my American colleague Marion S. Miller has written, Italy is the prism through which I have attempted to refract, reconstitute, and analyze the political reality that reached it from beyond the Alps and beyond the seas. Italy in the sunset of the eighteenth century was truly a prism, varied and multifaceted, wise about the past and curious about the future, in full recovery of its scientific spirit, and attracted, although with detachment, to political experiments being made by others, from the America of Jefferson to the Russia of Catherine II.

My friend Aldo Garosci, to whom I was relating the contents of this volume, told me one day that I risked writing not one volume but two. It was a risk indeed. At times the thread connecting distant events to the echoes that responded to them in Italy seemed thin and fragile. But how could one resist the temptation to consider more deeply the discussion that developed in Siena about the political models of England or America? How could one not listen to the voices that came from Peru in the years of Tupac Amaru? How could one not notice the deep but unexpected ties that linked Italian culture to the new Spanish national consciousness? A figure like Filippo Mazzei was both Tuscan and American. To help to know this man properly, we now have a book by Edoardo Tortarolo. But meanwhile, how could one not pay attention to this Florentine who gave himself over to a generous effort to draw everything possible, politically and ideologically, from the experience of the American Revolution? The reforms of Joseph II are, naturally, also the history of Italy. But a consideration of their European dimension adds to an understanding there. Belgium rebelled, and Lombardy did not. The position taken in Italy in these years was thus decisive for its history. As for the Russia of Catherine II in the eighties, there was no longer the immediate political interest that we witnessed in the seventies, especially in Venice and Naples. Still, intellectual curiosity was growing. Venice, second perhaps only to Paris, reflected the debate on the historiography of Russia's past, on the legends and realities of Muscovy, and on the significance and value of the work of Peter I. As for Sweden, there was no other witness as brilliant as Michelessi, but the political voices coming from Stockholm continued to be significant. Father della Valle's eulogy of Gustavus III was a strange fruit of the Roman arcadia, one of the many signs that the world was changing rapidly, both in the north and in the south. Perhaps the Italian prism risks at times being too varied and diverse to entirely contain the developing situation. But reading the gazettes, letters, and works of these years still confirms in me the conviction that this is a useful way of understanding the cosmopolitan world of the Enlightenment. If nothing else, it is still able to inspire today's historians with the vivid sense of curiosity that we feel present in many documents of the eighteenth century, which is, unfortunately, frequently lacking in our own historiography.

I intend to insert this volume, like the preceding one, into the pattern traced over the last hundred years by Albert Sorel in his work *L'Europe et la révolution française*, by Jean Jaurès in the part of his *Histoire socialiste* that he dedicated to *La révolution et les idées politiques et sociales de l'Europe*, and by R. R. Palmer in his two volumes entitled *The Age of the Democratic Revolution: A Political History of Europe and America, 1760–1800*. The general tendency of the pattern is clear: the French Revolution seems increasingly less alone and isolated and increasingly a part of a general process that one is tempted, with Gibbon's formula, to call the decline and fall of the old regime. This volume, like its predecessor, is dedicated to the effort to clarify the rhythms and characteristics of this general process, from America to Russia.

Too large to appear as a single volume, it thus appears as two, with consecutive pagination and one index of names at the end. *The Great States of the West* is the title of the first volume, and the second is titled *Republican Patriotism and the Empires of the East.* But the two parts are so closely united, and the Italian prism used in both is so similar, that I have preferred to keep them together under a single comprehensive general title: *The End of the Old Regime in Europe, 1776–1789.*

If writing a history book is the work of an individual, and not a group effort, research is always collective, because it is conditioned by the situation in which we find the necessary materials. It is difficult to be optimistic in this regard. In one's blackest moments one would like to conclude that the libraries, archives, museums, and so on, in Italy and abroad, tend now to follow exactly the opposite path to what I have attempted to describe in this volume: progression from privileges to rights was one of the essential trends of political life at the end of the eighteenth century. Now the rights of the scholar tend more and more to be replaced by multiple and mysterious privileges.

For this reason I thank still more warmly all those who have permitted me, nonetheless, to work. Colleagues in the Institute of History of my faculty in Turin are naturally first in line for this recognition. To cite only a single case, I mention the effort Massimo Firpo has made to render the facts contained in these volumes clear to both students and myself.

The text was, sometimes several times, typewritten from my certainly imperfect handwriting by Signora Carla Riassetto, whom I am glad to thank here.

Of the many libraries I would like to list and remember with thanks I select as an example those of Venice, so hospitable and so rich for those who depart through them to explore the European world of the eighteenth century.

This volume, born through a long labor, is naturally dedicated to Gigliola, at the beginning of the fortieth year of our life together.

Turin, the beginning of 1984.

Abbreviations

A   Archivio

AMAE   Archives du Ministère des affaires étrangères (Paris)

AS   Archivio di Stato

B   Biblioteca

BN   Biblioteca nazionale

PRO   Public Record Office (London)

RAF   Rubiconia accademia dei filopatridi (Savignano sul Rubicone)

SPFO   State Papers, Foreign Office (in the PRO, London)

The following works are indicated in abbreviated form:

DBI   *Dizionario biografico degli italiani*, Enciclopedia Italiana, Rome

DBN   *Dictionary of National Biography*, London

Efemeridi   Giuseppe Bencivenni Pelli, *Efemeridi*, Florence, BN, Mss N.A. 1050/1ff.

Riformatori   *Illuministi italiani*, vol. 46 of the collection *La letteratura italiana: Storia e testi*. Milan and Naples: Ricciardi, 1958–65. Vol. 3: *Riformatori lombardi, piemontesi e toscane*, ed. Franco Venturi. Vol. 5: *Riformatori napoletani*, ed. Franco Venturi. Vol. 7: *Riformatori delle antiche repubbliche, dei ducati, dello Stato pontificio e delle isole*, ed. Giuseppe Giarrizzo, Gianfranco Torcellan, and Franco Venturi.

Italian journals listed in the *Bibliografia storica nazionale* and non-Italian journals listed in the *International Bibliography of Historical Sciences* are abbreviated as follows:

Arch. stor. lombardo   *Archivio storico lombardo. Giornale della società storica lombarda*. Milan.

Eng. Hist. R.   *English Historical Review*.

Rass. arch. stato   *Rassegna degli archivi di stato*. Rome.

R. stor. ital.   *Rivista storica italiana*. Turin and Naples.

Sirio   *Sbornik Imperatorskogo russkogo istoričeskogo obščestva* (Miscellany of the Imperial Russian Historical Society).

Notizie del mondo [V.] indicates the gazette entitled *Notizie del mondo* published by Graziosi in Venice to distinguish it from the gazette of the same name that appeared in Florence.

The End of the Old Regime in Europe, 1776–1789

I: THE GREAT STATES OF THE WEST

———————————

I

Libertas Americana[1]

WITH THE DECLARATION OF INDEPENDENCE, ON 4 JULY 1776, THE attention that everywhere in Europe for years had turned to the "blustering" events beyond the ocean tended naturally to change. Above the political and economic debate appeared the problem of insertion of the new American nation into the sphere of diplomatic and military relations. The war, which continued for seven years, from the civil conflict that it was at its origins, took on more and more the aspect of an international struggle, involving France, Spain, and Holland. It continually risked transforming itself into a world war. Attention was focused on the effort of Great Britain—an effort that later proved fruitless—to transport to the shores of America sufficient men, arms, and means to crush the revolt in the colonies. French policy aroused interest everywhere and tried to take this opportunity to resume the duel interrupted in 1763. Dutch, and then Spanish, intervention, as well as the wavering neutrality of Prussia, the Empire, and Catherine II, contributed much to transform the initial affirmation of the right of the British colonies to self-government into a general war. From this, to be sure, most of Eu-

---

[1] This was the motto on the medal that Franklin designed and Augustin Dupré executed in 1782 at the end of the revolution and the war. See Winfried Schleiner, "The Infant Hercules: Franklin's Design for a Medal Commemorating American Liberty," *Eighteenth-Century Studies*, no. 2 (Winter 1976–77): 235ff. The Venetian gazette *Notizie del mondo [V.]* spoke of it in no. 22, 15 March 1783 (Paris, 28 February): "A medal with the symbol of liberty and the inscription *Libertas americana*." The *Gazzetta universale*, no. 19, 8 March 1783, p. 146 (Paris, 18 February), had already announced the following: "At the expense of the United States of America Mr. Franklin has had coined here a medal, in which on one side one sees the symbol of liberty with the inscription *Libertas americana* and on the other side a child who is in the act of crushing two serpents under his feet in the presence of a furious leopard, from which he is protected by a beautiful lady who covers him with her mantle all covered in lilies." See also what is said about this medal in *Correspondance littéraire, philosophique et critique par Grimm, Diderot, Raynal, Meister, etc.*, ed. Maurice Tourneux (Paris: Garnier, 1880), vol. 13, pp. 293ff.

rope was excluded, but still the most wealthy, powerful, and active states of the continent were involved. The war lasted for seven long years. Only when it ended, in 1783, did political discussion assume a new vigor from the effort to understand what had happened, to penetrate into the unknown reality that was emerging in America, and to discuss again the principles that, although not without difficulty, governed the new republic. The debate was particularly important in America, culminating in the *Federalist* and in the new constitution of 1787. This was a period of such intense political creativity that many contemporaries thought of it as a prodigy, a miracle. In Europe, the difficult process of assimilating—as well as failing to assimilate—the experience of the American Revolution was important in the fate of the last years of the old regime between 1783 and 1789.[2]

Both the period of the war and the constitutional transformation were dominated by what was written and done in France. Many of the ideas through which Europeans perceived the dissolution of the British Empire, the birth of the new American nation, and the extraordinary effort of readjustment in old England were germinated and diffused in Paris. From here and from Holland—whose political and intellectual evolution was linked to France—came a large part of the flood of news and interpretation that lent a deep coloring to the European debate on the Britannic world. Franklin, Jefferson, Adams, Price, and Mazzei presented themselves to Europe in Parisian clothing. And those works that did not put on this cloak, like the *Federalist* itself, and many other important elements in the debate of English radicals and American constitutionalists, finished somewhat obscured, to reemerge only after the great events of the French Revolution and Napoleonic era.[3]

The effectiveness and limits of this French mediation were clear in Italy from the beginning of the war. One name dominated at the time, that of the Abbé Raynal, the most widely known publicist of those years. In Siena a small and an active group of professors, translators, and editors made his principal work, *Histoire philosophique et politique des établisse-*

---

[2] A long series of works has recently responded to the growing interest in everything regarding the cosmopolitan reflections of the American Revolution. Among the more problematical works is that entitled *Scotland, Europe and the American Revolution*, ed. Owen Dudley Edwards and George Shepperson (New York: St. Martin's Press, 1976), whereas the most learned is by Horst Dippel, *Germany and the American Revolution, 1770–1800* (Wiesbaden: Franz Steiner, 1978). For a comprehensive view, see Lawrence S. Kaplan, "The American Revolution in an International Perspective: Views from Bicentennial Symposia," *The International History Review* 1, no. 3 (July 1979): 408ff.

[3] Although it is strongly tinged with French nationalism, see the work by Bernard Fay, *L'esprit révolutionnaire en France et aux Etats Unis à la fin du XVIIIᵉ siècle* (Paris: Champion, 1925).

ments et du commerce des Européens dans les deux Indes, known, whose most important part concerned the English colonies in North America. The first French edition of this work came out in 1772, followed soon by numerous other more or less revised and enlarged reprints. In the spring of 1776 the Sienese booksellers Luigi and Benedetto Bindi promised an Italian version of the Amsterdam edition, "one volume per month, beginning in April next," to be sold for two paoli each.[4] Eighteen volumes appeared in 1776 and 1777, the work, read the cover, of "Remigio Pupares, noble patrician of Reggio."[5] In the sixth book of his work, the Abbé Raynal had spoken of the discovery and conquest of America by the Europeans. The editor of the Sienese version also emphasized the importance of this moment in the "history of the human species." Whereas Asia and Africa were fairly well known, "the history of America and its political and economic systems can be said to be, from our point of view, a virgin untouched by the philosophic pen." Even the tragic history of conquest of the American continent was full of indispensable lessons for modern man. "History, the master, unfortunately teaches that to punish us in this mortal exile, peace, quiet, comfort, wealth, pleasure, have always resulted from war, disquiet, hardship, discomfort, and the ill-treatment of others." After so many conflicts and contrasts, it was left to "our age to provide for the happiness of these places and our own," making good use of "precious liberty and philosophic light." Violent means were necessary. "But now the sad part of these fatal crises is finished, and through an as yet uncompleted convalescence those vast and rich lands are acquiring a vigor that will protect them from further calamities." The future of America thus presented itself as a happy outcome of a difficult past. Therefore, there was even more need to know this distant place, which was ready to open itself to "precious liberty . . . the sweetest fruit of philosophical enlightenment."[6] With book 14 began a broad description of the English colo-

---

[4] *Notizie del mondo*, no. 21, 12 March 1776, p. 167 (Siena, 9 March).

[5] "Under the name of Remigio Pupares is hidden that of Giuseppe Ramirez of Reggio," one reads in an old manuscript catalogue in the Biblioteca comunale of Siena. Traditionally this version was attributed to Francesco Becattini, on whom see the article by Gianfranco Torcellan in the DBI, vol. 7, pp. 400ff. But the attribution to Giuseppe Ramirez seems more probable. He was some years later the author of the version of *L'amico degli uomini, ovverso trattato della popolazione*, translated from the French by Alessandro Mucci, Siena, 1783. No notes accompanied this work of Marquis Victor Riqueti de Mirabeau. Francesco Rossi, another important Sienese bookseller of these years, was associated with Raynal's version. See *Nuove di diverse corti e paesi*, no. 20, 13 May 1776, p. 160, "Avviso," and *Gazzetta universale*, no. 58, 21 July 1778, p. 464, "Avviso."

[6] *Storia filosofica e politica degli stabilimenti e del commercio degli europei nelle due Indie. Opera dell'abate Raynal . . . tradotta dal francese da Remigio Pupares nobile patrizio reggiano* (N.p. [but Siena: Bindi], 1776), book 6, "Prefazione," pp. 3ff.

nies on the islands and the American continent. The civil and religious life of New England was examined in detail, underlining how "intolerance" had filled "those lands with calamities" just as at present an exceptional "severity still reigned in the laws of New England." Raynal printed polemically the "plea before a magistrate, not long ago, of a girl convicted of having given birth to her fifth illegitimate child."[7] It was the famous speech of Polly Baker in defense of the right to conceive children outside of legitimate matrimony.[8] This was a myth of the Enlightenment with a remarkable history. It was born secretly in the forties, from the pen of Franklin, and then spread in gazettes and journals through the whole British world. It was utilized by the deist Peter Annet and was then destined to pass later, through Raynal, into the hands of Diderot, who included it in his *Supplément au voyage de Bougainville*, using it against all those who insisted on relating "moral ideas to physical actions, which do not correspond at all."[9] A libertarian exaltation of nature was already present in essence in the tale of Franklin, but in his work predominated a simpler popular compliance with the Christian precept of growing and multiplying in a land where growth of population was a vital element of survival. Even a "happy ending" was not lacking, half ironic and half compassionate, with the judge marrying the woman who had been condemned by law to be whipped and shamed.[10] There was something authentically American in the figure of Polly Baker. Nor was the Abbé Raynal wrong in replying to Franklin—who chided him for having inserted into his *Histoire* an incident that was anything but accurate, but instead the fruit, as he revealed after many years, of his own journalistic invention—that he did not intend to remove it, "preferring the telling of your tales to the truths of others." A myth like this was better than a true history.[11]

Only after telling the whole story of Polly Baker did the Italian translator feel obliged to warn his readers, by attributing all the shame of her words to Protestantism. "One must remember that these sentiments are those of a woman raised in a sect that has embraced a thousand errors, even with regard to fornication." "The court pardoned Polly Baker," that was the name of the accused, "from penance or castigation, and it was even better for her that one of the judges married her. Nonetheless,

[7] Ibid., book 16, pp. 115, 123ff.

[8] Max Hall, *Benjamin Franklin and Polly Baker: The History of a Literary Deception* (Williamsburg, Virginia: The Institute of Early American History and Culture, and Chapel Hill: University of North Carolina Press, 1960).

[9] Ibid., p. 66.

[10] One version of this story, which seems difficult to attribute to Franklin, added that to this marriage were born fifteen children. See ibid., pp. 25ff.

[11] Ibid., p. 81.

public disapproval kept the upper hand, either because political and social order required it, or because under English government, where religion does not promote celibacy, illicit commerce between the sexes is more condemned than in states where nobility, luxury, misery, and the scandalous example of the great and even of some priests corrupt, hinder, tarnish, and discourage marriage."[12] Franklin's tale was, in short, even more effective in Catholic lands than in Protestant ones.

But there were not many more references to recent events in the English colonies in the Sienese version of the work of Raynal, or to their growing opposition and resistance. Only with the new policy of Versailles in favor of the insurgents, and above all with the development of the revolution after 1776, did this work become the vehicle of heated declarations of sympathy and admiration for the colonies beyond the ocean. In 1776, when a version of book 8 appeared in Siena, the Italian editor could not help noting how out of place were Raynal's judgments of England, which he still believed to be a threat to the Spanish empire. "If our author had written his history a few years later he would certainly have restrained himself from menacing Spain with so many threats from the English. The disorders arisen in the colonies of this nation, which are known to the whole world, lead one to think that it will not remain long in control of its own possessions, so distant is it from being able to disturb those of other powers."[13] As one sees from this example as well, the Sienese version of Raynal's *Histoire* permits one to follow the rapid mutation of interest in Italian readers in what was happening beyond the ocean: from a curiosity about history and customs, there was a change, about the year 1776, to a more lively political participation.

The idea of abstracting the pages Raynal had written about the British colonies in America soon appealed to booksellers beyond the English Channel. A *History of North America* appeared in London in 1776, which concealed the name of the French author.[1] The same year, in Edinburgh, a similar compilation appeared, in two volumes, which presented itself openly as a translation of Raynal. In 1779 a second edition was

---

[12] *Storia filosofica e politica*, book 16, pp. 128ff.

[13] Ibid., book 8, p. 15.

[1] *The history of North America, containing an exact account of their first settlements, with the present state of the different colonies and a large introduction* (London: Millar, 1776).

published.[2] It would be hard to think that there was no consideration in
Venice of making a similar effort to translate and publish a work that
aroused such great interest and discussion elsewhere. Indeed, one of
the major Venetian publicists, Vincenzo Domenico Caminer, and a
younger journalist and historian, Vincenzo Formaleoni, joined forces to
publish, in 1776, something very similar to what had appeared in Great
Britain. Many passages were left out, particularly those about religious
history, tolerance, and Protestantism. By contrast, there were relatively
few omissions for political reasons, although naturally even distant al-
lusions to Venice were omitted. Raynal had echoed a commonplace
found everywhere in the Europe of the seventies: "One sees a few republics without brilliance or vigor sustain themselves by their very weakness amid the vast monarchies of Europe, which sooner or later will
swallow them up." He had even alluded to the atmosphere of suspicion
and surveillance that weighed on these archaic republics. No trace of
this is found in the text of Caminer and Formaleoni.[3] Nor was it permitted for the Abbé to prophesy that "the Corsicans will sooner or later
chase the French from their island" or for him to attack the Papal States.
But despite this censorship, the Venetian edition provided important
information about the problems raised by the "civil war between Great
Britain and the united colonies." It presented itself above all as an illustration of the geography of a little-known land. Dedicating his work to
officials in Padova, Domenico Caminer wrote: "The war burning presently in the Anglo-American provinces and the northern part of the
continent, which keeps European spirits intent and in suspense, has led
me to present to the eyes of the reader the theater of these distant undertakings with more precision than the maps of London and Paris, not
to mention Augusta and Livorno." "But since the field of geography is
sterile," he hastened to add, "when history does not seed it, I have arranged to make this Atlas more fruitful and pleasurable through the
Abbé Raynal's history of these provinces, translated from French, adding the events that have occurred up to the present."[4] Nor did the editor
feel the need to sing the praises of the work he was producing, given

___

[2] *A philosophical and political history of the British settlements and trade in North America,
from the French of Abbé Raynal, with an introductory preface not in the first edition, to which is
annexed an impartial history of the present war in America from its commencement to the present time*
(Edinburgh: C. Denovan, 1779).

[3] See the in-depth inquiry by Piero Del Negro, *Il mito americano nella Venezia del Settecento*. 2d ed. (Padova: Liviano editore, 1989), ch. 2, "Raynal nel Veneto," pp. 81ff.

[4] *Storia dell'America settentrionale del signor abate Raynal continuata fino al presente, con carte
geografiche rappresentati il teatro della guerra civile tra la Gran Bretagna e le Colonie unite* (Venice: Antonio Zatta, 1778). The dedication is not paginated. The preface is dated 27 February 1778.

the "applause with which it has been received in all of Europe." "This is demonstrated by the many reeditions that have appeared." He thought it useful to provide a complete version, although accompanied with "annotations correcting the excessive liberty of modern philosophy, which can mar the most precious and useful products of the human spirit."[5] Caminer attempted to return to the origins of the extraordinary developments in America. For this it was necessary to look at the history "of each one of these provinces." Strange and impressive was the past of these lands, not only because of the struggles among the English, French, and Spanish, and the continual encounters with the natives, but above all because of the marks left by the European religious developments of the sixteenth and seventeenth centuries. Enthusiasm had dictated the legislation of New England. "A singular mixture of good and evil, of wisdom and folly" was evident there everywhere. "No one could participate in government without being a member of the established church. The death penalty was decreed for witchcraft, blasphemy, false testimony, adultery, and for sons who cursed or struck their parents." "Pleasure was prohibited in the same way as vice or crime." Penalties were prescribed for swearing and working on Sundays. "It was a grace to be able to expiate an omission of prayer or an indiscreet oath with money." "But what one can hardly believe is that the cult of images is prohibited . . . under pain of death." Intolerance is maintained "with the sword of the law."[6] Thus the Quakers were persecuted. The case of the witches of Salem was deemed a typical consequence of such policy. Great, although superficial, was the admiration Raynal showed for the "capricious, but humane and peaceful, sect" of the Quakers, and he provided a detailed picture of Pennsylvania.[7] Diverse and contorted were the roots from which this new and unexpected plant had grown, that Raynal attempted to assess in some *General Reflections on the Anglo-American Provinces.* This was surely a curious mosaic where ingrained prejudices were set beside the most recent and authentic reports. Thus he repeated the theory that "under that foreign sky the spirit is enervated as well as the body. Lively and penetrating in youth, it perceives quickly, but does not succeed in lengthy meditation or become accustomed to it." It was thus not surprising that "America has not yet produced a good poet, an able mathematician, or a man of genius in any art or science." "They [the Americans] almost all have a facility for everything, but show no decided talent for anything in particular. Adults mature before we

---

[5] Ibid., p. ix, "Avvertimento dell'editore."
[6] Ibid., pp. 32ff.
[7] Ibid., p. 38.

do, but remain backward when we are reaching our prime."[8] Still, the
future seemed tinted with rosy colors. "We expect that more cultivation
may enlighten the new hemisphere, and better education correct the
penchant of the climate for weakness and voluptuousness. Might not a
new Olympus, an Arcadia, an Athens, a new Greece perhaps arise on
the continent and the islands around it: Homers, Theocrituses, and
above all Anacreons? Will a new Newton perhaps arise in New England?" The English colonists meanwhile were preparing the ground.
Perhaps one day, "in a singular reversal, if in the Old World the arts
have passed from south to north, in the New World one may see the
north illuminate the south."[9]

The deportation of criminals and the temporary or permanent slavery of whites and blacks nonetheless raised great obstacles to such
hopes. Nor could one close one's eyes to the fact that the colonists,
"healthy, robust, big men," did not yet make up a nation. Tenacious in
preserving the "principles and customs" of their homelands, they risked
causing the ruin of the American colonies with their "internal dissentions."[10] Everything would depend on the "method of government."

[8] Ibid., p. 61. On the persistent legend of the degeneration of nature and men in
America see the always fundamental work by Antonello Gerbi, *La disputa del Nuovo Mondo.
Storia di una polemica, 1750–1900* (Milan: Ricciardi, 1955), which has appeared in English
with the title *The Dispute of the New World: The History of a Polemic, 1750–1900*, tr. Jeremy
Moyle (Pittsburgh: University of Pittsburgh Press, 1973).

[9] Already the editor of *A philosophical and political history of the British settlements and trade
in North America*, pp. viff., was scandalized by Raynal's prejudices on the culture and value
of the Americans. "At the present day" the new continent had an abundance of philosophers, politicians, generals, and soldiers "resisting with success one of the greatest nations
in Europe whose arms were lately victorious in every quarter of the globe." In 1779 we
are already far from the Anacreons of Raynal. The war changed the ideas of Europeans
about North America very rapidly, as one sees.

[10] *Storia dell'America settentrionale*, pp. 61, 63ff. On the importance of the different national origins of American colonists see Willi Paul Adams, "The Founding Fathers and the
Immigrants," in *La révolution américainne et l'Europe. 21–25 février 1978, Paris-Toulouse*
(Paris: Editions du CNRS, 1979), pp. 133ff. This tells, on p. 141, of a committee in the
summer of 1776, whose members included Franklin, Jefferson, and John Adams, which
approved a project for a future great seal of the United States in which would be seen,
along with symbols of each of the American states, a harp (Ireland), a thistle (Scotland), a
lily (France), an Imperial eagle (Germany), and a Belgian lion (Holland). The motto, taken
from the *Gentleman's magazine*, would be *E pluribus unum*. The proposal was that of a Genevan exile beyond the seas, collector and traveler Pierre-Eugène Du Simitière. Among
the other proposals was one by Franklin, who coined for the occasion the motto "Rebellion
to tyrants is obedience to God," attributing it to John Bradshaw, the president of the commission that had condemned Charles I to death. Jefferson thought for a moment of the
judgment of Hercules as figured by Shaftesbury, or of the sons of Israel in the desert and
the two brothers Hengist and Horsa who had guided the Saxons to the British Isles "from
whom we claim the honour of being descended and whose political principles and form

The problems to be resolved might seem insoluble. In America, as elsewhere, "rich and poor, proprietors and mercenaries, masters and slaves, form two classes opposed unfortunately to that of citizens. . . . Everywhere the rich seek to obtain much from the poor at little expense; everywhere the poor seek to have their labor rewarded at a high price; but the rich will always set the rules of this unequal market." This was "the original evil of society," to which only more or less successful remedies cound be applied. In America all would depend on the "distribution of land" and on the civil laws, which tend "for the greater part to preserve property" and should at least be "simple, uniform, precise." This was made difficult particularly by the "initial vice" in the English colonies of having inherited the "old constitution of the metropolis." "Since the present government [of Great Britain] is only a modification of the feudal one . . . many customs have remained which, being initially only so many abuses of slavery, are all the more felt because of their contrast with the present liberty of the people." A fragile compromise was born from giving "so many rights to the nobility," while "feudal rights diminish, are cancelled, and change." "Thus so many laws provide exemptions for a single principle, there are so many interpretations, and so many new laws are entirely opposed to the old ones. For that reason there is no law code so confused and handicapped in the whole universe as the civil laws of Great Britain. The wisest men of that enlightened nation have often raised their voices against such disorder. But their cries were not heard, or the changes born from their protests have only increased the confusion."[11] In the colonies the evil had only become worse.

These were pertinent observations, which grasped the core of the British problem: a transformation arising not from planned reform, but instead from a continual readaptation carried out in an environment of

of government we have assumed." Only in 1782 was the two-headed eagle of Austrian origin replaced by the American eagle. Thirteen stars and the same number of stripes were substituted for the symbols of national and local distinctions. As one sees, the seal of the United States underwent a long and significant development in the political, historical, and literary world of the eighteenth century before reaching its maturity. See *The Eagle and the Shield: A History of the Great Seal of the United States*, ed. Richard S. Patterson and Richardson Dougall (Washington, D.C.: Department of State, 1978), pp. 6ff. Local particularism was also very strong. A recent historian has recalled the words of patriot James Otis: "Were the colonies left to themselves, tomorrow America would be a mere shambles of blood and confusion," and how Franklin was of the opinion that "union is not merely improbable, it is impossible," an opinion shared by Turgot and Frederick II. As for Josiah Tucker, he advanced the idea that "their fate seems to be—a disunited people, till the end of time." See James H. Hutson, "Tentative Moves toward Intercolonial Union," in *Aspects of American Liberty: Philosophical, Historical, and Political* (Philadelphia: American Philosophical Society, 1977), p. 81.

[11] *Storia dell'America settentrionale*, p. 65.

extraordinary liberty. Raynal was quite skeptical about the effectiveness of this method. In the American colonies, he said, it seemed that a breaking point had come.

Reviewing the chronicle of conflicts in the sixties and seventies, he emphasized that England had always shown that it was incapable of those timely concessions which might have avoided an armed confrontation. By taxing the colonies it had denied one of its own fundamental traditions, that of "not consenting to state impositions if not by consent: of oneself, or through one's representatives." "To defend this right the nation has shed its blood many times, deposed its kings from the throne, raised and weathered an infinity of storms. Did it perhaps want to deny to its two million sons an advantage that had cost it so much, or that was perhaps the only foundation of its independence?" On both sides of the ocean there was a conviction that "a nation is always enslaved when it has no more assembly, no body to sustain its rights against the encroachment of the power that governs it." "The spirit of liberty that has prevailed thus far in the English colonies" made the colonists ready to defend themselves against oppression "even in peril of their lives." "Extremes of expediency or violent means" had no justification "if not after vainly attempting reconciliation." But "this people . . . already knows that when reduced to a choice between servitude and war," any hesitation was unacceptable. Its "resistance" should thus not be considered a rebellion, but rather a defense of its rights.[12]

Raynal posed the problem of whether it was appropriate "for the nations of Europe to cooperate in rendering the English colonies independent from their metropolis." His reply contained an echo of obscure fears widely diffused at that time on the old continent: would not independence provoke a "great revolution" whose "time one was not permitted to foresee" but that appeared more and more threatening on the horizon of Europe? "All tended to this, both the progress of well-being in the New World and the evils of the Old one."

Alas! The rapid decline of our customs and strength, our crimes, and the misfortunes of peoples will make fatal perhaps that catastrophe which may detach one world from the other. A mine is prepared under the foundations of our abuses, the materials for the collapse are gathered together and heaped up, formed out of the relics of our laws, of the clash and ferment of our opinions, of our lack of valor, of the luxury in our cities, of the misery in our countrysides, of irreconcilable hate between vile men who possess all the riches, and the vigor of those who have nothing to lose but their lives. While our peoples become weak and submit, one group under the other, in America population and agriculture increase, the arts will grow rapidly, carried there by our eagerness. This

[12] Ibid., pp. 69ff.

land has come out of nothingness to find its place on the face of the globe and in the history of the world.[13]

This was an invitation, pessimistic but not despairing, to confront the evils of Europe with similar concern. The American Revolution was distant and perhaps not to be imitated. But it cast a new and vivid light on the very bases of the states and society of Europe.

More in the nature of a chronicle was the *Continuazione della storia dell'America settentrionale fino all'anno 1778* with which Caminer followed these pages of Raynal, not without warning that it was the "work of another hand."[14] The developments that had led from the Tea Party of 1773 to the treaty of 1778 between France and the "rebel subjects" of George III were amply documented. The world was menaced by a great war, "which proves even more that our century is superior to all previous ones, both in the advancement of philosophy and in the diffusion of reason and all sciences and letters, but that it is not less superior in the deplorable facts that create sad lugubrious periods for the human species."[15] These were the contradictions of the century, to which the news that arrived from beyond the ocean continually added new elements. The will of the colonies to fight *"pro aris et focis"* (for altars and hearths), which was explicit from 1774 on, and the echoes that resounded more and more loudly of the voices raised in the "Congress of the Anglo-American provinces" held in Philadelphia in September 1774, were transforming "the American cause" into an "object of universal attention." News of the first encounters in 1775, the more and more explicit will of the colonists to "live free or die," and the solemn general proclamations of the General Congress in Philadelphia in July of the same year, along with the agitated debates of the English Parliament, interspersed with military reports, gave the chronicle cumulatively an exemplary value.[16] The selection of documents might surprise us: the Declaration of Independence was missing, whereas the "instruction sent by the city of Boston to its delegates in the provincial Congress of New England" was included, filled, as we read, "with all those expressions that demonstrate an unbounded enthusiasm for liberty." The "rebellion of the Anglo-Americans" seemed at the point of formulating maxims "capable of subverting all nations."[17] Less explosive, but cer-

[13] Ibid., pp. 71ff.

[14] Ibid., p. ix, "Avvertimento dell'editore." Even in *A philosophical and political history of the British settlements and trade in North America*, p. 303, one finds "An impartial history of the present war in America." But the text is entirely different.

[15] Ibid., p. 123.

[16] Ibid., pp. 76, 83, 87ff.

[17] Ibid., p. 99.

tainly not less important, were the Articles of Confederation of 4 October 1776, which were reported in full.[18] The acts of government that followed these basic texts permitted one to follow the unfolding of the revolution, although from a distance and without a true and proper perspective and interpretation.

A long list of subscribers to the edition of maps that served as the basis for the text of Caminer and Formaleoni showed the liveliness of the interest that their editorial initiative aroused in Italy. The geographical distribution was skewed: 56 in Bologna and 2 in Genova, 18 in Imola and 2 in Naples (one of whom was the bookseller Domenico Terres, who ordered four copies). In many places the names are those we might expect a priori: in Milan, out of 5 subscribers one was Gianrinaldo Carli, another the Abate Parini, while the bookseller Galeazzi ordered five copies and Baldassarre Oltrocchi, the librarian of the Ambrosiana, ordered one. The only unexpected name is that of Signor Antonio Acerboni. In Jesi the list of 5 subscribers was headed by the governor, Francesco Maria Cacherano di Bricherasio. In Civitavecchia the only subscriber was Monsignor Gio. Battista Baldassini Crivelli, the governor of the city. In Turin the librarian Francesco Berta, and two booksellers, Michel Angelo Morano and Giacomo Antonio Rabby, each ordered two copies. The largest number of subscribers was naturally in Venice: 343, with many of the finest names of the patriciate. No city outside of Italy was listed except Zagreb.[19]

After this first fortunate undertaking, Domenico Caminer was not one to let fly an opportunity that continued to arise from the general curiosity about developments beyond the sea. Already in 1778, in the presentation of his edition of Raynal's *Histoire*, he had promised his readers "many other literary productions regarding America that would certainly be interesting." "Among others, we can announce to learned men the *Lettere americane*, an unpublished work from a good pen," where one can find a confutation of the *Ricerche filosofiche sugli americani* of the "celebrated Mr. Paw [Du Pauw]." "Erudition" would have a "large part" in the promised work, making it "delightful reading." Readers would also find "critical observations on four volumes entitled *Histoire de l'Amérique de Mr. Robertson*, translated from French and printed in 8vo in Mastricht in 1777."[20] The work that was advertised, written by Gian Rinaldo Carli, came out, as we shall see, elsewhere, and some years later.

[18] Ibid., p. 108.

[19] *Catalogo dei signori associati ascritto alle carte geografiche*, in an appendix, with separate page numbers.

[20] *Storia dell'America settentrionale*, p. ix, "Avvertimento dell'editore."

But it still traced its roots, as Domenico Caminer well knew, to the large erudite curiosity of the Venetian world.

Meanwhile, in 1779, Caminer kept abreast of events, informing his readers of the increasingly clear and important intervention of France in American events.[21] The same date saw a reedition of his *Storia dell'America settentrionale*, which was advertised as printed in Venice, although the cover carried the following advertisement: "Found in Genova in the establishment of Agostino Olzati." The interest raised by developments beyond the ocean induced a well-known Genoese bookseller to reprint these large volumes as a whole.

In Venice there was no lack of discussion. The ecclesiastical reaction against Raynal had begun to spread in 1776, and it assumed tones of cutting condemnation in the work of Father Valsecchi, in *La religion vincitrice*, which appeared in that year in Padova.[22] His was an effort to unite the church and "thrones," religion and politics, in a common attack on "recent philosophy." In the numerous works of modern unbelievers, one reads, "religion appears only under the name and guise of superstition. Principates have only the colors of despotism."[23] Raynal's *Histoire philosophique*, read in the 1773 edition, was presented as the last and most developed fruit of this *philosophie*. The polemic was too general to be truly effective. A more precise discussion appeared in the version of a work translated from French by François Bernard, *Analisi della Storia filosofica e politica degli stabilimenti degli europei nelle due Indie*, published in Venice by Tommaso Bettinelli in 1779.[24] Another bookseller attempted to substitute the *Storia d'America* by William Robertson for "the

[21] *Storia dell'America settentrionale in continuazione di quella del signor abate Raynal continuata fino alla primavera del 1779, nella quale, oltre alla guerra civile tra la Gran Bretagna e le Colonie Unite si descrive anche quella tra la prima e la Francia* (Venice: A. Zatta, 1779). This was reviewed, together with the first two volumes, by Giovanni Ristori in the *Memorie enciclopediche*, no. 13, April 1781, pp. 95ff. On p. 103 he contrasted America, "where all can have the means of subsistence," to Europe, where "a few sedentary indolents snatch the fruits of their labor from the languid arms of miserable peasants." On p. 104 he apologized for the length of this review by noting that the history of America "is too interesting at the present time, and is the latest fashion in all the cultivated conversations of Europe." On the same page he gave detailed information on the "articles of confederation" that had given birth to the "United States of America."

[22] See Del Negro, *Il mito americano*, pp. 89ff.

[23] Antonio Valsecchi, *La religion vincitrice . . . relativa ai libri de' fondamenti della religione e dei fonti dell'empietà* (Padova: Nella stamperia del seminario, appresso Giovanni Manfré), pt. 1, pp. 59, 44, 54.

[24] In the "Avvertimento del volgarizzatore," p. iii, we read: "The philosophical fever that inflames so many writers beyond the Alps and beyond the seas in our century has unfortunately through their works, which are avidly sought out and translated, passed to Italy where, propagated with rapidity, it has become a deathly and nearly universal contagion."

one of the too-famous ex-Jesuit Raynal." But fate continued to smile on Raynal, who succeeded in obtaining 1,014 subscriptions for a total of 1,249 copies, while the publisher of Robertson had to content himself with 281 subscribers and 518 copies.[25]

Despite the religious and political obstacles, the ferment that surrounded the *Storia dell'America settentrionale* continued in the following years. This was due to the merit of Raynal, but above all to American reality, which attracted more and more interest from readers. In 1780, in Padova, the *Descrizione geografica ragionata dell'America settentrionale e meridionale* by the noted geographer Anton Friedrich Büsching was published.[26] Two years later came to light a *Storia della rivoluzione dell'America inglese. Tradotta dal francese ed illustrata colle carte del teatro della guerra di M. Bellin di M***, americano* (this was in fact the Frenchman Pierre Ulric Dubuisson). The bookseller and writer Vincenzo Formaleoni, who introduced the work, inserted several pages taken from Raynal and others that he himself had edited. Thus, from his hands came, as P. Del Negro has written, "the first effort to present to the Italian public materials concerning the entire revolutionary decade from 1774 to 1783."[27] He was evidently convinced, to use the words of Voltaire which he printed at the beginning of the work, that

le temps de l'Amérique est enfin venu

. . . .

Chaque peuple à son tour a brillé sur la terre

. . . .

Ce peuple généreux, trop longtemps inconnu
laissait dans ses déserts ensevelir sa gloire.
Voici les jours nouveaux marqués par la victoire.[28]

"For eight years the eyes of nations have been fixed on the northern continent of America. Too-powerful colonies, armed against their metropolis, dare to try to create there a new and independent people, a people of farmers and warriors destined perhaps one day to dominate

---

[25] Del Negro, *Il mito americano*, pp. 93ff.

[26] See ibid., pp. 188ff.

[27] Ibid., p. 598.

[28] "the time of America has finally arrived / . . . / Each people in its turn has shone on the earth / . . . / This generous people, too long unknown / let their glory be buried in their deserts. / Behold new days marked by victory." *Storia della rivoluzione dell'America inglese. Tradotta dal francese ed illustrata colle carte del teatro della guerra di M. Bellin di M***, americano* (Venice: Vincenzo Formaleoni, 1782), vol. 1, p. 1. The year before the same editor published, also by Bellin, the *Teatro della guerra marittima e terrestre fra la Gran Bretagna, le Colonie Unite, la Francia, la Spagna ed Olanda che comprende la raccolta della carte nautiche e terrestri. Necessario per l'intelligenza de' fogli periodici per uso dei novellisti.*

the whole American hemisphere."[29] To the author of this work the interplay of ideas and passions that had given birth to this unexpected
reality seemed revealing. "The sciences and arts," we read in the para-
graph dedicated to Boston, "more intimately tied to the politics of empires than is commonly thought, prepared and brought the revolution
with them."[30] It was now necessary to make a basic revision of the most
accepted political convictions. "Montesquieu . . . admirer of the English
government . . . what would he have said, what would he have thought,
to see the sad results of a system of government that seemed to him so
wisely designed?"[31] The documentation Formaleoni provided in the
three volumes of this work (the Declaration of Independence of 4 July
1776 was not omitted)[32] provided a broad basis, even if incomplete, for
anyone who wanted to reflect on the problems confronting the United
States in 1784, immediately after the end of the war. The States, one
read, "after having quieted some small internal difficulties, are taking
measures to improve the condition of the inhabitants and form a solid
and flourishing republic."[33]

These hopes and enlightened certainties in Venice met not only the
obstacle of rejection by renewed Catholic apologetics, but also a more
original autonomous reaction, rooted in local tradition, which found its
most typical expression in the thought of the philosopher and economist Giammaria Ortes. America at the beginning of the seventies presented for him as well a symbol of humanity quite different from the
Italian one, and thus capable of providing a contrast to Europe of the
most candid sort.[34] Ten years later the growing conflict with the mother
country changed his perspective entirely. The will of the colonists to
preserve "their natural liberty" seemed to him legitimate and natural.
Their struggle appeared to him a defense of tradition and of a political
and economic reality menaced by the dominance of the English who,
"to preserve a superiority of power and trade among other nations,"
had ended up by "bloating the rich among them" and placing "the poor
in greater peril." It was time for the colonists to emancipate themselves
"from their mother country, which had become a burden, something no
mother or father can deny to children who renounce their legitimate
inheritance."[35] The form of government, and the "constitution" to

---

[29] Ibid., p. 1.

[30] Ibid., p. 35.

[31] Ibid., p. 62.

[32] Ibid., pp. 227ff.

[33] Ibid., vol. 2, p. 182.

[34] Giammaria Ortes, *Riflessioni d'un filosofo americano*, ed. Gianfranco Torcellan (Turin: Einaudi, 1961).

[35] Id., *Della religione e del governo dei popoli per rapporto agli spiriti bizzarri e increduli de'*

which the Americans had appealed, seemed to him, in 1777, to correspond to a politics "that I call *natural*, suggested to all men . . . by their
common reason." He held that the "easiest and most direct means to . . .
populate nations" was to "divide the greater into lesser, and thus reduce
the range while increasing the number in a determined land, with the
condition of there being a confederation among them, so that the interests of each relate to the whole community." If "the United Provinces of
Holland, or Switzerland" were imitated and "extended to all of Europe,"
this would become "all confederated and united, and thus all peaceful
and unarmed, all free, and all happy." Such would be a "natural" constitution, always checked by the will of each member to prevail over the
others. It was a vision of prosperity and peace continually "imagined,
but never realized among men."[36] The colonists beyond the ocean also
had this destiny before them. "The conflict between American and English ambition can have no other effect than that of subjecting the
Americans to the ambition, or even despotism, of a Congress in Philadelphia, just as they were earlier subjected to the ambition and despotism of a Parliament in London." This political logic was made all the
more inevitable by the purely human intent of the American insurgents
and by their lack of guidance in religion. "Those who think that the
current English colonies in America might set themselves up better than
any other nation are mistaken; they can constitute nothing better than
the English whom they emulate, for the precise reason that neither their
nor the other constitution is guided by the principle of religion, so necessary, as has been said, to the just and regular formation of a nation."
Franklin, "the man reputed among these colonists to be the chief philosopher," had understood and proposed a cult of the divinity and had
spoken of the Trinity and of biblical revelation, but still leaves "everyone
in full liberty to interpret things in the sense they most like, and to pro-
fess any other religion, however different from this." Without a religion,
like that of the Indians of Paraguay or even the Quakers of Pennsylvania, which found its perfect incarnation in Catholic tradition, it was vain
to hope or undertake to bend "the laws of ambition and force."[37]

His "natural" federalism thus remained a paradox, sufficient only to

---

tempi presenti libri tre (n.p., 1780). Cited in Del Negro, *Il mito americano*, p. 225. See ibid., p.
263, which contains a letter by Ortes to Cecilia Davies, openly in favor of the colonies. See
also Carlo Mangio, "Illuministi americani e rivoluzione americana," in G. Spini, A. M.
Martellone, R. Luraghi, T. Bonazzi, and R. Ruffilli, *Italia e America dal Settecento all'età
dell'imperialismo* (n.p.: Marsilio, 1976), pp. 50ff.

[36] G. Ortes, *Lettere sull'economia nazionale*, letter 8, dated Venice, 11 October 1777,
never published in the life of the author. See the critical edition edited by Gianfranco
Torcellan in *Riformatori* 7, pp. 56ff.

[37] Ortes, *Della religione e del governo*, in Del Negro, *Il mito americano*, p. 224.

demonstrate that men were incapable of finding a way to an equitably distributed and administered prosperity. If he had followed the tormented struggle of the Americans to give life to their new constitution (and Ortes was now too old and retired to do so), he would have rejected it a priori: it was not possible—he was convinced—to change the nature and destiny of human society through simply political means and instruments. Thus, religion remained at the center of his thought.

What Ortes—and many with him in Italy and abroad—refused to see was nonetheless evident at the beginning of the eighties. The ligature in religion that he sought in Catholic tradition was now largely substituted, on both sides of the ocean, by the ideas and passions that animated and illuminated the final crisis of the old regime and by the emerging religions of revolution. Ortes was not unaware of the formulation Rousseau had given to these ideas and passions in his *Contrat social*, nor, as we have seen, had he denied the value of Franklin's effort to give a religious form to the American desire for tolerance and liberty. But here Ortes stopped. His understanding of the American Revolution came to a halt, like so many other of his impulses and intentions, on the static margin of Catholic tradition.

The Venetian view of developments beyond the sea would be incomplete if we limited ourselves to Caminer's elegant books and to Ortes's more or less clandestine writings. In reality, the American Revolution was known—even in the Republic of St. Mark—above all through news transmitted by the gazettes. In Venice, as elsewhere, the passage between the seventies and the eighties was a moment of marked development in journalism. Already in the summer of 1778, Antonio Graziosi, one of the major booksellers of the city, who had distinguished himself in the preceding years in political and economic polemics, asked permission of the authorities of the Studio of Padova to "reprint the gazette of Florence, reorganized and enlarged with maps."[1] At the beginning of 1779, the first issue of this Venetian edition of the *Notizie del mondo* appeared. It carried a dual date, that of the Florentine and that of the Venetian edition. In number 1, for example, one reads "2 January 1779" and "23 January 1779." This was a curious formula, leading one to think that it was a "larger" reprint of the Florentine gazette, as one reads in the subtitle. But in reality it was an entirely different journal. The coincidence and similarity between the two sheets depended, when

---

[1] Venice, AS, *Terminazioni per stampe in data forestiera*, filza 338, 22 August 1778.

there was any, on a common origin, on the same foreign journal from which the news was taken. And after 1780 even the dual date was dropped. Thus was born the *Notizie del mondo*, published in Venice by the editor Antonio Graziosi. The gazette had its admirers even abroad. When a "cabinet de lecture" was started in Hamburg in 1783 promising "public newspapers . . . in the four principal languages of Europe," these included "the Italian gazette of Venice, the most esteemed of Italy," which provided "announcements and news from that beautiful part of the world."[2]

Echoes of the developments in America were not lacking in the first issues of the new gazette. From Paris, in January 1779, came the image of "Mr. Washington, adored by his troops."[3] In February came in turn a polemic against England by the "celebrated Adams."[4] The treaty of alliance "between France and the United Provinces of America" was printed in full.[5] La Fayette, returning from America, announced "that the affairs of the United States are in the best posture, that there is a most perfect union between the members of the General Congress and the commanders of the troops."[6] From "a French sheet in Germany" was taken a "History of the revolution of the United States of North America that we publish as a compendium."[7] In Pennsylvania, "amid bursts of cannon from the city" in February, "thirteen toasts" were raised: "That the alliance between France and the United States of America be eternal. . . . To General Washington and the army. . . . To the friends of liberty in all parts of the world." France was presented in the Venetian gazette as the "most powerful [nation] in the old hemisphere," whereas the rising American state was "the most reputable in the new."[8] Economic difficulties were not lacking: "One of the chief obstacles the American union has encountered in the establishment of its new republic," we read in the summer, "has been the lack of specie, which has obliged the Congress to resort to paper money."[9] But the image that came from America was still that of "a wooded country, filled with ports and rivers full of vessels, and of cities rising in the midst of forests, with a bright sun rising above a shining horizon and the motto 'New worlds arise from chaos,' " while England appeared more and more as a plain

---

[2] *Nouvelles extraordinaires de divers endroits*, Leiden, no. 41, 23 May 1783, in the footer.

[3] *Notizie del mondo [V.]*, no. 5, 16–27 January 1779, p. 22 (Paris, 8 January).

[4] Ibid., no. 8, 27 January–6 February 1779, p. 58 (London, 19 February).

[5] Ibid., no. 16, 23 February–6 March 1779, p. 136 (Leiden, 22 February).

[6] Ibid., no. 17, 27 February–10 March 1779, p. 141 (Paris, 19 February).

[7] Ibid., no. 22, 24 April–5 May 1779, p. 275 (Utrecht, 22 April), and continued in the following issues.

[8] Ibid., no. 39, 15–26 May 1779, p. 324 (Pennsylvania, 10 February).

[9] Ibid., no. 62, 3–14 August 1779, p. 520 (Amsterdam, 2 August).

strewn with ruins.[10] Even the religious aspect of American life attracted the attention of the Venetian gazette. The chaplain of the French troops delivered an address in a church in Philadelphia "on the occasion of the anniversary of American independence." "God has struck those who oppressed a free and peaceful people with an illusive and blind spirit that makes the unjust the creators of their own misfortunes." "A young monarch" had come to support those who defended their own liberty. A "glorious revolution" had "placed the sons of America among the free and independent nations scattered over the earth." "God will not deny our prayers: they have no other object than the fulfillment of the decrees he has already revealed."[11] These were informed and detailed accounts of military defeats and of the echoes they evoked in England.[12] Discussions of the "destiny of America" current in Holland were also reported.[13] The economic effects of the war on the Old World were followed attentively. The "American Revolution" had, among other things, "daily increased the commerce" of the "Russian Empire." The export of hemp alone had increased from 36,000 bales in 1777 to 139,800 in 1778. The account for 1779 was not yet closed, "but we estimate that it has increased this total by not a little."[14]

Often news about the internal situation of the American states was disquieting. Thus, in the spring of 1780 one read: "Our internal tranquillity has been troubled by disturbances that always affect free states. We consider these as passing excesses of liberty rather than as results of license or disrespect for public authority." Particularly disturbing was the "depreciation of currency."[15] The circular letter of John Jay, the president of the Congress, dated 3 September 1779, was printed in full. It vividly depicted the whole picture of America at war.[16] An "extract of an authentic letter from Philadelphia" arrived a few issues later to add a few more details of intense emotion: "We have never been more united, or more determined to complete the edifice of our independence." "Thanks to the Most High," Congress had been "purged" of "some outspoken" members among the "factious." Now there was "as much unanimity as can be expected in such bodies." "Attachment to the alliance with France" and "the standard of Whiggery" continued to

---

[10] Ibid., no. 74, 14–25 September 1779, p. 621 (Nantes, 29 August).

[11] Ibid., no. 94, 16–27 November 1779, p. 780 (Nantes, n.d).

[12] See, for example, ibid., no. 1, 8 January 1780 (London, 21 December), and no. 3, 15 January 1780, p. 19 (London, 31 December).

[13] Ibid., no. 6, 26 January 1780, p. 47 (Cleves, 29 December).

[14] Ibid., no. 11, 12 February 1780, p. 86 (Amsterdam, 30 January).

[15] Ibid., no. 16, 1 March 1780, p. 130 (London, 8 and 15 February), "Affari dell'America."

[16] Ibid., no. 24, 29 March 1780, p. 190 (Nantes, 29 February).

guide the Americans.[17] The publication in full of the *Declaration of rights of the inhabitants of the State of Massachusetts*, in October 1780, provided a concrete idea of what this "Whiggery" consisted and of the constitutional ideal motivating one of the states that were protagonists of the revolution.[18] Precisely these months in Venice saw the tired conclusion of the "correction" that had arisen from the reform efforts of Zorzi Pisani. He was now in prison and his followers were dispersed. (To be sure, one looked in vain for any echo of these facts in the Venetian gazette we are examining.) The news that came from beyond the ocean must have seemed far away but all the more interesting.[19]

Looking at Europe as a whole, an increasing penetration of American ideas was now evident, particularly in Ireland and Holland. "The insurgence in North America and the principles of liberty it has established have begun a ferment in our European heads, and a revolution has begun, in the mind of which it is easy to see what consequences may result in the future."[20] This was all the more true because the moment of victory for the revolution was nearing. On 5 February 1783 a letter arrived from Paris "by special courier" announcing that a few days before, on 21 January, "two preliminary conventions were signed separately to initiate the great work of peace."[21] The independence of the "Americans" was "recognized."[22] To be sure, the face of that land had changed during the long years of terrible conflict. "We all have reason to marvel at the change of spirit that has occurred since the beginning of the present war," one read in a communication from Boston. "This state, once the home of enthusiastic and fanatic Puritans, now permits a tolerance unknown in any other Protestant land." The alliance with

[17] Ibid., no. 29, 15 April 1780, p. 234 (Amsterdam, 7 April).

[18] Ibid., no. 81, 14 October 1780. See Mary F. and Oscar Handlin, eds., *The Popular Sources of Political Authority: Documents on the Massachusetts Constitution of 1780* (Cambridge, Mass.: Harvard University Press, 1966). For a recent interpretation see Ronald M. Peters, Jr., *The Massachusetts Constitution of 1780: A Social Compact* (Amherst: University of Massachusetts Press, 1978).

[19] On the "correction" attempted by Giorgio Pisani in 1780, see Del Negro, *Il mito americano*, pp. 122ff. In the following months and years the *Notizie del mondo* of Antonio Graziosi entered more and more widely into the variegated journalistic world that was then creating itself throughout Italy. Beyond the Veneto, Lombardy and the Papal States became zones of this gazettes greatest diffusion. There were some copies in Tuscany, in Piedmont, and beyond the Alps. See *Notizie del mondo [V.]*, no. 7, 23 January–3 February 1779, in the footer, "list of distributors": "Mantova, Modena, Bologna, Firenze, Lucca, Pisa, Roma, Sinigaglia, Ancona, Pesaro, Ravenna, Ferrara." In no. 63, 7–18 August 1779, in the footer, are also "Trieste, Fiume, Torino."

[20] Ibid., no. 68, 24 August 1782, p. 544 (The Hague, 12 August).

[21] Ibid., no. 11, 5 February 1783 (Turin, 20 January).

[22] Ibid, no. 12, 8 February 1783 (Paris, 29 January).

France, and the conflict sustained by the "citizens and subjects" of the two "confederated nations" together, had produced a similar result.[23] "It is said the Americans . . . have the idea of erecting in the center of the main square of Philadelphia a statue of the French monarch, with the inscription: 'To Louis XIV, liberator of the Americans.' " It was said that Franklin would soon return home to work on the "compilation of a code of laws for which he has promised to give his assistance." Meanwhile, trade between France and England resumed rapidly. Grain and wine were sought beyond the English Channel: "Now all the roads of Bourgogne, Champagne, and Picardy are full of carts, which, heaped with grain, are in motion toward Calais and Boulogne where they are to be loaded."[24]

The political life of America was tinted with mythical colors at the moment of triumph. Washington, "named lord protector of the new republic, has risen to a degree of glory that is the least to be expected from his prudence and extraordinary military talents. . . . Following the steps of Cromwell, his great master in politics, . . . he began this astonishing revolution in the theater of the world." "An architect has already designed a senatorial palace, or temple of fame, where the sessions of the legislative body of America will be held . . . a kind of amphitheater supported by thirteen columns. . . . In the center there will be a throne for the lord protector under a majestic canopy."[25] "The Marquis de La Fayette has given his portrait to General Washington." He was shown in American uniform, with his wife and children. Franklin was "full of vivid jubilation and contentment." Nothing as important as this had happened in history, the birth "of an independent empire in that part of the world." Mably continued his meditations on the political future of America. "To thus become the legislator of a great nation is the greatest honor to which a philosopher and political writer can aspire." Catherine II wrote to Vergennes calling him the "peacemaker of Europe."[26] Amid so much optimism, the most enthusiastic interpretation came from the Florentine *Notizie del mondo.* The war had brought liberty not only to America, but also to the whole world. "This peace can be finally seen as a general confederation for the benefit of humanity and commerce."[27] In April Franklin presented to Louis XIV a minted medal "to

[23] Ibid., Boston, 4 November.

[24] Ibid., no. 18, 1 March 1783 (Paris, 16 February).

[25] Ibid., no. 19, 5 March 1783 (London, 11 February).

[26] Ibid., no. 20, 8 March 1783 (Paris, 23 February). On the request made to Mably see *Nuove di diverse corti e paesi,* no. 10, 10 March 1783, p. 75 (Paris, 21 February), and also this volume, pp. 104ff., below.

[27] *Notizie del mondo,* no. 23, 22 March 1783, p. 183 (Paris, 11 March).

immortalize the memory of this great revolution."[28] From Philadelphia came the following report: "Peace, one might say, has invaded us so rapidly that we are all in a state of confusion."[29] Problems of credit, money, commerce, the navy, merchants were again emerging. The Americans counted themselves: there were 2,389,300 whites. A detailed picture of the finances of the new republic was distributed.[30] In Padova during the summer Franklin's *Political Works* was published; it could be bought "from Giovanni Manfré, Venetian bookseller, for the modest price of 3 lire."[31]

The atmosphere of enthusiasm and enchantment was not to last long. There was a brusque awakening when Venetian readers learned that soldiers, "after a disorderly rejection of the authority of their offi-cers . . . presented themselves in a session of the Congress in a violent and menacing way." The authorities had to take measures to preserve "the dignity and authority of the United States." The proclamation of the president of the Congress was dated "24 June 1783, the seventh year of our independence."[32] The rivalries among different states seemed to be growing.[33] "The American newspapers . . . announce a great fluctu-ation in the United States. . . . the different states, jealous of their inde-pendence, look with dismay on anything that seems to extend the au-thority of Congress. They maintain that the establishment of a permanent source of revenue under the control of this federative as-sembly is likely to form a dangerous aristocracy." One had to console oneself by thinking that "fears and jealousies are in the nature of repub-lics at their birth: they have to await the slow wise hand of time to see their government upheld by a solid basis of political harmony."[34] As in other similar cases, it is difficult to read these words without asking whether in Venice one was truly persuaded of the effectiveness of the "slow and wise hand of time" in obtaining "political harmony." The Most Serene Republic was at that moment embroiled in an acrimonious crisis of internal distrust. It was better to continue to fix one's gaze on distant America. There one saw "the immortal Washington with tears in

[28] *Notizie del mondo [V.]*, no. 35, 30 April 1783 (Paris, 14 April).

[29] Ibid., no. 50, 21 June 1783 (Philadelphia, 17 April).

[30] Ibid., no. 51, 25 June 1783 (Philadelphia, 22 April). See ibid., 28 June 1783 (Phila-delphia, 10 April), and no. 56, 12 July 1783 (Philadelphia, 17 April).

[31] Ibid., no. 60, 26 July 1783, in the footer. It was edited by Paolo Antoniutti. See Antonio Pace, *Benjamin Franklin and Italy* (Philadelphia: American Philosophical Society, 1958), pp. 128ff.

[32] Ibid., no. 67, 20 August 1783 (London, 5 August).

[33] Ibid., no. 69, 27 August 1783 (Amsterdam, 14 August).

[34] Ibid., no. 70, 30 August 1783 (London, 15 August).

his eyes" take "final leave of the thirteen states."[35] Commenting on the general's words on the need for unity and discipline, the gazette could not help but wonder if the republic the general had done so much to found did not risk following the example of the United Provinces and of taking a path that would lead to "inevitable dissolution."[36] The year of the peace, 1783, ended with these doubts. A new period of difficult reorganization and constitutional restructuring opened, which lasted until 1787.

In a way different from Venice, less broadly informed and more impassioned politically, the Neapolitan Enlightenment also showed its awareness of events in America. In the first two volumes of the *Scienza della legislazione* by Gaetano Filangieri, which appeared in 1780, developments beyond the ocean emerged against a background vision of pessimism and anxiety in Europe. The political life of the Old World seemed to be failing and agitated. "In less than two centuries we have seen four or five powers in turn dominate, be dominated, and pass in an instant from greatness to little account."[1] Spain, "a nation that could have been the happiest and wealthiest on the globe," had rapidly fallen into ruin. "Its legislators, with little reason and little cosmopolitanism," had not understood that "the prosperity" of their country "was dependent on the prosperity of the other European nations."[2] France had made the same mercantile errors. The expulsion of the Protestants and the policy of Colbert had "done more harm than all the benefits derived from its forty years of victories, its celebrated warriors, its academies, its great men in letters and arts, and its despotic influence over Europe."[3] England, which had profited much from the errors of its rivals, was itself in crisis. "This nation, after having ruled for so long over all the seas, all ports, and all coasts, and having dominated all the flags of Europe, after having influenced the commerce of two hemispheres, is now on the brink of ruin." Its flow of emigrants, and the birth of more and more new colonies, had finally exhausted its strength. "It has to content itself with those establishments absolutely necessary for its commerce . . . and remember that a man who leaves his country to serve it beyond

[35] Ibid., no. 73, 10 September 1783 (Paris, 24 August).

[36] Ibid., no. 74, 13 September 1783, continuation of Washington's letter.

[1] *La scienza della legislazione del cavalier Gaetano Filangieri* (Naples: Stamperia Raimondiana, 1784), vol. 1, pp. 75ff.

[2] Ibid., p. 77.

[3] Ibid., p. 79.

the seas does not stop being a citizen, that oppression is all the more
unjust when it comes from the hands of a free people, that moderation
is the only guarantee of detached possessions, and that restricting the
colonies to trade exclusively with the capital was an injustice that would
only embitter them." England had made other grave errors by depriving the colonies of the right to be judged "by their own juries" and subjecting them to "arbitrary taxes." "To take from them the right to tax
themselves was to deprive them of a prerogative that an Englishman can
never lose in whatever part of the earth he finds himself, a prerogative
that is perhaps the only guarantee of the liberty of England, a prerogative for which, to protect it, its citizens have so many times shed their
blood and dethroned their kings."[4] Nor did the causes of the English
crisis arise only from a wrong relationship with the colonies. The financial policy of Great Britain was a grave error, based as it was on "national
debts" and on the "infinite" increase in the "circulation of paper, representing money that does not exist." Consequently, there had been a
"devaluation of money." On the other hand, taxes had led to a rise "out
of proportion of the prices of commodities and labor, an inflation that
could do great damage to England in competition with whatever other
nation, and that would not delay the ruin of its industries." The final
judgment was hard: "England has reached its dotage; it increases taxes
rather than diminishing them, it loses its influence in Europe for having
wanted to extend it to America."[5]

Equally negative was the idea Filangieri had conceived of the political structure of Great Britain.[6] He devoted an entire chapter to a critique of "mixed government" and of Montesquieu's interpretation of
the English constitution. It was based chiefly on the work of Blackstone.
The critical elements of his judgment came from contemporary French
publicists, particularly Linguet.[7] The power entrusted to the king was
too great and undefined. "The laws have not foreseen the case of a king
who might want to destroy the political liberty of the English people." If
that happened, "there would be no other remedy than an insurrection
of Cretans."[8] Even without supposing that such an extreme would be
reached, the power of the monarch was dangerous. Filangieri thought
his right to veto was legitimate, because the constitution required that
the two houses and the king "exercise political power in agreement."
But a negative consideration was that the king was considered "the sin-

---

[4] Ibid., pp. 80ff.
[5] Ibid., pp. 82ff.
[6] The pages that Filangieri wrote on these problems are printed in *Riformatori* 5, pp.
674ff.
[7] See chapter 5, below.
[8] *La scienza della legislazione*, vol. 1, p. 157.

gle distributor of both civil and military offices" and "the single administrator of national revenues," putting into his hands all means necessary
"to buy, whenever he wants, a majority of votes."[9] English history, especially during the reign of Henry VIII, showed the use the king could
make of Parliament. Another grave vice of the English constitution resulted from the "continual fluctuation of power among different bodies" and the impossibility of ever reaching a true stability.[10] "The present vigor of the Parliament" was not "the result of a solid and
permanent condition, but of passing circumstances which render it precarious." If circumstances should change in the near future, "the pretended chains on the royal dignity would again become flexible, Parliament would lose its vigor, and the throne would again make itself
omnipotent."[11] If the independence of magistrates had limited the excessive power of the monarch, no reform had removed the other defects
of the constitution. It would be futile to try to take from the king the
right to nominate candidates to civil and military office. "We know how
little it benefited Poland and Sweden to diminish the royal prerogative
in this matter." There was no other way than to increase the powers of
Parliament, of the "assembly that represents sovereignty."[12] Electoral reform was also indispensable. Filangieri asked "that legislation not limit
itself to preventing the corruptibility of the members of this august assembly, but that it also seek to prevent it in the electors; through education, incentives, and honors so as to perfect manners and revive a love
for glory, which is always close to the patriotic sentiments of citizens."
"The indigence that always leads to venality" should be excluded "from
the body of electors" (by raising the minimum tax requirement for electors from two to twenty pounds). "The nation will be truly free . . . when
the possibility of substituting an assembly of citizens for a congress of
courtiers is finally realized."[13] Through this and other reforms the roots
of the political ills from which the English suffer would finally be removed, as well as the "most absurd barbarities of your fathers, that is,
what in the old feudal system was most strange and contrary to the liberty you think you possess." Previous legislation had not foreseen this.
Only comprehensive "new legislation" would be able to remove the vices
of "your constitution."[14]

England was only an example, although a fundamental one, of that

[9] Ibid., pp. 158ff.

[10] Ibid., pp. 163ff.

[11] Ibid., pp. 165ff. In a passage of Machiavelli, from the *Discorso sopra il riformar lo stato di Firenze a istanza del papa Leone*, Filangieri sought to confirm his judgment on mixed governments and their perpetual instability.

[12] Ibid., pp. 174ff.

[13] Ibid., pp. 177ff.

[14] Ibid., pp. 181ff.

general reform that was being proposed as necessary in all the nations
of Europe. Two roads were open to those who knew the corruption of
modern nations: reforming absolutism, of which Joseph II and Catherine were the best and most effective examples, and the new hope appearing on the horizon through the news that arrived from across the
ocean. In America the gaze of Filangieri fixed itself on Pennsylvania,
"the fatherland of heroes, the refuge of liberty and the envy of the universe." He held William Penn in great esteem; Penn had understood
that "the great object of legislation is to join public and private interests"
and that "the only way to succeed in this enterprise in free governments
is to assign to the people the distribution of offices." By doing this Penn
had undone the knot left tangled by the British constitution and had
thus succeeded in setting "the first foundations of a republic which today attracts the attention of the whole world."[15]

A precious element this, which came from America, but had now
entered, when Filangieri wrote these words, the international struggle
of the great powers, their "jealous commerce" and the "rivalry of
nations."[16] The "exclusive patriotism" of the English had finally created
a European coalition generally against them. Nevertheless, the consequences of a possible future victory of the Americans were preoccupying. "All members of greater European society, not less than the English, should be horrified by the disasters that threaten us through the
independence of the colonies." If Great Britain should emerge ruined
by the war, weakened in its commerce, and still more, oppressed by its
"national debts"; if it finally collapsed and "the vacillating liberty sustained by its wealth should be changed into the most oppressive servitude," making itself "prey to a conqueror or victim of a despot," there
would be grave consequences for the other European nations as well.
"France, to be sure, would free herself from a frightening neighbor"
and from the competition of English manufacturing. Spain "would see
again in its hands the presumed keys to the Mediterranean." Holland,
despite the loss of large sums it lent to England, could consider itself
freed from a fearful rival. Russia, finally, and Denmark and Sweden
would perhaps see with pleasure the collapse of a power that had wished
to "dominate their seas." But at least equally difficult would be the negative consequences. "Once the lightning of independence has struck in
British America, would it not make its thunder heard in the rest of that
vast continent? Would not then all of America become independent
from Europe? What would then happen to our commerce?" Not only
agriculture, but also industry would soon develop in the New World.

[15] Ibid., p. 195.
[16] Ibid., vol. 2, p. 218.

Manufacturing "flourishes already in Pennsylvania despite the clash of arms and the horrors of war." Commerce with the West Indies would soon pass into the hands of Americans. "The spirit of rivalry" had, in short, blinded Europeans and prompted them to aid their future imitators and rivals. "Some European nations are eager to prepare the materials that will serve one day to fashion their ruin and to offer an intrepid hand to the artificers of their chains."[17] Even for the colonies, it would have been more advantageous to make an honest compromise with the mother country, once England had finally ended any "absurd distinction between the interests of its citizens in America and those of its citizens in Europe." This would be advantageous for the economy of the colonies, which would thus find a necessary guarantee "against the perils to which total independence might expose them," and they would no longer need to fear "the ambition of some ardent active spirit, or the internal discord, that might arise in the lull after the peace, or reciprocal dissentions among themselves."[18]

The fundamental evil of modern politics consisted thus, according to Filangieri, in the mercantile system. The liberal solution was the only one that could avoid new perils and rivalries. "Freedom of industry and trade, this is the only treaty a commercial and industrious nation should establish at home or search for abroad. All that favors this freedom is beneficial to commerce, all that restrains it is harmful."[19] As for the internal politics of the American colonies, Filangieri was still deeply entrapped by the criticisms traditionally directed against republics, always menaced by internal discord, by the ambition of tyrants, and by their inability to form firm confederations. Ancient Greece and modern Holland were the examples by which he measured the new reality of the United States, which he judged economically vigorous, even menacing, but fragile from the political and constitutional points of view.

This last judgment was rapidly modified after the publication of the two first volumes of the *Scienza della legislazione*. His more and more acute discontent when confronted with the reality that surrounded him, and his increasing desire to flee the world of the Neapolitan court, turned his soul toward distant American reality, toward the new republic that seemed capable of victory and reform. In the winter of 1781–1782 he contacted Franklin and in the summer of 1782 sent him copies of the first two volumes of his work. He was writing the third and fourth, which came out a year later, concerning "the procedural system" and the "penal code." "The novelty of my ideas on these subjects does

[17] Ibid., pp. 230ff.
[18] Ibid., pp. 233ff.
[19] Ibid., p. 240.

not frighten me." He would have developed them, he said, even if his conclusions served only "to diminish the ills of a single people" or to "prevent a single injustice."[20] In December 1782 he announced his desire to leave the Neapolitan court behind him and to pass his days in the "refuge of virtue," the "fatherland of heroes," the "city of brothers." "Since my infancy, I have been attracted to Philadelphia. I am so habituated to considering it the only place where I can be happy that my imagination cannot rid itself of this idea. . . . Dear and esteemed Franklin, who but you could facilitate this enterprise?" It would have been a voyage with no return. "After having known and valued the society of citizens, could I desire the company of courtiers and slaves?"[21]

The dream of emigrating to America was not realized, but the relationship between Franklin and Filangieri continued in the following years. Thus arrived in Naples in October 1783 "the code of the American constitutions," which a year later was reviewed at length in the periodical *Scelta miscellanea*.[22] The third and fourth volumes of the *Scienza della legislazione* were sent to Paris as soon as they appeared, also in 1783.[23] Franklin could have found in the fourth volume a passionate

---

[20] Pace, *Franklin*, pp. 398ff., letter from Naples, 24 August 1782; and *Riformatori* 5, p. 773.

[21] Pace, *Franklin*, p. 400; and *Riformatori* 5, pp. 776ff.

[22] *Scelta miscellanea*, no. 1 (January 1784): 67ff.: "The new empire born in North America with the Confederation of the Thirteen Provinces certainly merits every attention from the Europeans." The continuation of this *Estratto del nuovo codice della costituzioni dei tredici stati dell'America settentrionale* is in no. 2 (February 1784): 131ff. (p. 133 on the freedom of the press), no. 3 (March 1784): 192ff., and no. 4 (April 1784): 257ff. The review is taken (or derived from another source) from the *Notizie del Mondo*, nos. 2 and 3, 6 and 10, January 1784, pp. 21, 32ff. Of the *Constitutions des Treize Etats-Unis de l'Amérique* (Philadelphie et se trouve à Paris, chez Ph-D. Pierre Pissot père et fils, in 8º) there was more discussion in no. 8 (April 1784): 558ff.

The celebrated Act of Independence . . . after having been published with a kind of ardor on 4 July 1776, was then sustained with much courage and constancy and ratified on 5 September 1783. . . . An American already known for his philosophical discoveries, for the laws he designed, and for the negotiations he has conducted has edited this edition. . . . But this great man had need of a French translator who knew the two languages well and understood the subject deeply; he found him in a distinguished personage, M. le Duc de R . . . [François-Alexandre-Frédéric de La Rochefoucauld-Liancourt], who has also illustrated the original with fine notes. [These were in fact explanatory notes, certainly useful in making a distant reality known, but hardly original.]

On the surroundings that produced the *Scelta miscellanea*, on the Duca di Belforte, Carlo Vespasiano, and so on, see Franco Venturi, "Tre note sui rapporti tra Diderot e l'Italia," in *Essays on Diderot and the Enlightenment in Honour of Otis Fellows*, ed. John Pappas (Geneva: Droz, 1974), pp. 348ff. See Jean-Dominique de La Rochefoucauld, Guy Ikni, and Claudine Wolikow, *Le duc de La Rochefoucauld-Liancourt, 1747–1827* (Paris: Perrin, 1980).

[23] Pace, *Franklin*, p. 401, letter from La Cava, 27 October 1783. In this book one also finds, on p. 153, the echo of the tradition preserved in the family of Filangieri according to which he had annotated his own thoughts in the margin of the volume of the American

discussion of American law. The United States demonstrated, Filangieri wrote, how difficult it was to always remain faithful to the spirit of reform. In France, at the time of Turgot, a law had abolished the death penalty for deserters.[24] Instead, "the Congress of the United Provinces of America has imposed it on its brave and free defenders." "Should the vices of our laws thus penetrate the city of brothers, into a field decorated with the banners of liberty, and among the ardent defenders of a contested independence! The empire of errors will thus pass from one hemisphere to another and overcome the barriers of enlightenment and virtue! The standard of liberty will be as tinged with blood as the scepter of despotism! The men who have broken with one hand the chains of servitude will not disdain to take up with the other the dagger that arms the executioner!" But hope still remained in the soul of Filangieri. "No, the respectful Assembly that offers this terrible sanction will surely not stain the new code it is preparing with such unjust laws. It will find in patriotism and honor the support of courage, constancy, and valor and place in infamy the penalty opportune to vileness and desertion."[25] Great was the task that awaited the Americans and greater still was their responsibility. "Free citizens of independent America, you are virtuous and enlightened, you have taken up in the eyes of the universe the sacred duty of being wiser, more moderate, and happier than all the other peoples. You must give account to the tribunal of the human species of all the sophisms your errors might effect against liberty. Thus, be careful not to make its defenders blush or give the word to its enemies."[26]

In 1784, just after the war, Filangieri hoped for a moment to become the representative of the kingdom of Naples in the United States. The idea had been suggested to him by Franklin. But no diplomatic contact was established between the two countries. *La scienza della legislazione*

constitutions and had sent them to Franklin, who had added his own observations. But the volume, if it ever existed, is lost.

[24] Franco Venturi, *The End of the Old Regime, 1768–1776, The First Crisis*, trans. R. Burr Litchfield (Princeton, N.J.: Princeton, University Press, 1989), p. 367.

[25] *La scienza della legislazione*, vol. 4, pp. 386ff. See Don Higginbotham, *The War of American Independence: Military Attitudes, Policies, and Practice, 1763–1780* (Bloomington: Indiana University Press, 1971), pp. 268ff. (containing a study of the legislation intended to suppress the various forms of loyalism), 398ff. (on the indiscipline of the republican army), and 413 (on the relative indulgence of Washington in his punitive measures). The problem of desertion always remained open. With the organization of the new army the penalties became more severe. Deserters were tried and sent to the galleys. Then there was a return to a less harsh policy: one execution out of ten per month. See John S. Pancake, *Seventeen Seventy-Seven: The Year of the Hangman* (Birmingham: University of Alabama Press, 1977). The problem remained serious even later, after the peace. See Richard H. Kohn, *Eagle and Sword: The Federalists and the Creation of the Military Establishment in America, 1783–1802* (New York: Free Press, 1975), pp. 63ff.

[26] *La scienza della legislazione*, vol. 4, p. 390.

continued to absorb all the philosopher's time. To Franklin, who had
returned to his country old in years, he augured the enjoyment "of the
laurels that your talents and virtues have merited."[27] There was just time
for him to receive on his deathbed, together with a letter from Franklin
dated 14 October 1787, the new constitution of the United States of
America.

Despite the doubts and criticisms he formulated, the American Revolution always retained a strongly exemplary character in Filangieri's
thought. Among Piedmontese reformers instead, and especially in
Vasco, the element of distance, of the difference between American and
European reality, was emphasized. The very idea of a "new" nation that
we find often from their pen served to indicate the possibility of carrying out those changes and realizing those reforms beyond the ocean
which were particularly difficult or impossible among us. Equality in
particular, which for Giambattista Vasco was at the center of his vision
of rural life, seemed to be able to find possibilities in America that were
lacking in Europe.[1] He examined for a moment the hypothesis of forming "a new society of men, or at least a new plan of government, with
the consent of the people," rather than annexing "new uncultivated
lands" to an already organized nation. Then, and only then, would it be
possible to proceed with a true and proper distribution of land. In general, however, in Europe, for example, it would be necessary to apply
"indirect laws," intended to establish the necessary equality slowly and
by other means.[2]

We find a certain curiosity for what happened in America in the only
effort of these years to found a gazette in Turin, or rather something
between a news sheet and a journal. It was called the *Giornale di Torino
e delle provincie* and the *Journal de Turin et des provinces* (it had, in fact, an
Italian and a French edition) and lasted for only one year, 1780. It began with brief reports of local events, book announcements, court notices, economic affairs and scientific information, and a "lost and
found." Political reportage slowly increased to the extent of giving this
Giornale the aspect of a modest gazette. There were numerous communications from the Empire, Russia, and France. But it was necessary to

---

[27] Pace, *Franklin*, p. 403, letter from La Cava, 24 December 1785.

[1] Piera Ciavirella, "L'opinione piemontese di fronte alla rivoluzione americana e alla
formazione degli Stati Uniti," in G. Spini et al., *Italia e America*, pp. 86ff.

[2] Giambattista Vasco, *La pubblica felicità considerata nei coltivatori di terre proprie* (Brescia:
Giammaria Rizzardi, 1769), pp. 92ff.

wait until 5 May 1780 to learn that in North America "commerce flourishes better in the present war than ever before, being protected by
French ships in those seas."[3] A few days later a "Historical portrait of
George Wasington [*sic*], the grand commander of the American army,"
was offered for sale. La Fayette had brought the original to France, and
it had now been engraved. "This general is represented on foot before
his tent . . . holding in his hands some papers concerning the history of
America, and one sees some scattered on the ground and torn, and others folded in different ways on a table; behind the tent is a man occupied with saddling a horse, and in the distance are troops on parade."
"The resemblance to the general and the truth of his stature can be
guaranteed."[4] From London and Paris news of naval encounters continued to arrive. With nearly six months' delay one heard from Philadelphia that "the Congress, grateful for the services given by Brigadier
General Count Pulawski and aware of the valor he has demonstrated in
different circumstances, and in particular in the attack on Savannah,
where he was mortally wounded, has resolved to erect a public monument to the memory of this officer. The execution of the monument
will be entrusted to the best French artisans."[5] Rochambeau embarked
again at the head of his troops. Charlestown was in peril (but "taking
this city, however important," one heard in London, "will not end matters in America, and will hardly induce the United States to renounce
their independence").[6] On 12 May the city effectively capitulated.[7] But
"now, far from believing the hope of soon seeing the whole of America
return to obedience," one read some time later, "it is feared that Virginia cannot be subjected so quickly. There are bets of 40 guineas to 100
that the king will not yet be in control this summer." At the same time,
"the Marquis de La Fayette arrived in Boston in April; he remained a
week in the camp of General Washington, where he has resumed his
military rank. He will be in command of one third of the operations
against New York." He had declared, to "the greatest satisfaction of the
Americans," that "his sovereign king was determined to support their
cause and make war vigorously in this state, as much along the coasts as
on the islands, and that with his fleet on its way to America there was a
good quantity of munitions, uniforms, and money for America."[8] The

---

[3] *Supplemento al giornale di Torino*, no. 18, 5 May 1780, p. 145 (Paris, 21 April).

[4] *Giornale di Torino e delle provincie*, no. 19, 12 May 1780, p. 155.

[5] Ibid., no. 24, 16 June 1780, pp. 195ff. (Philadelphia, 17 January).

[6] Ibid., no. 25, 23 June 1780, p. 202 (London, 27 May).

[7] Ibid., no. 27, 7 July 1780, p. 220 (Brussels, 20 June), and no. 28, 14 July 1780, p. 226 (London, 20 June).

[8] Ibid., no. 32, 11 August 1780, p. 258 (London, 24 July). "The Marquis de La Fayette

naval battles multiplied, but the English court continued to refuse "any negotiation."[9] The Giornale di Torino was now filled with news from America. To the hopes and illusions in London and Paris were added the firm and faithful words of the Congress, on which a circular letter dated 11 May was reported at length.[10] From Paris "rumors" of a "total abandonment of the insurgents" and of a "general reaction against republican principles and the articles of the constitution" could be dismissed completely. In reality, the Americans "were preparing to celebrate the anniversary of their independence with the greatest pomp ever employed in this act that they hold sacred."[11] In September the conclusion from London was that "the taking of Charlestown served only to reignite a fire that seemed quenched. The spirit of independence has never shown itself with that much force in all the United States. There is no more hope of impeding the union of the militias with the continental army. All Americans have been urged to join their units at the first sign of the general or Congress. Wasinghton [sic] is at the head of a large army that is growing daily. The arrival of Ternay and his troops in Rhode Island has revived the cause of America, where the most perfect harmony between the French and the subjects of the United States exists."[12] In Boston a new "plan of administration" had been "presented to the people, and it obtained a majority of votes." "Today this plan has been declared the constitution of the Republic of Massachusetts. The last Wednesday of the month of October past was the day designated to put it into effect."[13] In Philadelphia "all members of the government, merchants, and other classes of citizens" formally accept "paper money." The Bank of Pennsylvania was formed on 17 June 1780 and bound itself to contribute to the war, "on whose good outcome depends our liberty and the independence of the United States."[14] America was now a reality from which it was not possible to turn one's gaze. In Lyon it was said that the Abbé Raynal had proposed a prize for those who "demonstrated most satisfactorily: . . . whether the discovery of America has been useful or harmful to the human species. If it has produced advantages, what are the means of preserving and increasing

has been welcomed with joy in Boston" (ibid., no. 36, 8 September 1780, p. 289 [Paris, 29 August]).

  [9] Ibid., no. 33, 18 August, p. 267 (London, 26 July).

  [10] Ibid., no. 34, 25 August 1780, pp. 273ff. (Paris, 15 August, and London, 2 August).

  [11] Ibid., no. 35, 1 September 1780, p. 281 (Paris, 22 August).

  [12] Ibid., no. 39, 29 September 1780, p. 314 (London, 12 September).

  [13] Ibid., no. 40, 5 October 1780, p. 323 (London, 16 September).

  [14] Ibid., no. 41, 12 October 1780, p. 330 (United States of North America, Philadelphia, 5 July).

them? And if the discovery has caused any harm, what are the means of remedying it?"[15]

At the end of 1780 the seesaw of news continued, always more fully reported. It was noted with surprise that even when the news was favorable to the British, it did not succeed in inspiring hope or in raising the stock exchange.[16] Lord Westmorland, replying to the speech from the Crown, ended "with proposing to the House the great example of the Romans who adopted the maxim of never negotiating with the enemy when one had the lower hand, and of never making peace except after a victory."[17] The year ended without the position of the British or Americans appearing to come closer. This was a modest chronicle, as one sees, but one that still carried to Turin a resounding echo of the great military and political conflict that divided the world in the first years of the eighties.

The only Piedmontese voice that showed enthusiasm for the idea of liberty advocated by the Americans was that of Vittorio Alfieri, who in fact, when he wrote his American odes, was far in spirit from his native Piedmont. He was always more affiliated with Tuscan culture and busy with trips to Rome and Venice.[18] For Alfieri, as for Filangieri and Diderot, America was an exception, a land of innocence, justice, and prosperity in a world everywhere wearied by an evil that was all the more anguishing the less it was recognized and defined,

> del mal che nostra Europa tutta ingombra.

This was a negative evil, an absence, a deprivation of liberty, a long sleep in servitude, which Italians, more than any other people, should understand, having experienced it for centuries,

> l'Italia, che in catene
> abborrite e sofferte, indi mertate,
> tragge sua lunga etate.

But how could the English, who had known and experienced liberty up to recent times, be struck by such a similar deep malady? The whole first ode is an effort to respond to this question. In this discussion he thought that "the causes of the war," which continued between England and the American colonies and their allies (he wrote in 1782), were still hidden. He knew very well that the American Revolution was above all an inter-

[15] Ibid., no. 43, 26 October 1780, p. 346 (Lyon, 18 October).
[16] Ibid., no. 45, 9 November 1780, p. 366 (London, 20 October).
[17] Ibid., no. 47, 23 November 1780, p. 387 (London, 3 November).
[18] Vittorio Alfieri, *Vita*, ed. Giampaolo Dossena (Turin, 1967), pp. 195, 208. See Piero Bairati, "Alfieri e la rivoluzione americana," in Spini et al., *Italia e America*, pp. 67ff.

nal drama of the British world. It was "Cupidigia fella," "ira di re d'ogni bell'arte ignudo," the mistakes of ministers and sovereigns, and corruption of the people itself, who had descended so low as to sell their own votes. This had shaken Parliament and menaced the institutions of free England. The spirit of commerce had then come to push Great Britain against

> gli american tuoi figli.

The "sconsigliato stuolo / di mercatori armati" had moved against the colonies. Mercenary troops, "mal compri tedeschi," had been sent beyond the ocean, in hatred against the Americans. But these had risen at the blow.

> Ma che perciò? Vegg'io
> tremar quei prodi, o sbiggotir? Dolenti
> li veggio ben, ma impavidi: lor dio
> è Libertà. . . .

How could they not succeed?

> . . . non fieno in lei vincenti?

These were classical images, of Xerxes and Thermopylae, which weighed down, but did not extinguish, the intuitions of Alfieri on the transformation of a mercantile war into a war for freedom.[19]

In the second ode the conflict undergoes a further transformation and becomes international. How could it be that insurgent America, so different and so far from the passions of Europe, had found on the old continent a "luce inaspettata," ready

> a rischiarar l'americana notte?

One might have anticipated that assistance would come from the Dutch, that is, from the descendants of those who in the sixteenth century had fought for their freedom against the Spain of Philip II. But this was illusory: even the Dutch were now ruined by the mercantile spirit, and thus incapable of any virtue.

> Straniere a lor già fersi
> povertade, e virtú; già il ferro in oro

[19] "by the evil that encumbers all of our Europe." "Italy, which in chains / abhorred and suffered, and later merited, / drags out its long age." "vile cupidity" "a king's artless ire" "your American sons" "heedless swarm / of armed merchants" "ill-bought Germans" "But why? Do I see / those prows tremble, or take fright? / I seem them sad, but fearless: their God / is liberty . . ." ". . . will they not be victorious in Her?" *L'America libera. Odi. Ode prima,* "Accenna le cagioni della guerra," in Vittorio Alfieri, *Opere,* vol. 4: *Scritti politici e morali,* pt. 2, ed. Pietro Cazzani (Asti: Casa d'Alfieri, 1966), pp. 77ff.

ed in alga l'alloro,
e capitano invitto in signor molle,
ed unione e forza hanno cangiata
in rea, ma disarmata
discordia inerte che del par lor tolle
pace che guerra. Oh folle
chi spera in lor! . . .

One could hope for better from Spain, impoverished, depopulated, and the instrument of oppression in its own colonies, but which still maintained, contrary to what had happened in other lands, a sense of honor and a will to fight.

Gente lieve, e non cruda
benché non sciolta mai
da' regi lacci; mal servir cieco accoppia
onor verace; e in cor, piú ch'altra assai,
di tromba al suon l'impeto primo addoppia.

The greatest surprise came from France.

E il crederem? Fia ver che un re sottrarne
a servitude or voglia?

How could one forget that little more than a decade had passed since the time when France had crushed the free Corsican nation of Pasquale Paoli?

Re, che di ceppi apportator pur dinanzi
là dove il corso impavido s'inscoglia
tanti a Stige mandarne
fu visto, ed ora i lor dolenti avanzi
vuol servi tener, anzi
che a virtute lasciarli ed a bell'opre?
Suo dispotico brando, ancor grondante
di quel sangue anelante
vendetta, or fia per noi francar si adopre?[20]

---

[20] "unexpected light," "to illuminate the American night?" "Foreign to them became / poverty and virtue; already iron [turned] into gold / and laurel into seaweed, / and the undefeated captain into a soft gentleman, / and they have changed unity and force / into shameful, but disarmed / impotent discord that takes from them / peace as well as war. Foolish / he who hopes in them! . . ." "A fickle, and not crude folk / although never freed / from royal bonds; they blend blind service with / true honor; and in their hearts, more than others, / at the first sound of the trumpet, they double their initial ardor." "Shall we believe it? Can it be true that a king / wants to rescue us from servitude?" "A king who brings shackles, and recently / where the fearless Corsican lies / was seen sending so many to Hell; / now wants to keep the sad survivors / in slavery, instead / of leaving them to virtue and good works? / How could his despotic sword, still dripping / with that blood

This was not a rhetorical question, and it changed to another: who were those in France who showed a readiness to help the Americans? The answer was in the third ode, which "speaks of signor de La Fayette."

Ecco, di tromba americana al primo squillo . . .

disappears the image of "un giovin, schiavo, signor, gallo," replaced by the vision of the

. . . nobile ardente spirto,

of a Latin adolescent, or a reborn Greek, impatient to fight for American liberty, ready to

> . . . sossopra voltar da sommo ad imo
> tutto di corte il limo
> perché gli sia concesso
> scelti colà portar franchi guerrieri.

"Figliuol novello" of the "dea di Sparta sola" he left behind "le rive contaminate / di Senna, ove non è chi a libertade / sgombrasse mai le strade." With this detachment, with this break and neoclassical transformation, signor de La Fayette becomes a hero

a Marte caro, e a libertate. . . .[21]

Washington, to whom the fourth ode is dedicated, appears surrounded with so many memories of antiquity as to become unrecognizable, if not perhaps in the verses that celebrate his constancy and tenacity. Washington is the symbol of a reality more guessed at than known by Alfieri, of such shining virtue that it does not permit even a guess at the outline of a concrete political personality.

The last ode, the fifth, was written in 1783, when the peace was already concluded. Nevertheless, it is not a song of joy. Certainly America could be proud of the "full liberty" it had known how to obtain after so many years of struggle. But not even independence was a pledge for tranquillity in future times. The deep evil of the world reappears in a menacing way, attempting to prevent Europe from being renewed and purified from the "tempesta fremente / che a noi salvezza e libertate apporta." The breath of the American Revolution is blocked by a "torvo

---

crying / for vengeance, be working to free us?" *Ode seconda*, "Annovera i popoli belligerati," ibid., pp. 82ff.

[21] "Behold, at the first blast of the American trumpet . . ." "a young, enslaved, Gallic, lord" "noble ardent spirit" ". . . turn over from top to bottom / all the mud of the court / to be permitted / to take French warriors there." "New son" of the "only goddess of Sparta" "the poisoned banks / of the Seine, where no one ever / broke open the way to freedom." "dear to Mars and liberty. . . ." *Ode terza*, "Parla del signor de la Fayette," ibid., pp. 87ff.

genio profano" that encumbers Europe, a bloody deformed monster, the root of all evils and vices.

> Tu sei quel mostro rio, cui vita dienno
> pingue ignoranza, e scarno
> timor, che il fuoco il piú sublime agghiaccia
> con sua squallida faccia.
> DISPOTISMO t'appelli, e sei custode
> tu solo ormai di nostre infauste rive,
> dove in morte si vive . . .
> dov'è sol reo quel'uom, che il vero dica.

This was Alfieri's incarnation of despotism, which had assumed many forms in the eighteenth century. It had something Oriental about it:

> nell'Asia, come in suo terreno, alligna.

But above all it resulted from privilege, from badly distributed wealth, from baseness, envy, all the disequilibriums of old Europe. It derived from the despotism evoked by Nicolas-Antoine Boulanger, and as such could take its motto from Virgil: "Monstrum horrendum, informe, ingens. . . ."[22] Now it set itself up as an obstacle, as a margin to the successful revolution. It was cruel by its own nature, and also by the mission it had now undertaken to suffocate

> . . . ogni aura felice
> che a noi mandasse occidental piaggia.
> Malnata forma, oh! chi sei tu, cui lice
> far che ogni nostra speme a terra caggia?

The war itself, which was now finished, the economic causes (among them the "erba vil, che odora / infusa in bollente onda" [tea]) that had provoked it, now seemed gray and small, and the diplomatic reasonings that had accompanied it uncertain. The decisive struggle had not yet reached its end.

> Fia libertà, quella che or là protegge
> chi assoluto qui regge?

It was better to take refuge in classical memories.

---

[22] "shuddering tempest / which brings us salvation and liberty." "grim profane spirit" "You are that wicked monster, born of / bloated ignorance and gaunt / fear, who freezes the most sublime fire / with your squalid face, / DESPOTISM is your name, and you alone now / guard our unhappy shores, / where one lives in death . . . / where the only criminal is that man who speaks the truth." "In Asia, its own land, it takes root." From Virgil: "Monster, horrible, shapeless, enormous. . . ." This was the theme of the *Recherches sur l'origine du despotisme oriental*, which appeared in 1761. The motto in the version of V. K. Trediakovskij was taken up by A. Radiščev in his *Viaggio da Pietroburgo a Mosca*, ed. G. and F. Venturi (Bari: De Donato, 1972), p. 59.

Maratona, Termopile, l'infausto
giorno di Canne stesso;
guerre eran quelle. . . .
Pace era quella, che d'Atene in grembo,
con libertade ogni bell'arte univa. . . .[23]

We find another echo of America at the end of the eighties, during
the Indian summer of Piedmontese culture in the second half of the
eighteenth century, in the age of the academy generally called the San-
paolina. In the verses of Alfieri, the European republican tradition was
clothed in the armor of the ancients. It returned now, in the pages of
the *Biblioteca oltremontana*, under the pressure of the more concrete and
nearby events of America and Holland. The occasion was the publication in Paris in 1787 of a book by Charles-Joseph de Mayer, *Les ligues
Achéenne, Suisse et Hollandoise et révolution des Etats Unis de l'Amérique com-
parées ensemble . . .* , in two volumes, of which the second was entitled *Les
Etats Unis de l'Amérique Septentrionale comparés avec les ligues Achéenne,
Suisse et Hollandoise.* When Mayer's book came out, John Adams was
writing his *Defense of the American constitutions* and he did not fail to view
with irony the interest the models of ancient republics aroused. That of
the Achaeans, he said, had become quite celebrated in recent years. But
how could one forget that the history of the Achaeans had ended in a
catastrophe, that in those ancient cities the ratio of freemen to slaves
had been one to ten, "that the slaves did all the work and that free citizens had no occupation other than that of stuffing their gullets?"[24] If
one really wanted to follow such examples—as even Turgot seemed to—
why not give complete autonomy to each city in the United States?—
Adams concluded ironically. "Soon these cities will make war on one
another and form, like the Greek towns, combinations, alliances, and
political intrigues." And why not divide citizens between freemen and
slaves? "One would soon see what brilliant prosperity would result for
the whole republic from such a reasonable system, so easily adopted, so
favorable to equality, to liberty, and to the happiness of the generality
of citizens."[25] Mayer, in pages that impressed Felice di San Martino, the
reviewer in the *Biblioteca oltremontana*—he said they were written "in a

---

[23] ". . . any happy breeze / that western shores send us. / Cursed form, Oh! Who are
you, to cause / all our hopes to be crushed?" "vile herb, that smells / when infused in
boiling water" (tea) "Will it be true liberty, that is protected there / by the same one who
reigns absolute here?" "Marathon, Thermopylae, the unhappy / day of Cannae itself; /
those were wars. . . . / Peace was that, which in the lap of Athens, / joined liberty with all
great art. . . ." *Ode quinta*, "Pace del 1783," in Alfieri, *Opere*, pp. 96ff.

[24] John Adams, *Défense des constitutions américaines ou de la nécessité d'une balance dans les
pouvoirs d'un gouvernement libre* (Paris: Buisson, 1792), vol. 1, p. 429.

[25] Ibid., pp. 430ff.

vibrant and elegant style"—had emphasized instead that Achaea was born "an independent democratic republic, resulting from the needs of its own defense." After narrating its story, he concluded that only the Romans, "with their power and deep politics," had been able to defeat it.[26] He criticized the parts that Mayer dedicated to Switzerland and the United Provinces. "And free Switzerland? There is more independence there, but it is not fully free."[27] As for Holland, it was "the most defective" of all such republics.[28] Finally considering the United States of America, Mayer was struck by the rapidity of its growth. Persecutions and obstacles had only favored its development. It had suffered terribly during the war. "It was not only the English who committed horrible cruelties; no less cruel were the confederates against their compatriots, who had remained neutral or were suspected of being Royalists."[29] The "wise politics of Franklin" had contributed greatly to the victory of the Americans.[30] Washington had demonstrated, now that the conflict was ended, that he was "a good citizen in the simplicity of his expression, and the spirit of legislation in the solidity of his reflection."[31] His letter to his fellow citizens before retiring to Virginia was summarized at length, as well as his suggestions for attempting to end and limit the political and economic disputes that shook the young state. "The author believes that in time the Americans will recognize the need to adopt the system proposed by Washington, and that their republic will be the most perfect that has yet existed." This conclusion raised doubts in the reviewer. "A perfect republic (which he thought impossible) would be the ruin of all other kinds of government."[32] In the end the comparison between ancient and modern republics brought even Mayer to a defense of monarchy, to a reexamination of the ideas of Rousseau and of Mably, not without showing his preference for Mably's ideas regarding the United States.[33]

[26] *Biblioteca oltremontana ad uso d'Italia*, 1787, vol. 8, pp. 151ff.

[27] Ibid., p. 160.

[28] Ibid., p. 168.

[29] Ibid., vol. 9, p. 268.

[30] Ibid., p. 271.

[31] Ibid., p. 273.

[32] Ibid., p. 277.

[33] In this same period, in August 1787, Thomas Jefferson, in Paris, put some observations on paper, briefly intending to have them published in the *Journal de Paris*, which he did not do. What had struck him was the erroneous vision of Mayer of the origins of the American Revolution and of the events of 1776. See *The Papers of Thomas Jefferson*, ed. Julian P. Boyd (Princeton, N.J.: Princeton University Press, 1955), vol. 12, pp. 61ff. The interesting review published in the *Supplément au No. 197 du Journal de Paris*, 16 July 1787, and no. 241, 29 August 1787, pp. 1051ff., underlined the monarchical character of this

Even the review by Giuseppe Pavesio of the celebrated *Lettres d'un cultivateur américain*, by Michel-Guillaume-Jean Saint-John de Crève-coeur, in the three-volume Parisian edition of 1787 dedicated to the Marquis de La Fayette (the first edition was dedicated to Raynal), began with information about the most recent publications on America, from Robertson to Mably and De Pauw, not without, naturally, insisting on Raynal.[34] What struck the reviewer most was the American atmosphere, the "benevolence," the "hospitality," the "country virtues," the "happiness" that issued from those countrysides of small proprietors, from those "producers of rustic wealth able not only to support numerous families of laborers, but even to improve their condition."[35] "Civil war" had touched those lands, but it was now ended and transformed into a memory. New realities demanded attention. In the book one found information on "two kinds of men, of some interest to readers, that is to say, Negroes and savages, whose characters are depicted masterfully, with a faithful description of customs, and continual pathetic declamations against the barbarous slavery that oppresses the former."[36] This was a complex reality from which it was difficult to avert one's gaze. "What part of the world can now appeal to the soul, so to speak, or touch the imagination more than can America?"[37] Surprise and amazement went hand in hand. It was enough to think of the Quakers, of the University of Pennsylvania, and of the celebrated doctor Benjamin Rush, professor of chemistry there, who was intent on "*civilizing* and *Christianizing* the savages."[38] "Great and inestimable are the advantages that redound to the American from the kind of government under which he measures out his days, in which no strange or exclusive institution, no prejudice of education or birth impedes his designs or interrupts his aims. He can call himself truly the absolute ruler of himself, whether in choosing the situation of life that is most favorable and suitable to his talents, or in carrying out all his projects."[39] Free in an "immense continent," the American does not see only crops and other products grow around him. Culture, in this land, was rapidly becoming more widespread. "Gazettes, once introduced in America to promote

book and reminded that "the ancestors of M. de Mayer have long been in the service of Prussia."

[34] See Jean Beranger, "Un auteur, deux publics: Étude des versions françaises et anglaises des Lettres d'un cultivateur américain de St. John de Crèvecoeur," in *La révolution américaine et l'Europe*, pp. 309ff.

[35] *Biblioteca oltremontana ad uso d'Italia*, vol. 11, pp. 175ff.

[36] Ibid., p. 179.

[37] Ibid., pp. 181ff.

[38] Ibid., p. 198.

[39] Ibid., pp. 199ff.

novelties, have for some time become objects of increased importance and advantage. One could almost say that they have become warehouses for the deliberations of legislation in the sessions of magistrates. One reads in them newly proclaimed laws, sentences of tribunals, instructions contained in the speeches of governors on the opening of the courts, and news extracted from the gazettes of Europe and the United States. History has its place, as well as news about agriculture, medicine, commerce, mechanics, mathematics . . . ," without neglecting naturally "the invention of machines."[40] There was a diffusion of cultural societies (above all agricultural ones). "The typographic arts make admirable progress among Americans, and after the peace many printers have published most interesting works, for example, the voyages of Cook, the history of America by Robertson, and other similar works." Politically, government founded on the principle of "popular sovereignty" was in full operation. The administration was excellent. "The regulations for extinguishing fires, and for public security in the daytime and at night, are wonderful." There was no lack of "spacious hospitals." "The prisons are constructed with foresight in solitary arid places. . . ." Over this world of tolerance and labor still hung the venerated image of "the most respectable Doctor Franklin, printer, philosopher, and statesman."[41]

In Genova American affairs did not fail to arouse curiosity and interest. In 1779, as we have seen, Raynal's *Histoire* was reprinted there. What was missing was a local gazette, although this was substituted, it is true in some ways, by the dispatches of Francesco Ageno, the representative of the Republic in London, which were read and discussed, like other diplomatic correspondence, in the Serene Councils, and thus came to the knowledge of more or less all of the ruling class. Ageno, like other patricians, was convinced that any "rebellion" should be crushed as soon as possible, if for no other reason than that "the example is always pernicious."[1] What had happened in Corsica was more than sufficient to demonstrate the truth of this maxim. The first news, arrived in London in June 1775, about the encounters near Boston between insurgents and the king's troops, persuaded him immediately of the particu-

---

[40] Ibid., pp. 200ff.

[41] Ibid., pp. 203ff., 208ff. See the review of this work that appeared in the *Journal de Paris*, no. 229, 17 August 1787, pp. 1003ff.

[1] Giuseppe Colucci, *I casi della guerra per l'indipendenza d'America narrati dall'ambasciatore della repubblica di Genova presso la corte d'Inghilterra nalla sua corrispondenza ufficiale inedita* (Genova: Tipografia dell'Istituto sordmuti, 1879), vol. 1, pt. 1, "Prefazione," p. xxxviii.

larly cruel nature of the conflict that had begun beyond the ocean. "The Americans have demonstrated quite a few barbarities by mutilating some English prisoners, even making them undergo the operation of 'scalping,' that is to say, cutting off the arms, which is customary among the American savages when they are at war." "This iniquity . . . confirms the example of all times, that is to say, a greater incitement to fury and atrocity is present in civil wars than in those involving enemies of a foreign nation." The contemporaneous "popular commotion in New York" showed, meanwhile, that "the spirit of rebellion was spreading more and more among Americans." Under the pretext of "legitimate defense" they were forming "a general confederation."[2] In the summer, at the "General Congress of Philadelphia," the figures of Samuel Adams and John Hancock, "wealthy and boisterous men," emerged. Many clerics were involved with these politicians; "the most recalcitrant colonies are of the Presbyterian faith. They admit no superiors in the ecclesiastical hierarchy, and tacitly exclude them in the civil sphere."[3] Economic motives had a great weight: "Freedom of commerce is the principal aim of the inhabitants of the colonies."[4] With the beginning of 1776 it was evident that the colonists wanted "absolute independence."[5] The lesson for England was clear: it should be "more cautious in the future when acquiring too-distant and too-extensive establishments."[6] This was an ideal of prudence that made Ageno, like the readers of his dispatches, ill suited to understand the American Revolution, and which made both deaf to the stubborn will that moved Great Britain. The Declaration of Independence was transmitted almost without comment. As for the motives that inspired Franklin's work in Paris, these were viewed with particular diffidence. Was he "a negotiator, or a simple philosopher?"[7] "The motive of his voyage to France is not thought to be accidental, although many attribute it to the reserve that philosophers generally employ to withdraw from dangerous enterprises after having advised them. The man being, however, a schemer with a reputation, he might easily be entrusted with a secret commission favoring the Americans, to whom he will undoubtedly attempt to be useful in this casual and mysterious pilgrimage."[8] The free political life of emerging America, as well as that of England, where he lived, remained opaque and obscure to Ageno's eyes. He believed the rumors suggesting that Washington had

---

[2] Ibid., vol. 1, pt. 2, pp. 70, 73, 16 June 1775.
[3] Ibid., p. 101, 4 August 1775.
[4] Ibid., p. 137, 20 October 1775.
[5] Ibid., p. 181, 12 January 1776.
[6] Ibid., p. 193, 2 February 1776.
[7] Ibid., p. 328, 20 December 1776.
[8] Ibid., p. 344, 3 January 1772.

been nominated "Lord Protector of the Confederated Provinces," "as if he were a temporary dictator."[9] Only with French support did the fate of the colonies seem assured to him.[10] In Genova the government repeated to the English consul that the Republic had no intention of deviating "from the strictest neutrality." Any attempt by the French to recruit seamen for their war would be stopped energetically. As it was, even the Corsicans attempted to escape such a levy, "those people being heartily tir'ed of their new masters and terrified at the loss of their countrymen who were out with Monseigneur d'Estaing: few of them returned."[11] From London Colucci sent uncertain news in the summer of 1779 of the internal situation of the rebellious colonies: "Here it is said that they are reduced to final extermination, although some believe they still have strength."[12] It would be better for the Genoese government to pay attention to the possible concrete reflections of American developments in the daily life of the Republic. Why not profit from the rise in prices and the commercial difficulties England encountered in procuring "goods from Italy," especially oil, which was indispensable to the army and fleet, and for that reason could be of "rather poor" quality? A "Venetian ship" had already arrived in Great Britain with "products of the Levant." "Nautical experience," which even the English recognized in the Genoese "nation," was a strong incentive to such initiative.[13] In the spring of 1778 the gazette of Leiden assured its readers that Genova "had concluded a treaty of friendship with the Congress after negotiations to this end with an individual from Charlestown in southern Carolina, named Savage, who has resided in Genova in the last two years."[14] There was a rumor that a ship with sixty cannons from South Carolina was "commanded by a captain with a disguised name, but recognized as Genoese, together with some of his ship's seamen who belong

---

[9] Ibid., p. 391, 21 March 1777.

[10] Ibid., vol. 2, p. 78, 31 March 1778, and pp. 179ff., 21 August 1778.

[11] London, PRO, *SPFO* 28, *Genova 1776–80*, dispatches of John Collet, 31 March 1778 and 21 March 1779.

[12] Colucci, *I casi della guerra*, vol. 2, p. 428, 13 July 1779.

[13] Ibid., vol. 1, pt. 2, p. 417, 23 May 1777.

[14] *Supplément aux Nouvelles extraordinaires de divers endroits du n. XXVIII*, 7 April 1778. This strange piece of news is not confirmed in contemporary documents. On Savage, member of a rich family of merchants, see George C. Rogers, Jr., "The Charleston Tea Party," *South Carolina Historical Magazine* 75, no. 3 (July 1974): 156, 161. John Savage had amassed "the largest Charleston fortune." See Lawrence Park, "The Savage Family," in *The New England Historical and Genealogical Register*, vol. 67 (1913), pp. 309ff. I thank Professor George C. Rogers, Jr., of the University of South Carolina for the information he kindly furnished on these persons. The official denial of the Republic of Genova is reported in Nino Cortese, "Le prime relazione fra gli Stati Uniti d'America e gli stati italiani," *Rassegna Storica del Risorgimento* 63, fasc. 1 (January–March 1971): 6.

to the same nation." Many cannons were apparently "marked with the arms of the Republic."[15] In September 1779 one read in the London gazettes that the Americans were attempting to obtain a loan from Genova.[16] Accusations were spreading of the partiality of Genova for France and Spain. The opposition, above all the Duke of Richmond, mentioned it often, "in an effort to provoke censure and to discredit the ministry," thus increasing the "spirit of acrimony and alienation that exists among these nationals toward the Republic."[17] Internal developments in Great Britain in 1780, from the growing pressure of radicals and the disorder created by George Gordon, to the dissolution of Parliament, as well as the news that came from Ireland and Holland—together with what continued to arrive from the United States—now provided Francesco Ageno, when his mission to London ended, with a broad and varied picture for meditation on the contagious character of rebellions. His shortsightedness nonetheless prevented him from arriving at more general conclusions.

The first direct contact between the port of Genova and America, once independence was established, if we can believe a Florentine gazette, occurred in the spring of 1784. "Last Saturday, toward evening, a small ship arrived here with the American flag, and it is the first to arrive with such a flag in this port, coming from New England in America, from where it departed on 4 December last year, and from Martinique last February."[18]

The American world was also far removed from the Enlightenment in Lombardy, both in the years of the slow maturation of the revolution and in the period of war and consolidation. The men of *Il Caffè* were too busy discussing local problems for their attention to turn beyond the ocean. Instead, the example of England was always present to them. Expansion and emigration had created a situation that became increasingly difficult there. "After two or three generations," we read in the *Meditazioni sulla economia politica*, by Pietro Verri, "colonists lose their affection for their old fatherland, and if it is not renewed through the continual sacrifice of population, it is to be feared that they will degenerate into cold allies of little use, or that, impatient with dependence,

---

[15] Colucci, *I casi della guerra*, vol. 1, pt. 2, p. 475, 19 September 1777.
[16] Ibid., vol. 2, p. 478, 10 September 1779.
[17] Ibid., p. 523, 14 December 1779.
[18] *Notizie del mondo*, no. 41, 22 May 1784, p. 360 (Genova, 19 May).

they will become the enemies of their old fellow citizens."[1] The dramatic character such problems assumed among British writers (among others, in the thought of General Henry Lloyd, a friend of Verri's) was supplanted here with a kind of natural law of the detachment of colonies.

Still, a curiosity about events in America was not lacking in Lombardy. In the year that Verri's *Meditazioni* was published in Livorno, in 1771, a curious little book came out in Milan from the bookseller Reycends, the first, not only in Italy but in the entire European continent, to echo the protests and vindications of the British colonies. It was entitled *Précis de l'état actuel des colonies angloises dans l'Amérique Septentrionale par M. Dominique de Blackford.*[2] It contained an account about America, and in the appendix, a summary of Franklin's interrogation before the House of Commons in 1766. The work was a particularly characteristic example of the cosmopolitanism of the eighteenth century. The author and translator were Germans. The language was French. The place of publication was Milan. Dominick von Blackford was an international journalist who in this period edited for publication in Livorno, in French, another little work, the first history of Russian literature ever published.[3] Giambattista Vasco, who lived at that time in Lombardy and was responsible for the *Gazzetta letteraria*, the bulletin edited by Galeazzi, was struck by Blackford's work. "This little book," he wrote, "contains most useful information on the sciences of politics and economics." It transcribed at length the testimony of emigrants who, finding it impossible to pay for their voyage to America, sold themselves to an employer, "whom they are obliged to serve in exchange for their livelihood alone for a determined number of years, after which they are free." Peasant serfs in German lands subjected themselves to such contracts, if only to escape their harsh conditions. "Since in many principalities of Germany the peasants, commonly serfs, are oppressed by impositions and gravely disturbed in their cultivation of the land by wild game, which they have to protect for the sport of their lords, moved by desperation, they often leave their paternal fields to continue their unhappy days in another hemisphere, and they go to America, despite their reluctance to leave their homes. They embark from Holland and elsewhere, and at Rotterdam from time to time one sees vessels crowded with three or four hundred such unfortunates." Through an interest in America, the

---

[1] Pietro Verri, *Meditazioni sulla economia politica* (Livorno: Nella stamperia dell' Enciclopedia, 1771), p. 148.

[2] A German translation (Turin and Bern: Typographische Gesellschaft, 1772) is cited by Horst Dippel, *Americana Germanica, 1770–1800. Bibliographie deutscher Amerikaliteratur* (Stuttgart: J. B. Metzlersche Verlag, 1976), p. 17 n. 40.

[3] See Venturi, *The End of the Old Regime, 1768–1776*, pp. 91, 92n.

reality of Europe and the need for reform reappeared with greater clarity from the pen of Giambattista Vasco. "The surest and simplest way of
preventing such clandestine emigration would be to improve the peasants' standard of living and treat them more kindly." The declarations
of Franklin, which closed the work, instead presented the problems of
Americans in all their starkness. "From the responses not less frank than
erudite of this renowned Pennsylvanian one can know perhaps better
than from any book the form of government established in the colonies
of North America, the maxims of the Americans, who seek to break the
yoke of England, and those of the English, who seek only to draw the
greatest profit from the colonies."[4]

The "most renowned Pennsylvanian" remained, in the years that followed, the most important intermediary between America and Lombardy. Technical and scientific problems and moral and political concerns intersected in him so closely as to attract the attention of all
cultivated men, whatever their speciality. Even for Lombards, Franklin
was a kind of living American encyclopedia.[5] To give only one example,
the *Scelta di opuscoli interessanti da varie lingue,* published by Giuseppe
Morelli in Milan, was launched in 1775 with a kind of special issue dedicated to him. As the *Gazzetta letteraria* wrote, "two memoirs taken from
the work of the celebrated Mr. Franklin occupy the larger part of this
first volume. The first is the *Description of the Pennsylvania stove.* . . . The
second is *Poor Richard become wealthy.* It contains wise economic advice
and has contributed much to the generous resolve of inhabitants of the
English colonies in America to import no manufactured goods from England until Parliament revokes the acts displeasing to them, and also the
acts that the colonists' unanimous and constant agreement has rejected,
one might say, from the metropolis. This alone is sufficient for his eulogy."[6]

When the open conflict began, debate resumed on a central question: what was the value of the highly prized British liberty? Profiting
from the publication of the French version of Blackstone's famous *Com-
mentaries on the Laws of England,* an anonymous reviewer attempted to
answer without ambiguity. "Does the liberty the English nation so prizes
make it as powerful and happy as it could be?" It was enough to look at
the situation of the colonies to have doubts. "What a conflict! Liberty set
against liberty! The enemy of tyranny has become a cruel tyrant! A people oppressed by the effort to avoid fanaticism; an ambition to greatness
declares itself the oppressor of its brothers, who are good patriots!"[7]

---

[4] *Gazzetta letteraria,* no. 3, 15 January 1772, pp. 21ff.
[5] Pace, *Franklin,* pp. 120ff.
[6] *Gazzetta letteraria,* no. 2, 11 January 1775, p. 9.
[7] Ibid., no. 35, 30 August 1775, p. 275.

During the long years of war, *La gazzetta di Milano* also referred to events beyond the ocean. But these were scarce notices, not only when the columns are compared with those of Dutch, Swiss, and French gazettes, but also with the Florentine gazettes, and the *Nuove di diverse corti e paesi*, the journal of Lugano. The Lombardian world was too involved in the internal transformations of the last years of Maria Theresa, and above all of the first years of Joseph II, to become truly passionate about American affairs. Observing the political and cultural temperature of Europe from Milan, one perceives clearly the dividing line between the Hapsburg world and the rest of the continent. This was a world in full development, intent on the effort to bring the experience of enlightened despotism to a conclusion, but removed from the reality of Paris, London, and Philadelphia, even when, in the end, a similar political language was employed.

It is enough to open the most famous book on the New World written in Lombardy between the seventies and the eighties, the *Lettere americane*, by Gianrinaldo Carli, to be aware of the closeness to British and French debates, but at the same time of the substantial differences. The problem of equality was also central for Carli and even assumed utopian aspects in his pages, but this was an equality arrived at from above, under the influence of a power that was absolute and despotic. The guiding ideas of the state made it into a theocracy. The America of which Carli spoke was not the north in ferment, but the world of great primitive empires, the monarchy of the Incas, a kind of archaeological transformation of the government of Maria Theresa and Joseph II. Still, the Cremona edition of the *Lettere americane*, of 1781, was not dedicated to the emperor, but rather to Franklin, the glorious member of the republic of philosophers who had done much to create the new consciousness of Americans. Both the editor Manini and the writer Isidoro Bianchi influenced Carli's presentation of his work. Nor did Franklin miss the opportunity to benefit from the opening that came from Lombardy to spread his own ideas and works.[8] The *Lettere americane* was distributed widely in German and French, and reappeared, with a preface by Isidoro Bianchi, in volume 11 of Carli's *Opere*. It became a classic, which today still permits us to measure what is similar and what is different in the French, American, and Imperial visions of the New World in the first years of the eighties.

We must seek in Tuscany, among the different centers of Italy, for the most vivid interest in American developments. Here there was a

---

[8] Pace, *Franklin*, pp. 135ff.; *Riformatori* 3, pp. 432, 464ff.

larger number of gazettes, journals, and other works, even in comparison with the ample publications of Venice. There were frequent translations and polemics, even where we least expect them, in Siena, for
instance. We can reconstruct from the Tuscan press a vivid chronicle of
the revolution and war in America, as well as of the first years of the
United States, and follow step by step what was offered to readers in the
Grand Duchy between 1776 and 1789.

In September 1776 the *Notizie del mondo* and the *Gazzetta universale*
had published the Declaration of Independence.[1] In the winter of 1776
and 1777 disquieting news filtered in from London. "Perils and difficulties multiply in America. The progress of our troops thus far promises little; they cannot distinguish themselves without exposing themselves to great risk," one read in October.[2] The seesaw of defeats and
successes was followed attentively by Florentine gazettes in the following
months, as well as by the *Nuove di diverse corti e paesi*. But political developments attracted attention the most. Beside very detailed descriptions
of battles, the *Notizie del mondo* focused in November on the activity of
"Mr. Adams, who is the soul of the American Congress."[3] In December
the state of mind of the combatants was depicted vividly. "Fanaticism
has reached the point of excess among the Americans. Many of the soldiers wear the word *Liberty* on their uniforms as a sign, and preserve
this with extreme jealousy. The clergy are inflamed with zeal for liberty.
Even unwarlike women share the general enthusiasm."[4] In February
1777 the gazette began a full publication of the *Articles of confederation
and perpetual union of the thirteen united colonies of America*. "This document has been written with much knowledge and mastery, as have many
others sent out before by the American confederation, a sign that if
something is lacking from a military point of view it certainly is not lacking in politics or in the worthy ability of an illustrious legislative body."[5]
The *Articles* carried the dateline of Philadelphia, 5 October 1776. It had
taken almost five months for them to arrive in Italy. But there was no
doubt about the interest they aroused. In March 1776 the gazette of
Lugano gave nourishment to this curiosity by publishing the constituton

---

[1] Venturi, *The End of the Old Regime, 1768–1776*, pp. 436–37.

[2] *Notizie del mondo*, no. 81, 8 October 1776, p. 621 (London, 13 September).

[3] Ibid., no. 89, 5 November 1776, p. 688 (London, 15 October).

[4] Ibid., no. 98, 7 December 1776, p. 764 (Livorno, 4 December).

[5] Ibid., no. 15, 22 February 1777, p. 114 (London, 13 January). The publication of
this text follows in no. 16, 25 February 1777, pp. 123ff. (London, 4 February). The *Articoli*
are also inserted in the *Nuove di diverse corti e paesi*, no. 8, 24 February 1777, p. 62 (London,
4 February); no. 9, 3 March 1777, p. 70 (London, 11 February); no. 10, 10 March 1777,
p. 76 (London, 14 October). See Jones, "The Articles of Confederation and the Creation
of a Federal System," in *Aspects of American Liberty*, pp. 126ff.

of Delaware. "Among the solemn acts of the American Assemblies, which demonstrate the animating spirit of their insurrection, perhaps none shows as much energy as that of the Province of Delaware, with which on 11 September these colonists expressed the will to constantly follow the maxims contained in the following 23 articles." Here was the first: "All government comes from the immediate right of the people, it is founded on a compact that has no other object than the common good." The second article read: "Every man has an inalienable right to worship the most high in accordance with the determination of his own judgement and the persuasion of his conscience." Article 5 read: "Persons entrusted with legislative and executive power are the holders of public trust." Article 6: "Liberty is founded on the right of the people to participate in legislation." Other articles fixed the form of trials before justices and showed the inveterate distrust of Americans for standing armies, which were considered "perilous for liberty" (Article 19). Article 23 affirmed that "the freedom of the press must be inviolably preserved."[6]

Returning to the Articles of Confederation, on 1 March 1777 the *Notizie del mondo* provided a most enlightened interpretation.

One can reasonably, with a great philosopher of our time (M. d'Alembert), consider this century to be one of the most fertile in literary, moral, and political revolutions. While Europe rested, so to speak, on its laurels, a new nation is being created in the New World, which at its birth is no longer content to provide a most unexpected spectacle of courage, prudence, and patriotic spirit. It applies itself also, through a prodigal and unique phenomenon, to spread culture, diffuse useful sciences, and increase the mass of physical knowledge, without at all losing itself in sterile curiosity or lazy pleasure. One could say that letters are passing from Europe to make a new home in the remote regions of America.

It was enough to read the *Philosophical transactions* of the Academy of Philadelphia to be persuaded of this.[7]

The citizens of what was now commonly called the United States had chosen: "*Potior est visa periculosa libertas*" (Once seen, liberty though dangerous is preferable).[8] They would continue to fight even if "the Euro-

---

[6] *Nuove di diverse corti e paesi*, no. 11, 17 March 1777, p. 87 (London, 28 February), with a continuation in the following issue. See *Notizie del mondo*, no. 20, 11 March 1777, pp. 155ff. (London, 18 February).

[7] *Notizie del mondo*, no. 17, 1 March 1777, p. 130 (London, 4 February).

[8] In reality, as Harry W. Jones reports in "The Articles of Confederation," p. 133, "the term 'United States of America' appears once, . . . but it signifies not a political entity but an aggregate of separate sovereignties 'united' only in a shared purpose to break off all ties with an imperial power that had oppressed them all." But the international echo con-

pean powers, and particularly France," persisted "in their pacific system."[9] Philadelphia was in peril. Appeals and declarations multiplied
and were "avidly" read, even in Italy, precisely for their general character, because one saw in them "delineated the fundamental principles
of civil society, principles that are almost universally recognized among
all enlightened peoples, and are taught by those very writers which the
British nation has added to the number of great men admired by Europe."[10] The news from Paris was fairly optimistic from a military point
of view, and it was particularly attentive to the work of ideas. "Some wise
Americans, along with a number of our philosophers, are currently
working to compile a code of natural law that can apply to all men."[11]
In the following issue of the *Notizie del mondo* the speech of Washington
at the Battle of Trenton was published.[12] Discussions and feats of arms
intersected more closely in the spring of 1777. *The American Crisis* was
the title of a work "published a few months ago in the colonies." "It was
attributed to the author of the work entitled *Common Sense*, which paved
the way for the Declaration of Independence." The brother of the "celebrated author of the *Letters from a farmer*" had become General Dickinson. Franklin responded to General Howe.[13] An almanac came out in
Boston, from which was removed an "observation of the birth of the
king of Great Britain and of his accession to the throne; instead, certain
epochs of the rule of Cromwell were commemorated. On the frontispiece were the words 'The Year of the Lord 1777 and the first year of
American independence.' "[14]

Linguet launched his prophesy: "One day these Americans will conquer Europe with the arts they will perfect. . . . The time of that revolution is uncertain, but it is inevitable."[15] The echo of events beyond the

---

tributed, as one sees, to give a different and fuller meaning to the name of the emerging
American confederation.

[9] *Notizie del mondo*, no. 18, 4 March 1777, p. 137 (Paris, 17 February).

[10] Ibid., no. 20, 11 March 1777, p. 155 (London, 18 February).

[11] Ibid., no. 24, 25 March 1777, p. 186 (Paris, 10 March).

[12] Ibid., no. 25, 29 March 1777, p. 195 (London, 7 March).

[13] Ibid., no. 37, 10 May 1777, pp. 291ff. (London, 18 April). *The American Crisis*, no.
1, came out on 23 December 1776. No. 2 appeared in January 1777. These pamphlets,
with which T. Paine accompanied the American Revolution, are collected in *The Complete
Writings of Thomas Paine*, collected and edited by Philip S. Foner (New York: Citadel Press,
1945), vol. 1, pp. 47ff. John Dickinson had written his *Letters from a farmer in Pennsylvania*
between 1767 and 1768. His brother Philemon was named commander in chief of the
militia of New Jersey in June 1777 and participated actively in the political and military
events of the revolution.

[14] *Notizie del mondo*, no. 42, 27 May 1777, p. 331 (London, 6 May).

[15] Ibid., no. 45, 7 June 1777, p. 354 (London, 16 May). See Lester G. Crocker, "Lin-

ocean resounded more and more widely. The new government of Pennsylvania was saluted with toasts not only to the United States of America, but also "to the friends of liberty in all parts of the world," to the "arts and sciences," to "agriculture," to "commerce and navigation," and ended with the hope that "the human sciences, virtue, and happiness may receive their highest level of perfection in America." The long series of toasts concluded with one addressed to "Dr. Franklin."[16] Volunteers came forward in France.[17] There were even Italians, who were said to be numerous in Boston. "There are among others the nephew of the famous Cardinal Alberoni who possesses, as General Washington says, all the genius of his father. He is admitted to all the councils. The nephew of Marchese Monti is also here in the quality of a colonel with a large number of engineers."[18] In Paris, through the work of Franklin, the "republican spirit" advanced more and more:

> Il est beau d'asservir la nature au génie
> Il est plus beau di triompher des rois.[19]

In New England La Fayette was received "with the enthusiasm that a great name and great courage can inspire in a people fighting for liberty."[20] In Philadelphia he declared to the Congress that he thought of "his coming as a happy prefigurement of the alliance and amnesty that will necessarily establish themselves one day between his country and the United States of America."[21] In the name of Washington the insurgents took to themselves all the great traditions of English liberty. They intended to fight for that "constitution for which Hampden fought and died, for which our ancestors abandoned a decadent country that they could no longer defend, having escaped the shipwreck of English liberty ... the eternal palladium of freedom and happiness."[22] Every passing day added an element to the fusion of British republican tradition and the ideas of the European Enlightenment. Freedom of commerce, vindicated by the "Assembly of Massachussetts," translated this development into economic terms, concluding the long struggle with the mer-

guet's Prognostication for the American Colonies," *The French American Review* 2, no. 1 (January–March 1949): 45ff.

[16] *Notizie del mondo*, no. 49, 21 June 1777, p. 388 (London, 30 May).

[17] Ibid., no. 42, 27 May 1777, p. 331 (Paris, 12 May).

[18] Ibid., no. 51, 28 June 1777, p. 403 (London, 6 June). This correspondence was presented as a "Lettera del volontario Duplessis" (and thus could be from Thomas Antoine Maudit du Plessis).

[19] "It is nice to subject nature to genius / It is better to triumph over kings" (ibid., no. 54, 8 July 1777, p. 427 [Paris, 23 June]).

[20] Ibid., no. 62, 5 August 1777, p. 493 (Amsterdam, 19 July).

[21] Ibid., no. 64, 13 August 1777, p. 506 (Dunkirk, 22 July).

[22] Ibid., no. 83, 18 October 1777, p. 659 (London, 26 September).

cantilism of the mother country. "Commerce must regulate itself; one can never put up obstacles without ruining it; it always flourishes when left in freedom. In a word, commerce can be precisely compared to a well-educated mistress: she must be captivated with a delicate love, but one is finished with her by trying to force her affections."[23] These words undoubtedly must have seemed persuasive to Tuscans involved in the reforms of the grand duke Peter Leopold. The grand duke himself contributed, at a date difficult to establish, to this confrontation of European reality with political and economic ideas arriving from beyond the ocean. His *Observations sur les constitutions de la république de Pensylvanie* were a step in the preparation of a constitutional project for Tuscany; from this point the American experience was for him an indispensable part of the work of reform in which he was engaged.[24] He began with the *Contrat social*, and he placed liberty and equality at the base of his system of legislation—even if, he immediately added, in a monarchy equality must be understood not in a political, but in a civil sense, making all equally subject to law, without exception.[25] The constitution of Pennsylvania responded to the same problem of establishing a right to change government so as to make it adapted to ensuring the inalienable natural rights of all. Life, liberty, and property were guaranteed to everyone. All would obey only those laws to which they had consented. Convinced that happiness depended on good penal laws, the authors of the constitution had synthesized in a single article the principles on which they should be based. Indicating that they knew which and how many perils menaced governments at a certain level of perfection, the Americans based theirs on the only possible guarantee, free consultation with those who had every interest in being governed in the best way possible. In the past, Roman tribunals, parliaments in England, and now a separation between legislative and executive power in America had arisen against the prevailing deterioration induced by the passions of those in power. Despotism was a peril for both monarchies and republics. The Americans attempted to avoid it by insisting on the rights of the people. Many dispositions foreseen in the constitution of Pennsylvania—such as the publicity of elections and debates—were intended to

[23] Ibid., no. 93, 22 November 1777, p. 739 (London, 31 October), *Instruzioni date ai rappresentanti di Boston per l'assemblea di Massachuset ad oggetto di stabilire nel governo la più perfetta eguaglianza e di favorire efficacemente il commercio.*

[24] Adam Wandruska, *Pietro Leopoldo. Un grande riformatore* (Florence: Vallecchi, 1968), pp. 394ff. The test of these *Observations*, preserved in the State Archive at Vienna, has been translated into English by Gerald H. Davis, "Observations of Leopold of Habsburg on the Pennsylvania Constitution of 1776," *Pennsylvania History* 29, no. 4 (October 1962): 373ff.

[25] The passage of Rousseau transcribed by Peter Leopold opens book 1, chapter 11.

address the same problem. In particular, the nomination of censors every seven years, to control the constitutionality of laws and the legitimacy of policies implemented, seemed to Peter Leopold an excellent institution, capable of preventing the ruin of the constitution by uprooting the abuses that had penetrated it. In the complex constitutional effort that occupied him and his adviser Francesco Gianni between the seventies and the eighties, American examples were set for a moment beside Hungarian and Belgian ones and the exigencies arising in Tuscan society. Pennsylvania inserted itself like yeast into their project, both as a point of arrival and as the limit of the reforming experience of Peter Leopold.

This was all the more true because, as the grand duke meditated, American reality continued in full swing. The "total defeat" of General Burgoyne at Saratoga came, at the end of 1777, to put its seal on the great initial hopes of the Americans. In the House of Commons the news "caused the perplexity and confusion caused in the Roman Senate by the news of the famous defeat of its army at Cannae. One read pain and surprise on the faces of all, and no one uttered a word."[26]

English public opinion became increasingly attentive to the problems raised by the American Revolution. "Public sheets" multiplied on both sides of the ocean. The interpretations they furnished became more and more divergent. According to one gazette, after the fall of Philadelphia, "nothing can equal the present happiness of the inhabitants of that city where one swims in joy and abundance." "But according to contrary news, Philadelphia is deserted and its suburbs present only a scene of desolation and ruin."[27] The *Giornale fiorentino* of February 1778 noted the "general ferment of the British Parliament." A true "fanaticism" moved the American colonists. How could one now hope to defeat them? The "lovers of liberty" followed them, in "three parts of Europe." "We flatter ourselves that they would find partisans even among the English."[28] France appeared increasingly well disposed. "There is practically no longer any doubt that our ministry has finally determined to make a treaty of commerce with the United States of America, and consequently to recognize their independence."[29] How one should move in

[26] *Nuove di diverse corti e paesi*, no. 52, 29 December 1777, pp. 404, 408 (London, 5 December).

[27] *Notizie del mondo*, no. 10, 3 February 1778, p. 74 (London, n.d.).

[28] *Giornale fiorentino*, February 1778, pp. 80, 86. In the January issue this periodical mentioned, on p. 14, an *Atlante dell'America contenente le migliori carte geografiche e topografiche delle principali città, luoghi, fiumi e fortezze del Nuovo Mondo* (Pescia: Tommaso Masi, 1777). This was also an indication of the interest Tuscans felt for developments in America.

[29] *Notizie del mondo*, no. 25, 28 March 1778, p. 197 (Paris, 28 March).

this new reality aroused strong debates in America.[30] But now the shape of the future was becoming fixed. "There is no longer any doubt that France under Louis XVI will become the friend of the thirteen United States of America, as under Henry IV it was of the Seven United Provinces of the Low Countries."[31] But in reality France only "followed the example of England under Queen Elizabeth toward the Seven United Provinces of Holland." It was now the turn of Holland itself, and of Russia, to determine their positions.[32] Franklin, "who more than anyone contributed to the independence of North America, left nothing untried to sustain it."[33] In the summer the Florentine chronicles echoed the "acclamations" with which the treaty with France was greeted in America: "Let the liberty and independence of America perpetuate itself to remote posterity." "The security of slavery is not preferable to liberty, even amid perils." "Let the glorious resistance of the Americans convince all despotisms that it is not possible to subject a people pushed to the resolution of breaking their chains." "Let the free and independent states of America become the refuge of all whom cruel tyrants have taken the pleasure to oppress." "Let the internal enemies of America never enjoy the sweetness of liberty." "Let the American union last to the end of time."[34] "New articles of confederation" had been voted on 5 December 1777 and the *Notizie del mondo* considered them a document "too essential" not to print them in full. There had been opposition, especially in Boston, but these were still the insurgents' most important effort to confront the new situation in which they found themselves at home and abroad.[35]

A testimony of the atmosphere in America in the summer of 1778 came to Florence from Carlo Bellini, a Tuscan and a resident of Virginia, and it was printed in both gazettes of the city.[36]

I am finally a free and an independent man. Due to the liberty and independence of this vast country no one is so base as to have the insolence to think himself superior to another. The only superior is the law, law made by all the people, so that an individual obedient to the law does nothing but obey himself. The legislator himself cannot break the law without making himself unhappy

---

[30] *Nuove di diverse corti e paesi*, no. 12, 22 March 1779, p. 93 (Paris, 8 March).

[31] *Notizie del mondo*, no. 27, 4 April 1778, p. 214 (The Hague, 19 March).

[32] Ibid., no. 33, 25 April 1778, p. 261 (Paris, 7 April).

[33] Ibid., no. 40, 19 May 1778, p. 317 (Paris, 5 May).

[34] Ibid., no. 56, 14 July 1778, pp. 445ff. (Paris, 30 June).

[35] Ibid., no. 42, 26 May 1778, p. 336 (London, n.d.); no. 43, 30 May 1778, p. 344 (London, n.d.); no. 44, 2 June 1778, p. 352 (London, n.d.); no. 45, 6 June 1778, p. 361 (London, n.d.); no. 46, 9 June 1778, p. 368 (London, n.d.).

[36] *Gazzetta universale*, no. 94, 24 November 1778, pp. 752ff., and *Notizie del mondo*, no. 95, 28 November 1778, pp. 780ff. (Florence, 27 November).

and ridiculous. The governor or first magistrate in whom executive power resides is elected by the people: still he cannot do anything without a council of nine persons also elected by the people, and the people united together in an assembly examine, decide, approve, or disapprove according to what is reasonable.

After examining the continual change of magistrates, Bellini went on to the "cruel war" he judged now to be "near its end, thanks to our magnanimous ally and protector of humankind Louis XVI, and to the valor, prudence, and constancy of the American General Washington." "We are three million men who fight for ourselves, for the liberty of our country, our wives, and our children, and we are determined to live in liberty or to die gloriously with arms in our hands, and we detest any who think differently." "I am a common soldier, a noble and glorious occupation! But I am also secretary of this state of Virginia for foreign affairs and professor of modern languages in this University of Williamsburg." The "commander of the Virginia armies" had publicly praised him because, having "barely arrived in the country," he gave himself "voluntarily to defend it as a soldier." Now completely accustomed to Virginia, without having had to pass through "those humiliations that are usual in other climates," he "had managed to buy a house, male and female slaves, horses, cows, and so on." "The revenue of my employments could be calculated at two thousand scudi a year." "This was a small revenue," also because "furniture and other items are at an excessive price." "The money of these lands is only paper for the larger part. . . . This is also used in some of the magnificent capitals of Italy." These were, as one sees, the first impressions and first enthusiasms of an emigré.

It was also significant that in Florence in 1780, falsely identified as Philadelphia, was published "at the expense of the Society of Stecchi and Del Vivo" the Italian version of the work of a French antiquarian and polemicist, Guillaume Emmanuel Joseph Guilhelm de Clermont-Lodève, Baron de Sainte-Croix (he is generally known by this last name), the author of numerous interpretations of obscure elements in religions of antiquity and a student of the federal constitution of the Cretans. The book, which appeared in French in Paris in 1779, was entitled in Tuscan: *On the state and condition of the colonies of ancient peoples*. As in antiquity, in modern times "the scepters of iron" of colonial nations, he said, were destined to be broken "into so many tiny pieces." He openly defended the actions of France, reserving all his animosity for the English. The rebellion against them in North America had become "the cradle of a people in whom it is uncertain which is to be admired more: frugality, customs, probity, prudence, valor, or good administration." Like Pericles, Chatham had tried in vain to oppose the "devouring and convulsive ambition" of his country. "From the fire of your light," he concluded addressing himself to the "proud and unquiet Britains," "from which have emanated rays that have sometimes enlightened the world, now come only flames to incinerate it."[37]

Many unusual and significant aspects of American reality continued to appear in Italian gazettes between the seventies and the eighties. Here, for example, were "the principles and articles of the Constitutional Society of Philadelphia," a true club of the supporters of the Congress.[38] And above all an extensive discussion began in the *Notizie del mondo* in February 1780 on the finances of the United States. "In governments founded on general principles of egalitarian liberty, in which heads of state are the servants of the people and not lords over those from whom they derive their authority, it is the precise duty of the same to inform their fellow citizens of the state of their affairs," making them see "the wisdom of measures taken in public administration."[39] After having furnished the essential information on loans, balances, and so on, the document concluded by reporting that "the expedients of the United States depend on two things, the first is the success of the present revolution, the second is the sufficiency of natural wealth and compensation of the country." The first point, "independence," was "now fixed in destiny." "Is there perhaps any reason to fear that the supreme sovereign of human affairs, after leading us from the land of slavery and across a sea of blood toward the land of liberty and the promised land, would leave the work of our political redemption unachieved . . . ?" The "close alliance" with France, the "friendship with many other nations, and finally the benevolence of all" were secure guarantees for the future.[40]

It is interesting to see how the Americans sought to translate their great hopes into diplomatic language, as if they were forcing themselves

[37] *Dello stato e della storte delle colonie degli antichi popoli, opera nella quale si tratta del governo delle antiche repubbliche ecc., con delle osservazioni su le colonie delle nazioni moderne e la condotta degli inglesi in America* (Philadelphia [Florence: Stecchi and Del Vivo], 1780), pp. 249, 272, 275, 278. See chapter 2, below.

[38] *Notizie del mondo*, no. 68, 24 August 1779, p. 549 (London, 3 August).

[39] Ibid., no. 17, 26 February 1780, p. 131 (Leiden, 11 February). The declaration from which these words were taken was dated 13 September 1779 and signed by President John Jay.

[40] Ibid., no. 20, 7 March 1780, p. 156 (Leiden, 20 February). From the point of view of economics this vision of the American future was anything but discouraging: "Immense deserts . . . await nothing else but to be cultivated . . . vast lakes and rivers . . . only ask to feel the stimulus of industry, and offer themselves to the service of commerce swelling with pride to see built on their banks the buildings and high towers of spacious cities" (ibid., no. 22, 14 March 1780, p. 173 [Leiden, 25 February]).

to find a common language with the reforming monarchies of Europe. Here, for instance, is the reply of Samuel Huntington, president of the Congress, to the ambassador de La Luzerne when he presented his credentials. "The Most Christian King, in appointing himself the protector of the rights of humankind, had to become the protector of a downtrodden people and fly to its assistance. Equity and truth are precious ornaments in the diadem of this monarch, who, awaiting alliance with His Catholic Majesty [Charles III of Spain], has delivered a fatal blow to the common enemy."[41]

But the situation was less straightforward than such words seemed to promise. "Extreme" was "the need for specie in which the United States finds itself."[42] In Philadelphia there were riots caused by the loss in value of paper money. "The taking of Charlestown put the whole United States in a state of greatest consternation." It seemed that the people were "now tired of war, and General Washington was obliged to send 2,000 men to protect the Congress, which had already retired to Connecticut, from the fury of the people who threatened to massacre all its members." The same Marquis de La Luzerne, it was said, was obliged to "flee Philadelphia by night to escape the vengeance of the inhabitants who had sworn his death for having, as is said, suggested that the Congress govern the people with more rigid laws than those of that place."[43] From London the news spread that Washington had "renounced command of the American army," while the people "were in general inclined to make peace with the mother country."[44] From Amsterdam came the news via "a private letter" that Philadelphia, once the most flourishing city of all America, "had now become a place of confusion, and offers little more than a spectacle of disorder and anarchy. . . . Crimes go unpunished. All live as they please, and can abandon themselves to their own passions. In a word, no one is assured for an instant of what he possesses, or that in the next moment he will not become prey to the stronger or more daring."[45] Some days earlier the *Gazzetta universale* reported that "the American army is much diminished, the remainder is malcontent and badly paid, and the credit of the nation is ruined."[46]

There were many efforts to calm the waters and to restore tone and

[41] Ibid., no. 22, 14 March 1780, p. 171 (Philadelphia, 18 December).

[42] Ibid., no. 49, 17 June 1780, p. 385 (Paris, 2 June).

[43] Ibid., no. 56, 11 July 1780, p. 445 (Hamburg, 27 June). The communication was taken from the *Courier d'Europe* of 19 April. See also *La gazzetta di Milano*, no. 29, 19 July 1780 (Hamburg, 30 June).

[44] *Notizie del mondo*, no. 58, 18 July 1780, p. 459 (London, 29 June).

[45] Ibid., no. 70, 29 August 1780, p. 556 (Amsterdam, 14 August).

[46] *Gazzetta universale*, no. 64, 8 August 1780, p. 507 (London, 20 July).

vigor to the actions of the Americans. Washington and Rochambeau emphasized the collaboration between the Americans and the French. La Fayette in the province of Connecticut issued a proclamation "by order of the king."[47] "Madame Washington," wife "of the American general of that name," appealed to the "pure patriotism" of American women.

Disdaining the yoke of a tyrannical government, we will participate in the grandeur of those reputable queens who have carried the scepters of the greatest kingdoms with so much splendor, the Bathildes [queen of the Franks, wife of Clovis II], Elizabeths, Catherines, who have extended the empire of liberty, have reigned with moderation and broken chains of slavery forged by tyrants in times of ignorance and barbarity. We have before our eyes the recent example of Spanish women who have contributed goods to provide the monarchy with the means for making war. That sovereign is a friend of the French; they are our allies. We must also remember that a Frenchwoman lighted the flame of patriotism in her compatriots, that is, the maid of Orléans who drove the ancestors of those same English, whose odious yoke we have broken, from the kingdom of France, and whom we must now drive from our continent.

To the "brave Americans" she recommended "less luxury" and reminded them of their "generous sisters" who had renounced the use of tea, "however tasty it was to their palates, rather than receive it from our persecutors."[48]

The attacks on Washington still did not cease. He was accused of being a "dictator," the "Tarquin of Congress," "an astute Nicodemite." "He attempts to establish his power over the ruins of our old king, like Cromwell, but more cleverly than he."[49] Such internal conflicts left large traces even in the Tuscan press and in that of other Italian states, as we have seen with the gazette of Venice. The last year of war was followed with particular attention, as much in internal politics as in its battles, above all the naval ones, which at the end seemed again to leave in doubt the victory of independence.[50]

---

[47] Ibid., no. 91, 11 November 1780, p. 718 (Paris, 24 October).

[48] *Nuove di diverse corti e paesi*, no. 18, 30 April 1781, pp. 140ff. (Philadelphia, 20 February). See *Notizie del mondo*, no. 35, 1 May 1781, p. 276 (Amsterdam, 16 April), which says this letter was "read in all the churches of Virginia." On "Madame Washington" and the "American women," see also the *Notizie del mondo [V.]*, no. 76, 27 September 1780, p. 610 (Amsterdam, 14 September), and 28 April 1781, p. 268 (London, 13 April). *Le politique hollandais*, the weekly of A. M. Cerisier published in Amsterdam, noted that "there is nothing comparable in this sublime and delicate eulogy to the august sovereign of Russia, written by women and citizens incapable of flattery" (vol. 1, no. 10, 16 April 1781, p. 159).

[49] *Notizie del mondo*, no. 35, 1 May 1781, p. 278 (Amsterdam, 16 April).

[50] See, for example, the verses of Compagnoni on the victory of Admiral Rodney: ". . . tutto in lui sta d'Inghilterra il fato / . . . Salve, o Rodney! A te tutto già cede / e

In 1783 it was time to give an accounting of the seven long years of war and to confront the difficult period opening before the United States. "The war," one read in the *Notizie del mondo* in June 1783, "has cost America 80 thousand men, a considerable portion of whom have perished in prisons and casements aboard vessels."[51] A year later the account appeared even more tragic. "The population of the United States of America is notably diminished; of the 3,137,869 inhabitants counted in 1775, in the census taken by order of Congress in January 1784 there are only 2,369,300."[52]

Desolation and misery contrasted with the extraordinary victories America had won in the realm of ideas and hopes. There were many sacrifices, but the United States had nonetheless succeeded in giving to themselves, and maintaining, a constitution "that has added the external strength of a monarchy to the internal benefits of a republican government," to cite the words of a small and vivacious Florentine journal at the end of 1782. The words of Raynal might now séem "vague declamations."[53] The "great revolution" of America had succeeded. A little later, at the beginning of 1783, another, more important Florentine journal, the *Corrispondenza universale*, which was born from a French model provided by Brissot de Warville but was largely compiled by Italian collaborators, started its first issue with a long article on *L'Indipendenza americana*. "A new sovereignty is now established in the New World. . . . To this spectacle all friends of truth feel their eyes fill with delicious tears and their hearts rise with joy." It was now a question "of investigating the causes of this strange singularity, if one can thus call the emancipation of a land populated with philosopher citizens." It had originated in an error of calculation. "In the beginning England, proud of the revolutions of its own country, did not see all the elements of peril and danger in the storm that threatened its distant possessions." The repression had been carried out "with the slowness usual in lands calling themselves free." "To the public spirit that reigns in England more than in other nations of Europe was joined a party spirit, perhaps the first

l'imperio del mar Londra riprende" (. . . in him rests the fate of England / . . . Hail, O Rodney! All cedes to thee / and London regains its rule of the sea) (*Memorie enciclopediche*, no. 25, August 1782, p. 208).

[51] *Notizie del mondo*, no. 48, 17 June 1783, p. 381 (Philadelphia, 12 April).

[52] *Notizie del mondo*, no. 48, 17 June 1784, p. 181 (London, 21 May). For a modern vision of these problems, see Jim Potter, "The Growth of Population in America, 1700–1860," in David Victor Glass and David Edward Charles Eversley, *Population in History: Essays in Historical Demography* (Chicago: Aldine, 1965), pp. 630ff.

[53] *L'osservatore. Opera periodica da servire di continuazione degli 'Annali politici, civili e letterari del secolo decimoottavo del Sig. Linguet.' Tradotto dal francese con aggiunte per uso degli italiani* (1782), vol. 1, no. 2, p. 157.

limb of a republic." The soldiers of England were not automatons. "The influence of the constitution is so strong that it extends to the troops . . . the English soldier preserves a passion for political liberty which is difficult to imagine in our land." The corruption, luxury, and gallantry with which the English had recently been infected by French and Italian models had done the rest. England had ended up demonstrating that it was incapable of arresting the Americans' desire for independence.[54] The article was signed R. (Ristori?) and was substituted for the text of the French original, attributed to "a writer now known to all of Europe, perhaps more for his misfortunes than for his literary talents," that is, Linguet.[55] In the following issue the *Corrispondenza univerale* provided an *Idea generale delle Tredici provincie americane* asserting that "these great revolutions of liberty are so many precious lessons for despots. . . . This is the source of the vivid interest that makes wars of liberty arise among us all. It was this, one must confess, that inspired us with the Americans. Our imagination is inflamed in their favor." Would these "three million persons, including four hundred thousand blacks," be capable in the future of resisting the temptation of luxury and conquest, of inequality, even among different religious groups?"[56] In number 3, the *Corrispondenza universale* seemed for a moment to let itself be overtaken by doubts, discouragement, and a sense of uselessness, even in the victory it attributed to the Americans. Uncertainty clouded the world when the cannons finally stopped sounding. But not even then could one forget that the Americans had renewed "the example, now long lost, except among the Corsicans, of a nation fighting for its liberty."[57] Some heartening news still appeared in the gazette: "The new republic is being re-

[54] *Corrispondenza universale in ogni genere di letteratura. Opera periodica scritta da una società di letterati oltremontani* (1783), no. 1, pp. 8ff.

[55] Ibid., p. 12n.

[56] Ibid., no. 2, pp. 51ff. This article recalls, and here and there translates, the *Révolution de l'Amérique by the Abbé Raynal* (London: Lockyer Davis, 1781), pp. 174ff.: "These great revolutions of liberty are lessons for all despots. . . . This is the source of the vivid interest which engenders wars of liberty in us all. That is what inspired us in the Americans. Our imagination was aroused by them. We associated ourselves with their victories and with their defeats." Even the figures, in rounded form, are taken from this work, p. 180. We find a hymn to Pennsylvania in the first issue of the Florentine *Corriere europeo*, 1782, pp. 62ff.: "This song of the land where humanity, faith, liberty, concord, and equality have been in refuge for more than 300 years. . . ." "The princes of the north," looking at it, should have had the courage to abolish "slavery in their own lands, or to give peasants at least their personal liberty." "Why ever do they not hear the cry of humanity which invites them to this glorious act of beneficence? And with what right do they bury in odious servitude against their best interests the most industrious part of their subjects when they have before their eyes the example of these Quakers who have granted liberty to all their Negro slaves?"

[57] Ibid., no. 3, p. 69.

populated," one read in the spring of 1783 in one of the Florentine sheets, "by numerous colonists who arrive from Poland, Prussia, Germany, Holland, France, Italy, the Antilles, and the Spanish mainland." "It will some day become formidable to Europe and perhaps give laws even to its liberators. . . . The activity of the Americans is surprising."[58]

In general, however, the news in the gazettes diverted the attention of readers to the difficulties that the Americans had to confront daily in the first months of their conquered liberty. It was necessary to construct "strongholds" against the aborigines.[59] As was reported from Pennsylvania in the *Nuove di diverse corti e paesi*, "the savages continue to infest the frontier of that province with attacks and massacres, and lately they have massacred two families." It was indispensable "to wage a campaign, to enter their territory, to erect good strongholds against them; this is the only way to provide for the security of our frontiers."[60] The economic situation remained difficult. The gazette of Lugano reported letters "from Mr. Morris, intendant of finance of the United States of America, sent to the president of the Congress." "If these letters have sufficient authenticity to be believed, the affairs of that republic are in a very critical state."[61] Word came from London that European merchants should not delude themselves. "Blinded by enthusiasm," they let themselves be seduced in vain by "the deceptive prospect of a quick fortune" in the "young republic."[62] Word came from Philadelphia that difficulties were in fact not lacking. "We must struggle for some time still to consolidate the young fortunes of our republic." Many were "the insidious and hidden practices through which attempts are made to stop the course of our prosperity."[63] The political news was no better. In an *Estratto di una lettera di Filadelfia* dated 21 July came the report that "dissention has been introduced into our states, and it will not be easy to overcome the difficulties that have arisen." The army was restive. Taxes weighed heavily. "The Americans who have taken arms against the mother country so as not to pay some miserable taxes, now that they have become independent do not wish to hear of paying higher ones."[64] Already in September 1783 the discontent had taken a political form that could not help but interest Italians. From Paris came echoes of doubts regarding the actions and words of Washington. Had not perhaps Julius Caesar, Cromwell, "and other similar astute men" ended by

[58] *Notizie del mondo*, no. 41, 24 May 1783, p. 328 (London, 1 May).

[59] Ibid., no. 57, 19 July 1783, p. 453 (Philadelphia, 17 May).

[60] *Nuove di diverse corti e paesi*, no. 28, 14 July 1783, p. 214 (Philadelphia, 20 May).

[61] Ibid., no. 20, 19 May 1783, p. 150 (London, 2 May).

[62] Ibid., no. 23, 9 June 1783, p. 174 (London, 20 May).

[63] Ibid., no. 26, 30 June 1783, p. 199 (Philadelphia, 9 April).

[64] *Notizie del mondo*, no. 72, 9 September 1783, p. 573 (Philadelphia, 21 July).

"renouncing the command in order to induce the troops to force them to resume it?" But personal ambition was not sufficient to explain the words and attitudes of Washington. "He is one of the most zealous partisans of Congress, and believes that without the federative union of all thirteen states the American republic will either go to its ruin or certainly not achieve the degree of power to which it seems destined." He still encountered strong opposition, above all among Virginians. Some thought the rivalries and contrasts were new proof of the political vitality of the new state. "In republics, peace and harmony, they say, are a bad sign and indicate a rapid progress toward despotism." "To confirm this strange and unprecedented proposition they cite the example of the Dutch." But the experience of Italians seemed to prove the opposite. It was sufficient to think of the "most serene liberty of Venice, which was able, with high prudence, to keep its republic pure in the calamitous period for Italy of the cruel factions of the Guelfs and Ghibellines, Whites and Blacks, and it had continued to flourish for many centuries while almost all other Italian republics went miserably to their ruin."[65] The appeals of Washington seemed to confirm a similar conviction. "When in republics sovereign liberty degenerates to license and anarchy, then tyrants . . . make themselves absolute rulers of the state." To "ensure the enjoyment of the fruits of the revolution and the basic advantages of civil society," a "free government was needed, pure and uncorrupted."[66]

But was this possible for the "confederated republic" that had emerged from the long war? Many doubted it in the autumn of 1783. "Given the small accord that reigns among the United States and their jealousy of the authority of the Congress, if the system does not change, soon the thirteen United States will become instead 30, 40, or 100, all disunited, as were the ancient republics of Greece and Italy, of which, as one of our gracious poets said,

> Ogni porta sconnessa e rovinata
> Scrivera Libertà sulla facciata.[67]

Continually, in fact, "the authority of the American Congress" was "contested in different states: its resolution to impose a customs tax of 5 per cent on all European merchandise was rejected by Virginia, by the two Carolinas, and by Georgia, which refused to subscribe to it."[68]

The need to reconsider the fundamental constitutions of the new

---

[65] Ibid., no. 73, 13 September 1783, p. 583 (Paris, 26 August).

[66] Ibid., no. 75, 20 September 1783, p. 597 (Philadelphia, 26 August).

[67] "Every separate and ruined door / will write Liberty on its portal" (ibid., no. 80, 7 October 1783, p. 640 [London, 19 September]).

[68] *Nuove di diverse corti e paesi*, no. 4, 26 January 1784, p. 29 (London, 6 January).

state was increasingly evident. The English example was placed at the center of many debates. Should the future American Congress model itself on the British Parliament, in the form in which English radicals had wanted and hoped to reform it? The replies were generally in the negative. "It appears," one reads in a communication from New York, "that the Americans are resolved to make a great difference between the Congress and the Parliament of England, and between American and English electors. They want those represented to have a direct influence over those who represent them."[69] The gazette of Lugano announced the following in October: "United America has finally fixed the system of legislation by adopting a Declaration of Rights that forms the basis of the particular governments of the respective states . . . composed by order of Mr. George Mason, one of the most prominent citizens of Virginia."[70] The text was taken up by the gazette of Venice, which published the first eight articles of the Declaration, promising that it would be "continued." But for a reason unknown to us nothing is found in the following issues.[71] Two months later, at the beginning of 1784, the Florentine *Notizie del mondo* published a *Supplimento* to provide its readers with a fundamental document on these debates, an *Estratto del nuovo codice delle costituzione de' Tredici Stati Uniti dell'America Settentrionale.* "The new empire born in North America from the Confederation of the Thirteen United Provinces certainly merits the attention of Europeans, and since legislation is the soul and first mover of any regulated government, for anyone who wants to understand the news of a state fully, it is above all necessary to examine its current laws." Thus was presented that collection of American constitutions edited by Franklin, which Filangieri received, and that the Neapolitan journal *Scelta miscellanea* had quickly reviewed, taking its words from the *Notizie del mondo.* This collection was, as we see from this example as well, the most important intermediary between American political life and that of Italy in these years. It is enough to look at the documents furnished by the *Notizie del mondo* to understand the vivid interest with which they might have been read in Tuscany. "The first care of American legislators, or of those bodies charged with legislative power, has been to establish and fix the natural and civil rights of the people clearly and invariably." The articles of the constitution of Massachusetts exemplified these principles. "It is necessary to state that in the confederated colonies there is

---

[69] *Notizie del mondo,* no. 85, 25 October 1783, p. 667 (New York, 7 September). See Edmund S. Morgan, "The Problem of Popular Sovereignty," in *Aspects of American Liberty,* pp. 95ff.

[70] *Nuove di diverse corti e paesi,* no. 41, 13 October 1783, p. 318 (Philadelphia, 20 August).

[71] *Notizie del mondo [V.],* no. 90, 8 November 1783 (Philadelphia, 20 August).

no religion that one can call dominant . . . (Article 1)." "The idea of a man born a magistrate, a legislator, or a justice is absurd and against nature (Article 6)." "It is established that Englishmen are judged by their peers and the United States have wisely preserved this system (Article 11)." "Freedom of the press is essential to ensure the liberty of the state, and thus it cannot ever in any guise be restricted (Article 16)." A significant comment followed: "The government of a free people does not fear being censured or examined; on the contrary, it invites everyone to aid it with their reason. The more that is written on this point, the easier it will be to arrive at the end that is the happiness of society." Massachusetts thought "piety, justice, moderation, temperance, industry, and frugality" were all indispensable to "preserve the advantages of liberty and maintain a free government (Article 18)." The constitutional mechanisms were illustrated in detail, not without emphasizing the common and different elements with respect to English legislation, and explaining where the American states were in agreement or disagreement. Thus it reported Article 27 of the constitution of New York, which was intended to guarantee the honesty of contracts with indigents, and mentioned the initiative Philadelphia took to establish "censors who would watch over the conduct of different magistrates." South Carolina had excluded from its legislature "tax collectors, financiers . . . bloodsuckers of the people." "Clergymen, of whatever denomination, cannot enter any of the councils of legislation." A sense of profound admiration emerged from this minute examination of American constitutional life. "It would certainly be difficult to take more precautions to ensure for this new people a liberty acquired with the price of so much blood." The Americans had the wisdom to leave open the way to future reforms; thus, "the legislation of America will follow the course of political and moral developments, that of knowledge and opinion. In an enlightened century America will not be governed, like the majority of European states, by laws made of cobwebs from barbaric and dark ages."[72]

Washington's letter of farewell, which received widespread attention in Italian gazettes, symbolized the beginning of actions and political ceremonies intended to place their future into the hands of the American people. The memory of past sufferings showed the need for and the possibility of a solid and rational system, capable of confronting the greatest difficulties, just as the victorious army of the republic had arisen among "the most extreme miseries." "Who has ever seen a disciplined army formed suddenly from men entirely new to military operations?" And who would have believed that "men from different parts

---

[72] *Notizie del mondo*, no. 2, 6 January 1784, pp. 21ff., and no. 3, 10 January 1784, pp. 33ff., *Supplimento. Estratto del nuovo codice delle costituzioni de' Tredici Stati Uniti dell'America Settentrionale.*

of the continent, predisposed by habit and education to quarrel with and scorn one another, would become in a minute a society of brothers united by patriotism?" By retiring from active life and returning to his farm Washington showed the exemplary value for the future of "such a blustering revolution."[73] He also dismissed the "mistrust of those who suspected him of designing to aspire to a permanent dictatorship and to make himself the enemy of American liberty, after having been its defender."[74] "In a tavern in New York the principal officers of the army" gathered to take their last farewell from their adored commander Washington. "The scene was most moving. The passions of human nature were in tender agitation in that moment, which was as painful as it was interesting."[75]

The extremely simple and homely ceremonies with which Washington took his farewell were transformed, across the ocean, into an extraordinary festival symbolic of the new republican spirit. "In the great hall where the entire body of legislation was united there rested on a majestic throne the book of the laws, or rather the constitutions of America collected into this book, as a majestic sovereign, to which all took an oath of fealty. This was covered with a precious jeweled crown. The session ended, during which General Washington took leave of his command of the army; this great man took the crown, went to a balcony in the hall, and broke it into a thousand pieces, throwing them to the large crowd gathered to view the ceremony, almost as if to announce that beyond the book of the law they would have no other king. Doubtless the ancient history of past and present republics offers nothing comparable with the grandeur and magnificence of this ceremony."[76] The gazette of Venice also brought to light the exceptional quality of this "festival of liberty" and spoke of the "prodigious crowd that waited on the plain" to admire the actions of Washington.[77]

---

[73] *Nuove di diverse corti e paesi*, no. 3, 19 January 1784, pp. 19ff. (Paris, 5 January).

[74] Ibid., no. 10, 8 March 1784, p. 77 (from United America, 16 December).

[75] The *Address to Congress on resigning his commission*, of 23 December 1783, is a description of the dinner that followed, in which the participants were so absorbed in the "pleasures of imagination" that "not a soul got drunk," and also of the ball where the ladies had the pleasure "of touching him." See *The Writings of George Washington*, ed. John C. Fitzpatrick (Washington, D.C.: U.S. Government Printing Office, 1938), vol. 27, pp. 284ff.

[76] *Notizie del mondo*, no. 25, 27 March 1784, p. 229 (Paris, 9 March).

[77] *Notizie del mondo [V.]*, no. 26, 31 March 1784 (Paris, 13 March). One is tempted to compare these strange fables, and true republican legends that flourished during the war and the American reconstruction (and it would be interesting one day to know the route they followed in reaching Florence and Venice), with modern narratives of this concluding act of the life of Washington as general. After having narrated in detail the disorders and conflicts born from the discontent of the army, James Thomas Flexner writes: "Washington advanced slowly to Annapolis, where Congress was now sitting. The question how to receive His Excellency's resignation threw Congress into an agony of dignity, all the more

The egalitarian conclusion that for the moment seemed to prevail in the long controversy raised by the creation of an honorific order among officers of the republican army, the Order of Cincinnatus, also emphasized the fundamental principles for which the long years of war had been fought and won. "This institution, thought appropriate for the in-

fierce because (due to a continuing lack of quorum) it was otherwise impotent." "On the appointed day, December 23, 1783, Washington was ushered before Congress with appointed formality. His physical eye saw a tiny, powerless body of some twenty men, hardly worth, Napoleon would have thought, the whiff of grapeshot that would so easily have sent them flying; but in his mind's eye, Washington saw gathered before him the power that was to grow down the centuries, the dignity of a great nation. Bowing in all humility as the tall and short politicians took off their hats, he held in a trembling hand the paper on which he had written his address. In order to read, he was forced to steady his right hand with his left" (James Thomas Flexner, *George Washington in the American Revolution* [Boston: Little, Brown, 1967], p. 526). Douglas Southall Freeman writes: "A little before 12 he started for the State House and, on the hour, presented himself with two aides at the chamber where the Congress was sitting. . . . Escorted by Charles Thomson, the general entered the room . . . nineteen or twenty members only were present, seated and with their hats on. Washington passed among them and took a seat pointed out to him. . . . Doors of the chamber and of the gallery then were opened; favored ladies quickly filled the gallery; public servants, former officers and Maryland's most eminent citizens packed closely along the wall. . . ." After having cited the words of Washington and described the emotion that struck him in pronouncing them, he concludes:

Mifflin [president of the Congress] then answered on behalf of Congress in a brief, finely phrased tribute to Washington's leadership and constant respect for civil authority. When he had finished in about three minutes [and in a note, 'The answer is in approximately 350 words'], Thompson ['senior official' of the Congress] came down from his position at the President's elbow and handed Washington a copy of the answer. Washington took it and bowed once more to the President and delegates, who uncovered again but did not lower their heads. Then, followed by his former aides, George Washington, Esq., walked from the chamber. A minute later, after he had stepped into an anteroom, the spectators were dismissed, and, when they had left, Congress formally adjourned. Washington thereupon reentered the place of meeting and, completely the master of himself again, shook hands and said goodbye to each delegate (Douglas Southall Freeman, *George Washington: A Biography*, vol. 5, *Victory with the Help of France* [New York: Charles Scribner's Sons, 1952], pp. 475ff.).

Before this cinematographic precision and exactness, disturbed only by a shadow of recurring anti-parliamentarianism, one is tempted to prefer the eighteenth-century myth of the shattered crown, which flows out of the whole long republican tradition of the British world.

F. Mazzei, in his *Recherches historiques et politiques*, pt. 4, p. 124n (see also pp. 117ff.), protested against this fable of the crown, which he had read in the *Histoire impartiale des événemens militaires et politiques de la dernière guerre dans les quatre parties du monde*, by M. de L. [Pierre de Longchamps] (Paris: Chez la veuve Duchesne, 1785, published in three volumes, and then continued in two augmented editions, the third of which was published in 1787). The episode is not found in the first edition but rather on page 185 of the continuation. Mazzei had already criticized this work in the *Mercure de France* on 11 March 1786. See Edoardo Tortarolo, *Illuminismo e rivoluzioni. Biografia politica di Filippo Mazzei* (Università di Turino, Dipartimento di Storia: Franco Angeli, 1986), and id., "Filippo Mazzei e la rivoluzione Americana: Alcuni documenti inediti," *R. stor. ital.*, year 93, fasc. 1 (March 1781): 353ff. (I would like to thank the author for the assistance he gave me in this work on the relations between America and Italy in the Revolutionary period.) See *The Papers of Thomas Jefferson*, vol. 10, p. 580, letter to Jean Chas, Paris, 7 December 1786.

troduction in the new republic of a kind of patriciate, has greatly offended the idea of equality presented as the basis of the Constitution and the genius of the nation."[78] As the gazette of Lugano said, the Americans expected to obey "the noble aim of equality which, having to form the basis of the new republic, would be offended and lost if a place for personal distinctions were made." Their decision was new proof of the "wisdom of these new republicans" who had pledged themselves "to

[78] *Notizie del mondo*, no. 41, 22 May 1784, p. 357 (London, 30 April). See *Nuove di diverse corti e paesi*, no. 1, 5 January 1784, p. 3 (Paris, 26 December), and *Notizie del mondo*, no. 57, 17 July 1784, p. 484 (Paris, 29 June). Some of the most important political men of the revolution were strongly opposed to the Order of Cincinnatus and particularly to the hereditary arrangements it wanted to establish. Among them were John and Samuel Adams, Thomas Jefferson, and John Jay. See Edward Erskine Hume, "Early Opposition to the Cincinnati," *Americana* 30, no. 4 (October 1936): 597ff. The controversy was public and soon crossed the borders of the nascent republic. The pamphlet of the judge Aedanus Burke, which appeared in Philadelphia in 1783, was translated and commented on by Honoré de Mirabeau. The writers and thinkers led by Condorcet, among whom was Filippo Mazzei, were hostile to the Cincinnati, whereas many French military men who had taken part in the war of the insurgents were in favor of it. The list of their names represents, as has been said, "the very élite of the French nobility." See Edward Erskine Hume, *General Washington's Correspondence Concerning the Society of the Cincinnati* (Baltimore: Johns Hopkins Press, 1941), p. xix. In the work cited one finds an ample documentation of the atmosphere in which this order was born and developed. Particularly interesting are the letters of Chevalier de La Luzerne to the Conte de Vergennes dated 14 February and 12 April 1784, in which the Cincinnati were accused of being a group of nobles who wanted to establish a feudal system and a patriciate similar to that from which Catiline, Sulla, Caesar, and even Tiberius and Nero had emerged. In vain they were compared with Freemasons, among whom there was no primogeniture, who did not involve themselves with affairs of state, and who did not constitute a nobility. The order was, in short, considered contrary to republican principles and perilous to liberty. "I think these fears are not chimerical," La Luzerne concluded (ibid., pp. 77ff.). Washington proposed important changes in the statutes and explained in detail his motives in a very interesting document, a kind of confession of the state of his mind and of that of his companions in the war. "In the moment of triumph and separation," he said, in the last both "pleasing" and "melancholy" scenes of their military drama, penetrated by sentiments "which can be more easily conceived than described," they had naturally been motivated by a desire to perpetuate their friendship in the future. It was "extremely natural" for this state of mind to be "perpetuated by our posterity to the remotest ages." "With these impressions and with such sentiments, we candidly confess we signed the institution." There remained the fact that it could indicate "an unjustifiable line of discrimination between our descendants and the rest of the community." They had presumed too much in assuming "the guardianship of the liberties of our country." They should not in the future arouse any anxiety or worry in those "whose happiness it is our interest and duty to promote." Even assistance to the needy, which had been proposed, should be exercised in such a way as to eliminate any doubts in the minds of fellow citizens. (Ibid., pp. 172ff. The text had been prepared by John Dickinson of Pennsylvania, Henry Lee of Virginia, and David Humphreys of Connecticut.) In reality these resolutions, voted in the Philadelphia meeting of May 1784, were not accepted. One after another the different states showed their willingness to maintain the principle of inheritance. The French section of the order was also split on this matter. And thus the Order of Cincinnatus survived the egalitarian tempest that saluted its birth.

maintain and perpetuate that liberty whose importance they learned in the school of hardships suffered in the long and difficult war they sustained."[79]

These symbols and affirmations of principle could not hide the need to reconsider the entire edifice of the American constitution, but rather accentuated it with their lack of precision. Fortunately, it was said in Philadelphia, "the different states . . . had not tied their hands with indiscreet obligations or absurd oaths: they have always reserved the right to make any modifications and improvements that circumstances and new combinations might render necessary."[80] From Philadelphia, by way of The Hague, arrived in Venice echoes of the increasingly animated constitutional debate. Virginia, Carolina, Massachusetts, "together with Pennsylvania," requested that "executive power" "be given to General Washington." This was a "necessary revolution in their government," which nonetheless encountered strong opposition. "The other provinces, always wanting equality, are obstinate in preserving the prerogative that is the delight and, in a certain sense, even the recompense of liberty." Equality and liberty were difficult to preserve in a "dispersed society" like that of America, spread over a vast space.[81] The news that came from America confirmed each state's tenacious defense of its own laws and interests. Thus, the same news from Philadelphia reported at the end of 1784 that "the constitution of that republic" would remain "as it was established when it was founded."[82] Suggestions that came from outside, even from Paris, were little appreciated. "The Abbé Mably has been hardly applauded by Americans for his work on the legislation of the thirteen United States of America. His book has been banned and publicly torn after he had received a thousand invectives from the common people, and the author has been hanged in effigy."[83] In the summer of 1785 in Madrid the dissolution of the young state was said to be certain. "There reigns in the United States a terrible discord. They would have us think that the union is already broken and that some provinces, especially Connecticut, seek assistance from Great Britain; that Carolina is also about to revolt and join with the inhabitants of the region of Vermont" (who in fact rebelled).[84]

These conflicts became more bitter with the difficult economic situation, which was often emphasized in the Italian gazettes. "The most

[79] *Nuove di diverse corti e paesi*, no. 29, 19 July 1784, p. 229 (Paris, 9 July).

[80] *Notizie del mondo*, no. 40, 18 May 1784, p. 347 (Philadelphia, 12 March).

[81] *Notizie del mondo [V.]*, no. 25, 27 March 1784 (The Hague, 10 March).

[82] *Notizie del mondo*, no. 7, 22 January 1785, p. 50 (London, 31 December).

[83] Ibid., no. 11, 5 February 1785, p. 83 (Paris, 21 January).

[84] Ibid., no. 70, 30 August 1785, p. 555 (Madrid, 9 August).

recent news from North America," it was said in a communication that not by chance came from England, "indicates that the affairs of these new republics are in a deplorable state, caused by the new form of government and by their independence. Trade in several items is much diminished."[85] The news that arrived in Venice from Paris was clearly better. "The actual state of United America," it said in June 1784, "contradicts the prediction of those who only see in that form of government a mere jumble, if not anarchy and confusion, and predict that the Americans, finally arrived at independence, will shortly destroy themselves. Letters from that part of the world announce only harmony, well-being, and happiness. Commerce flourishes and American ports are frequented by ships of all Europe. The Congress, for its part, has been busy up to now with regulations to enlarge the Confederation."[86] A vivacious correspondent some months earlier had described Philadelphia as being in search of new business. "The city is at least double the size of Dijon or Tours, but the streets are precisely as the Abbé Raynal described them. The people do not seem to me very enthusiastic about their independence: they don't complain of it, but at the same time they don't eulogize it."[87] Optimistic tones, however, became rarer and rarer as months passed without the economic and constitutional problems being confronted or resolved.

At the beginning of 1787 a correspondent from Boston described "this province that all, and particularly the Italians, have believed most suited to heaping up riches through commerce" as now miserable and unhappy. Agriculture was "exposed to the pillage of the savages." There was little state protection. "Congress prolongs discussion to the extent that even legislation regarding commerce has not been approved." Should one perhaps conclude that America was not in a position to live separate from England or "without the support of an allied power?"[88] Soon after economic problems and threats of civil war were pointed out in a letter from New York.[89] In August, from London, it was said that "great confusion reigns in Congress."[90] The problem of slavery contin-

---

[85] Ibid., no. 12, 12 February 1785, p. 99 (London, 21 January).

[86] *Notizie del mondo [V.]*, no. 57, 17 July 1784 (Paris, 27 June).

[87] Ibid., no. 44, 2 June 1784, "Estratto d'una lettera di Filadelfia del 5 aprile."

[88] *Notizie del mondo*, no. 16, 24 February 1787, p. 128 (Livorno, 21 February), "Estratto di lettera scritta da Boston in America in data del 2 dicembre dell'anno scorso." The same report, with some variations, is found in the *Gazzetta universale*, no. 16, 24 February 1787, p. 126 (Livorno, 21 February).

[89] *Notizie del mondo*, no. 20, 10 March 1787, p. 155 (London, 15 February), "Estratto di una lettera della Nuova York." See no. 32, 21 April 1787 (London, 30 March): "The discontent of the people is at its height and there is much fear of a general revolt."

[90] *Gazzetta universale*, no. 63, 7 August 1787, p. 498 (London, 20 June).

ued to divide the Americans. The Quakers gave "proof of virtue and generosity." But "South Carolina and Georgia, on the other hand, show the will to be regulated by the opposite ideas."[91] This question could not be avoided. "It seems that the European nations, which pride themselves on their culture and enlightenment above that of other people of the earth, cannot find a commerce so infamous or contrary to humanity as that of black Africans." But now something worse was invented: a commerce of European children sold in America. The government of Ireland had to intervene.[92] As for the general situation, rumors of a kind of defeat of the United States were not lacking. "The rumor has spread that the Americans have proposed to Great Britain that it permit them to return to its rule: the news is not surprising . . . since anarchy reigns among them; the small credit they enjoy among the other nations of Europe, and the almost total destruction of their trade, has much disgusted them with their independence."[93]

In October 1787 a "letter of our fellow citizen," published in the *Gazzetta universale*, gave the first news of the convention in Philadelphia. "In the month of May there will be an assembly in Philadelphia to which all the states are to send their representatives. This will establish a new plan of government, statutes, and commerce for the United States." But our fellow citizen was skeptical: "Since the results of this assembly must be approved by all the states individually, it is believed that it will not accomplish anything."[94] In November it was announced nonetheless that in Philadelphia "deputies of the different provinces resolved that the Congress would be regarded as a true National Assembly, that an army and a navy would be established, and that taxes would be levied to meet current expenses."[95] Before the end of the year the projected new constitution advanced by the Congress was published.[96] "The people in general applaud the new code of legislation compiled by the Convention in Philadelphia," even if commerce continued to languish, and there were persistent rumors of an "approaching war with the savages."[97] What dangers threatened but were averted appears clearly from the news circulating in Europe before the end of 1787: "Newsmen bring the

[91] Ibid., no. 54, 7 July 1787, p. 426 (London, 15 June).

[92] Ibid., no. 55, 10 July 1787, p. 435 (London, 22 June).

[93] *Notizie del mondo*, no. 84, 20 October 1787, p. 667 (London, 28 September).

[94] *Gazzetta universale*, no. 83, 16 October 1787, p. 664 (Livorno, n.d.), "Fine dell'articolo di lettera di un nostro concittadino scritta ultimamente dalla Nuova York."

[95] Ibid., no. 92, 17 November 1787, p. 730 (London, 30 October).

[96] Ibid., no. 95, 27 November 1787, p. 755 (London, 7 November), and no. 96, 1 December 1787, p. 763 (London, 9 November).

[97] *Notizie del mondo*, no. 97, 4 December 1787, p. 770 (London, 16 November).

interesting rumors that General Washington has been named dictator of the American States for four years."[98]

The next year the situation was clarified. "We hear from America," one read in the *Gazzetta universale*, "that the new government established in the United States begins to have support. Eleven states have formally consented to the new agreement. North Carolina is the only one that has refused to adopt it. . . . Despite this appearance of success, the partisans of the proposed government, who are known by the name of *Federalists*, must still overcome infinite difficulties before executing it." Washington had been made president "and he will be given privileges and rights very similar to those of the king of Great Britain, except, however, that the office will be elective and cannot be held by the same person for more than four years."[99] The American Revolution presented itself not as a simple vindication of liberty and equality, but as a point of encounter between these principles and British tradition. The news, at the beginning of 1789, was good, and confirmed "the prediction of wise men of the consolidation and growth of that republic." The harvest had been so good that part of it had been exported. "The low cost of labor has contributed wonderfully to the establishment of various manufactures." It was thus true that "only free peoples have solidly increased their industry and commerce. . . . The execution of Charles I and the immortal navigation acts can surely be regarded as the foundation of British greatness . . . industry is the only barrier against the absolute power of the great."[100] In the spring of 1789 there were reports in The Hague "of the happy provinces of America now that those brave republicans are at the point of unanimously adopting the new form of federal government preserving the individual liberty of each province, which will give them more prompt and more vigorous attention of their defense against common enemies."[101] And by way of London news arrived from New York that the "old Confederation of the States of America had been replaced by the new Federal body . . . thus giving more activity to the strength of the association as a whole."[102] A few issues later it was said that "the party of the anti-Federalists was losing influence in America in measure as the new federal constitution takes effect."[103] Now "the new legislative assembly of the American Confederation is in full operation." John Adams, the vice president, gave a speech

[98] *Gazzetta universale*, no. 102, 22 December 1787, p. 815 (Augsburg, 12 December).
[99] Ibid., no. 92, 15 November 1788, p. 731 (London, 24 October).
[100] Ibid., no. 16, 24 February 1789, p. 123 (London, 6 February).
[101] Ibid., no. 29, 11 April 1789, p. 227 (The Hague, 27 March).
[102] Ibid., no. 41, 23 May 1789, p. 323 (London, 5 May).
[103] Ibid., no. 45, 6 June 1789, p. 354 (London, 19 May).

in the House of Representatives and his words were printed in the *Gaz-zetta universale*.[104] Washington, the first magistrate of the United States, "accompanied by the representatives and the Senate, swore before the people, according to the constitution, an oath to maintain this as the actual form of government. On the occasion this virtuous citizen gave new proof of his patriotism and magnanimity by solemnly renouncing, in an elegant speech given on the first day of his presidency, any salary attached to his office."[105]

One year later, in 1790, there appeared in Milan the most important Italian book on the new reality that was arising and consolidating itself on the other side of the ocean. Like Brissot, Chastellux, Saint-John de Crèvecoeur, and so many others, Luigi Castiglioni, a member of culti-vated society in the Lombardy of the Enlightenment, was also "moved," as he said, "by curiosity to see the political birth of a republic composed of different nations, distributed among various provinces distant from others, and varied in climate and products."[1] A nephew of Pietro Verri, he was not yet thirty (he was born in 1757), when he began his voyage in the summer of 1784, through Genova, Montpellier, Paris, and Lon-don, with the intention of visiting the American states and Canada in detail for three years.[2] Like Mazzei, he was convinced that the diffusion of European science and technology on the American continent had opened the main means of contact between the two so-distant realities. The adoption of American vegetables in Europe seemed to him the best basis for establishing a solid relationship between the Old World and the New. Parallel to the diffusion in America of European technology, con-tacts in the large fields of agriculture and botany became more intense.[3] In these exchanges Luigi Castiglioni played his part (we owe the diffu-sion in Europe of robinia to him). He collected above all "the surest information about [American] agriculture, being persuaded that, al-though our most industrious system of cultivation should not be com-

---

[104] Ibid., no. 50, 23 June 1789, p. 393 (New York, 22 April).

[105] Ibid., no. 53, 4 July 1789, p. 417 (New York, 1 May).

[1] *Viaggio negli Stati Uniti dell'America settentrionale fatto negli anni 1785, 1786 e 1787 da Luigi Castiglioni, patrizio milanese, cavaliere dell'ordine di S. Stefano P.M., membro della Società filosofica di Filadelfia e della Patriotica di Milano. Con alcune osservazioni sui vegetabili più utili a quel paese* (Milan: Giuseppe Marelli, 1790), vol. 1, "Prefazione," p. v. In 1983 an English version edited by Antonio Pace appeared at the University Press of Syracuse, New York.

[2] See the article on him by Carlo Capra, in DBI, vol. 22, pp. 166ff.

[3] Piero Bairati, "Per il bene dell'umanità. Benjamin Franklin e il problema delle mani-fatture," *R. stor. ital.*, year 40, fasc. 2 (June 1978): 262ff.

pared with the first efforts of a land that could be said to be populated
for the first time, it was still good to know the methods of cultivation
used in a climate so similar to ours."[4] He thought the experience he had
gained was indispensable not only to technology, but also to politics. He
had no doubt that "the revolution that has occurred in past years in
North America is one of the most memorable events of this century, and
can with time produce important consequences for Europe."[5] He had
thus left Milan ready to receive anything new and experimental over-
seas, even in this area. In his passage through Paris he had been "graciously received" by Condorcet and participated in the academic and
scientific life of the capital, discussing magnetism with Mesmer, aerostatic spheres (Paolo Andreani was also in Paris in those days), the chemical experiments of Lavoisier, and contacts he expected to make with the
Philosophical Society of Philadelphia.[6] Naturally political problems were
brought to his attention. He was at dinner with the ambassador of Joseph II and went to find Franklin in Passy, who "received him with every possible cordiality." Buffon was away, but Condorcet introduced
him to "M. de Malesherbes, once a minister and now an agriculturist
and a farmer." These were the very days when the death of Diderot was
"deeply felt by all men of letters in Paris."[7] Once in America, his *Viaggio*
alternated between natural and political observations. He closely examined the "new constitutions" that had been adopted in Massachusetts at
the beginning of 1780, and he noted what it was in them that had been
established "in imitation of the House of Commons in England."[8] It
seemed to him that "many grave impediments" resulted from the constitution of the "republic of Massachusetts," as from the others adopted
in the northern part of the United States. The model, "always flattering
but perhaps often ideal, of a perfect democratic government," had been
rejected. There were two houses, as in England. But sufficient account
had not been taken of the different circumstances in the two countries.
"If the delegates of the different cities and districts of an ancient and
powerful nation such as England can be instructed in politics, who are
men of sense, and wealthy enough to sacrifice part of their particular
interests for the well-being of the republic—this is not true of the new
and poor American republic." Here it was a question of Irish peasants,

---

4 *Viaggio negli Stati Uniti*, vol. 1, "Prefazione," p. vii.

5 Ibid., p. v.

6 He wrote a kind of diary of his stay in Paris in a series of letters to Paolo Frisi preserved in Milan in the B. Ambrosiana, Y. 153 Sup., f. 105, 30 July 1784; f. 107, 2 August
1784; f. 109, 4 August 1784; f. 113, 13 September 1784; f. 115, 23 September 1784. On
this correspondence see Pace, *Franklin*, pp. 133ff.

7 Milan, B. Ambrosiana, Y. 153 Sup., f. 109, 4 April 1784.

8 *Viaggio negli Stati Uniti*, vol. 1, pp. 78ff.

"as deprived of money as they are of knowledge," who had recently arrived from the "poor countryside of their miserable fatherland." Having
selected among them a "representative to the General Assembly," this
man "leaves his axe" and goes to Boston "unhappy to interrupt his work
in the fields that are still on his mind amid his political duties." His mistrust prompts him to refuse any military expenditure or new tax. The
representatives who are less ignorant than he are "perhaps even more
dangerous." "Raised in the countryside with ideas of unlimited liberty,
and knowing of relations among the great powers only from the gazettes, which they read avidly, they take potshots at even the most complex public affairs, and become politicians without instruction or guidance. They often attach themselves obstinately to opinions from which
it is impossible to shake them." "Educated individuals," although they
exist, are deprived of power and influence. They are the hostages of
"malcontents," intent on "opening the door to unrestrained license."[9]
The fragility of the social and political equilibrium of Massachusetts was
evident in the summer of 1786. "Some inhabitants of the most interior
part" had rebelled against the fiscal and judicial organization of the state
and "had demanded a reform of different articles of the constitution of
the General Assembly."

Their principal demands were to lower the salary of the Governor, to abolish
the Senate as useless, to remove the tribunals of first instance, or, as they say,
courts of common pleas, and finally that there be an equal distribution of land
among all inhabitants of the republic, and that all debts incurred to this point
be forgiven. That is to say in clear terms that the industrious man should lose
the fruit of his labor and share with the do-nothing, and that the debtor should
defraud his honest creditor of the money that perhaps assisted him in his misfortunes. For many months, almost a whole year, the revolt continued, and it
might have had sad consequences for the state if the government had not finally
determined to remedy the situation by sending a regiment under the command
of General Lincoln. In a little skirmish with the insurgents, four of them were
left on the ground, and since the others dispersed and the leaders fled to Canada the others later returned to obedience to the government.[10]

This was a hostile, but by no means blind, interpretation of what is generally known as "Shays' Rebellion." The social roots of the revolt, the
contrast between the internal region, which was poorer and more backward, and the rich and commercial region of the coast, on which the
modern historian Jackson Turner Main has much insisted, the ideal of

[9] Ibid., pp. 81ff. On these problems see Stephen E. Patterson, *Political Parties in Revolutionary Massachusetts* (Madison: University of Wisconsin Press, 1973), and Dirk Hoerder,
Crowd Action in Revolutionary Massachusetts, 1765–1780 (New York: Academic Press, 1977).
[10] *Viaggio negli Stati Uniti*, vol. 1, pp. 83ff.

equal distribution flickering on the horizon of the United States in these years, was echoed, as we see, in the pages of Luigi Castiglioni.[11]

He saw the origins of the American discontent and difficulties after 1783 in the uncertain peace with the English, the disputed frontier with Canada, and above all, in a general slackening of the nation once independence had been gained.

With the war ended and the peace signed, the only word of the people was liberty. The soldiers who had served in their defense were badly paid and the people only waited the moment of their dismissal to rid themselves of this expense, out of fear as well that their defenders would become their tyrants. This idea grew when it was almost suspected that the great Washington wanted to make himself a sovereign, and his refusal was received with applause. This destroyed the nerve of the republic and its growing military discipline; everyone returned to their homes, as if their ceded provinces were located in the midst of a stormy sea, far from any inhabited part of the globe, and thus secure for centuries to come.[12]

But the new state did not even succeed in coming to a just accord with the savages. This was all the worse because the "original inhabitants of America, although lacking in education in the European sense, have a natural talent superior to what is commonly attributed to them." They were quite different from the Africans "educated in the misery produced by slavery." They were "courageous and intelligent" and "abhorred even the word *slaves*." To the invasion of their territory, and the colonists' increasingly serious molestation, they had finally responded with a "cruel vendetta" and the "massacre of entire families."[13]

These constitutional doubts, and criticisms of the internal and external politics of the United States, still did not hide in the eyes of this "Milanese patrician" what he thought was an essential fact, that a new solid and an active society was planting itself in these states, such as in Massachusetts, where there were difficult contrasts and conflicts. In the city of Boston as in the village of St. Georges there was clearly "a certain equality of comportment even among people of different rank, which by not vilifying the poor man, makes him less servilely dependent on the rich." There was clearly "an avid interest in knowing the affairs of others, provoked less by vain curiosity than by a desire to instruct oneself, a strong inclination to involve oneself in public administration and government, and finally a vivid love of liberty, joined with firmness and courage." "There is a general ability to read and write, and schools for

---

[11] See Jackson Turner Main, *The Antifederalists: Critics of the Constitution, 1781–1788* (New York: Norton Library, 1974), pp. 59ff.

[12] *Viaggio negli Stati Uniti*, vol. 1, pp. 85ff.

[13] Ibid., pp. 96ff.

this purpose are maintained at public expense in every city, town, and village." Religious sects, which had produced much conflict in the past, "have now been rendered innocuous and peaceful through complete freedom of choice."[14] Distinctions among classes were more visible in New York, a city of twenty-two thousand inhabitants. The "owners of manors" who under the English government had "bought certain privileges" and, together with the most wealthy merchants, could think of themselves "as the noble order of the city," had lost "much of their superiority since the recent revolution, when persons of little renown arose to occupy the most conspicuous offices of the new republic." After these came the categories of "less proud or wealthy merchants," "artisans," and finally the "people." Everywhere the revolution had left its mark. "European culture, combined with American cordiality, makes society very agreeable, and the gentle sex is equally pleasing. Although more refined than in Boston, this last city lacks nothing in beauty of form or complexion."[15] In Virginia, a visit to Monticello, and a eulogy to Thomas Jefferson, absent in those days from his estate because of his appointment as ambassador to Versailles, was one of the apexes of this naturalist-political pilgrimage. "The house, designed by the owner, is in the Italian style, with high and spacious rooms, and perhaps a too-grandiose plan, which is why it is not yet completed. On the side of the hill there are a quantity of vines, a large orchard with the best fruit trees of Europe, and a collection of singular plants and bushes, collected by himself in the woods of Virginia. What makes Monticello most agreeable is the large library of the best and rarest books, in English, French, Italian, Greek, and Latin, collected by Mr. Jefferson not for luxury, but for his own study, since he knows the languages." Mention of his *Notes on Virginia* was not lacking.[16] When Castiglioni came to write of Pennsylvania, political problems were at the center of the picture. He quoted in its entirety the preamble of the "constitution" "which breathes more than others the ideas of a pure democracy," intended as it was to "fix those principles of government that best tend to establish the happiness of the people of the state and their posterity, and to provide for their future progress without any partiality in favor or prejudice against any particular class, sect, or denomination of men."[17] To this end was directed not only the mechanism of the constitution, which Castiglioni described in detail, but also penal legislation, which had recently been reformed and codified. "It can only be pleasing to my fellow citizens to know," he has-

[14] Ibid., p. 89.
[15] Ibid., pp. 178ff.
[16] Ibid., pp. 354ff.
[17] Ibid., vol. 2, pp. 20ff.

tened to add, "what an influence the book *Dei delitti e delle pene* has had in the establishment of penal laws in the different American constitutions." The "attorney general of the State of Pennsylvania, William Bradford Jr.," had confirmed this in a letter from Philadelphia dated 10 August 1786, which is translated in full in these pages. "The efforts of Beccaria to extend the empire of humanity," he wrote, "have been crowned on the new continent with the greatest success. Well before the recent revolution this book was known to literary men in Pennsylvania; they admired its principles without daring to hope that these would be adopted in legislation, since while subordinate to England we merely copied their laws. As soon, however, as we were free from political tutelage, this system of humanity, long venerated in secret, was adopted publicly and incorporated into the constitution of the state itself." Too busy at first "to undertake this beneficent reform," the legislative bodies had recently "put their hands on this important work." "Already the plan has been drawn up, approved, and published to receive the vote of the citizens, so that only the new session of the General Assembly is awaited to give it the force of law. Then when this change in our penal laws has occurred forced labor for different terms will be substituted for flogging, branding, mutilation, and death, and instead of the one hundred and seventy capital crimes of the country from which we have just been separated, there will be only four in Pennsylvania." To Beccaria one had to ascribe

principally . . . the honor of this revolution in our criminal code. . . . The name Beccaria has become familiar in Pennsylvania, his authority is great, and his principles, spread through every class of the people, have impressed deeply the hearts of our citizens. You will have observed the influence of his maxims in other American states. The empire of injustice is ruined, and the voice of a philosopher has put an end to vulgar clamor. Although the old bloody system may persist in the laws of many of our states, nonetheless the beneficent spirit spread by Beccaria works secretly in favor of the accused, moderating the rigor of the laws, and tempering justice with pity.[18]

A more vivid tribute to Beccaria would be difficult to imagine. Finangieri's dream of being asked to reform the laws of Pennsylvania seemed to have become a reality through the diffusion and persuasion of ideas. Already in 1774 William Bradford had written to Madison that Pennsylvania was in relation to America what America was to the whole world, a special "land of freedom."[19] Now it presented itself as a symbol of the spirit of reforms. The name of Castiglioni's correspondent was

[18] Ibid., pp. 23ff. n. a.
[19] Cited by Gordon S. Wood, *The Creation of the American Republic* (New York: Norton Library, 1972), p. 86.

symbolic. In the seventeenth century William Bradford, one of the founders of New England, had incarnated the spirit of Puritanism. Now his namesake spoke for the Enlightenment.

However, this shining vision did not prevent the Milanese traveler from becoming aware that the constitution of Pennsylvania was also in crisis. It provided "an almost unlimited liberty to the people" and foresaw only "one legislative body." The result was "a weak and fluctuating administration." "Seeing the defects, some seek to give greater energy and stability to the government by reviewing and correcting the constitution, while others reject change as useless." Franklin had arbitrated the dispute "with all the authority of an ancient legislator." "Inclined to the proposed reform he showed that laws excellent in the turbulence of war can be dangerous in peace, and that it is right to act like a good gardener, who to obtain more fruit from a tree cuts the same branches he preserved before with so much care, to make them grow roots." Perhaps a conciliation between the two parties was impossible, but still on this occasion the vigorous octogenarian had demonstrated he was "a true father of his country."[20]

As one sees from his pages on Pennsylvania as well, there was a clear influence on Luigi Castiglioni of political currents that originated in the convention of 1786 and in the new constitution of the following year. The last chapter of his book announced the victory of the tendencies he had seen at work in the different states and was entitled "Del nuovo governo federativo." The inability of the Revolutionary Congress to confront and resolve the problems of the country was evident. "Among the various disorders," it had permitted "commerce to languish," while "public credit" had not been supported with sufficient energy. Under the presidency of Washington the assembly met in Philadelphia and "in September 1787 presented the new constitution to the Congress, which was examined by the delegates of the people of each state and being approved by more than two thirds of them will probably soon have the force of law." Castiglioni did not doubt the need for reform or the means adopted to accomplish it. "In my belief the United States will gain much utility by adopting this constitution, in which," as he emphasized, "the rights of the individual states are guaranteed as much as possible, and the interests and security of the Union are secured by giving Congress the exclusive power to make war, peace, and treaties, to levy general taxes, and to regulate commerce."[21]

Without tracing the intellectual roots of the new constitution, that is,

---

[20] Ibid., pp. 40ff. On the constitutional discussion in Pennsylvania, see Main, *The Antifederalists*, pp. 41ff.

[21] *Viaggio negli Stati Uniti*, vol. I, pp. 113ff.

without citing the *Federalist*, which to his eyes, like those of many observers of these years, remained completely in shadow, Castiglioni furnished a version of the new text of the constitution, convinced that it was "the basis on which the independence and prosperity of the United States rest."[22] At only one point was his version influenced by what happened later beyond the Alps: the word *impeachment* was translated "crime of *lesa-nazione* [*lèse nation*], this significant expression having been adopted also by the French Assembly during the revolution."[23] In the letter on the new constitution, as in all of his long voyage, he did not hesitate to foresee a strongly optimistic future for the United States of America. Ideas about the degeneration of man and nature on that continent had become ridiculous after what happened. The new nation was "capable of nourishing an immense population, particularly at its center, where there are vast plains irrigated by numerous navigable rivers under a temperate and salubrious sky. Animated by such advantages, under the auspices of the new government, the United States would flourish and arrive more easily at the happy epoch to which they aspire, and in which they will distinguish themselves among the wealthiest and most amiable of nations."[24]

We catch glimpses, through the too-scarce information that has come down to us, of the figures of two other Lombardian gentlemen, who like Castiglioni were fascinated with the fate of the United States at the moment of independence and who participated in its decisive years of internal transformation: Francesco Dal Verme and Gaudenzio Clerici, the first recommended by Franklin to Robert Livingston in 1783 as a great traveler, desirous to come to America "merely to see the country and its great men," and by John Adams to John Langdon, the same year, as "a nobleman of Milan in Italy and a near relation to Prince Carminico [Caramanico], an ambassador at the court of London." They were both correspondents of Jefferson and served as his guide when he was in northern Italy in the summer of 1787.[1] Jefferson wrote to Dal Verme, when he returned to Paris, not only of the most recent books

---

[22] Ibid., p. 114.

[23] Ibid., p. 120 n. a.

[24] Ibid., pp. 167ff.

[1] Pace, *Franklin*, p. 133; *The Papers of Thomas Jefferson*, vol. 12, p. 43n, pp. 38ff., to Gaudenzio Clerici, Paris, 15 August 1787, and pp. 42ff., to Francesco Dal Verme, 15 August 1787: "I cannot begin with an act of greater justice than that of expressing to you all my gratitude for your attentions and services while in your capital and to which I am indebted for the best informations I received there."

published in the United States, but also of the most important political problems now to be confronted. "You must have observed when in America that time and trial had discovered defects in our federal constitution. A new essay, made in the midst of the flames of war, could not be perfect. The states have appointed deputies, who are now sitting at Philadelphia to consider what are these defects and to propose new articles to be added to the instrument of confederation, for amending them." He explained in detail the mechanisms through which this constitutional transformation would be effected. It was made necessary, among other events, by the recent revolt in Massachusetts.[2]

There is something dilettantish in the elegant cosmopolitan curiosity of these two Milanese noblemen.[3] A more profound and experienced adhesion to the American Revolution was expressed through the long life of Filippo Mazzei, that Italian who more than any other in the eighteenth century took an active part in the life of the new republic beyond the sea. His experience as a reformer, diplomat, journalist, and polemicist was quite exceptional.[4] He had grown up in Tuscany under the Regency for Francis Stephen, among doctors, literary men, and jurists attentive to the daily intrigues against superstition and open to new ideas, above all those coming from England. A student at the Hospital of Santa Maria Nuova, he engaged in discussion with various priests, and with the father inquisitor himself, on doubts raised in his mind by a case of "two babies who died soon after birth, one of whom went to paradise because the nurse, seeing him in peril, baptized him, and the other to hell because the other nurse, out of stupidity, or from being

[2] *The Papers of Thomas Jefferson*, vol. 12, pp. 42ff., Paris, 15 August 1787.

[3] Typical in this regard is the lively letter of Francesco Dal Verme to Jefferson from Milan, 12 February 1788, ibid., pp. 587ff. More interesting is the letter of Gaudenzio Clerici from Milan, 2 February 1788, where the vision of the free American world is the background for a growing dissatisfaction with all aspects of life in the years of Joseph II. "Demolishing churches, new thoughts about suppressing convents and making money for war; restricting the number of parsons and parishes, reformation of ecclesiastical education, I am sure are no news to you. *Opere, feste da ballo, mascherate* is every thing we have and we wish at the present season *di carnovale*. We want dancing and raree—shows and ramadans to forget miseries and wretchedness as much as the africo-americans want the banjar to digest with their kuskus the hardships of their lives and the unsafe treatments of their overseers" (ibid., p. 556).

[4] *Memorie della vita e delle peregrinazioni del fiorentino Filippo Mazzei, con documenti storici sulle sue missioni politiche come agente degli Stati Uniti d'America e del re Stanislao di Polonia* (Lugano: Tipografia della Svizzera italiana, 1845), in two volumes, remains, despite the haste with which it was written and the many inaccuracies it contains, the natural point of departure for any study of him. More than a century later *Memorie*, edited in the first edition by Gino Capponi, was republished by Alberto Aquarone (Milan: Marzorati, 1970) in two volumes (cited henceforth as *Memorie*). The most recent, complete, and penetrating work on him is by Tortarolo, *Illuminismo e rivoluzioni*.

asleep, had not baptized him." The dispute ended only when he announced that he was persuaded by the orthodox position and when the inquisitor, for good measure, rebaptized him ("this doesn't cost anything, and it can't be a bad thing"). But in reality he had taken in his heart the decisive step toward an irreversible detachment from religion. "After that time I have had no more doubts and consequently not even a desire to disturb confessors or inquisitors."[5] The definitive break came when he was accused of taking communion "after having drunk warm water with sugar (because of a cold)" and was therefore expelled from his medical studies.[6] Close to the group of Antonio Cocchi and his son Raimondo, in contact with cultivated Jews in Florence, in continual conversation with artisans and doctors, he felt rise in him, also due to quarrels with his family, a desire to go out and get to know the world. On 4 March 1754, in the act of selling the farms he had inherited three years earlier, he declared to the notary that he intended to make "some voyages to better adapt himself to his profession as a surgeon."[7] Having arrived in Livorno he was dissuaded from going to South America. He left for Smyrna, passing through Vienna, Budapest, and the Banat, and arrived in Constantinople in 1755.[8] The Moslem world struck him in its various aspects, as he described them in his characteristic episodic and disconnected manner a half century later in his *Memorie*. In Smyrna he was soon retaken by the desire to change scene: "I felt too restricted in that land and a need to see more of the world than I had."[9] War was about to erupt in Europe, a war that would last for seven years. Embarked on an English ship equipped as a corsair he hoped to receive part of the booty. He arrived in London at the beginning of March 1756. The defense and demonstration of Italian, and instruction in our language, soon took him to the heart of English intellectual life: he had as pupils, among many others, the famous Doctor Matthew Maty, who was keeper of the British Museum, and the historian Edward Gibbon, with whom he read the *Istorie fiorentine* and the *Discorsi sopra la prima deca di Tito Livio* by Machiavelli.[10] He knew the writer Samuel Sharp and the publisher David Mallet. Among diplomats he was particularly close to the Genoese Pietro Paolo Celesia and the Neapolitan Domenico Carac-

---

[5] *Memorie*, pp. 38ff.

[6] Ibid., p. 50.

[7] Act cited by Guelfo Guelfi Camajani, *Un illustre toscano del Settecento. Filippo Mazzei medico, agricoltore, scrittore, giornalista, diplomatico* (Florence: Associazione internazionale toscani nel mondo, 1976), p. 229.

[8] Tortarolo, *Illuminismo e rivoluzioni*, p. 15.

[9] *Memorie*, p. 107.

[10] Salvatore Rotta, "Il viaggio in Italia di Gibbon," *R. stor. ital.*, year 39, fasc. 2 (June 1967): 229.

ciolo.[11] Meanwhile he learned English, even if, as he recounts, he always
pronounced it so as to make it instantly obvious that he was Tuscan.[12]
What made him decide to remain in England and renounce his plans
for voyages and adventures (he hesitated again between South America
and Smyrna), was his growing interest in the political life of Great Britain. It was finally possible for him to experience in person what he had
heard about this land at home. In effect, the law was applied with an
almost unknown rigor. A "peer of the realm, whose family descended
from royal blood," had been hanged for having killed "one of his farmers." "In most of the states of Europe a great lord who had committed
such a crime would be kept for a while in one of his villas." "I saw that
personal liberty in England was established on an even more solid basis
than in Holland." Even foreigners were protected by British laws. "Personal liberty," he concluded, "is more important than public to an individual; thus I decided to remain and took a house."[13] English lessons
certainly could not have been sufficient to satisfy his need for action. He
became involved with trade in Italian products, particularly wines,
which he organized personally, returning for some time to Tuscany and
visiting Mantova, Milan, Venice, and Naples, which opened to him
broad, if not easy, possibilities of earnings and employment. The principal obstacle against which he protested was a denunciation by the Holy
Office, after he had left London on 24 September 1765, which accused
him of having "loaded an immense quantity of banned books onto a
ship destined for Genova, Livorno, Civitavecchia, and Messina, to sup-
ply all of Italy." Pietro Molini, the well-known Livornese editor living in
England, was clearly his "right arm."[14] The list of books that Mazzei was
accused of having sent to Italy, "the only place" now in Europe "remaining untouched by the common corruption," included the works of La
Mettrie and above all Voltaire, from the *Pucelle* to the *Philosophie de l'histoire*, besides more or less imaginary titles of libertines and deists: *The
Material God, Paradise Destroyed, Hell Burned Out, Purgatory Spurned, The
Saints Banished from Heaven, Priapus the Creator*, and many others of a
similar nature in French, now a common language. The vicar of the
Inquisition in Livorno added, for his own part, heavy accusations
against the bookseller Marco Coltellini, who was in effect a friend of
Mazzei's, for "the commerce he maintained in most perilous books, giv-

---

[11] Tortarolo, *Illuminismo e rivoluzioni*, p. 16, and Salvatore Rotta, "L'illuminismo a Genova: lettere di P. P. Celesia a F. Galiani," in *Miscellanea di storia ligure*, year 3 (n.s.), nos. 1
and 5 (n.s.), no. 1, 1968 (Firenze: La Nuova Italia, n.d.), in the index.

[12] *Memorie*, p. 115.

[13] Ibid., pp. 116ff.

[14] Ibid., p. 151.

ing them to anyone to read, and taking the profit of renting them out."
From Rome Cardinal Neri Corsini supported these accusations, with an
invitation to Incontri, the Archbishop of Florence, to press the young
Grand Duke Peter Leopold, arrived in Florence only a few months before, to take appropriate measures, or as the prelate expressed himself,
to put into operation a "remedy, as secret and prompt as it is suited, to
the spiritual health of the subjects God has entrusted to him."[15] Coltellini and his collaborator Giuseppe Aubert were warned. Mazzei was
obliged to leave Tuscany. At first he said he wanted to go to Rome to
defend himself, but his friends dissuaded him from taking so hazardous
a step. He retired to Lucca, remaining there for three months, and then
went to Naples, where Galiani and Tanucci defended him and acted on
his behalf. The exile from Tuscany, to which he was condemned, terminated on 15 June 1766. The grand duke accorded him on that day
"return and residence in the state" and added that "Senator Rucellai
had seriously warned the Inquisitor at Pisa to abstain in the future from
such hasty acts."[16]

Mazzei hoped much from this change of direction in Tuscan politics,
which not only concerned himself, but also affected the whole internal
and external situation of the grand duchy. In fact, he hoped too much
and attempted in vain to be appointed the official representative of Peter Leopold in London, as the Abate Niccoli was in Paris a little later.
Maria Theresa, through her ambassador at the Court of St. James, imposed a kind of veto against a man as "irreligious" as Mazzei.[17] His commercial activity constituted another insurmountable obstacle.[18] Having
returned to London, to his shop "across from the theater of the Italian
opera," he hoped to become at least an agent of Peter Leopold in Great
Britain.[19] But precisely this modest ambition opened another road for
him, which was decisive for his fate. The grand duke asked him to find
two stoves of the kind Franklin had invented, and Mazzei obtained them
directly from the colonial agent of Pennsylvania, thus entering into contact with the active and vivacious group of Americans in London, such
as the Virginian Thomas Adams, "a great friend of Mr. Jefferson." As
we read in the *Memorie*, "he and I had known each other a few years
before we met." "Some of these Americans began to buy goods in my
shop for their use, and even for export to their country . . . especially

[15] Florence, BN, *Manoscritti Tordi* 546.90 cited by Tortarolo, *Mazzei*, pp. 48ff.

[16] Florence, B. Marucelliana, *Manoscritti Frullani* 41, pp. 888ff.

[17] *Memorie*, p. 183.

[18] Many interesting details about this are in Tortarolo, *Illuminismo e rivoluzioni*, pp. 19ff.

[19] *Memorie*, vol. 1, p. 181.

oil, wine, pasta, parmesan cheese, sausages, and anchovies."[20] In this
warehouse atmosphere, and amid the preoccupations of commercial
life, he had his first political discussions about America. His "new
friends," "especially Doctor Franklin and Mr. Thomas Adams, advised
me to go and live among them. I doubted that their government was
more than a poor copy of the English one, and consequently that liberty
was on even less solid ground."[21] London resounded in those days to
the cries of "Wilkes and Liberty." There were violent protests against
the abuse of power of Parliament, the desire for reform encountered
obstacles that seemed insuperable, and a pugnacious new radicalism developed precisely in the group of merchants among whom he lived. Liberty seemed everywhere much threatened.[22] But still, something solid
remained at the basis of English society, that profound respect for the
law rooted in the souᴸs of all, even where one least expected it. Even in
the midst of the worst scuffles no one dared touch a judge, as he himself
had witnessed on the occasion of an encounter he reported in a brief
and curious bilingual pamphlet, in Italian and English, which appeared
anonymously in the first months of 1768.[23] "The English people don't
kill. I have seen many riots, and against some who were much more
hated by the public than those who have injured individuals, and no one
has ever been killed." Judges, for their part, did not hesitate to hold firm
to the certainty of the law, even when this could seem to have a negative
result. "If a minister of justice were allowed not to hear accusations
when he believed there was strong calumny, this would open the way to
corruption, and there would be no denying that it is less evil to be subjected to inconvenience proceeding from severity, or from some defect
in the law, than to mistakes or malevolence in interpretation of the
same, when there is no obligation to follow it *ad litteram*."[24] Beccaria had
said the following: "A disorder arising from a rigorous observation of
the letter of the penal law is not to be compared with disorders arising
from interpretation."[25] "If there were not this certainty, impartiality,
and rigor," Mazzei added, "then the people would seek to do justice

[20] Ibid., p. 186.

[21] Ibid., p. 192.

[22] Venturi, *The End of the Old Regime, 1768–1776*, pp. 397ff.

[23] *A letter on the behaviour of the populace on a late occasion in the procedure against a noble lord* (London: W. Bingley). On the attribution to Mazzei, the occasion of this work, and the editor W. Bingley, a noted radical, see Tortarolo, *Illuminismo e rivoluzioni*, p. 20.

[24] *A letter*, p. 12.

[25] Cesare Beccaria, *Dei delitti e delle pene, con una raccolta di lettere e documenti relativi alla nascita dell'opera e alla sua fortuna nell'Europa del Settecento*, ed. F. Venturi (Turin: Einaudi, 1965), p. 15.

themselves, and wreck all civil order."[26] The equality of all before the law was at the basis of English liberty. But liberty still threatened to make private interests prevail over public ones. Thus the India Company was "a body separated from its country," perilous for England as for any other nation, like Tuscany, that might enter into relations with it, he wrote to Peter Leopold on 3 May 1769.[27] In general, civil liberty was safe, political liberty in danger.[28]

His American friends maintained in their discussion that the injustices he was so impressed with in London did not exist in the colonies beyond the ocean. "Franklin as well as Adams showed me that there was no aristocracy, that the people did not have their sight dazzled by the splendor of the throne, that every family head cast his vote in elections and could be elected, that they had their own municipal laws and had adopted only those English laws convenient to them."[29]

He found a new fatherland in America in 1771, when he decided to emigrate, which promised liberty and happiness. He wanted to take with him silk, olives, and vines, fifty expert peasants, ideas on agronomy of men like Cosimo Trinci, and the intellectual fruits of the first harvest of Italian reforms, Beccaria above all. He protested from the beginning against a variety of mercantilist prejudices. Ludovico Barbiano del Belgioioso, the ambassador of Maria Theresa in England, did everything possible to prevent the emigration from Lombardy of able cultivators and artisans. Similar efforts were made by the Conte di Scarnafigi, the representative of Carlo Emanuele III from Turin. In Livorno, instead, where he returned to organize his expedition, he received some support from Peter Leopold, who was most interested in the possibility of receiving grain from America, and more inclined than other sovereigns to export Tuscan plants, "excepting, however, mulberry trees."[30] Meanwhile, the expedition began to take on a clearer political perspective in Mazzei's eyes. As he explained to the grand duke, a break between the American colonies and the mother country was inevitable, and this

[26] *A letter*, p. 14.

[27] Tortarolo, *Illuminismo e rivoluzioni*, p. 23.

[28] He summarized these conclusions twenty years later in writing that he soon became aware in England that "with regard to public life, liberty was an illusion. But I followed the execution of Lord Ferrex that led me to reflect on the bases of personal liberty, which reconciled me to this country." *Lettere di Filippo Mazzei alla corte di Polonia (1788–1792)*, ed. Raffaele Ciampini (Bologna: Zanchielli, 1937), vol. 1, p. 38, 13 October 1788. On the condemnation and execution of Lawrence Shirley, Earl of Ferrers, see Leon Radzinowicz, *A History of English Criminal Law* (London: Stevens, 1948), vol. 1, in the index.

[29] *Memorie*, p. 192.

[30] Livorno, AS, *Fondi del governatore*, no. 574, cited in Tortarolo, *Illuminismo e rivoluzioni*, p. 28.

could produce profound political and economic changes in America as well as in Europe.[31] But the number of persons who departed with him was smaller than he had planned, only about ten. Absent was Giovanni Fabbroni, a youth in whom he had placed great hopes, who in fact became an important Tuscan reformer at the turn of the century, but who never went to America. Mazzei, in reality, could count on only himself when he disembarked in Virginia on 2 September 1773.

He found in America what he had sought in vain in England, a society in which respect for the law, an egalitarian will, and an openness in human relationships was joined to a spirit of enterprise, even of adventure, and where intense economic activity was joined with a political vision that was exalting and new. The many problems that had prevented him up to then from escaping his merchant condition and becoming a part of the ruling class did not exist. Access to offices, and to responsibility, seemed rather a natural duty in Virginia. The electoral procedures were there to aid him in transforming himself into a citizen of a new land, in which there was everything to construct, including the nation itself. The men with whom he made friendly relations were exceptional: it is enough to remember Thomas Jefferson and George Mason. There was much work to do. But his farm, Colle, as he called it, near Jefferson's Monticello, remained all his long life the symbol of the liberty he had acquired by emigrating to America.[32]

He continued to have close relations with Tuscany. Grain and tobacco were sent to Livorno, and from there came different kinds of plants so that Jefferson could see whether their transplanting would improve the quality of the local vegetables: "garlic from Terracina," "radishes from Pistoia," "French broccoli from Pisa," "strawberries," and so on. Agricultural implements crossed the ocean, and there was even "a live hare, to see the difference between ours and the hares there." The books ordered had their roots in the centuries: Lucretius in the version of Marchetti, Ariosto "in the correct edition," "Guicciardini, *Storia d'Italia*, the most recent edition," Davila, *Guerre civili*. To Mason was sent the *Elettricismo* by Father Beccaria. To Jefferson went at least one of the three copies of *Dei delitti e delle pene*, which he read and utilized, in fact,

---

[31] *Memorie*, p. 203. He said to Peter Leopold, as he himself assures us, that "Your Royal Highness should not be surprised to see a revolution astonish Europe in fewer years than many philosophers and politicians predict, who think it will take centuries" (*Lettere di F. Mazzei*, p. 35, 13 October 1788).

[32] See "Plan of Philip Mazzei's Agricultural Company," of 1774, in *The Papers of Thomas Jefferson*, vol. 1, pp. 156ff. On the general problems of the state, see Rhys Isaac, *The Transformation of Virginia, 1740–1790* (Williamsburg, Virginia: Institute of Early American History, and Chapel Hill: University of North Carolina Press, 1982).

during the second part of 1775.[33] Ten years later, from this first Tuscan transplant in America sprouted, certainly unexpected, even a new language, Italo-American. Jefferson was already in Paris, as the representative of the new republic. The letters he received from home, from the gardener Antonio Giannini, must have aroused his curiosity. "Honored Sir, . . . You write me to tell you news of how are the trees and other things of your estate. . . . The apples in the *orchard* [*sic*] that is below the garden are very well and produce much fruit. . . . The apricots are well, but a few are dead, and I have replanted them. The almonds are still alive, but do not *improvano* [improve] much. . . . What should I say of the vineyard? The vines *improvano* marvelously." He even promised to send wine soon to France.[34]

In 1775 one was on the eve of war. The news from Massachusetts reported the first encounters. Mazzei, who had followed passionately the events of the year and a half that had passed since his arrival in Virginia, sent home a long report, which was published in four installments in the *Gazzetta universale*.[35] As he himself said, one should write a book on a subject of this nature. These pages were in fact the seed of the *Recherches* that he would publish ten years later. In them he strongly emphasized, repeating the ideas of Jefferson, the private, not royal, origin of the colonies, their autonomy from the earliest times, and their present close union in response to efforts of the English monarchy to divide them. Their governments "although dissimilar" were, "however, almost all on the same footing as that of England." The initial consensus of "the leaders," the Assembly, and the governor had soon broken down under the pressure of the policy of Great Britain intended to create a situation of privilege for itself. But the Americans had proved to be "most courageous and enterprising in protecting their rights and privileges." Boston had taken arms. Virginia had started a committee of correspondence with the other colonies and had begun to mobilize. In Philadelphia the General Congress met. "Can one imagine a greater or more singular Senate?" "It was elected and approved by the people in general, without the least contradiction, and asked to attend to the public good, permitting all and each to solemnly inform themselves and act in all things in conformity with the deliberations of respectable magistrates." This was a "magnanimous union" like the one Salem had made

[33] Tortarolo, *Illuminismo e rivoluzioni*, p. 42.

[34] *The Papers of Thomas Jefferson*, vol. 9, p. 623, Albermarle, 9 June 1786 [in Italian].

[35] "Lettera della Virginia che passa per scritta da un forestiero stabilito in quella provincia e che dà il dettaglio piú esatto del governo e delle attuali circostanze delle colonie," in *Gazzetta Universale*, no. 46, 10 June 1775, p. 382 (London, 19 May), and in the following numbers. See Venturi, *The End of the Old Regime, 1768–1776*, p. 428 and footnote, where the author is not identified.

with Boston, which was disposed on its own part to sacrifice itself to the
other colonies, an "admirable concord and unity of spirit that distinguishes this people from any other," and that was also confirmed in Williamsburg on the occasion of the conflict with the governor of Virginia.
The "spilling of blood" would be terrible if England remained obdurate
in attempting to break the union of the Americans.[36] In these words
sounded, sometimes literally, the ideas of Jefferson, and they derived
otherwise from Mazzei's personal experience in the committee of correspondence in which he had actively taken part, and in the council of
his parish, which was also elective and engaged chiefly in assisting the
poor. Even in the midst of the Revolutionary epoch Mazzei was involved
in political action, and in working to improve and reform everyday life.
He was a man forever inclined to leave aside great debates to occupy
himself, for example, with deaf-mutes, and then return to the most difficult military or diplomatic undertakings. What he did and saw in 1775
and 1776 can be thought decisive for him, as it was for the birth of the
American nation. The break with traditional English political forms was
completed. He saw the nominal liberty of selecting one's own magistrates replaced by a more substantial liberty, based on the equality of all
citizens, and on the continual control by the people of their own representatives.[37]

He did not later abandon these principles, from time to time obliging himself to place them in the international reality that surrounded
him. The more he felt taken by the ideas and passions of his new country, the more he attempted to act in a cosmopolitan way, in Tuscany,
France, and Austria. With this double impulse he transformed himself
into a *militia diplomat*, as they were called at that time, into one of those
adventurous representatives of the United States who attempted in any
way and all directions to persuade the world of the value of the American cause. In August 1777 Jefferson became convinced that it would be
worth the trouble to request assistance through Mazzei from Tuscany,
certainly a "minor" state, but one that had been at peace too long to not
have had the possibility of setting aside some savings. He had been told
this by Carlo Bellini, the Florentine who had emigrated to Williamsburg
and whom we have already encountered. Certainly the grand duke of
Tuscany was "somewhat avaricious," but the place was "favorable to our
cause."[38] Mazzei, in April 1776, had written *Osservazioni di un cittadino del
mondo in risposta ad un americano*, really addressed to Peter Leopold,

---

[36] "Lettera dalla Virginia," pp. 382ff.

[37] Tortarolo, *Illuminismo e rivoluzioni*, pp. 43ff., contains the heretofore unedited texts
of May and June 1776.

[38] *The Papers of Thomas Jefferson*, vol. 2, p. 27.

which appeared in English translation in the *Virginia Gazette* on 24 August of the same year.[39] He had said what in his opinion was the importance of the intervention of France on the side of the colonies. Independence had given a new turn to commerce in the Atlantic. France had the first place, "Italy the second, Spain the third, and only a small remnant would be left for England." Tuscany would profit also from the great possibilities that were offered by the decision of Americans "to sacrifice everything to the enjoyment of liberty and free trade with all nations."[40] Jefferson, in August 1778, proposed that Mazzei be paired with William Lee, the agent of the Congress in Vienna and Berlin, and that he be charged with relations with Tuscany, Rome, and Naples, where "his acquaintance with capital men is great." "If his integrity did not of itself ensure his zeal, his strong and pure principles of republicanism would do so."[41] Richard Henry Lee was of the same opinion as Mazzei. And why not attempt to obtain a good loan even in Genova? "To cultivate a good understanding with the nations in South Europe is undoubtedly wise policy, and may produce the more profitable consequences."[42]

Despite the esteem with which he was surrounded, and the support of men of the first importance, Mazzei still did not succeed in obtaining a mission from Virginia until 8 July 1779, when he was charged with requesting a loan and acquiring "goods in Italy for the use of the armies." It was a difficult mission, as he well knew. Still he left for his adventure, which was soon interrupted by the capture of the ship on which he found himself by the English. He succeeded in ridding himself of all documents, but remained a prisoner until September 1779. One month later he was in Europe without money and credentials. He arrived in Paris at the end of February 1780, and immediately contacted Franklin, Caracciolo, La Fayette, and other persons of the first importance, informing himself minutely about the state of Virginia and all that could involve the war and the revolution. He did not receive any money. His diplomatic mission was opposed by Franklin, who was clearly hostile to *militia diplomacy*. But he was still able to enter the center of military and political discussions, confronting different men: from the minister Vergennes to Genoese bankers, from Peter Leopold to Jean

[39] The text of the English version is reported in full in Tortarolo, *Illuminismo e rivoluzioni*, p. 50, and partially, with comments, in id., "Mazzei e la rivoluzione americana," pp. 198ff.

[40] Tortarolo, *Illuminismo e rivoluzioni*, pp. 60ff.

[41] *The Papers of Thomas Jefferson*, vol. 2, p. 210, to Richard Henry Lee, 30 August 1778.

[42] Ibid., pp. 214ff., 5 October 1778.

Luzac.[43] As always in the past, even in these critical years, he confronted the most general problems in a parallel way, the fundamentals of world politics, and more concrete social questions, such as mendacity, public assistance, and local administration. The first result of his extraordinary activity—which we can follow better by guessing his part in the anonymous pages of the Florentine gazette to which he says he contributed—was to change his position with regard to the grand duke Peter Leopold. It was altogether, on the part of Mazzei, a tacit recognition of a defeat and a rebellion. For years he had attempted to persuade the grand duke of the necessity of establishing commercial, financial, and political relations with the colonies beyond the sea. Now he had to realize that nothing could be done. The explanation for this insensitivity lay, he became more convinced, in the character of Peter Leopold and the nature of his power. Many pages of his *Memorie* are devoted to explaining how the initial ability of the grand duke changed into duplicity, how his absolutism degenerated into police power, his desire to know and understand into an unhealthy common curiosity. The true life of Tuscany in the eighties—the constitutional effort, the penal legislation, the effort to organize a national church—eluded Mazzei. He felt, and now was, an exile in his own country. He had participated in the birth of American liberty too passionately to be able to further adapt himself to the closed world of enlightened despotism. Detaching himself from Peter Leopold he turned his course more decisively toward the world of the revolution. He had seen its birth in Virginia, and now it took new forms in Holland, and in France itself. Even with regard to Joseph II he tried to arrive at the center of the political problems of those years, and to persuade him as well of the utility of supporting the emerging American republic.[44] Mazzei never gave up completely the idea that government by one man alone might be a useful instrument for making indispensable reforms. But his experience in America and in Europe detached him radically from those who were carrying out a vigorous effort to instill new life into absolutism in Florence and in Vienna. The model that inspired him

[43] On the initial problems of American diplomacy see James H. Hutson, *John Adams and the Diplomacy of the American Revolution* (Lexington: University of Kentucky Press, 1950).

[44] Piero del Negro, "Mazzei e gli Absburgo. Una versione della rivoluzione americana 'ad usum principum,' " in *Atti del I congresso internazionale di storia americana. Italia e Stati Uniti dall'indipendenza americana ad oggi (1776–1976)* (Genova, 26–29 May 1976) (Genova: Tilgher, n.d.), pp. 235ff., which contains (on pp. 241ff.) the work of Mazzei of 1781 entitled "Ragioni per cui non può darsi agli Stati americani la taccia di ribelli." These pages, I suggest, are less purely diplomatic and apologetic than what P. Del Negro seems to think. Even here, at the center of the thought of Mazzei, is an affirmation of the original and natural liberty of the colonies. See Tortarolo, *Illuminismo e rivoluzioni*, p. 97 n. 70.

was now a quite different one. He gave the best of himself in the years immediately preceding and following the peace and independence of the United States to make known the American model, and to illustrate it in its larger contours and smallest details. The free government that was being born of common law, the long and tenacious vindication of rights, and the sacrifices of the war contrasted more and more in his eyes with the despotic and unreformable English parliamentary oligarchy, which was truly responsible for the economic and political ruin of Great Britain. In England, he wrote in April 1781, "the opinion of 99 per cent of the nation counts for nothing; the Parliament decides, and since the majority of members of both houses are devoted to the ministry, it is in substance absolute; those formalities which dazzle one into believing that the voice of the nation has a place in affairs of state serve only to make the operation of a minister and absolute sovereign more secure, since the sanction of Parliament provides a shield, like that of the Roman senate under the first Caesars."[45] Thus he wanted neither absolute monarch nor parliament. The only possible way was indicated by America. There Congress was anything but despotic, whatever might be said by the enemies of the republic in Europe. Washington was so little "an ambitious dictator avid for command" that his chief defect was precisely his excessive modesty. Many remained tied to the mother country, one must admit, even beyond the ocean. But "the partisans of England were generally wealthy and elderly people. There were few among the young or common people." Now a change of generations was taking place. "Daily a prodigious number of youths reach the age of bearing arms who have grown up amid wars and tumults, and with sentiments of disdain for enemies of whose actions they cannot hear without horror."[46]

A trip to Virginia that he took shortly after the conclusion of the peace, between 1783 and 1785, despite the practical difficulties he encountered (he was even arrested for debt), only confirmed his conviction that the greatest opportunities were opening before the American people. All that was needed was a great effort to instruct and illuminate them. "In a truly free country, where prosperity and national happiness provide the same basis for all, it is proper that those inhabitants who have not been able to obtain an education should have the right of instruction and counsel from those who have, like sons from their fathers." The people had defended the revolution. For the people should thus now rise those institutions like the "Constitutional Society" created

---

[45] "Riflessioni tendenti a pronosticar l'evento della presente guerra," in Tortarolo, *Illuminismo e rivoluzioni*, pp. 82ff.

[46] Ibid., pp. 83ff.

by the brothers Lee, by James Madison, and by John Blair, of which Mazzei had been one of the founding members. He had now decided to leave Virginia, but until the end he did not renounce the desire to participate in some way in the political life of his "adopted country." Present always in his mind, besides those who had brought the revolution to a good conclusion, were those French and Italians who represented the spirit of enlightenment and reform. "I would like you at the first meeting [of the Constitutional Society] to propose the admission of honored foreign members, . . . the Duc de la Rochefoucauld . . . , Marchese Beccaria . . . , Signor Fontana . . . , Signor Spallanzani."[47]

In 1785 he returned to Paris. Poor, to the extent of not being able to buy the wood he needed, he was always ready to undertake new commercial ventures (and for this reason he was also in Holland), but above all he discussed with himself and with French philosophes the value and significance of the American Revolution. He knew the United States as few other publicists resident in France did. He felt close to political men such as John Adams and Jefferson. He shared with Mably, Condorcet, and Dupont de Nemours a vivid interest in everything that had happened and was happening beyond the ocean. Expert like the Americans, philosophical like the French, this Tuscan came to find himself at the crossroads of the most important discussion of political ideas that developed in Paris between the time of Turgot's fall and the French Revolution. It was a cosmopolitan crossroads, where Mazzei succeeded in erecting, between 1786 and 1788, a kind of encyclopedia of the American Revolution in four volumes entitled *Recherches historiques et politiques sur les Etats-Unis de l'Amérique septentrionale, où l'on traite des établissemens des treize colonies, de leurs rapports et de leurs dissentions avec la Grande-Bretagne, de leurs gouvernemens avant et après la révolution, etc.* par un citoyen de Virginie. *Avec quattre Lettres d'un bourgeois de New-Heaven sur l'unité de la législation.* Printed in Paris "chez Froullé, libraire, quai des Augustins, au coin de la rue Pavée" in 1788, these volumes carried the place of "Colle," his farm in Virginia, almost as a reminder of how deep the roots were that tied him to the United States.

The problems Mazzei discussed aroused great interest. In 1788 Mirabeau completed his *Considérations* on the Order of Cincinnatus with the publication of a letter Turgot had written to Price ten years earlier, a letter that can effectively be considered the point of departure for the

---

[47] *Memorie*, pp. 504ff., to John Blair, 12 May 1785.

ten-year confrontation between Americans and philosophes.[1] Turgot thought that the superiority of France over England in the most important of all the sciences, "that of public happiness," was evident. Except for A. Smith and J. Tucker, no one in Great Britain knew how to reason with force and clarity on the problems of the colonies and war. Perhaps national pride, perhaps precisely that British empiricism, had pushed Burke to describe as "vain metaphysics, all those speculations which tend to establish fixed principles on the rights and true interests of nations." The fact was that a land like England, which even had freedom of the press, had not succeeded in arriving at a just notion of liberty. Only with the writings of Price had progress been made beyond traditional concepts of natural rights of individuals and nations. The Enlightenment—if we want to translate things into modern terms—had been born late and with difficulty in Great Britain. Confronted with the great problems of the American revolt, the country had hesitated to recognize principles that alone would have been able to construct a solid basis for the two nations, and that is, "that a nation should never have the right to govern another nation, and that such a government can have no other basis than force, which is also the basis of piracy and tyranny; that the tyranny of a people is of all tyrannies the most cruel and intolerable." By denying these principles England had been defeated. Instead, the conquest of independence by the Americans was firm. But "this new people, situated so well as to give to the world the example of a constitution in which man enjoys all his rights, exercises freely all his faculties, and is governed only by nature, reason, and justice; would they adopt such a constitution," avoiding those divisions and corruptions that threaten all other forms of government? Were the Americans, in a word, tall enough to face the task the situation they were in imposed on them?[2]

These stakes were so high that the attempts the insurgents had made thus far to reach them did not seem to Turgot at all appropriate. "I am not at all satisfied, I must confess, with the constitutions that have been written up to now by the different American states." It was enough to think that one of them even required faith in the divinity of Christ. Turgot had such a lofty idea of the task awaiting the thirteen colonies that he completely forgot he was minister of a kingdom where Catholicism

---

[1] *Considérations sur l'ordre de Cincinnatus ou imitation d'un pamphlet anglo-américain*, par le comte de Mirabeau, suivies . . . d'une lettre de feu monsieur Turgot, ministre d'état en France au docteur Price sur les législations américaines (London: J. Johnson, 1788), pp. 181 ff. The English version of this letter had been published by Richard Price in 1785 in the London edition of his *Observations on the importance of the American revolution*.

[2] Ibid., pp. 186ff.

was the state religion and where Protestants continued to be persecuted. He had done much in the past to change this situation but had had little or no success. Now he was surprised that the separation between church and state was not perfect in all of the American states. His political criticisms were even more serious. It seemed to him that the rebel colonies had remained too faithful to British tradition. He saw everywhere "the useless imitation of English customs." "Rather than making all authorities one (that of the nation), they establish different bodies: a body of representatives, a council, a governor, because England has a house of commons, an upper house, and a king." Balance of powers, held necessary where the powers of a monarch predominated, became useless "in republics founded on the equality of all citizens." By combatting chimerical fears, "one engenders real ones." Similarly, by making members of the clergy ineligible "one has made these a body outside of the state." The only solution was "true toleration, that is to say, absolute lack of powers of the government over the conscience of individuals."[3] He also thought the relationship established between political and administrative organs was unsatisfactory. At the very base of the constitutional edifice he saw an error that particularly struck him, that is, the lack of distinction between "two classes of men, the landowners and the landless." How could taxes be levied without making this distinction? The fiscal and customs system of the American states seemed to him "still lost in the maze of European illusions" for having failed to proclaim that "the law of absolute freedom of all trade is a corollary of the right of property." These were physiocratic formulations that, as one sees, hindered Turgot's acceptance of the idea of equality, which, in however confused and contradictory a manner, was growing in the American Revolution beyond any limit of property.[4] Even on a political level his criticisms struck at the form the American confederation assumed. "This is only an aggregation of parties, always too separate and always preserving a tendency to diverge by the dissimilarity of their laws, their customs, their opinions, by the inequality of their actual powers, and still more by the inequality of their future development. It is no more than a copy of the Dutch republic." Even here the prejudices of the past, in military, political, and economic matters, impeded the birth and development of a nation that radically destroyed exclusivities and traditional rivalries and completely abandoned "a very ancient and traditional idea of political life." America needed to be, as one sees, a state not only based on different principles, but moved by passions and hopes different from those of the past. It was a state that we might call naturally

---

[3] Ibid., pp. 188ff.
[4] Ibid., pp. 191ff.

anti-Machiavellian. Renaissance and modern republics had already held
that they were different from monarchies, directed as they were to well-
being, peace, moderation, and virtue, rather than to power and conquest. They were thus exceptions to the politics of Machiavelli.[5] The
nation arising beyond the ocean should not only realize the principle of
a perfect political and economic liberty, but renounce any military rivalry, and any desire to excel even in the area of culture or science.
"Glory of arms" and "that of arts and sciences" should be repudiated by
them.[6] As in archaic republics, now even in the new America favorable
circumstances appeared that seemed to make plausible a program in
which, as one sees, strong utopian elements were not lacking. Turgot
took as given the fall of the mercantilist system and the triumph of the
"sacred principle of freedom of trade." Thus, what enemy or rival did
the young republic have to fear? "The presumed interest in possessing
more or less territory will vanish with the principle that territories do
not belong to nations, but to individual landowners."[7] The problem of
borders would be automatically resolved. The intolerance of the Puritans, the economic inequalities in the southern states, the slavery of
blacks, "incompatible with a good political constitution," the prejudices
in political and cultural matters inherited from Great Britain (among
these a repulsion for a standing army) were grave obstacles, but not insurmountable ones. The American people were and remained "the
hope of the human race." "They could become the model. It must be
proved to the world, by facts, that men can be free and peaceful and do
without the chains that tyrants and charlatans of all kinds have attempted to impose on them under the pretext of the public good. There
must be an example of political liberty, religious liberty, liberty of commerce and industry. The refuge they offer to all the oppressed of all
nations will console the earth."[8]

With the peace, the strong faith that the United States had evoked
in the mind of Turgot was naturally again in question. The mercantile
system did not dissolve, and the political, economic, and cultural rivalries did not disappear; they weighed even more on the internal and external life of the new nation. The destiny of America seemed to depend
on Europeans even after the end of the war. Raynal, always ready to
reap the spirit of the moment, launched a public competition on the
significance of America in the modern world. Had it been worth discovering it? Or to put this in a more academic manner, "Has the discovery

---

[5] Franco Venturi, *Utopia e riforma nell'illuminismo* (Turin: Einaudi, 1970), pp. 29ff.
[6] *Considérations*, p. 192.
[7] Ibid., p. 193.
[8] Ibid., pp. 197ff.

of America been useful or harmful to the human species?"[9] For internal matters, Raynal did not suggest anything besides the quiet fate of a land that did not pretend to be the model for anyone, preoccupied, as it should be, by the task of preserving its own sacred mediocrity. Europeans fleeing oppression and intolerance would find ever fewer lands: "There will be nothing to offer them besides sterile deserts, unhealthy marshes, deforested mountains. . . . If ten million men succeed in finding sure subsistence in those provinces, that will be enough. . . . Before long the country will be self-sufficient, provided that its inhabitants know how to find happiness in economy and mediocrity."[10] The utopian absence of conflicts Turgot pictured implied giving up making oneself a model for other peoples or nations. The shadowy existence of republics that had outlived the age of absolutism was foreseen for the United States. The burning concrete political problems born of the independence and federation of the new states of North America were diluted and drowned in the larger problem of utility or harm that humanity had derived from the discovery of the whole American continent.[11] There were few replies to Raynal's inquiry, almost as a demonstration of how constitutional debates were increasingly replacing the general considerations of a passionate, but generic, philosophy of history.

One of the replies marked nonetheless a significant moment in the development of the Parisian political debate. In 1787, in a small work, the Marquis de Chastellux drew the conclusions of his varied experience as a philosophe and his active participation in the American Revolution. With great passion, and not without imitating the emphatic style of Raynal, he reversed Raynal's fundamental thesis, defended commerce, and preached economic development against any temptation to take refuge in a utopia of peace and mediocrity. "Look around us, take things as they are, what happened undoubtedly had to happen: now is not the time to remake the world."[12] The polemic against the evils born in America and the world from property and commerce clashed with a reality in movement that it was necessary to know and accept. From the formation of capital was born commerce, agriculture, and everything else in modern society. "Thus, become accustomed, you harsh moralists, to that inequality of wealth that makes you moan and no longer think it

[9] *Révolution de l'Amérique*, par M. l'abbé Raynal, p. xl.

[10] Ibid., pp. 180ff.

[11] On the advertisement of this competition in the *Giornale di Torino e delle provincie*, no. 43, 26 October 1780, p. 346 (Lione, 18 October), see above, pp. 34–35.

[12] François-Jean de Castellux, *Discours sur les avantages ou les désavantages qui résultent pour l'Europe de la découverte de l'Amérique. Objet du prix proposé par M. l'abbé Raynal par M. P. ***, vice consul à E. **** (London and Paris: Prault, 1787), p. 7.

an infirmity of the political body."[13] Vain was any effort to turn back, to return to the infancy of humanity. In the past stood in reality "all the barbarity of the feudal system," as seen in Bohemia, Poland, and Russia.[14] "Industry assisted by capital" and international trade had now created a different reality elsewhere, an "almost magical picture" that made all "denunciation of luxury" useless.[15] The conquest of America had cost cruelties and horrors. But now the question had changed. One had reached, even there, that "precious age, marked by destiny for the satisfaction of the New World," in which America had become "the sanctuary of reason, liberty, and tolerance."[16] Nor was it true that the colonization of the new continent had been paid for by the depopulation of Europe, especially Spain. There were other causes: "The expulsion of the Moriscos and the Jews, the terrors inspired by a fanatic tribunal, the superstition that has multiplied monks and bachelors. . . ."[17] Intensification of commerce and industry had finally changed the situation of black slaves, those "unhappy victims of our greed." "The more that commerce flourishes, the more it creates capital, and this capital is used to multiply the number of Negroes and for the progress of agriculture." The logic of economics itself, in rendering "the Negro happier, makes him more useful." "Legislation has not yet and perhaps will not for some time be able to abolish slavery, but it begins to make it less harsh, and making it less harsh is to work towards abolishing it."[18] Even in this area, what counted were not Raynal's exhortations, but the study and comprehension of a reality in development. "The Abbé Raynal has taught men what they should do, I am telling them what they will do one day."[19] It was enough to observe the situation in Europe and in "old nations" such as France, England, and so on, to understand that colonies constitute a necessity that no moralism can eliminate. "Where the population is numerous, riches are considerable and unequally distributed, the subsistence of part of the people is difficult and precarious . . . colonies are a discharge, the necessary outlet into which the overflow can drain."[20] Thus he lamented the loss of Canada and exhorted France to remake itself by cultivating Guiana and by transforming Cayenne into a center of improvement, offering in that land "an asylum as

[13] Ibid., pp. 8, 11.
[14] Ibid., p. 12.
[15] Ibid., pp. 19, 21, 30.
[16] Ibid., p. 33.
[17] Ibid., p. 40.
[18] Ibid., pp. 52ff., 55, 57.
[19] Ibid., p. 55.
[20] Ibid., pp. 6off.

healthy as it is productive."[21] Examples from antiquity were not useful in the present situation (without forgetting Cato's exhortations against colonies, accompanied by his cruel and low-minded advice on how to treat the slaves). There could and should be only one example for all, precisely those United States of America, which by themselves were sufficient to lead one to respond positively to the question Raynal posed on the greater or lesser utility of the discovery of the new continent. "Oh land of Franklin, of Washington, of Hancock, of Adams!—Who could want that you had never existed, for them and for us. . . ."[22]

"The prize offered by the Abbé Raynal on the good or evil resulting for Europe from the discovery of the New World has aroused my interest," wrote the Marquis de Condorcet in 1786, adding immediately that he had soon abandoned treating such a broad theme and preferred to concentrate on the more lively political question of what influence the American Revolution had had on Europe.[23] With 1776, he said, something basic had changed in the world. One had passed from ideas written in the "books of philosophers" and impressed "into the hearts of virtuous men" to a political vindication of the rights of man. An example had been needed. "America gave us that example. The act that declared its independence is a simple and sublime exposition of these sacred and long-forgotten rights." Slavery continued, it is true, to mar this shining purity. But even in the United States "all enlightened men feel the shame of this danger, and the spot will not stain the purity of American laws much longer." Similarly, the economic understanding of the new republic still reflected "English prejudices." "The wise republicans . . . have not learned sufficiently that prohibitive laws, the regulation of commerce, and indirect taxes are impediments to the right of property." Even with regard to tolerance, the Americans had not always remained at the height of the principles they had proclaimed. "In establishing a broader toleration than any other nation, they have given in to some limitations required by the people." Traces "of a fanaticism too great to succumb to the first efforts of philosophy" had not entirely disappeared.[24] But beyond such limitations, what counted was the fact that the foundations on which the new republic was rising had remained intact. "They are the only people among whom one does not find either

[21] Ibid., p. 62.

[22] Ibid., p. 68.

[23] "De l'influence de la révolution d'Amérique sur l'Europe." A M. le marquis de la Fayette, qui à l'âge où les hommes ordinaires sont à peine connus dans leur société, a mérité le titre de bienfaiteur des deux mondes, par un habitant obscur de l'ancien hémisphère. 1786," in *Oeuvres de Condorcet* (Paris: publiées par A. Condorcet O'Connor et M. F. Arago, Firmin Didot, 1847), vol. 8, p. 4.

[24] Ibid., p. 12 and, on the economy, pp. 41ff.

Machiavellian maxims erected for political reasons, or in their sincere leaders of opinion a feigned impossibility of perfecting the social order and reconciling public prosperity with justice." Thus here was neither Machiavellianism nor renunciation of creating a society based on the rights of man. The defeat of England had meant the victory of liberty, not only for the colonists, but also for Great Britain itself. "If America had succumbed to the arms of England, despotism would soon have forged irons for the mother country, and the English would have experienced the fate of all republics who cease to be free because of having wanted to have subjects instead of only citizens." The "French philosophes," who, like the poor of all the world, were continually attacked and denigrated, now found a model and refuge in the United States.[25] Freedom of the press beyond the ocean was an example to all. "One has seen public discussions destroy prejudices and prepare in the wise views of legislators a support in public opinion." A religious tolerance, broader than anything ever seen in the past, "far from raising discord in America, makes peace and fraternity flourish." The horrible collection of military laws through which European armies operated had been demonstrated to be not only harmful, but also useless before the "example of a free people, supporting peacefully both military and civil laws." "The spirit of equality that reigns in the United States, and ensures its peace and prosperity, could be useful in Europe." America had demonstrated what could be done by "men of all conditions" as long as they were not made vile by "unjust opinion" and oppressed "by bad laws."[26]

The American Revolution seemed to have made humanity take a step toward a better international equilibrium and thus toward a more stable peace. Liberation from English domination seemed to promise a more rapid development of reason in America, and there was no other way to "improve the condition of humanity."[27] All the peoples of Europe had profited from "the healthy ideas of Americans on the rights of property and natural liberty," France perhaps more than any other, because it had "more need of these ideas than the English nation" and found itself "in a degree of enlightenment which will permit it to profit from this and join it to a constitution where useful reforms would find few obstacles to overcome, and also many fewer than in England."[28] As for the economy, there were no doubts, in the eyes of Condorcet, about the great advantages that had resulted from the commercial develop-

---

[25] Ibid., pp. 13ff.
[26] Ibid., pp. 16ff.
[27] Ibid., p. 30.
[28] Ibid., p. 31.

ment of America. He did not have the optimistic enthusiasm of Chastellux but nurtured a solid and reasonable faith in the future of principles of economic liberty as well as the political liberty of the United
States.

One year later, in 1787, Condorcet returned to the problems of
America, concentrating on constitutional issues. Thus, one decade later
he took up again the critique of his master Turgot and provided a
deeper and more detailed judgment of the governments issuing from
the revolution.[29] The central object of his polemic was the English constitutional tradition, the illusion that one could "increase the number of
powers by considering them in mutual balance." His principal aim was
to examine in its different aspects the functioning of a constitution
based on "a single legislative body" and "on the natural rights of man
anterior to social institutions."[30] Such a government had never existed.
First of all, women were deprived of electoral rights and excluded from
governing functions in the state. Everywhere (and in England in a particularly scandalous way) electoral legislation violated the principle of
equality and equity. The limits and character of the power of legislative
assemblies was not fixed precisely in any nation. The division between
legislative and judicial power, although very important, was uncertain
and vague. The whole system of collecting taxes and state finance
should be rationalized. The constitution should reconsider from its
roots the powers of government in matters of foreign policy, war, and
peace. These problems became more complex in the case of a "federal
republic," formed "among states independent of one another." But this
growing complexity made necessary a reaffirmation of the general principles at the basis of any rationally organized government. "The more
complex the constitution becomes, the more one perceives how to ensure the security of liberty, protection of citizens, internal peace of each
state, and union among members of the confederation by excluding
treaties of alliance in time of peace and restriction on trade, by considering absolute freedom of trade and industry as a right to be respected,
that is to say, a necessary adjunct to the right of property and personal
liberty: and finally by declaring that a property tax proportional to net
yield is the only just one."[31] Thus, only by ending traditional policies of
raison d'état and by substituting for them principles of economic liberty
of a physiocratic type could one fully satisfy, according to Condorcet,

[29] "Lettres d'un bourgeois de New-Haven à un citoyen de Virginie sur l'inutilité de
partager le pouvoir législatif entre plusieurs corps. 1787," in *Oeuvres de Condorcet*, vol. 9,
pp. 1ff.

[30] Ibid., pp. 10, 14.

[31] Ibid., pp. 53ff.

the needs created by the American Revolution. Any federal republic incapable of this, and maintaining the old controls and economic and fiscal restrictions, would place itself on the road of its own ruin. "Any federative republic that adopts other principles will risk disunity and loss of liberty."[32] Natural rights and reason alone could provide the uniformity among different states that would permit and guarantee unity. "Mercantile principles" were the worst enemies of free states.[33] Any recourse to "old habits," to the "pretended conventions of custom," to "vague principles of utility for encouraging agriculture or commerce," to the "amassing of riches and power" would lead to dissolution. "The constitution, the civil or criminal code, the police laws, the forms of justice" should become, if not identical everywhere, at least as uniform as possible.[34] And this would not be possible if one did not return to "maxims of natural right, universal justice, and reason."[35] It was the task of the "enlightened men of Europe and America" to indicate the means and instruments adapted to effecting such a grandiose transformation.[36] In great detail he suggested regulations for legislative assemblies and the policies they should follow in different areas, from taxation to armies. Everywhere the principal obstacle that should be done away with as soon as possible was the English example. Liberty existed effectively in Great Britain. This had been made to seem a merit of its constitution, which it was often desirable to imitate and follow as a model, with the illusion of transforming the principles on which it was based into "general maxims."[37] Bicameralism, the division of powers of the king, ministers, and the army, were found, in different forms and proportions, in other nations where monarchy was mixed with aristocracy, as in France, Spain, Hungary, Poland, and Sweden. Montesquieu had said that the archaic republics were incapable of liberty precisely because they had not succeeded in establishing that separation of the three powers whose model was furnished by England. But this type of reasoning from examples was repugnant to Condorcet. "One must argue independently of examples here." Why not criticize instead traditional republics for having been incapable "of organizing a representative democracy where it was possible to have peace and equality at the same time?"[38] This was precisely what was now demanded of the new American constitutions. The true problems to resolve were, for example,

[32] Ibid., p. 55.
[33] Ibid., p. 45.
[34] Ibid., p. 56.
[35] Ibid., p. 63.
[36] Ibid., p. 56.
[37] Ibid., p. 76.
[38] Ibid., p. 84.

those of the limit and character of the "spirit of faction" that was fatally forming itself in a free country, and which Condorcet, like almost all of his contemporaries, refused to accept or legitimate.[39] And then returned the problem of social inequality. The conclusion was always the same: no sumptuary laws, censors, "complicated constitutions, or all the inventions of traditional politics, would prevent the establishment of social inequality." The only possible remedy was the "freedom of commerce" and "good civil laws." This was the great lesson of the past and present of America, when compared with what had happened and was happening in Europe, and in England in a particular way. "Republican liberty cannot exist," he concluded, "in a land where the civil laws, the laws of finance, and the laws of commerce make possible the long continuation of great fortunes."[40]

The weight of the past was even heavier in the judgment the Abbé Mably pronounced in his *Observations sur les lois et le gouvernement des Etats Unis d'Amérique*, which appeared in 1783, written, as was insistently claimed at the time, on the request of the American government. It remained at the center of the Parisian debate on the American Revolution of these years. The old philosophe, the only survivor of the great generation of the French Enlightenment, had intervened ten years earlier in the crisis of the Polish republic. He turned now to pronouncing his opinion on the constitution of the thirteen American states, and on the federal bond that united them.[1] At the root of the new nation he saw—

---

[39] Ibid., pp. 87ff. See Richard Hofstadter, *The Idea of a Party System: The Rise of Legitimate Opposition in the United States, 1780–1840* (Berkeley: University of California Press, 1972).

[40] "Lettres d'un bourgeois de New-Haven," p. 93.

[1] The official American request, which made its rounds in the European gazettes and chanceries, is a legend. See, for example, *Notizie del mondo [V.]*, no. 20, 8 March 1783 (Paris, 23 February). What actually happened resulted from the initiative of John Adams, both in soliciting *Observations* and in procuring its publication in Holland, in the autumn of 1783, through his French correspondent and collaborator Antoine Marie Cerisier (see the index of part 2, volume 2). See *Adams Papers. Diary and Autobiography of John Adams*, ed. L. H. Butterfield (New York: Atheneum, 1964), vol. 3, p. 101. See also *The Works of John Adams, Second President of the United States*, vol. 9, p. 522, letter to Cerisier from The Hague dated 22 February 1784, in which he called the Abbé Mably "my friend" and said he was particularly sensitive to his approval, "as I know his principles to be pure and his spirit independent." He exhorted Cerisier to write the preface of the Dutch version of *Observations* and was pleased to see "the pen of a De Mably, a Raynal, a Cerisier, a Price turned to the subject of government. I wish that the thoughts of all academies in Europe were engaged on the same theme, because I really think that the science of society is much

exactly the opposite of what Condorcet claimed—British tradition interpreted as a repudiation (even if rather out of ignorance than of mature
judgment, at least in its origins) of the "unhappy politics of Machiavelli."
The Americans had done well not to create a new state but to have given
life to a federal republic, a true Switzerland beyond the sea. Their vast
territory, the austerity of their life, and the smallness of their inhabited
centers had permitted them to avoid the destiny of republics in antiquity, of falling into a tumultuous citizens' democracy. The judicial institutions inherited from Great Britain, above all the jury, also constituted
a precious guarantee against democratic degeneration. "You will see, I
believe," he wrote addressing himself to John Adams, "that democracy
must be managed, tempered, and established with the greatest prudence."[2] Perils were not lacking. The passage from a state of subjection
to one of liberty had perhaps been "too quick." The preparation of
minds had been insufficient, all the more so because the war had not
lasted long enough to correct "their prejudices" and give them "all the
qualities that should be shown by a free people." Seven years of the
American war seemed few in comparison with eighty for the Dutch.
Now the United States faced difficulties even worse than those Rome
had confronted after the expulsion of the Tarquins, and these were ag-
gravated by the fact that everywhere in the world ancient virtues were
on the verge of extinction, "and I don't know if a war of seven years was
sufficient to restore them in America." The danger of dissolution menaced the new nation. "I fear that the rich will want to form a separate
order and control all authority, while the others, too proud of the equality with which they have been flattered, will refuse to consent." The
"revolution" which could be painless and peaceful if the weakness of the
nation permitted it, would probably give rise instead to grave confrontations and conflicts.[3] Were the American constitutions sufficiently solid
barriers against such a danger? It was enough to observe the constitution of Pennsylvania to be convinced of the contrary. "The law of Pennsylvania favors an uncontrolled democracy, but this proclivity will only
incense the rich, who will never consent to not having different rights
and prerogatives from the multitude of the poor." Against democracy
stood British tradition and all of American reality. "For myself, I think

behind other arts and sciences, trades and manufactures—that the noblest of all knowledge is the least general and that a general spirit of inquiry would produce ameliorations
of the administration of every government in every form." As to the reaction Mably's book
aroused in America, the news that one reads in the Florentine *Notizie del mondo* is curious
and legendary (no. 11, 5 February 1785 [Paris, 21 January]); see above, p. 70.

[2] "Observations sur le gouvernement et les lois des Etats Unis d'Amérique," in *Oeuvres
complètes* (Paris: Bossange, Masson et Besson, 1797), vol. 8, pp. 222, 229.

[3] Ibid., pp. 233ff.

America is pushed toward aristocracy by a superior force that will destroy the laws set up against it." The force opposing legislators would serve for nothing other "than to inflame intractable passions that will precipitate the republic into either anarchy or oligarchy."[4] The history of Florence confirmed this prediction. From the stalls and shops of Pennsylvania would arise the new American Medicis. "To what will ambition, genius, money, and popular favor not lead?"[5] The electoral laws of Pennsylvania, the unicameral character of its legislative assembly, the very publicity of debates would impede that equilibrium between aristocracy and democracy, that mixed government, which had been the strength of Sparta and Rome.[6] Massachusetts had been much more wise to reproduce, with new names, the political structure of Great Britain, improving it in various respects.[7] Thus the governor, who had taken the place of the king, had been justly deprived of any right of veto. "On a democratic basis, which assures the multitude its liberty without giving it too audacious hopes," Massachusetts had "established an aristocracy," giving life to a government otherwise much more stable than that of Pennsylvania. Founded on "metaphysical speculation," it took a fundamental fact into consideration: corruption, which had originated in Europe and had now invaded the new continent as well. The citizens of Georgia had done even better, and their constitution was halfway between the one of Pennsylvania and that of Massachusetts. "What good circumstances for establishing a republic among a people still only occupied with searching out their wealth by clearing lands near their habitations."[8] But this was an exception. In general, all the American states, concerned with pressing political and economic questions, had failed to occupy themselves sufficiently with the need to stabilize and maintain customs, and not give in to the seduction of well-being and wealth. Did not even the laws on religious tolerance risk leading to a kind of "indifference"? A "moral and political catechism" was indispensable. "It would be worthy of the wisdom of the Continental Congress to compose such a work." Nor should one forget "that it is very dangerous to establish by law an absolute freedom of the press in a new state that has acquired its liberty and independence before having use of the arts or sciences."[9] To be sure, scientists had to be absolutely free in their research, but how could one permit any citizen able to write the "impunity

---

[4] Ibid., p. 238.
[5] Ibid., p. 239.
[6] Ibid., p. 248.
[7] Ibid., p. 255.
[8] Ibid., pp. 251, 255.
[9] Ibid., pp. 270, 272.

to entertain the public with his dreams, or attack the fundamental principles of society?"[10]

These were symptoms of the incurable evil that attacked "all free states where riches are unequally distributed."[11] What should be done? The fatal character of the disease made any revolutionary outcome impossible: how could one imagine a revolt of the poor to attain social leveling? He was also doubtful when confronted with the life the United States was seeking to open for itself of broader and broader liberties, an enlargement of suffrage, a more and more complete freedom of the press and religion, a democracy, in short, that without pretending to make social differences disappear tended to make them less rigid and self-conscious. This was a development precisely contrary to the one indicated by Mably. The history of ancient republics seemed to suggest only one possible solution. There had always been a transformation from democracy to oligarchy. All one could do was try to slow the process by institutionalizing political and constitutional forms and by fixing the existing equilibrium in a mixed government. The Swiss provided an example. "Why has the democracy of some cantons experienced none of the caprices and confusion natural to democratic government?" Berne was a "paternal government." The "simplicity of Swiss customs" had made it possible to maintain equality joined with "wise aristocracy."[12] The military system of the Swiss, "the people armed," had contributed significantly to solidifying their confederation.[13] But how could one hope that the United States would benefit from such favorable circumstances? Commerce and industry were already beginning to develop there. One could foresee that sooner or later the seas would be covered with American ships. "The greatest prosperity" was on the horizon. "For myself, I confess," he said turning to the Americans, that "this prodigious fortune makes me tremble before the fate awaiting you." Plato had foreseen it intuitively, the modern economist Cantillon had described it, and the English writer John Brown had deplored it: "The most sordid interests that reign in banks and counting houses" had invaded, corrupted, and distorted society as a whole.[14] The principles set as the basis for the constitutions of the new states would be unable to resist such pressure. With what eyes would the sons of the rich, in the second or third generation, look on "that equality that your laws have sought to establish among citizens? They will understand nothing

[10] Ibid., p. 273.
[11] Ibid., p. 280.
[12] Ibid., pp. 281, 284.
[13] Ibid., p. 285.
[14] Ibid., pp. 287, 299.

of the inalienable rights of sovereignty you have attributed to the people."[15] As for the inhabitants of the countryside, how would they accept
the formation of this new aristocracy of money? "A Graccus, that is,
some adroit ambitious person, or an inspired orator, will be enough to
raise citizens against each other." Washington had declined power, "and
still showed the antique virtues of the Roman republic."[16] But would he
always be imitated and followed? The example of the United Provinces
showed clearly what could happen in a land where commerce was allowed to multiply the needs of men. "It is now only the pale shadow of
a republic."[17] In the United States it would not even be possible to appeal to the authority of a stadholder to limit the foreseeable bitter internal struggles. Only greater powers given to Congress might be useful.
"Menaced by the troubles, divisions, and domestic discords of which I
have spoken, you will not be able to do without a supreme magistracy to
prevent or stop them."[18] Fear of pressure from below, and a desire to
institutionalize the conflicts of American society, ended by pushing him
in the direction later taken by the Federalists. "I see only," he concluded,
again addressing John Adams, "one single remedy for the Americans:
that is to make the Continental Congress the supreme judge of all differences that might arise among different orders of citizens in the states
of the Union."[19] The reestablishment of lost integrity, and the concord
of interests and sentiments, should be celebrated, Mably added, in a
great annual festival: "Let illuminations, games, and dances summon all
citizens to enjoy themselves, let the magistrates and rich mix with the
multitude in this kind of Saturnalia, let the great be shown the image of
equality, while the people learn to love their country and their superiors." In the name of God and in the presence of the people, delegates
of the different republics would swear "to adhere to the laws rigorously,
to defend the union, and to submit their judgments to the rules of justice."[20]

   In this debate—of great interest, as we have seen, and which tended
continually to transcend American problems and touch on the most
heated questions agitating France and Europe—Thomas Jefferson ac-

[15] Ibid., pp. 294ff.
[16] Ibid., p. 296.
[17] Ibid., p. 300.
[18] Ibid., p. 309.
[19] Ibid., p. 310.
[20] Ibid., p. 314.

tively intervened, beginning in the autumn of 1784 when he was named
American plenipotentiary minister in France. Beside him, from July of
that year, was Filippo Mazzei. Already in the summer, when Mazzei was
still in America, he had traced a picture of persons who might support
the American cause in Paris: the Duc de La Rochefoucauld, who had
edited the collection of American constitutions (and had thus made
known to a close group of Europeans documents that the American
Congress on 29 December 1780 had decided, with exceptional modesty,
to have printed in two hundred copies); the Duc de La Vaugouyon, the
French ambassador at The Hague (who was connected to the patriot
party); Marmontel and Morellet, two Encyclopedists; Francesco Favi
(who was in Paris to fill the place of the representative of Tuscany,
which Mazzei had hoped might be his); and naturally, Vergennes, the
minister of foreign affairs, along with some other functionaries, besides
Neapolitan diplomats and officers, such as Don Diego Naselli d'Ara-
gona, who was in favor of solidifying commercial relations with the new
country. Even if one adds the lesser personages indicated, the list is
poor. A great work opened before Mazzei and Jefferson in drawing attention to the United States, which remained a distant and an isolated
land, despite the enthusiasm raised during the revolution.[1] When
Raynal predicted that the new nation would soon close in on itself, he
only indicated a possibility that must have been obvious to many observers. Officers of the French units that had fought in America were of a
different opinion, indeed an opposite one. Saint John de Crèvecoeur,
Chastellux, and naturally La Fayette, established contact with Jefferson
immediately; they wrote books and projects and provided their own interpretations of America, insisting on the future place of the United
States in the commerce and economic life of the world.[2] Reading
through Jefferson's correspondence one cannot fail to notice that his
efforts were directed, at least at first, toward lands in some sense on the
margin of the great currents of trade: Tuscany, Naples, the Mediterranean, the lands of Barbary, and Morocco. Great Britain and France,
despite their long struggle, remained at the center of the picture and
did not seem to admit intrusions into their sphere of influence. Despite
victory and independence, America remained in a sense still a colonial
nation. The situation was either denied or accepted, but it could not be
ignored.

[1] *The Papers of Thomas Jefferson*, vol. 7, "Philip Mazzei's Memoranda Regarding Persons
and Affairs in Paris," pp. 386ff.

[2] On the judgment that Jefferson gave of La Fayette, a man of "unmeasured ambition,
but the means he uses are virtuous," see ibid., vol. 8, p. 39, to James Madison, Paris, 18
March 1785.

Thus, Jefferson's effort was directed toward international opinion, rather than at commerce, to defend the good name of the new republic, to combat the incessant propaganda of English gazettes, and to persuade the world that the political creature born beyond the ocean was alive and well. At first this was an especially polemical and defensive effort (how, for example, could one speak of anarchy in the United States when in Great Britain Lord Gordon had turned London upside down just a few years earlier?).[3] On this basis a solid relationship became established between Jefferson (and Mazzei) and Jean Luzac, the editor of the gazette of Leiden, the best journal in Europe.[4] In France, Jefferson found enthusiasm and sympathy for the United States. But there was no philo-American political organization. In Holland a first nucleus was formed through journalistic polemics, which had a notable influence on the development of the patriot party in the United Provinces. In Paris, Jefferson acted out the role of a philosophe, correcting without offending, persuading without imploring, making clear and near places and problems that seemed exotic and mysterious.[5] He discussed the constitutional questions at the center of his politics with his compatriots, and even with some Englishmen, such as Richard Price.[6] With the French he was an Encyclopedist, focusing on natural and political history, on humanity and on economics. He made a wise distribution of his *Notes on the state of Virginia*, which was written in 1781, revised the next year, and published at Paris in two hundred copies. It appeared in French in 1786, and at London in 1787. He transformed this limpid book on the choreography of his native land into a kind of membership card for a semisecret confraternity, the symbol of a brotherhood of believers in a religion of America and nature. The pages in which he refuted once again the theory of inferiority or biological degeneration in lands beyond the sea were transformed by his pen into a manifesto against Buffon, in favor of science and of life marked with a lucid rigor.[7] In vain Jefferson attempted to procure a faithful and exact French translation. Morellet did again for the *Notes* what he had done for Beccaria; he rewrote the book in translating it. Jefferson had to give in to

[3] Ibid., vol. 7, pp. 540ff.

[4] For a typical example of the collaboration of Jefferson, Luzac, and Mazzei, in the winter of 1785–1786, see ibid., vol. 9, pp. 4ff. See also *Memorie*, pp. 303ff., 306ff.

[5] See, for example, the letter to Chastellux, from Paris, 24 December 1784, *The Papers of Thomas Jefferson*, vol. 7, pp. 580ff., and all their subsequent correspondence.

[6] Ibid., pp. 630ff., Paris, 1 February 1785, and the reply of R. Price, 21 March 1785, vol. 8, pp. 52ff.

[7] "Notes on the State of Virginia," in *The Complete Jefferson*, assembled and arranged by Saul K. Padover (New York: Duell, Sloan and Pearce, 1943), p. 567. See Antonello Gerbi, *The Dispute of the New World: A History of a Polemic, 1750–1900* (Pittsburgh: University of Pittsburgh Press, 1973), pp. 252ff.

seeing it published "mutilated in it's freest parts."[8] Mazzei wrote to Stanislaus Augustus, king of Poland, offering him a copy in the name of the author: "The Abbé Morellet has translated it into French, not too accurately, and has changed its method, in the style of French authors who want to be original even in translations."[9]

Rigorous with himself, Jefferson knew how to be generous and understanding with the political writers multiplying in the eighties. He welcomed the collaboration of the heirs of the physiocrats, and above all Dupont de Nemours, the chief among them. He was open with men such as Honoré de Mirabeau and Jacques-Pierre Brissot de Warville, even when the spirit that moved them to rebel and look toward the United States of America was different from his. Through Mazzei he contacted the youngest of these writers, such as Giovanni Ferri, whom we will find in the Dutch revolution, and Jean-Antoine Gallois, Filangieri's translator.[10] Religious liberty was a terrain where followers of the Encyclopedists, admirers of Joseph II, and dissidents from beyond the ocean often met. Jefferson's formulations were particularly effective and persuasive, even in this area, and Mazzei did not miss distributing them even in Italian versions.[11]

---

[8] *The Papers of Thomas Jefferson*, vol. 9, p. 265, letter to James Madison, Paris, 8 February 1786. Writing to William Carmichael, on 15 December 1787, Jefferson said of the translation of Morellet: "The whole order is changed and other differences made, which, with numerous typographical errors, render it a different book, in some respects perhaps a better one, but not mine" (vol. 12, p. 426). The parallel with what had happened twenty years earlier is striking. Jefferson rejected the French travesty. Beccaria gave in to it.

[9] *Lettere di Filippo Mazzei*, vol. 1, p. 9, letter to Maurice Glayre, Paris, 1 August 1788.

[10] *Memorie*, pp. 306ff. Jefferson sent a curious description of a reunion of "friends of America" and the Marquis de La Fayette "to hear a discussion on American politics and commerce by Mr. Warville" to David Humphreys on 17 March 1786. It listed "the duke de Rochefoucault, the marquises Condorcy and Chattelus, messeurs. Metza, Crevecoeur etc." and said that the atmosphere re-created "the freedom of investigation in America," concluding that the remarks of Brissot were good, "some of the observations new, many of them just and ingenious: but perhaps there is too much declamation blended with them" (*The Papers of Thomas Jefferson*, vol. 9, pp. 329ff. In the misspelling of the names one almost hears this American colonel speak. With "Metza" one recognizes Mazzei).

[11] *The Papers of Thomas Jefferson*, vol. 10, p. 200n. Jefferson was particularly satisfied with the echo that had responded everywhere to the diffusion of the Virginia laws on religious tolerance.

The Virginia act for religious freedom has been received with infinite approbation in Europe and propagated with enthusiasm. I do not mean the governments, but the individuals which compose them. It has been translated into French and Italian, has been sent to most of the courts of Europe, and has been the best evidence of the falsehood of those reports which stated us to be in anarchy. It is inserted in the new *Encyclopédie* and is appearing in most of the publications respecting America. In fact it is comfortable to see the standard of reason at length erected, after so many ages during which the human mind has been held in vassalage by kings, priests and nobles and it is honourable for us to have produced the first legislature who has had the courage to declare that the reason of man may be trusted with the formation of his own opinions (vol. 10, pp. 603ff., letter to James Madison, Paris, 16 December 1786).

His defense and illustration of free America never fell to the level of pure propaganda or to that of routine diplomacy. His philosophical and political convictions were too deep and clear for that to happen. The spectacle of European politics, and the news that came to him daily, deepened his detachment and reinforced the sense of superiority that he nourished in this distant land, so new and different from his own. He arrived in Paris when the decision of Joseph II to reopen navigation in the Scheldt seemed to threaten outbreak of a new war. The situation in the East, between Russia and Turkey, was also threatening. The old king of Prussia was a symbol of the uncertainty and weariness of the Old World. Before such realities, any comparison with America could only highlight the weight, vanity, and fragility of the ancien régime. Holland, even if it escaped war, risked an "internal revolution." The English remained deaf to reason in their commercial policy. And what would France do?[12] "I am watching with anxiety the part which this court will act," he wrote to James Monroe. It would be to abandon all faith in "national rectitude" if, as it appeared, France continued to be inspired in its actions by the "rascality of the 16th century." Of what use were the "enlightened men" of this country or the good intentions of its king?[13] It was not only a question of inbred Machiavellianism. European life as a whole caused a profound reaction in him. He wrote to Carlo Bellini, the Tuscan emigré in Virginia, to confess that he found "the general fate of humanity here most deplorable." Voltaire had been right in saying that everyone in Europe had to be either an anvil or a hammer. It seemed a scene of hell and paradise, with God and the angels in glory and "crowds of the damned trampled under their feet." A huge mass of people suffered "under physical and moral oppression" while the great were looked up to by all with admiration. The comparison with the "degree of happiness which is enjoyed in America by every class of the people" was impressive. With "tranquil permanent felicity" beyond the ocean was contrasted tense moments of "extasy" and long periods of "restlessness and torment" in Europe. This imbalance also showed itself in the world of knowledge. "In science, the mass of the people is two centuries behind ours, their literati half a dozen years before us." There was no need to run behind the latter: with time what was authentic in the progress of science would come to America. Meanwhile, frankness continued to prevail over "European politeness."[14] So deep did this distrust become in him that it induced him to recommend

---

[12] Ibid., vol. 8, pp. 38ff., letter to James Madison, Paris, 18 March 1785.
[13] Ibid., p. 42, Paris, 18 March 1785.
[14] Ibid., pp. 568ff., Paris, 30 September 1785.

Geneva as a place of education for young Americans (although it was ruined by the tyranny that France, Savoy, and Berne had established after the defeat of the revolution of 1782), and above all Rome, for its classical models and its distance from Paris.[15] As for political life, Jefferson, who was always sensitive to the difficult problems that accompanied American liberty, still concluded: "all this is better than European bondage."[16] It seemed more and more incredible to him that there continued to be people convinced "that kings, nobles, or priests are good conservators of the public happiness." A visit to France would soon persuade them of the contrary. It was enough to think of the French people, intelligent and happy in a fertile land, but still oppressed and reduced to misery. The situation was better in England. But even there the ground was prepared for the establishment of a despotism. "Nobility, wealth and pomp are the objects of their adoration." Learned men were fewer than in France, and "infinitely less emancipated from prejudice." "Let our countrymen know that the people alone can protect us against these evils": Americans should never forget this.[17]

In Paris Jefferson's most important political and editorial discussions were with Jean Nicolas Démeunier, the compiler of the four volumes on *Economie politique et diplomatique* of the *Encyclopédie méthodique*, one of the largest editorial undertakings of those years.[18] Dedicated to the Baron de Breteuil, minister and secretary of state, these volumes were intended to be the last word on ideas and political realities of the world. Published between 1784 and 1788, they became a balance sheet and portrait of the last years of the ancien régime. One understands why Jefferson tried to assert his own vision of the United States. The Duc de La Rochefoucauld had recommended the author to him when the first volume had already appeared with the articles "Amérique," of a geographical nature—referring to *Etats-Unis* for "everything relating to the constitution, products, politics, commerce, and so on, of the thirteen colonies which have just broken the yoke of England"—and "Caroline," with a long historical and constitutional account, and a discussion of what Locke and Mably had said about it.[19] Démeunier was aware that

---

[15] Ibid., vol. 9, pp. 58ff., letter to Thomas Elder, Paris, 25 November 1785.

[16] Ibid., p. 215, letter to John Jay, 25 January 1786.

[17] Ibid., vol. 10, pp. 244ff., letter to George Wythe, Paris, 13 April 1786.

[18] See Robert Darnton, *The Business of Enlightenment: A Publishing History of the Encyclopédie, 1775–1800* (Cambridge, Mass.: Harvard University Press, 1979).

[19] *Encyclopédie méthodique. Economie politique et diplomatique . . .* par M. Démeunier, avocat et censeur royal (Paris: Panckoucke et Liège, Plomteux, 1784), vol. 1, pp. 139ff., 444ff. The information on the constitution of the Carolinas derived in large part from the collection of American constitutions edited by the Duc de La Rochefoucauld. See *The Papers*

he knew very little about the real problems of the new state and thus asked for assistance, assuring Jefferson that his "zeal for the glory and prosperity of your new republics" was "very much alive."[20] Verbally, and in writing, the ambassador brought him up-to-date on American problems, and then agreed to revise the text of the article. Still more questions appeared: for instance, what position should one take with regard to the problem of the Order of Cincinnatus?[21] The outcome was far from satisfactory to Jefferson. He continually objected to ideas and phrases derived from Raynal, and the more he reread him, the more convinced he became of this author's ignorance and lack of solidarity. Démeunier cited him continually, together with Crèvecoeur, Mably, Turgot, and Price, and he did not hesitate to add to the mosaic entire phrases of Jefferson when these were open affirmations of republican and federal faith. The result was a composite, eclectic, from which factual errors were not entirely eliminated. The ideas lacked a solid coordinating principle. These ninety tightly packed pages, in two columns, were a vivid testimony to the interest developments in America aroused in France, just as they reflected the gaps, limits, and abstractness of the discussion carried on during the previous ten years. They were certainly distant from the clarity of the *Notes on Virginia* that Jefferson had before his eyes as a model and were mentioned as such just at the end of Démeunier's article. But still, there was a thrust, which Jefferson, perhaps for reasons of diplomacy and perhaps because of a natural philosophical detachment, tended to restrain and channel: the thrust of what had prompted the colonists to rebel (and here Tom Paine and even Raynal furnished an undeniable testimony, along with the Declaration of Independence, which was naturally published in its entirety); a thrust toward democracy, equality, and liberty; a thrust to profoundly transform the civil and penal laws. A great example came directly from Virginia, with its law on religious liberty which, to be sure, we find in these pages. But, as for equality, the formation of the Order of Cincinnatus touched a sore point. The problem of relationships with the "unhappy population" of savages remained open; in vain, one reads, there had been an attempt to obscure them: "Truth and justice will make themselves heard amid the forests of the New World." Clear, however, was the imprint of Jefferson's thought on what had now become a central political problem (we are in the year 1786), that is, the need for changes "to make in the

of Thomas Jefferson, vol. 9, p. 150, letter of the Duc de La Rochefoucauld from Paris, 4 January 1786.

[20] *The Papers of Thomas Jefferson*, vol. 9, p. 155, Paris, 6 January 1786.

[21] Ibid., pp. 382ff., Paris, 9 April 1786. The material on these discussions is in vol. 10, pp. 3ff.

federative act of the Americans." This would undoubtedly be a constitution better than the one that had united the Achaean states, and that
still united the Swiss and Dutch. The "act of confederation having been
written in haste and in the middle of the war, it should not be astonishing that it is susceptible to a higher degree of perfection and that the
federal bond does not have the necessary force to ensure the prosperity
of the United States and to maintain its tranquillity."[22] Revision of the
constitution was now at the center of American problems and debates.
Jefferson knew this. Démeunier instead remained distracted by a thousand questions of geography, economy, and society.

In the dialogue between the ambassador and the Encyclopedist a
third party was continually present, Filippo Mazzei. To him Jefferson
unburdened his disappointment at not having been able to keep Raynal's shadow completely at bay. He sent his pages to him as soon as they
were written.[23] This passionate collaboration contributed to prompting
Mazzei to put together the work on the United States of America that
he had planned for so long. This was also to be a kind of encyclopedia;
but unlike the one of Démeunier, it was intended to give a specific interpretation to the revolution and its results. He wrote it in Italian and
found a capable and willing translator in "a certain M. Faure, a youth
from Normandy, a lawyer at the Parlement." The version was in fact a
collective work of an entire group of friends composed of Jefferson,
"Ferri, Gallois, Condorcet, Dupont, and the Abbé Morellet," as Mazzei
himself listed them. "The pretty Marquise de Condorcet was the only
one," he added, "who was not content with the translation of M. Faure
and wanted her husband to join with her in redoing it. . . . Condorcet
was very busy, yet did not have it in his power to oppose his wife's wish.
But it was not appropriate for me to intervene, and thus I went away,
leaving the manuscript she had in hand, which contained two chapters,
one on the Order of Cincinnatus (which was translated by her) and the
other on the relationship of General Washington and the Marquis de La
Fayette to that society, which was translated by her husband. One sees
in the first the style of a truly sensitive soul, and in the second geometry
speaking."[24]

As Mazzei told us, "this work was written in large part and the printing started in 1786."[25] In May, Jefferson, who had just returned from a

---

[22] *Encyclopédie méthodique. Economie politique et diplomatique*, vol. 2 (1786), pp. 345ff.,
433, 372.

[23] *The Papers of Thomas Jefferson*, vol. 10, pp. 10ff.

[24] *Memorie*, pp. 307ff.

[25] *Recherches historiques et politiques sur les Etats-Unis de l'Amérique septentrionale, où l'on
traite des établissemens des treize colonies, de leurs rapports et de leurs dissentions avec la Grande-
Bretagne, de leurs gouvernemens avant et après la révolution, etc.*, par un citoyen de Virginie,

trip to London, wrote that Mazzei "will soon publish a book on the subject of America."[26] "The author is an exact man," he said again many years later.[27] "He is well informed and possesses a masculine understanding," he wrote in the summer of 1786 to his Dutch friend Van Hogendorp in announcing the coming publication of Mazzei's work. But obstacles were not lacking. The book was more adapted to free Holland than to France: "I believe it cannot be printed here."[28] For a moment an edition in the original language, in Tuscany, was considered.[29] Finally, with much delay, the Parisian edition came to light, at the beginning of 1788.

He dedicated his work "to the people of the United States of America." From his first words to his "dear fellow citizens" he declared his polemical intentions. "The prejudices I have found in Europe regarding our governments and our present situation inspired in me the desire to destroy them." He would not be an apologist, but a historian of the new republic, "exact and true" in exposing the facts, open and frank in his judgments, "as is appropriate to a citizen of a free country." He would not follow in the footsteps "of certain European writers" who wrote of the American constitutions without having seriously studied them. Nor would he insist on the internal polemics of citizens of the United States. There governments were perfectible, whereas the defects "that reign in others" were greater and more irreducible. "Despite what remains for you to do, you have great objects of consolation in what you have already done." "The progress of philosophy" had guided them along the road that opened before them.[30]

It was necessary before all else to dismiss those imaginary or inexact histories that impeded a true comprehension of the American Revolution. The eloquence of Raynal, the "tone full of warmth and energy" with which he evoked the truth, did not at all prove that he was faithful to it. The zeal of Mably was stranded on the weakness of his old age, "a time of life little suited to scrupulous research on new topics," and on the inaccuracy of the sources he had used. "If ignorance is preferrable to error, it must be admitted that the actual state of opinion in Europe

avec quattre lettres d'un bourgeois de New Haven sur l'unité de la législation (Colle et Paris: Froullé, 1788), pt. 1, "Avertissement," p. v. See Tortarolo, *Illuminismo e rivoluzioni*, pp. 119ff.

[26] *The Papers of Thomas Jefferson*, vol. 9, p. 446, letter to John Page, Paris, 4 May 1786.

[27] *The Complete Jefferson*, "Notes on Professor Ebeling's Letter of July 30, 1795," p. 79.

[28] *The Papers of Thomas Jefferson*, vol. 10, p. 299, Paris, 25 August 1786.

[29] On 15 August 1787 Jefferson wrote to Gaudenzio Clerici: "Mazzei is still here. His book is in the press. He proposes going on to Florence in the winter, where I imagine he will print his work in Italian" (*The Papers of Thomas Jefferson*, vol. 12, p. 39).

[30] *Recherches historiques et politiques*, pt. 1, pp. 1ff.

about America is worse than before the revolution, and the observations of the Abbé Raynal have singularly contributed to sanctify numerous dreams that are still believed on the continent to be to the disadvantage of the United States."[31] His errors were all the more pernicious because of his renown and his relationship in Paris with "some of the most illustrious citizens of the United States."[32] Particularly awkward were the rumors of an official request for a constitution from the old *philosophe*. The United States were themselves a model; they did not need to be restructured by anyone. Any doubts about this (and the allusion to John Adams was clear) only helped to confirm the legend of the "pretended anarchy" that was said to be tearing at the young republic. The English version of Mably's work supported these calumnies. "This is why the errors of the Abbé Mably have had greater consequence than those of the Abbé Raynal, and require a formal and more extended refutation."[33]

Thus having established his objectivity as a polemicist, Mazzei returned to the theme that had inspired him from the time of his first encounter with America, the very origin of the colonies. He repeated that one should never confuse "men who have nothing else in view than the hope of making a fortune with those who only seek the advantage of enjoying liberty."[34] Precisely for this reason he did not intend to return to the history of Christopher Columbus and the conquistadors, and he thus clearly separated the development of the Spanish and Portuguese world from that of the free British colonies. For these only liberty, not avidity, was at the root of existence. Whatever the opinion of Hume, "whom many people consider to be a courtier," cupidity was not the origin "Of the Foundation of Virginia."[35] The great fortune of North America consisted precisely in the fact that the ambitious, and adventurers, had been mistaken: they sought riches where there were none. "Speculators had formed a false idea of the country. Instead of imagining it as a most advantageous asylum for the enjoyment of liberty, they thought they would be able to draw great wealth from it. Their views were founded on commerce and on the hope of finding mines of precious metals; they perhaps feared competition and wanted to have a monopoly." "By good fortune for us the precious metals were never found, and any American who is sincerely attached to his country should be

[31] Ibid., "Introduction," pp. viiiff.
[32] Ibid., p. ix.
[33] Ibid., pp. xiiiff.
[34] Ibid., "Des colonies qui ont donné naissance aux Treize Etats-Unis de l'Amérique," p. 2.
[35] Ibid., p. 8 n. 1.

happy that nature had not thus poisoned the happy soil."[36] Free and
uncorrupted, Virginia saw its liberty threatened only in the mid-seven-
teenth century by the hand of the "usurper Cromwell, who had become
the tyrant of England with the imposing title Protector of the republic."[37] But its original liberty returned in the epoch of the Restoration
and provided a first indispensable basis for the vindication of the sixties
and seventies. From this point of view Mazzei reviewed the different
American colonies one after the other: Massachusetts, where the laws
"conformed to the austerity of religion and customs," Rhode Island,
Connecticut, New York, Pennsylvania, and so on.[38] He wrote one hundred or so pages of history of the colonial period, where polemical
points against Raynal were not lacking, and where the conclusions were
preemptory: how could one doubt, after what one had learned, what
was the "true cause of the revolution"?[39] Europeans, who continued to
speak of the deportation of criminals as an important element in the
formation of modern America, only detracted attention from the true
origins of the United States: all had arisen from the mistaken and unjust
policy that Great Britain had attempted in vain to impose on its colonies,
and this policy originated in the constitution of the United Kingdom
itself. "A minister can act as he likes against the law, provided that he
has the majority of Parliament devoted to him. One is mistaken to believe that the first minister of England is obliged to pay attention to public opinion. He is less subject to its effects than the minister of an absolute prince, because the sanction of Parliament serves him as a shield,
just as the Roman senate served as a shield to the ministers of the first
Caesars."[40] The obstinacy of the colonies had succeeded in breaking this
legal enchantment. "The happy star of the colonies saw that obstinacy
won over politics."[41] Experience taught that "the greatest misfortune
that can happen to a nation" consisted in "becoming the subject of a
republic."[42] Independence and liberty had become the cardinal points
of American politics, so much so as to ransom the future, Mazzei assured. It could be that one day the inhabitants of the United States
would help their neighbors become free. But this would never be a conquest: "It is improbable that they will give in to the no less imprudent
than unjust desire to have subjects."[43] The colonists had been extraor-

[36] Ibid., p. 13.
[37] Ibid., p. 18.
[38] Ibid., pp. 38ff.
[39] Ibid., pp. 111ff.
[40] Ibid., p. 129.
[41] Ibid., p. 125.
[42] Ibid., p. 126.
[43] Ibid., p. 126 n. 1.

dinarily patient in resisting the incursions of the English government. Their constitutions themselves, "a composite of monarchy, aristocracy, and democracy," predisposed them to this.[44] Finally, they showed that they were capable of giving life to institutions that alone could be useful to their cause. America owed its liberty to committees of correspondence in the various colonies.[45] Most vivid then was his reevocation of the birth of the new state, the preparations for war, the formation of a people, and their actions. He said that even the most imperfect of governments born at this time was "less distant from the principles of liberty than those of any other ancient or modern republics" even if the best "did not yet approach the point that could satisfy the philosopher or legislator."[46] Nor should the Americans become proud of the superiority they had acquired in the struggle of all nations to obtain liberty. The circumstances in which they had operated had been particularly advantageous. "There is only one class of citizens."[47] The idea of the rights of man was deeply rooted. The press was free and there were no obstacles to the exercise of religion. "One must consider further that the American people are very gentle and that they have the greatest confidence in those in whom they entrust the care of their own affairs." These circumstances took on a new significance when seen in the light of a central fundamental truth, "that our century is one of philosophy." No republican government, ancient or modern, had taken so many steps to guarantee "the rights of man"; "we did not have to fight against distinctions of rank, the most terrible obstacle to the establishment of a free and just government." It was even surprising, with so much experience, that they had not succeeded in creating governments even closer to "the perfection of which they are capable." Improvement would come "from the free and healthy way of thinking of our youth." The elders were not able to abandon their prejudices or detach themselves from the maxims of the "old government." Young men arriving at places of responsibility showed "their disposition to do the best possible."[48]

It was not easy for the elders, or for the new generation, to live at the height of principles at the base of all the American constitutions: "All men are born equally free and independent."[49] Electoral requirements varied, the prejudice that made the rich better citizens than others continued to be widely diffused, while the poor were deprived of

---

[44] Ibid., p. 136.
[45] Ibid., p. 141.
[46] Ibid., "Gouvernements des Etats-Unis," p. 166.
[47] Ibid., p. 168.
[48] Ibid., pp. 173ff.
[49] Ibid., "Du droit de suffrage et d'être représentant," p. 175.

many of their rights. But still history showed how erroneous such pre-
conceptions were. There were infinite examples "of the tepidness and
pusillanimity of the rich. . . . There were other examples of the heroic
courage of indigent or poorer citizens." This was true in America, and
the situation was similar elsewhere. "The revolution of Genova, in the
war of 1745, provided a surprising example." The government was
aristocratic. The patriotism of the people was pure and disinterested,
while the noble sovereigns "accepted the loss of their authority with an
astonishing resignation." "Only the people could not accept the idea of
losing the name *Republic*, and of no longer seeing the dear word *Libertas*
on the gates of the city and in other places." It was the people who saved
Genova, while the nobles "did not become involved" and "even lowered
themselves to the point of pretending to disapprove of the conduct of
the people," limiting themselves to providing provisions to the city's defenders.[50] For the patricians wealth had proved to be more precious
than liberty. For the people the illusion of liberty had been a sufficient
motivation. In America experience confirmed that equality should be
the sole basis for just politics, and that if this were deviated from, it
should be to intervene in favor of the poor, alleviating the weight of
their burdens, rather than depriving them of their rights as citizens, as
had been done. The hope of seeing any limitation of electoral rights
abolished in the future was alive and active.

In developing an assertion that we have already found in a page inspired by Jefferson, Mazzei affirmed that the drafting of the American
constitutions had been done with too much haste and that it was now
time to revise them. The entire "legislative power," like the "executive"
power, should pass through the winnow. The need to revise the judicial
function "following the advice of Beccaria" seemed urgent to him. The
legislature should be "indulgent and humane," while "executive power
should for its part become inexorable."[51]

These were passionate themes which he developed in the second
and third parts of his *Recherches*, intending to polemicize against his adversaries and with the group that was forming around Jefferson. He
began with Mably's *Observations* and sought to demonstrate—quite effectively—that the whole terminology inherited from the classical and European past was now useless and even dangerous for understanding the
new American reality.[52] It was enough to look at the society of ancient

---

[50] Ibid., pp. 189ff.

[51] Ibid., "De la puissance exécutrice," p. 209.

[52] The whole of the more democratic wing of the American Revolution was anticlas-
sical, critical of myths of Athens, Sparta, and Rome. Interesting in this regard is the essay

Rome and of the United States to persuade oneself of this. "The Romans were divided into two very distinct social classes. We, on the contrary, are formed into only one."[53] Patricians, aristocrats, plebeians did not exist beyond the ocean. "The word *slave* was never applied, and I am speaking not only of those in service to colonists, but also of criminals transported from England to America before the revolution."[54] To speak of democracy and aristocracy was also an error. "Our governments are really neither aristocratic nor democratic."[55] "Since there exists among us no distinction of rank and no particular privilege, since no citizen is absolutely excluded from whatever employment may exist in the republic, and the citizens as a whole confer on their agents almost all the power they exert personally in governments called democratic, neither of these two terms is appropriate to us, unless one wants to call them limited, or rather corrected and reasoned, democracies."[56] In this formula was a reflection of the experience of Geneva or Holland rather than an interpretation of the classical past. "The author [Mably] has compared our people with the common people of other nations and assuredly he is wrong." Even those in America who were obliged to live "in a state below others" did not constitute "a distinct class, and it is certain that this portion of our people resembles in no manner the peoples of other nations, ancient or modern." These differences did not depend at all on environment, climate, or such. "The real difference comes from morality, not from natural philosophy." This was a fruit of the revolution. "There had never been a republic where the mass of the people has so influenced the government, or where ways have been as open to them to all the honors and advantages of the nation as in the United States."[57] With his gaze turned continually to the past, Mably had ended by making himself a zealous partisan of republican government, but at the same time he upheld principles "diametrically opposed to those appropriate to republics."[58] It was enough to think of what he had written on freedom of the press and the rights of citizens. His very conception of antiquity was wrong: the Gracchi had not been the ambitious rebels he thought they were, but rather "two virtuous citizens whose

by A. Owen Aldridge, "Thomas Paine and the Classics," *Eighteenth-Century Studies* 4 (June 1968): 371ff.

[53] *Recherches historiques et politiques*, pt. 2, "Réponse aux Observations de l'Abbé de Mably à l'occasion desquelles on discute plusieurs points importans relatifs au gouvernement des Etats-Unis," p. 21.

[54] Ibid., p. 17.

[55] Ibid., p. 28.

[56] Ibid.

[57] Ibid., pp. 31ff.

[58] Ibid., p. 55.

name should be forever revered by any good republican." Marmontel
was right on this point.[59] As for the other fear of Mably, the rich Florentine merchant, Mazzei dedicated one page to explaining the profound difference separating Tuscany in the age of the Medici from the
America of Franklin and Jefferson. "Initially, the government of Florence was aristocratic. It continued to be so, even after its plebeian families uprooted the nobility. It seemed to have been arranged purposely
to produce dissensions. Those who comprised the sovereignty of the
state assembled at the sound of a bell. . . . They were united within the
walls of a city, and a great hall could contain them all. The state and
government of Pennsylvania are well enough known; thus the reader
will easily recognize the error of comparisons made with the republic of
Florence."[60]

Forcing Mably's thought, but setting into relief some undeniably traditional aspects, Mazzei interpreted it as dominated by a "predilection
for the rich" and incapable of hiding "his sovereign distrust for the
poor." Hence his approval of the measures taken in the constitution of
Massachusetts to keep the disinherited distant from public functions.
The precaution was useless, Mazzei rebutted. "Poverty itself would be
quite sufficient, unless there were very favorable circumstances, joined
with extraordinary merit."[61] "The constitution of Massachusetts"—that
is, the one with the strongest imprint of the thought of John Adams—
did nothing but prepare "the inevitable passage from a republic to an
aristocracy." The excessive authority attributed to the governor, and
thus to executive power, was also liable to criticism. Massachusetts suffered from an evil opposite to the one weighing on Pennsylvania, where
"the balance of political power is too much on the side of legislative
power exercised by a single house." But in America, constitutional formulas did not decide all: even Massachusetts had demonstrated, during
the revolution and after, the value in "the spirit of equality." Thus, Mably's acceptance of aristocratic ideas and forms was all the more dangerous.[62] "Happily, my fellow citizens are convinced that the egg of the
serpent should be destroyed at its origin. Thus, I hope they will never
let themselves be persuaded that aristocracy should, if one can express
oneself in this way, be inoculated, like smallpox vaccine."[63]

It was also necessary to consider the criticisms and suggestions Mably
had offered to Americans in matters of education in this light. Mazzei's

[59] Ibid., p. 66.
[60] Ibid., pp. 70ff.
[61] Ibid., p. 73.
[62] Ibid., pp. 76ff.
[63] Ibid., p. 80.

thoughts returned to his Virginia (which was, as he recalled, "the largest and most populated of the thirteen United States"),[64] to the college in Williamsburg, and to projects maturing throughout the Union to create "colleges and universities" everywhere.[65] He did not conceal the enormity of the task awaiting Americans in this area. More difficult still was their backwardness in judicial reform. With all his optimism Mazzei could not help but confess that much remained to do. Mably's rigor required the impossible of Americans, and that is "to be one day exempt from weaknesses that are only too common among men." All that could be done was "to improve our governments until they reach that degree of perfection which it is permissible to attain."[66] The spirit of reform in Tuscany here returned to the center of his polemic against Mably's utopianism. In some central issues, among them religious liberty, he leaned on what Jefferson had written, "one of my friends and fellow citizens, the author of the Declaration of Independence and of many other writings of importance." After having cited a page of *Notes on Virginia*, "a book not yet published," he concluded by citing in full the preamble of a law of 1786, in a "translation that is as literal as can be, given the difference between the two languages." This was a splendid text, a true act of faith in reason and of an anathema against anyone so criminal or tyrannical as to "compel a man to furnish contributions of money for the propagation of opinions which he disbelieves." "Truth is great and will prevail if left to herself, . . . she is the proper and sufficient antagonist to error, and has nothing to fear from the conflict, unless by human interposition disarmed of her natural weapons, free argument and debate, errors ceasing to be dangerous when it is permitted to contradict them."[67] Mazzei was right to want a literal translation. He knew this was a sacred text of the religion of enlightenment. Mably had tried to reduce the problem of religious liberty to a question of lesser or greater tolerance, the limits, that is, within which political power might use religion for its own ends. But he left this power quite limited. "The sad death of Socrates is enough to keep alive an unhappy memory in us. The barbarity and atrocities that this has caused in all times are so numerous and so revolting that humanity shivers when dreaming of them. . . . The enthusiasm of religion may serve as an instrument for the ambitious or for scoundrels to assist them in their designs. A virtuous man would never

[64] Ibid., pp. 81ff.

[65] Ibid., p. 86.

[66] Ibid., p. 99.

[67] Ibid., pp. 115ff., 118ff. Chapter 11, "De la loi écrite et des tribunaux d'équité," is a version of a text whose original is in *The Papers of Thomas Jefferson*, vol. 9, pp. 67ff., November 1785.

have recourse to it." One could only predict "that there will never be a
government in America so barbarous and impious as to dare use religion as a political means."[68] The Mohammedans were not to be feared;
it was necessary to stop persecuting and despising the Jews. Experience
had demonstrated "that novelties in religion are like a torrent that does
harm in proportion to the dams set up against them."[69] Mazzei sealed
this invocation with other pages from *Notes on Virginia*.[70] The chapter
on religion was one of the most successful in this expert work of interpretation and compilation.

To contrast American reality with the distant visions of ancient republics, as Mably had done, was not only an error, but also a fault. Classical times had been much less happy than ours. Nor had they been
more heroic than periods closer to us, as, for example, Florence in the
time of Cappone Capponi. The pedantic admiration that antiquity continued to inspire was in reality an impediment to understanding the ancient world as much as the modern one. [71] It was enough to think of the
way in which Mably had treated the most pressing issue, that of confederations. It was repugnant to Mazzei to attribute new powers to Congress, thus making it the center of an absolute authority. "Liberty is dear
to us."[72] It would also be perilous to prolong the interval between one
election and another. It was absurd to compare, as the French philosopher had done, the constitutional needs of Geneva with those of the
United States, proposing "to make Congress the supreme judge of all
the differences that could arise among different orders of citizens in the
states of the Union."[73] The conflict between Federalists and anti-Federalists that would dominate the second part of the eighties began to
emerge in these pages, if in a distorted and an uncertain manner. When
this polemic was published the lots were already cast, and the new constitution was already adopted. Even more significant was the defense
Mazzei made of the principles gained by the revolution, from the rapid
change of deputies to local autonomy.

The force that motivated him was a profound faith in the nature of
the society and state born from the revolution. This had happened at
the right time, when England was no longer in a position to crush it,
and when it had not yet had time to "introduce among us a distinction

[68] Ibid., p. 126.
[69] Ibid., p. 128.
[70] Ibid., pp. 133ff. See also pp. 239ff.
[71] See the interesting appendix, pp. 252ff., in defense, always against Mably, of Gibbon and Machiavelli, the latter being considered a "zealous republican."
[72] Ibid., p. 151.
[73] Ibid., p. 156.

of families, and thus a diversity of interest, and divisiveness."[74] The result was a society resistant to the privileges of aristocracy and wealth. Any comparison with Greece and Rome was erroneous. "Before the American Revolution a republic founded on reason had at no time existed, as history shows." America had been able and had known how to profit from the English experience. "The English who emigrated to America took with them republican sentiments."[75] The American Revolution was made by the majority of the population, and "the majority had no need to employ violence to effect a change."[76] Mably was wrong in predicting for the United States "the fate of Florence and Geneva, and all the disorders of ancient republics." America was a new reality.[77]

The third volume of *Recherches* was dedicated to Raynal and what he had said "about the United States of America" in his *Histoire philosophique*. His "imposing tone" and "the magic of his style" made this confutation indispensable.[78] "In America," he said, "a dogmatic tone and declamation are not in fashion, whether among philosophers or among historians. True philosophers reason and do not declaim. . . . The people, accustomed to see that the most enlightened men are almost always afraid to make mistakes, regard an apparent haste in wanting to articulate on everything as proof of being informed of nothing."[79] He thus disputed the facts, where Mazzei had no difficulty showing which and how many were the lacunas and mistaken views of the celebrated Raynal. His true and proper ideological and political reflections were few, even if they were interesting. What had the French alliance with the American republics meant? It was no longer a question of a traditional alliance of the Bourbon monarchy with places like the Swiss cantons, in an age when it was not yet understood that "alliances can influence the interior administration of different governments."[80] As Tom Paine had correctly noted, also in polemic with Raynal, the intervention of England and France in the American Revolution signaled an entirely new development. The great European states had emerged transformed.

The defense of America became more refined and detailed in the fourth volume. Here there was no longer a question of cutting down the classical vision of Mably or the enthusiastic one of Raynal. It was

[74] Ibid., p. 141.

[75] Ibid., pp. 173ff.

[76] Ibid., p. 176.

[77] Ibid., p. 178.

[78] Ibid., pt. 3, "Observations sur l'Histoire philosophique des deux Indes relativement aux Etats-Unis d'Amérique," pp. 1ff.

[79] Ibid., p. 28.

[80] Ibid., p. 120.

necessary instead to speak of the "pretended anarchy of the United States," a theme, as we have seen, dear to all the European gazettes in the mid-eighties. The conflicts among different states, and "the pretended discord on the subject of the division into states," were the war horses of English journals.[81] The question of paper money and of the public debt hung like a Sword of Damocles over the whole economic future of the country.[82] Commerce between France and America developed less quickly than had been anticipated.[83] The problem of emigration continued to interest Europe as a whole.[84] The Society of Cincinnatus remained central to the fears of the "friends of liberty."[85] Debating with Aedanus Burke and Mirabeau, Mazzei concluded once again by placing all his hopes in the candid opinion of the American public, which alone was capable of effective reforms and enlightened politics.[86] Washington expressed this reality. If he had believed "that the Society of Cincinnatus might one day be a danger to liberty, he would certainly have sought to stop its institution with wise and moderate councils." But this was not a reason to deify him. "General Washington is a man and it is as such that we love him."[87] A still more important question for "all those who love justice and humanity" was slavery. "Small evils are easy to correct; great ones take time and prudence; too much haste often makes the remedy even worse than the disease. It is certain that the evil of slavery in the five southern states is the most serious, the most humiliating, and the most difficult to reform." Nevertheless, it was necessary to educate the Negroes before liberating them. Even here Mazzei ended by referring to Jefferson and his *Notes on Virginia*.[88] As for the "savages," Mazzei paid much attention to them in this and in his other volumes. The brilliance of his mind and his always fresh effort to find a solution, even for the most unexpected and complicated problems, reveals itself also in these pages.[89]

He ended his work by taking into account those who were writing about America at the same time as he. The *History of South Carolina* by David Ramsay was a work of great value to him, as well as for Jefferson.[90] Full of interest was Chastellux's *Voyages*, permeated with a preoc-

---

[81] Ibid., pt. 4, "Continuation des recherches politiques," pp. 11ff.
[82] Ibid., pp. 23ff.
[83] Ibid., pp. 54ff.
[84] Ibid., pp. 76ff.
[85] Ibid., pp. 102ff.
[86] Ibid., pp. 115ff.
[87] Ibid., p. 121.
[88] Ibid., pp. 127ff.
[89] Ibid.
[90] When the editor Froullé, who printed Mazzei's *Recherches*, published in 1787 the

cupation with the transformation of Virginia in an aristocratic sense. But the French author was mistaken, Mazzei answered. The agricultural and social life of that state did not justify such fears.[91] Mazzei, as I have already mentioned, did not forgive the eclectic character of Démeunier's article in the *Encyclopédie méthodique*.[92] He gave more importance, naturally, to the *Apologie des constitutions des Etats Unis d'Amérique* by John Adams, which he read in English, although its translation was "currently in press and is to be published immediately." "The aim of the author is to prove, contrary to the opinion of Turgot, the Abbé Mably, and Doctor Price, that in the constitutions formed up to now by the different American states, it was proper to establish the different bodies found in them, so as to balance the three powers as much as possible and thus create the equilibrium necessary to maintain liberty."[93] His personal relations with John Adams were excellent up to when the two had worked together in America. "In that land," Mazzei noted, "diversity of opinion does not diminish friendship or esteem."[94] But basic differences remained. Adams wrote in criticism of Turgot and of the Enlightenment interpretation of the American Revolution. In the second volume of his *Defense*, already written in the summer of 1787, he had accomplished a work somewhat similar to that of Mazzei and intended to demonstrate the inadequacy of classical republics as models for modern America. But he had not stopped with Mably; he had dug, as he said, "into Italian rubbish and ruins." And he was convinced he had found "enough pure gold and marble . . . to reward his pains."[95] He had found, that is, the republican tradition, the distant roots of those ideas of liberty and balance of powers to which he remained faithful, intending to safeguard them through the revolution and independence. Thinking of Turgot and Condorcet, he fixed his opposition to government by an assembly, insisting instead on government by a "natural aristocracy" and that mutual control and balance of powers without which any liberty or equality was impossible. "In what did such a confidence in one assembly end in Venice, Geneva, Biscay, Poland but an aristocracy and an oligarchy?" It was useless to delude oneself; America was not a world unto itself.

Histoire de la révolution d'Amérique par rapport à la Caroline méridionale, the *Journal de Paris*, no. 139, 18 May 1788, p. 605, spoke of it as the "work of a truly educated man."

[91] *Recherches historiques et politiques*, pt. 4, pp. 185ff.

[92] Ibid., pp. 204ff.

[93] Ibid., p. 214.

[94] *Memorie*, p. 289.

[95] John Adams, *A defense of the constitutions of government of the United States of America against the attack of M. Turgot in his letter to Dr. Price dated the twenty-second day of March 1778*, vol. 1, letter 25, to Doctor Franklin. I have used the third edition (Philadelphia: Budd and Bartram, 1797), p. 121.

"There is no special providence for Americans and their natures are the same with others." Against all the rationalistic and geometric extolling of Parisians, against all illusion that a new and different nation had been born beyond the seas—a conviction nourished in varying degrees by the followers of Jefferson—traditional British good sense resounded in the pages of John Adams.[96]

The central question, that of the federal constitution, remained open. At the end of volume 4 readers were invited to resume discussion with Condorcet, whose text *Influence de la révolution de l'Amérique sur l'Europe*, which we have already examined, was inserted.[97] A *Supplément* followed, which the editors of Condorcet's works have included among his works, but which contains so many details on events in America as to suggest at least a close collaboration with Jefferson and Mazzei.[98] It was written on the occasion of the "uprising that has occurred in the state of Massachusetts," that is, the rebellion that took its name from its leader, Shays, and that occurred in the autumn of 1786. It was the only uprising in the eleven years of life of the thirteen American states, Condorcet noted.[99] Nor had there been acts of violence, except for this encounter, which left four dead and many wounded among the insurgents. From the first the repression had even taken into account the circumstances, while always avoiding the rumor or suspicion of any weakness on the part of the government.[100] In Europe this episode was seized upon as

[96] See Zolitan Haraszti, *John Adams and the Prophets of Progress* (New York: Grosset and Dunlap, 1964).

[97] *Recherches historiques et politiques*, pt. 4.

[98] Ibid., pp. 237ff., and *Oeuvres de Condorcet*, vol. 8, pp. 43ff.

[99] How largely the state of mind aroused by this revolt was diffused in New England is documented by Jackson Turner Main, *The Antifederalists*, pp. 59ff.

[100] From London on 30 November 1786 John Adams exhorted Jefferson not to let himself be disturbed by the "late turbulence in New England . . . this commotion will terminate in additional strength to government" (*The Papers of Thomas Jefferson*, vol. 10, p. 557). John Jay wrote on 14 December: "The government of Massachusetts has behaved with great moderation and condescension toward the insurgents. . . . These people bear no resemblance to an English mob—they are more temperate, cool and regular in their conduct, they have abstained from plunder." He feared nonetheless that England might benefit further from the discontent (p. 597). As usual, the most solidly optimistic was Jefferson, who wrote to Ezra Stiles on 24 December 1786: "The commotions which have taken place in America, as far as they are yet known to me, offer nothing threatening. They are a proof that the people have liberty enough, and I would not wish them less than they have. If the happiness of the mass of the people can be secured at the expense of a little tempest now and then, or even a little blood, it will be a precious purchase. *Malo libertatem periculosam quam quietam servitutem.* Let common sense and common honesty have fair play and they will soon set things to rights" (p. 629). Writing to Francesco Dal Verme, on 15 August 1787, he still held that "the commotions which had taken place in Massachusetts" were "the only ones which had ever taken place since the declaration of independence" (vol. 12, p. 43). As one sees, the pages inserted in Mazzei's *Recherches historiques*

an occasion of "declamations against popular governments." It would have been sufficient to make a comparison with the governments of Turkey, France, and England, despotic, monarchical, and mixed, to see how many disorders had arisen in the previous ten years. Attention could have been paid to the state to which London was reduced by the "Lord Gordon riots." "The results of the insurgence in Glasgow, about two months ago, which has hardly been mentioned, were much more disturbing than those that have occurred in the state of Massachusetts, about which so much noise is made in Europe." In Glasgow there were five dead and many wounded, among them "the first magistrate of the city and others who had gone to quiet the tumult."[101]

If there were no disorders in the United States on a scale comparable with those of states of the old regime, the cause was political. "It is time to convince oneself that a nation with equality of rights will support its government, if it is thought good, and will change it when it is thought bad, or correct it when it is defective; thus the majority has no need of violence, and the violence of a small minority will be powerless." In America the people, as the word was understood in Europe, did not and could not exist. Nor could roots grow among them, for "national dissensions" arise only where "odious and unjust distinctions" exist. Only those excluded "from the rights of citizens" were indifferent or enemies of the "established system." "In the end the only way to attach the people to the preservation of good order is to make the only good order consist of their happiness and security."[102]

Little more than ten years had passed since the Declaration of Independence. The right to change one's own government had become

---

et politiques—whether they came from the pen of Condorcet or not—reflect from nearby the preoccupations and conclusions of Jefferson's friends.

[101] Recherches historiques et politiques, pt. 4, pp. 284ff., and *Oeuvres de Condorcet*, p. 47.

[102] Ibid., pp. 291ff., 49ff. Mazzei's *Recherches* was judged "one of the most useful and best executed works that have appeared for some time" by the *Journal de Paris*, no. 180, 28 June 1788, p. 786, "Lettre de Paris," 20 June 1788. But it was criticized by the *Gazzetta universale*, which was scandalized by Mazzei's free criticism of writers such as Mably and Raynal: "This is an immense compilation of facts, in which one finds some good ideas and precious documents in the midst of an immense number of entirely useless observations. The anonymous author conceals himself behind the title citizen of Virginia. One knows, however, with certainty that under this American cloak hides Signor Mazzei of Florence who, after having wandered through our whole continent, after having practiced medicine in Constantinople and speculation in London, went to America to seek his fortune, and has now returned here to attack writers who enjoy the greatest reputation in Europe." *Gazzetta Universale*, no. 31, 15 April 1788, p. 241 (Paris, 1 April).

the duty to create a government that would no longer need to be torn down and remade. This was the trend and result of the revolution. The will to reform, the search for a more effective relationship between political structure and society, thus took first place. Religious tolerance, rights of succession, the first steps against slavery, judicial guarantees, relationships between creditors and debtors, the means for carrying out the peace treaty with England, had animated the life of the thirteen states in the few years that had elapsed since the conclusion of the war. Mazzei's book ended with Washington's letter, which proposed the new constitution of the United States by unanimous order of the convention, on 17 September 1787. It was printed word for word in the concluding pages. Five hundred copies of the letter had been printed. Washington himself had hastened to send one to Jefferson as soon as it appeared, "not doubting but that you have participated in the general anxiety which has agitated the minds of your countrymen on this interesting occasion."[1] John Adams had another copy. It was still a rare and precious document when it was inserted into the work of Mazzei in the winter of 1787–1788. The twenty or so pages of comment that accompanied it reflected the passionate discussions that had arisen immediately. Even Jefferson, along with the larger part of the American governing class, was convinced that the constitution would be changed. "My idea is that we should be made one nation in every case concerning foreign affairs, and separate ones in whatever is merely domestic. That the federal government should be organized into legislative, executive, and judiciary as are the state governments, and some peaceable means of enforcement devised for the federal head over the states."[2] But the way in which the convention in Philadelphia had proceeded in modifying the fundamental law of the state had not pleased Jefferson at all. Why ever, in "amending some defects in the instrument of confederation," he wrote to Gaudenzio Clerici, had one arrived, as he said also to John Adams, at prohibiting any publicity for the debates of the convention, creating from the beginning "so abominable a precedent as that of tying up the tongues of their members?"[3] And to think that this had been an "assembly of demigods," a gathering of extraordinary personalities, capable of taking wise and effective measures, who had nonetheless shown their artlessness and their indifference to "the value of public discussions" by acting in this way.[4] From Philadelphia James Madison wrote

[1] *The Papers of Thomas Jefferson*, vol. 12, p. 149, Philadelphia, 18 September 1787.

[2] Ibid., p. 28, letter to John Blair, Paris, 13 August 1787. The same letter mentions a correspondence with Mazzei that cannot be found now.

[3] Ibid., pp. 39, 69, Paris, 15 and 30 August 1787.

[4] Ibid., pp. 36, 69, Paris, 15 and 30 April 1787.

to him that the gravity of the moment justified secrecy and silence. "If the present moment be lost it is hard to say what may be our fate."[5] John Jay expressed to him his cautious faith in the result of the deliberations, affirming that there was nothing else to do but continue in the way taken.[6] Jefferson sometimes seemed to allow himself to be persuaded by the advantages of such calm and coolness, worthy of philosophers, while other nations—and he evidently thought of Holland, Belgium, and Poland—took up arms "to amend or to restore their constitutions."[7] But the United States had operated in their reform with such reserve as to give it the appearance of a plot. It was a plot of the elite that had issued from the revolution, who hid even from Jefferson the most important documents of their own internal debate, those Federalist papers which today are considered the masterpiece of their time and a model of political thought but were then veiled and little known, almost as if they were the esoteric code of this political operation. In Paris much was published, as we have seen, on American problems. But Froullé, the editor of Mazzei, Condorcet, Dupont, Adams, and Ramsay, did not provide an edition of the *Federalist*. Jefferson does not even mention it in his correspondence of this period. When he read the text that had emerged from the convention in Philadelphia he did not delay studying the debate that had generated it or discussing the theories of Madison, Hamilton, and Jay, whose precise formulation he did not know. He threw himself immediately into a lively political polemic against the project for a new constitution, rejecting it energetically and declaring himself an anti-Federalist even before he had time to become a Federalist. Madison and Jay were very prudent and careful (perhaps we should call them hypocritical) when they touched on the heart of the problem with him. At the end, Jefferson put together his criticisms and gave his general judgment in writing to John Adams: "I confess there are things in it which stagger all my dispositions to subscribe to what such an assembly has proposed." The new federal Congress seemed to him inadequate as much for international as for internal affairs. The president seemed to him "a bad edition of a Polish king." The fact that he could be reelected after every four-year term fatally transformed his position into "an office for life." Foreign influences of all kinds would soon focus on him. "It will be of great consequence to France and England to have America

---

[5] Ibid., p. 103, 6 September 1787. In this letter as well regards were sent to Mazzei, from whom he had received a book that may have been one of the first volumes of *Recherches*, not yet in circulation at the time.

[6] Ibid., p. 105, New York, 8 September 1787.

[7] Ibid., p. 113, to C.W.F. Dumas, Paris, 10 September 1787.

governed by a Galloman or Angloman."8 The convention had profited
from the general fear of falling into anarchy to create a kind of stadholder. What was happening in Holland was enough to demonstrate
what an error was being made. This was all the more clear because the
anarchy in fact did not exist. The revolt in Massachusetts had remained
entirely isolated. There was nothing to be afraid of. "What country can
preserve its liberties if their rulers are not warned from time to time
that their people preserve the spirit of resistance?" It was up to the government to know how to pacify revolts. "What signify a few lives lost in
a century or two? The tree of liberty must be refreshed from time to
time with the blood of patriots and tyrants. It is its natural manure."9 In
a more pacific tone (the news he received from America was generally
favorable to the Federalists) he summarized his thought in writing to
Madison on 20 December. The division of powers was rightly included
in the new constitution. He declared he was "captivated" by the compromise it had established among the "opposite claims of the great and
small states." Thus he accepted the keystone of the new Federalism. But
how many things were absent or lacking in the work of the convention
of Philadelphia! There was not "a bill of rights providing clearly and
without the aid of sophisms for freedom of religion, freedom of the
press, protection against standing armies, restriction against monopolies, the eternal and unremitting force of the habeas corpus laws and
trials by jury in all matters of fact triable by the laws of the land and not
by the law of nations." It was a mistake to say that the new constitution
made such declarations of principle unneeded. "A bill of rights is what
the people are entitled to against every government on earth, general
or particular, and what no just government should refuse or rest on
inference." This was all the more true because the figure created in the
president justified fears. "Reflect on all the instances, in history ancient
and modern, of elective monarchies and say if they do not give foundation for my fears, the Roman emperors, the popes, while they were
of any importance, the German emperors till they became hereditary in
practice, the kings of Poland, the deys of the Ottoman dependencies."
Against such threat the oath to maintain the constitution would serve
for little or nothing. In general, he concluded, "I am not a friend to a
very energetic government." It was not in this way that one responded

8 Ibid., p. 351, Paris, 13 November 1787.

9 Ibid., p. 356, letter to William Stephens Smith, Paris, 13 November 1787. The response from London on 3 December also emphasized the perils of the American situation,
comparing it with Holland and Poland, but rejected the very thought that the new constitution would not be accepted (pp. 390 ff.).

to the perils of seditions and revolts. It was enough to look at France or Turkey to be persuaded.

These objections and fears would still not have prevented him from accepting the new constitution if it were confirmed by the people. In the end, what was important was the nature of the nation. "I think our governments will remain virtuous for many centuries, as long as they are chiefly agricultural, and this will be as long as there shall be vacant lands in any part of America. When they get piled upon one another in large cities, as in Europe, they will become corrupt as in Europe. Above all things I hope the education of the common people will be attended to, convinced that on their good sense we may rely with the most security for the preservation of a due degree of liberty."[10] The frontier and education, in short, would always regenerate America.

It would have been better, as he repeated and as Mazzei's *Recherches* expressed, to maintain the old constitutional framework, making the necessary modifications to it. The initial confederation should have been preserved, "which any society of sensible and virtuous men could be proud of having brought to light," "a respectable monument" that should have remained "the fundamental basis of our union."[11] It was certainly right to establish a different relationship between the legislative and executive powers, but the bicameral system that was chosen did not seem sufficient. The modes of election to the Congress and Senate were too rigid. Certainly, the problem defied easy solution. "Whoever finds the true solution and presents it in a clear and decisive manner will do a great service to America and perhaps also to Europe, where the considerable progress of philosophy raises the hope of one day seeing a confederation established, which could infinitely diminish the evils of humanity." It was a bad idea to give Congress the power to determine the salaries of deputies. "A dangerous abuse might result in the future." In no case, contrary to what had been decided, should one be able to suspend habeas corpus. Federal powers in financial matters were too great. The arrangements for the election of the president were poor, which tended "to prefer the subject who makes the most noise to the one who has the most merit." Nor should he be given the power to command troops, but instead only the selection of officers. Indefinite reelections were inadmissible, even when this might involve "the greatest man that nature could create" (thoughts ran naturally to Washington, who still had not been nominated). "It would be better to do without the advantage of having such a prodigy at the head of the confederation than to accustom the people to seeing the same individual always in that

[10] Ibid., pp. 440ff.
[11] *Recherches historiques et politiques*, pt. 4, pp. 340ff.

place. With another step, one would soon have a king of Poland, with the terrible danger of seeing him change himself one day into a hereditary stadholder."[12] The clause that fixed the necessary age for the two houses was "injurious to youth and diametrically opposed to our experience." Scipio Africanus was remembered as an example and, even more surprising and curious, the case of William Pitt, who at the age of twenty-two had demonstrated his superiority to his father in the House of Commons: "One sees him now conduct the affairs of Great Britain with applause to which envy itself has been forced to cede." And how could one not speak of the "young heroes who, at twenty-nine years at most, crossed the ocean to offer their help in the most critical time of the revolution?"[13] "Among the young Americans I know I can name a great number who justify my feelings." That which was considered the defects of youth, as of women, derived in reality from a "faulty education."[14] The right given to the president to grant pardons was also unjust, and it would still be unjust if it were given to Congress. "Beccaria clearly demonstrates that that kind of poorly understood humanitarianism is no other than an asylum opened to impunity, and consequently a source of crimes." The means for ratifying the new constitution could be criticized: nine states out of thirteen were not enough. It would have been better to require three fourths, "otherwise there would be too much to fear if four of the most populous ones consider breaking away."[15]

Mazzei—and with him Jefferson and Condorcet—ended up accepting what the men of the convention had decided; they were too wise and capable not to have good reasons to act as they did. One could not fail to give in to the "powerful motives" that had moved "so many men filled with zeal, reason, and wisdom." "One who was not part of that assembly is hardly in a state to judge the motives that must have led each one to give to that act their full and entire consent, although there was no one perhaps who thought it was without imperfections."[16] The new constitution, as one sees, was not judged on the basis of the ideas on which it was founded, but as a supreme political opportunity. The work of the convention was not based on the ideas of the "Federalist," which were unknown, but on local and momentary circumstances and exigencies. Even in matters regarding the economy Mazzei withheld the objections that would have been natural from his pen, as he himself recog-

[12] Ibid., pp. 346ff.
[13] Ibid., pp. 350ff.
[14] Ibid., pp. 351ff.
[15] Ibid., pp. 353ff.
[16] Ibid., pp. 354ff.

nized, where the "power given to the Congress to regulate commerce and to raise sums of money in the respective states" was mentioned. "There is no doubt that commerce should be perfectly free and unencumbered by any tax. . . . But the circumstances in which we find ourselves demand that there be, for some time, the right to raise a tax and to levy duties on foreign merchandise." This was a temporary situation, due to circumstances and not to nature. "For example, a direct tax on real property could not be the only revenue of the state of Genova, where nature, instead of land, presents so to speak no more than rocks, nor in the state of Holland, where it offers on all sides masses of water."[17] In the United States, at least as long as the low price of land impeded "the establishment of manufactures," and foreign debts weighed on the country, "it will be appropriate to add a modest tax on foreign merchandise to direct taxes, not only to raise public revenue, but also to oblige the consumer to make the least possible use of this merchandise, because without much economy in this regard the product of our exports will be insufficient to balance their cost and to pay the existing debt. . . . Our system thus requires that we make a few exceptions to the general principle."[18] We can conclude that the returning trend toward mercantilism, which followed the great attack of the American Revolution and the liberalism of Adam Smith, needed to be and could be contained, but it could not be ignored. Mazzei said it should be explained to the people that this was an exception and an evil made necessary by circumstances. Even more important, looking to the future, was ensuring and guaranteeing the publicity of debates, and not losing sight of general and fundamental principles.

These were all political and economic problems reflected in the concluding speech of Franklin, when he explained the motives for his final acceptance of the constitution. "I repeat, there are certain articles that I oppose, and I have already made known my doubts. But I declare that, beyond these walls, no one will hear me speak of them; otherwise I think that in total the proposed constitution is the best that can be formed in the present circumstances."[19] Certainly he also hoped to see soon reformed the article of the constitution that made the president the commander of the army and transformed him into a kind of Polish king. To be sure, in the case of Washington, who was only fifty-five years old and "sane and robust," his words were an invitation to vote for him.[20] The international situation of the United States—one should not

[17] Ibid., p. 355.
[18] Ibid., p. 356.
[19] Ibid., p. 358.
[20] Ibid., p. 360.

forget this—remained difficult. England did everything possible to be a hindrance, including probably a long hand in the disorders of Massachusetts. But there was good news about this affair. "One hears that no one suffered the highest penalty on the occasion of the uprising in Massachusetts; two or three of the guiltiest were led to the gallows, where, contrary to expectation, their pardon was read to them. The conduct of the government diffused a general satisfaction, and calm is perfectly restored."[21]

The publication of the *Recherches* polarized, at the beginning of 1788, the interest and enthusiasm for what was happening in America. Condorcet reviewed it for the *Mercure de France*, not without endangering the situation of the bookseller Panckoucke, who held the privilege for this journal but was threatened with its withdrawal for having permitted celebration "with too much compliance all that the citizen of Virginia [Mazzei] dared say in favor of the broad liberty of conscience established in that province by the law of 1786, drawn up by Mr. Jefferson."[22]

The long warm review of the *Recherches* that appeared at the beginning of 1788 in the *Journal de Paris* took up again the considerations of Jefferson and Condorcet, and gave further evidence of the weight Mazzei had in the formation of French public opinion on the United States of America. There was admiration for this man "born in Europe, having part of his life traveled through different states with the intention of choosing as a fatherland the one whose constitution was most in agreement with the idea he had formed on the rights and happiness of man." The author of the *Recherches* was "almost always right" in his polemic with Mably, even if he was undoubtedly very severe. He had responded properly to the excessive cult of antiquity of the elder *philosophe* by citing facts and incidents of the American Revolution, where one could see, "for the first time, perhaps, heroism and love of country obey a quiet reason without losing anything of their heat or energy. This is a phenomenon unique in the history of man, and it is due to the progress of reason." Condorcet showed he was capable, in the texts inserted into the *Recherches*, of discussing fundamental problems and revealed "a superior mind, which has studied well men and governments, and is able to introduce a rigorous precision into the most abstract theories." Wise were the considerations in the *Recherches* on the "federative constitution" adopted in Philadelphia, which could be "criticized at the same time for having narrowed dangerously the independence of single states and copied the English constitution with too much servility." Why not give

---

[21] Ibid., pp. 363ff.
[22] *Correspondance littéraire*, vol. 15, p. 251.

Americans the opportunity to differ from the British constitution, against which they had fought in their revolution victoriously?[23]

Despite this and other voices of dissent at the beginning of 1788, a general acceptance seemed to reign when Mazzei's book on the political operation of the Philadelphia convention appeared. The Federalist plot had succeeded. Appeal to realism, circumstance, and immediate necessity had changed the constitution. Madison, Jay, and Hamilton had known how to be practical, lucid, and Machiavellian. They had won on the political level where they wanted to succeed. But the first victim of their politics had been precisely the deepest and most genuine ideas of the American Revolution, which they had hastened with so much care to put aside, limit, and contain, referring instead to British models, the tradition of free countries in Europe, and the experience of America in the ten years that had elapsed since the Declaration of Independence. Federalism, which they had examined with so much mastery in the journals, would take on a vigorous life in the practical constitution of the United States. But at the level of ideas it was eclipsed. America did not become a model for the revolution already in full development in the European world in the year 1788. Federalism remained a kind of specter, about which little or nothing was known. It was the task of the anti-Federalists, and above all Jefferson, to keep alive the principles of the American Revolution he and his adversaries shared.[24]

The polemic of men close to Jefferson against John Adams was not only a dutiful rearguard action between North and South, Virginia and Massachusetts, but now chiefly an effort to take from the hands of the Federalists the instruments that had contributed to channel the American Revolution into the traditional riverbed of free countries, of England and ancient and modern republics, and that prevented it from emerging as a more or less pure and direct democracy. In 1789 appeared, again from the bookseller Froullé, the final Parisian intervention in the debate, which was entitled *Examen du gouvernement d'Angleterre, comparé aux constitutions des Etats-Unis, où l'on réfute quelques assertions contenues dans l'ouvrage de M. Adams, intitulé: Apologie des constitutions des Etats-Unis d'Amérique et dans celui de M. Delolme intitulé: De la constitution d'Angleterre*, par un cultivateur de New-Jersey. Ouvrage traduit de l'An-

---

[23] *Journal de Paris*, no. 29 (29 January 1788): 135ff.

[24] The book by Aldo Garosci, *Il pensiero politico degli autori del "Federalist"* (Milan: Comunità, 1954), has been for me, and I hope also for others, the natural point of departure for thought on these political and historical problems. The contemporary polemic has been collected by Herbert J. Staring, *The Complete Anti-Federalist* (Chicago: University of Chicago Press, 1981).

glois et accompagné de Notes.[25] "At a time when all nations are employed in seeking principles of a good constitution for society," one read
in the "Avertissement des éditeurs," "it is a service to dissipate the prejudices they might have about some constitutions that now exist." Examples from the past could be deceptive. "One always runs the risk of
error when trying to follow the steps of others in a servile manner. Reason, justice, and deep study of the rights of man never mislead." The
English model was typical of such deception and error. Voltaire and
Montesquieu had allowed themselves to be seduced in observing that
"the fate of the human species was a little less bad in England." Now
even Adams, "so laudable for the great services he has done for the
United States of America," had allowed himself to be attracted and had
accepted De Lolme's defense of the British constitution.[26]

An American, which the "Avertissement" identified as Livingston
but in reality was John Stevens, had polemicized with Adams. Dupont
de Nemours now provided a version of this work, making it possible to

[25] Londres et se trouve à Paris: Froullé, 1789. The translator was here again the Norman lawyer Louis Joseph Faure. See Tortarolo, *Illuminismo e rivoluzioni*, pp. 16off. The
"notes" were thought "very judicious" and written "by good political writers" by Brissot in
his *Nouveau voyage dans les Etats-Unis de l'Amérique septentrionale* (Paris: Buisson, April
1791), vol. 2, p. 23n. On pp. 190ff. he spoke of his encounters with Mazzei, the "Italian
author" who was the collaborator in this *Examen du gouvernement d'Amérique*.

[26] *Examen*, pp. iiiff. Mazzei himself said that this "Avertissement des éditeurs" was the
work of Dupont de Nemours (*Memorie*, p. 289). There is a strong imprint of this physiocrat on the entire work. Thus, it is surprising not to see it inserted in the photostatic
reprint of his *Oeuvres politiques et économiques* (Nendeln, Liechtenstein: KTO Press, 1979). It
was precisely Dupont who in 1770 emphasized that economic freedom was not only an
advantage and a necessary means of increasing production, but constituted a true and
proper right. He had concluded his *Observations sur les effets de la liberté du commerce des
grains et sur ceux des prohibitions* (Basel and Paris: Lacombe, Roset, 1770), p. 181, by saying:
"Liberty is thus necessary, but it is necessary whole, complete, general, equally unburdened with restrictions, limitations, inspections and interference of authority, which, by
its nature, is made only to protect useful works; it cannot undertake them itself without
banishing liberty and prohibiting true competition. Liberty is the right of man. It is the
nourishment of societies. It is the first source of all production and of all wealth." This
passage of liberty from a means to a right was the point of contact of late physiocracy with
the late Enlightenment, of Dupont with Condorcet, as we see in the *Examen* of 1789.
There is nothing also in *The Correspondence of Jefferson and Du Pont de Nemours, with an
Introduction on Jefferson and the Physiocrats*, ed. Gilbert Chinard (Baltimore: Johns Hopkins
Press, 1931). Dupont's letter from Paris, of 5 November 1787, published in *The Papers of
Thomas Jefferson*, vol. 12, pp. 325ff., is very important for the relationship between Dupont
and Jefferson. "I have always had difficulty understanding how one could expect to extract good constitutional principles from ancient republics where slavery was ingrained,
and those who did useful labor in agriculture and the arts were not members of the state,
or from modern republics founded with fanaticism and the sword in centuries of general
barbarity. Yours is the only one clearly influenced by reason. How can one reach perfection? Through a still deeper search for what is reasonable and just."

add those comments necessary for transplanting to Europe a text that was originally intended exclusively for readers beyond the ocean. The notes were to be "like little separate treatises," without pretense of formal perfection, but still intended "to increase the happiness of the human species." "One will encounter in them different pens, but very similar principles, since truth once arrived at is the same for all good minds." "Several American, Italian, and French writers have contributed to this work, which thus serves to show that the progress of reason has become general." The great republic of learned men would in this way be "the natural ally of all other republics, and all empires, where a serious effort is made for the public good. It is the natural enemy of all arbitrary and oppressive government. . . . May that fraternal republic conquer the world."[27]

John Adams had been in London when he wrote the book that was being challenged. It was natural that he should see "everywhere riches and power in the hands of a few."[28] But how could he forget that he was born in a quite different society, that of America, where it was useless to try to balance nobility against monarchy in order to maintain liberty. For that matter, it was not necessary to try to establish a purely democratic government, said the American author. "A perfect democracy" will always be impractical. "A numerous people, assembled in a tumultuous manner, is by its nature incapable of deliberation."[29] But it was by no means impossible to find the means to delegate the power of the people effectively. Juries and a bicameral system addressed this need. It was an open question, the annotator replied, referring to the letters of Condorcet published in the *Recherches*.[30]

This was the beginning of a long series of notes, more ample altogether than the work of John Stevens himself, written, as we have seen, by a cosmopolitan group: the Italians were Mazzei and Piattoli, the French, Dupont de Nemours, Gallois, and Condorcet. They were all intent on discussion with the Americans.[31] With great respect for John Adams, and recalling his merits during the revolution (the author of the first salutation was Mazzei), they told him that his defense of British tradition had ended by skirting the very problem of political principles

[27] *Examen*, pp. viff.

[28] Ibid., p. 27.

[29] Ibid., p. 37.

[30] Ibid., p. 58n.

[31] As Mazzei wrote to Stanislaus Augustus of Poland, on 27 April 1789, "The notes are principally by Mr. Dupont and myself; some of the Marquis de Condorcet, by the Abbé Piattoli, and by a certain Mr. Gallois, a youth of great merit, who translated the famous work of Filangieri, to which he added very interesting notes" (*Lettere di F. Mazzei*, vol. 1, p. 121).

on which any society should be based, from religious liberty to the liberty of thought, from freedom of trade to personal freedom. "The constitution of England," one should never forget, "has not sufficiently ensured the liberty of men."[32] In the United States of America instead "freedom of the press is a fundamental law," while "in England it is only a tolerance based on custom."[33] The cases of Annet, Shebbeare, and Wilkes demonstrated this. And the same could be said for all other liberties. There were, for instance, frequent cases of oppression of Scotland by England, not to mention the "counties of Wales, inhabited by the ancient race of Britons who, to their detriment, experience an inequality of representation."[34] And how could one forget Ireland? The inequalities in the electoral laws of England were well known. Under the system of criminal justice in Great Britain, "where the list of capital crimes is immense, one is hanged for thefts of any sum exceeding a shilling!" "There was no doubt about this matter because it was developed with much clarity by M. le Marquis Beccaria, in the *Traité des délits et des peines*, which Mr. De Lolme himself calls 'an admirable work.' "[35]

In conclusion, it was true that "personal liberty is much better secured against abuses of authority in England than in any other government of Europe, and vices of administration, although great, are also much less there than elsewhere, but that does not prove that in any other country one could not do better without much difficulty. The great error consists in the pretended perfection found there. The only thing that could excuse the English for not having made better use of circumstances favorable to liberty is ignorance of principles that have not been well known until recently."[36] The English constitution should be seen in the light of the "progress of reason." "The first man to eat grain would look at acorns with distaste. The one who then invented cakes baked under the coals would not think one should remain content with eating uncooked wheat. But once bread was known, it became equally impossible to limit men to unleavened cakes, uncooked wheat, or the acorns of the forests."[37] This was a splendid metaphor of the changes taking place in the idea of liberty in the age of the American Revolution.

Nor could England claim that its system of liberty and balance was entirely original. "The constitution was representative in almost all the

[32] *Examen*, p. 75.
[33] Ibid., p. 81.
[34] Ibid., p. 89.
[35] Ibid., pp. 97ff.
[36] Ibid., p. 114.
[37] Ibid., p. 120.

lands of Europe; it seems always to have been so in Sweden, it was in the Low Countries long before the revolution in Holland, one finds it in the Estates General of France, in its estates, and in many of its provinces; it existed in Castille." A city could restrict the right of citizenship within itself. But if a free people is "dispersed over a great territory, a representative constitution is born of necessity itself."[38] The problems arose when it became necessary to establish means for putting this representation into practice. Inspired by that "profound thinker" Quesnay, the commentator (and we might think he was the physiocrat Dupont) said that "all regulation has a touchstone: Is it in conformity with the declaration of rights or is it not?"[39] In America a search had begun for the means of applying this principle. The Marquis de Condorcet had already contributed to these thoughts as much in his *Recherches* as in his *Essai sur l'application de l'analyse à la probabilité des décisions rendues à la pluralité des voix*. It was necessary to continue in this sense in political life as well as in the administration of justice.[40] Why not take up and put into practice the idea of a committee of six persons suggested at the end of the first volume of the *Récherches*?[41] The very concept of a political contract should be restudied, to review what this word meant in England, Holland, and Sweden. "The people of the United States of America are the first nation and still the only one that has understood that legislation should not begin with a 'contract,' as among enemies who negotiate and come to an agreement, but with the 'exposition of the principles of all contracts,' as among wise men who first examine the 'what' of a question." A declaration of rights was thus indispensable for a good constitution. "The declarations of rights made by the different states of America united are neither complete nor sufficiently systematic, but the truths they contain are indubitable. Their stroke of genius was to put them first. It is sufficient for reason and logic to develop the consequences, to return to the true principles, and to arrange the ones and the others in a methodical order. In the future it may be possible to arrive at such a degree of perfection that the declarations of rights of all the world will not differ among themselves by a single word. Where then would be arbitrary governments?"[42]

[38] Ibid., p. 175.

[39] Ibid., pp. 179ff.

[40] Ibid., pp. 183ff. See Keith Michael Baker, *Condorcet: From Natural Philosophy to Social Mathematics* (Chicago: University of Chicago Press, 1975), p. 228.

[41] *Examen*, p. 190.

[42] Ibid., pp. 200ff. In June 1789 there appeared in Paris a small bilingual work entitled *Declaration of Rights: Déclaration des droits*, where these ideas were taken up again and publicized. It was a work by Condorcet. The English version was by Mazzei. Jefferson succeeded in having inserted in the *Gazette de Leyde* of 19 February 1788 an explicit request

The application of such ideas to a hereditary nobility did not offer particular difficulties. More interesting was the effort to examine in their light rights to bequeath property, to which is dedicated an ample and a curious note that may have been by one of the Italians.

But it was time to return to the actual problems at hand, and thus above all to the new federal constitution. The concluding note, written by Mazzei, addressed just this question. That changes were necessary was undoubtedly true. But it would be dangerous to make mistakes. "If the proposed constitution were received unanimously, without making the needed changes and without even speaking of its defects, there could be tragic results for liberty." The best citizens might be denounced as enemies of public peace. "The death of a few distinguished citizens, the prejudice of the people toward the work of so many virtuous men, a natural penchant toward indolence, the delayed bad effects of a vicious system might make the remedy impossible." There should be "many essential changes" before approving the new constitution.[43] The means it adopted for resolving conflicts among the states were insufficient and ineffective, as Mazzei had already said in *Recherches*. "It is wrong to flatter oneself that one is able to reconcile contradictory principles."[44] Wilson was wrong, "one of the deputies from Pennsylvania, a man much distinguished in talents," when he affirmed that a declaration of rights was superfluous.[45] One would seek in vain to put into operation institutions designed to take the place of and substitute for the active and frequent participation of citizens in public life, if one did not give "general sustained attention" to maintaining "the spirit of equality, and to increasing and spreading enlightenment."[46] It was evidently an illusory possibility to always find a man like Washington to take in trust such extensive powers as were foreseen in the constitution. While for the moment accepting what had been decided, it was necessary to think of revision in the future. For the moment it would be unjust to require the unanimity of all thirteen states. "That would be the *liberum veto* of the Poles."[47] Nor was the situation different in the United Provinces. "All the bad things that happen to you, someone said not long ago to

that the new constitution contain "a bill of rights, that is to say, an act in which the government common to all the confederation determine and state the fundamental principals of the liberty of citizens in a republic, and that these be such in fact and not only in name" (*The Papers of Thomas Jefferson*, vol. 12, p. 584n, letter to C.W.F. Dumas, Paris, 13 February 1788).

[43] Ibid., p. 229.
[44] Ibid., p. 230n.
[45] Ibid., p. 231.
[46] Ibid., p. 234.
[47] Ibid., p. 239, cited in relation to the opinion of Count Wielhorski.

Dutch patriots, come from that error in your *so-called* constitution, which, in many important instances, requires perfect unanimity."[48] America would not make a similar mistake.

A *Supplément* announced that now only South Carolina and Rhode Island had not ratified the constitution, which was published in its entirety in the final pages of the book: "We the people of the United States, in order to form a more perfect union, establish justice, insure domestic tranquility, provide for the common defense, promote the general welfare, and secure the blessings of liberty to ourselves and our posterity, do ordain and establish this constitution of the United States of America."

[48] Ibid., p. 239.

II

Great Britain in the Years of the American Revolution

IN 1776, THE YEAR OF THE DECLARATION OF INDEPENDENCE, A quite exceptional moment in the moral and political life of Great Britain was marked. In that year Gibbon's work began to be published. Adam Smith's *The Wealth of Nations* appeared. Hume's death closed an entire epoch in British philosophical, political, and historical thought. Two centuries later, the date seems also to symbolize the watershed of another deep transformation, the industrial revolution, which made England "the first industrial nation," to use the words of Peter Mathias, a historian of our own days who has deeply observed and described it.[1] For historians of diplomacy and warfare 1776 marked the moment when the conflict with the American colonies became irreversible. Great Britain was now inexorably involved in another seven years' war, a much more serious one than the other was at midcentury and one destined to have quite a different outcome. Isolated, Britain confronted the growing strength of a group of enemies and rivals.

Also, in the eyes of contemporaries, the center of this stormy and complex picture still remained, in 1776, the political problem of the value and function of the constitution, which was a perpetual source of amazement and admiration for continentals and a source of more and more heated disputes for the inhabitants of the British Isles, as well as for colonists beyond the ocean.

Enlightenment Europe had been passionately interested in Wilkes's campaign between the sixties and seventies and continued to follow with great interest what was said in the English Parliament in the seventies and eighties, in the age of Shelburne and of William Pitt the younger.

---

[1] Peter Mathias, *The First Industrial Nation* (London: Methuen, 1969); id., *The Transformation of England: Essays in the Economic and Social History of England in the Eighteenth Century* (London: Methuen, 1979).

An empire was crumbling, and Great Britain had to confront not only the revolt of its colonies, but also the hostility of France and Spain. In 1779 it even seemed that it might be invaded. Fleets superior to those of Britain dominated the English Channel for several months. Seven years of war, which daily seemed to become more serious, had to elapse before England became convinced that logistical barriers opposed its will to send a sufficient military force beyond the ocean to crush the Americans, while in Europe much courage, often heroism, was needed to defend key positions, such as the Rock of Gibraltar. Even in this situation England not only showed no sign of discouragement or acquiescence, but, what counted most, offered the extraordinary and unique spectacle of a free country, where political discussion not only did not cease but became more and more vigorous, and where the constitutional struggle between the king and Parliament took on more and more intense and vibrant forms. The American Revolution had broken out in the midst of a wave of reform efforts in the mother country and in the full development of radicalism and utilitarianism. The Enlightenment, which had not flourished in England in the years of the *Encyclopédie*, emerged in London in the affirmation of Price, Priestley, and Bentham. The constitutional debate—on electoral representation, the duration of Parliaments, the rights of deputies, relations with the Crown, the responsibility of ministers—remained at the center of the political and intellectual life of the nation. The old political structure resisted the most diverse obstacles and incidents—from the revolt in the colonies to the madness of the king, from rising radicalism to the brutal blows of religious fanaticism of the London plebs, from the difficult financial situation to exigencies that derived from increasing economic expansion.

The result of this elastic but active political conservatism, from this typically British endurance in liberty, was on close inspection paradoxical. There was no political revolution. The industrial revolution developed in a land of traditional political structures where radicalism and the need to reform did not succeed in cutting deeply into customs or things, and where an agile and mobile aristocracy continued to dominate with a spirit that was both conservative and republican. The industrial revolution—we must not forget—was accomplished in a land dominated by the ideas of Burke, in a land guided by men like Lord North, William Pitt, Charles Fox, in a land, finally, not little influenced by George III, the king who brought the tensions between American colonists and internal radicals to their highest point. The contrast with France is clear from all points of view. Great Britain was the first nation in the world to undergo industrialization; it was "the first industrial nation." It was also the land, it must be emphasized, that desired and was at the same time able to maintain and preserve its own political and institutional traditions.

   In 1774 the Encyclopedist Alexandre Deleyre published his *Tableau de l'Europe* "to serve," one reads in the title, "as a supplement to the *Histoire philosophique et politique des établissements et du commerce des Européens dans les deux Indes*." A few years later, in 1778, a Tuscan translation appeared. The author forced himself to explain British government historically, shaken as it had been through the course of centuries, but always successful in surviving. "The mysterious government of the English," Deleyre wrote, "is composed of monarchy, which is the form of government in almost all of Europe, of democracy, which tends to anarchy, and of aristocracy, which participates in both, uniting in itself the advantages of the three types of power, examining, changing, and smoothing to a new level, and thus tending naturally to the national good."[1] It was a constitution unknown to the ancients, founded on "reasoning" and "experience," which still left observers perplexed about its apparently precarious internal equilibrium. Usurpations of the Crown were certainly no longer to be feared. "In other monarchies, one seeks to gain the goodwill of the king; in England, the king seeks to gain the Commons."[2] Nor was the aristocracy able to equivocate, because of its internal mobility ("commerce keeps riches continually circulating, so that one does not see wealth and dignities accumulate in the hands of a few persons"), and because of the continual emergence of contrasts among individuals and groups. ("There will always be heads of factions who in serving the nation observe, accuse, and frighten Parliament itself.") But still, dangers were not lacking. The perversion of national customs, "the vain idea of a false greatness," errors in the choice of enemies and allies, the risk of losing colonies "in the attempt to extend

   [1] *Prospetto attuale dell'Europa*. Opera dell'abate Raynal, A spese della società (London, 1778), p. 32. This carries the date 1777 when it constitutes the eighteenth volume of the *Storia filosofica e politica degli stabilimenti e del commercio dell'Europa*, published in Siena by the booksellers Luigi and Benedetto Bindi. It was recirculated the following year with the title given here. The translation is very approximate and censored here and there. In the corresponding French text we read: "Le gouvernement placé entre la monarchie absolue, qui est une tyrannie, la démocratie qui penche à l'anarchie et l'aristocratie qui, flottant de l'une à l'autre, tombe dans les écueils de tous les deux: le gouvernement mixte des Anglois, saisissant les avantages de ces trois pouvoirs qui s'observent, se tempèrent, s'entr'aident et se rèpriment, va de lui même au bien national." *Tableau de l'Europe pour servir de supplément à l'Histoire philosophique et politique des établissements et du commerce des Européens dans les deux Indes* (Maestricht: Jean-Edme Dufour, 1774), p. 22.
   [2] *Prospetto*, p. 33.

them," the incapacity to transform "love of patriotism" into "love for humanity," to seek inspiration, that is, in motives that transcended local and particular ones, could plunge England again into a situation "from which it emerged only through torrents of blood and the calamities of two centuries of turbulence and war."[3] Deleyre concluded that if this happened "despotism, which weighs universally on subdued and degraded souls, would rear its head alone amid the ruins of arts, customs, reason, and liberty."[4] England, in other words, would either succeed in carrying out a revolution of universal value or would fall back heavily into its own past. The phrases seemed too strong for the translator, who suppressed them. The echo of Deleyre, one of the most original and sensitive of the philosophes, although smothered and deflected in places, was, as one sees, significant even in Italy.[5]

In the same city, and with the same date as the edition of this *Prospetto*, in Siena in 1778, Francesco Rossi, another bookseller of the city, published the Italian version of the most fortunate and diffused work on England in the second half of the eighteenth century, the *Constitution de l'Angleterre*, by the Genevan Jean-Louis De Lolme.[6] Obliged to leave his fatherland in 1770 because of the internal struggle between citizens and patricians, in which he had taken the side of the first, he arrived as a twenty-year-old in Great Britain and gave himself over to a passionate study of the political constitution. "I had been a witness to the dissentions that for some time had troubled the republic where I was born and the revolution that ended them." "Such great changes in a state that, however small, was independent and contained within itself the principles that made it function, naturally gave me some notion of the theory of government," he wrote in presenting the work and dedicating it to the king of France in the years of the revolution.[7] The first editions

---

[3] Ibid., pp. 34ff.

[4] *Tableau*, p. 24.

[5] See Franco Venturi, "Un encyclopédiste: Alexandre Deleyre," in id., *Europe des lumières. Recherches sur le 18ᵉ siècle* (Paris and The Hague: Mouton, 1971), pp. 51ff. On the other side of Europe, in St. Petersburg, on 30 August 1774, Catherine II thanked Grimm for sending the *Tableau de l'Europe* and told him that she would read it as soon as she had it in her hands. Sirio, vol. 13 (1874), p. 440.

[6] On the beginnings of his adventurous life see *Mémoires de Brissot membre de l'Assemblée législative et de la Convention nationale sur ses contemporains et la Révolution française*, publiés par son fils (Paris: Ladvocat, 1830), vol. 2, p. 153. See Nicola Matteucci, *Jacques Mallet-Dupan* (Naples: Istituto italiano per gli studi storici, 1957), in the index, and Jean Pierre Machelon, *Les idées politiques de J.-L. De Lolme (1741–1806)* (Paris: PUF, 1969).

[7] *Constitution de l'Angleterre ou Etat du gouvernement anglais, comparé avec la forme républicaine et avec les autres monarchies de l'Europe, par M. de Lolme, membre du Conseil des Deux Cent de la république de Genève*. Nouvelle édition entièrement revue (Geneva: Barde et Manget, 1793), vol. 1, "Avertissement," p. ix.

appeared in French in Amsterdam in 1771, and in English in London
in 1775.

Giambattista Vasco reviewed the first edition with enthusiasm. Too
numerous were the useless books, which were multiplying. But this, "although small, will compensate in part for the sterility and uselessness of
so many others and restores a part of its lost honor to the press of this
century. It is no less than a reasoned analysis of the present government
of England, considered from the point of view of its fundamental constitutions." Mixed government had been discussed for a long time. Tacitus had "thought it a passing phenomenon, or unlikely to succeed."
"The English have disproved the views of Tacitus, and their government is celebrated not only by the common people, but by philosophers
of many nations, although none that I know of before Mr. De Lolme
has penetrated the secret mechanisms of such a complex machine or has
traced, as our author has done with such fine notation, the insensible
actions and reactions that have given and preserve this illustrious body
in such a splendid life." These pages demonstrated the appropriateness
of giving "all executive power to the single person of the king, and legislative power together to the king and the two houses." "The perfect
liberty that each citizen enjoys in his goods and person" was ensured
"principally by the singular form of administration of criminal justice."
The English people were "deprived of any influence in government, except for the terrible censure they exercise through the freedom of the
press and their election of representatives in the House of Commons."
De Lolme's book was a refutation of the *Contrat social* and the idea that
"sovereignty, or rather legislative power," was situated "essentially and
inalienably in the whole body of the people." Rousseau had concluded
"that the English people believe they are free but are deceived. They
are not so in the act of electing members to Parliament. Because they
are electors they are enslaved: they are no longer anything." "One could
not read anything more solid or illuminating," Giambattista Vasco concluded, "than the arguments with which Mr. De Lolme shows how illusory and sad a sovereignty is in which the people pride themselves only
on having the right to give an affirmative or a negative vote in public
affairs, in comparison with the more reasonable and useful power exercised by the English through the election of their representatives."
The full adhesion of the Genevan to representative government, as one
sees, struck the Piedmontese economist deeply. "The style is clear, energetic, and copiously adorned with allegories taken from the physical
sciences." If he had emphasized "the merits of national liberty" conquered at the expense of "royal power," he had also brought to light
"the greater activity of absolute government" intended to adjust "that
liberty which is so prized, more so than of any republican type." It was

not surprising that so much "enthusiasm" was shown by an author who was "republican by birth, although not English, and who lives in England and writes of that government."[8] De Lolme's work was like a mirror for Vasco. Piedmontese by birth, but permeated with the culture of Lombardy, where he lived, he recognized himself in the vivid pages he had before him on the constitution of England.

The Tuscan translator was Pietro Crocchi, one of the most cultivated and cosmopolitan men of Siena in the second half of the eighteenth century. A member of the Accademia dei Rozzi since 25 September 1757, he became a few years later professor of Italian to Lord Mountstuart, the eldest son of John Stuart, Earl of Bute, the celebrated favorite of George III, who was in exile for some years in Italy. Crocchi dedicated a version of William Robertson's *Notizie preliminari alla storia di Scozia*, one of the great masterpieces of Scottish historiography, to his quarrelsome pupil. "Few historians," he wrote in his preface to readers, "have been able to exhibit a more exact and an impartial criticism in their research, a more just maturity in their judgments, more clarity, nobility, and elegance in their style." Italy, "the fatherland of many famous historians," would certainly welcome with interest a work like this, in which the "system of feudal government is depicted with no less mastery than force and truth, so that this picture, so worthy of fixing the attention of a thoughtful reader, can also serve to make known the state of almost all monarchies founded on the ruins of the Roman Empire, that is to say, almost all of Europe during those centuries when feudal institutions were in force."[9]

To another "Mylord," "John Child Tylney," was dedicated a few years later the Italian version of the thesis of John Brown on the progress and decline of the arts, a curious and tormented attempt to connect moral and artistic life, which explained the sense of decadence that oppressed the author and drove him to suicide.[10] Particularly interesting

[8] *Gazzetta letteraria*, no. 12, 18 March 1772, pp. 89ff.

[9] *Notizie preliminari alla storia di Scozia avanti la morte di Giacomo V, nelle quali si contiene un succinto ragguaglio dell'origine, de' progressi e della decadenza del sistema del governo feudale*, del sig. dottore Guglielmo Robertson, rettore dell'università di Edimburgo, tradotto nella lingua italiana dall'originale inglese (Amsterdam [actually Siena], 1765), "Avviso al lettore," unpaginated. On this work see Gianfranco Tarabuzzi, "Le traduzioni italiane settecentesche delle opere di William Robertson," *R. stor. ital.*, year 91, fasc. 2–3 (June 1979): 487ff.

[10] *Dell'origine, unione e forza, progressi, separazoni e corruzioni della poesia e della musica.* Dissertazione del dottor Giovanni Brown, tradotta in lingua italiana dall'originale inglese, del dottor Pietro Crocchi senese accademico fisiocritico, a qui si aggiunge *La cura di Saule*, ode sacra dell'istesso autore tradotta fedelmente in poesia italiana di metro irregolare a confronto del testo inglese da Oresbio Agieo, P. A. (Francesco Costetti) (Florence: Stamperia Bonducciana, 1772). In the dedication chiefly the voyages of John Child Tylney

was section 4, "Of the natural consequences of a supposed civilization," and a note on Ossian.[11] Politically more compelling was the version, which appeared five years later, of the *Principî di legislazione universale,* by Georg Ludwig Schmidt d'Avenstein, one of the sources of Filangieri, an author widely known in Italy.[12] In the preface, P. Crocchi spoke of this work as a "precious book" that he had wanted to translate "for diversion and to better imprint it in my mind. . . . The desire to be useful to my nation and make this work known to the community of readers induced me to bring it to press." "A man of good sense does not translate a work he does not esteem," he added, criticizing "those mercenary translators who live from the trade and translate badly so many romances and histories that flood Italy. . . . These translations, instead of instructing, serve to corrupt customs, or at least to ruin the Italian language."[13] He polemicized against those who abused the word *reason,* whereas religion and revelation "are not, and can never be, contrary to that precious gift of the creator intended to serve for our happiness."[14] In the notes he added that he was in favor of "some limits" on the freedom of the press and explained the difference between the "feudal system" beyond the Alps and that in Italy. The very origin of the nobility was different in Italy, he said, where citizen aristocracies were common. "In Italy one could say that being rich is the same as being noble, because if any of the rich are outside the nobility, especially if they have landed possessions, they can easily enter and in fact do mostly enter this class. . . . Nobility in Italy is reduced in substance to ancient and sustained wealth."[15] In 1778 the four volumes of the *History of Scotland* by W. Robertson appeared, published in Siena by Francesco Rossi.[16] "The translator was Pietro Crocchi of Siena," one reads in an old catalogue in the Biblioteca Comunale of Siena. He evidently "esteemed" all these works. He had established a profitable contact with the most lively culture of his age, chiefly in England.

Clothed in the sententiously elegant Italian style of Pietro Crocchi, the work of De Lolme was thus presented to Italians in 1778. Great Brit-

were emphasized: "You saw Naples, you saw Florence, where for many years making it your alternate home you made continual efforts of humanity, liberality, and greatness."

[11] Ibid., pp. 11, 135.

[12] *Principî di legislazione universale.* Opera tradotta dal francese in linguaggio italiano (Paris: Presso la Vedova, 1777). Se vendono in Siena da Vincenzo Pazzini Carli e figli e Luigi e Benedetto Bindi, opera di Shmidt d'Avenstein. On this last see Franco Venturi, "Su alcune pagine d'antologia," *R. stor. ital.,* 71, fasc. 2 (June 1959): 321ff.; and id., *Europe des lumières,* pp. 206ff.

[13] *Principî di legislazione,* vol. 1, p. v.

[14] Ibid., p. viii.

[15] Ibid., vol. 1, p. 263, and vol. 2, p. 169.

[16] Tarabuzzi, "W. Robertson in Italia," pp. 488ff.

ain appeared in De Lolme's eyes as a nation where there had been a historical development in the last two centuries opposite to that of his native Geneva, where citizens had seen diminish more and more the value of their legislative power "to find themselves in the end deprived of it, almost without remedy." And if Genevans had recently been able to recover somewhat, it had been by appealing to the laws of the past, "with the assistance of what remained from their prerogatives."[17] In England instead there had been a continual broadening and consolidation of liberty. In comparison with France, Great Britain showed how a quite different monarchy could develop from similar roots. With a similar feudal origin, France had remained a muddle of disparate elements, "of pieces placed beside one another without mutual adhesion," whereas England "was made up of pieces united with the strongest bonds, and royal authority, seemingly an immense weight, had succeeded with its pressure in making them an indissoluble whole."[18] This was due not only to the historical circumstances of England's development, from the Norman Conquest onward, but also to the development of new and more perfect forms of liberty. "The torrents of feudal servitude that flowed over the continent did not produce any advantage beyond the damages they in fact caused, and in receding they left only aristocracy and despotism." In England, on the other hand, "the same feudal rights, after collecting, deposited and continued to deposit noble seeds of the spirit of liberty, union, and wise resistance." "Little by little" the edifice of the English constitution was raised, and from the time of Edward I, at the end of the thirteenth century, "the eye already perceived the green summits of that fortunate horizon where one day philosophy and liberty would reign as inseparable companions."[19] England, in short, had succeeded in avoiding the fate that carried other states toward absolutism. Elimination of the power of the nobles had not meant the end of all liberty. "In France, where as a consequence of the provincial power of nobles, the people had counted for nothing, when the nobles were defeated the task was complete. But in England, through a variety of circumstances, when the nobles were defeated, the people arose firm and united."[20] Even the effort to substitute republican government for monarchy in the seventeenth century was but an episode. The English "rested finally in the only constitution appropriate to a great state and a free people, that is, one where a small number deliberates and one alone executes, and where, at the same time, through the disposition of

[17] *Costituzione dell'Inghilterra*, del sig. De Lolme, tradotta dell'ultima edizione francese coretta e accresciuta dall'autore (Siena: Francesco Rossi, 1778), p. 150 n. 1.
[18] Ibid., p. 11.
[19] Ibid., pp. 26ff.
[20] Ibid., p. 33 n. 1.

things, general satisfaction is made a condition of the duration of government."²¹ The revolution of 1688 had finally arrived to put a seal on
this evolution. "With the expulsion of a king who had violated his oath,
the doctrine of resistance was vindicated, and this is the final refuge of
the people when oppressed. With the exclusion of a dynasty hereditarily
disposed to despotism, it was affirmed that nations do not belong to
kings. All the principles of passive obedience, of indestructible authority, in a word, all the apparatus of distressingly untrue ideas on which
royal authority had rested to that point, was destroyed and replaced
with the solid and lasting support of love of order and the appeal that
government necessarily has among men."²²

   With his minute examination of the complex political mechanism of
England De Lolme intended to show—recalling like Machiavelli the
struggles that had led Florence to disaster—how the English constitution did not permit "those accumulations of power that have ruined so
many republics."²³ Instead, the limits of power were quite evident in
England, and evident as well were the "advantages of a constitution in
which the people act only through their representatives."²⁴ Also certain,
and fundamental, were the "advantages of a single head of state," that
is, a monarch.²⁵ The bases of public opinion, nourished and stimulated
by a free and vigorous press, were solid. "When the laws gave free play
to the expression of public sentiments, those who governed could not
ignore the displeasing truths resounding from all sides. . . . Like the lion
in the fable, they receive the blows of the enemies they most despise and
are finally obliged to renounce their unjust projects. . . ."²⁶ Guarantees
ensured by law to the liberty of the press were the basis from which had
developed the "great interest that everyone in England takes in everything related to government." The "public sheets" had multiplied. In
their columns "particular news of the capital and provinces" had been
added to political and parliamentary news. The circulation had even extended to the countryside, "where everyone, even peasants, read them
with apprehension"; thus "each individual is informed daily of the state
of the nation, from one end to the other, and communication is such
that the three kingdoms seem to make up a single city."²⁷

   ²¹ Ibid., pp. 35ff.
   ²² Ibid., p. 40.
   ²³ Ibid., p. 121. An entire chapter, the sixteenth, is dedicated to illustrating the necessary failure of governments founded on assemblies of the people in modern and ancient
republics (ibid., pp. 160ff.).
   ²⁴ Ibid., p. 141.
   ²⁵ Ibid., pp. 165ff.
   ²⁶ Ibid., pp. 178ff.
   ²⁷ Ibid., pp. 175ff. He explained in a note that the *Middlesex Journal*, for instance, and
the *Public Advertiser* were "essential wares for every peddler."

From history, and the laws of England, had thus been born a nation profoundly different from others, not dominated by rigid and mechanical relationships of command and obedience, but alive, and always ready to exercise its right of resistance. "The nation forms, so to speak, an *irritable* whole, of which no part can be touched without arousing a general *reaction*." "The cause of each is the cause of all; to attack the least of the people is to attack the whole people."[28] When instead, in other countries, the people attempt to act directly, without representatives, they fail in their intent and soon end by "finding themselves all at once subject to a small number of leaders, as absolute as their title is unclear. . . ." Only with "the ordinary legal course" of political life are they ensured effective power. "Do you want the people to love and defend its laws and its liberty? Then give them time to know what is law and what is liberty."[29]

Not on arbitrary power, not on "ostracism, dictators, or state inquisitors," was "founded the government of England," but on liberty: "Liberty, having such great effects on public opinion, and consequently on the basis of all government, is disdained by those who, moderate in other respects, depend on a less solid basis." "It would be a mistake, for example, to think that one could find it in republics."[30]

For centuries liberty had been "the *dea incognita*," venerated by all peoples, but never truly known by them. "Invoked on all sides," she had finally found her temple in England.

Excluded from those places she seemed at first to prefer (among the "ingenious peoples, who inhabit the southern parts of Europe"), pushed to the extreme of our western world, even driven from the continent, she took refuge in the Atlantic Ocean. . . . Having taken refuge as in a fortress, she reigns over a nation as worthy to possess her as it is to extend her empire, and she carries with her, above all, equality and industry. . . . Surrounded . . . by the deep moat of the ocean, bounded by outworks, which are its vessels, and by the defense and courage of its mariners, she preserves that important secret of the human race, that sacred fire, so difficult to light, and which when extinguished cannot be rekindled. When conquerors overturn the earth, she teaches men anew not only the principle that should unite them, but, just as important, the form of what they should do when they are joined together. And philosophers—when they reflect that strong reasons seem to make despotism a necessary end of society, but that man does not obey the instinct leading him to his fellow men only to find himself almost irredeemably abased—reassure themselves in seeing that LIBERTY has shown her secret, and has finally found a refuge.[31]

[28] Ibid., p. 189.
[29] Ibid., p. 190.
[30] Ibid., p. 199ff.
[31] Ibid., pp. 138ff. A brief and eulogistic notice of De Lolme's book is in the *Gazzetta universale*, no. 76, 22 September 1778, p. 608.

These were the words of prophetic knowledge that concluded the work in which De Lolme succeeded in replying to the much diffused fear of these years, that modern societies were tending more and more toward despotic forms. Through a critique of absolutistic states, as much as of the republican tradition, arguing with Montesquieu as well as with Rousseau, he had shown that England was the only possible example of liberty founded on the laws, on public opinion, and on the complex interplay of institutions and social groups. It was a vision both exalting and static. De Lolme was as little convinced of the importance of political parties as more recent historians—the followers of Namier—have been. Nor did he deign to even glance at the radical forces operating in the late eighteenth century. The problem of America passed by in silence. In his eyes England was a closed world, which nonetheless preserved—and it is difficult to deny it—a peculiar and unique element: liberty grown through its own history.

The revolt of the American colonies and the difficult war it produced soon came to cast a candid light on the much admired British liberty. For a decade there was discussion almost everywhere in Europe not only of the causes that had led the Americans to take arms, but also of the political and constitutional roots that had prevented Great Britain from resolving the crisis of its empire peacefully. Beyond the many juridical, commercial, and economic causes, the "circumstance that seems of greatest weight" in the evolving conflict was sometimes found, "however strange it may seem to some, in the nature of liberty in the British constitution." Political writers taught that free governments could "be fairly happy for those who participate in their liberty," but that they were "ruinous and oppressive for their provinces." Monarchs instead tended not to create ruin among their subjects, whether they were old or new. The ancient Romans, "throughout their republic, were most cruel tyrants toward their subjects." The Carthaginians did the same. Modern examples proved this rule. "The provinces conquered by France are better cultivated and more populous than Ireland, and if Corsica remains under the government of France, it will in a short time probably enjoy a greater prosperity than it could have hoped for under the rule of a republic."[1]

Meanwhile, other and more pertinent voices arrived from England. Critics and adversaries of the colonial policy were certainly not lacking;

---

[1] *Notizie del mondo*, no. 39, 17 May 1777, p. 308 (London, 25 April).

for example, Josiah Tucker, according to the *Notizie del mondo* in 1777, was "one of the most distinctive authors among those who have written against the colonies."² Two years later, the Florentine journal showed him engaged in an effort to reassure his fellow citizens at a moment when a Franco-Spanish invasion was threatening, while continuing to explain to them that "the most advantageous policy for the nation would be to abandon the Americans to their fate and separate from them forever." The "national disquiet" became ever greater. Nor should one forget that "England has always been a land of uproar, even of the greatest revolutions."³ Echoes of the words of Richard Price soon began to be heard in Italy. Already in the spring of 1777 he was seen to challenge the bases of the government's policy with figures in hand.⁴ In Parliament Chatham thundered: "America is lost. England, I fear, is ruined forever."⁵

A quite different voice, placid and clear, echoed in Italy at the end of 1776, the voice of Adam Smith, the greatest scholar and critic of the mercantile origins of the war in which England found itself. It might seem surprising, but it is true that the first and most important review of the *Wealth of Nations* appeared in Rome, in the periodical of Luigi Riccomanni, the *Diario economico di agricoltura, manifatture e commercio*.⁶

---

² Ibid., no. 23, 22 March 1777, p. 178 (London, 28 February). In reality, "his anti-imperialism was based wholly upon British interests, not at all upon American rights," Robert Livington Schuyler explained in the introduction to *Josiah Tucker: A Selection from His Economic and Political Writings* (New York: Columbia University Press, 1931), p. 35. "With the radical democratic movement that began in England and with the political theory to which it appealed, he was wholly out of sympathy," one reads further on p. 39. The popular movements of his generation, from the struggles against Walpole through his violent opposition to the reform of the calendar, and protests against concessions made to Jews in 1753, persuaded him that it was necessary to oppose those who sought extension of the electoral franchise. In his eyes, the masses were stupidly conservative in internal matters and incorrigibly bellicose and imperialistic in external matters. "*Vox populi, vox dei* was for him a blasphemous motto" (p. 40). There is an intelligent interpretation of Tucker's thought in John Derry, *English Politics and the American Revolution* (Glasgow: J. M. Dent, 1976), pp. 162ff., and see W. George Shelton, *Dean Tucker and Eighteenth-Century Economic and Political Thought* (London: Macmillan, 1981), pp. 182ff.

³ *Giornale fiorentino*, September 1779, pp. 332ff.

⁴ *Notizie del mondo*, no. 25, 29 March 1777, p. 196 (London, 7 March), where the financial debate in the Commons is reported at length. Price had already been spoken of (no. 23, 22 March 1777, p. 179 [London, 28 February]). On the actions of Richard Price see Colin Bonwick, *English Radicals and the American Revolution* (Chapel Hill: University of North Carolina Press, 1977); Henri Laboucheix, *Richard Price théoricien de la révolution américaine. Le philosophe et le cosiologue, le pamphlétaire et l'orateur* (Paris: Didier, 1970), pp. 29ff., and Robert E. Toohey, *Liberty and Empire: British Radical Solutions to the American Problem, 1774–1776* (Lexington: University Press of Kentucky, 1978).

⁵ *Notizie del mondo*, no. 50, 24 June 1777, p. 395 (London, 4 June).

⁶ See Oslavia Vercillo, "Della conoscenza di Adamo Smith in Italia nel secolo XVIII,"

The Roman reformer drew from the great book of the Scottish economist not only reason to reconsider all the problems that most interested
him—such as the division of labor, the economic history of the lands
that had been subject to the Roman Empire, the consequences of feudal
rights—he was also particularly attracted to what he found on the "system of commerce and agriculture," citing at length the celebrated pages
on mercantilism and physiocracy.[7]

English policy on the American colonies was, to be sure, a fundamental example of mercantilism that Adam Smith criticized and opposed. On the reverse of the medal of the much admired Great Britain,
the war against the insurgents changed the image of the sanctuary of
liberty that De Lolme admired and exalted. The historical roots of the
contrast were deep: they had emerged earlier in the century to find examples and instances in the conflict that risked not only dissolving the
British Empire, but also of changing the relationship between Europe
and the world. Sparta, Athens, Carthage, and Rome were asked to reveal the secrets of their empires and to explain the origin and decline
of their colonies. Italy was particularly attentive to the echoes of this
international discussion. In 1780 a revealing book, as we have seen, appeared in Florence: *Dello stato e della sorte delle colonie degli antichi popoli,
opera nella quale si tratta del governo delle antiche repubbliche ecc., con delle
osservazioni su le colonie delle nazioni moderne e la condotta degli inglesi in
America.*[8] The author, Emmanuel Joseph Guilhelm de Clermont-Lodève, Baron de Sainte-Croix, was known to have touched on a strongly
controversial issue.[9] The year before, in 1778, the *Histoire de la fondation*

Economia e Storia, no. 3 (July–September 1963): 416, and Franco Venturi, "Elementi e
tentativi di riforme nello Stato pontificio del Settecento," *R. stor. ital.*, year 75, fasc. 4 (December 1963): 800ff.

[7] *Diario economico di agricoltura, manifatture e commercio*, no. 5, 1 February 1777, pp.
22ff. The discussion continues in no. 6, 8 February 1777, pp. 41ff.

[8] A spese della Società Stecchi e Del Vivo, Filadelfia (Florence), 1780. The French
original was entitled *De l'état et du sort des colonies des anciens peuples. Ouvrage dans lequel on
traite du gouvernement des anciennes républiques, de leur droit public etc., avec des observations sur
les colonies des peuples modernes et la conduite des Anglois en Amérique* (Philadelphia: 1779). In
the Italian version the dedication to the "savant confrère" Abbé Barthélemy is missing.
The translation is accurate and complete, except for the omission of some notes in the last
pages of the book, which referred to books one might assume were less known or unknown to Tuscan readers, like the *Lettres d'un fermier de Pensylvanie* by Dickinson or the
Observations on the present State of the waste lands in Great Britain by Young, "a famous English
economist," where he maintained "that it would be infinitely more advantageous for Great
Britain, which has much uncultivated territory, to cultivate its own lands than to make
new plantations in Ohio" (pp. 328 n. 1, 329 n. 2. See p. 330 n. 1). See also chapter 1 above.

[9] See "Notice historique sur la vie et les ouvrages de M. de Sainte-Croix," by M. Dacier,
in Baron de Sainte-Croix, *Recherches historiques et critiques sur les mystères du paganisme*, se-

des colonies des anciennes républiques adaptée à la dispute présente de la Grande Bretagne avec ses colonies américaines was published in Holland.[10] The author, William Barron, had not shown "that profound erudition, that exact logic which his compatriots know how to employ when national pride or spirit of party does not blind them."[11] Thus he had defended British policy, refusing to accept the broadening of perspective and view that historians such as Raynal and Robertson adopted.[12] He had sought to justify the "vexations" Great Britain imposed on the Americans by basing his argument on the "example of ancient republics." "Our zealous realistic Tory, not content with having tried to prove through the conduct of the ancients that the conduct of the English ministry toward the Americans is just and legitimate, threatens to frighten the latter with a fate equal to what confronted the Greek colonies when they tried to recapture their liberty." Even England could not want "such a distressing outcome from its war with the Americans as the one that resulted from the ambitious designs of Sparta and Athens on the Greek cities of Asia." How could it want a "total subversion" of their governments? This had served only to prepare Sparta and Athens to accept "the chains of Macedonians and Romans." Nor was it right to compare these "seditious republics, sometimes vile slaves of tyranny, sometimes incapable of repulsing the attacks of their metropolis," with the "Anglo-Americans." These, after declaring themselves independent through "a memorable act that consoles humanity after so many centuries of tyranny, had hastened to adopt a federative constitution against which the lightning bolts

conde édition revue et corrigée par M. le baron Sylvestre de Sacy (Paris: De Bure, 1817), vol. 1, pp. xxff.

   [10] Utrecht: Chez J. van Schoonhoven, 1778. It was the translation, with notes and additions by Antoine Marie Cerisier, of the *History of the colonization of the free states of antiquity applied to the present conflict between Great Britain and the American colonies. With reflections concerning the future settlement of these colonies* (London: T. Cadell, 1777).

   [11] *Dello stato e della sorte delle colonie*, p. 5. John Symonds, the historian at Trinity College, Cambridge, who published against Barron the important *Remarks upon an essay intitled The history of the colonization of the free states of antiquity* (London: J. Nichols, W. Bowyer, T. Payne, 1778), finally wrote to J. Bentham to accuse Barron of having obtained a pension from the ministry for writing this political defense of the government. See *The Correspondence of Jeremy Bentham*, ed. Ian R. Christie (London: University of London, Athlone Press, 1971), vol. 3, p. 323, Cambridge, 28 April 1785. In this work John Symonds cited and praised Adam Smith, underlining the superiority of modern politics and economics over those of antiquity. "The republicks of antiquity . . . were, for the most part either licentious democracies or tyrannical oligarcies, extremes equally unfavourable to liberty." They were free when compared with Oriental despotisms, "but compared with the constitution of this island, they were arbitrary and violent" (*Remarks*, p. 5). On the author, see Mauro Ambrosoli, *John Symonds. Agricoltura e politica in Corsica e in Italia (1765–1770)* (Turin: Fondazione Luigi Einaudi, 1974).

   [12] *Dello stato e della sorte delle colonie*, p. 6.

of their metropolis break."[13] Now Chatham, like Pericles, talked of
peace. But, like him, he could not obtain it because it was contrary to his
own policy, which England had followed thus far. Like Carthage, Great
Britain no longer made colonies "to support the indigence of her citizens, but rather to subdue foreign nations. The harshness of her yoke
grows with her opulence: her reversals make her cruel, and her successes make her insolent."[14] The whole experience of ancient republics
led one to predict the decline of a modern nation that imitated them.
"The fickleness of ambition, after having raised and then lowered Athens, Sparta, and Rome, swallowed up those conquering cities. Tyre,
Carthage, and other commercial states were wrecked on the rocks of
avarice, from which all the art of their avid pilots could not save them.
Did modern peoples expect a better fate?" The revolt in the colonies
predicted a deep and radical change in the fortunes of the world. Modern peoples seemed to dominate "the whole surface of the globe," but
their domination was undermined by incessant discord, and now it
seemed threatened. "Your implacable hatreds and eternal jealousies
have raised storms that will soon provoke a commotion healthy to the
peace of the universe. The moment comes on apace when your iron
scepters will be broken into a thousand pieces. . . . All the nations you
subjugate, under the pretext of protecting and providing what is necessary for them, will cease to obey your laws." In the future, if "they
permit you to participate in their wealth, they will do it to corrupt and
destroy you."[15]

Escape from such a destiny would be possible only through a complete transformation of English politics. "The sanctuary of liberty has
become for you an asylum for despotism; there it pronounces its murderous oracles, and there it arms you against your brothers. It infects
your souls with the contagious breath of corruption and tramples the
rights of nations. . . . Open the annals of Carthage, open those of Athens, etc., read there your destiny. Ask the peoples of Europe: they all
hope for the happy moment when your power will founder in the very
wave that gave it birth."[16]

The daily chronicle of events seemed to confirm a continual worsening of this contrast. The opposition tried in vain to prevent the war

[13] Ibid., pp. 271ff.
[14] Ibid., p. 67.
[15] Ibid., pp. 249ff.
[16] Ibid., p. 278.

from becoming more bitter. David Hartley, one of the chief exponents of radical views, had given "a speech of two hours in which he related all the evils and the deplorable state to which our nation was reduced by the distressing American war."[1] Parliament became more divided, while the people "began to revive the names Whig and Tory with new bitterness, an odious distinction that seemed forgotten since the reign of George II." "Democracy" reappeared also in the speeches and pamphlets of the Count of Abington.[2]

These were journalistic statements, which came spontaneously from the pens of newsmen but touched one of the most sensitive and important points of the English situation in the seventies and eighties: at this moment of change what was the effective value of political ideas, and the role of reemerging political parties, in determining the events of these important years? For fifty years now—since Namier's first works—this problem has been at the center of all historical discussion of England in the age of the American Revolution. The conclusion is now clear: a reemergence of parties and an accentuation of discussion of more general problems ultimately dominated the horizon of these years. The revolt in the colonies changed the very character of the debate within and outside of the British Parliament. It is true that in the last years of George II the governing class had taken the form of an elastic federation of family and local groups—as Namier described—but as soon as the choices became more difficult and the consequences of any decision more severe, political life was reorganized along the old lines of division between Whigs and Tories, while new and more virulent ideas and passions grew. Traditional diffidence toward the very idea of party did not end, but the need for more strict organization within and outside of Parliament became more attractive, while the ideological debate heightened.[3]

It is not difficult to recognize the growing political tensions in En-

[1] *Notizie del mondo*, no. 2, 6 January 1778, p. 12 (London, 14 December). On David Hartley see Bonwick, *English Radicals*, in the index. On the complex and sometimes ambiguous position the Whig followers of the Marquis of Rockingham assumed when confronted with the problem of American independence, see Frank O'Gorman, *The Rise of Party in England: The Rockingham Whigs, 1760–82* (London: George Allen and Unwin, 1975), p. 362: "It would be innacurate to describe them in the session of 1777–78 as positive advocates of American independence. Rather, they were advocates of peace."

[2] *Notizie del mondo*, no. 15, 21 February 1778, p. 113 (London, 30 January). On Willoughby Bertie, Earl of Abingdon, see Bonwick, *English Radicals*, in the index.

[3] There is a lively exposition of the historiographical debate of the last decades on this nexus of problems in the work of O'Gorman, *The Rise of Party in England*, pp. 13ff. See now Ian R. Christie, *Wars and Revolutions: Britain 1760–1815* (London: Edward Arnold, 1982).

gland, even from afar, through the news that arrived in Italy. Chatham wondered: "Is it possible that we are the same people who sixteen years ago were the object of admiration and envy of the whole world? What a change! What a distressing catastrophe!"[4] In the House of Lords, in the winter of 1778–1779, discussion became more heated and gloomy. The Bishop of Peterborough asked to have removed, "if possible, from the English name, the too humiliating charge of immunity, of cruelty done unnecessarily."[5] The Marquis of Rockingham asked for reforms and referred to the "genuine British constitution."[6] The gazette of Venice, from which these words are taken, promised to print in full, in a supplement, "the speech of Mr. Wilkes in the House of Commons, in the last sitting . . . which provides a picture as lively as it is disquieting, where nature is shown in all its parts, as well as the actual state of England with regard to the American colonies."[7] In June a speech by Burke on these problems was transmitted by way of Amsterdam and printed in three packed columns.[8] In the summer thoughts on the "general situation" by the "Dean of Gloucester, Joshua Tucker," also became widely known.[9]

Nor did the agitation of these months remain within the ruling class. The echo of what was happening in Ireland was anything but reassuring. The unemployment of weavers and other artisans threatened "perilous disorder" already in June 1778. "Recently, for several days and nights, the drum has been heard in Dublin calling for liberty, and large disorderly crowds have gathered insisting on the means to procure their livelihood."[10] Soon the political and social agitation in Ireland deepened and broke out, as we shall see, in a complex and vigorous movement.[11] In London, the following spring, "popular ferment" also increased. "The low people, with whom were mixed various persons of distinction,

---

[4] *Notizie del mondo*, no. 36, 5 May 1779, p. 286 (London, 17 April).

[5] *Notizie del mondo [V.]*, no. 4, 12–23 January 1779, p. 28.

[6] Ibid., no. 6, 19–30 January 1779, p. 44.

[7] Ibid., no. 5, 16–27 January 1779, p. 36 (London, 6 January).

[8] Ibid., no. 50, 22 June–3 July 1779, p. 400 (Amsterdam, 22 June).

[9] Ibid., no. 66, 17–28 August 1779, p. 556 (London, 10 August).

[10] *Notizie del mondo*, no. 45, 20 June 1778, p. 393 (London, 2 June). The source was the *Courier de l'Europe*, no. 44, 2 June 1778, p. 351 (London, 2 June): "All letters from Dublin augment the disquiet of the government; everything there is in disorder, and the tumult has increased every day tending to turn into a worker's revolt since the 15th to 20th of May . . . the sound of the drum has been heard in the place called Liberty and thousands of unfortunates have been seen to assemble, who as yet only shake with misery and ask for bread, but worse has happened in other places . . . mutinous committees have been formed in which it has been resolved to receive no goods of English manufacture."

[11] Robert Brendan McDowell, *Ireland in the Age of Imperialism and Revolution, 1760–1801* (Oxford: Clarendon Press, 1979), pp. 23 ff.

committed great excesses," the gazette of Lugano reported on 8 March 1779. The two ministers, North and Germain, "to save their lives from the fury of the people, had to flee in haste in the deep of night."[12]

In the winter of 1778–1779 the international situation became more difficult, with the first defeats in America and the increasingly grave threat of a prolonged conflict with France. In February one could read in the gazettes about the "treaties of this nation with the United Provinces of America."[13] In the summer the situation became tragic. Spain, along with France, threatened the British Isles. From London on 2 August came the following report: "We receive the distasteful news that the combined enemy fleet, one hundred ships strong, has not only resisted the winds and entered the Channel, but is now before Plymouth to bombard this port." "This is a terrible development, which could become fatal for the entire British Empire."[14] In London the news filled "spirits with most terrible and threatening views toward humanity."[15] A landing was awaited and the best means of defense were discussed.[16] Against these uncertainties and fears prevailed, even in Italy, a strong admiration for the energy with which the islanders kept their heads in adversity. "The critical situation in which England finds itself, confronted by so many enemies and the fear of an approaching invasion of our realm," one reads in the gazette of Lugano, "has aroused and restored the courage of the nation to defend the country in an extraordinary way. The war with America was undertaken and carried out with a kind of indifference as long as it was only a matter of castigating perverse sons of the mother country, with the hope of returning them to duty. The hostility with France was approached slowly, with the hope that the differences would be negotiated amicably, but the declaration of Spain proves that the health of the nation requires vigorous doubled efforts, and these seriously occupy the government."[17] The gazette of Venice fol-

[12] *Nuove di diverse corti e paesi*, no. 10, 8 May 1779, p. 80 (London, 19 February).

[13] *Notizie del Mondo [V.]*, no. 16, 23 February–6 March 1779, p. 136 (Leiden, 22 February). The text continues in the following issues.

[14] Ibid., no. 69, 28 August–7 September 1779, p. 582 (London, 20 August). In Amsterdam at this time Dérival de Gomicourt, a philo-French polemicist, compared the situation England found itself in to that of Venice at the time of the League of Cambrai. The ambition and pride of both these states had made it so that all other nations regarded "with indifference" the deadly peril that weighed on them both. "Lettres hollandaises, ou Correspondance politique sur l'état présent de l'Europe, notamment de la République des Sept Provinces Unies," vol. 2 (August 1779), pp. 79ff.

[15] See Franco Venturi, "Le avventure di generale Henry Lloyd," *R. stor. ital.*, year 91, fasc. 2–3 (September, 1979): 415ff.

[16] *Notizie del Mondo [V.]*, no. 70, 31 August–11 September 1779, p. 290 (London, 27 August).

[17] *Nuove di diverse corti e paesi*, no. 29, 19 July 1779, p. 230 (London, 2 July).

lowed the British revival attentively, concluding in August that "the fleet was full of spirit and awaits only the moment to do battle with our enemies, however powerful they are. The true patriotism that animates them will certainly make them fight with the greatest vigor. A free nation promises much before others who are deprived of this advantage."[18]

The two enemies, England and France, seemed in a sense to come together in this duel, both inspired by a common mirage of liberty. "The English nation," one reads from a Parisian correspondent in the Venetian gazette, "counts on the advantages of a republican government, and with good reason, but the French call themselves happy to live under a moderate monarchical government, like their present one, ruled by a young sovereign who has no other aim than to command a free and generous people."[19]

It was useless to delude oneself: the causes that had brought England to the brink of ruin continued to operate, generating more and more serious conflicts. That mercantilist policy, a mixture of an obtuse defense of privileges and an uncertainty in putting any decision into effect, which had done much to incite the revolt of the American colonies, now reignited conflicts within England itself. Ireland was an example that became more significant daily.[1] The gazette of Venice was quite attentive to voices that came from there. "The great contest between Great Britain and Ireland," one read in a communication from Dublin dated 15 October 1779, "on the question of whether the interests of the second should always be subordinated to those of the first, seems about to break out in a manner that, in all probability, will be decisive." The spokesman of Ireland was Henry Grattan, who, "after having ferociously censured the conduct of the British government with regard to Ireland, and the shameful attachment of those who favor his aims through motives of interest, proposed a total change of direction" and asked for "free and unlimited trade in all the ports of Ireland."[2] More and more concern was raised by the voluntary militias' being raised to

---

[18] *Notizie del mondo [V.]*, no. 71, 4–15 September 1779, p. 598 (London, 27 August).

[19] Ibid., no. 71, 7–18 September 1779, p. 604 (Paris, 3 September).

[1] On the precedents see Francis Godwin James, *Ireland and the Empire, 1688–1770: A History of Ireland from the Williamite Wars to the Eve of the American Revolution* (Cambridge, Mass.: Harvard University Press, 1973).

[2] *Notizie del mondo [V.]*, no. 89, 30 October–10 November 1779, pp. 743ff. (Dublin, 15 October).

support such protests. An English minister assured that these were in reality "a troop of vagabonds and evildoers" that he would be able "to destroy at his will." Meanwhile, they were doing "irreparable damage to the British Empire." The Irish were presented as "better-mannered persons than the inhabitants of Boston." But good manners, and "civilization," did not diminish the "injustice" they were doing. And what were their intentions? "Is Ireland on the point of separating from us?"[3] This problem was discussed in more than three packed columns.[4] The origins of the militiamen, or "military associates," were reported from "a sheet printed in London on 29 October."[5] "The public sheets," we read soon after, "are full of lively paragraphs on this subject." It was not surprising to learn that "forty thousand men are presently under arms in Ireland, not only without any need," but without any authorization.[6] At the end of 1779 the movement seemed to have reached its culmination: "The ferment that reigns in Ireland, particularly in the capital, has begun to break out."[7] The grievances of Dublin had a large part in the debates that began on 25 November in the House of Commons, which were reported in detail in the Venice gazette, one issue after another, for a total of thirteen columns.[8] Trade difficulties multiplied. Increasingly English goods were stopped and sequestered. "We have worked for Great Britain too long," it was said in Dublin; "now we want to work for ourselves." [9] The religious dimension of the Irish conflict began to attract more attention. The first hasty and imprecise news was published about this great problem.[10] But constitutional and economic questions remained at the center of the picture, always actively upheld by volunteers. [11] At the beginning of 1780 came the first news of the "plan" Lord North proposed "to remedy the present calamity of Ireland."[12] These were uncertain and contradictory measures, as soon became apparent, which left ample scope for old and new grievances. The naturalization

---

[3] Ibid., no. 90, 2–13 November 1779, pp. 750ff. (London, 26 October).

[4] Ibid., no. 97, 27 November–8 December 1779, pp. 808ff. (London, 22 November).

[5] Ibid., no. 91, 6–17 November 1779, p. 758 (Dublin, 25 October).

[6] Ibid., no. 95, 20 November–1 December 1779, p. 790 (London, 9 November).

[7] Ibid., no. 99, 3–15 December 1779, p. 822, "Estratto d'una lettera di Dublino del 18 Novembre."

[8] Ibid., no. 102, 11–22 December 1779, "Camera dei communi. Prima sessione di giovedí venticinque novembre." Continued in the following number.

[9] *Nuove di diverse corti e paesi*, no. 1, 3 January 1780, p. 7 (Dublin, 4 December).

[10] *Notizie del mondo [V.]*, no. 12, 16 February 1780, p. 92 (London, 25 January–1 February), "Affari d'Irlanda."

[11] Two resolutions of the latter are reported in ibid., no. 13, 19 February 1780, p. 101 (London, 1–4 February), "Affari d'Irlanda."

[12] *La gazzetta di Milano*, no. 2, 12 January 1780 (London, 12 December). See also *Gazzetta universale*, no. 1, 1 January 1780, p. 5 (London, 10 December).

of English merchants, who thus avoided obstacles set up against their trade, and above all "the absurd restrictions and differences in matters of faith," discontented the Irish, who feared they would ultimately have to emigrate and "leave this island of delights." But there was still some hope, it was said in Florence. "Heaven wills that the Royal Stock Exchange [of Dublin], this noble edifice," become the symbol of a new fraternity "from the burning sands of Africa to the forbidding mountains of Canada, and that the great commandment be written in letters of gold on its portico: Love one another." The creation of an Irish national bank might operate in the same way.[13] The proclamation of the decree granting Ireland free trade "with the American colonies, the West Indies, and the coast of Africa" was received with enthusiasm. "The cannon of the fortress was fired, the garrison lit a bonfire, the palace and other public buildings were illuminated, as were some private houses."[14] "With regard to commerce, the Irish have obtained what they wanted." "It is more than probable that they do not have the least intention of separating from Great Britain," was the conclusion in Venice.[15]

As a recent historian of these incidents has written, "Lord North had hoped that after the commercial concessions were granted it would be possible to keep constitutional issues 'out of sight.' "[16] But Lord North was mistaken even on this. The "arrangements of the British government" in economic matters were giving "that country a new aspect." But Ireland continued "to insist with force on a revocation of the act that subjects it to the laws of England."[17] "There is no doubt that Ireland aspires to the most absolute independence from Great Britain, except for having in common the same sovereign."[18] The speech with which Grattan, speaking in the Irish House of Commons, demanded "legal independence from the English Parliament" was printed in full in number 14 of the periodical *Progressi dello spirito umano*, a "literary journal" parallel to the *Notizie del mondo* that the bookseller Graziosi published in Venice, which could be bought, as was reported, "from the distributors of the present gazette."[19] Economic grievances, like the emerging religious ones, impressed anyone observing Ireland at the beginning of the

[13] *Notizie del mondo*, no. 26, 28 March 1780, p. 204 (Dublin, 26 February).

[14] Ibid., no. 28, 4 April 1780, p. 219 (Dublin, 4 March).

[15] *Notizie del mondo [V.]*, no. 13, 19 February 1780, p. 101 (London, 1–4 February).

[16] McDowell, *Ireland in the Age of Imperialism*, p. 270.

[17] *Notizie del mondo [V.]*, no. 19, 11 March 1780, p. 151 (London, 22–25 February).

[18] Ibid., no. 22, 22 March 1780, continuation of the news from London of 3–7 March.

[19] Ibid., no. 48, 21 June 1780, p. 316, continuation of the news from London of 30 March. On the celebrated speech of 19 April 1780, which "gave liberty to Ireland," as the man who made it later said, see Stephen Gwynn, *Henry Grattan and His Times* (New York: Freeport, Books for Libraries Press, 1971), p. 91.

eighties. But even here, as in England, the center of all tension remained political and constitutional. In a parallel situation, the American colonies had broken out in a war for independence. Would it be possible to manage the Irish instead with a formula of autonomy, of independence guaranteed by a common sovereign?

The interest with which these debates were followed in Venice cannot help but strike one. Once again one wonders to what extent this curiosity reflected the internal crisis of the Republic of St. Mark, which just in those months was embroiled in Zorzi Pisani's attempt at "correction." Certainly the patricians who intervened at this moment in the internal struggles of Venice were not unaware, as we see, of how many and what difficulties stood in the way of any renewal, any reform of the constitution of Great Britain. The English example was present in this significant moment for the Most Serene Republic.[20]

We must ask a similar question in returning our gaze to London, the center of the British drama. Here as well, economic, religious, and political elements sought a difficult, and perhaps impossible, relationship and balance. But what produced them? Financial measures? Transformations in the life of Parliament? A deep and obscure movement of a religious nature? The first alternative, the economic one, was sustained by Burke, the chief representative of the more moderate reformist tendencies. He presented himself as a British Necker. He wrote a eulogy on the "economic policy of France" and the savings this had succeeded in accumulating. "In whatever form of government public frugality is a part of the national strength; this is a kind of strength of which our enemies were in possession before us." "In the name of God, don't say that economy is the only French fashion we don't succeed in adopting."[1] But as in France, even in Westminster the prospect of economic reform soon ended in conflict with the traditional centers of power. Just as Necker was blocked by the French court and parlements, so Burke could not avoid the problem of the relations between the king and the

---

[20] See Piero del Negro, *Il mito americano nella Venezia del '700* (Padua: Liviana, 1986), pp. 122ff.

[1] *Nuove di diverse corti e paesi*, no. 14, 3 April 1780, p. 109 (London, 17 March), and no. 15, 10 April 1780, p. 118 (London, 24 March). See *Notizie del mondo [V.]*, no. 21, 18 March 1780, p. 196, continuation of the news from London of 29 February and 3 March: "Mr. Burke has made a speech in the House of Commons on the necessity of public economy which lasted more than three hours and was applauded even by the ministry." See John Ashton Cannon, *Parliamentary Reform, 1640–1832* (Cambridge: Cambridge University Press, 1973), pp. 72ff., where the policy of Necker is noted.

House of Commons. The civil list was the largest stumbling block in his path.

Thus, only by reforming Parliament would it be possible to overcome the most serious obstacles. During the sixties the agitation of Wilkes had aired this problem. Now again, with much more breadth and passion, there was discussion of the electoral circumstances and powers of the House. The more moderate sought to broaden representation and proposed a triennial term for Parliament; others, who were less numerous but not less active, wanted the term to be annual. At least one of the radicals, the Duke of Richmond, opted for universal suffrage.[2]

The origins of these grievances went back to the English revolution of the seventeenth century, and to the century of debate that had followed it. But now, about the year 1780, new and different ideas flanked and gave impetus to such requests. Radicalism became more philosophical, electoral problems presented themselves as aspects of the rights of man, and constitutional guarantees appeared as civil and political liberties. The daily political struggle was too lively, and the dispute among ministers, the votes, and the powers of the king too enclosed for it to be possible to put aside historical precedents, the traditions of the past, or legal disputes. Even for extremists, like the Duke of Richmond, whom I have mentioned, the experience of liberty inherited from the past remained firm and unshakable.

Also, if reform was wanted, one had to ask oneself what was to be changed and with what means. The Duke of Richmond, for example, knew well that one could not ask Parliament to vote universal suffrage. The Commons would never have voted "such a self-denying law." "I am convinced," he said, "that nothing but an irresistible cry from without the doors could induce them to vote it. . . . Reform was up to the people themselves." But how was this popular pressure to be exercised? James Burgh, one of the most energetic reformers, held that the army might be employed "to force Parliament by popular acclamation."[3] It was difficult not to think of what was happening in these years in Ireland and America, where militias were so important, or of what soon happened in Holland. Nor, except in a few instances, was there an appeal to generic popular pressure. Organization and politics were emphasized by these radicals, not violence or mass movements. None of them had the slightest partiality for tumults. Wilkes had unleashed such and attempted to manipulate them. Now instead the reformers paid attention

---

[2] Alison Gilbert Olson, *The Radical Duke: Career and Correspondence of Charles Lennox, Third Duke of Richmond* (Oxford: Oxford University Press, 1961), pp. 54ff.

[3] Ibid., p. 55.

above all to the possibility of organizing the provinces, thus leaving the
field of London in which Wilkes had moved, and giving life to large
associations outside of Parliament and potentially opposing it, by creating local committees as true and proper nuclei of a reform party that
would be able to find its supreme expression in a national convention,
an assembly of deputies of the sovereign people. This would declare the
House of Commons corrupt and unrepresentative and would supplant
it by voting a new constitution.[4] The "Grand nation association for res-
tauring [sic] the constitution," James Burgh called this movement (and
even for him, as one sees, it would be a matter more of restoration than
of institution).[5] Adherents were many and often enthusiastic, even if
there was no lack of disagreement among the reformers. For Burke a
"popular election" remained "a mighty evil." Fox also was rather critical.
But the push was there. Other organizations were born in the wake of
the reform "associations." In April 1780 the Society for Constitutional
Information was created. Wider and wider became the divergence between economic and political reform.[6] Despite all doubts, the Association, as it was ultimately called, led, above all in York, to the formation
of a political force distinct and detached from local notables and traditional parliamentary ties.[7]

The gazette of Venice offered its readers a detailed and vivid picture
of this movement. In March it printed the speech of Fox "on the corruption for the most part of Members of Parliament, and on appropriate remedies to prevent this." The celebrated politician took to himself
the arguments that had led to the formation of the Association. The
people had nothing to expect "from the current administration . . . except indigence and ruin." The decision was in their own hands. "If they
only said 'we are our own liberators' they would be free. The examples
given to encourage them were lively and recent. They have seen America and Ireland demonstrate how to act, although different and reduced
by perverse men to extremes. Do we not, perhaps, have a common origin with these men? Are life and liberty less dear than appear to them?
. . . Have we not ourselves received, like them, an education that inspires us to despise life when our liberty is in peril?" All distrust for the
new instrument of defense must be eliminated. "Let not the word *asso-*

---

[4] Albert Goodwin, *The Friends of Liberty: The English Democratic Movement in the Age of
the French Revolution* (London: Hutchinson, 1979), p. 59.

[5] Ibid., p. 53. From the beginning of 1780 the *Courier de l'Europe* printed documents
of the "National Association" with breadth and frequency, following closely their development and polemics.

[6] Cannon, *Parliamentary Reform*, pp. 82ff.

[7] See Eugene Charlton Black, *The Association: British Extraparliamentary Political Organization, 1769–1793* (Cambridge, Mass.: Harvard University Press, 1963).

ciation frighten you: it is in no way opposed to the spirit of the constitution; instead it persuades with a relevant truth, which is, that by means
of the Association independence is preserved; without the Association it
will perhaps succumb to the influence of the Crown, an influence that
has reached an excess unknown in any other period of our history."[8] A
few issues later it was said that the "plan for a patriotic association . . .
has planted strong roots in the larger part of the kingdom . . . in York
freeholders in the assembly of 30 December 1779 have unanimously approved the form of the present Association." Its program was reported
in full in three columns in the gazette of Venice. The aim of the Association was "to reestablish the liberty of Parliament by peaceful and legal
means through a general union of citizens in all the kingdom." Starting
from the assertion that "an inequitable distribution of the right to
choose representatives in Parliament is at present the principal cause of
a great number of our public ills," there was a demand for "economic
reform," a "triennial parliament," and finally a change of policy with
regard to the colonies. Only in this way could one avoid "the total destruction of the British Empire."[9]

Francesco Ageno, the minister of the Republic of Genova in London, was also impressed. "Internal disturbances and discontent," he
wrote in January 1780, "are growing in the provinces of this kingdom."
The opposition was advancing "proposals of reform that are flattering
to the people and impractical for the government." "The County of
York, which is the most powerful and considerable of this kingdom,"
had sent "a solemn representation to Parliament, and many other provinces have followed suit." Even in London there had been "public meetings." "These have been given the name General Association to promote
by expedient and legitimate means a reform of public expenses and
suppression of the corruption attributed to the court." He concluded:
"One cannot foresee the consequences of this General Association."[10]

A crisis developed in the spring session of Parliament, which opened
in days of intense discussion of the General Association. The opposition
lashed out with particular venom against Lord North, "author of the
American war," accused of "corruption practiced through the creation
of a quantity of new offices in the civil, military, and finance depart-
ments, and in the India Company." This was a true parliamentary "tempest," which did not fail to mention the great names of the "celebrated
Hume" and "illustrious Justice Blackstone," and there were violent

---

[8] *Notizie del mondo [V.],* no. 20, 15 March 1780, pp. 16off. (London, 25 and 29 February).

[9] Ibid., no. 32, 26 April 1780, p. 255 (London, 7 April).

[10] Colucci, *I casi della guerra,* vol. 2, p. 554, 25 January 1780, and p. 560, 9 February
1780.

threats of "an admonitory castigation of the authors of the ruin of the British Empire."[11] Despite the efforts of the Marquis of Rockingham, the attempt of the parliamentary opposition to resume control of the movement and have political reforms approved by the Commons ended in failure. There were reversals even in the provinces. The methods the Association used resembled too closely those of the American colonies to be widely accepted when, in the most difficult period of the war, a defensive tide was rising.[12]

Then in the spring of 1780 a quite unexpected development momentarily froze all attempts at reform. In June the greatest and most violent disturbance that the streets of the capital had witnessed since the days of Wilkes broke out in London. Hatred of the Irish and general xenophobia, anti-Papist fanaticism, protests against the efforts of Parliament to enlarge the area of toleration of Catholics, and a visceral uprising against misery and degradation in the poorer quarters of the capital combined in the explosive missile manipulated by George Gordon, a Scottish deputy, a cultivated but evidently unbalanced man, who was convinced that Lord North was the center of a vast plot organized by Catholics to corrupt and pervert the moral and political life of the nation.[13] His organizational capacities had already been demonstrated in his native Scotland, where he had led a broad action to intimidate Catholics and anyone favorable to greater religious tolerance (among them the historian William Robertson).[14] With some support by the radical

---

[11] *Nuove di diverse corti e paesi*, no. 18, 1 May 1780, pp. 141ff. (London, 14 April). The report of the "very interesting session of the House of Commons" continued in the two following issues. Then there was a vote, with 233 for and 215 against the celebrated motion of John Dunning on the fact that "the influence of the crown has increased, is increasing and ought to be diminished."

[12] Cannon, *Parliamentary Reform*, p. 84, and Goodwin, *The Friends of Liberty*, p. 61.

[13] On the political action of Gordon, an exponent of "rigid Protestantism," see the *Gazzetta universale*, no. 18, 29 February 1780, p. 139 (London, 4 February). Francesco Ageno, the minister of the Republic of Genova in London, called him in his dispatches an "illustrious fanatic" (Colucci, *I casi della guerra*, vol. 2, p. 656, 6 June 1780). The *Courier de l'Europe*, of March 1780, paid much attention to the propaganda and manifestations of Gordon, inside and outside of Parliament, in London and the provinces. It is enough to follow this gazette to see the parallel development, in 1780, of the four forms of protest and revolt that shook the British world: the National Association, the Protestant associations, the Irish associations, and, more and more broadly reported, the declarations and constitutions of the insurgent Americans. All these moved in assault on the government but, far from being coordinated, tended to contradict one another. The goodwill of the Whig tradition was insufficient to avoid either war with the Americans or conflicts between reformers and Protestants.

[14] Black, *The Association*, pp. 131ff., and J. Paul de Castro, *The Gordon Riots* (London: Oxford University Press, 1926), p. 13. The factory of a "Catholic potter" was destroyed. A detailed study of the activity of Gordon in Scotland and of the opposition that he encountered is found in Richard B. Sher, "Church, University, Enlightenment: The Mod-

elements, and by John Wesley, the creator of Methodism, Gordon succeeded in injecting his fanaticism into London as well, by organizing a great anti-Catholic demonstration that led to a violent tumult.[15]

The irony of history has it that the London plebs attacked the House of Commons precisely on the day when the Duke of Richmond, the partisan of universal suffrage, presented his motion favoring a profound electoral reform. He insisted on speaking for almost an hour, "though with frequent interruptions from the thundering of the mob at the doors of the House." Then the tumult constrained him to silence. There was nothing left for him to do but reaffirm the principle of toleration, "determined always, to defend liberty of conscience in all sects of religion: those were his unalterable sentiments; no fears, no hopes should ever make him change them." But a chance to open the way to reform was lost.[16] Gordon, "at the head of fifty thousand men, appearing before the House of Commons," as the gazette of Florence narrated some days later, "presented a petition of the inhabitants of London and Westminster signed by 150,000 Protestants to seek revocation of the Act of 1778 made in favor of Roman Catholics." On the refusal of Parliament, the "crowds gave in to the greatest excesses, insulting and maltreating different members who favored civil toleration." The "drunken multitude," as Francesco Ageno called them, then launched itself against the centers of the Catholic cult.[17] "The chapels of the ministers of Sardinia and of Bavaria were the victims of their fury."[18]

---

erate Literati of Edinburgh, 1720–1793" (Ph.D. thesis, Department of History, University of Chicago, June 1979), pp. 455ff., "The 'No Popery' Affair of 1778–1779." And see Richard B. Sher, *Church and University in the Scottish Enlightenment* (Princeton, N.J.: Princeton University Press, 1985), pp. 284ff.

[15] See George Rudé, "The Gordon Riots: A Study of the Rioters and Their Victims," *Transactions of the Royal Historical Society*, 5th ser., vol. 6 (1956): 93ff. An engraving placed in circulation on 2 June 1780 directed "To the respectable Association of protestants, and to every worthy supporter of both Church and State," shows the Pope distributing indulgences from the heavens; a naked truth remembers from on high the English massacred and burned in the epoch of Queen Mary, as well as Parisian victims and those of the "Valleys of Piedmont"; Lord North is pictured trying to find money for the American war; George III is shown blindfolded; Lord Gordon, in Scottish attire, leads John Bull; on the left a flock of Anglicans are "asleep." It is reproduced in de Castro, *The Gordon Riots*, opposite p. 12. Samuel Romilly, writing to his friend John Roget on 5 June 1780, said: "The methodists, the followers of Wesley and the sectaries of Whitefield were the first if not to raise, at least to join, the cry against popery" (*Memoirs of the life of Sir Samuel Romilly, written by himself, with a selection from his correspondence*, edited by his son in three volumes [London: John Murray, 1840], vol. 1, p. 114).

[16] *Memoirs of the life of Sir Samuel Romilly*, vol. 1, p. 116, letter to John Roget, 6 June 1780.

[17] Colucci, *I casi della guerra*, vol. 2, p. 660, 6 June 1780. On p. 663 he speaks of the "disordered mob that takes the name and representation of the British people."

[18] *Notizie del mondo*, no. 52, 27 June 1780, p. 411 (London, 6 June).

These events were narrated in the *Giornale di Torino e delle provincie* with many details.

A blue ribbon was the symbol of the anti-Papists; anyone who did not wear it or refused to accept it was insulted and maltreated. . . . Finally some political officers dispersed in the midst of fifty or sixty thousand men to tell them to withdraw. Their exhortations producing nothing, the cavalry was brought up with naked sabres. . . . But while quiet seemed to be restored at the gates of Parliament, the multitude turned to the different Roman chapels. It was no longer a question of kicks and punches; this was an unleashed rabble armed with cudgels and torches that nothing could contain. The first object of their fury was the Sardinian chapel. The building was razed, the sacred ornaments were pulled from the altar and burned in a heap in the middle of the road and at the door. The excellent picture by Cavaliere Cazoli, which had cost 2,500 pounds sterling, was also abandoned to the flames. By midnight the whole chapel was a heap of ashes. In vain the trumpet had sounded to save it.[19]

It was difficult to set limits to the disorder: "It was observed that the troops refused to fire on the mutineers," reported the gazette of Lugano. The insults to deputies, "threats to the person of the king," and "abominations" of all kinds continued to spread.[20] In the following days the "seditious" did not cease to "commit pillage and cruelly exhibit their fury against different members of the ministry, many citizens, and the majority of the Roman Catholics. . . . Newgate prison, the palace of Lord North, and various public edifices were attacked." The government reacted slowly and with difficulty, concentrating bodies of troops "in Hyde Park and St. James Park," and setting patrols in some quarters. It could not prevent, as the gazette of Turin noted, "the razing of Newgate prison and the setting free of three hundred prisoners." And to think it had been "newly built" and had cost "in fourteen years 140,000 pounds sterling."[21] Even two thousand imprisoned debtors were liberated. Citizens were obliged to defend themselves. "The inhabitants joined forces with those of the court, and everywhere hands were laid on the seditious, of whom one hundred were killed. Anyone taken in the act of committing violence was hanged on the spot." It was "the most vile type of plebeian uprising," "which for that matter did not prevent the presence at their head of some persons of higher rank."[22] *La gazzetta di Milano*, like those of Florence and Venice, emphasized that "public order was finally restored" thanks to the wisdom of the ministry, seconded and supported "by the principal bourgeois of this city who took

---

[19] *Giornale di Torino e delle provincie*, no. 26, 30 June 1780, p. 210 (London, 4 June).

[20] *Nuove di diverse corti e paesi*, no. 26, 26 June 1780, p. 204 (London, 6 June), and no. 27, 3 July 1780, p. 210 (London, 21 June).

[21] *Giornale di Torino e delle provincie*, no. 27, 7 July 1780, p. 218 (London, 16 June).

[22] *Notizie del mondo*, no. 53, 1 July 1780, pp. 418ff. (London, 13 June).

arms in their own defense." All three journals, as well as the *Gazzetta universale*, hastened to bring to light the action in the disturbance of a figure with whom they had been concerned more than ten years earlier as a leader and instigator of London crowds. "Among other magistrates Mr. Wilkes distinguished himself by preserving the Bank [of England] from the fury of the mutineers and by arresting the authors of some ill-intentioned writings tending to remove the people from loyalty to the sovereign." "The conduct of the said Mr. Wilkes received the full approbation of the court."[23]

Gordon, arrested, was imprisoned in the Tower of London and his trial began. The repression continued violently. "We have learned that by virtue of military law 17 of the Protestants associated with him were hanged today," it was said in the *Courier de l'Europe* as reported in the *Notizie del mondo* on July 1.[24] "The suburbs are filling with troops and the inhabitants are armed as military companies," narrated the *Giornale di Torino e delle provincie.*

Several bodies of militia have arrived from nearby counties, and 24,000 troops are counted in the city. On the same evening cannons from the arsenal at Woolwich were brought to the Bank. Many houses and public buildings are kept from harm by troops, who have garrisoned St. Paul's, where prisoners are being kept. The palace of the Lord Mayor, the palace of the City, the Tower, the Bank, the Mint, the palace of St. James, Whitehall, the palace of the Queen, the country house of Lord Mansfield are safeguarded; nonetheless, one still sees the City in flames in seven different places from Blackfriars Bridge. The house where tolls are collected on the bridge was torn down by the people, who say they no longer want to pay this duty . . . the house of a rich Catholic distiller is reduced to flames, and his liquors run in streams down the streets. The low people are drunk with them and this drunkenness by good fortune has disarmed more mutineers than the arms of the troops. . . . On Thursday morning thirty-three were counted dead in different quarters and a great number wounded. . . . The rumor spreads that disorders extend to the counties of Lancaster, York, Corn-

---

[23] *La gazzetta di Milano*, no. 27, 5 July 1780 (London, 13 June). See *Notizie del mondo*, no. 53, 1 July 1780, pp. 418ff. (London, 13 June). *Notizie del mondo [V.]*, no. 50, 28 June 1780, p. 398 (London, 13 June), where there is a long report of the "horrible London uprising." This sheet explained that it printed the news with some delay in preference to the vague and uncertain news in other gazettes. The *Courier de l'Europe* provided its readers with ample material on the tumult, in which "the president of the Protestant Association crowned all his farces with a tragedy," one reads in no. 45, 6 June 1780, p. 368 (London, 2 June). On the use of the army in the repression of the "Gordon riots" see Tony Hayter, *The Army and the Crowd in Mid-Georgian England* (London: London School of Economics and Political Science, 1978), pp. 147ff.

[24] *Notizie del mondo*, no. 53, 1 July 1780, p. 423 (Hamburg, 10 June), "Estratto di una lettera inserita nella gazzetta intitolata il 'Corriere d'Europa' in data del 9 del corrente."

wall, Devonshire, and Wiltshire. The news was disclaimed immediately. . . . The damages are valued at 1,200,000 pounds sterling.[25]

Some days later the *Gazzetta universale* could finally breathe a sigh of relief. "The wise conduct of the ministry, the distribution of many troops through different quarters of the city, the almost immediate arrest of Lord George Gordon, head of the mutineers, the successive imprisonment of so many of them, the rapid justice given to so many others left on the edge of the gallows by the terror of the plebs, the zeal of good people in taking arms against them, all has produced good effects for the safety and quiet of the nation. Above all the effort of students of the courts to stop the uprising was noted: they requested leave to unite into a corps and arm themselves. . . . The chief justice . . . was there to see the military development of this body." Even the news that came from America in these days was favorable to the English cause. "At the same moment that we saw this peril averted there finally arrived consoling news of the taking of Charleston, the capital of South Carolina. . . . This glorious victory was quickly announced by a volley of artillery in the Park and from the Tower, and by illuminations in the City."[26]

There could be many consolations, but the problem remained: how could such a tumult occur? To be sure, it was easy "in this moment of giddyness" to place all the blame on the "Louis d'or of France" or the "American agents."[27] But Parliament did not content itself with such explanations. Before June had ended a serious debate began on this impressive outbreak of fanaticism. "Mylord North, Mr. Fox, Burke, and all the principal members declared to be in favor of general toleration in matters of religion to the extent permitted by public safety."[28] This was the only possible response to fanaticism. "Do we persecute Roman Catholics?" Fox asked, and responded immediately: "The days of delirium are passed." "The principles of their religion are not incompatible, as is sought to believe, with the government or with civil liberty." Disdain for the ignorant and fanatic plebs reinforced Fox in his aim to include even Catholics within a tolerance that found its roots in a common civility.

[25] *Giornale di Torino e delle provincie*, no. 27, 7 July 1780, pp. 218ff. (London, 16 June).
[26] *Gazzetta universale*, no. 54, 4 July 1780, pp. 427ff. (London, 15 June).
[27] *Notizie del mondo*, no. 53, 1 July 1780, p. 423 (Hamburg, 10 June), "Estratto di una lettera." The *Courier de l'Europe*, no. 47, 13 June 1780, p. 385 (London, 13 June), polemicized against those who attributed the responsibility for the uprising to "French insurgents." It was much easier to blame it on the "plebs." Certainly London "offered the image of a city taken by an assault of Indians and delivered to pillage." As one sees, the formulas employed by the journalist reveal the formation, in the minds of people, of local as well as American images.
[28] *Notizie del mondo*, no. 56, 11 July 1780, p. 444 (London, 22 June).

"Who are the enemies of toleration?" he asked. "Who are those who, instead of interesting themselves in the ills that actually oppress the nation, employ themselves only in demanding persecution of their fellow citizens?" It was enough to read the petitions of the fanatics and observe the signatures on them to know who they were. "It is enough to see the subscriptions to notice more crosses, more signs than signatures: they are thus for the larger part the most ignorant, who can neither read nor write."[29]

For the whole summer of 1780 such efforts to defend tolerance intersected news about "the criminals kept in prison as fomenters of the past sedition." Many were condemned to death, "not sparing even those of minor age." "From time to time convoys of the condemned left the prisons, which, after justice had hanged the first, returned to collect others. On 20 August came the turn of the Jew Salomon Salomons for having joined with others in demolishing the house of Christopher Connor and burning the furniture."[30]

Among more timorous and traditional observers, for instance, Francesco Ageno, the representative of the Republic of Genova, the London riots confirmed doubts always held about the English political system. This, "under the appearance of liberty, permits the most unbridled license." Certainly "the reasonable and sensible part of the nation" had observed what had happened "with horror" but also had to confess how difficult it was to oppose effective limits. "The municipal laws are too favorable to the excesses of the people." "Magistrates do not dare exe-

[29] *Nuove di diverse corti e paesi*, no. 29, 17 July 1780, p. 231 (London, 30 June). See *Notizie del mondo*, no. 57, 15 July 1780, p. 452 (London, 24 June), which reports the speech of Fox as follows: "There is no need to look into the proffered petitions deeply, one observes in them more crosses than signatures. These therefore are honest Protestants who know neither how to read nor write. It is natural that these fine people will never pardon a Roman who knows how to read and write." How horror of popular fanaticism contributed to make the governing class more united in Parliament is illustrated by John Norris, *Shelburne and Reform* (London: Macmillan, 1963), pp. 132ff. Samuel Romilly compared the appeals of Gordon against Papists, his incitements to revenge, and the reevocation of the persecution of Protestants in past centuries to the war cries of Red Indians that Robertson had made known in his history of America. His horror when confronted with a regression into primitive and elementary instincts is clear. *Memoirs of the life of Sir Samuel Romilly*, vol. 1, p. 136, letter to John Roget dated 28 October 1780. As for Burke, see Frederick Dreyer, "Burke's Religion," *Studies in Burke and His Time* 17, no. 3 (Autumn 1976): 199ff. His critics often thought of him as a virtual Catholic, because he was tied to Irish families, and because he strongly favored the emancipation of Catholics in Ireland. In truth he was a latitudinarian and an energetic supporter of tolerance.

[30] *La gazzetta di Milano*, no. 33, 10 August 1780. On this episode see Rudé, "The Gordon Riots," p. 111: "Salomon Salomons . . . risked his neck during the riots to settle accounts with a Roman catholic publican because he thought him to be a 'thief-taker' who had lived 'by the price of blood.' "

cute measures valuable for limiting violence." Troops could fire only if authorized by the justices, who were threatened and intimidated by the people. Otherwise disapproval of what had happened was all but unanimous. "The opposition to the ministry profits from this disorder," even if it could not "decently refuse to cooperate with beneficial projects" required by the "common tranquillity." The revolt against toleration was only one aspect of a deeper opposition, expressed recently above all in the reformist organizations in the provinces. "The actual persecution of Catholics has been only a pretext for the perpetrators of the rebellion, since all other associations of inhabitants promoted by Members of Parliament to overturn the state and defeat the ministry had failed." Salvation came from the energetic intervention of the authorities. "It is certain that the king, assisted by the ministers of state and those of the law and military, has saved this metropolis and the whole nation from universal ruin." It was enough to think what might have happened if the Bank had been taken: "It would have collapsed public credit, that of many foreign nations, and the possessions of two thirds of these inhabitants." "It must be agreed" that the measures the government took had been "marvelous in suppressing an internal rebellion, for which the persecution of Catholics had provided a pretext." "Now the court is the only one to govern, through martial law," if with some limitations.[31] There was talk of cancelling and attenuating the easements given to Catholics in the past. But England now knew well how useless were concessions made to a people in revolt. "The example of what had happened in America, which did not fail to rebel despite the obtained removal of those regulations that had troubled it, was too recent and distressful to be forgotten." The situation seemed unavoidable. But the conclusion remained that "the too-free constitutions of this licentious and independent people, while influencing and authorizing tumults, seem equally ineffective in suppressing them."[32]

The *Giornale di Torino e delle provincie* reported that the English Houses of Parliament had reconfirmed tolerance for Catholics. "The opinion was that it should not be revoked, following the seditious cries of the people unleashed." Otherwise "mutineers would imagine that every time Parliament passed an act displeasing to the people, they would not have to do anything other than attack and besiege it in the very place it met to revoke it."[33] It would be even more dangerous when it was not a question of laws regarding religious tolerance, but social con-

[31] Colucci, *I casi della guerra*, vol. 2, pp. 657ff., 6 June 1780, pp. 666ff., 9 June 1780, and pp. 668ff., 13 June 1780.

[32] Ibid., p. 680, 27 June 1780.

[33] *Giornale di Torino e delle provincie*, no. 30, 28 July 1780, p. 243 (London, 10 July).

flicts, and the right of workers to create their own organizations. This was precisely the threat appearing in Dublin. "There was much fear for a while," one read in the Piedmontese gazette, "that there might be a renewal in Ireland of the scene that occurred lately in London, many thousands of artisans having gathered in Phoenix Park after the Parliament to present a petition to prevent the effect of an act tending to impede organizations among tradesmen." But the armed volunteers were drawn up on the side of Parliament, as the London militia had been shortly before. "The volunteers of Dublin," the same sheet reported, "remained united, and 1,000 were under arms to support the civil authorities. The Lord Mayor, on his part, notified the mutinous artisans that he would not give permission for more than six of them to enter the city at the same time, and this precaution of the magistracy, supported by the afore-mentioned subjects, had all the effect that could be desired."[34]

These episodes and reactions provided a vivid and disconcerting image of events that was particularly difficult to interpret at a distance, far from the British Isles, for those who did not share the public passions of the English of this period. Even the work of historians two centuries distant, although providing precious information and minute details, have not entirely untied the tangled knot of the "Gordon riots." Thanks to the work of George Rudé we know that there were 210 dead among the troops, 75 were sent to hospital, and 173 were wounded. This gives us an idea of the violence of the tumult. There were 450 arrested. Of these, 62 were condemned to death and 25 were hanged. This confirms the impression of contemporaries of the harshness of the repression.[35] The damages were in reality less serious than had appeared at first. It is more difficult to assess the importance of religious motives in the incident. One should not forget that "anticatholicism remained a part of the political tradition of the people," nourished "by republican-whig or nationalist agitation and closely linked with abiding memories of 'the good old cause.'" But according to the historian who has studied these events most closely, fanaticism was not the determining element. The quarters with the most dense Catholic population were not attacked. In the attack on the Bank of England the motives propelling the mutineers could have been quite different. Undoubtedly there was an element of social protest, the "groping desire to settle accounts with the rich."[36] From the political point of view there was no lack of those who, as E. C. Black has observed, thought they saw in the London tumult "the Oliverian and

---

[34] Ibid., no. 29, 21 July 1780, p. 234 (London, 27 June).

[35] On 20 June there was talk in London of 285 dead and 175 prisoners or wounded (ibid., no. 28, 14 July 1780, p. 227 [London, 20 June]).

[36] Rudé, "The Gordon Riots," pp. 111ff.

republican spirit. . . . Religion is a mere pretence for subverting the government and destroying the constitution." Lord Bute said the attack concealed "a deliberate design to destroy monarchy and establish some wild scheme of democratic government."[37]

Tradition, even from the Protestant Reformation and the revolution of Levellers, might have had a weight in the London violence. But what counted most was that the past was evolving and becoming modified in the estimation of contemporaries. The last wave of revolutionary anti-Papalism and republicanism was unleashed exactly when the radical tradition, under the influence of the Enlightenment and the American insurgence, was transforming itself into an increasing faith in liberty and religious toleration.[38] In 1780 Priestley, the celebrated scientist and writer, published a pamphlet in defense of Catholics. Referring to the example of Maryland, he opposed the idea that Catholicism was necessarily hostile to civil liberty and cited Franklin in defense of toleration. Richard Price moved in the same direction. Through animated discussion and the formation of clubs that were in continual movement (the "Honest Whigs" was typical), a new idea of religious toleration was being affirmed, which was detaching itself from the traditional grievances of "dissenters" and coming closer to considerations that were diffused contemporaneously on the Continent in the years between the suppression of the Jesuits and the laws on toleration of Joseph II.[39] Economic and

[37] Black, *The Association*, p. 165. Contemporary prints, reproduced in de Castro, *The Gordon Riots*, provide a vivid image of the different political and social elements that came together in these events. We see the assault and fire on Newgate Prison (opposite pp. 88 and 90), dancing, arms, and flames in contrast with the solemn bulk of this edifice, an image that makes one think irresistibly of the French Revolution (p. 92), images of insurgents inspired more by fear than by mockery (pp. 104 and 138), with the inscription "No pope, no ministry." A Dutch print shows Gordon in prison despairing when he knows that his followers are being hanged (p. 208). There are other witnesses and illustrations in Christopher Hibbert, *King Mob: The Story of Lord George Gordon and the Riots of 1780* (London: Longmans and Green, 1958). One sees opposite p. 101 his portrait when he converted to Judaism and called himself Israel bar Abraham Gordon; the last chapter, "Gordon and Liberty!" pp. 152ff., narrates his long imprisonment at Newgate for debt and his death in the cell where he had continued to receive so many friends and admirers and where he had maintained a broad political correspondence with different lands (he wrote among others to Franklin and other Americans that John Adams, then ambassador of the United States in England, was preparing "a liberticide plot to subvert the republican government by raising up an emperor and senate like that of Rome dependent on France, upon the ruins of the betrayed commonwealth under the auspices of the Washington Convention" [p. 168 n. 1]). He died on 1 November 1793, up to the end forcing himself to sing the *Ça ira* (p. 172).

[38] Michael R. Watts, *The Dissenters: From the Reformation to the French Revolution* (Oxford: Clarendon Press, 1978), pp. 471ff.

[39] Bonwick, *English Radicals*, p. 201. See W. C. Crane, "The Club of Honest Whigs: Friends of Science and Liberty," *William and Mary Quarterly*, 3d ser., vol. 23 (1966): 210ff., and Russel E. Richey, "The Origins of British Radicalism: The Changing Rationale for

political problems took precedence over religious ones. In this light the Gordon riots appeared as an outbreak of fanatical and reactionary rage, dominated by religious prejudices and superstitions worthy only of the most miserable and ignorant classes.[40] From the first encounters the gazette of Leiden called this a tumult "whose cause itself makes it detested by the wiser part of the nation."[41] The gazette of Amsterdam wrote that in France the impression and revulsion were such as to make the war forgotten for a moment "with the thought only of the frightful ills that seemed about to afflict its rival, which was thought of at that time only as a part of suffering humanity."[42] This was an eloquent testimony of the emergence of a new sensibility that united the governing classes before the obscure perils of popular revolts and phantoms.

The desire for tolerance also raised a shield against the cruel repression that followed the London riots. As the gazette of Venice noted, "It seems that the measures taken by the government to put an end to the excesses of the people are generally not entirely approved." "To put the fate of citizens in the hands of troops" seemed to many to put "national liberty in peril." Thus the protest made by the York Association, signed by his leader, Christopher Wyvill, and dated from a "tavern in York, 2 August 1780," was reproduced in full.[43]

Dissent," *Eighteenth-Century Studies* 7 (1973–74): 179ff. Particularly important is the chapter entitled "The Dissenting Interest and the Campaign for the Abolition of the Test and Corporation Acts, 1787–1790," in Goodwin, *The Friends of Liberty*, pp. 65ff., where one can follow the battle for toleration in England. As for electoral laws, even in this case the movement was very advanced; more was demanded than on the Continent, but the practical results remained small. Old institutions resisted, supported by a reaction that collected around the motto "church and king." But the dissenters' struggle still remained important. They asked for toleration and ended up more clearly wanting liberty for themselves and for all. Over them weighed, a pamphlet of 1789 read, "a civil and not an ecclesiastical oppression." "They complain of being injured as citizens, as being wronged as Englishmen," hope for a "restauration of their rights" and a "participation" in the life of the community. (This last word was used for the first time during these discussions, by Lord North, in a speech of 8 May 1789.) The humanitarian and tolerant position of Lord Mansfield, the best representative of English legists whose house was burned and his life imperiled in the Gordon riots, was characteristic. See Edmund Heward, *Lord Mansfield: A Biography of William Murray, First Earl of Mansfield, 1705–1793, Lord Chief Justice for Thirty-Two Years* (Chichester: Barry Rose, 1979), pp. 150ff. He presided over the tribunal that judged Lord Gordon and obtained his absolution.

[40] See the interesting full study by Martin Fitz-Patrick, "Joseph Priestley and the Cause of Universal Toleration," in *The Price-Priestley Newsletter* (1977), pp. 3ff.

[41] *Supplément aux nouvelles de divers endroits*, no. 47, 13 June 1780, "Extrait des nouvelles de Londres du 2 et 6 Juin."

[42] *Gazette d'Amsterdam*, 30 June 1780, cited in Turin, AS, *Materie politiche estere in genere*, mazzo 66, 1780.

[43] *Notizie del mondo [V.]*, no. 71, 9 September 1780, p. 566, continuation of the news from London of 16 August. See the article "Wyvill, Christopher," by Gilbert Cabill, in

In the summer a new test awaited the government and the opposition. Parliament was dissolved and new elections were called for September 1780.[44] The opposition emerged stronger than before. Something magical, as William Pitt said, emanated from the personality of Charles Fox. Rockingham was undoubtedly an able and a patient manipulator. The reflections of Burke compactly expressed the preoccupations and hopes of those who awaited the end of the American war for a solid economic reform.[45] During the winter even more urgent problems weighed on England. On 25 January 1781 the war with Holland was announced in Parliament. This was a "break," wrote the gazette of Venice, "that could perhaps have distressing consequences for all of Europe." The war risked spreading like an oil slick. "France advances a considerable army toward the frontier of the Low Countries to shield and defend the republic from English attack. The States General might request the assistance of the king of Prussia and try to involve the powers of the north."[46] The United Kingdom had to confront new serious threats. A London "public sheet" published "wise reflections" that were soon translated in the gazette of Lugano: "Great Britain, attacked on all sides without being able to count further on the king of Prussia or on the emperor, after their assumption of neutrality, remains alone, and it is not to be hoped that she could preserve much longer a pride like that of Medea, who when asked on what her hopes depended when confronted with so many enemies, responded: 'on myself.' " [47] In February the opposition multiplied its attacks. It counted a number of deputies nearly equal to the partisans of Lord North. So long as there was some hope of success beyond the ocean, these succeeded in remaining in the saddle, supported and spurred on by George III. But still, the news, arrived in November, of the defeat of General Cornwallis in Yorktown put the difficult political equilibrium in doubt. An acute "parliamentary crisis" opened at the beginning of 1782. This led to a true and proper repudiation by the House of Commons of the American war in February, in collision with the king, who insisted on his decision not to concede independence to the rebel colonists, and finally, in March, to a

Biographical Dictionary of Modern British Radicals, ed. Joseph O. Baylen and Norbert J. Gossman (Hassocks, Sussex: Harvester Press, 1979), vol. 1, *1770–1830*, pp. 558ff.

[44] Ian R. Christie, *The End of North's Ministry, 1780–1782* (London: Macmillan, 1958), pp. 20ff. On the general election that followed and the structure of the new Parliament, see ibid., pp. 46ff., 167ff.

[45] Ibid., pp. 219ff.

[46] *Notizie del mondo [V.]*, no. 4, 13 January 1781, p. 28, continuation of the news from London of 26 December.

[47] *Nuove di diverse corti e paesi*, no. 2, 21 January 1782, p. 23 (London, 28 December).

minority for Lord North.[48] For a day or two George III held firm and talked of abdication. But on 20 March the Parliament, threatening a vote of censure, obliged the government to resign. The way was opened for peace and for a new political arrangement.[49]

The picturesque and virulent campaign of Charles Fox, the "man of the people," was particularly striking. "Liberty and independence" was written on his banners. Great hopes were raised even in him by the "glorious revolution" that had occurred in Parliament. But "we cannot conceal that, for being too slow, it was effected at a moment of crisis little adapted to dispel all apprehensions." The only route seemed to be the one he had had the courage to indicate and put in practice: his alliance with North against an incapable opposition. "We are about to see what this unhappy earth has not seen for a long time, a perfect alliance between the government and the people." "The revolution that has procured me this singular honor [of entering the government] is your work entirely," he said turning to his electors. He even promised to act in favor of Ireland. At the end of his speech "four gigantic Irishmen carried him in triumph on their shoulders, ran him through the streets, and finally brought him down at the door of a tavern, where he dined with many of his friends." [50] "Generally speaking," one read a few days later, "the enthusiasm for the new ministers is without limit. At a dinner with 200 persons of the winning party the toasts began with the majesty of the people followed by that of the king."[51] It was finally possible to end "the shameful contest arisen between ourselves and our fellow American citizens," "to finally determine the constitution" of Ireland, to restore peace "in the East Indies . . . and establish a just and honorable system of government," "to make some progress in the constitutional project to reduce the influence of the Crown," and finally to restore "alliances on the continent with the old friends of Great Britain."[52]

The reform effort reemerged with the nearing of peace.[53] Under the guide of Christopher Wyvill, one of the most noted and active radicals, two petitions were prepared in March 1781 on the "public economy" and on the "reform of Parliament."[54] But in May the House of

---

[48] Christie, *The End of North's Ministry*, pp. 299ff., 319ff., 340ff.

[49] O'Gorman, *The Rise of Party in England*, pp. 427ff.

[50] *Notizie del mondo [V.]*, no. 35, 1 May 1782, pp. 176ff. (London, 12 April).

[51] Ibid., no. 37, 8 May 1782, p. 293 (London, 19 and 23 April).

[52] Ibid., no. 40, 18 May 1782, p. 313 (London, 30 April). See John Cannon, *The Fox-North Coalition: Crisis in the Constitution, 1782–84* (Cambridge: Cambridge University Press, 1969).

[53] See the interesting chapter "The Friends of America" in the book by Derry, *English Politics and the American Revolution*, pp. 129ff.

[54] See Simon Maccoby, *English Radicalism, 1762–1782: The Origins* (London: George Allen and Unwin, 1955), pp. 348ff.

Commons refused to discuss them. In the following months the close struggle around the central problem of continuing the war with the Americans or not attracted all the political energy of the nation. Still, the question of the reform of Parliament soon returned to the foreground. Thus in June 1782, "in a meeting of electors of the County of Middlesex," there were denunciations of "the unjust inequality existing in rights of suffrage and representation. . . . It is hardly believable that such an enlightened nation permits such an injurious error to exist in the true foundations of liberty. In a kingdom that contains nearly eight million inhabitants, more than half of the Members of the Commons are elected by fewer than 6,000 votes." The "inhabitants of the County of Middlesex who should elect a sixth of the House of 513 members, elect only 8." This was a "monstrous inequality" that resulted from the change over centuries in places more or less inhabited. "The population of the city of London has grown prodigiously, but its right of representation is the same." In vain it was repeated "that our excellent constitution, like a venerable old edifice, has withstood the shocks of centuries, and it is perilous to try some innovation for fear of ruining it." The nation, in reality, moved only when pushed by need. "America owes its liberty to this, and Ireland has known how to profit from it." It was now England's turn. "England, united, industrious, and content with its constitution, when this is reduced to its first principles, has need of only itself to be happy." In truth, a part of the governing class seemed to open to the projects for reform. William Pitt and Charles Fox were thought favorable. "In the house of the Duke of Richmond it was agreed to have printed a plan for reform and to distribute it throughout the kingdom." Remembering again the examples of America and Ireland, the gazette concluded that the reformers were not at all fearful of their adversaries: "The English nation will certainly not want to be less than its two sisters."[55]

These threats did not seem small in the early winter of 1782–1783. The crisis was not only political, but also one of social customs. "There have never been seen in this capital," came a communication from London, "such frequent and excessive disorders as in the past months, the natural consequence of the unrestrained license everywhere. Despite all the horrors and ills of the war, the most voluptuous luxury and the most ruinous love of pleasure and libertinage have reached a peak. The shows, lewd places announced openly in the public sheets, and taverns for all kinds of games of chance multiply excessively." It was an atmosphere that could not help but be politically dangerous. "The corruption of morals is the surest basis for establishing an arbitrary power over

[55] *Notizie del mondo*, no. 50, 22 June 1782, pp. 395ff. (London, 4 June).

the ruins of true liberty, reducing citizens to misery and slavery. The government has not yet paid attention to this aspect of public administration. The ministry even looks with indifference on Members of Parliament taking their pleasure in the coffeehouses around Westminster Abbey so that they can run quickly to vote when necessary." But now, finally, the government had taken some measures.[56]

The social disorder of England struck even a distant observer, an editor of the Bolognese *Memorie enciclopediche*. "Excessive riches and monstrous inequality" characterized England. "The discontented and divided citizens have not even the artfulness to hide their concern for private interest and their penchant for theft and betrayal behind a veil of public utility." The colonies had rebelled and fought "with fierce enthusiasm." Now it was time for England to change itself. "For a nation so favored by commerce and the arts and sciences, we would sincerely like to predict a revolution leading to a better future."[57]

The chessboard of Parliament became more and more complicated. The gazette of Lugano provided a guide to this labyrinth in the spring of 1783. Here in first place was "the Portland party," "called variously the Whig party, the Newcastle party, the Rockingham party, and the Portland party. It is composed chiefly of descendants of persons whose attachment to both civil and religious liberty procured the act of succession and established the present royal family on the throne." Fox and Burke belonged to it. "The North party" was known instead under the different names of "Scottish party, Tory party, and North party." "The Betford party" was formed "partly at the beginning of the present reign." "It has sufficient strength to be important for supporting the royal prerogative or defending the majesty of the people, as is most appropriate to its own interests." Finally, there was "the Shelburne party." "This has been heard of for only about twelve years." Among others

[56] *Nuove di diverse corti e paesi*, no. 47, 25 November 1782, p. 376 (London, 2 November).

[57] *Memorie enciclopediche*, no. 31, October 1782, pp. 249ff. Review, signed Osti, of the *Riflessioni sopra la elevazione e la tendenza delle antiche repubbliche adattate al presente stato della Gran Bretagna*, del kavalier Odoardo Montagu, tradotte dall'originale inglese (Undine: Gallici, 1781). The English original, *Reflections on the rise and fall of the ancient republicks, adapted to the present state of Great Britain* (London: A. Millar, 1759), had numerous editions. It was translated into German in Breslaw in 1769 and appeared later in French: *De la naissance et de la chute des anciennes républiques*. Traduit de l'anglois, par le citoyen Cantwel (Paris, 1793). On the strange personality of the author, son of the noted traveler and writer Mary Wortley Montagu, see DNB, vol. 38, pp. 237ff. He was the first European to be vaccinated against smallpox; he converted to numerous religions, lived for a long while in the Levant, and died in Italy, in Padova. On his reviewer, perhaps really Giuseppe Osti, see Carlo Capra, *Giovanni Ristori da illuminista a funzionario, 1755–1830* (Florence: La Nuova Italia, 1968), p. 80 n. 85.

William Pitt belonged to it. "But the leading figures are beginning to tire of this union. . . . Still, there are in his party some men of ability and talent, who have no reason to complain," even concerning the "gifts" that come to them "from the public purse."[58]

The participation of Lord Shelburne in the Rockingham government from March to July 1782 marked the highest point of British parliamentary reform.[59] It seemed that finally Burke's ideas had found a political leader capable of putting them into practice. He was a man of great culture and linked, through Morellet in particular, to the French philosophes. Shelburne had many adversaries and carried out his complicated and sinuous operations with great difficulty. But his words were received with notable interest even far from England.[60] At home, he succeeded in mcriting even singular praise from Bentham. "He was the only minister, to his knowledge, not to fear the people." One saw this when it was a question of permitting the use of personal weapons and eroding in some measure the old monopoly of landed proprietors. "The hunting laws," we read in the *Notizie del Mondo*, "tended to repress and enslave the people of the countryside more than any other from the time of the court of Charles I to the present. Under them no unqualified man was permitted to keep a gun. If an enemy should land in some part of our coast tomorrow, the people would not have arms and not know how to use them. . . . The circular letter of Lord Shelburne to arm the people is the most certain proof one could give of the mutual confidence between government and people."[61] The measure was accepted also because it appeared in the climate of tension at the end of the war. But when, instead, the will to reform began to touch the bases of the powers of Parliament, all hope for change foundered.

William Pitt himself, arguing with North when the war was barely over, spoke of the "great inconvenience, manipulation, scandals, and corruption in the election of members of the House." Fox declared he was of the same opinion.[62] In the spring of 1783 a heated constitutional debate thus began in the "houses of Parliament," which was prolonged

[58] *Nuove di diverse corti e paesi*, no. 13, 31 March 1783, pp. 99ff. (London, 7 March).

[59] Norris, *Shelburne and Reform*.

[60] His speech of 27 November 1781 is printed in the gazette of Venice, which said it preferred to print it late than provide only fragments, as other gazettes had done. See *Notizie del mondo [V.]*, no. 5, 16 January 1782, pp. 37ff.

[61] *Notizie del mondo*, no. 45, 4 June 1782, p. 355 (London, 16 May). On an important period in the hunting laws, see Edward Palmer Thompson, *Whigs and Hunters: The Origin of the Black Act* (London: Penguin, 1975), and above all P. B. Munsche, *Gentlemen and Poachers: The English Game Laws, 1671–1831* (Cambridge: Cambridge University Press, 1982).

[62] *Notizie del mondo*, no. 43, 31 May 1783, p. 344 (London, 13 May).

for many months.[63] Many wanted "a more equal representation in Parliament." When Pitt took his stand "it was a long time since the House had been so full." Even he, like all the English, looked on the constitution "with venerable respect." It was "the fruit of the most consummate wisdom . . . at the same time both the envy and the pride of the universe." "Europe learned from it that liberty is the basis of true greatness." But it was necessary to "defend it from decadence." Certainly "innovations at any time were dangerous." He did not intend "to innovate" but "to revive and consolidate the spirit" of the constitution. "The time was ripe for reform." The nation found itself "in a state of humiliation." It was necessary to remedy the "radical vice of the constitution," the influence, that is, of the Crown, which "ruins the foundations of liberty through corruption." As for Parliament, this too was in a difficult situation. "According to the constitution it should be the custodian of the liberty of the people, a barrier against executive power," but it always risked "degenerating into an instrument of tyranny and oppression to destroy the constitution in fact." Even with regard to "rotten boroughs" one should proceed with caution. "I think they cannot be removed without making the whole crumble."[64] A few days later came Fox's turn. It was hopeless to try to revive, he said, proposals for reform now definitely rejected by the House.[65] Meanwhile, fears of a renewal of disorder in London increased. "The state of uncertainty and anarchy in which the nation now finds itself appears unequivocally. The spirit of sedition revives in the people and in the land and sea troops. Seditious circulars have been distributed in the city, inviting the inhabitants to take arms for the defense of their rights and to gather in St. George's fields. These incendiary notes, written in the lowest language, caused great concern."[66] In the winter of 1783–1784 the uncertainty was even greater. On 18 December the king dismissed the North-Fox government. "We are in a critical situation," came a report from London. "A divided Parliament about to be dismissed and prorogued, without a minister beside the president of the council and chancellor of the exchequer, and no one disposed to accept the vacant places."[67] In vain Fox called for "an administration promising some stability."[68] Parliament remained obstinate in defending its own traditions, without ceding any of its rights. A further effort at reform was rejected with 157 votes against

[63] *Nuove di diverse corti e paesi*, no. 27, 7 July 1783, p. 206 (London, 20 June).

[64] *Notizie del mondo [V.]*, no. 44, 31 May 1783 (London, 13 May).

[65] Ibid., no. 46, 7 June 1783 (London, 20 May).

[66] *Notizie del mondo*, no. 31, 19 April 1783, p. 247 (London, 1 April).

[67] *Nuove di diverse corti e paesi*, no. 2, 12 January 1784, p. 13 (London, 23 December).

[68] Ibid., no. 4, 26 January 1784, p. 28 (London, 6 January). See John W. Derry, *Charles James Fox* (London: B. T. Batsford, 1972), pp. 169ff.

77.[69] A reaffirmation of the powers of the Crown, even before the dissolution of the House, on 25 March 1784, raised more violent objections. The deputy Sheridan said: "I have found in history only two examples of the use of this prerogative, but one cost the head of Charles I and the other the crown of James II."[70] "The actual situation of England," the gazette of Lugano reported, "is perhaps the most singular that has appeared in its history since the revolution." Two parties were in balance, with neither being able to dominate. "The king himself is reduced to a witness of these maneuvers." "Meanwhile, the treasury is empty, subsidies are uncertain, and all the laws that serve to maintain the national forces are on the point of expiring."[71]

Meanwhile, amid violent contrasts, the popularity of William Pitt grew, a man apparently open, as we have seen, to proposals of reform, but dominated in reality only by the logic of power and politics. Extraordinarily young and self-possessed, he dominated the tumultuous and violent scene more and more. Here he was, for example, at a "banquet of merchant druggists enjoying a magnificent dinner to install him as a citizen of London." Even Wilkes was there. The banquet changed quickly into a riot. Stones were thrown at houses that were not illuminated. The partisans of Fox, "leaning from the windows of a tavern," insulted the people. "The carriage of Mr. Pitt was overturned, and it was his great good fortune to be able to save himself in a coffeehouse," while the "Lord Mayor was slightly wounded in one hand."[72] But the young deputy did not seem troubled by this.

The struggle between Pitt and the coalition of his adversaries for the seats of Westminster soon reached an exceptional intensity.[73] Fox trailed behind him a crowd of variegated followers, from the most well-spoken and brilliant noblewomen (for this he was called "the man of the fair sex") to "a troop of butchers, porters, and other low people." They were united under the banner "Fox and liberty."[74] In May knives appeared among "the companions of Mr. Fox and those of Sir Wray" (Cecil Wray, Pitt's candidate). "Some mariners on the side of Wray, wanting to stop a symphony the butchers made every evening sharpening their knives before the tavern where Mr. Fox meets, went into a fray in which the butchers and porters attacked the mariners with such vigor that these

[69] *Notizie del mondo*, no. 1, 3 January 1784, p. 3 (London, 11 December).

[70] Ibid., no. 16, 24 February 1784, p. 151 (Paris, 30 January).

[71] *Nuove di diverse corti e paesi*, no. 8, 23 February 1784, p. 60 (London, 3 February).

[72] *Notizie del mondo*, no. 25, 27 March 1784, p. 229 (London, 5 March), and *Nuove di diverse corti e paesi*, no. 12, 22 March 1784, p. 91 (London, 5 March).

[73] Derry, *Fox*, pp. 206ff., and Loren Reid, *Charles James Fox: A Man for the People* (London: Longmans, 1969), pp. 199ff.

[74] *Nuove di diverse corti e paesi*, no. 17, 26 April 1784, p. 131 (London, 9 April).

were obliged to retreat into a tavern and shut the door." There followed "a new kind of battle . . . a hail of glass bottles, which seriously wounded many heads." Even the ancient Romans, the correspondent from London concluded, never arrived at such shameless violence."[75] Referring to another such incident the Florentine gazette finally concluded: "This liberty that we much prize and is much envied by other nations is really a terrible thing. . . . Who can count the arms and legs broken, or the wounds caused, just in the election of a member from the city of Westminster? But these are times of license and disorder, in which the laws themselves, given the greatness of ills, are obliged to stay quiet and let things pass."[76]

But now the political balance, despite all the disorder, weighed on the side of the party of the ministry and Pitt (even the electoral victory of Fox was contested). It was a defeat for the reformers, which a modern historian has attributed not to their advanced grievances, but on the contrary, to their excessive moderation and prudence. They refused to follow the logic of their position. "For all their adulation of the Glorious Revolution of 1688, the thought of emulating it in practice did not occur to them."[77] Thus the victory remained in the hands of the king. The great crises of the last years of the war and the first years after were being resolved, even if in a far from painless way. New taxes, and above all one on shops, again caused riots in London, leading on 14 July 1785 to a "kind of revolution in this capital." "Many shops were closed and the people went in crowds to others that were open, insulting those who accepted the tax." Pitt himself was "villainously insulted by the people." George Gordon returned to action, "inciting the people to greater fury."[78] "The entrances to Parliament" were occupied by a crowd.[79] A kind of lockout by the owners of three hundred barges loaded with coal

[75] *Notizie del mondo*, no. 43, 29 May 1784, p. 372 (London, 7 May). Even the gazette of Lugano, when Fox was finally assured of his seat of Westminster, described "the great parade, with more than a thousand persons," that accompanied him in triumph. One noted "the two duchesses of Devonshire and Portland, all adorned with laurels, surrounded by their livery in gala, and preceded by a standard on which was written in big letters FEMININE PATRIOTISM" (*Nuove di diverse corti e paesi*, no. 23, 7 June 1784, p. 181 [London, 21 May]).

[76] *Notizie del mondo*, no. 35, 1 May 1784, p. 307 (London, 9 April).

[77] Cannon, *The Fox-North Coalition*, pp. 223ff. For an extensive discussion of the significance of the electoral contest between Fox and Pitt and the function it assumed in public opinion, see Paul Kelly, "Pitt versus Fox: The Westminster Scrutiny, 1784–1785," *Studies in Burke and His Time* 14, no. 2 (46) (Winter 1972–73): 155; Lucyle Werkmeister, "Pitt versus Fox: A Response to Paul Kelly," ibid. 15, no. 1 (48) (Autumn 1973): 45ff., and Paul Kelly, "Reply to Lucyle Werkmeister," ibid. 15, no. 2 (49) (Winter 1973–74): 169ff.

[78] *Notizie del mondo*, no. 54, 5 July 1785, p. 426 (London, 17 June).

[79] Ibid., no. 56, 12 July 1785, p. 442 (London, 21 June).

made any provisioning of London impossible and reduced two or three thousand workmen to "unemployment." These reacted violently against the coal dealers.[80] Such events show how difficult it was to exercise government in the age of William Pitt, but they were not enough to shake its foundations.[81] Even at its summit the character of the political struggle was changing, focusing chiefly on abuses and scandals in the administration of India, and then on the delicate problem of a regency at the moment of the madness of George III.

For a half decade, between 1780 and 1785, the most varied blows seemed to carry Great Britain toward revolution. A war lost; the winning of independence by America; the increasingly acute need to review relations with Ireland, and also Scotland; a deadlock among parties that seemed to have appeared only to prevent any action or decision; the frequent dissolutions of Parliament with consequent elections; the reemergence of old contests between Parliament and the Crown; the blindness of a conspicuous part of the ruling class; the formation of a reform movement capable of attracting the attention of all and creating an effective organization, but not capable of obliging the government to accept its proposals, and a deep sense of discontent and repulsion for growing corruption; the reemergence of religious fanaticism that had seemed spent; the outbreak of popular revolts in the very heart of the nation; the scarce but cruel measures of repression; the continual agitation of all classes, made more acute by public opinion, the press, and the more vivid and intense discussion: how could one not consider in the assemblage of such facts the possibile occasion for a deep transformation of the political, social, and moral order of the nation? Examples were not lacking, models, derived from the British past or created in these years by the American Revolution.[82] But still, in 1785, with many bumps that made many observers in the British Isles and on the Continent catch their breath, the venerable coach of the English constitution was again in movement on its old tracks.

Was this a failed revolution? H. Butterfield thought so when he affirmed that "our French revolution is in fact that of 1780—the revolu-

---

[80] Ibid., no. 67, 20 August 1785, p. 532 (London, 29 July).

[81] See Paul Kelly, "British Politics, 1783–84: The Emergence and Triumph of the Young Pitt's Administration," *Bulletin of the Institute of Historical Research* 54, no. 129 (May 1781): 62ff.

[82] Of great interest is the collection of essays *Three British Revolutions, 1641, 1688, 1776*, ed. J.G.A. Pocock (Princeton, N.J.: Princeton University Press, 1980).

tion that we have escaped."[1] To this Richard Pares, also a great expert in this period, objected that it was not in 1780, but rather in 1782, or again in 1783, that George III seized control of the House of Commons. Nor did the Irish movement reach its point of culmination between 1779 and 1780. The crisis before the election of 1780, like that of 1784, remained parliamentary, and it is thus an exaggeration to call it revolutionary.[2] John Cannon has rightly recalled, intervening in this discussion, that in the years 1783–1784 "the extraparliamentary associations were still vigorous, the loss of the thirteen colonies was an undoubted fact, public credit was at a low ebb, there was serious disaffection in the army and navy, Parliament and executive government were paralysed by constitutional deadlock." Cannon also underlines the importance of the extraordinary development of public opinion. The followers of Rockingham appealed to it in 1782 to force the hand of the king, and it vindicated them in 1784.[3]

Nor can the discussion on the rhythm of the crises of the first years of the eighties be said to be closed among English historians. John Cannon has taken some steps in a direction that might prove fruitful. Events in England need to be compared with those of other countries in the same period. Cannon has indicated how George III was compared by contemporaries with Gustavus III of Sweden, and how the struggle between the English parliamentary aristocracy and the king can be compared with encounters between nobles and monarchs in continental Europe. Undoubtedly the Great Britain of the Gordon riots, of Fox and of Pitt, is not comprehensible if the general crisis of the old regime is not taken into account. And already a contemporary—it was, in truth, Honoré de Mirabeau, a man with revolution in his blood—understood and said that, in this perspective, England, despite delays and defeats, was more advanced than any other European nation, and that on the Continent it was necessary to begin by asking if one really wanted to surpass it. "A tumult, a sedition in London does more good to the heart of an honest man than all that imbecile subordination one is so proud of elsewhere." The risk the English ran was great, but, precisely for this they were to be preferred to others who accepted their own slavery. "Slaves, with their feet and hands in irons, mock the dangers faced by tightrope walkers." Europeans had to begin by understanding England: "Philosophy should try that revolution before wanting another." The political

---

[1] Herbert Butterfield, *George III, Lord North and the People, 1779–1780* (London: Bell, 1949), p. vi.

[2] *The English Historical Review* 65 (October 1950): 526, review by Richard Pares of the book by H. Butterfield cited in note 1.

[3] Cannon, *The Fox-North Coalition*, pp. xiff.

message of Great Britain consisted in the fact that "the constitution is the best that is known, the administration the worst possible." Only a reaffirmation of liberty would resolve this contradiction. "The constitution, although incomplete and defective, saves and will continue for some time to save the most corrupt people of the earth from their own corruption."[4] A few years later Mirabeau was persuaded that only a general plan for reform, promoted by thinkers of the whole world, would be able to save England. The consolidation of the political situation seemed to him a symptom of sclerosis, of immobility. This is what a constitution based on counter-balances, such as Montesquieu and De Lolme had praised, led to. "*Ponderibus librata suis*" (Freed from her burdens), the latter author had called it.[5] This could result in nothing but "the fatal inertia of servitude." [6] The power of the king remained immobile, and Parliament continued to be chosen on the basis of an unjust electoral law. Still present was "the House of Peers, the remnant of feudal hierarchy."[7] All hope seemed lost, "unless all sages of all nations, moved by the great examples England has given to the universe, and the even greater examples she owes to it, do not join together to show her a plan of reform. The sages represent providence here below. They alone can rejuvenate states approaching old age."[8]

When compared with this cosmopolitan vision, the recent book by Ian R. Christie, *Stress and Stability in Late Eighteenth-Century Britain: Reflections on the British Avoidance of Revolution*, can be considered a step backward historiographically, a return to the "deep isolationist English love of country," to use the words of this English scholar.[9] He thus does not miss criticizing the work of R. R. Palmer and in general pays little attention to efforts made to insert the British crisis into the context of European and world developments. What interests Ian R. Christie are the social, political, and religious forces that slowed down and stopped the subversive tendencies that nonetheless affected Great Britain in the epoch of the Gordon riots and the Associations, not the emergence of new ideas and forces that to be sure ended by being checked, but still existed, and contributed to creating the revolutionary climate of these years on the continent and on the other shores of the ocean.

England was no exception. All the revolutions that shook the world

---

[4] W. R. Fryer, "Mirabeau in England, 1784–85," *Renaissance and Modern Studies* 10 (1966): 75ff.

[5] Cited in *Aux Bataves sur le stadhouderat, par le comte de Mirabeau* (n.p., 1788), p. 183.

[6] Ibid., p. 106.

[7] Ibid., p. 185.

[8] Ibid., p. 107.

[9] Ian R. Christie, *Stress and Stability in Late Eighteenth-Century Britain: Reflections on the British Avoidance of Revolution*. The Ford lectures (Oxford: Clarendon Press, 1984), p. 218.

at the beginning of the eighties had failed, except, of course, the one of
the American colonies. In England at this moment crystallized attitudes
that were important in determining reactions to the French Revolution
a few years later. At this moment that "basic patriotism" and that "basic
loyalty to the Crown" which flooded the British press and took to itself
one of the most popular forms of political propaganda, satirical prints,
was consolidated.[10] After 1780 these were almost unanimously favorable
to Protestant agitation and hostile to the whole republican tradition.
Take, for example, "Britannia's Assassination; or, the Republican
Amusement," in which Wilkes, John Dunning, and Charles Lennox,
Duke of Richmond (the supporter of universal suffrage), appear as assassins. It did not even miss the memory of Algernon Sidney's work *On
Government*.[11] Fox was elsewhere compared to Cromwell.[12] Religious toleration was considered "an outrage."[13]

No one doubted the "low state" in which England found itself. Its
policy could be only peace and neutrality, while internally a sense of
impotence spread. It was necessary to keep in mind, as the gazette of
Lugano wrote, that "since the revolution of 1689, the nation has sacrificed 750 million pounds sterling in wars." "It is truly deplorable that
this enormous sum was spent to keep the balance in Germany and subject America, since if the twentieth part were employed in agriculture,
commerce, fishing, and other objects of internal economy, exceptional
advantages would have resulted to the nation." And in fact, "these objects, neglected and obscured, are now the occupations of the current
ministry."[14]

Thus, the varied echoes of the defeated revolution spread. The English had not followed the example of the Americans; nor did they win
the war against them. But what would Ireland do? The threat from that
part was the greatest one remaining when the situation seemed some-
how stabilized in England. The constitution had held. But what would
be the fate of the United Kingdom if the national pressure of the various elements composing it increased?

Beginning in 1778 as a defensive measure against a possible French

[10] M. Dorothy George, *English Political Caricature to 1792: A Study of Opinion and Propaganda* (Oxford, Clarendon Press, 1959), vol. 1, pp. 159ff.

[11] Ibid., plate 61.

[12] Ibid., p. 178, plate 67.

[13] Ibid., p. 159, plate 56. See also Herbert M. Atherton, "The 'Mob' in Eighteenth-
Century English Caricature," *Eighteenth-Century Studies* 12 no. 1 (Autumn 1978): 47ff.

[14] *Nuove di diverse corti e paesi*, no. 5, 31 January 1785, p. 34 (London, 11 January).

attack and recruiting a large number of volunteers among local Anglicans (as opposed to Catholics or even Presbyterians), the Irish movement, as we have seen, took the form of a defense of rights of the local parliament and of a struggle against the commercial privileges of England. The volunteers had acted through great meetings, similar to those of Dutch patriots some years later, and succeeded in getting some concessions from the government of Lord North, which was preoccupied with the struggle against the United States.[1] In the spring of 1782 the program elaborated by the volunteers of Ulster seemed mature. They wanted: "I) Free trade with the whole universe, II) A clarification of the rights of Ireland, with formation of a statute containing all these rights, III) An act of Habeas Corpus, IV) A statute through which judges would be declared independent from the Crown, as in England. . . . VIII) A repeal of penal laws against dissenters and Roman Catholics."[2] "The Irish nation is now so well united and strongly resolved to sustain its rights that any effort to prevent them will be absolutely useless."[3] The government in London was in fact obliged to give in. It conceded a parliament at least theoretically independent, even though still under British sovereignty (the so-called Gratton Parliament, from Henry Grattan, one of its creators). The concessions did not remove from the minds of the volunteers a propensity to follow the example of the colonists beyond the ocean. "The Irish seem inclined to be in good harmony with the Americans. . . . The Hibernian Union has decided that our corps [of volunteers] will greet the first ship that enters the port of Dublin carrying the American flag with three salutes."[4] "Some letters from Ireland indicate that various families of that realm are inclined to go to North America. This prospect is surprising because it has been seen that England has granted what the Irish have demanded almost entirely. One must believe that American liberty has good breeding indeed for the freest people of the Old World to seek out another, so distant one." Certainly the new laws on immigrants of the Congress of the United States were seductive: "Three years of residence and payment of public impositions will suffice to acquire the right of citizenship

---

[1] See Butterfield, *George III, Lord North and the People*, pp. 71ff., and the clear explanation of these problems by Robert Roswell Palmer, *The Age of the Democratic Revolution* (Princeton, N.J.: Princeton University Press, 1959), vol. 1, *The Challenge*, pp. 289ff. A more recent general picture is by Edith Mary Johnston, *Ireland in the Eighteenth Century* (Dublin: Gill and Macmillan, 1974), pp. 132ff.

[2] *Notizie del mondo [V.]*, no. 32, 20 April 1782, p. 254 (Dublin, 22 March).

[3] *Nuove di diverse corti e paesi*, no. 18, 6 May 1782, p. 141 (London, 19 April). On the "revolution" of volunteers, see no. 20, 19 May 1783, p. 150 (London, 2 May).

[4] *Notizie del mondo*, no. 22, 18 March 1783, p. 175 (London, 25 February).

in the different provinces, and all the advantages relating to the same."[5] But if the vision was seductive, the desire of the Irish to hold on to the liberty they had obtained at home was stronger still. "The people are well disposed toward the sovereign and the British nation, but are resolved to maintain their independence and legislation. It is said they even intend to establish a separate army and navy for the defense of the realm and the protection of its commerce." A "parliamentary reform" would follow and there would be "a tax on absent citizens," so as to oblige "all Irish proprietors who live outside the country . . . to return and consume their revenues there."[6] "The armed association, rather than dissolving at the conclusion of peace, as the government had hoped, remained in existence and did not hide its intention of asking the Parliament for a reform of various pieces of legislation, such as the composition of and election to the House of Commons, the duration of Parliament, the terms on which subsidies would be granted, and the like."[7] A great assembly held in Duncannon, "two days' distance" from Dublin, "to pass in review" was the occasion of a violent demonstration in the city of artisans left without work because of English competition. Profiting "from this distance, they united into a crowd. They violently stopped anyone they encountered and tore from their backs whatever they found of foreign cloth, pulling from their shoulders and necks even the handkerchiefs of ladies, but leaving any native cloth they had on. To justify their violent action they dragged along the road two corpses, exclaiming that these were the bodies of two unfortunate artisans who had died of hunger for lack of work. The uprising lasted for three days and was not quieted until the return of the volunteers."[8] These had meanwhile voted thirteen resolutions against the threat they thought pending "of an *absolute monarch*, and the still more odious government of a *tyrannical aristocracy*." They declared they were admirers of "those illustrious men" who "in England and Scotland" had courageously, even if thus far fruitlessly, intended "to obtain the redress of such wrongs." "Let the example of those nations who are mutually sisters animate the inhabitants of each to persevere with tireless devotion until this glorious work is finally completed."[9] Their demands were rad-

---

[5] Ibid., no. 29, 12 April 1783, p. 233 (London, 25 March). On the "spirit of emigration" that had taken hold of the Irish, see *Nuove di diverse corti e paesi*, no. 33, 18 August 1783, p. 254 (London, 1 August).

[6] *Nuove di diverse corti e paesi*, no. 37, 15 September 1783, pp. 284ff. (London, 26 August). The same correspondence is in *Notizie del mondo [V.]*, no. 72, 6 September 1783 (London, 21 August).

[7] *Notizie del mondo [V.]*, no. 83, 15 October 1783 (London, 29 September).

[8] Ibid., no. 75, 17 September 1783 (Dublin, 14 August).

[9] Ibid., no. 88, 1 November 1783 (Dublin, 13 October).

ical. "Men of the province of Ulster, one of the four large provinces of Ireland, have recently held an assembly where there was unanimous adoption of several resolutions, the very reading of which makes the first principles of the American Revolution come to mind, and Great Britain has every reason to fear that absolute independence might not be the final result if the situation in Ireland is not much different from that of America." They departed from the principle that "liberty is an unalienable right of Irish and Britons, derived from the author of their being, and of which no earthly authority, and even less a delegated authority, has the right to deprive them." They demanded popular elections and an annual parliament. Departing from these "fundamental principles," they had formed a "great convention, assembly, or national congress, composed of five representatives from each county and charged to obtain a plan for parliamentary reform." Thus "the inhabitants of Ireland and Great Britain," like those of Scotland, had acquired "the title of *free men*."[10] It would be the task of the assembly of volunteers to control the parliament, keeping an eye on it "so that it will not become a parliament of the ministry, in the same way that ephors in ancient Sparta supervised the conduct of their king." This was undoubtedly a preoccupying situation in the eyes of the English. How could one not fear the "pompous phrases of these pretended republicans, who by making the people childish with dreams of liberty, incite them to revolt and sedition that will end in the ruin of states?"[11] It was not surprising that "the affairs of Ireland continue to embarrass our ministry," was communicated from London.[12] "We are on the eve of some blustering scene in Ireland . . . new disturbances seem to menace that state," one read again at the beginning of January 1784. A "great national convention has adopted the resolutions taken by the delegates of volunteers concerning the reform of Parliament." An "ardent resolution" on its rights and duties, "against any usurpator of its autonomy," was presented and "approved with a majority of 150 votes against 68."[13]

During the same winter, beyond the ocean, a "good number of Irish immigrants who had come to establish themselves in America" paid homage to General Washington. "We members of the Association of

---

[10] *Nuove di diverse corti e paesi*, no. 42, 20 October 1783, pp. 327ff. (Dublin, 23 September).

[11] *Notizie del mondo*, no. 74, 16 September 1783, p. 592 (London, 28 August).

[12] Ibid., no. 92, 18 November 1783, p. 735 (London, 30 October).

[13] Ibid., no. 1, 4 January 1784, p. 3 (London, 11 December). It appears that the "Grand National Convention" of Dublin in November 1783 was "the first body calling itself a 'national convention' in a world that was to know many such conventions in the next fifteen years" (Palmer, *The Age of the Democratic Revolution*, p. 303). On this "convention," see McDowell, *Ireland in the Age of Imperialism and Revolution*, 303ff.

Volunteers and other inhabitants of the kingdom of Ireland" offer the
"most sincere felicitations on the glorious conclusion of the recent cruel,
unnatural, and oppressive war. . . . Nations have been enlightened, universal liberty and the security of subjects have been made permanent
and respectable by your work." They expressed their "gratitude for the
great advantages that our land, oppressed for so long, owes to you."[14]

In Ireland itself the problem of toleration was posed again, even as
a way of enlarging the base of the Irish movement, which was restricted
in the beginning to the Anglican minority of the island. The gazette of
Florence underlined how Irish Catholics "merited universal admiration
for the prudence that has characterized their conduct." They had already obtained much. "Perhaps only political offices will be forbidden
to them." Meanwhile, in all the Catholic churches, "one heard fervent
exhortations to inspire in each Catholic a love of peace, obedience, and
resignation to the government."[15] Religious toleration appeared, even
in Ireland, to be the best way to untie political knots that were becoming
more and more tight and difficult.

"The news from Ireland continues to be very disquieting," came the
report from London in the spring of 1784. The movement assumed
increasingly a popular, working-class character. "The government is
taking every precaution to prevent disturbances on the part of the people, and particularly of workmen. The quarter where the largest number of them live [in Dublin] is guarded by a battalion, and sentinels are
posted in all the streets."[16] To calm the "ferment" and maintain the
"public peace," it had become necessary to take "violent and distasteful"
action. The agitation had extended "to the provinces, which are even
more discontented with the conduct of Parliament." "The people in
general see the present House of Commons as an enemy to its rights
and privileges."[17] Three possibilities had opened before the Irish, the
gazette of Venice wrote, and all three had failed: "parliamentary reform," the "more equal distribution of taxes," and "encouragement
given to manufactures of the country." The constitutional possibility,
the financial, and the economic one were like three "blows" into the

[14] *Nuove di diverse corti e paesi*, no. 7, 16 February 1784, p. 54 (New York, 15 December). The response of Washington follows: "If the example of Americans fighting happily
for the cause of liberty can be of some utility to nations, we have still another motive to
rejoice." He then insisted on "an equal liberty" and a "commerce without restrictions"
between the two countries and said that America had "opened its bosom to welcome not
only wealthy and respectable foreigners, but also the oppressed and persecuted of all
nations and all religions."

[15] *Notizie del mondo*, no. 1, 3 January 1784, p. 3 (London, 11 December).

[16] *Nuove di diverse corti e paesi*, no. 20, 17 May 1784, p. 156 (London, 27 April).

[17] Ibid., no. 21, 24 May 1784, p. 164 (London, 4 May).

void. Not even "the spirit of toleration" seemed "to gain ground."[18] Protests against unemployment and hunger dominated the horizon. The defense of local industries seemed the only remedy, if one did not want to accept a more intense emigration. "In the city of Belfast an association of the principal inhabitants has been formed, who have solemnly obliged themselves to buy no further articles of wool, silk, cotton, or mixed cloth that is not of Irish manufacture." "It has even been recommended to the ladies of the city to unite themselves with this resolution and contribute what they can to encourage the manufactures of the country so as to provide subsistence to the inhabitants and prevent emigrations, which become more and more numerous and frequent, even from the Irish capital."[19] Protests became more violent and numerous. "A new corps of volunteers has adopted the name the 'Invincibles of Dublin,' with the motto 'Liberty or Death.' "[20] "The people enter the shops of cloth merchants and scrupulously examine the cloth for sale to see if it is of English or of Irish manufacture." Boycotts were extended even to the press. "The distributors of gazettes and public sheets have united and formed a body, making a solemn and public decree not to sell or distribute any sheet that contains the least article favorable to the viceroy, and the people, entering into this plan, have effectively prohibited all writings favorable to the British government."[21] In August the Irish people "had reached such a degree of license that it was impossible to leave them unpunished." Two parties that had taken the name Sons of Ormond and Sons of Liberty were committing "ferocious atrocities."[22] In Dublin "scenes of anarchy and disorder" multiplied.[23] The movement began to take on a clearer political connotation. "During an inspection of a corps of more than 5,000 men, among the banners were found some with the arms of France or the XIII United States of America, and one with these words: *Liberty or Death*."[24] In Dublin the director of the *Journal of Volunteers*, who had incited revolt, was imprisoned. Encounters with army detachments grew in number. "This may be the mo-

[18] *Notizie del mondo [V.]*, no. 39, 15 May 1784 (London, 27 April).

[19] *Nuove di diverse corti e paesi*, no. 21, 24 May 1784, p. 164 (London, 4 May).

[20] Ibid., no. 23, 7 June 1784, p. 181 (Dublin, 15 March).

[21] *Notizie del mondo*, no. 58, 20 July 1784, p. 494 (London, 23 June).

[22] Ibid., no. 64, 10 August 1784, p. 540, "Estratto di una lettera da Dublino del 13 luglio." On the movements of "Ormond and Liberty Boys," bands of peasants who made whole zones of the country impassable, see McDowell, *Ireland in the Age of Imperialism and Revolution*, pp. 81ff.

[23] *Notizie del mondo [V.]*, no. 67, 21 August 1784 (Dublin, 14 July). See *Nuove di diverse corti e paesi*, no. 32, 9 August 1784, p. 253 (Dublin, 16 July).

[24] *Notizie del mondo*, no. 71, 4 September 1784, p. 600 (London, 13 August).

ment of the great revolution predicted for some time."[25] If the government does not take steps, it was said in the autumn, "it will be impossible to stop the sedition." Rumors spread that "the Marquis de La Fayette would take command of a national corps, together with many other French officers."[26] The situation in the following months remained disturbing. Offers of the government in commercial matters had to be withdrawn. A general illumination celebrated this victory, obtained, it was said, by the "resolute courage of the nation."[27] Discontent spread more and more in the provinces and in the countryside, directed "against the exactions of the clergy and injustices committed by officials of police, who are accused of exercising a tyranny that inflames the spirit." "The viceroy has marched troops against the malcontents to return them to their duty, but it was in vain, and it has been concluded that they should first examine their grievances and correct abuses, so as to restore the tranquillity of the people."[28] The government of Pitt was trying to get the situation again in hand, despite a thousand difficulties. At the end of the year the situation was depicted thus in the gazette of Lugano: "Although the spirit of party is diminished in Ireland, the people still wait with weapons in their hands expecting the promises made to them to be carried out; thus, fire gleams below the ashes and will break out with greater violence if the wrongs done to the Irish are not remedied. It is not enough to grant them participation along with Great Britain in the trade of the West Indies; they also want participation in the trade of the East Indies, and with China, Africa, and what the English carry out with all the nations of Europe."[29] "Regulation of commerce," even when it was imposed in May 1785, continued to "encounter the greatest difficulties," as much in England as in Ireland. "The minister Pitt encounters constant resistance from the opposition party."[30]

But now in the forefront were no longer the moves and organizations of volunteers, but rather the close contest between Irish and English merchants. North, Fox, and Burke intervened in the debate.[31] "In peril was not only the popularity of Mr. Pitt, but also his career in the ministry." The compromise he proposed "has turned against him the numerous class of merchants, builders, and manufacturers throughout

---

[25] *Nuove di diverse corti e paesi*, no. 39, 27 September 1784, pp. 307ff. (London, 10 September).

[26] *Notizie del mondo*, no. 91, 13 November 1784, p. 775 (London, 22 October).

[27] Ibid., no. 74, 13 September 1785, p. 589 (London, 26 August).

[28] Ibid., no. 64, 12 August 1786, p. 506 (London, 25 July).

[29] *Nuove di diverse corti e paesi*, no. 2, 10 January 1785, p. 16 (London, 17 December).

[30] Ibid., no. 22, 30 May 1785, p. 172 (London, 13 May).

[31] Ibid., no. 23, 6 June 1785, p. 181 (London, 21 May).

Great Britain." He had also "put into a ferment the even more numerous class of retail merchants." George Gordon reappeared: "He excites and blows upon the revolution of the people and does not cease to incite them to their usual fury." Now "the perilous symptoms of popular disturbances" were visible.[32] "The tax on shops" continued "to excite turbid mutineers. . . . Tuesday the low people burned the minister Pitt in effigy in several quarters. A carpenter was arrested for making a gallows to hang a dummy of the minister."[33] All parties hastened to the opposition. Failure of the project for a commercial agreement was predicted. "This could be the happiest event Ireland could desire." It would be all the more so if "that encouragement to its infant manufactures which have been so useful to other nations" were substituted for these liberal measures. "For a long time Great Britain has made every effort to ensure an exclusive monopoly, so it should not take it ill now that its example is taken as a model."[34] The Irish grievances seemed to have returned to their point of departure, to a narrow defense of local privileges.

In reality an economic compromise between Great Britain and Ireland was reached. Despite many fears, it did not ruin English manufacturing, which maintained its supremacy. The Irish crisis reopened only under the pressure of events in France, some years later. In 1785 this much feared revolution, which had raised many hopes, failed. However, it had been precisely the Irish, as we have seen, who came closest to the American model. Protests and demonstrations on many different levels of the population were particularly heated in Ireland. The volunteers appeared to provide an active and a lively direction to the movement. But even their energies fell back into shadows.

It seemed for a moment that even Scotland was about to take the road to rebellion. "The Scottish nation," we read in the gazette of Lugano in February 1782, "has always been regarded as invariably attached to the ministry, whose members in good part, and particularly the secret heads of the cabinet, are natives of Scotland." The shade of Lord Bute seemed still to float above them, twenty years later. The insistence with which "the utility and even necessity of the war with America [was] always supported there" then confirmed such an image of Scotland. But things were changing. The "sentiments" of those who were

[32] Ibid., no. 27, 4 July 1785, p. 212 (London, 17 June).
[33] Ibid., no. 28, 11 July 1785, p. 219 (London, 22 June).
[34] Ibid., p. 220 (Dublin, 12 June).

"dependent on the ministry" were no longer "common to the whole Scottish people." In Edinburgh a "numerous assembly of inhabitants" had voted a motion sustaining that "this American war must be promptly terminated because its prolongation will totally annihilate all ties of blood, from religion to commerce, and it is absolutely necessary to procure a federative union with America."[1] A similar position had "embarrassed the ministry and Parliament," all the more so because it was accompanied by the affirmation that "Scotland had the right to enjoy all privileges attributed to England and particularly that of internal and constitutional defense." There was more and more insistent talk of "arms," of "voluntary corps," and of "constitutional militia." Were similar requests "compatible with the spirit of union"?[2] "Spirits are in ferment," wrote the gazette of Venice. The disquiet that had always marked the Scots before the "union of the two kingdoms" seemed to return.[3] "The night of the 8th current, the low people of Edinburgh, the capital of this kingdom, marching to the sound of a drum and armed with sticks, etc., took themselves to Cannonmills. The military guard opposed the mutineers and killed a few. . . . The same night other malcontents in the same mood collected at Forde, 10 miles from Edinburgh, and went to set fire to the large factory of a distiller of whiskey, alleging as a pretext that the quantity of grain used in the said distillery caused the excessive price of flour."[4] "Other news from Scotland," it was reported in Florence in August, "reports that the inhabitants have taken resolutions similar to those of the Irish and threaten to pass to similar excesses, particularly because of impositions established on cloth and cotton."[5] The figure of George Gordon appeared again, attacking William Pitt violently on this issue. In the winter of 1784–1785 "everywhere the people appear determined to uphold their rights with firmness." It was necessary to conclude that "the spirit of reform has reached such a point that it seems difficult to stop its progress." This was all the more

[1] Ibid., no. 6, 11 February 1782, p. 46 (Edinburgh, 7 January). On the complex problems of the relations between Scotland and America, see Andrew Hook, *Scotland and America: A Study of Cultural Relations, 1750–1835* (Glasgow: Blackie, 1975), and J. M. Bumsted, *The People's Clearance: Highland Emigration to British North America* (Edinburgh: Edinburgh University Press, 1982).

[2] Ibid., no. 36, 9 September 1782, p. 288 (London, 23 August). See Cannon, *Parliamentary Reform*, pp. 107ff. One notes that the electoral system in Scotland was more restricted and oligarchical than in the other two components of the United Kingdom. In England there was 1 elector for every 10 persons, in Ireland 1 in 30, in Scotland 1 in 100. Edinburgh counted 11 electors.

[3] *Notizie del mondo [V.]*, no. 71, 4 September.

[4] *Nuove di diverse corti e paesi*, no. 27, 5 July 1784, p. 213 (London, 18 June). The same correspondence is in the *Notizie del mondo*, no. 54, 6 July 1784, p. 400 (London, 18 June).

[5] *Notizie del mondo*, no. 69, 28 August 1784, p. 586 (London, 9 August).

the case because prices rose and necessities lacked. More than anything the Scots seemed to suffer from a scarcity of tea. "There is reason to fear that this spirit of ferment may strongly oppose the aims of the government regarding new taxes."[6] Even in Scotland, however, as in England and Ireland, a crisis beginning with fiscal problems on the American model, which for a moment risked transforming itself into a national revolt, now, in the middle of the eighties, was being reabsorbed.

[6] Ibid., no. 104, 28 December 1784, p. 878 (London, 5 December). The Venetian gazette concluded: "The disturbances in Scotland are less violent than those in Ireland, but still they could become equally dangerous. . . . Under the cinders there is a fire that glows to break out with greater violence whenever a remedy for the grievances of the country is lacking" (*Notizie del mondo [V.]*, no. 3, 8 January 1785, continuation of the news from London of 17 December).

III

Portugal after Pombal, the Spain of Floridablanca

AS IN THE BRITISH EMPIRE AND THE FRENCH MONARCHY, EVEN IN
the states of the Iberian Peninsula the year 1776, and those that immediately followed, marked a political turning point. Turgot fell on 16 May
1776. On 4 July came the American Declaration of Independence. On
27 August Tanucci, the minister who for decades had kept the kingdom
of Naples in Spain's orbit, fell. On 7 November Girolamo Grimaldi, the
artificer of Madrid's foreign policy, was sent as ambassador to Rome and
was replaced in Spain by Floridablanca, who for more than a decade
remained at the helm of the monarchy of Charles III. The new year,
1777, saw Joseph I, the king of Portugal, disappear on 22 February. In
March Pombal, who for more than thirty years had been as much dictator as minister of Portugal, resigned. On 6 February 1778 the alliance
between France and the United States was signed. The hostilities began
in June. On 3 April 1779 Spain declared war on England. On 12 April
Floridablanca agreed to the treaty of alliance between Spain and France.
In three years the entire political scene in the West had changed, under
the pressure of revolts and revolutions, especially, the American one,
but also the *guerre des farines*, and the more and more acute political
conflicts developing everywhere.

Even Portugal—the state of the Iberian Peninsula that succeeded
best in escaping the long conflict at the end of the seventies and first
years of the eighties—could not avoid the problems of the age. It reacted by closing in on itself and by trying to reverse the work of the
Marquis of Pombal. Portugal had been the first Catholic country in Europe to unleash the struggle against the Jesuits.[1] It was now the first to

[1] Venturi, *Settecento riformatore* 2, pp. 3ff. See Samuel J. Miller, *Portugal and Rome, c.
1748–1830: An Aspect of the Catholic Enlightenment* (Rome: Università Gregoriana, 1978),

try to reverse that tendency and to close off the road the minister had opened with much force and scandal, and not without bloodshed. Like the beginning of the struggle, even this retreat aroused vivid interest. In Naples in 1776 a large work was published, translated from the French, that was still apologetic and full of praise for Pombal. It marked a certain tardiness in Neapolitan publishing and an intent to close the door against the concerns and doubts spreading more and more everywhere. The conclusion was still clearly positive: "After Carvalho took the reigns of government, the nation was generally more enlightened, agriculture improved, and commerce extended its roots." Pombal's program had been grandiose, designed "to bring Portugal to the level of the currently most flourishing states of Europe." It had to be recognized that "the spirit of legislation was not able to finish such a great work in a few days." "All the glory to which a great minister can aspire is to lay foundations for the greatness of a state. The rest is done in time."[2]

In centers closer to the Portuguese court, and better informed, optimism was much less. It was known that Joseph I, the faithful king, was gravely ill, and that with his disappearance Pombal's situation would become very difficult. Still, Felice Nepomuceno Fontana, the Piedmontese minister at Lisbon, wrote, "Pombal, following his usual custom, since the illness of his master the king, has appeared in public more frequently, but with an unembarrassed air." To consolidate his own power he had suppressed the office of secret treasurer to the king, thus obliging the sovereign to "ask him directly for money he needs from the royal treasury." "Unbelievable at any time, the behavoir of the Marquis of Pombal is not less so at this moment."[3] The heavy veil of mystery that surrounded the life of the Portuguese court became even thicker. It was still possible to assume that the conflict with the Roman Curia would continue uninterrupted, and that Pombal was glad of the differences between the pope and the Republic of Venice.[4] In Lisbon publications

and J. S. Da Silva Dias, *Pombalismo e teoria política* (Lisbon: Centro de história da cultura da Universidade nova de Lisboa, 1982).

[2] *Ragionamento che contiene l'elogio di sua eccellenza il signor marchese di Pombal ecc. ecc., primo ministro di S.M.F. ecc. ecc., tradotto dal francese in italiano e dedicato a S.E. il signor Francesco d'Almada e Mendonza . . . del consiglio di S.M.F. e suo ministro plenipotenziario presso la S.S. ecc.* (Naples, 1776). The dedication, dated 2 August 1776, is signed F.A.N.P.

[3] Turin, AS, *Lettere ministri, Portogallo*, mazzo 8, no. 2, 6 February and 20 January 1776.

[4] Ibid., 30 April 1776. Pagliarini, the well-known Roman bookseller who was exiled to Portugal, informed the minister Fontana of this. Count Cataneo, the Portuguese consul in Venice, was charged with providing details on the quarrel between Rome and Venice. In Lisbon Pombal profited from the tension with the pope in order to "make use of the revenues of a quantity of vacant benefices for works he called pious, but which really only concern the improvement of the city, the commodity of its port, and in part his own interest." On Pagliarini, see Venturi, *Settecento riformatore* 2, in the index. On Count Giovanni

full of "excessive adulation" and "the lowest flattery" for the omnipotent minister continued to circulate.[5] Some books contrary to his religion or critical of the government were publicly burned.[6]

The king lingered on for long months, and Pombal continued to exercise his weighty power through 1776. The Cardinal Patriarch died in November. "The different objects of humiliation which this prelate has suffered contributed much to his demise, among them being reduced to extreme misery and not being able to pay his debts." For sixteen years he had received no income "from his benefices in the patriarchate."[7] Pombal controlled the army with an iron fist, given the recurrent threat of a conflict with Spain and the increasingly difficult international situation.[8] He showed that he did not fear "an uprising" in the capital, which might have been provoked by more intense forced recruitment. A tumult broke out nonetheless among fishermen beyond the Tago; the troops sent to repress it burned "all the cabins of the mutineers, and nearly forty did not have time to escape."[9] In December the news from Italy produced a profound impression. Marchese Tanucci had fallen from power in Naples. The cause did not seem to be entirely the queen, Maria Carolina. Pombal declared he was convinced that "the Court of Rome had also contributed much to this development." "The minister did not fail to add that the intrigues of the ex-Jesuits had set things in motion." Pagliarini said he was persuaded that an outcome similar to that of Naples awaited even Portugal. "The Court of Rome will undoubtedly regain a large part of its old influence." The words and actions of the nuncio in Lisbon made known clearly "how glad he was."[10] The Piedmontese minister, an intelligent man who was anything but clerical (he even ended up marrying a Protestant when he was sent to the German non-Catholic world), concluded at the beginning of 1777 that the crisis of Pombal's government had surprised the minister in midcourse, when his work was not yet finished. The "discipline" he had tried to introduce in the army was still uncertain. The "good measures

Cataneo, see Roland Mortier, "Un adversaire vénetien des 'lumières,' le comte de Cataneo," *Studies on Voltaire and the Eighteenth Century* 32 (1965): 91ff., and the comment by Gianfranco Torcellan, *Settecento veneto e altri scrittori storici* (Turin: Giappichelli, 1969), pp. 323ff.

[5] Turin, AS, *Lettere ministri, Portogallo*, mazzo 8, 12 March 1776.

[6] Ibid., 8 October 1776.

[7] Ibid., 7 November 1776. His successor, chosen by Pombal, was "mentally limited" (24 December 1776).

[8] When Rome requested that he "send new Italian missionaries to all the Portuguese establishments beyond the seas where there are hardly any," Pombal responded that there "one had more need of soldiers than of monks" (ibid., 28 October 1777).

[9] Ibid., 19 November 1776.

[10] Ibid., 10 December 1776.

1. No one in the late eighteenth century knew better than Benjamin Franklin how to keep reason and politics, science and liberty, united. When Charles Willson Peale painted this portrait in 1787 Franklin was a universally recognized symbol of the new American nation and of the constitution just then being defined.

Lord GEORGE GORDON,
President of the Protestant Association

2.   The disquieting figure of George Gordon, a Scottish noble, president of the Protestant Association, and instigator of the violent London riots of 1780, is represented here treading Popery under foot and indicating with his staff the Protestant petition, containing thousands of signatures that he collected against any concession to or toleration of Catholics. In the background are the troops called up to quiet the plebs of the capital, who from their attempt to impose the petition on Parliament, passed rapidly to an assault on the prisons, the Bank of England, and the houses of deputies and judges, not to mention the embassies of Catholic countries. Hundreds were killed, wounded, or tried. Arrested, Lord Gordon was soon released and continued his tumultuous life as an agitator for decades. He took refuge in Holland, converted to Judaism and was again imprisoned, and died singing the *Ça ira*.

3.   The Protestant Association marches toward the House of Commons on Friday, 2 June 1780, demanding the revocation of recent laws favoring Catholics. This was ostensibly a traditional and respectable demonstration, in the name of "civil and religious liberty" and the "Protestant cause," but it soon was transformed into a violent popular sedition. Who was to blame? Catholic provocators and "mischievous emissaries of Papists," the author of this engraving said.

The Devastations occasioned by the RIOTERS of LONDON Firing the New Goal of NEWGATE, and burning Mr. Akerman's Furniture, &c. June 6. 1780.

4.   Whatever the origins of the riots, the subversive character they soon assumed was evident. This was the burning and looting of Newgate Prison. The people liberate the prisoners. On the banners are again the words of Lord Gordon: "no Popery."

NO POPERY or NEWGATE REFORMER.

Tho' He says he's a Protestant, look at the Print.
The Face and the Bludgeon, will give you a hint,
Religion he cries, in hopes to deceive,
While his practice is only to burn and to thieve.

Published as the Act Directs, June 6, 1780 by I. Catch of Middlesex

Real Character

5. A protagonist of the London riots in a contemporary print: "No Popery or Newgate reformer." "Tho He says he's a Protestant, look at the Print. / The Face and the Bludgeon will give you a hint. / Religion he cries, in hopes to deceive, / While his practice is only to burn and to thieve." On his cockard: "no popery." His cry is "down with the Bank."

6. Amid fires and looting the "real character" of a London rioter is revealed, crying, "No Popery. No Ministry. Dam my Eyes."

C.J.Fox. Ld Shelburn. D. Richmond Jan 23 1782.

MALAGRIDA & Conspirators, consulting the Ghost of OLIVER CROMWELL.

Gillray.

7.   The conclusions attributed two years later to the Whig leaders Fox, Shelburne, and Richmond, true conspirators against monarchical authority, as Malagrida had been in Portugal, were not that different. In this reactionary print they are represented consulting the ghost of Oliver Cromwell, who advises them to "Arm the People," "trample on [the Royal] Prerogative," and thus follow the "republicans' favoured plan." All in vain: "The spirit of the Constitution never dies," concludes even Cromwell's ghost.

8. José Moñino, Count of Floridablanca, son of a notary, raised in the world of the law, a diplomat and an expert functionary, in Rome played a significant part in the destruction of the Company of Jesus and then dominated the political life of Spain for a decade. This portrait by Goya shows him in all his glory with technicians and artists.

9. King of Naples and then of Spain, Charles III, of the House of Bourbon, knew better than many other contemporary monarchs how to ensure dynastic continuity in a period of growing political difficulties. His virtues (his greatest passion was hunting), his moderation, and his ability to adapt himself to changes of the times helped him to avoid sharp breaks during his long years as head of state. The crises of Spain came immediately after his death. The portrait is by Goya.

Vista del Tumulo construido en la Yglesia de Santiago de la Nacion Española de Roma en las Honras del Rey Carlos III.

10.   Designed by Nicolás de Azara the obsequies of Charles III were performed in Rome, in the Church of San Giacomo, and in a clearly neoclassical form almost as if to make one forget a past that it was now desirable to obliterate, and to immobilize and crystallize the passions and aims of the new generation of Goya and Jovellanos.

GUILLAUME THOMAS RAYNAL.

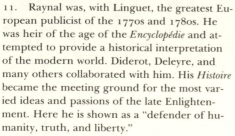

Un Défenseur de l'Humanité, de la Vérité, de la Liberté. ELIZA DRAPER.

Soyez libres: vivez.

11. Raynal was, with Linguet, the greatest European publicist of the 1770s and 1780s. He was heir of the age of the *Encyclopédie* and attempted to provide a historical interpretation of the modern world. Diderot, Deleyre, and many others collaborated with him. His *Histoire* became the meeting ground for the most varied ideas and passions of the late Enlightenment. Here he is shown as a "defender of humanity, truth, and liberty."

12. Soon after his release, after two years of imprisonment, Linguet published, at the beginning of 1783, his famous *Mémoires sur la Bastille*, in which he invited Louis XVI to pull down this gloomy fortress, liberate all the prisoners, and abolish lettres de cachet. The caption accompanying this graphic representation of his proposal, "Soyez libres: vivez," is taken from Voltaire's *Alzire*.

taken to extricate the land from the lethargy into which superstition had plunged it" were fragile. They had remained "sketches, partly because he did not have the time to look after them himself, partly because his jealousy did not permit him to entrust them to persons whose merit was proportionate to the importance of their offices."[11]

On 22 February 1777 the trickle of liberations and rehabilitations of those whom Pombal had persecuted began.[12] It was said that perhaps eight hundred prisoners were held without trial. "The revolution we can foresee in this government is proportionate to the absolute despotism (and without precedent in history) of the minister, whose fall has spread an inexpressible joy in the public."[13]

Naturally, there was "contentment with the crisis in Portugal" also in Rome, Galiani reported from Naples on 12 April 1777.[14] From Rome itself Alessandro Verri said they were going about saying "things from the other world about the Marquis of Pombal," and "the minister of Portugal, Count Almada, who because he is a relative of the Marquis of Pombal was treated in Rome with consideration, is now frankly treated with the greatest coldness in anticipation of his being recalled." Queen Maria of Portugal hastened, as soon as she reached the throne, to ask "license of the pope to introduce in her kingdoms a new Portuguese rite dedicated particularly to the heart of Jesus."[15]

Everywhere in Europe there was speculation about the truth of the many contradictory voices that arrived from Lisbon. The *Courier de l'Europe*, taking in hand the small volume by Dumouriez, *Etat présent du royaume de Portugal*, written in 1775 ("badly written ... but the most instructive work that has appeared on this subject"), ended by concluding that Pombal was "a man of genius, but at the same time a despotic minister." It was true that "young gentlemen have begun to give themselves over to literature and are passionate above all about Voltaire, Rousseau, and the new philosophy." It was to be hoped that "the Portuguese would extricate themselves from ignorance sooner than their neighbors the Spaniards."[16] As for Pombal's work, Dumouriez had no doubts: "He is

[11] Ibid., 21 January 1777.

[12] Ibid., 24 February 1777.

[13] Ibid., 4 March 1777. On 18 March 1777 Fontana referred to 1,040 state prisoners. For a clear and detailed picture of the fall of Pombal, based on the dispatches of Robert Walpole, the English ambassador in Lisbon, see Kenneth R. Maxwell, *Conflicts and Conspiracies: Brazil and Portugal, 1750–1808* (Cambridge: Cambridge University Press, 1973).

[14] *Opere di Ferdinando Galiani*, ed. Furio Diaz and Luciano Guerci (Milan and Naples: Ricciardi, 1975), p. 1145, to Francesco Sanseverino.

[15] *Carteggio di Pietro e di Alessandro Verri*, ed. Giovanni Seregni, vol. 9 (Milan: A. Milesi, 1937), p. 26, 26 April 1777. On Almada, see Venturi, *Settecento riformatore* 2, in the index.

[16] *Courier de l'Europe*, no. 60, 27 May 1777, p. 511 (Paris, 19 May).

the one who has extricated his nation from barbarism, and the ignorance and brutality into which it had fallen."[17] As the same *Courier de
l'Europe* noted, the queen mother herself did everything possible to slow
the pace and importance of the rehabilitations of individuals, and to
stop attacks on the work of Pombal, knowing how much the memory of
King Joseph, who had been the creature of the imperious minister,
would suffer.[18] But the high nobility, grouped around the family Távora, pressed for restoration of the power and wealth Pombal had
eroded. And Rome pressed more and more for a return to the old state
of relations with the church.[19] The Piedmontese minister in Lisbon
wrote: "It is generally believed that the government has already taken
measures to restore the Inquisition to its old standing, which is all the
more to be feared because of the influence of the clergy and the history
of this country, where there have always been excessively severe tribunals. This leads one to believe that the Tribunal of Suspicion may well
replace the Inquisition."[20] The use Pombal had always made of the old
instruments of power, including the Inquisition, now turned against his
work, and everything seemed to return to the situation *quo ante*. The
weakness of his government itself tended in this direction. Great was the
ascendancy the nobility regained "and that it has always strongly
abused."[21] Immobilized by contradictions within the royal family, the
government instituted, and then immediately forgot it had instituted, a
commission of magistrates to examine "the grievances of all those who
believe they have received some wrong or damage from the Marquis of
Pombal during his ministry."[22] Otherwise Pombal began to find defenders. "There are people, even among the Portuguese, who have begun to
realize that the Marquis of Pombal procured several real advantages to
the country, which may not now be maintained. This is already clear in
the case of some despotic measures taken by the nobility, and by the
license of the people."[23] The nuncio succeeded in removing the sums
assigned to it at the time of the expulsion of the Jesuits from the University of Coimbra, demonstrating "clearly that the country is about to
fall again into its old ignorance." Even the commercial companies and
the manufactures of silk Pombal instituted were threatened, and not

[17] Charles François Dumouriez, *Etat présent du royaume de Portugal en l'année 1766* (Lausanne: François Grasset, 1775), p. 294.
[18] *Courier de l'Europe*, no. 3, 1 June 1777, p. 17 (Lisbon, 2 May).
[19] Turin, AS, *Lettere ministri, Portogallo*, mazzo 8, 11 March and 1 April 1777.
[20] Ibid., 15 April 1777.
[21] Ibid., 13 May 1777.
[22] Ibid., 3 and 10 June 1777.
[23] Ibid., 24 June 1777.

without the involvement of the English. [24] The only positive element of the new government, derived more than anything from its weakness, was the treaty concluded with Spain in October 1777 that put an end to the long dispute between the American colonies of the two countries. [25]

Great curiosity continued to center on Pombal, now deprived of all power, confined to his fief, and menaced by new accusations and inquiries. The incidents reported of his serenity and energy were surprising and aroused new admiration. It was told how he had gone to visit the bishop of Coimbra, who was staying in a nearby Franciscan monastery. "At the appearance of the bishop the Marquis threw himself on his knees and could only speak the words: 'Your Excellency is my bishop, give me blessing.' The bishop told him to get up, and he refused to do so. The monsignor then replied, 'If Your Excellency does not get up I will kneel down too.' Thus, the ex-minister got up and entered the apartment, where he stayed for half an hour, and then left most contentedly. . . . Pombal held him by the arm and cheerfully led him back to his carriage, where he knelt. The bishop blessed him, and he left. It was noticed that the prelate's eyes were bathed in tears." This moving scene takes on meaning when one reads the comment that accompanied it in the *Gazzetta universale*. "Everyone recalled that the said bishop of Coimbra was unjustly kept in the Fort of St. Julian for twenty years by the said ex-minister." [26] Also released, at the beginning of 1778, were "the natural brothers" of the defunct sovereign, the "Archbishop of Braga, primate of the realm," and the supreme commander of the army, "imprisoned for so many years by order of the Marquis of Pombal." [27] The request of the queen was heard: the pope conceded "the rite and mass of the heart of Jesus." [28] After the aunts of the king were released came the turn of "His Excellency Don José de Seabra, once minister and colleague of the Marquis of Pombal and then his victim." When he disembarked in Lisbon, there was a great "concourse of all ranks of people. . . . In the great square . . . people shouted greetings . . . the carriage did not have room to advance." Such "innovations" did not impress "the Senhor de Carvalho." "He listens to them with great indifference, and although old, enjoys perfect health . . . fearing no sinister development of fate, since he is certain that everything done by the past minister appears to be entirely authorized by the defunct king." [29]

---

[24] Ibid., 22 July 1777.

[25] Ibid., 8 October 1777.

[26] *Gazzetta universale*, no. 5, 17 January 1778, p. 33 (Pombal, 8 December).

[27] Ibid., no. 11, 7 February 1778, p. 81 (Lisbon, 6 January).

[28] Ibid., no. 12, 10 February 1778, p. 96 (Rome, 4 February).

[29] Ibid., no. 73, 13 September 1778, p. 577 (Lisbon, 11 August), and no. 75, 19 September 1778, p. 591 (Lisbon, 18 August).

In the summer of 1788 Pietro Verri received direct news from Portugal from Michele Blasco, the brother of Teresa, Beccaria's first wife. He had been a "captain of engineers in Brazil for ten years" and had ruined his career by leaving it without permission. For this he had spent eight months in prison and was finally liberated by the new queen.[30] "He does not speak as badly as others of the Marquis of Pombal; he admires him because he believes his plans were to liberate the Portuguese from the tyranny of hidalgos and friars. Under him the army was put on a better footing, and the university taught with fewer errors." But he had amassed too much wealth. And how could one approve a policy based on making "the king tremble like an imbecile on his throne, believing he was surrounded by conspirators and rebels, and having only a despotic minister as faithful tutor"?[31]

Linguet, in his *Annales*, also painted the portrait of the fallen minister in strongly contrasting colors. "We have seen him govern for twenty years," read the Tuscan translation, and "govern that kingdom as a most potent monarch. His vigorous but dark and bloody administration was quite similar to that of our Cardinal Richelieu. . . . In this guise he dragged his enemies to the scaffold; in this guise he exercised his vendettas with the sword of justice, acting under the pretext of *raison d'état*. . . . As soon as the arm he leaned on weakened all his power drained away. The institutions he abolished were revived, and those he gave existence to were annihilated. His creatures were thrown into the same prisons from which his enemies were released. In the struggle that he unleashed against the Jesuits there prevailed "fanaticism on one side and the other," without reason being able to "show itself."[32] A little farther on Linguet furnished information about the penetration of more modern ideas into Portugal: "Some persons of wit have formed, it is said, a small clandestine academy, which furtively reads and translates our recent and most spicy works." But he did not fail to foresee the worst consequences for such "accelerated maturity" developing in Portugal any more than in Russia.[33] Undoubtedly Pombal had fought a good fight in favoring the establishment of manufactures and opposing "another tyranny, less frightful in appearance than his own, but really more dangerous, that of English merchants, who are one of the sources of the degradation of Portugal." If the people had "the eyes of reason"

---

[30] *Carteggio di Pietro e di Alessandro Verri*, vol. 10, p. 61, Milan, 22 August 1778, and p. 123, Milan, 10 November 1778. Alessandro asked for his news from the noted bookseller Pagliarini (p. 263, Rome, 1 May 1779).

[31] Ibid., p. 61, Milan, 22 August 1778.

[32] *Annali politici, civili e letterari del secolo decimottavo* (The Hague [Florence]: Filippo Stecchi, 1778), vol. 1, pp. 106ff.

[33] Ibid., p. 224.

they would consider him "their benefactor" for what he did after the Lisbon earthquake with the abolition of the Inquisition, "whose yoke oppressed all orders in the state," while "the tribunal he substituted for it was dangerous only to the class of nobles." Instead, immediately after his fall, the people threw themselves into destroying his medallion in the statue of King Joseph.[34] And now a law of the new government prohibited any criticism, under penalty of death. "Some disinterested witnesses will observe perhaps that after having destroyed tyranny it is unnecessary to preserve its forms."[35] This was all the more true because at the same time the old forms of religious intolerance reemerged. An auto-da-fé was celebrated in October, "not in the public square as it once was, but in a great hall in the palace of the presiding cardinal." There were "ten accused, for the most part materialists, and they were condemned to various spiritual punishments and confiscation of property; only a certain José Martino Texiera, who studied canon law at the University of Coimbra, of 24 years, was exhibited with a placard on his head as a defender of the sect of Freemasons, and then whipped in the public square, given five years in the galleys and other punishments."[36]

When, more than a year later, Cavalier de Pollone, the new representative of the kingdom of Sardinia, arrived in Lisbon, he could report immediately that "the nuncio exercises his jurisdiction in all its extent, without any trouble or opposition from the government." A half intention to give an official character to Pagliarini in Rome, in the name of His Most Faithful Majesty, was dropped immediately "on the first difficulties" the pope raised.[37] In general, "the situation of this court," the same diplomat said some time later, was "always the same, that is, of an impotent power."[38]

In the summer of 1779 the gazette of Venice summed up the consequences of the inquiry arisen in Portugal and elsewhere concerning the dictator fallen in disgrace. "The despotic Marquis of Pombal teaches posterity with his example to respect the property of all, and this is all the good he has done in the world."[39] At the end of the year news ar-

---

[34] Ibid., pp. 226ff.

[35] Ibid., p. 228.

[36] *Gazzetta universale*, no. 89, 7 November 1778, p. 705 (Lisbon, 6 October).

[37] Turin, AS, *Lettere ministri, Portogallo*, mazzo 10, 7 December 1779.

[38] Ibid., 23 May 1780.

[39] *Notizie del mondo [V.]*, no. 60, 27 July–7 August 1779, p. 512 (Lisbon, 18 July). There are many details of the "Pombal investigation" in no. 96, 23 November–4 December 1779, p. 800 (Lisbon, 26 October). The gazette published in Florence entitled *Le courier français en Italie*, no. 21, 26 May 1780, p. 161 (Venice, n.d.), spoke of the queen who had "avenged the great of her kingdom of the horrible crimes against their persons committed by the

rived in Milan that the old Marquis had not failed to defend himself:
"Nothing is yet published," one reads in the gazette, "but still it appears
that writings printed in London are an apologia the said Marquis has
made for himself. He asserts that Portugal was in a deplorable state under past reigns, and particularly under John V, and in contrast that it
was at the summit of happiness under Joseph I." The queen was wrong,
he said, to "liberate so many victims." "One sees in these writings the
thousand lies, the thousand exaggerations of a madman."[40] He was
thought to be dying a few days later: "He has written a letter to his son
the Count d'Oeyras, which is said to be a masterpiece and that will probably come to light."[41] From Rome, Alessandro Verri thought "certain
the news that the Marquis of Pombal has been condemned to be be-
headed, but the queen has pardoned him."[42] To this his brother Pietro
responded that he would have liked "less clemency and for the head of
the old man to be cut off, if he had the infamous cruelty to abuse power
and sacrifice innocence with so much opprobrium," having sent the
Duchess of Távora to the scaffold. What most struck him was the usur-
pation Pombal committed in substituting himself for the legitimate sovereign. "Despotism is never fatal when exercised by a prince; he works
on his own property and it is not to his advantage to devastate it." "Cruel
despotism, atrocious despotism, occurs when a timid monarch, weak
and indolent, blindly abandons everything to a minister of atrocious ill
nature." "The name of Pombal and an executioner's knife seen in a
dream" should in the future be "a warning to bad favorites."[43] A few
months later, the concentration of all power in the hands of Joseph II
in Vienna after the death of the empress Maria Theresa seemed to confirm Verri in his conviction and, in contrast, reminded him of the Portuguese minister. "In my opinion, subjects should never fear the power
of a sovereign when he himself exercises it and does not abandon any
essential part of it to other hands . . . intermediate power alone is to be
feared, and I think and feel that the best of all political systems will
always be despotism, on the condition that the sovereign acts and super-
intends and does not abandon any part of his sovereignty."[44] Pombal
had terrified the king, making him "pusillanimous and fearful at the
sight of any subject, almost as if he feared an assassin." He had thus

last minister" and who even wanted "to give an equal satisfaction to the exiled Jesuits in
recalling them and reestablishing them in their positions."
　　[40] *La gazzetta di Milano*, no. 4, 26 January 1780 (Lisbon, 22 December).
　　[41] Ibid., no. 5, 2 February 1780 (Lisbon, 29 December).
　　[42] *Carteggio di Pietro e di Alessandro Verri*, vol. 11, p. 96, Rome, 12 July 1780.
　　[43] Ibid., pp. 101ff., Milan, 19 July 1780.
　　[44] Ibid., p. 228, Milan, 6 January 1781.

become "an opaque body interposed between the father and sons, between the king and the people." Pombal, who twenty years before had appeared, if still amid heated discussion, as the champion of reforms, was now expunged from the list of enlightened, or as Verri preferred to say, legitimate, despots.

In Lisbon, despite the renewed resistance of the queen mother, a sister of Charles III of Spain, the trial of Pombal continued. The Countess of Atouguia was declared "publicly innocent with regard to the execrable crime of attempted regicide" and appeared "at court with the son with whom she was pregnant when she was arrested and imprisoned by order of the Marquis of Pombal." A pension was granted to her and to two of her daughters "forced to become nuns." The same was done for the young Duke of Aveiro, "being educated with the greatest attention; he had been so long in prison from his earliest years that when he was freed he was entirely ignorant." Pombal, again in good health, was given orders not to leave his fief, "and meanwhile proceedings continued in the greatest secrecy."[45] "Many prisoners, as many ecclesiastical as secular ones," continued to emerge from the "horrible prisons" in which they had been held, one of the Florentine gazettes announced. The prisons, which "the Marquis of Pombal had built to vent his fury," those "odious monuments of his ministry," were dismantled by order of the queen. "Antonio Freire d'Andrada-Enserrabodez, who had been minister to many courts and then imprisoned for twenty years, was suddenly made first chancellor of the realm."[46] Now even the *Notizie del mondo*, which had never been in favor of curial or ecclesiastical pretensions, warmed to the defense of Jesuits whom Pombal had persecuted twenty years earlier. A minute chronicle of these now distant events, translated into Italian and "distributed throughout the Roman Curia," was reproduced in three whole pages in the Florentine gazette. The words "barbarous cruelty" and "horrible prisons" paraded before the eyes of readers.[47] The progress of the trials to rehabilitate condemned Jesuits and nobles was followed in detail by the gazette of Milan.[48] When it was known that all sentences given on the occasion of the plot to assassinate the king of Portugal in 1759 had been revoked, some were surprised by the silence

---

45 *La gazzetta di Milano*, no. 37, 13 September 1780 (Lisbon, 4 August).

46 *Notizie del mondo*, no. 80, 3 October 1780, pp. 638ff. (Genova, 27 September).

47 Ibid., no. 20, 10 March 1781, pp. 153ff. (Cologne, 2 February). There was nothing in this period, as we have ascertained in the gazette of Lugano, which reported from Lisbon only marine and court news. The anti-Jesuit tendency of this sheet is well known. But there was detailed information in Venice in the *Notizie del mondo [V.]*, no. 19, 7 March 1781, p. 149 (Cologne, 11 February).

48 *La gazzetta di Milano*, no. 20, 16 May 1781 (Lisbon, 10 April).

on this matter the Florentine *Notizie del mondo* maintained. But soon after a "Lettera scritta all'estensore di questo foglio da uno suo corrispondente" was printed: "I knew earlier," one read, "of the outcome of the
unfortunate and well-known affair in Lisbon regarding the revocation
of sentences from the supposed plot of 1759. Later, not seeing it reported by you, I thought immediately that your silence arose from a
proper caution in announcing such surprising news before its authenticity was certain." Now that one could and should refer to the gazette of
Madrid, how could there be any doubt of the occurrence? "What will
Europe say of it?"[49] At the beginning of October the decree that threatened Pombal with an "exemplary punishment" was printed in Milan,
not further specified, with the addendum that, given his "decrepit age,"
he had been spared "corporal punishment."[50]

He died at the age of eighty-four on his estates, on May 7 of the
following year. "One says," the Piedmontese envoy reported to Turin,
that "he again declared in his last moments his recognition that, as a
man, he had committed sins against God, but that his conscience did not
reproach him for anything he had done as minister of state."[51] But not
even death put an end to the half measures that for years had surrounded him and to his family and collaborators. Members of the clergy
faithful to him and his son received "a light reprimand for having permitted a burial thought to be too pompous."[52] Nor was the problem of
those Pombal had sent to the scaffold confronted more decisively. Revocation of the sentence against members of the Távora family was decreed by the tribunal, but the sentence was never published because of
the opposition, formulated in as many as 280 articles, by the procurator
general, a rigid, intransigent magistrate: "That affair having been dor-
mant since that time, it is only lately that the families involved have revived and obtained, through a new appeal to the queen, that a second
commission of justices be authorized to rule definitely."[53] And thus, year
after year, the question of the attempted assassination of the king of

49 *Notizie del mondo*, no. 54, 7 July 1781, p. 432, in the footer. Further details are in no.
58, 21 July 1781, p. 464, in the footer.

50 *La gazzetta di Milano*, no. 42, 10 October 1781 (Lisbon, 7 September). This time even
the gazette of Lugano published this edict of 16 August 1781. *Nuove di diverse corti e paesi*,
no. 40, 1 October 1781, pp. 316ff. (Lisbon, 4 September). The *Gazzetta universale*, no. 6,
19 January 1782, p. 41 (Lisbon, 26 November), spoke of economic penalties with which
Pombal was threatened, but concluded nonetheless: "He is meanwhile recovering from
his weakness of health and awaits good weather to go to his villa."

51 Turin, AS, *Lettere ministri, Portogallo*, mazzo 10, 14 May 1782.

52 Ibid., 9 July 1782.

53 Ibid., 20 January 1784.

Portugal in 1759 passed from the hands of politicians to those of justices and finally to those of historians, who have not, it seems, yet pronounced a clear and definitive sentence.

Discussion of Pombal's work became lively, particularly in Italy. Already in 1781 a *Vita* of him appeared in five small volumes.[1] Anonymously published, it was the work of a certain Francesco Gusta, a most active young ex-Jesuit of Catalan origin who had emigrated to Italy after the expulsion of the Jesuits from Spain.[2] The work was quite successful.[3] Its motto, taken from Pope, was well chosen: "See C*** damn'd

---

[1] *Vita di Sebastiano Giuseppe di Carvalho e Melo, marchese di Pombal, conte di Oeyras ecc., segretario di stato e primo ministro del re di Portogallo D. Giuseppe I* (n.p., 1781). The place of publication was Florence, as it was also for the second edition, on which see *Notizie del mondo*, no. 78, 29 September 1781, p. 624, in the footer: "The first and second volumes of the reprinting of the life of Pombal are being distributed, volume 4 will soon appear, and it will be completed in volume 5."

[2] See Miguel Batllori, *Francesco Gustá, apologista y crítico (Barcelona 1746–Palermo 1816)* (Barcelona: Editorial Balmes, 1942), p. 11. His name was originally Gustá, as one sees, which was Italianized as Gusta, the form the author always used in his exile.

[3] A third and fourth edition carry the place Yverdon and the date 1781 and were printed in Siena: *Vita di Sebastiano Giuseppe di Carvalho e Melo, marchese di Pombal. Edizione riveduta e corretta dall'autore, di nuovi aneddoti arricchita e di alcuni rami singolari corredata.* (The engravings at the end of the first and second volumes had to do with the executions that followed the conspiracy against King Joseph I.) See *Gazzetta universale*, no. 24, 23 March 1782, p. 192, "Avviso." The editor was Vincenzo Pazzini Carli. In Florence these were sold by Anton Giuseppe and Gioacchino Pagani for three paoli for the unillustrated volumes, and four for those with the engravings. A French translation by the ex-Jesuit Claude Marie Gattel came out with the title *Mémoires de Sébastien-Joseph de Carvalho et Mélho, comte d'Oeyras, marquis de Pombal*, with the place and date "A Lisbonne et à Bruxelles, chez B. Le Franq," 1784, in four volumes, and was published in Lyon in the same year.

In 1783 a volume of nearly five hundred pages entitled *Anecdotes du ministère de Sébastien-Joseph Carvalho, comte d'Oyeras, marquis de Pombal, sous le règne de Joseph I, roi du Portugal*, appeared, with the place Warsaw, "chez Janos Rovicki." The work "was sold out with a surprising rapidity," we are told by the editor of the "nouvelle édition," which appeared in "Varsovie, Janosrovicki" (this spelling makes one think of a printer distant from the Polish world. It was in fact a Dutch printer). In the *Avertissement* of this second edition, the *Mémoires du marquis de Pombal* by F. Gusta was bitterly criticized. The author had given too much credence to "absurd maxims" and to "impassioned gazettes" for everything that involved the attempt on the king and its consequences. "The author of the *Mémoires*" had "borrowed the tone of the philosophes in his judgment of the suppressed Society" and had shown he was incapable of defending its history and rights without bringing sufficiently to light the "odious despotism" that had crushed it. "It was undoubtedly a ruse on his part to get himself read." But how could one "employ the language of the philosophes

to everlasting fame!" No one would ever be able to forget the acts that had made the Portuguese minister eternally famous. His name now stood next to those of Peter the Great, Catherine II, Voltaire, Frederick II, as well as—we read without surprise—that of "Madame d'Eon." No one could forget the part Pombal had played in the "great affair that occupied the most powerful and enlightened cabinets for years, with the desecration of a body, which, when living, made their tranquillity impossible." In his fight against the Jesuits he had shown "a truly extraordinary character," comparable only with that of men like Ximenes, Sully, Richelieu, Colbert, Alberoni, and Chatham.[4] To be sure, circumstances had assisted him: "Joseph I was filled with timidity and credulity," "miserable was the decadence in which Portugal lay"; the land was backward ("there are nations that should belong to other centuries, rather like buildings where some relic of ancient customs still lingers").[5] In the mortal struggle in which the Jesuits found themselves, they had little outside assistance, and least of all from "those Roman Abbés used to observing minutely the steps of others and turning any action graciously to ridicule."[6] But the "barbarous, proud, and self-interested soul" of Pombal had not manifested itself only in his hate of the Jesuits.

and then return to his own to present a mass of praises and accusations, plaudits and sarcasms? An author should be consistent in the truth." His "affected dissimulation" and his "timid stratagems" had ended by subjecting him, if only for a moment, to the "philosophic influence of our day" (pp. viff.). This still did not prevent the editor of the new edition of the *Anecdotes* to draw from the *Mémoires* numerous facts and episodes so as to make his work as complete as possible. "A smaller volume" could have contained "many more facts and details than are in the four volumes of the *Mémoires*" (pp. viff.). In 1787 the *Aneddoti del ministero di Sebastiano Giuseppe Carvalho, conte di Oeyras, marchese di Pombal sotto il regno di Giuseppe I re di Portogallo*, came out in Venice from the publisher Pietro Savioni. Here it was said explicitly that this was to "serve as a supplement to the *Vita* of the same." It polemicized against Gusta's *Mémoires* and the work of Pierre-Marie-Félicité Cormatin-Desoteux, *L'administration de Sébastien-Joseph de Carvalho et Melo* (Amsterdam, 1786), in 2 volumes, and ibid. (1788), in 4 volumes.

A German translation of Gusta's *Mémoires*, edited by Christian Joseph Jagemann, *Das Leben Sebastian Josephs von Carvalho und Melo, marquis von Pombal*, appeared in Dessau, "auf Kosten der Verlagskasse für Gelehrte und Künstler," in 1782, in two volumes. A Spanish translation never appeared, because of opposition from Jovellanos. See Miguel Batllori, *El abate Viscardo. História y mito de la intervención de los jesuitas en la indipendencia de Hispanoamerica* (Caracas: Istituto panamericano de geografía e história, 1953), p. 279 n. 175. The *Mémoires* was again reprinted in Orange, by Jules Escoffier, in 1843.

F. Gusta had great success, as one can see. Among new editions, attacks, and critiques his *Mémoires* takes us to the heart of the intricate and tenacious underground world of the Jesuits in the decades that followed their suppression.

[4] *Vita di S. G. di Carvalho*, vol. 1, p. v.

[5] Ibid., pp. 20, 23, 65.

[6] Ibid., vol. 2, p. 207.

From the first years of his government he had made himself "insuffer-
able to the nobility and people of Portugal with his arrogance." The
king, John V, had justly said that "Carvalho had hair on his heart" (a
classical memory of the *"cor exactum pilis"* of Valerius Maximus).[7] Infinite
were his contradictions: he had abolished the auto-da-fé and organized
a solemn one for Malagrida; he had struck down the Inquisition and
replaced it with a more inept censorship; he had tried to improve the
economic situation and at the same time had terrified everyone "with
the terrible Tribunal of Suspicion."[8] He had to confront "a government
truly susceptible to great disorders, pervaded by greed, venality, fraud,
and subtle plots," but the ideas he had utilized to wage his battle were
in his eyes worse than the very evil he wanted to end. He opened the
door to polemics against the Jesuits and burned a pastoral letter with
which the bishop of Coimbra had condemned the *Encyclopédie*, the *Contrat social*, the *Discours sur l'inégalité*, the *Despotisme oriental*, and the *Dic-
tionnaire philosophique*. He should have occupied himself with these and
not with the "obscure points of seventeenth-century thought" that he
prohibited.[9] The protection of Pagliarini and condemnation of Verney
were clear signs of the mistaken road he had taken.[10] His economic policy was equally brutal. Who did not remember "the metal buttons on the
coats of ministers of justice being cut off in public streets because they
were not made in the kingdom . . . or clothes made of prohibited cloth
torn and cut from the backs of persons"?[11] Positive, undoubtedly, had
been his reform of the University of Coimbra, where for too long indolence, ignorance, and "useless if not shocking peripatetic opinions"
had reigned. It had been wrong, "out of fear of novelty, to refuse to
recognize the progress of the sciences, which are truly the splendor of
the century in which we live, amid the errors with which false philosophers drain the heart of any thought of religion or good customs."[12]
The "great lights of the century," he concluded in the following volume,
were not impressed by the bluster and violence of Pombal. But these
would flower again after his official condemnation by the queen, under
"her protection and encouragement."[13] While in Lisbon the "incautious
plebs" cried "death to the tyrant," this Catalan Jesuit exiled in Italy

[7] Ibid., vol. 3, p. 5.
[8] Ibid., pp. 20, 24. He is called "an inhumane as well as a contradictory character"
(vol. 4, pp. iii, iv), and "changing and unintelligible" (p. 3).
[9] Ibid., pp. 91, 104.
[10] Ibid., pp. 125, 166.
[11] Ibid., p. 180.
[12] Ibid., pp. 194ff.
[13] Ibid., vol. 5, pp. 34, iv.

placed his hopes in the maternal and moderate government of Maria Francesca I.[14]

In the summer an *Orazione funebre del marchese di Pombal* was published.[15] It was presented as the work of an ex-Jesuit moved by a sense of disgust for the "destroyer of my order," as well as by an insistent admiration for a figure with the originality of the recently defunct Portuguese politician.[16] He had utilized every means "to enrich himself" and "to create the happiness of Portugal." "Eighteen or twenty victims from among the great served to secure his power on that terrible day, full of massacres and horrors, . . . all was just and necessary to support and protect this Portuguese Sejanus. The death of this single man would be more dangerous to the state than the disgrace of many hundreds of citizens sacrificed, imprisoned, or exiled." The danger he faced of "falling into disgrace with his monarch," and the threats that continued to weigh on him from the great of the realm, constrained him to a naked exercise of power. "His continually buffeted ministry did not permit him to shine with generous actions and wise provisions, but instead he was obliged to make himself feared in order to preserve it." One should also recognize that although he had not "honored humanity," he had nevertheless "devoted himself to the strongest passions, appropriate to his character and rank."[17] When death came it was seen that his entire work consisted in "making himself feared." Someone like him who had been "the terror of a nation and the object of hatred for a royal family" could now, "in dying, compare his life to a dream." The courtiers were unfeeling. "The people, who are the least regarded part of the state, could not know enough of his worth to mourn him."[18] But still, everyone, rich and poor, was shaken by his disappearance. "The castle of Pombal was bathed in tears . . . all hearts were drawn to the funeral apartment; even those exiles, who because of his measures went to beg their bread through the streets of Italy, where they found a difficult asylum but still remain, directed their thoughts to his deathbed."[19] Everyone saw himself reflected in him. "The more one loves austerity, rigor, subtlety, power, a spirit of greatness and virtuous ambition, the more one must mourn the loss of this minister. If all of Portugal were

[14] Ibid., pp. 108, 166.

[15] It was mentioned in the *Notizie del mondo*, no. 54, 6 July 1782, p. 432, in the footer. It cost a half paolo.

[16] *Orazione funebre in morte del marchese di Pombal recitata li 10 maggio 1782 nel suo castello di Pombal*. Dat Deus immiti cornua curta bovi (Pombal: A spese dello stampatore, 1782), p. vi.

[17] Ibid., pp. ivff.

[18] Ibid., pp. viff.

[19] Ibid., p. viii.

not dressed in mourning, the cries of nature would still rise amid the general grief of the nation."[20] His end was admirable, without the "weakness of spirit," without "remorse of the heart," without "reproach of conscience." He regretted only that he was no longer "the arbiter of Portugal and thus no longer able to make his fellow citizens happy and secure." "Had he not filled the place assigned to him by nature?"[21] His political task had not been that of "humanity" or "sweetness." "The Portuguese nation had more need of rigor and castigation than of rewards and benefits." He had not worked in a paradise, but in an arid desert. "He held that if Cain had been born in Lisbon after the death of Joseph I, at the moment of his fall God would not have condemned him to roam the earth, but would have punished him severely by forbidding him to leave his country. Thus Portugal, which at the height of its honors he thought of as an earthly paradise, appeared in his eyes in recent times similar to the most horrible desert in Africa."[22] "His greatest disgrace, his greatest grief, was to be obliged to pass the remainder of his days in this castle, in peace, silence, and repose. He had the nature of a salamander, which takes its life from fire."[23] The fire had something infernal about it: "To long for ambition and power to the point of becoming their victim, to sacrifice to them all that one holds most dear, to have no fear of the reproach of conscience and to despise the castigation of heaven and earth, this is a heroism found in only a few privileged souls. Such heroism is all the more admirable at the end of the eighteenth century—the century of true philosophy!"[24]

Who wrote this singular exaltation of pure ambition and politics without regrets? Who was the author of this apology for a despot that makes us think, beyond Machiavelli, of Linguet or even Alfieri? An unsigned document, "but clearly by the hand of Riguccio Galluzzi"—I am assured by Maria Augusta Timpanaro Morelli, who discovered it in the Florentine archives—tells us. "The funeral oration on the death of the Marquis of Pombal is the work of Francesco Catani, who to give it credibility artfully made it seem the work of an ex-Jesuit by imitating the style of the oration that was written by Father Stratico on the occasion of the death of Ricci, the last general of the Jesuits."[25] "Irony triumphs in this oration from beginning to end, so that by mixing eulogy and

---

[20] Ibid., p. ix.
[21] Ibid., p. xi.
[22] Ibid., pp. xiiff.
[23] Ibid., p. xv.
[24] Ibid., p. xxii.
[25] He alluded to the *Orazione funebre recitata in Breslavia nei funerali di Lorenzo Ricci ultimo generale della Compagnia di Gesú celebrati nella chiesa della stessa Compagnia*, tradotta in italiana favella dall'originale tedesco (n.p., 1776).

satire the true character of this minister is not clearly revealed. The
same artifice was utilized with success by Father Stratico, because it is
not clear whether his oration was a eulogy or a satire of Ricci and the
Jesuits."[26] This was a singular convergence, as one sees, of the traditional accusations of Machiavellianism made against the Jesuits and the
new exaltation of politics in the Enlightenment. The Florentine censor
ultimately concluded that Catani's paradox had not entirely succeeded.
The "bad little book," in his view, was "miserable, boring, disconnected,
and pointless throughout." It was nonetheless reprinted.[27] The intended ambiguity of these pages deceived even a man like Ristori, one
of the most astute publicists of these years. He was scandalized by the
acid and critical tone of the oration. How could the "Sully of Portugal"
become an "object of horror and distaste"? "The style of our author
instantly reveals that he is the one who wrote the *Vita* of Carvalho in five
volumes," that is, the ex-Jesuit Francesco Gusta. And in general, why
"unload oneself villainously against the memory of an unhappy old
man"?[28] Already for some time both the *Vita* and the *Orazione* had been
called "parts of a strong malignity" by the *Novelle letterarie*, one of the
most lively Tuscan periodicals with which Giuseppe Maria Galanti was
in contact at that time. It was precisely the "malignity" of the *Vita* and
the *Orazione*, the review continued, that "decided a friend of the truth
to write an *Elogio di Giuseppe Sebastiano de Carvalho e Melo, marchese di
Pombal*," a work of forty pages, which presented itself as printed in Aletopoli, but was found in Florence at the bookseller Bonaiuti. The "principle and perhaps unique merit" of this work was its "impartiality."[29]
Aletopoli here stood for Siena, from where the booksellers Luigi and
Benedetto Bindi had requested permission to publish, on 29 July
1782.[30] Giuseppe Bencivenni-Pelli had judged that it was "poorly" written and that it did not contain "anything at all new"; that its polemic was
done "in so much haste and with such an air of confidence that it will
do no great damage to the opinion of enemies of the memory of the
minister Pombal." But there was no reason to prohibit this *Elogio*, he
concluded. In fact, the grand duke consented to its publication on 3
August 1782. Even in this work the principal object of dispute was the
work by F. Gusta. The *Vita* in five volumes, one reads, "when it first

[26] Florence, AS, *Reggenza*, f. 626, ins. 155.

[27] *Orazione funebre in morte del marchese di Pombal recitata li 10 maggio 1782 nel suo castello
di Pombal*. Seconda edizione riveduta e corretta. Dat Deus immiti cornua curta bovi (Cosmopoli, 1782).

[28] *Memorie enciclopediche*, no. 39, December 1782, p. 319, Cosmpoli, n.d.

[29] *Novelle letterarie*, no. 39, 27 September 1782, col. 813.

[30] Florence, AS, *Reggenza*, f. 626, ins. 155. I owe this piece of information as well to the
courtesy of Maria Augusta Timpanaro Morelli, whom I gratefully thank again.

appeared nauseated men of good sense." In Siena even the calendar "printed with the title *Mangia* this year" had criticized it. As for the *Orazione*, it could be called "with the name Dr. Goldoni gave to the work the librarian planned to write in his *Cavaliere di buon gusto*, that is to say, the name *posticcio*" (counterfeit). "The introduction is a version of the beginning of the *Eulogy of the Duke of Sully* written by the celebrated M. Thomas, and the rest, entirely disorderly and disconnected, is a formless medley of other eulogies written by the same writer, all miserably translated, and sewn together worse still."[31] The accusation of plagiarism concealed, as one sees, the debate on the central point, the significance of the thirty years of Pombal. The same Bencivenni-Pelli, in his *Efemeridi*, could not escape the paradoxical and contradictory tone the minister of Joseph I often aroused: "I thought he was an illustrious scoundrel who had done both good and bad for Portugal."[32]

These polemical skirmishes surrounded the most important defense of Pombal to appear in Tuscany. Utilizing a well-known formula, it was entitled *Testamento politico*, and it contained, in reality, quite varied considerations on the Portuguese minister and Europe in his time. "I have collected under this title," the author said, "many political ideas of this great man, which could be published only after his death." It was a kind of posthumous dialogue, or as the author made clear, a "sketch of a portrait" of the ideas of Pombal, colored by his "actions."[33] It was a portrait of a man who had been "more an elegant writer than an able minister," who "wrote much better than he thought," who "had a pen that was better than his head, and who nurtured the weakness of esteeming the glory of an author."[34] He was a writer in the end persecuted and oppressed, as one could see in reading the decree of 15 August 1781 that was printed at the beginning of the biography. He had been the "Richelieu of Lisbon." His power had been absolute. How could one doubt that he had abused his authority by carrying out "offenses to the

[31] *Elogio di Giuseppe Sebastiano de Carvalho e Melo marchese di Pombal primo ministro di Giuseppe I re del Portogallo* (Aletopoli, 1782), pp. ivff.

[32] *Efemeridi*, vol. 10, 2d ser., 11 June 1782, carta 1814v.

[33] *Testamento politico del marchese di Pombal o sieno ultime istruzioni al conte d'Oeyras suo figlio trovate fra i suoi manoscritti e tradotte dal portoghese* (Italia: A spese di Ranieri del Vivo, 1782), p. 5. "The *Testamento politico* of the defunct Marquis of Pombal is about to be published, which will please the public and cost two paoli. This advance notice is intended for those who were associated with his life so that they can take up this as well and make the proper subscription to Anton Giuseppe Pagani and Ranieri del Vivo in Florence," one reads in the *Gazzetta universale*, no. 80, 5 October 1782, p. 748, in the footer. In no. 82, 12 October 1782, p. 664, "Avvisi," it was added: "It has already appeared." In no. 94, 23 November 1782, p. 760, "Avvisi," the publication of a second edition of this work was announced.

[34] Ibid., p. 6.

laws and to justice"? Desiring "courageously to restore a kingdom where the fury of nature fought with ignorance, prejudice, the independence of the great, habit, custom, and even the laws to prolong disorder and ruin," he had certainly not intended to make "this terrible effort without tyranny." "An absolute and independent minister must often of necessity be cruel and unjust." The sovereign might take his great power from his hands. It was unjust to punish him with the threat of a "shameful end." There had been much discussion of the reasons for the long and solemn trial carried out against him. The one responsible had perhaps been "a religious confessor of the queen and a partisan of the Jesuits." Thus, were confessors even in Portugal "what gravity is for the Newtonians," the explanation for the "many revolutions" of "modern history"? What Pombal had done in 1759 was sufficient to explain the reaction unleashed against him, without its being necessary to search other more or less obscure causes. "Lisbon was horrified by such repeated punishments, its prisons were always open and always full, the general terror of great and small and so much violence from a bloody and mysterious despotism already announced the fate of its author when he was abandoned by his royal supporter." From a family of "mediocre patrimony," he died in possession of "extraordinary riches." He was thus not only "stained with the blood of a crowd of innocents," but also "enriched with their remains."[35] But still the moment for a definitive judgment had not yet come.

When history places on the scale the talents and passions of this illustrious disgraced man, his virtues and vices, his errors, his injustices and their motives, the good he did for Portugal and the harm he did to individuals, then perhaps he will be presented to the public as more worthy of respect than of execration. He will be put in the ranks of Sulla, Guise, Cromwell, Richelieu, etc., etc., great characters rather than great men, celebrated in the opinion of the world, which admires what surprises it and what it fears. They knew how to use power with utility, for the glory of an empire rather than for its happiness, in a way that makes one shudder with the thought of seeing such men near the thrones of kings.

He had "the same kind of enemies" as Richelieu and fought them "with exile, imprisonment, and punishment, exterminating the great who tried to obscure him, and never gave pardons. . . . Both cultivated letters with pedantry and had the ambition to appear as *belli spiriti*." But here the comparison had to stop. There was nothing of a courtier in Pombal; nor did his character show "the mixture of force and uprightness that characterized Richelieu." And, above all, the latter "used his genius to

[35] Ibid., pp. 10ff.

oppose the enemies of France more than to reform abuses." Pombal paid significant attention to economic problems, "to commerce and agriculture." In his disgrace he showed extraordinary firmness. Old and persecuted, "he looked with a compassionate eye on Portugal, which was immersing itself anew, according to him, in the confusion and disorder from which he had extricated it." Abandoned by all, he had not even found support from the people, "the only order of the state toward which he had not turned his persecution and revenge," but which nonetheless looked on "his ruin and peril with great indifference." One of Pombal's greatest merits was that he made Lisbon rise again after the terrible earthquake of 1755. But "the sword of an executioner could have made the head of the restorer of Lisbon fall without the multitude's shedding a tear over his body."[36]

The trial initiated against him, with its delays and uncertainties, was the result of *raison d'état* rather than of an authentic desire for justice. "Discoveries, searches, punishments, and tales of plots are always wrapped in shadows." It was enough to think of the attempt to assassinate Stanislaus Augustus in Poland to be persuaded of this. "We have heard of enlightened Poles who were absolutely incredulous of the horrible attempt the Confederates of Bar made against their king, despite the publicity of the crime and the confessions of the criminals made known to all of Europe." Many uncertainties, undoubtedly, had accompanied this strange event. Now Puławski had died "serving the insurgents," that is, the Americans, and the last curtain had fallen on this "collection of curious adventures."[37] The events of Portugal were still mysterious and difficult to interpret.

In this political drama, one of the principal points was the relationship with the legitimate sovereign.[38] From two centuries of distance what had happened in Portugal seems like a variation on what also happened in France. Turgot and Necker fell when Louis XVI abandoned them. Pombal saw his work end with the death of Joseph I. The author of the *Testamento*, perhaps again Catani, compared the Portuguese minister to Cromwell, but the comparison did not hold. Only with the French Revolution was there a break in traditional legitimate authority,

---

[36] Ibid., pp. 14ff.

[37] Ibid., pp. 20ff.

[38] The submission of the king of Portugal to his minister Pombal struck all contemporaries. "I have seen in Portugal a king enslaved to his first minister to the point of believing that he would cease to be king if this minister failed him. I have seen Joseph de Bragance prostitute his august rank to become the first spy of his kingdom, and denounce to his minister those who seemed to him to not love him," wrote, for example, Giuseppe Gorani (*Dal dispotismo illuminato alla rivoluzione*, ed. Alessandro Casati [Milan: Mondadori, 1942], vol. 3, p. 49).

allowing new enlightened despots to dominate on their own. Pietro
Verri, as we have seen, still hoped for a personal union between sovereign and reformer, and in this case, as we have seen, he accepted despotism. But what happened in Lisbon showed how perilous this coincidence was. Charles III, in Madrid, was still able to support men like
Aranda and Floridablanca. But already in Naples, Ferdinand IV was
inept in supporting vigorous technicians and enlightened politicians.
Pombal's example demonstrated how such uncertainty might lead to a
political drama. The power of an absolute monarch now appeared precarious and uncertain, even to the author of the *Testamento*. "Political
and civil government depends on chance," he had Pombal say. "Treaties
of alliance, sieges, battles, and above all the influence of ministers depend almost always on the death or life of a single prince. ... A
crowned head more or less transforms the face of a monarchy. The formality of a marriage establishes a regime, that of a funeral destroys it."
Like others of his century, even Pombal, when confronted with such a
situation, seemed to be taken for a moment by the dream of being born
"in the woods of America, among the savages, without a political system," before throwing himself with all his force into the attempt to
change his country. Portugal, "when I was put at the head of its government," he said, "seemed to me to come out of nothing; its politics, arts,
finances had remained in infancy. I held to the principle that it would
take at least twenty centuries to put it at the same level as other European states." "I found ambition subordinated to laziness." "Laziness" was
a "violent passion" there. "Drowsiness was universal."[39] "To reestablish
the monarchy," he thought, it was necessary "to abolish the Inquisition,"
"diminish the number of clergy," "close the mines: the gold taken from
them was the source of the general indolence," "abandon America: that
new part of the world will sooner or later be the destruction of our
own," "cultivate the fields," "encourage industry," "protect letters," "increase manufactures," "multiply commerce." "Political power" also had
to be put in order. But how could one do all this in a land where "inaction is not a vice"? "Here, as in almost all nations of the world, when a
man can exhibit 500 years of indolence and laziness, from father to son,
he acquires nobility with all the honors and distinctions attached to it."
"Here there is a general emulation that consists of not having any at all."
"Religion, politics, customs go in perfect accord to establish this comfortable system." Among nobles and friars there were "three hundred
thousand Portuguese totally useless to the state."[40] In vain was the effort
to write and spread books and ideas. "Great men were punished with

[39] *Testamento politico*, pp. 28ff.
[40] Ibid., pp. 32ff.

loss of life or liberty for having had the courage to be a little more enlightened than the others." "One saw the abuses, one knew about the
disorders, one could distinguish the defects of administration, but nothing was done about them because of the habit of letting things pass."[41]
Portugal, at the moment when Pombal began his work, became a kind
of perfect example, according to the pen of the author of the *Testamento*,
and almost a caricature, of the difficulties and resistance that all reformers at that time encountered. "All the governments of Europe," he made
the Portuguese minister say, "have made reforms in their political and
civil systems. Perhaps only Portugal has not changed." "No particular
capacity is needed to leave things as they are, but much is needed to
carry out reforms. Meanwhile, the old abuses are perpetuated, which is
a common disgrace of governments that decide nothing."[42]

The result was clear in the "Portuguese countryside": "A few old
castles always on the point of falling into ruin, fields badly cultivated,
orchards that present a few immature fruits. . . ." "One sees in this countryside animals walking on two feet who call themselves men but hardly
have a human form. They have thin, emaciated bodies. Nature is about
to expire in them for lack of subsistence. These miserable beings . . .
inhabit gravelike openings dug in the earth, which in the language of
the place are called houses. . . . These wild Portuguese don't speak any
language, but mutter a jargon understood only by themselves. . . . The
greater part live on roots and acorns. . . . Every Portuguese village is an
infirmary, every hut a hospital." Precisely such a reality as this engen-
dered in the mind of Pombal a violent desire to "get in a position to
permit the remedy of an abuse that degrades humanity."[43] A great distance separated the social life of Portugal from that of the other nations
of Europe. "Men are insufficiently educated, the earth is insufficiently
cultivated, the arts are insufficiently developed. America in comparison
with Portugal is what Portugal is in comparison with France and Italy."[44]
A look at the maritime, financial, and commercial situation of Portugal
proves the need for and possibility of transforming the country. The
failure of the conspiracy against the king, and then above all "the total
extermination of the Jesuits, who thought of themselves as omnipotent
in the kingdom and were destroyed without causing the least revolution," had finally shown the way to indispensable reforms, and "that an
absolute king can attempt anything in his dominions."[45] There had

[41] Ibid., pp. 39ff.
[42] Ibid., p. 43.
[43] Ibid., p. 43.
[44] Ibid., p. 59.
[45] Ibid., p. 79.

been, to be sure, laments and criticisms, but monarchal power had prevailed. Imagining the "last wishes of the Marquis of Pombal," the author concluded: "One is rarely a prophet in one's own country; but I have contradicted this proverb." "When I take a careful look at my past conduct, I reflect that I would do again what I have done." Nor did he fail to deal a last blow to the Jesuits. "The ex-Jesuits who still remain will perhaps be political enough to dissimulate my persecution of them and imagine themselves generously pardoned, especially because they have no force or credit." A "tombstone inscription" finally presented again the image of a Richelieu or a Sully in a troubled and stormy time: he died "leaving ample material for the praise and astonishment of future centuries, as a philosopher, a hero, and a Christian."[46] His merits were Lisbon "rebuilt," manufactures "established," letters "restored," laws "confirmed," hypocrisy "unmasked," and fanaticism "repressed." He was "filled with glory, crowned with laurels, oppressed by calumny, praised by foreign nations, and satirized in his own country."

The *Testamento* was translated into German by Christian Joseph Jagemann, the cleric and writer who had played a large role in establishing and maintaining relations between Tuscany under Peter Leopold and the German-speaking world.[47]

But what remained of all this after the fall and death of Pombal? To judge from the gazettes of the period, Portugal seemed to have fallen back into its age-old inaction. "On different occasions anyone has been able to see," one read in the gazette of Venice, "that the ideas that, particularly in the last half-century, have spread generally in Europe about the true duties of religion toward civil society have not yet been adopted in Portugal." Everywhere convents were being suppressed. New ones were being built only in Portugal.[48] But even observations of this kind were rare. The silence about Portugal became increasingly heavy, broken only by information about matrimonial events in the ruling family.[49] As for intellectual life, it is enough to remember that the rectorship of José Francisco Miguel António de Mendonça of the University of Coimbra, between 1780 and 1785, has been called the "reign of stupid-

[46] Ibid., pp. 94ff. The *Iscrizione sepolcrale*, "an ironic eulogy of the deceased Marquis of Pombal," is also in the *Gazzetta universale*, no. 64, 1 August 1782, p. 513 (Lisbon, 9 July).

[47] *Politisches Testament des marquis von Pombal, oder Sein lezter Unterricht an den Graf von Oeyras, seinen Sohn, aus seinen hinterlassenen Papieren gezogen* (Dessau: Buchhandlung der Gelehrten, 1783). There was a reedition in Leipzig by the bookseller G. E. Beer, in 1787. On Jagemann see Venturi, *The End of the Old Regime, 1768–1776*, p. 97n.

[48] *Notizie del mondo [V.]*, no. 100, 13 December 1783 (Lisbon, 28 October).

[49] See, for example, *Nuove di diverse corti e paesi*, no. 24, 14 June 1784, p. 189 (Madrid, 18 May).

ity."[50] There was little encouragement in the manifesto that the general intendant of police put out on 14 March 1781 against the "infected and abominable doctrines" and against "satirical and defamatory libels" that seem to have circulated at that time in Portugal.[51] Until the Real Mesa Censoria, the Royal Board of Censorship, was abolished, in 1787, the situation remained very closed.

More ardent thoughts and more vivid ferment continued to live on in this or that figure of an *estrangeirado* at the end of the eighteenth century, cosmopolitan Portuguese who were all different from one another and thus were typical of the Lusitanian world of the age of the Enlightenment.[1] We have encountered one, Luís Antonio Verney, in following the formation of Genovesi and studying the preparations for the religious crisis of the sixties in Rome.[2] Francisco Xavier de Oliveira pushed the desire for religious reform to the point of becoming an Anglican, after having written a whole series of works and books through his long life (he died in 1783). Burned in effigy by the Inquisition in 1762, he wanted to respond to the question, How and why? adding "Anecdotes and Reflections on This Subject." He then tried to find a point of linkage between his Protestantism and the policy of state supremacy that then flourished in Portugal, and he continued to polemicize later on themes of religious and political reform.[3] The chief among these estrangeirados—a word meaning "admirer, cultivator of what is foreign"—was António Nunes Ribeiro Sanches, a Jew who had converted to Christianity. His career as a doctor and schemer took him from Coimbra to Salamanca, from London to Leiden, where he studied with Herman Boerhaave, Jacob Gravesande, and Peter Burmann, and thus with some of the chief scientists and erudites of the first half of the eigh-

[50] Mario Brandão and M. Lopes d'Almeida, *A universidade de Coimbra. Esbôço da sua história* (Coimbra: Por ordem da universidade, 1937), p. 114.

[51] It was sent to Turin in an Italian version with the dispatch of 20 March 1781 by Cavalier de Pollone. Turin, AS, *Lettere ministri, Portogallo*, mazzo 10.

[1] Manoel Cardozo, "The Internationalism of the Portuguese Enlightenment: The Role of the Estrangeirado, c. 1700–c. 1750," in The *Ibero-American Enlightenment*, ed. A. Owen Aldridge (Urbana: University of Illinois Press, 1971), pp. 141ff.

[2] Venturi, *Settecento riformatore* 2, in the index. In *Notizie politiche*, no. 86, 26 October 1790, p. 581 (Rome, 20 October), one reads: "Cavaliere Luigi Antonio Verney was one of the first and perhaps the first for many years with his works and example to promote new study in Portugal and to introduce a taste for the beautiful in the sciences and arts."

[3] See Cavaliero Francisco Xavier de Oliveira, *Opúscolos contra o Santo-Oficio*, publicação e prefácio de A. Gonçalves Rodrigues (Coimbra: Atlântida, 1942).

teenth century. He was in Moscow and St. Petersburg, until he was chased out of Russia by the anti-Semitism of the new czarina, Elizabeth. Catherine assisted him financially, and he was able to live in Paris until his death in 1782. He was a friend of Holbach and Diderot, a collaborator in the *Encyclopédie*, and he collected a library, which contained, together with many books from different countries, some of the most representative works of the Italian Enlightenment, from the *Vero despotismo* of Gorani, to the *Meditazioni sull'economia politica* of Pietro Verri (the sixth edition published in Livorno), *Della moneta* and the *Dialogues* of Galiani, *Della vera influenza degli astri* of Toaldo, and so on.[4] The scientist João Hayacinto de Magalhães (or Magellano, as Italians called him), in London, was also a cosmopolitan Lusitanian.[5] Isaac Pinto, even though he was of Portuguese origin, a counselor, as we shall see, to the stadholder, and a writer on economic matters whose ideas even attracted the attention of Diderot, instead should be considered a cosmopolitan Dutchman.[6]

Eleonora Fonseca Pimentel was a Portuguese estrangeirada and an Italian patriot. With her few precious works, and her martyrdom at the hands of the Santa Fede (the clerical and popular reaction at Naples), she made a narrow but solid bridge between the age of Pombal and that of the Neapolitan republic of 1799. She was still a child, born on 13 January 1752, when her family had to leave Rome, in 1760, at the moment of greatest tension between Lisbon and the Roman Curia, at the time of Pagliarini's arrest. The order to leave came from Pombal and there was no possibility of hesitation. Thus Eleonora grew up and studied in Naples, in a world in which young men such as Pagano and Filangieri were natural points of reference. The summer of 1776 was the moment of her first cosmopolitan flowering: she wrote a letter to Meta-

---

[4] David Willemse, *António Nunes Ribeiro Sanches, élève de Boerhaave et son importance pour la Russie* (Leiden: E. J. Brill, 1966), in the appendix, nos. 98, 100, 117, 122, 140. On his ideas on religious toleration, which also reflected his experience in Holland and Russia, see Cardozo, "The Internationalism of the Portuguese," pp. 181ff. Particularly interesting is the study by Pierre Van Bever, "La religion du docteur Antonio Nunes Ribeiro Sanches," *Studies on Voltaire and the Eighteenth Century* 41 (1966): 277ff. On p. 281 he cites a note "en marge de Pilati" taken from his papers conserved in the Ecole de médecine of Paris, on the function of great men and on natural law, as well as a note taken from Jean Manzon.

[5] Venturi, *Settecento riformatore* 2, p. 11.

[6] See Moses Bensabat Amzalak, "O economista Isaac de Pinto e seu 'Tratado da circulação e do crédito' e autros escritos económicos," extract from *Anais do Iscef*, tomo 2, vol. 28 (Lisbon, 1960), and Alan J. Freer, "Isaac de Pinto e la sua 'Lettre à Mr. Diderot sur le jeu des cartes,'" *Annali della Scuola normale superiore di Pisa*, 2d ser., vol. 33, fasc. 1–2 (1964): 104ff., and id., "Ancora su Isaac de Pinto e Diderot," ibid., vol. 35, fasc. 1–2 (1966): 121ff.

stasio, which he called "poetic, moral, metaphysical, seductive, rather incendiary," and, in a Sienese journal, exchanged verses with Voltaire.[7] At the same time she drew up the struggles, obstacles, and victories of Pombal's policy in a scenic representation entitled the *Trionfo della virtú*. In the preface she explained in detail how such a perfect collaboration had been born between the sovereign and his minister. The king was "the image of divinity, because he is the distributor of justice and eternal providence." The minister was not only the reflection and transmitter of sovereign power, "but also the image of the people, by whose means their needs and prayers are raised to the throne." "Public happiness" was born and depended on his "double, delicate task." Pombal thus had the function of holding legitimacy and popular will firmly together. This function found its roots in the history of Portugal, a nation born of war, but where military power had never stood above civil authority, and thus it "was never subjected to the abuses of feudal law." "Sufficient unto itself," Portugal had assumed the task of "watching over the security and greatness of Europe, still torn by divisions," and had thrown itself into the discovery and conquest of other continents. "A nation jealous of its own honor," it succeeded in recapturing its own independence even when it was annexed to Spain. Its weakness, which had finally led "to the decadence of commerce, and to the prejudices and disorders that oppress the internal virtues of the body politic," had been intellectual sterility, and "above all negligence of the science of mathematics,"

---

[7] Metastasio's response is published in Joaquim de Araujo, *Eleonora Fonseca Pimentel. Il trionfo della virtú* (n.p., 1899), p. 10. This insert is part of the work of Antonio de Portugal de Faria, *Portugal e Italia* (Livorno: Tipografia Raphael Giusti, 1898), vol. 1, pp. 417ff. (This, like the other two volumes, is a book of rare disorder.) See *Giornale letterario di Siena* 2, no. 1 (July 1776): lxxi, "Versi del Sig. di Voltaire responsivi ad un sonetto della nobile ed egregia donzella Eleonora Fonseca di Pimentel abitante a Napoli": "Beau rossignol de la belle Italie / votre sonnet cajole un vieux hibou / au mont Jura retiré dans un trou, / sans voix, sans plumes et privé de génie. / Il veut quitter son païs morfondu: / après de vous à Naples il va se rendre; / s'il peut vous voir et s'il peut vous entendre / il reprendra tout ce qu'il a perdu." ("Beautiful nightingale of Italy / your sonnet coaxes an old owl / hidden in a hole on Mount Jura, / without voice or feathers, deprived of genius. / He wants to leave his chilly land: / and come to you in Naples; / if he can see and hear you / he will recover all he has lost.") In number 4, dated October 1776, pp. ccxlvff., of the same *Giornale letterario di Siena*, there is a review of the *Etat présent du royaume de Portugal* of Dumouriez, which we already have had the occasion to cite. It was an exaltation of Pombal and his work. The style does not seem to be that of Fonseca, but it is in tune with her enthusiasm for the reforms of the minister. "Never has a minister been more resisted or more glorious than he. A thousand perils surrounded his dignity and he needed all his courage to overcome them. The more critical things became the more he showed his great and sublime soul. In the course of many tempests he did not lose the thread of his vast projects: his universal genius embraced all their parts, attacked all abuses, remedied all evils, plucked out all bad roots, and planted better and deeper ones."

so necessary and useful in the period of colonial expansion. Thus "the force of the state was weakened, the constitution altered, its activity enervated, and the opinion of citizens vitiated." A "kind of inertia" had taken hold of the country. "And other peoples, proud of their new learning," hastened to forget that "the Portuguese had been the discoverers of India." The recovery came with Joseph I and with "Carvalho," the latter armed "with that magnanimity that announces men chosen to change the face of nations, capable of infusing the energy of a creative mind into the internal springs of the kingdom."[8] "The rebuilding of Lisbon" was proof of the capability this "intrepid philosopher, indefatigable minister, sensible citizen" had shown in confronting the terrible misfortune of the earthquake. The reform of the university, the abolition of slavery within Portugal, and the "new honors" given to colonists in America were evidence of his value among "all peoples and in all centuries."[9] The equestrian statue of Joseph I, adorned by a medallion with Pombal's portrait symbolized the work carried out by the sovereign and minister. At the feet of the "superb colossus . . . rests the sculptured image of the minister . . . and while it seems that he lowers his head respectfully, there as well he is a support for the king."[10] The happy results of the economic policy of Pombal are sung by nymphs of the Tagus:

[8] The first scene, where "hatred," "betrayal," "envy," and so on, intervene, alludes to the attempt made against Pombal on the day of the inauguration of the equestrian statue of the king, on 6 June 1775, in the central square of Lisbon, which had been rebuilt after the earthquake. On this statue and its symbolic value see Jose-Augusto França, *Une ville des lumières. La Lisbonne de Pombal* (Paris: SEVPEN, 1965), pp. 163ff. And this is how Francesco Gusta narrated it: "In the midst of the preparations for the magnificent function the Marquis of Pombal found himself much perturbed because of a denunciation made by a certain Luigi Giuseppe de Figueiredo against an unknown man by the name of Gio. Batista Pele, a Genoese, who was accused of having threatened his life with a secret mine hidden in the magnificent carriage he was to use on the day of the inauguration of the statue. The unhappy accused Pele was immediately arrested by order of Carvalho and subjected to a rigorous examination. After four months of questioning he was condemned by the Tribunal of Suspicion to die torn apart by four horses, after both his hands had been cut off. This inhumane punishment (which horrified all of Europe) was carried out with all rigor on the unhappy Pele on 9 October 1775" (*Vita di S. G. di Carvalho e Melo*, vol. 5, pp. 65ff.). The preface of the poetic composition of Eleonora Fonseca Pimentel is dated 15 March 1777. For reasons unknown to us she delayed writing and publishing her work until it was anachronistic: Joseph I was dead, as we have seen, at the end of February, and everyone in Europe knew that Pombal's political situation was strongly shaken.

[9] *Il trionfo della virtú. Componimento drammatico dedicato all'eccellenza del signore marchese di Pombal primo ministro, segretario di stato ecc. ecc. del re fedelissimo* (Naples, 1777). Republished in E. di Fonseca Pimentel, *Il Monitore repubblicano del 1799. Articoli politici seguiti da scritti vari in versi e in prosa della stessa autrice*, ed. Benedetto Croce (Bari: Laterza, 1943), pp. 200ff.

[10] Ibid., p. 213.

Nei nostri campi Cerere
era da Bacco oppressa.
Cerere or sorge anch'essa
i campi a ricoprir.
Le merci a noi veniano
pria da stranieri regni,
or vanno i nostri legni
i regni ad arricchir.[11]

The chorus of arts and disciples of virtues, instead, sing of the reform of the University of Coimbra:

Prima l'error coprivasi
col manto del saper
ora le scienze svelano
i puri rai del ver.[12]

Asia, America, and Africa also celebrate the triumph over the "hard slavery" that had oppressed them earlier. Finally the chorus urges:

Tutti corriamo adunque
del sacro bronzo al piè.
Ivi il ministro onorisi,
ivi si adori il re.[13]

The reality was different now: precisely in those days Pombal's medallion was carried off amid shouts from the crowd. The ruin of the minister and his policy did not touch Fonseca, whom we see in the following years continuing along the way that led from anticlericism to a broader program of reforms. The great tradition of independence in the country of Giannone was evoked by her in her preface to the translation from Latin, which appeared in 1790, of the work of Nicolò Caravita, *Niun diritto compete al sommo pontefice sul regno di Napoli*.[14] Thus, along with Gennaro Cestari, she wanted to make known the work of Antonio Pereira de Figueiredo, a great enemy of papal infallibility, and one of the most typical figures in the policy of state supremacy of the age of Pombal.[15]

[11] "In our fields Ceres / was oppressed by Baccus. / Ceres now raises herself / to cover the fields. / Goods came to us / before from foreign kingdoms, / now our ships go out / to enrich kingdoms" (Fonseca Pimentel, *Il Monitore repubblicano*, p. 221).

[12] "Before error covered itself / with the mantle of knowledge / now the sciences unveil / the pure rays of truth" (ibid., p. 222).

[13] "All flock therefore / to the foot of the sacred bronze. / There the minister is honored, / there the king is adored" (ibid., p. 224).

[14] Ibid., p. 247.

[15] De Araujo, *Eleonora Fonseca*, pp. 11ff., 16. On A. Pereira, see Venturi, *Settecento riformatore* 2, in the index.

At the end of the nineties a new and an enthusiastic vision was laid over the hard and arid reality that surrounded her. The sad events through which she passed, the death of her only son, an abortion frankly reevoked in what seem to be the best of her verses, and her separation from her husband detached her more and more from the hopes of her youth. In 1777 she had imposed the luminous vision of a definitive triumph of virtue on the Portugal of Pombal. Now, in 1799, with her whole soul, she identified herself with the cause of liberty and democracy in Italy. Her *Monitore repubblicano* is the splendid testimony of her full and intelligent dedication.[16] And once again, as in distant Portugal, reality turned against her. The reaction of the Santa Fede overcame her, carrying her, after a long and courageous struggle, to the scaffold. All her life she had sought a fatherland worthy of that name, creating one in imagination when she did not find one in reality. Her death alongside that of the republican revolutionaries of Naples sealed that tendency, that dream of a Portuguese estrangeirada.

With always fresh curiosity she had followed the scientific life of Portugal along with that of Italy in the years before the revolution. In one of her few letters that have survived we see her enthusiasm for the discovery of fossilized elephant bones near Verona, and also an inquiry to her correspondent, Bishop Fr. Manuel de Cenaculo: "What is now being done by the academy of natural history founded in Lisbon under the patronage of the Duke of Lafoẽs?" In general, she hoped to receive scientific works from what she insistently called "my mother country."[17]

The diffusion of the Enlightenment was in fact an essential element in the difficult life of Portugal in the eighties, after the fall of Pombal. Around academies similar to the one Fonseca recalled a Portuguese elite slowly gathered and was formed. This elite was certainly not a homogeneous and compact governing class, but it was not a group of estrangeirados either, even if many individuals had lived long years abroad. One of the best examples of the generation formed in the epoch of Pombal came to live in Turin in 1778. This was Pombal's godson, Dom Rodrigo de Sousa Coutinho, the son of Francisco Innocencio, who had been governor of Angola and ambassador in Madrid. He had studied along with the crown prince, under the guidance of Michele Franzi, an Italian, and it was even said that Pombal thus intended to prepare him to follow in his own footsteps one day, capture and dominate the future sovereign. After attending the *collegio dei nobili*, he had traveled and was struck above all by what he had seen in France. In August 1779 he went to visit the Abbé Raynal, and he gave an account of their conversation

---

[16] *Il Monitore repubblicano*, ed. Mario Battaglini (Naples: Guida, 1974).
[17] Fonseca Pimentel, *Il Monitore repubblicano*, p. 261. The letter is dated by B. Croce "the beginning of 1786" (ibid., p. 259 n. 1).

in a letter to his sister. France had a revenue of 160 million cruzados, that is, much more than Spain and Portugal together, the celebrated writer told him. The French monarchy, he answered, would be quite unbearable to the rest of Europe if it were "raised to the point of strength that its situation and greatness permit." Raynal had interrupted. "It is for this reason, sir, that an Italian Abbé among my friends said to me one day: providence has made all equal by giving to some what it has denied to others. It has given France power, but denied her common sense." The irony of Galiani—it is difficult to think it was not he—thus inserted itself into the dialogue between the young cosmopolitan Portuguese and the author of the *Histoire philosophique*. The fiscal situation preoccupied both. The discussion on the subject of Necker resumed. But the conclusion was still the same: "France is always in the situation described by the Italian Abbé." The dilemma, for Europe, was always open: would it be better to be a branch office of the English, or a slave of the French? The only consolation came from the impossibility of France's reforming its own government, thus making vain any pretension of hegemony over Europe. But, as the historian who has most recently paused on the youthful reflections of the Portuguese diplomat has noted, "reforms in France, in the form of revolution, were not slow in coming." The choice between France and England also weighed on Portugal in the late-eighteenth and early-nineteenth century. Rodrigo de Sousa Coutinho was destined to play a role of first importance when it became a question of choosing between Napoleon and his enemies, and between Brazil and Portuguese territory.[18]

Meanwhile, for many years, Dom Rodrigo found something more than a diplomatic post in Piedmont.[19] He married Anna Gabriella Asi-

[18] Marquês da Funchal, *O conde de Linhares, dom Rodrigo Domingos António de Sousa Coutinho* (Lisbon: Typographia Bayard, 1908), p. 191, letter to the sister of Mariana de Sousa Coutinho, Fontainebleau, 4 August 1779 (the book is devoted chiefly to the period after 1798 and contains little on the Piedmontese years of Dom Rodrigo), and Maxwell, *Conflicts and Conspiracies*, pp. 206ff.

[19] See *Gazzetta universale*, no. 95, 28 November 1778, p. 753 (Lisbon, 27 October): "Tomorrow Sig. Dom Rodrigo de Souza Coutinho, son of the Portuguese ambassador in Spain, who was minister of this court at Turin, leaves for Madrid. He will remain some days in Madrid with his father, then on to Paris to the ambassador of this court, and then to his destiny." When he returned the first time, in the summer of 1780, Felice Mossi di Morano, the Piedmontese ambassador in Madrid, noted that he had "made the trip from Turin here in 19 days and some hours" (Turin, AS, *Lettere ministri, Spagna,* mazzo 90, 25 July 1780). John Trevor, the British ambassador in Turin, spoke of Sousa Coutinho as a "person of no common merit." "He is very ambitious of going hereafter to England; he is master of our language and of all our best authors and a great admirer of our Constitution and the wonderful efforts which he sees it produce in philosophy, politics and commerce" (London, P.R.O.F.O. 67.4. Sardinia, 12 January 1786). Attached to the dispatch of 20 January 1786 is a copy of the essay on Piedmontese money by Sousa Coutinho.

nari di San Marzano, interested himself vividly in the agricultural problems of the country, and discussed economic questions of importance
with Giambattista Vasco, even publicly.[20]

None of the Piedmontese diplomats who went to Lisbon were of the
high station of Dom Rodrigo de Sousa Coutinho. But their testimonies
about Portugal in the eighties remain significant. Giovanni Giuseppe
Spirito Nomis de Pollone repeatedly pointed out the notable economic
advantages that neutrality brought to the country during the long war
of the French, Spanish, and Dutch against Great Britain. "It is unques-
tionable that the commerce of this country has grown considerably since
the war," he wrote at the beginning of 1782. He had to add that the
government and the people of Portugal had not known how to take advantage of the situation. All that was needed was "a little more activity
in the nation, fewer restrictions and more encouragement from the government." Nonetheless, despite these obstacles, seventeen ships were
ready to leave for India, something never seen in the past. Trade with
Africa would also have developed rapidly "if through the spirit of indolence inherent in the character of the nation it had not been entirely
ignored." Trade with European countries was increasing, even if Portuguese ships did not yet dare pass through the Strait of Gibraltar. In
Brazil everything was at a standstill, and the mines yielded less than before.[21] Great hopes were set on commerce with Russia, which Cavalier
Pinto, "the envoy of this court in London," had proposed. St. Petersburg
was willing. The Portuguese ships arriving there were not numerous,
but "always more than one has ever seen."[22] But then difficulties increased. Pinto, having arrived in Lisbon after his mission at the end of
1783, was much occupied, with perhaps even arranging a treaty with
the United States of America. He finally confided his bitterness to the
Piedmontese envoy: "Here nothing but projects are made, and nothing
is ever concluded."[23] The news arriving from northern Europe suggested daily parallels with the situations in which more commercially
active and prosperous nations found themselves. Holland, under pressure from the Emperor, was menaced by "some great revolution, which
it is thought will not be too far away." And we might add that in the
Austrian Low Countries, Antwerp and Ostend also were confronted
with problems of rapid transformation, after the war of American independence had changed the old equilibrium even there. But revolu-

[20] Gianno Marocco, *Giambattista Vasco* (Turin: Fondazione Luigi Einaudi, 1978), pp.
126ff. On the problems of that age, see Giovanni Levi, "Gli aritmetici politici e la demo-
grafia piemontese negli ultimi anni del settecento," *R. stor. ital.*, year 86, fasc. 2 (June
1974): 201ff.

[21] Turin, AS, *Lettere ministri, Portogallo*, mazzo 10, 15 January 1782.

[22] Ibid., 20 November 1781.

[23] Ibid., 23 December 1783.

tions in Portugal were not to be feared. Nothing seemed to threaten "the spirit of slowness and indecision that is commonly seen to dominate all the operations of this ministry."[24] From the dispatches of the Piedmontese representatives unfolds a long tale of fearful and inept ministers and of wasted and stunted members of the royal family, dominated by their confessors and by the crowds of monks surrounding them.[25] Maria I reigned along with her husband, Peter III, from 1777 until May 1786, when he died, and then alone until 1791, when she went mad. Her son John assumed the regency in 1792. An elder brother, José, died in 1788. The end of Peter III was particularly typical of the atmosphere in Queluz, the Versailles or Sans Souci of Portugal. "A quantity of monks of all kinds have taken him in hand recently," wrote Count Philippe Saint Martin de Front in May 1786.[26] A few days before, "His Majesty the King had a serious seizure while he was discussing a good death with a Piedmontese monk; he stammered for half an hour without being able to utter a single word; I have this from the very monk who was with him."[27] Less than two weeks later the sovereign died.[28] A serious struggle developed at the court over the nomination of the confessor for the queen and new ministers. There was a bitter contest between nobles and non-nobles, and between followers and adversaries of Pombal. The *fidalgos* wanted neither Pinto nor Seabra, because they did not belong to their party and because their formation associated them with the period of the defunct dictator. As a result, all business was neglected, including the commercial agreements that were to be made with Russia. Nothing was done to extricate the country from the disastrous economic situation in which it found itself. "Portugal," de Front wrote, concluding his dispatches for 1786, "could be self-sufficient and in time have flourishing manufactures if the high cost of labor here did not prevent it. This is a necessary result of the intolerable prices of basic commodities, because agriculture is entirely neglected due to the terrible taxes here on the harvest, which arrive at nearly 90 percent, of which only the smallest part is returned to the royal treasury and the rest goes to the tithes of the church and tithes of the knightly orders, taxes for education, and the cut of mendicant friars." Two hundred years before, Portugal had exported grain.[29] Now it did not even have enough for itself. The many projects that continually accumulated remained merely dreams, for example, the possibility of using Brazilian

---

[24] Ibid., 30 December 1783.

[25] On the "decrepit state" of the ministry, see, for example, ibid., mazzo 12, 13 February 1787.

[26] Ibid., mazzo 11, 23 March 1786.

[27] Ibid., 11 May 1786.

[28] Ibid., 25 May 1786.

[29] Ibid., 12 December 1786.

cotton "to clothe a part of the Americas," thus capturing a lucrative traffic "from the factories of Manchester."[30] News coming from outside instilled an increasingly acute sense of preoccupation and fear. The emperor Joseph II followed an increasingly dangerous policy. The revolts of Holland, Brabant, and Spanish America were followed by increasing disquiet. The year 1789 came without any limit being set to the "kind of anarchy that reigns in this country," Isasca, the Piedmontese chargé d'affaires, wrote.[31] When the ambassador, the Count di Pollone, returned in the summer, he could not help stating that "the crisis of domestic affairs in France occupies public attention, and the result of matters in the Estates General and the court is awaited with curiosity."[32] But still, before echoes of developments in France became more insistent in Lisbon, the first initiative of a change, a transformation, appeared in Portugal with the more and more clear reemergence of men from the epoch of Pombal, among them his active and capable son; with the abolition in July 1787 of the Mesa Censoria, the heavy censorship which for many years had weighed on the country; and, finally, after years of uncertainty, in January 1789, with the nomination of Pinto and Seabra as secretaries of state, one for foreign and the other for internal affairs.[33]

The renewed cultural interests, the creation of academies, and the resumption of scientific discussion had an important central place in this however slow and modest renewal. Much time and energy would be required "for a revolution which this land needs much," to put on its feet again a country where everything is lacking, and where there is above all a need for enlightened individuals with a firm character. The only possible road was the one that finally seemed to be opening.[34]

The agrarian academy created by the Duke of Lafoës, a patron and politician—the one of whom Eleonora Fonseca Pimentel had requested

---

[30] Ibid., 13 March 1787.

[31] Ibid., 3 March 1789.

[32] Ibid., 21 July 1789.

[33] Ibid., 17 July 1787 (on the reorganization of the censorship, entrusted, at least in part, to the university and to magistrates), 21 April 1787 (on the growing influence of the prince royal, "educated according to the system of Pombal," and on the "young Marquis of Pombal"), 28 August 1787 ("the high nobility, which is much more powerful than appropriate to a monarchical state and to which the words and deeds of revolution are a bit too familiar, fear, with reason, that the prince royal might follow the system of Pombal on his own accord and act against them. Those of the church, and particularly the monks, fear this very much"), and 31 January 1789 (the nomination of Pinto and Seabra: "Portugal will not be slow, I think, to feel the good effects of their choice"). On these personages and facts, see Maxwell, *Conflicts and Conspiracies*, pp. 177ff.

[34] Ibid., 28 August 1787 (need for "an enlightened person with a firm character"), 27 November 1787 (appeal to the "most enlightened" bishops and "desire to draw this land from the lethargy in which it is immersed").

news—began to publish at the Royal Academy of Sciences, in 1789, a series of memoirs discussed and approved in the immediately preceding years.[35] The motto selected for this and the following volumes was "*Nisi utile est quod facimus stulta est gloria*" (Unless what we do is useful our glory is empty). A last wave of the great European movement of agrarian societies, a late reflection of physiocracy, thus came to erode and intersect the traditional and closed fortress of Portuguese mercantilism erected on the great memories of discoveries and conquests of the past and defending Lusitanian privilege and immobility. The interest in agriculture also traced its origins to the age of Pombal. The name of Genovesi, who was destined to have much success in Portugal and Brazil (the philosophy of the Neapolitan reformer was official in these lands for decades), resounded also through their economic writings, as José Verissimo Alvares da Silva noted in 1782 in his *Memoria historica sobre a agricultura portugueza considerada desde o tempo dos romanos até ao presente*. It was effectively Genovesi, with his warm and generous spirit, who made the first bridge between the religious conflicts of the age of Pombal and later hopes for reform. As Alvares da Silva emphasized, Genovesi had prophesied in 1765—observing the care with which Lisbon selected catechisms distant from the traditional Jesuit ones as worthy of "Christian educators"—that "the Portuguese employ every means to be wiser than other European nations."[36] Then a year later, in 1766, the Portuguese translation of the *Eléments de commerce* by Forbonnois appeared, which contained, as Alvares da Silva noted, the first details about the "Norfolk method," that is, the beginnings of the agricultural revolution in Great Britain.[37] Some other works, actually very few, were

[35] *Memorias economicas de Academia real das sciencias de Lisboa, para o adiantamento da agricultura, das artes e da industria en Portugal e suas conquistas* (Lisbon: Na officina da Academia real das sciencias, 1789), vol. 1. On agrarian problems in Portugal see the monumental work of Albert Silbert, *Le Portugal méditerranéen à la fin de l'Ancien régime. XVIIIe - début du XIXe siècle. Contribution à l'histoire agraire comparée* (Paris: SEVPEN, 1966), with a detailed bibliography (pp. 17ff.) and an important conclusion on the importance and decline of agrarian collectivism. On the Duke of Lafoês, see Marc-Marie de Bombelle, *Journal d'un ambassadeur de France au Portugal, 1786–1788*, ed. Roger Kann (Paris: PUF, 1979), in the index and pp. 351ff.

[36] Antonio Genovesi, *Lezioni di commercio o sia d'economia civile* (Naples: Simone, 1765), pt. 2, ch. 10, n. A. See José Verissimo Alvares da Silva, "Memoria historica sobre a agricultura portugueza considerada desde o tempo dos romanos até ao presente," in *Memorias economicas*, vol. 5 (1815), pp. 194ff. (A work of 1782 under this title is on p. 194.) See p. 243, "Haverá desaste annos que o profundo Genuense, escrevendo em Napoles, dizia, . . ." with a translation of the phrases cited here. This "Memoria" reflects and discusses on pp. 224, 242, and 250 n. 1 other parts of the *Lezioni di commercio*. On the philosophical fortune of Genovesi in the Portuguese world, see Mariana Amélia Machado Santos, "Os filósof 'recentiones' do século XVIII em Portugal," *Biblos* 21 (1945): 207ff.

[37] *Memorias economicas*, p. 255. The *Elementos do commercio, traduzidos livremente do francez* by José Manoel Ribeiro Pereira, published in Lisbon in 1766, is cited in Kenneth E.

taken from the immense European library of agronomy of these years and translated into Portuguese. The chief one, *Tratado theorico e pratico de agricoltura*, in four volumes, was by a Padovan, Giovanni Antonio Della Bella, a professor of physics, first in the Collegio dei Nobili, and then for seventeen years, until 1789, at Coimbra. A student of electricity and magnetism, an active collaborator of Pombal, he participated in the radical reform of the university, in 1772, which had seen the dismissal and replacement of almost the whole body of instructors. When he returned to his fatherland he dedicated his old age to agriculture.[38] From Padova also came Domenico Vandelli, a doctor, naturalist, and botanist. Because, as his biographer says, "he loved movement and work," he gave himself over to travels through Italy collecting plants and minerals, he was appreciated by Linnaeus, and he created the nucleus of a museum he eventually gave to the University of Coimbra.[39] His experiments led him to polemicize with Haller, and his growing fame won him an invitation to St. Petersburg, which he refused, accepting instead that to Portugal, where he arrived at the beginning of 1765.[40] He was also a professor at Coimbra, the first for that university in natural sciences and chemistry, and he planned, along with Della Bella, a grandiose botanical garden. "I have always thought," Pombal answered, "that things are good not only because they are costly and great, but because they correspond to the ends for which they are intended." Those principles, he added, had been adopted in England, Germany, Holland, and Padova. But in those places "Portuguese gold" was not being spent.[41] Nonetheless, a botanical garden arose at Coimbra, although without the magnif-

Carpenter, ed., "Luzo-Brazilian Economic Literature Before 1850: A List of the Kress Library's Holdings," *Kress Library Bulletin*, no. 13 (1978), to which one can refer also for other works cited earlier. In the same year, 1766, with the place of Brussels, the Portuguese version of the famous essay on a general grain policy by Claude Jacques Herbert was published.

[38] See Mario Gliozzi, *Elettrologia fino al Volta* (Naples: Loffredo, 1937), vol. 2, pp. 43ff., and Giovanni Costanzo, "Fisici italiani in Portogallo," in *Relazioni storiche fra l'Italia e il Portogallo. Memorie e documenti* (Rome: Reale Accademia d'Italia, 1940), pp. 380ff.

[39] Louis Gabriel Michaud, *Biographie universelle. Supplément* (Paris: Beck, 1862), col. 85, p. 2. His cosmopolitan curiosity is reflected well in the "Dissertatio de studio historiae naturalis necessario in medicina, oeconomia, agricultura, artibus et commercio," in his *Dissertatio de arbore draconis seu dracaena* (Olisipone: Apud Antonium Rodericum Galliardum, typographum Regiae curiae censoriae, 1768), pp. 11ff. See pp. 31ff. *Conspectus musei Dominici Vandelli Patavii 1783*: "Hoc museum originem habuit ab itineribus vario tempore a Vandellio peractis per hetruscos, bononienses, mediolanenses, patavinos montes, per mare Thyrrenum et Adriaticum," (This museum had its origins in the voyages made by Vandelli at various times through the mountains of Tuscany, Bologna, Milan, Padua, and in the Tyrrhenian and Adriatic seas.)

[40] Smith, *Memoirs of the Marquis of Pombal*, vol. 2, p. 168.

[41] Biagio Longo, "Domenico Vandelli e la fondazione del primo orto botanico nel Portogallo," in *Relazioni storiche tra l'Italia e il Portogallo*, pp. 403ff.

icence dreamed of by the two Italians, and Vandelli directed it until 1792.[42] He was active in the agrarian academy of the Duke of Lafoēs. Many of his writings are contained in the first volumes of the *Memorias economicas*. Speaking of olives, he remembered "Abbé Fortis, the famous naturalist," and he referred to the well-known *Cours d'agriculture* by the Abbé Rozier.[43] He confronted a larger and more central theme in a memoir on the situation of agriculture in Portugal, Europe, and the world. He said the many volumes on agronomy published in "all learned nations" were insufficient. Wise policies were being carried out in Great Britain. In France agrarian academies were active. In Portugal, as elsewhere, books would be useless without "well-executed particular legislation," capable, that is, of removing obstacles and providing encouragement. Like Eleonora Fonseca Pimentel, he also reflected that "this kingdom was born amid the clash of arms." "The total decline of agriculture" had begun with the conquests and then perpetuated itself with exorbitant privileges, taxes on basic necessities, and the "prohibition of export of agricultural products." Abandonment of the land and depopulation of the country had resulted from the "total lack of observance" of "wise agrarian laws." Taking up again the ideas of Jean Bertrand on legislation favorable to agriculture, which had such a large echo even in Italy, Vandelli made a rapid sketch of a rural code, whose application would be entrusted to "agrarian censors" capable of recognizing, honoring, and giving prizes to "good workers." The improvement of means of communication, and consequently a greater circulation of agricultural products, was to accompany their work. Nor would one any longer see, although it was still present in Alentejo, peasants' limiting cultivation to only what was "necessary for the support of the inhabitants" or transforming cultivated land into pasturage.[44] Agriculture should be preferred to factories, he insisted in another work.[45] But he did not forget to study crops that would be capable of providing raw materials for industries.[46] The same tone was adopted in the memoirs

---

[42] See his "Memoria sobra a utilidade dos jardins botanicos," in D. Vandelli, *Diccionario dos terminos technicos de historia natural* (Coimbra: Na real officina da universidade, 1788), pp. 293ff., and *Dominici Vandelli . . . viridarium Grisley lusitanicum linneanis nominibus illustratum, jussu Academiae in lucem editum* (Olisipone: Ex typ. R. Acad. Scientiarum olisiponensis, 1789).

[43] "Memoria sobre a ferrugem das oliveiras," in *Memorias economicas*, vol. 5 (1815), p. 8.

[44] "Sobre a agricultura deste reino e das suas conquistas," ibid., pp. 184ff.

[45] "Memoria sobre a preferencia que em Portugal se deve dar á agricultura sobre as fabricas," ibid., pp. 244ff.

[46] "Memoria sobre as producções naturaes do reino e das conquistas, primeiras materias de differentes fabricas ou manufacturas" (ibid., pp. 223ff.). On the problems Vandelli raised in this and other writings, see Jorge Borges de Macedo, *Problemas de história da*

of other collaborators in the same first volume of the *Memorias economi-cas*. Rodrigo di Sousa Coutinho, the politician and economist who had been the Portuguese ambassador in Turin, wrote about mines. Others polemicized against luxury or inquired into the cause of their compatri-ots' small desire to work. Genovesi and the physiocrat Boesnier de l'Orme were cited in similar simple and solid anti-mercantilist sermons. More technical, but still interesting, were the two memoirs of Vandelli inserted in the second volume, which appeared in 1790, on plants that could serve for the manufacture of hats and on the bitumen and petrol that could be extracted in Portugal.[47] There was also a long memoir by Giovanni Antonio Della Bella on the manufacture of oil. One year later Vandelli was occupied with dredging a river and cited Italians who had been occupied with the same problem: Zendrini, Michelotti, Alberti, Frisi, and Fantoni.[48] The rock salt of the islands of Cape Verde attracted his attention in volume 4, which came out in 1812.[49] It was little more than a page. But even this seemed to him a subject worthy "of a citizen philosopher." As one sees, the spirit of the naturalist, curious about ev-erything that could be useful, did not abandon him when the Portu-guese government, considering him too enthusiastic about France and Napoleon, confined him to the island of Terceira in the Azores. Then he went to London and returned to Lisbon in 1815, where he died past the age of eighty, on 27 June 1816.[50]

At the end of 1776 Pombal focused for a moment on what was hap-pening in the kingdom of Charles III: after thirteen years of rule Gri-maldi had fallen. To be sure, this was not done to displease him. But

---

indústria portuguesa no século XVIII (Lisbon: Associação industrial portuguesa. Estudos de economia aplicada, 1963), pp. 217ff.

[47] Vandelli was vividly interested in mining problems, especially in Brazil. In 1790, he collaborated actively in the effort to train up-to-date technicians by sending youths to Sax-ony, Bohemia, and Hungary. See Maxwell, *Conflicts and Conspiracies*, p. 178.

[48] "Memoria sobre o encanamento do rio Mondego," in *Memorias economicas*, vol. 3 (1791), p. 22 n. 1.

[49] "Memoria sobre o sal gemma das ilbas de Cabo Verde," ibid., vol. 4 (1812), pp. 65ff.

[50] Longo, "Domenico Vandelli," p. 407. Facing p. 406 of this article is a letter from Lisbon dated 2 April 1777 in which one sees how Vandelli accepted with good grace the changed situation after Pombal's death: "The beginnings of a happy government," he said. It was in fact the beginning of the period in which he hoped to have more influence on the economic policy of the country and he worked, as we have seen, in this direction. There is little of interest in "Del dottore Vandelli iuniore modenese," in *Notizie biografiche in continuazione della Biblioteca modenese del cavalier abate Girolamo Tiraboschi* (Reggio: Rotti-giani, 1835), vol. 4, pp. 423ff.

who would be his successor? The name that came most spontaneously to everyone's lips was the Count of Aranda. This was precisely "one of those whom he feared the most."[1] Everyone, foreigners and Spaniards, in the embassies and chanceries, from the sovereign to dignitaries in the provinces, knew that the selection of the successor to Grimaldi would weigh heavily on the fate of Spain, which was now nearing the onset of war. Grimaldi's successor would have to confront serious and complex problems within the country and abroad: the future of the struggle against the Inquisition and the excessive power of the clergy, and the future of the economic and administrative reforms that had been undertaken, but certainly not concluded in the twenty years that had passed since King Charles had arrived from Naples in 1759. These questions were closely connected with the consolidation and perhaps expansion of Spain's role in the world: against pirates in the western Mediterranean, and beyond the seas in its immense American colonies. In Europe, the kingdom of Charles III now seemed to have reached the conclusion of the long and difficult period of revival and reaffirmation that had begun in the period of the War of Spanish Succession, in the first years of the century.[2] Now it was no longer just a question of retaking Gibraltar and Minorca (even if the attention and passions of many Spaniards were fixed on these limited objectives), but also of opening a way between hostile England and France, which was both a model and a rival. At the bottom of this quest was a more general need, an insistent search, appearing under different forms, for the mission of Spanish life of the past and the future. This was no longer simply, as in the first part of the century, a search for causes of the decline of Spain. The emphasis was now on revival and on an effort to penetrate more deeply into the nature and history of the nation. The crisis of reforms was developing as a crisis of identity. This was the complex problem that Grimaldi's successor would have to confront.

The choice of Aranda would mean giving preference to the most European and cosmopolitan candidate, the central figure in the struggle against clerical interference who was tied to the military nobility. It would mean choosing the leader of the Aragonese party, a group with indefinite boundaries but that appealed to that sense of independence and pride which was an irreducible element in the life of the nation. Legends have gathered around this man: it is not true that he was the

[1] Turin, AS, *Lettere ministri, Portogallo*, mazzo 8, 19 November 1776.

[2] Henry Kamen, *The War of Succession in Spain, 1700–1715* (London: Weidenfeld and Nicholson, 1969). On the Italian presence in Spain in the early eighteenth century see Franco Venturi, "L'Italia fuori d'Italia," in *Storia d'Italia*, vol. 3, *Dal primo settecento all'unità* (Turin: Einaudi, 1973), pp. 1004ff.

creator of the central Masonic lodge of Madrid; nor is it exactly true
that he had shone in Parisian salons (he was never sufficiently familiar
with French for this to have been possible). But his libertine tendencies
were appreciated by Voltaire, who did everything to attempt to attract
him as a follower. And, above all, it had been Aranda—as everyone remembered—who, *manu militari*, had banished the Jesuits from Spain on
the night of 2–3 April 1767.[3] This was a central event of eighteenth-
century Spanish history, corresponding to and paralleling to what Pombal had done in Portugal. But Pombal, after having destroyed the Jesuits, had continued to govern his country for twenty years, while Aranda
had soon been distanced from the center of power and made ambassador to Paris. In 1776 the ruin of the Jesuits was a thing of the past,
discussed or admired, but no longer serving as the basis for a new policy. To the hard and violent impression that Pombal had made in Portugal there was no similar act by Aranda or by any other political figure
in Spain. A variety of tendencies always remained in the reform movement. Its continuity was ensured by Charles III, through the stormy
incidents of his reign. Aranda did not have the place of prime minister,
but rather that of head of the opposition, to the extent that this could
exist in an absolute monarchy, the man, that is, through whom intrigues
directed against those in control of the government tended to be focused.[4] Only in 1792, when the sovereign changed, did he return to the
center of political life. But by then the situation had become quite different.

Fifteen years earlier, in 1776, not to choose Campomanes, the other
great personage in Spanish life, meant rejecting the only man capable
of showing a way to resolve the polemic on the property of the clergy
and the relationship between church and state, or of undertaking a new,
more harmonious reform program. Among the different possible candidates Campomanes was the most learned and intelligent.[5] He stood
for the agrarian academies appearing everywhere, and he was a focus
of the desire for political improvement and economic transformation.
Culturally, Campomanes was broadly open to European thought and
strongly attracted to the study of the past of his country. He had great

---

[3] Venturi, *Settecento riformatore* 2, pp. 56ff. Numerous recent works on Aranda are
listed in José A. Ferrer Benimeli, *La masonería española en el siglo XVIII* (Mexico D.F.: Siglo
veintiuno editores, 1974), pp. 481ff. See above all Rafael Olaechea and José A. Ferrer
Benimeli, *El conde de Aranda. Mito y realidad de un político aragonés* (Saragossa: Colección
Aragón, 1978).

[4] See the interesting dispatch of Count Masino, Turin, AS, *Lettere ministri*, Spagna
mazzo 89, 9 March 1778.

[5] See the lengthy review of recent studies by Girolamo Imbruglia, "Qualche nota sul
conte di Campomanes," *R. stor. ital.* year 94, fasc. 1 (April 1982): 204ff.

experience and had already shown a firmness in difficult situations, like the one that accompanied and immediately followed the expulsion of the Jesuits.[6] One could say without attempting to be paradoxical that he was too vigorous a reformer to govern in a period of reform crises.[7] Spain in 1776 was preparing not for a new effort in its institutional transformation, but rather for a difficult and risky war, which would oblige it to detach its attention from internal problems and concentrate instead on its immense empire, threatened by English attack and by the example of the British colonies beyond the sea.

Thus Count Floridablanca was chosen; he had not fought against the Jesuits but had contributed to persuading the pope to suppress the Company of Jesus. He was a diplomat and financial expert, obstinate and hardheaded, well thought of at court and among the embassies, but largely unknown to European public opinion. The son of a notary, educated in the world of the law, a typical petty lawyer (or, as the Spanish say, *golilla*), José Moñino had been made ambassador to Rome in 1772, and because of his success there the king had made him Count of Floridablanca.[8] The *Courier de l'Europe*, the French gazette in London, thought these were two different persons when it reported the succession of Grimaldi, and then it publicly apologized.[9] Italians saw him making his voyage from Rome toward Madrid and received with honor in Bologna and Parma. In Genova, despite his being incognito, many nobles courted him, and offered him a "splendid banquet."[10] Nothing about the ideas or plans of this great figure appeared. The reports from Spain in Italian gazettes did not touch on him. There was disquieting

[6] Venturi, *Settecento riformatore* 2, pp. 44ff.

[7] See Laura Rodríguez, *Reforma e Ilustración en la España del siglo XVIII. Pedro Rodríguez de Campomanes* (Madrid: Fundación universitaria española. Seminario Cisneros, 1975). For a general picture of the economic and administrative problems of Spain in the seventies, see the fine pages by Raymond Carr, *Spain: 1808–1975* (Oxford: Clarendon Press, 1982), pp. 22ff.

[8] Venturi, *Settecento riformatore* 2, pp. 45ff. On Floridablanca see Cayetano Alcázar, "Ideas políticas de Floridablanca. Del despotismo ilustrado a la revolución francesa y Napoleón (1766–1808)," *Revista de estudios políticos*, no. 79 (January 1955): 35ff. It is difficult to speak of Floridablanca without thinking of the extraordinary portrait of him by Goya: a court mannequin with a solid and an intelligent head. See José Gudiol, *Goya. 1746–1828. Biografía, estudio analítico y catálogo de sus pinturas* (Barcelona: Ediciones Polígrafa, 1980), vol. 1, plates 135–36.

[9] *Courier de l'Europe*, no. 15, 20 December 1777, p. 21 (Bologna, 6 January), and no. 18, 31 December 1776, p. 137 (Madrid, 3 December). On his appointment, see *Notizie del mondo*, no. 95, 26 November 1776, p. 733 (Madrid, 10 October).

[10] *Notizie del mondo*, no. 3, 11 January 1777, p. 21 (Bologna, 6 January); no. 33, 18 January 1777, p. 37 (Parma, 9 January), and p. 38 (Genova, 11 January). It seems that he took this long land journey because he was afraid of the sea. Turin, AS, *Lettere ministri, Spagna*, mazzo 88, 16 December 1776.

news. From Madrid the following report came: "We have learned not without surprise from some public sheets that several respected public figures have been arrested," among whom was Campomanes himself. But these were lies. "This wise and learned minister enjoys the full support of His Catholic Majesty and continues in his high office."[11] In the summer the assurances were reconfirmed by an illustrious Venetian patrician traveling across Spain. "The minister Campomanes, who is well known in Italy for his largesse," Cavalier Francesco Pesaro wrote in the summer of 1777, "is a man who unites with the solid principles of his profession a vast learning, great knowledge of history, and deep knowledge of different languages: Hebrew, Greek, Latin, Arabic, besides French, English, and Italian. I see him almost every evening in the house of the Duke of Medina Sidonia, where a small company of erudite men meets, by whom I am honored with admittance." In Spain, "good books" were "very well known." "There is no lack of singular talents, which would develop more if they were not impeded by superstition and fear of the Inquisition."[12]

Two years earlier Campomanes had succeeded in having a Castilian version of Beccaria published. Now, in the summer of 1777, the counteroffensive of the Inquisition grew stronger.[13] The *Courier de l'Europe* wrote that the struggle between the Council of Castile and the Holy Office was being decided in favor of the latter. "Consequently, in all the parish churches a long list of books is read that are forbidden or to be forbidden if their authors refuse to make corrections; among this second group one notices sadly the celebrated work of Marquis Beccaria on crimes and punishments. It is unclear how it could be corrected without taking what is most precious from it." Other prohibitions of the Inquisition had worsened "the languishing state" in which Spanish literature found itself. A sense of resignation was spreading. "Honest and enlightened men would like things to be different, but the general spirit of the nation opposes the granting of their wish."[14] Still, there were some symptoms of revival and vigor. William Robertson was elected a member of the Academy of History and there was talk of a translation

[11] *Nuove di diverse corti e paesi*, no. 7, 17 February 1777, p. 52 (Madrid, 28 January).

[12] *Alcune lettere inedite d'illustri veneziani a Clemente Sibiliato* (Padova: Cartellieri e Sicco, 1839), p. 7, Madrid, 29 July 1777.

[13] Cesare Beccaria, *Dei delitti e delle pene. Con una raccolta di lettere e documenti relativi alla nascita dell'opera e della sua fortuna nell'Europa del Settecento*, ed. F. Venturi (Turin: Einaudi, 1965), pp. 567ff.

[14] *Courier de l'Europe*, no. 18, 1 August 1777 (Madrid, 29 June). On the methods and results of the Holy Office, see Marcelin Defourneaux, *L'inquisition espagnole et le livre français au XVIIIe siècle* (Paris: PUF, 1963).

of his *History of Charles V.* "He is thought to be the first Protestant to whom Spain has given literary honors," the *Courier de l'Europe* noted.[15]

But what did this matter in comparison with the catastrophe of 14 November 1776, that is, the arrest and imprisonment by the Inquisition of Pablo Olavide? Some months before, the *Gazzetta universale* had sung his praises, saying that he was "born in Spanish America, in the kingdom of Peru, but had come to Europe and was much traveled in France, Holland, England, etc., a man of merit, and of much talent and education."[16] Then, for a long time, a heavy silence surrounded him. It was not until January 1779 that the gazette of Venice announced his condemnation. "At last sentence was pronounced on the 24th of last month in the famous affair against Sig. Pablo Olavide, one of the magistrates of the city of Seville, accused of novelties in matters of religion and as such declared a heretic and schismatic, condemned to lose his office and all the honors attached to it, and also to be exiled in perpetuity from the province where he lived, with the order to inhabit a monastery until new disposition is made."[17] The *Courier de l'Europe* felt "a terrible repugnance in publishing" the news. But now it had circulated in "all the public sheets of Europe." Why hide the fact that Olavide had been condemned to be publicly whipped, and that this sentence had been reduced to confinement in a monastery for eight years? "Two monks constantly keep him company to guide his conscience and make him recite the rosary, read holy legends, etc." How could this have happened? The court, the nobility, the "healthy part of the nation," was not responsible for what had happened. Letters from Spain agreed that "everyone shuddered, but. . . ."[18] Some time later, a correspondent attempted in vain to justify what had happened in Spain by recalling that there were numerous political prisoners in Venice, as there were at Vincennes and in the Bas-

[15] *Courier de l'Europe*, no. 41, 21 October 1777, p. 326 (London, 21 October).

[16] *Gazzetta universale*, no. 90, 9 November 1776, p. 718 (Malaga, 20 March 1776), letter written by Cav. D. Vincenzo Imperiali to the Duca di Belforte, his friend in Naples.

[17] *Notizie del mondo [V.]*, no. 1, 2–23 January 1779, p. 3 (Madrid, 6 December). The same correspondence was already published in the *Gazzetta universale*, no. 101, 19 December 1778, p. 801 (Madrid, 2 December). See no. 103, 16 December 1778, p. 817 (Madrid, 8 December): "The tearful departure for prison of D. P. Olavide should be a great example for his followers." He was confined in "a monastery of reformed Franciscan friars, located in the middle of a forest on a mountain called S. Pio di Sagim, where he must remain for seven years."

[18] *Courier de l'Europe*, no. 3, 8 January 1779, pp. 21ff. The reaction of the generation that had expelled the Jesuits and hoped for reforms is well represented by what Azara wrote from Rome: "Is it possible that we still see things like what happened to Olavide? I am not his friend, but my humanity makes me shed tears of blood" (*El espíritu de don José Nicolás de Azara descubierto en su correspondencia epistolar con don Manuel de Roda* [Madrid: J. Martín Alegría, 1846], vol. 3, p. 57, 5 December 1776).

tille.[19] Still, there was something absolutely exceptional in the case of
Olavide. When he finally succeeded in escaping to France he was not
extradited: even Vergennes and Louis XVI recognized that he was not
a criminal. Grimm and Diderot helped to make this victim of the Inquisition known everywhere.[20] We find his pathetic victimized figure even
in the chronicle of the Florentine *Notizie del mondo*: "In the walks of the
Palais Royale one sees with pleasure Sig. Olavide, the intendant of Sierra Morena, who is known not so much for his wit and talent as for his
misfortunes."[21] He refused to become a symbol of enlightenment and
finally gave in to that devotion which had surrounded him for many
years and eventually suffocated him. If not his ideas, at least his sufferings left an indelible mark on the image of Spain under Charles III.

An episode of much less importance, but that was also indicative of
the climate that was emerging at the end of the seventies, involved the
Bolognese monk Cesareo Pozzi. He was the son of Giuseppe, the personal doctor of Benedict XIV, president of the Institute of Bologna and
professor in the Sapienza of Rome, and had grown up in the most cultivated part of the Papal states, occupying himself with mathematics and
physics and creating an encyclopedic culture for himself. He had become part of the small select congregation of Benedictines of Monte
Oliveto, ultimately becoming the abbot. In 1769 he was asked to deliver
an oration in honor of Pope Ganganelli, Clement XIV. After long years
of reaction against the pressing anticlerical policies of different European states, this pope gave a hint of hope for a return to the policy of
Benedict XIV. Father Cesareo Pozzi was optimistic. "The prudence and
knowledge" of Clement XIV promised "to the universe to restore the
throne of Peter to the brightness of its ancient light, dissipating those
dark intervening clouds that lightly surround and obscure it, reducing
the present tempestuous and uncertain times to times of serenity and
concord."[22] "Our high pontiff," he assured his listeners, "is an enlightened genius, capable of seeing things in their true light."[23] He was proposing an entire program of renewal: "Restoration of roads, correction
of rivers, growth in number of inhabitants, favorable exchange rates,
equitable circulation of gold and silver." He indicated that the agrarian
societies were the best instruments to carry out this policy. The "illustri-

---

[19] *Courier de l'Europe*, no. 12, 9 February 1779, p. 89.

[20] Marcelin Defourneaux, *Pablo de Olavide ou l'afrancesado (1725–1803)* (Paris: PUF,
1951), pp. 399ff.

[21] *Notizie del mondo*, no. 52, 30 June 1781, p. 412 (Paris, 12 June).

[22] *Al beatissimo e santissimo papa e signor nostro Clemente decimoquarto, Orazione di D. Cesareo Pozzi . . . , detta in laude di lui e de' pregi suoi nell'Accademia delle scienze di Bologna il dí nove
di novembre dell'anno 1769* (Bologna: Lelio della Volpe, 1769), p. 4.

[23] Ibid., p. 19.

ous societies of Brittany, Paris, Berne, Zurich, and other most learned European academies" had emphasized the central importance of agriculture. Their call should not be without a response. "Even the academies of the Papal Sates, moved by such significant examples, apply themselves to physical and mechanical experiments with our climate and soil." Without forgetting "the ornament of the liberal arts," "we have as a primary objective the happiness and wealth of individuals." "The literary society of Dublin, with its agricultural maps, has changed the face of Ireland. . . . Does not our part of the Italian people think, reflect, calculate, strive?" "Many observations, considerable machines, and many books are needed for this."[24]

This rosy, bombastic, but clearly sincere zeal was still alive in the soul of Father Pozzi when, after being in Vienna in 1771, he arrived in Madrid at the end of 1778 in the suite of the nuncio Nicola Colonna di Stigliano.[25] The Spain of Campomanes must have seemed to him an excellent place to carry out his work as heir and continuer of the age of Benedict XIV. He took the motto of the work he was writing, which appeared at Madrid in 1778, from the *Industria popular*: "Men were born with the necessity to work."[26] A voluntary increase in work was in fact the central element in his thought, which was intended to reform the traditional preparation of monks so as to make them "useful to common society." It was not a great book. It had the defect of all improvements and compromises: it sought more concession than conviction. After many pages where the precepts of the Counter-Reformation were diluted in a flowery, cheerful style, one came to the second part of the work, an "Essay on Monastic Education with Regard to the Cultivation of the Sciences," where, even in religious matters, he recommended to put aside "a spirit of bias and partisanship." Youths should be persuaded that "truth almost always escapes the impetus of judgments founded on a party spirit, but it is never a stranger to modest reason, which advances slowly and passes successively through all the levels of

---

[24] Ibid., p. 21.

[25] *Notizie degli scrittori bolognesi, raccolte da Giovanni Fantuzzi* (Bologna: S. Tommaso d'Aquino, 1789), vol. 7, p. 91.

[26] *Saggio di educazione claustrale per li giovani che entrano nei noviziati religiosi, accomodato alli tempi presenti affinché colla pietà, coll'esempio e con le scienze ben coltivate si rendino utili alla pubblica società, dedicato a sua eccellenza reverendissima monsignor don Nicola Colonna de prencipi di Stigliano, arcivescovo di Sebaste e nunzio apostolico appresso S.M. il re cattolico Carlo III*, di don Cesareo Pozzi, abbate della Congregazione benedettina di Monte Oliveto, professore di mattematica nella università della Sapienza di Roma, esaminatore dei vescovi, bibliotecario della biblioteca Imperiali, corrispondente con le piú celebri accademie d'Europa (Madrid: Don Antonio de Sancha, 1778), p. ii.

light of which it is capable."[27] Such modesty would be a help in rejecting "frivolous, useless, and irreligious books."[28] Even in learning Latin one should put aside all useless erudition, following the example of what "Don Juan de Yriarte," a Spanish writer, librarian of the library of His Highness "and his nephew Tomás de Yriarte," had written.[29] This method had permitted "Signora Maria Emanuela Pignatelli Gonzaga, Duchess of Villahermosa," to arrive at a deep knowledge of the classics.[30] Latin, Greek, and Hebrew should thus be taught without pedantry. The concessions made to the opinions of the time in the pages devoted to moral and political philosophy were even stronger. "Happiness is that end to which men aspire, and politics is in general the art of arriving at this end."[31] Ecclesiastical and civil history was at the center of his program of education, and he did not close his eyes to heretics, not even to "the Socinian authors called Polish brothers," always, to be sure, with the end of "knowing better the force and solidity of those who have refuted them."[32] A lengthy bibliography was added to this eclectic pedagogical outline.

It was surprising that a book of this kind should provoke such a scandal. It had been published with the permission of academicians, ministers, and inquisitors. There had even been an official invitation to have it translated into Castilian. The gazette of Lugano announced that the king of Spain had awarded Father Pozzi "with the honorific post of adviser to the Inquisition, and he was added to the censors of the press, a position infrequently given to Italians."[33] But everything collapsed when Juan Baptista Muñoz, the chief cosmographer of the Indies, set about weaving what Father Pozzi called "a dirty intrigue" against him.[34] He accused him publicly of having plagiarized a whole series of irreligious authors and of having thus distributed in Spain the ideas of the century. He had correspondents write to him from England and France that he ran the risk of being burned as a heretic. He accused

[27] Ibid., pp. 128ff.
[28] Ibid., p. 135.
[29] Ibid., p. 143.
[30] Ibid., p. 144.
[31] Ibid., p. 179.
[32] Ibid., p. 194.

[33] *Nuove di diverse corti e paesi*, no. 49, 8 December 1777, p. 380 (Madrid, 11 November).

[34] *Apologia del p. Cesareo Pozzi abbate della Congregazione benedettina di Monte Oliveto d'Italia scritta in difesa del suo libro intitolato Saggio di educazione claustrale contro l'impugnazione del signor Giambattista Mugnos intitolata Juicio* (Perpignano: Claude Le Comte, 1780), unpaginated. The work of Muñoz was translated into Italian with the title *Giudizio scritto per l'onore della letteratura spagnola contro il trattato d'educazione di R.D.C. Pozzi* by Francesco Gusta, whom we have seen as the biographer of Pombal, and was published in Ravenna.

him of denigrating literature and the Spanish nation. Before such an attack Father Pozzi collapsed "into apoplexy, without words and with half of his body numb," as he himself wrote.[35] Denounced by the Inquisition, deprived of all support, he could find no other route than to abandon Spain, and he took refuge in Perpignan. From there he wrote to the Venetian, Austrian, and Sardinian ambassadors, to Floridablanca, to Campomanes, and even "to the literary men of Turin from whom he had always received the greatest kindness and honesty." He sought aid and protection from the theologians of Pisa, Padova, and Milan, not to mention his justification to the Spanish Inquisition. He could not understand why such a storm was raised by a work of which only three hundred copies had been printed and only forty-five or fifty had circulated in Spain. Without success, he continually advised himself to follow the example of the patience shown by Feijoo, also a Benedictine, when he had been attacked. All was in vain. When he finally reached Italy, also "to consult its chief doctors," he was unable to recover his position, and he died in 1782.[36]

It was a clash of temperaments. Father Pozzi never succeeded in understanding that there was "still in Europe a land where for some, although few, the example of the infinite goodness by which they are surrounded neither restrains nor corrects them, but they are nurtured, enjoy, and amuse themselves by doing evil to others."[37] It was a clash above all of national character. Father Pozzi had difficulties, for example, defending himself by assuring Campomanes of "the sincere attachment he had always had for Spanish literature, whose profundity and penetration he had perhaps unduly exaggerated." Such justifications were worthless. He found unleashed against him "malevolence, hatred, and fanaticism," and all this "for being a foreigner," as one attempting to defend him noted when he arrived in Italy.[38] The expulsion of Father Pozzi from Spain was, in short, an incident in the multiform dispute on the past and present of Spain becoming widely diffused in Europe of those years. There was undoubtedly an element of religious fanaticism. His placing himself under the protection of Campomanes was not an advantage, and was even considered "one of his greatest crimes." "Some miserable Valencians had the courage to tell me so to my face."[39] But

[35] Ibid.

[36] Fantuzzi, *Notizie degli scrittori bolognesi,* p. 92.

[37] *Apologia del p. D. Cesareo Pozzi.*

[38] *Estratto del libro intitolato Saggio di educazione claustrale del p. abate D. Cesareo Pozzi della congregazione benedittina di Monte Oliveto e della sua Apologia contro l'impugnazione del sig. Giovanni Mugnoz, cosmografo maggiore delle Indie levato tutto alla lettera da una gazzetta uscita in Italia a difesa dello stesso libro* (Mantova, 1780), p. 34.

[39] *Apologia del p. D. Cesareo Pozzi.*

what counted most was a personal and political rejection of that soft indulgence, that broad eclecticism, which Father Pozzi thought possible to transplant outside of Italy and which was so contrary to Spanish traditions and temperament.[40] Even José Nicolas de Azara, an open and a cultivated man who had been much involved in the struggle against the Jesuits, fully approved Muñoz's attack and said that "Pozzi will always be a disgrace to men of reason," thus reacting violently to the echoes that reached him in Rome from Bologna of the "horrors Pozzi relates about Spain and the Spanish."[41]

If the condemnation of Olavide and the persecution of Pozzi were defeats for the Spanish enlightenment, the rise and development of patriotic societies, or friends of the country, as they were generally called, instead marked its victories.[42] Reflecting in their origins the Academy of the Georgofili in Florence, and above all French and Swiss agricultural societies, the Spanish academies distinguished themselves for the great variety of their activities and, in relation to their origins and locations, the local roots they succeeded in developing.[43]

Italians, who were undergoing a similar experience, were from the beginning rather curious about what they learned about the "amigos del país." In 1773 their activity in Galicia was noted in Milan. "The Royal Academy of Agriculture of Galicia has awarded the prizes promised last year consisting of a gold medal one ounce in weight showing a bust of His Majesty with the legend *Carolus III Aug. P.P. Rei Rusticae Patron*. On the reverse is a chalice with a Host, over which one reads *In Ubertate*

---

[40] The condemnation by the Holy Office, "most vigilant in preserving the rights and maxims of the court of Rome," of Pozzi's *Saggio* and *Apologia* was reported in the *Gazzetta universale*, no. 47, 12 June 1787, p. 369 (Madrid, 29 May).

[41] *El espíritu de don José Nicolás de Azara*, vol. 3, p. 246, 13 May 1779, and p. 325, 6 April 1780.

[42] Gonzalo Anes Álvarez, "Coyuntura económica e 'ilustración': las sociedades de amigos del país," in *Economía e 'Ilustración' en la España del siglo XVIII* (Barcelona: Ediciones Ariel, 1969), pp. 11ff. There is a valuable collection of data by Paula de Demerson, Jorge Demerson, and Francisco Aguilar Piñal, *Las Sociedades Económicas de Amigos del País en el siglo XVIII. Guía del investigador* (San Sebastian, 1974). (The general bibliography naturally begins with Campomanes, and then details are provided for more than a hundred of these societies.)

[43] On the initial relations between the Florentine academies and those of Madrid, see the letter by Ricardo Wall da Aranjuez, of 8 June 1756, in which he gives thanks for information received from Florence on "the institution, method, and progress of studies" of the Georgofili, which he calls "an important idea," promising to utilize it for the "royal service" (Florence, Accademia dei Georgofili, Mss Bl I, sez. III, 11.

Felicitas (Happiness in abundance), which is the aim of the academy, and around it *Reg. Academia Callaica Anno VIII Industr. Proem.*"[44] In the *Efemeridi letterarie di Roma*, in the summer of 1773, there was a lengthy review of the "efforts of the general assembly held by the Basque Royal Society of friends of the country in the city of Bilbao in September 1772."[45] Echoes continued in the following years. "The Society of Biscay *de los amigos del país*," one reads in the spring of 1775 in a Florentine gazette, had obtained permission to form "a company for the purpose of fishing for cod along the Cantabrian coast."[46] The same sheet announced one year later that the "Economic society of Madrid of the *amigos del país* has recently established four patriotic schools to teach the method of spinning linen, hemp, cotton, and wool for the greater advantage of the public placed in four different quarters of the city."[47] As one sees, these were quite varied activities but united by a common spirit of enterprise. "In truth," we read further, the Society of Madrid was "called *patriotic* to encourage industry and labor." It was a patriotism that found an echo throughout the country. Thus, for example, a "praiseworthy project" begun in the capital had found imitators in the city of Jaén.[48]

Like all "patriotic" movements of the seventies and eighties—it is enough to think of one of the strongest and most active in Holland—the Spanish movement was born in the provinces and then taken in hand and utilized by the capital and the government. It developed with a not-always-easy relationship between periphery and center, between local and emerging national patriotism. The history of agrarian academies, in all of Europe, is a witness to this polarity. These organizations had given their first signs of life in Ireland and Great Britain—lands that were not central to the Enlightenment. Scotland and Berne had seen them grow and assert themselves. The French monarchy made them an instrument of government control and development. In Italy their local character was strong and their national character weak, while within individual states—Austrian Lombardy, the kingdom of Naples, even Tuscany under Peter Leopold—central control often risked im-

---

[44] *La gazzetta di Milano*, no. 13, 31 March 1773.

[45] *Efemeridi letterarie di Roma*, 28 August 1773, no. 35, pp. 275ff. This is the *Estractos de las Juntas generales celebradas por la Real sociedad bascongada de los Amicos del país en la villa de Bilbao por septiembre de 1772* (Vitoria: Tomás de Robles, 1773). On this society, the first (1763) and one of the most significant, see Demerson et al., *Las Sociedades Ecomómicas*, pp. 357ff. On the importance of these *Estractos*, see Ramón Carande, "El despotismo ilustrado de los amigos del país," in *Estudios de historia de España* (Barcelona: Ariel, 1969), pp. 154ff.

[46] *Notizie del mondo*, no. 38, 13 May 1775, p. 297 (Madrid, 25 April).

[47] Ibid., no. 64, 10 August 1776, p. 485 (Madrid, 23 July 1776).

[48] Ibid., no. 28, 8 April 1777, p. 218 (Madrid, 25 March).

poverishing and suffocating local spontaneous initiative. In Spain, the
friends of the country got under way in the Basque region, through the
work of Xavier Maria de Munibe, Count of Peñaflorida, who for his
culture and tenacity was the exemplary figure of the whole movement.
The local element was very strong (even the symbol of the Society, three
joined hands, bore the motto in Basque *Iruras bat*, Three are one), and
the regional organization, based on the alternate leadership of the centers Vitoria, San Sebastiano, Vergara, and Bilbao, was complex. The ed-
ucative attempt was considerable, and the ideas that circulated were
lively and modern, as the figure of Valentín de Foronda would soon
confirm.[49] But the element that impressed anyone who observed the diffusion of economic societies at the end of the seventies, more than any
specific coloration, was undoubtedly the patriotism that enfolded different local elements and extended to the country as a whole. The war
alongside France and the American insurgents evoked a deeper response than many expected. "The will of the nation to support the
rights of the Crown" was extraordinary, wrote the gazette of Lugano in
the summer of 1779. "We hear from all parts of the kingdom that measures are being taken to ascertain the extent to which patriotism dominates the nation. It extends even to women of rank, who, in imitation of
the ladies with whom they are allied, and the enemy 'Myladies,' prepare
ships for common defense."[50] This was the summer when the French
and Spanish fleets joined in the Channel to threaten invasion of Great
Britain. The news coming from beyond the ocean moved people's spirits. Closer by, domestic memories also raised the wave of patriotism.
This was all the more so because they were memories of failures, of
defeats valiantly suffered. In the summer of 1775 Algiers was assaulted
and bombarded, but without success in taking it. Such an important expedition against the Barbary pirates had not occurred for some time.[51]

[49] See the bibliography in Demerson et al., *Las Sociedades Económicas*, pp. 357ff. The
fundamental work remains that by Julio de Urquijo, *Los amigos del país (según cartas y otros
documentos inéditos del XVIII)* (San Sebastián: Imprenta de la Diputación de Guipúzcoa,
1929), where the refutation, already made by the author, of the ideas of Menéndez y
Pelayo on the heterodoxy of the educational institutions of the Basque society is taken up
again, and many curious details are provided about Count Peñaflorida and on the voyage
his son Ramón made in the seventies and the beginning of the eighties in France, Brabant,
Holland, Denmark, Sweden, Vienna, Rome, and Turin, where he was interested in many
things, but above all in science. The emphasis is chiefly on local elements in José de Aralar,
El conde de Peñaflorida y los caballeritos de Azkoitia (Buenos Aires: Editorial Vasca Ekin,
1942). A general picture is furnished in Antonio Elorza, "La Sociedad Bascongada de
Amigos del País en la Ilustración española," *Cuadernos hispano-americanos* 62, no. 185
(1965): 225ff.

[50] *Nuove di diverse corti e paesi*, no. 38, 20 September 1779, p. 300 (Madrid, 31 August).

[51] *Notizie del mondo*, no. 66, 19 August 1775, pp. 521ff. (Madrid, 1 August), "Relazione

An age-old conflict opened anew. "Everything suggests," the gazettes wrote, "that the poor success of the attack on Algiers will soon be reversed. The Tunisians, Algerians, and Moroccans, surrounded by the Mediterranean and the Ocean . . . do all they can to bring all the forces of Christianity down on them. Their corsairs attack and pillage." Against them Spain had risen: "A fine navy, a courageous and faithful nation, a wise and economical government."[52] The treaty of 1777 with Portugal concerning territories in America promised an ability to concentrate new and more important forces in the struggle against the Barbary pirates.[53] The figure of a captain came to symbolize the will of the Spanish to fight. "In Algiers the valor and bravery of Señor D. Barcelò has always been feared." Recent encounters had made him "formidable," one reads in the *Notizie del mondo* at the beginning of 1780.[54] The expertise and experience thus acquired would now be turned against the English. "The blockade of Gibraltar has been decided on by the court of Madrid," the *Courier de l'Europe* read in the summer.[55] In vain the Algerians had "attempted to enter the port of Gibraltar to unload provisions for the garrison of this place." "Few have been able to escape the vigilance of Sig. D. Barcelò, and there is such fear that none dare approach the strait where he is known to be."[56]

Thus began the obstinate battle for Gibraltar, which was destined to last for long years and to put the English ability to resist and the obstinacy of the Spanish to a hard test. It produced new naval and ballistic discoveries, involved some of the greatest names of the French aristoc-

fedele di quel che è accaduto relativamente all'apparecchiata spedizione contro gli algerini nel 1775." The following issue, 22 August 1775, p. 529 (Madrid, 8 August), contains a detailed account of the Tuscan participation in the expedition, at the cost of thirteen dead and seventy-four wounded, which merited "the greatest praise" from the commanding general.

[52] Ibid., no. 89, 7 November 1775, p. 707 (The Hague, 22 October), "Estratto d'una lettera di Madrid in data dei 19 Settembre."

[53] *Gazzetta universale*, no. 3, 10 January 1778, p. 17 (Lisbon, 9 December), "Trattato di pace de' limiti nell'America Settentrionale . . . 1 Ottobre 1777."

[54] Ibid., no. 14, 15 February 1780, p. 105 (Algiers, 3 January).

[55] *Courier de l'Europe*, no. 10, 3 August 1779, p. 73 (Cádiz, 28 June 1779). There are numerous official Spanish documents, before and after the entry into the war, in the *Notizie del mondo [V.]*, no. 84, 16–27 October 1779, p. 714, Bay of Gibraltar. At the beginning of the new year the Venetian journal emphasized how everywhere in Europe gazettes boasted of "providing information at the very moment when events occurred" and assured its readers that it had taken means to provide such expected news (ibid., no. 105, 21 December 1779–1 January 1780, p. 868, Spain). An example of reportage, from Gibraltar and on the difficulties overcome by the besieged, was a vivid and detailed diary by a woman published in the *Courier de l'Europe*, no. 14, 17 August 1781, pp. 109, "Siège de Gibraltar."

[56] *Notizie del mondo*, no. 14, 15 February 1780, p. 105 (Algiers, 3 January).

racy, among them the Count of Artois, brother of Louis XVI himself, and finally became a seemingly insurmountable obstacle for a moment in the conclusion of peace. It was the last great battle of the old regime in Europe, and in it, if one looked closely, could be perceived forces that would take on great importance in the years that followed: British intransigence, new technology, and especially the patriotism that moved the contenders, the Spanish above all with their singular mixture of aristocratic pride and popular tenacity. This surprised contemporaries and struck Europeans in general at the beginning of the new century.[57]

As the difficult years of war passed, deeper and deeper became the contradiction between the absolutism of Charles III and the ferment of revolt in the American colonies—for the independence of which this monarch nonetheless continued to fight. There was no effort in Spain— in contrast to what happened in France—to find a modus vivendi between propaganda and diplomacy, between the enthusiasm of liberation and *raison d'état*. In Spain an ever more heavy silence was imposed on this secret and burning issue. Jay, the American envoy, received "only limited politeness, being admitted nowhere." (Franklin, in this period, had become one of the poles of the intellectual and political life of Paris.) At the Spanish court the heavy reserve was sometimes theorized into an astute diplomatic expedient. A general confided one day to the Piedmontese ambassador: "The king my master will be content not to let himself be seduced by these gentlemen . . . the future peace must be made without considering their interests, but the French do not have this advantage, since they have taken them by the hand."[58] Even when peace neared Charles III continued not to want to "recognize these insurgents as a free nation."[59] Only in July 1781 did Jay, piloted by the French ambassador, begin to receive "invitations to dinners and other social events."[60] Louis XVI had made much use of La Fayette. Charles III, when it became a question of giving him Jamaica if it were seized from the English, as was expected, refused to make use of him, saying

[57] An echo of the battle for Gibraltar is in Francesco Becattini, *Storia del regno di Carlo III* (Turin: Società dei librai, 1790), vol. 2, p. 179: "In Paris, Genova, Rome, and Naples considerable bets were made against those who denied the possibility of its capture. It was interesting to see the differences of men in this matter, which reached the point of ridiculous passions and fanaticism agitating them." The *Nuovo giornale letterario d'Italia*, no. 10 (first quarter of 1788): 154, cited a work that appeared in Turin: *Elliot. Poema lirico d'un piemontese* (Stamperia reale, 1787), saying it was the work of Carlo Bossi. "The brave Elliot," it concluded, "certainly merited being celebrated by such a poet."

[58] Turin, AS, *Lettere ministri, Spagna*, mazzo 50, 3 July 1780.

[59] Ibid., 16 January 1781.

[60] Ibid., 17 July 1781.

that La Fayette "wasn't good for anything but dealing with rebels."[61]
And this was in 1782, when the "rebels" were on the eve of their victory.
Only then, in Paris, did Count Aranda "for the first time offer a dinner
to Mr. Franklin and Mr. Jay, commissioner of the Congress." "From this
our politicians deduce," the Florentine gazette read, "that Spain will not
delay in recognizing the independence of America."[62]

Despite these precautions and doubts, the worm of radicalism born
of the cobelligerence between Spain and the United States revealed itself south of the Pyrenees in a more serious way than to the north. The
French colonies were much smaller than the Spanish ones, and even if
they were discontented they did not take the route of open rebellion.
The immense possessions of Charles III were instead an enigma and all
the more disquieting for the deep silence that surrounded them.

In September 1780 news of uprisings and revolts in Spanish America began to arrive in Europe. With a letter from Montevideo, dated 3
June 1780, the *Courier de l'Europe* spoke of "a revolution broken out in
the interior of the country, because of the establishment of a royal customshouse." It was said that the natives "wanting to make *Inca* king,"
after having "cut down and trampled under their feet a portrait of
Charles III, had caused a thousand embarrassments to the Corregidors
and highly placed persons of those provinces." "One fears that the revolt," this correspondent continued, "will become general in the great
extent of this viceroyalty." Even a priest was found among the rebels.
There was only hope that the sovereign would withdraw the fiscal measures provoking the rebellion. "If he does not do so, he will lose America which cost so much blood."[63] How could one not remember how, a
few years before, fiscal and customs problems had pushed North America to revolution? In October the Venetian gazette passed on from London news of uprisings in the Spanish colonies.[64] The *Gazzetta universale*
of the same date dedicated five columns to describing what was happening there.[65] It was said two days later in Lugano that this was "very important news," if confirmed. But could it be believed? "This news, it is

[61] Antonio Ferrer del Río, *Historia del reinado de Carlos III en España* (Madrid: Matute
y Compagni, 1856), vol. 3, p. 395.

[62] *Notizie del mondo*, no. 60, 27 July 1782, p. 473 (Paris, 16 July). Little is contained in
Mario Rodríguez, *La revolución americana del 1776 y el mundo hispánico. Ensayos y documentos*
(Madrid: Editorial Taurus, 1976).

[63] *Courier de l'Europe*, no. 26, 29 September 1780, p. 205, "Copie d'une lettre d'un
habitant de Buenos-Aires à son frère résident à la Corogne datée de Montevideo, 3 Juin
1780."

[64] *Notizie del mondo [V.]*, no. 81, 14 October 1780, p. 648, "Continuation of the news
from London of 26 September."

[65] *Gazzetta universale*, no. 83, 14 October 1780, p. 661 (Arequipa in Peru, 6 March).

said, comes from Scotland by way of a Spanish ship heading from
Buenos Aires to Cartagena that was taken as a prize to Glasgow." It
seemed that the uprising had begun in La Paz on 25 March, "and from
there soon spread to Arequipa, Cuzco, Cochambamba, to Potosí, and to
all of Paraguay." Already an ex-Jesuit who had "excited the people to
revolt" had been captured and taken to Spain.[66] Soon there was a correction: "One begins to suspect that the reporter in Glasgow was amus-
ing himself by moving the scene of North America to the south."[67] In
Madrid, the "gazette of the court" admitted that "among the upland
people of this immense province" there had been "frequent disturbances of small consequence," which had given "some slight grounds to
the exaggerated reports given out in London," but it declared "totally
false" the reports of new customs or taxes imposed in these lands. "On
the contrary," there were "precise orders to remove various taxes and
abuses harmful to the inhabitants." "All the subjects of those parts are
currently happy with Spanish rule. In Lima, Cuzco, and other principal
cities there is the greatest tranquillity, and in the kingdom of Chile,
where previously the Araucanians had been hostile to European laws,
now for some time, having become more cultivated, they have begun to
send their eldest sons to Spanish schools and colleges, and in the present
war have offered to defend the coasts of the monarchy against any foreign invasion."[68] But it was not possible to sustain this official line of
defense. It soon became necessary to give in to the need to provide a
version of what had happened through the publication of a letter from
Arequipa dated 26 January, which the gazette of Lugano hastened to
translate. The customshouse was in fact assaulted, many papers were
burnt, and four thousand pesos were taken. On the following night,
"there was a disorderly uprising of plebs in the city and a sacking of the
house of the Corregidor that did not leave a stone standing." A cloth
shop was also attacked. "On the 16th the city, that is, the nobility, put
itself in the best state of defense, and a company of nobles was formed
under the command of Arrambide and another of grenadiers under the
command of Solares." Two watches were established. There were in fact
"two groups, one against the customshouse, and the other made up of
individuals and plebs against the Corregidor and other subjects." "Despite the defense established on the 16th, about 800 Indians of the pampas attacked at about ten at night" and were defeated only after several
encounters. "By one o'clock at night there were no more heads of Indi-

[66] *Nuove di diverse corti e paesi*, no. 42, 16 October 1780, p. 332 (London, 26 September).

[67] Ibid., no. 43, 23 October 1780, p. 342 (London, 6 October).

[68] Ibid., no. 47, 20 November 1780, pp. 371ff. (Madrid, 24 October).

ans in the pampas, and on the 17th, at dawn, four companies attacked the tepees of the pampas as far as Cerri, and many wounded were taken, while all fled." "Fire was set to all the tepees of the pampas and they were for the most part destroyed . . . six Indians were hanged and there are many wounded in the hospital or the prison."[69]

This was but one episode in the terrible revolution—the worst in modern Spanish colonial history—that had erupted in Peru. Slowly and in fragments came the news of Tupac Amaru, who was its leader. "He prides himself on being a descendant of the ancient Incas, and as such he is generally taken," read the Florentine *Notizie del mondo*.

Although he demonstrated an active and independent spirit, the viceroy at that time only tried to ensure his affection for the Spanish government, but as soon as he came to adulthood he withdrew to a part of the country called the Andes, between Lima and Quito, where he was recognized by an independent Peruvian tribe as their legitimate sovereign, and he has since reigned over them without being attacked or molested. Sixteen years ago he prepared an expedition against Lima, and two Jesuits were sent to prevent him; they negotiated with him for a week and in the end persuaded him to desist from his undertaking, on which occasion, being offered some small concessions, he accepted them, but he said, showing some of his own sons: "When these children become men I will not be able to content myself with so little." He occupied himself in preparing the youth of his land with military exercises.

The gazette added: "Now he is about fifty-five years old and has three sons, one of whom shows great courage and ability."[70]

He was descended in fact from the last Peruvian sovereigns and in the preceding years had done all he could to have his qualities generally recognized. His effort to protect the rights of the native caciques, whom the Spanish had preserved and inserted into their colonial structure, was thus of aristocratic origin. But from this broke out an indigenous revolt, aimed at undoing the old yoke the conquest imposed. There was no real intent of returning to the customs of the past. Tupac Amaru always sought the support and collaboration of the Creoles. Nor was the power of the church to be touched, not even, paradoxically, that of the Spanish king, whom Tupac Amaru recognized and in whose name he intended to act. His revolt was an attempt at reform. He tried to conquer what more enlightened governments held just and necessary: the

[69] Ibid., no. 48, 27 November 1780, pp. 380ff. (Madrid, 6 November).

[70] *Notizie del mondo*, no. 55, 10 July 1781, p. 433. "Extract of a letter from Bilbao in Galicia dated the seventh of the current month." *La gazzetta di Milano* had spoken of him in no. 27, 4 July 1781 (Madrid, 5 June). In Venice the *Notizie del mondo [V.]* of 14 July 1781, p. 446, published about him an "Extract of a letter from Buenos Aires dated 24 January."

reorganization of local administration, the abolition of the *mita*, forced labor, and finally the *reparto*, that is, the obligation to buy goods imported by the state, a kind of gabelle and the source of infinite abuses.[71] These were moments for Peru of both commercial development and economic crisis. The shadow of the past had not yet disappeared and new ideas had barely begun to penetrate. The contrast with the Creoles, the *criollos*, that is, local whites and privileged functionaries from Spain, was already bitter, but not enough to lead to a generalized movement for independence.[72] The revolution of Tupac Amaru was thus a *unicum* that was not later repeated. The whites, when they shook the government of Madrid from their backs forty years later, took care not to appeal to the myths of the Incas or to the rebellion of their descendants. The revolt of Tupac Amaru was an earthquake demonstrating the weaknesses of the old regime, even in the distant lands of Peru, rather than announcing a new era.[73]

Throughout Europe the events in Peru were viewed with surprise and curiosity. In Italy the ground had already been in some way prepared by the publication, in 1780, "in Cosmopoli," that is, Florence, of the *Lettere americane* by Gianrinaldo Carli, based on a rereading and reinterpretation of Garcilaso de la Vega (probably the most important text that inspired Tupac Amaru; so much so, that once he was tried the Spanish authorities attempted to prohibit its circulation). Peruvians were spoken of often even beyond this work. In 1778 Marmontel's "philosophical romance," *Les Incas, Ou la destruction de l'empire du Pérou*, had been translated. The author, the gazette that announced its publication added, "is perhaps the first among writers of second rank" and his book is "written with force, elegance, and sentiment."[74]

In Madrid, in October 1780, rumors began "of a very serious upris-

[71] For a particularly significant example of an enlightened reformer inspired by Genovesi, see Ricardo Levene, *Vida y escritos de Victorián de Vilava* (Buenos Aires: Penser, 1946).

[72] See Boleslao Lewin, "Les tendencias separatistas del movimiento de Túpac Amaru," in *Anuario del Instituto de investigaciones históricas* (Rosario: Universidad Nacional del Litoral, year 2, 1957), no. 2, pp. 175ff.

[73] See Daniel Valcárcel, *La rebelión de Túpac Amaru* (Mexico: Fondo de cultura económica, 1947), and Boleslao Lewin, *Túpac Amaru. Su época, su lucha, su hado* (Buenos Aires: Ediciones siglo veinte, 1973). For the relationship between reform and revolution see Stanley J. Stein, "Bureaucracy and Business in the Spanish Empire, 1759–1804: Failure of a Bourbon Reform in Mexico and Peru," *The Hispanic American Historical Review* 61 (February 1981): 1ff.

[74] *Gazzetta universale*, no. 75, 19 September 1778, pp. 593, 600. See Maryvonne Portal, " 'Les Incas.' De l'histoire au roman philosophique," in *De l'Encyclopédie à la Contre-Révolution. Jean-François Marmontel (1723–1799)*. Etudes réunies par J. Ehrard (Clermont and Ferrand: G. De Bussac, 1970), pp. 273ff.

ing that broke out during Holy Week in several towns in Peru, particularly at Potosi, where almost all the wealth of His Majesty is found," Cavaliere Mossi di Morani communicated in a dispatch to Turin. Officially the secret was kept, but soon the arrival of foreign gazettes brought even the Spanish up-to-date with regard to what was being said everywhere. Fantasies appeared: the revolt had extended to Paraguay, "particularly to Buenos Aires." At the head of the insurgents was a Jesuit, who, when arrested and put on a ship bound for Spain, had been liberated by the English. The only one who knew nothing about it was the king. "The king was left in ignorance of this revolution for several days since it was not known what measures to take to tell him of it." When the crown prince decided to speak to him about it, Charles III received the news "with all the Christian resignation he customarily shows."[75]

In effect, the revolt of Tupac Amaru began on 4 November 1780. The strangest legends circulated in European gazettes when they began to discuss it in the summer of the following year.[76] The Florentine *Notizie del mondo* talked at length of an English expedition to Buenos Aires, which did not succeed in contacting the insurgents.

Still in some interior provinces of Peru and La Plata there have been uprisings by subjects of low condition who, to deceive the incautious Indians, have given themselves out to be descendants of the ancient and noble caciques. There is authentic word from Buenos Aires that Field Marshal Don Giuseppe de la Valle, sent by the Viceroy Don Agostino de Járegui with a considerable body of troops, has dispersed the mutineers, who after committing many robberies, murders, and other ill deeds have gathered in good numbers in the nearly inaccessible mountains, with plenty of provisions, arms, and some artillery. Despite these obstacles, and its being the month of March, which is the hardest winter month in these regions, this general has so well disposed his troops, composed of Spaniards and indians, that the mutineers were obliged to abandon their Alps [and were defeated in the plain]. The principal leader of the insurgents, called Tupac Amaru, then fled across a river with his fast horse but was soon taken and consigned to the general by his own companions. [In a note it was said that his] true name was Joseph Cordoneanqui, Camino, and Negueruela, a native of Pampamarca in the province of Tinta, a carter by trade. To gather a party among the Indians he pretended to be a cacique from the distinguished family of Tupac-Amaru, which resides in Cuzco.[77]

Some more direct and authentic documents reached Italy, but through the chanceries rather than through the gazettes. One version of a Spanish report, for instance, reached Turin; it contained several

[75] Turin, AS, *Lettere ministri, Spagna*, mazzo 90, 24 October 1780.
[76] See, for example, *Notizie del mondo [V.]*, 14 July 1781, p. 446, "Extract of a letter from Buenos Aires dated 24 January."
[77] *Notizie del mondo*, no. 86, 27 October 1781, p. 682 (Cádiz, 30 September).

lies but also furnished the remarkable, but characteristic, text of a proclamation by Tupac Amaru of 25 November 1780. It was directed "to
Creole patriots." Thus were called, he explained, the "nationals of the
country." With them he wanted to "live as brothers united into one body
to destroy the Europeans." He threatened anyone who had not heeded
his appeal to "reduce this province to ashes." "The priests must think of
their own state, as must the religious and monasteries, its being my only
intention," he concluded, "to put an end to the bad government of so
many great assassins who rob the honey from our hives."[78]

According to the gazette of Madrid, which gave the official version
of the disturbances at the beginning of October 1781, "in some interior
provinces of Peru and the Plata region," the mutineers were "subjects of
low extraction, who to trick the gullible Indians pretended to be descendants of the ancient and noble Indian chiefs." Tupac Amaru himself was
in reality a half-breed who pretended to be a cacique and to belong to
the "distinguished family from Cuzco." The rebels had been driven out
of the mountains. Their leaders had been treated "according to the
enormity of their crimes."[79] Again in February 1782 news that an ex-
Jesuit had been the leader of the Peruvian insurgents circulated from
Cologne to Venice. "We are assured that this Pasquale Ausmendi is a
true ex-Jesuit from Cantabria." After having lived for "twenty-four
years in Chile, he currently lives quietly in the city of Pesaro in Italy at
the age of 70 years."[80]

It is clear that the revolt in Peru interested Spanish Jesuits exiled in
Italy. Many of them had come from America and continued to occupy
themselves with the historical and economic problems of that land.[81]
Through them Italians, and then Europeans, came to know the past and
present of lands like Chile, Mexico, and so on. One of them, Juan Pablo

---

[78] Turin, AS, *Materie politiche estere in genere*, mazzo 63, 25 November 1780.

[79] *Gazeta de Madrid*, no. 81, 5 October 1781, pp. 806ff. (Cádiz, 30 September). See
Notizie del mondo, no. 681, 27 October 1781, p. 687 (Livorno, 24 October). The mutineers
had been "broken on the battlefield by the imprisonment of their leaders, who were immediately hanged. One hears in the same letters that now all is in the hands of the army
and that on this occasion various barrels filled with precious jewels, gold in great quantity,
silver, and many documents fell into the hands of the Spaniards that will be of use in
drawing up accusations in the trial already begun against one of the principal subjects of
this realm."

[80] *Notizie del mondo [V.]*, no. 17, 27 February 1782, p. 136 (Cologne, 12 February).
There are many details also in the *Gazzetta universale*, no. 3, 8 January 1782, p. 17 (Paris,
25 December), and no. 9, 29 January 1782, p. 17 (Genova, 12 January). These concern
that "picturesque madman passing himself off as an ex-Jesuit," called Francisco José Mar-
cano y Arismendi, about whom there is information in Batllori, *El abate Viscardo*, p. 97.

[81] See John D. Browning, "Cornelius de Pauw and Exiled Jesuits: The Development
of Nationalism in Spanish America," *Eighteenth-Century Studies*, no. 3 (Spring 1978): 289ff.

Viscardo y Guzmán, refuged in Massa, was so struck by the news arriving from Peru, from whence he came, as to be induced to take the pseudonym Paolo Rossi and to contact John Udny, the English consul in Livorno, to propose to him a plan to assist Tupac Amaru. The letters he wrote at that time, in Italian, on 23 and 30 September 1781, are among the most lively and informative documents one can read "on the great revolution that has occurred in Peru."[82] Bonifazio Tupac Amaru, "cacique from Tinta," wanted to "liberate the Indians from the slavery of Spain and restore the empire of his ancestors." His victories had been rapid, so much so as to raise the hope of taking Lima "without blood," thus repaying the inhabitants of that city "for favors received in the period of his studies. In these he made such progress, above all in law, that he qualified with applause for several chairs." Behind this Inca lawyer, if we can use this term, developed the deeper movement of the natives. "Another cacique took the name of Francis I, ruler of the province of Charcas, and put everything to fire and blood without sparing either sex or age."[83] "The equilibrium among the different races making up the population of Peru" was broken. Up to that point reciprocal jealousies had suspended the "effects of the disgust and resentment everyone felt against the government." The Creoles had long felt "a secret resentment" for Madrid, which was accused of keeping them distant from offices and wealth, "for the purchase of which their fathers had spilled much sweat and blood." Even when they became nobles the Creoles were the object of the "insulting disdain of the Europeans." The "mixed class," that is, the half-breeds, oppressed by a "head tax that was infamous and difficult for them," followed the Creoles, who they felt were "more enlightened, robust, and courageous." There was a deep hatred by the Indians for Europeans, "while no damage was ever done to a Creole." "Born amid the Indians, nursed by their women, speaking their language, aware of their customs, having become naturalized through a stay of two and a half centuries so that they were almost the same people, the Creoles had mostly a beneficial influence on the Indians." "For the most part" Creoles were the parish priests. These "classes" no longer acted "separately"; they now formed "a political whole in which the Creoles, for the reasons given earlier, have the first place, the mixed breeds the second, and the Indians last." Tupac Amaru himself, Abate Viscardo was convinced, "would not have acted without being sure of a powerful party among the Creoles." His interpretation of the revolution—however penetrating it might have been—was strongly influenced by his desire to demonstrate to the English government that

---

[82] Batllori, *El abate Viscardo*, p. 204, Massa di Carrara, 30 September 1781.
[83] Ibid., p. 199, Massa di Carrara, 23 September 1781.

Peru, with its "seven million inhabitants of all races," was united against the Spanish government and that its leadership was in the hands of the most cultivated and capable of the Creoles. Based on this presupposition, Abate Viscardo could launch his prophesy: "All of southern America, from the Isthmus of Panama to Buenos Aires, will detach itself from Spanish domination. If these peoples are provided with sufficient arms and good leaders, they will have nothing to fear from the power of the Bourbons."[84] The Abate Viscardo continued to act in this way. The posthumous publication of his *Lettre aux espagnols américains* in London in 1801 made him in effect a precursor of the independence movement in South America. But his reasoning in this work was more generical than that of the letter he sent to John Udny in 1781, when the problem of "classes" and "races" in Peru were vividly reflected in the spirit of this Jesuit refuged in Massa. At that time he was in contact with other members of the dissolved Company of Jesus, such as Father Pietro Berugini, a Piedmontese and also a great expert in the Andean world, who was more than inclined to put his experience at the service of the British envoys in Livorno and Turin. Seeking to explain the "universal revolution" taking place in those lands, he insisted particularly on the "new taxes, that is, a capitation of a coined peso on all Indians, half-breeds, and mulattos," a "tax on foodstuffs," "taxes on ecclesiastics," but he did not forget to underline the importance of Inca tradition. "Joseph Casimir Boniface [actually José Gabriel] Tupac Amaru was the grandson eight times removed of the Inca Philip [Felipe] Tupac Amaru who was decapitated in the city of Cuzco by order of Francisco de Toledo, Viceroy of Peru." After two and a half centuries his descendant had been "crowned and proclaimed in Cuzco as legitimate sovereign and successor of the Incas." His chief battle and victory had been obtained by "20 thousand Indians, 8 million half-breeds, and some thousand Spanish Creoles. He showed that he was a monarch, and his victories were marked by humanity and sweetness."[85]

The war in Europe and the revolt beyond the ocean induced Spain to examine its conscience. The growing attention aroused everywhere by what was happening in the peninsula and in its colonies imposed it. With increasing insistence, in the seventies and eighties, one asked the meaning, weight, and value of Spain in the world. From a given fact, the Spanish nation was transforming itself into a problem, capable of

[84] Ibid., pp. 204ff., Massa di Carrara, 30 September 1781.
[85] Ibid., letter by John Udny, Florence, 14 October 1782.

arousing curiosity, but also anxiety; voyages and explorations, but also intense and deeply felt debates.

The departure point for this international discussion was curious and unexpected. It broke out as a dispute between Italian and Spanish ex-Jesuits. With a bit of irreverence one could say that it began as a scuffle among Renzo's chickens (as in Alessandro Manzoni's *The Betrothed*). Both one side and the other were but a shadow of what they had been; indeed, officially after the bull *Dominus ac redemptor* of 1773 they no longer existed. The Italians were often viewed with diffidence, and the Spanish were often thought undesirable and inconvenient guests. They both lived at the edge of institutions, far from the major centers of Italian culture, in little places in the Papal States or in Genova. Even the most famous Italians among them, such as Bettinelli or Tiraboschi, could not help feeling on the margin of the society in which they lived, more tolerated than accepted. The Ragusan Boscovich, admired everywhere, wandered through the world. For better reasons the Spanish felt they were exiles, persecuted, distanced from their country for reasons whose basic logic they could never accept. Their *destierro*, uprootedness from their country, was all the more strange and paradoxical to their eyes considering that they lived on pensions paid to them by Charles III, king of Spain, who continued to think of them as subjects, and they never renounced the hope that, after a certain testing period, they would one day be able to return to their country. They were not emigrés, but exiles, whose punishment was precisely the necessity of living in a foreign country. One could add that the pensions were very small, and that this pushed them to find any possible way of improving their situation a little. Many were quite young. They were pushed forward by the ambition that had induced them to enter the Company of Jesus and to give themselves and others proof of being capable of doing something better than living miserably, in idleness, in provincial corners. Frequently they were missionaries taken from their missions. Nor were these exiles few, about three thousand, and they came from the most distant parts of the Spanish empire, a true elite frustrated in its birth and exiled, which carried with it the ferments, contrasts, and hopes of a land that was both so immense and closed in on itself that it remained unknown and mysterious for many Europeans, even for Italians, who had been and remained particularly close to it.[1]

---

[1] A rapid but expert guide to the world of Spanish Jesuits is provided by Miguel Battlori, "La literatura hispano-italiana del Setecientos," in *Historia general de las literaturas hispánicas publicada bajo la dirección de D. Guillermo Díaz-Plaja* (Barcelona: Editorial Barna), vol. 4, pt. 1, pp. 4ff. By the same author there is also the collection of essays *La cultura*

In this world of memories and recriminations, of resentment and rebellion, fermented "le vieux mot de patrie," to use the expression of Voltaire. Bettinelli, struggling to put his works together in 1780, seized upon "belle lettere" and good Italian. He felt rise around him "the full flood" of books in "history, politics, morals, commerce, crimes and punishments, happiness, population."[2] His reform movement carried him back to the time of his youth, to the early eighteenth century, which he reevoked with precise colors. "By chance, in my first years of study, I happened on the revival of good taste, after the disorder of the seventeenth century, of which I experienced the last traces. I came to know in their old age Muratori, Maffei . . . , Abate Conti . . . the great Foscarini."[3] Travels in France and Germany, even contact with Voltaire, confirmed his vision of Italy. He continued to defend it against all the "foreign peoples" who did not cease to "dominate Italy," as did "many valiant Spanish," "many French," English, and so on.[4] A kind of patriotism was thus born under his hands from the research and rediscovery of good taste. Those responsible for the decadence of the seventeenth century were Spaniards guilty of "bad taste," as well as the "many customs, ceremonies, habits, and forms of speech" imposed by "Spanish domination, which extended in those times to many parts of Italy."[5] On the French, and above all Condillac, weighed the sin of having counterposed the "perfect" language of algebra to that of literature. "On the basis of metaphysics they wanted us to write everything in hieroglyphics."[6] The literary patriotism of Bettinelli ended up rejecting the whole program of enlightened reform, not excluding the effort to transform agriculture. Under this impetus, he wrote ironically, "all nations seem to want to return to the acorns of Saturn." But none of these agronomists or economists ever became peasants. "None of these many experts on agrarian matters began his salubrious reform by embracing a rustic life."[7] He had a wide knowledge of the world of the French enlighten-

hispano-italiana de los jesuitas expulsos, expañoles, hispanoamericanos, filipinos. 1767–1814. Biblioteca románica hispánica (Madrid: Editorial Gredos, 1966), and now the syllabus *Cultura e finanze. Studi sulla storia dei gesuiti da S. Ignazio al Vaticano II* (Rome: Edizioni di storia e letteratura, 1983). Among the numerous Italian writers, see Vittorio Cian, "L'immigrazione dei gesuiti spagnoli letterati in Italia," in *Memorie della R. Accademia delle scienze di Torino*, 2d ser., vol. 45 (1894–95), pp. 1ff.; Arturo Farinelli, "La Spagna, il Conti e altri italiani del '700," in id., *Italia e Spagna* (Turin: Bocca, 1929), vol. 2, pp. 287ff.

[2] *Opere dell'abate Saverio Bettinelli* (Venice: Zatta, 1780), vol. 1, "Prefazione dell'autore," pp. 23, 26.

[3] Ibid., p. 16.

[4] Ibid., vol. 5, "Discorso sopra la poesia italiana," p. 1.

[5] Ibid., p. 103n.

[6] Ibid., p. 26n.

[7] Ibid., p. 231.

ment, but before it he closed up, wounded by the desire for action he could not help but sense enclosed within it, offended by the part it had played in the disappearance of the Jesuits. "That *Encyclopédie* so prized by impartial philosophy will be shamed one day in the article 'Jésuites,' which recalls the time of the Holy League."[8] He called fanatics those who did not accept his resigned and sad vision of "poor and divided Italy," which he recalled historically and continued to observe around him.[9] To that "people and nation," which he saw born in the Middle Ages and which was "the trunk from which present Italians draw their source and origin," he intended to give the best of himself, hoping to "procure some good for poor Italy, or some part of it." "Without that hope, however small and far, I certainly would never have taken up my pen."[10] This was patriotism deprived of a will to reform in the present, of which Muratori, Maffei, Conti, Foscarini had been masters, but that still expressed the tepid agony always present in the "vieux mot de patrie."

The most massive response to Bettinelli and Tiraboschi came from the ex-Jesuit Saverio Lampillas, who had decided to "defend our Spain from those prejudices which make many think it an enemy of good taste and corrupter of literature."[11] He thus accepted the polemic at the level to which the two Italian critics had brought it and enlarged it through a broad discussion of writers born in Spain. He was so determined to be a "good patriot" that he did not even disdain eulogizing Marmontel, whom he discovered to be an ally in his passionate defense of the Spanish philosopher Seneca against Tiraboschi. Thus he ended up, in his fourth volume, with a book where the "erudite M. Diderot" had made "a history and an apology of the writings of this philosopher." "If the Abate Tiraboschi ever deigns to read this work, he will find good reason to praise the moderation of my 'ridiculous' apology."[12] Patriotism, as one sees, tended to bring together people who were in reality quite distant from one another. Lampillas, in fact, did not fail to thunder against "the torrent of irreligion that has flooded the republic of letters in our day." "The name philosopher, although worthy initially, has become a standard under which the declared enemies not less of religion than of customs have united."[13] In Italy, according to him, the fundamental er-

---

[8] Ibid., vol. 7, p. 144. The article "Jésuites," as is well known, was by Diderot.

[9] Ibid., vol. 3, "Il risorgimento d'Italia," p. xxxix.

[10] Ibid., vol. 4, pp. 337, 401.

[11] *Saggio storico-apologetico della letteratura spagnuola contro le pregiudicate opinioni di alcuni moderni scrittori italiani. Dissertazione del signor abate D. Saverio Lampillas* (Genova: Felice Repetto, 1778), pt. 1, "Della letteratura antica," vol. 1, p. 8.

[12] Ibid., p. ii, and pt. 2, vol. 2, p. 242 n. a.

[13] Ibid., pt. 1, vol. 1, p. 146.

ror was "an immoderate liking for pleasurable studies." "According to the way of thinking of some modern Italian writers, Italian literature is made up of only *belle lettere*." This was "the origin of the prejudice against modern Spanish literature." Why not consider the "theologians" and "jurists" that Spain had produced? Such was the fixation on good taste in Italy that works such as the *Discourses on Industry and Popular Education* by Campomanes were not known. "I can say, from what appears, that he is entirely unknown in this nation."[14] Lampillas, in writing this, reflected on the situation he saw around him in Genova. In other Italian cities the name Campomanes was not only known, but famous. It is enough to think of Naples at the time of Antonio Genovesi. But even here patriotism shook the traditional order. The Catalan ex-Jesuit cited Robertson as proof of the value of Campomanes, leaving in shadow his active and intelligent work against the Company of Jesus and his support of greater autonomy for the state with regard to the church. He was Spanish, and that was enough.

Continuing with his polemic, Lampillas tried nonetheless, even if not always successfully, to distinguish between "a noble national undertaking" and "puerile national wars."[15] More and more strange seemed to him Bettinelli's pretense of giving lessons in patriotism, he who had "run roughshod over the best brains Italy can pride itself on."[16] National tradition had to be accepted altogether; in Spain, for instance, it included scholastics.[17]

As for Tiraboschi, the critique of Lampillas was such as to induce readers to think he had written "his history of Italian literature only to fault the literature of Spain," as he himself ironically objected.[18] In his vigorous response he intended to reveal above all the sense of inferiority that seemed to dominate his adversary. The Spanish seemed restive for an open confrontation between their own writers and those of other countries. Good books were not lacking among them. But "the same was

---

[14] Ibid., pt. 2, vol. 1, pp. 22, 20, 32, 47.

[15] *Risposta dell'abate Saverio Lampillas alla lettera scrittagli dall'abate Saverio Bettinelli sopra il tomo I della parte II del Saggio storico apologetico della letteratura spagnola e pubblicata nel tomo XIX del 'Nuovo giornale di Modena'* (Genova: Felice Repetto, 1780), p. 18.

[16] Ibid.

[17] In Genova at the same time there was an effort to make known the encyclopedic writings of Feijoo, who was little known in Italy. "Our Italy is indebted to the constant work and penetration of the learned and illustrious Sig. Abate Antonio Eligio Martínez de Valdepegnos for a work that has merited all the applause of the learned men of Spain" (*Gazzetta universale*, no. 26, 28 March 1780, p. 208, "Avvisi").

[18] *Lettere de' sig. abati Tiraboschi e Bettinelli con le risposte del signor abate Lampillas, intorno al Saggio storico-apologetico della letteratura spagnola del medesimo, per servir di continuazione del medesimo saggio* (Rome: Luigi Perego Salvioni, 1781), p. 7.

true of good German, English, and even Russian books."[19] Cosmopolitanism seemed natural from the pen of an Italian writer, but forced from a Spanish one. Nor could Tiraboschi accept the insinuations of Lampillas against irreligious philosophers, which did not seem to him to have anything to do with the two patriotisms in formation, the Italian and the Spanish one.

The most limpid and harmonious voice in this debate was that of Juan Andrés, an ex-Jesuit from a noble family of Valencia of Aragonese origin, exiled when he was not yet thirty and never to return to Spain, who made himself in some ways an Italian.[20] He lived in Mantova, Pavia, and Naples, with important and even well-paid employments, far from the anguish of a *destierro*, but always tied to the memory of Spain. Likewise he was true to his order, without doubts or anguish. Patriotism and religion were parts of his nature, and he had no need to reaffirm them through a polemic with the world in which he lived. In Italy he admired, without jealousy, the variety, beauty, and richness of historical memories. But he was not unaware that others among his fellows in Italy were in quite different situations. "Passing through Ferrara, Bologna, and Rome I was moved to pity for so many men of talent and knowledge, some able to teach mathematics, others natural science, others ancient languages, others literature, and in seeing them deprived of comfort and means to pursue their studies and unable to give our nation the honor their cultivation would certainly bestow on it if they had greater opportunity."[21] He visited his colleagues one after another, following attentively their efforts to express themselves through study and books. The Italian ex-Jesuits were also natural points of reference for him. Anyone who reads the five volumes of his travel letters published in Madrid by his brother Carlo becomes aware that this was not so much a more or less secret organization as it was a society of learned men, who were active and most attentive to all their surroundings.[22] In Germany,

[19] Ibid., p. 150.

[20] See the article by Miguel Batllori, "Andrés, Giovanni," DBI, vol. 3, p. 155.

[21] *Cartas familiares del abate D. Juan Andrés a su hermano D. Carlos Andrés dandole noticia del viage que hizo a varias cuidades de Italia en el año 1785, publicadas por el mismo D. Carlos* (Madrid: Antonio de Sancha, 1786), vol. 1, p. 5. One notes that this work was dedicated to "Don Joseph Moñino, Count of Floridablanca," the Spanish prime minister who had done much to obtain from the pope the dissolution of the Company of Jesus.

[22] A second edition of these *Cartas familiares* was published by Sancha in Madrid between 1791 and 1793. Volume 3 was concerned with the "viagecito de 20 dias" that he took in the Republic of Venice in 1788, volume 4 saw him in Lombardy, and volume 5 in Piedmont and Genova. The copy preserved in Turin in the B. dell'Accademia delle scienze has the inscription "Prosper Balbus emit Barcinone anno 1799." On the circumstances of the trip to Barcelona of Prospero Balbo see the article by F. Sirugo in the DBI, vol. 5, pp. 420ff.

at the same time, ex-Jesuits were accused of having become a kind of Freemasonry. In Italy, erudition, culture, and literature prevailed. Andrés, along with Tiraboschi, was the chief exponent of this tenacious and elastic academy, which was also politically active and aware.

When he arrived in Italy from Spain in 1767, Andrés carried with him the echo of the most refined erudition and literary and historical culture that had flourished in Spain in the first half of the eighteenth century. Academies and universities had multiplied in Catalonia and the lands of Valencia. For decades the scholar Gregorio Mayans had embodied an encyclopedic attempt at renewal, from theology to linguistics. The roots of this were in a resistance against the Bourbon dynasty in the period of the War of Spanish Succession, and in a tenacious defense of local liberties against Madrid and Philip V.[23] Mayans had inherited this penchant from his family, but he was able to give it a broader meaning, which went beyond all dynastic contests or rivalries. He was in contact with the European erudition of his time, above all with the rigorous currents of state supremacy over the church of the age of Muratori and Giannone.[24] He did not have the breadth of views or the combative energy of either of these two Italian writers, although Mayans knew them both well. But his seriousness, his desire to find the reality of facts after so much rhetoric and sentiment, his deep faith in an exact and precise conscience, without frills, his immense curiosity about a world that had been closed for so long, made him a model and an inspiration for the most diverse intellectual energies. The title of his works was emblematic: *Censura de historias fabulosas*. Recent Spanish scholars, in publishing his correspondence with a wide spectrum of persons, have reconstructed a rich dialogue where Jesuits and critics of the Counter-Reformation met, and where there was a fleeting echo of Vico's *Scienza nuova*.[25]

[23] In this regard the following volume by Antonio Mestre is revealing: *Historia, fueros y actitudes políticas. Mayans y la historiografía del XVIII* (Valencia: Publicaciones del ayuntamiento de Oliva, 1970).

[24] See id., *Ilustración y reforma de la iglesia. Pensamiento político-religioso de don Gregorio Mayans y Siscar (1699–1781)* (Valencia: Publicaciones del ayuntamiento de Oliva, 1968); Vicent Peset, *Gregori Mayans i la cultura de la illustració* (Barcelona: Curial, and Valencia: Tres i quatre 1975); Antonio Mestre, *El mundo intelectual de Mayans* (Valencia: Publicaciones del ayuntamiento de Oliva, 1981), 2 vols. Of particular interest in the first of these are the articles by José Antonio Maravall, "G. Mayans y la formación del pensamiento político de la ilustración," and by Miguel Batllori, "Gregori Mayans y la cultura italiana," pp. 43ff., and 155ff.

[25] Gregorio Mayans y Siscar, *Epistolario*, vol. 1, *Mayans y los médicos* (Valencia: Publicaciones del ayuntamiento de Oliva, 1972); vol. 2, *Mayans y Burriel* (ibid., 1972) (one of the most interesting volumes; Burriel was a Jesuit, and historical criticism brought them together, then made them friends and close collaborators); vol. 3, *Mayans i Martí* (ibid.,

In these surroundings Juan Andrés was formed. In the library of Gregorio Mayans he found the rare books he sought and a warmth of sympathy he never forgot.[26] Like Boturini, he too could not help but sense against whom such an encyclopedic critical endeavor was directed. The infidels beyond the Pyrenees, whether named or passed over in silence, were always the principal adversaries of these wise Catalans. Mayans eliminated the writings of Pufendorf from his library, holding them "impious and abominable." He considered Montesquieu "a politician more diabolical than Machiavelli." Certainly in the *Esprit des lois* there were "many excellent things" and the author was "very erudite." But Mayans did not even trust himself to write an open and a public refutation: "I read it with attention so as to refute it secretly in my book on Christian wisdom." As for Voltaire, he was "one of the greatest atheists living today. I must study him to refute him when God wills that I write about natural law."[27] Even the *Filosofia morale* by Muratori, about which he was enthusiastic and which he had begun to translate "with joy," since it was a work "of greatest importance in its genre, incomparable," in the end proved too perilous to be published.[28]

When we move from these judgments and facts to the first works written and published by Juan Andrés in Italy, we sense that a generation had passed. Twenty or thirty years later certain things were not repeatable. But the more or less open polemic against the French enlightenment continued. What surprised him was that the Italians among whom he lived had not been able to marshal better and more effective arguments and means against the *lumières*. "Often thinking of the literary glories of Italy," he wrote in his *Saggio della filosofia di Galileo*, "I have not been able to do less than marvel." He was unable to understand why Italy had not "formed a party among the schools of philosophy, taking their Galileo as leader, and contested the glory of France with its Descartes, and England and Germany with their Newton and Leibnitz."[29] Galileo had established, before all others, the "true method of philosophy": "examining particular facts and not forming general systems, following the traces of nature through geometry, experiments, and observations rather than proposing vague ideas and airy plans . . . , in short making himself a disciple of nature." This was a method elaborated and

---

1973); vol. 4, *Mayans y Nebot (1735–1742). Un jurista teórico y un práctico* (ibid., 1975); vol. 5, *Escritos económicos* (ibid., 1976). On Vico see Franco Venturi, "Un vichiano tra Messico e Spagna: Lorenzo Boturini Benaduci," *R. stor. ital.*, year 87, fasc. 4 (October 1975): 770ff.

[26] Mestre, *Historia, fueros y actitudes políticas*, pp. 355ff.

[27] Id., *Ilustración y reforma*, p. 458.

[28] Ibid., p. 403.

[29] *Saggio della filosofia di Galileo, dell'abate D. Giovanni Andrés* (Mantova: Alberto Pazzoni, 1776), "Introduction."

later followed by Newton. But while Newton had in recompense "a kind of apotheosis," Galileo received for his work "only persecution, hatred, and oblivion."[30] Hume had been right in underlining the superiority of Galileo even over Bacon, and in lamenting "that Italy, still, either because it is separated in different governments or because of the boasting of its literary forces in ancient and modern times, has neglected the honor of having given birth to such a great man."[31] Thus d'Alembert had been wrong in exalting only "his Descartes," calling him "the Czar Peter of philosophy," while he should more likely have compared Galileo to the "wise and great Gustavus of Sweden, and Descartes to the valorous but timerous Charles XII."[32] Mosheim, for his part, had attributed to Gassendi the merits of Italian science. "The great glory of Galileo was not to create systems, and this was perhaps also his demerit and the reason for his merits' not being sufficiently appreciated."[33] It was both a political weakness of Italians in not recognizing their countryman and an excess of literature among them. There was finally a disparity in the age when Galileo lived, between his "too great merit and the too great obscurity of his times."

The excess, or as he now said, the "literary luxury" that had prevented Italians from affirming themselves in the seventeenth century among other nations, was then diffused everywhere in Europe, causing a kind of paralysis in the general progress of knowledge. *Belle lettere* had continued to flourish. It was enough to mention Voltaire, Metastasio, Gessner, Hume, Robertson, and Raynal. "Political eloquence found a Demosthenes in the famous William Pitt." "Didactics never appeared so gloriously triumphant as from the pen of Rousseau, Buffon, Bailly, Voltaire" (even if, naturally, the ex-Jesuit who wrote this was obliged to note his reservations on the position of these writers with regard to religion). In none of the sciences did one note "outstanding discoveries at this time," despite the fact that there had never been "such a display of physics and mathematics."[34] The cause of this paralysis was not "ignorance" and "lack of skill," or "roughness" and "barbarism," but rather the "spirit of culture, praiseworthy and universal though it was." In trans-

---

[30] Ibid., pp. 3ff.

[31] Ibid., p. 8.

[32] Ibid., pp. 9ff.

[33] Ibid., pp. 10ff. Of Mosheim, Andrés cited: "Hist. Chri, rec. saec. XVII," that is, Io. Laurentii Mosheimi, *Institutiones historiae christianae recensioris* (Helmstad: Christ. Fried. Weygand, 1741), "Saeculum decimum septimum historiae christianae," pp. 472ff.

[34] G. Andrés, "Dissertazione sopra le cagioni della scarsezza de' progressi delle scienze in questo tempo," recitata nella Real Accademia delle scienze e belle lettere di Mantova, in *Raccolta di opuscoli scientifici e letterari di chiari autori italiani* (Ferrara: Giuseppe Rinaldi, 1779), vol. 2, pp. 114ff.

forming itself into "literary luxury," this became no less "harmful" than "economic" luxury. The "abundance" of means "that should provide for progress" ended in reality by making it impossible. Learned men rather than concentrating on the problems of their own sciences dissipated their minds in a thousand different directions. This is what prevented d'Alembert from becoming "a new Newton." Why ever had he given himself over to being the secretary of an academy? They read much of learned men, but in a general manner, without consulting the essential books or referring to fundamental hypotheses. "Visits, conversations, games, theaters, diversions" distracted them continually. This led to "a soft and delicate life, and an incapacity for application or effort."[35] What was even worse, they hoped to find in machines, in calculation, what they would be able to realize only through reflection. "Literary luxury is also the great effort made at present to perfect machines and instruments, methods of observation and calculation, in short to accumulate and make a show of wealth and abundance of things that are merely means." Bibliography and algebra were typical examples. "The mind is nearly liberated from the need to think, becoming lazy and idle, and when the spirit does nothing it lets the hand work." "Galileo . . . Boyle did not have the use of machines that were so very delicate or perfect." "Too much respect for calculation, too much love for experiment, makes one forget observation, which should be cultivated above all else." The history of electricity showed it. Through reflection and experiment Father Beccaria had been able to bring to fruition the hypotheses of "the former Jesuits of China."[36]

These were past and present weaknesses which Andrés refused to project onto other peoples, as Bettinelli, Tiraboschi, and in general other recent Italian historians had done, not excluding Muratori. How could one blame Spain for the "corruption of taste" of the seventeenth century? It was enough to observe dates to convince oneself of the absurdity of such an accusation. One hundred years separated the conquests of Spain from the emergence of Achillini, Marino, and so on. "A century between Spanish domination and the new style is too great an interval for these two things to be thought connected."[37] How, then, could commanders and Spanish officers exercise such power over Ital-

---

[35] Ibid., pp. 128ff.

[36] Ibid., pp. 137ff. See the review of this work in *Magazin der Italienischen Literatur und Künste* by C. J. Jagemann published in Weimar, 1780, vol. 4, pp. 18ff. These themes were taken up and developed in Andrea Rubbi, *Rapporti del lusso colla vita sociale o sia del lusso politico, letterario, civile, domestico e sacro* (Venice: Pietro Marcuzzi, 1783).

[37] *Lettera dell'abbate D. Giovanni Andrés al sig. comendatore fra Gaetano Valenti Gonzaga, cavaliere dell'inclita religione di Malta, sopra una pretesa cagione del corrompimento del gusto italiano nel secolo XVII* (Cremona: Lorenzo Manini, 1776), p. 13.

ian literature? Sovereigns had done no more than favor poets, writers, and academicians. "One owes to the Spanish government the blooms of the best days of Italy."[38] Later then, when writers such as Lope de Vega had been able to have some influence, one might ask why Italians allowed themselves to imitate bad Spanish theater.[39] But even in this case there were exceptions. One should follow the example of Don Gregorio Mayans, the man who introduced "new taste into Spain in both prose and verse," and examine closely which Spanish books actually circulated in Italy at that time. The result would be that for some time good Spanish authors were translated, while no one thought of turning into Italian the writings of Calderón and Lope de Vega. Corruption came to both nations at the same time. "At the beginning of the seventeenth century the decadence of good literature in Spain began and at the same time Italy became corrupt."[40] This was a much more able and restrained defense of Spain than that of Lampillas. "My being Spanish, and having to employ myself in defense of my country, is the embarrassment that most restrains me," he declared at the beginning of this *Lettera*.[41] He had hoped to raise to a cosmopolitan and historical level what for others was a contest of national sentiment.

The result was immense: seven volumes in quarto, which appeared with the title *Dell'origine, progressi e stato attuale d'ogni letteratura* in Parma, from Bodoni, between 1782 and 1799. It was intended to be a kind of encyclopedia of world culture, and it was influenced, in the classification he adopted, by Baconism and the French *Encyclopédie*. But Diderot, rather than being his model, was his principal adversary, little named and even avoided, but always polemically present. In the midst of this enormous collection of facts, traditions, and reflections, one preoccupation returned insistently to dominate his vision: the relationship of men of culture to political power. Contrary to the *Encyclopédie*, his was not a defense of the liberty of intellectuals, but rather an examination of the process of adjustment between literature and power. In short, it was a history of patronage, or if one prefers a more modern term, of cultural politics. He never tired of repeating that neither climate nor liberty was the determining factor in the flourishing of literature, and that ancient as well as modern examples show instead that all lands and peoples are capable of intellectual development, above all when they have the benefit of being governed by "absolute monarchs." This had been true of "Alexandria, master of the sciences," as it was now for

38 Ibid., p. 17.
39 Ibid., p. 34.
40 Ibid., pp. 12, 41.
41 Ibid., p. 4.

"Prussia and Brandenburg." "The republic of letters loves liberty," he concluded, "but it is content with the literary more than with political liberty."[42] His neoclassical taste made this renunciation of a civil function for his literary encyclopedia particularly cold, polished, and measured. But the Spanish themes that continued to be at the center of his interests, and to which he dedicated many pages, raised elements that were difficult to reconcile with his harmonious construction. This was especially the case with Arab civilization, of which Andrés was a great admirer who never tired of praising its excellent schools, academies, libraries, and agricultural refinements. "Arabic literature" seemed to him to have had a great "influence on the rebirth of Europe," even through "Provençal poetry."[43] From Spain Andrés thus introduced a theme of historical thought that would have much weight in the nineteenth century and in the historiography of our own day. But this vision still remained an excursus in the great avenue he followed to reach the center of his story, the rebirth of Italy and Spain, which were closely allied in the search for formal perfection and for a balance between religion and philosophy. Certainly, there were deviations in the sixteenth century. In Erasmus and Machiavelli there was already something of modern disbelief. "Enormous errors and solemn madness" were in Bruno and Cardano.[44] "Perfection" was found only in writers like Bellarmino.[45] Italy, nonetheless, had at that time "felt true beauty and had restored to Europe the solid and perfect taste that had been banished for so many centuries." Beside it was Spain, "the first nation to follow the example of Italy."[46] The two nations, united in glory and decadence (even if their corruption was less emphasized in this work by Andrés than it was in his work of ten years before), now found themselves confronted with the modern world, before that "eighteenth century that was rightly called," he was forced to admit it, "an enlightened century." Only then was "the light of science" finally "spread universally throughout Europe." "In the sixteenth century the culture of traditional language in prose and verse was restricted to Italy and Spain, without being communicated to other nations. . . . In this century alone culture was made fully universal." From one "extremity of Europe" to the other, from Russia to Spain, the new philosophy had triumphed. In Spain itself, "the tenacious protector of scholastic subtleties," these had been "finally banished from her

[42] *Dell'origine, progressi e stato attuale d'ogni letteratura, dell'abate D. Giovanni Andrés, socio della R. Accademia di scienze e belle lettere di Mantova* (Parma: Stamperia reale, 1782), vol. 1, *Che contiene lo stato della letteratura nelle diverse sue epoche,* "Prefazione," pp. 27, 29.

[43] Ibid., pp. 156, 297.

[44] Ibid., pp. 394, 397.

[45] Ibid., p. 406.

[46] Ibid. (1785), vol. 2, *Che contiene le belle lettere,* pp. 8, 11.

schools," which turned "wisely to more useful knowledge."[47] As long as
religion was maintained intact and safe, Andrés was ready to make great
concessions. He did not hesitate to admit that one could, and even
should, prefer "the fine taste of Voltaire, the eloquence of Rousseau,
and the erudition of Freret" to the "mediocre talents of the larger part
of their adversaries."[48] Nor did he hide his astonished admiration for
Linguet, creator "of a new type of eloquence, different from the style of
Plato, Tully, and other ancient and modern writers," or his understanding of Raynal, despite his "arrogant philosophy," his "masterful and decisive tone," and above all his "affected detail and inexact scrupulous-
ness."[49] But when he confronted the prose of more typical
enlightenment writers, for instance, the Italian ones, his disdain became
invincible. The polemic against the Accademia della Crusca was not his
business, and he could not help but condemn those who, "carried away
blindly by the fire and vivacity of some moderns beyond the Alps, hurl
all kinds of blame at the masters of the Italian language, boasting of
their spirit and philosophy, and their love for facts, not words, who believe only in thoughts and conclusions, and seek a strong and vibrant
style, without taking care of the selection and arrangement of words and
the measured liquid flow of oratory."[50] He hardly mentioned Beccaria
in this third volume, echoing the "clamor" that had arisen "in all Europe" from his "philosophical and political" work.[51] Some years later he
revealed the political reasons for this reserve. "It should be observed,"
he wrote in 1794, "that what created the universal fame of Beccaria and
the veneration for him by superficial modern philosophers was not any
of his just and useful teachings, but rather a paradox arising from the
spirit of false humanity in this century, of little truth, but that too incautiously adopted by some governments has done perhaps more damage
than good to society." He judged Filangieri as being clearly better: "One
of the more moderate and wise writers who allow themselves to be carried forward from time to time by poetic enthusiasm, believing to perceive as strong evidence what hardly emerges in twilight, and to determine matters frankly and without hesitating with abstractions."[52] He
turned with greater pleasure to the figure of Genovesi, doing with him

[47] Ibid., vol. 1, pp. 456ff.

[48] Ibid., p. 453.

[49] Ibid., p. 474. He returned to Raynal at length in vol. 3, p. 369: "It is perhaps a good
work; it is certainly not good history." He wanted the removal of "the frequent and
lengthy digressions," as well as "the long pages of philosophy." It was, in other words, a
Raynal without Diderot.

[50] Ibid., vol. 3, pt. 2, *Delle belle lettere*, p. 55.

[51] Ibid., p. 115.

[52] Ibid. (1794), vol. 5, *La seconda parte delle scienze naturali*, p. 612.

what he had done for Galileo, that is, comparing him with the dangers of more recent developments in philosophical thought. By criticizing and expunging, Andrés ended up by fashioning the image of the eighteenth century in Italy that passed on to the following century, and in part still remains, an eighteenth century without Giannone, Verri, and Beccaria, while in first order stood Algarotti, Cesarotti, Bettinelli, even Tiraboschi, and Napoli Signorelli.

Spain too, in the eighteenth century, after having abandoned "scholastic thorns" and having decorated morality with "prettier flowers of philosophy and erudition," had taken the same road as Italy.[53] But Andrés seemed to want to stop in the first steps along this road. Besides the "much praised Mayans," and a few of his friends and collaborators, we find practically no one in the pages of this immense history.[54] Campomanes and Jovellanos are completely missing, as is the whole new generation of the eighties. Exile, and the growing reaction against enlightened ideas, had stopped him in the polemics and benevolent concessions of his youth. To speak the language of art history, he had stayed in the period of Mengs while others had already reached the years of Goya.

An admiration for Mengs was a common trait of many Italianized Spaniards of the late eighteenth century, a symptom and symbol of their neoclassicism. José Nicolas de Azara, the representative of Charles III in Rome and one of the most active critics of the policy of the Curia, brought this taste to his relationship with Italian artists and exiled Jesuits. He collected the works of Mengs and was the patron of the architect Milizia, and of Stefano Arteaga, a critic and historian of Italian music.[55] "I would have wanted, and certainly have wanted," Arteaga wrote in dedicating his book to him, "with the zeal that national love inspires and justifies, to consecrate my efforts to our beloved country." He would thus have been better able to lighten "the involuntary remorse of leading a life entirely useless to the glory of Spain." He turned to Azara as to one who, "in a city so much the master of religion and politics, sustained with such decorum the rights of a monarch" like Charles III and had also done so much for the glory of Mengs, "the greatest genius in painting of our century."[56] To another Spanish diplomat, "Don Miguel

[53] Ibid., p. 607.

· [54] Ibid., p. 694.

[55] See the article by N. Borsellino, "Arteaga, Stefano," in DBI, vol. 4, pp. 352ff. See *Opere di Antonio Raffaello Mengs primo pittore della maestà di Carlo III re di Spagna, ecc. ecc. ecc. pubblicate da Niccola d'Azara* (Parma: Stamperia reale, 1780), 2 vols.

[56] *Le rivoluzioni del teatro musicale italiano dalla sua origine fino al presente*. Opere di Stefano Arteaga madrileno (Bologna: Carlo Trenti, 1783), "Dedica a Giuseppe Niccolò di Azara," pp. viff., viiiff.

José de Torres y Morales, Marquis of Matagliana, plenipotentiary minister of His Catholic Majesty to His Royal Highness the Infante Duke of Parma," he dedicated another typical text on patriotism two years later, a kind of discussion with Matteo Borsa. In Arteaga, as in Andrés, there is a strong sense of the political value of culture, even if this was distorted by an insistent search for patronage. Colbert remained a great model in his eyes as the minister who had succeeded in persuading his sovereign "that it was not a lesser glory to the French name to be superior to other nations through the gifts of genius than to acquire a predominance in politics."[57] Floridablanca appeared to him as the man who, "under the auspices of the best of monarchs, opened roads for the chariot of Minerva in a peninsula that dominates two worlds at the same time, and pleases her with his wise political provisions." The same diplomat he was addressing seemed to him to have accomplished "a rare and admirable union of patriotism and philosophy," "departing from love of the nation as the center, and then extending in thought to the human species, becoming with nobility of spirit the contemporary of all ages and the citizen of all countries."[58]

This cosmopolitanism was soon put into crisis by the "melancholy" that Matteo Borsa, a student and relative of Bettinelli, felt when confronted with "foreign neologisms," and the weakness and subjection that had become an integral part of taste "current in Italy."[59] "We are under foreign domination on all sides: thus we are subjected to force."[60] The French "take from us the savor and taste of our language and style. . . . What greater sign of servitude than to lose even the characteristic sign that distinguishes us from other nations, that makes us a nation, and that creates us in the eyes of others?"[61] Arteaga could not help but assent to such discouraging considerations. He took the opportunity to warn that it was not Spain but France that had truly changed Italian taste. In the sixteenth and seventeenth centuries Italy had become "to a large extent Spanish" and "should have been proud (and was in fact) of

[57] *Del gusto presente in letteratura italiana. Dissertazione del sig. dott. Matteo Borsa regio professore nella università di Mantova, data alla luce e accompagnata da copiose osservazioni relative al medesimo da Stefano Arteaga* (Venice: Carlo Palese, 1785), unpaginated. See the article by R. Amaturo, "Borsa, Matteo," in the DBI, vol. 13, pp. 110ff., and above all Emilio Bigi, "Tra classicismo e preromanticismo: Matteo Borsa," *Lettere italiane* 11, no. 3 (July–September 1959): 320ff., and id., "Nota introduttiva a Matteo Borsa," in *Dal Muratori al Cesarotti*, vol. 4: *Critici e storici della poesia e delle arti nel secondo Settecento*, ed. Emilio Bigi (Milan and Naples: R. Ricciardi), pp. 393ff.

[58] Borsa, *Del gusto presente*, dedication to S. Arteaga.

[59] Ibid., p. 1.

[60] Ibid., p. 13.

[61] Ibid., p. 16.

the sonorous and masterful language of its rulers." Then, "the splendid and highly polished court of the immortal Louis XIV" permanently imposed "the Gallic tongue" on Italians. However, "neologisms" had not been the cause of the "weakening of the national spirit." The opposite was truer. "Whenever political circumstance makes men less fond of their country, or go against it, it makes them desire and esteem foreign things." It was enough to look around one to be aware of this. "The greater part of modern nations experiences (strictly speaking) only love of place. What the ancients called love of the fatherland is a daydream for us, a name without meaning, an old-fashioned word, which should be deleted from almost all dictionaries of living languages, along with the word *citizen*. This is particularly true of the Italian nation, but I will be careful not to say why."[62] It was useless to hide the situation by praising the perfection of the logic or literature of Italy. Who could be called the true model for Italian prose? "Perhaps Boccaccio? . . . perhaps Machiavelli?" "But although his depth of thought, and his style full of nerve and concreteness, is close to the current philosophical genius of our century, nonetheless the blackness of his maxims, which restrict him rightly to the hands of a few, has not yet permitted him, and will not permit him in the future, to have all the influence he should on the literary taste of Italy." Nor can any other writer of the sixteenth century replace him. "Only Galileo is in some sense adaptable to the current situation of Italy for the precision, elegance, probity, and robustness of his style; but confined as he is to matters of physics, he cannot serve as a model for those who want to express other things." Here was the true origin of that "kind of literary anarchy" which Borsa lamented. Returning to the relationship with the French language, it still had to be admitted that no one in Italy was "capable of exhibiting the appropriately vulgar style of a book like the *Tableau de Paris*." Neither romances nor letter-writing styles existed in Italy.[63] The "philosophy of the *Encyclopédie*" was the source of many evils, mixing and irremediably confusing poetry and spirit, literature and science. Nor could the remedies Borsa suggested—a new edition of the *Dizionario della Crusca*, the creation of Italian academies, and even an appeal to a vigorous and an intelligent satire modeled on Piron, Cervantes, and Swift—persuade Arteaga.[64] Perhaps, he concluded, some advantage would result if "the journals and other critical assemblies of one kind or another passed into the hands of venerable athletes, who, having won laurels more than once,

[62] Ibid., pp. 97ff.
[63] Ibid., pp. 102ff.
[64] *Dialoghi tra il sig. Stefano Arteaga e Andrea Rubbi in difesa della letteratura italiana* (Venice: Antonio Zatta, 1786), p. 7, "A miei amici Andrea Rubbi."

enjoy in the eyes of the whole nation an uncontested and peaceful glory": Bettinelli, Denina, Goldoni . . . Cesarotti . . . Parini . . . Tiraboschi should become the masters and arbiters of Italian taste. The eighteenth-century Italy that Andrés wanted to transmit to posterity would, as one sees, obtain literary power all at once if the academic utopia of Arteaga were realized.

Andrea Rubbi, another ex-Jesuit and a great champion of the Italian nation and above all a great enemy of enlightened France, responded to him. "My thought is to destroy this ferocious Gallomania," he wrote in 1786 in opening his troubled dialogue with Stefano Arteaga. How had this person been able to assert that in Italy love of country was "a word without meaning"? It was enough to glance at the "literary journals" published in Rome, Florence, Siena, Pisa, Vicenza, Bologna, Modena, and Milan to see with what interest these reviewed "our books and discoveries." And how could one not see that the "love of country had produced many general and particular literary histories"? Academic patriotism was thus counterposed, with ingenuity and sincere conviction, to the Spanish search for a different and more concrete patriotism. They thought the Italians were too literary, and not without effort Andrea Rubbi sought to demonstrate to them that this was false, that Filangieri had "made a law code" without bending a knee to "pedantry" or to the "idol of scholastic superstition." In their own fields Buonafede and Bettinelli had done the same.[65] These were not very numerous examples, or even persuasive ones, as one sees. On the grounds of the civic value of Italian literature, Andrea Rubbi felt uncomfortable in his defense. He cited *Il Caffè*, in passing, and tried in vain to counterpose the discourses of lawyers in Naples and Venice with the "parliamentary harangues of England."[66] He finally found a strong defense only by repeating what G. Compagnoni had written in the *Memorie enciclopediche* of Bologna. He cited Denina, Cocchi, Beccaria, Carli, Verri, Buonafede, Filangieri, and Albergati "for the glory of Italian letters." The movement for reforms emerged thus as the only authentic love of country in Italy.[67] "The truth from the mouth of Signor Compagnoni," he was able to conclude, "is truly Italian." Many things divided them, but Rubbi and Compagnoni had found a point in common, negating or attempting to fill that "void" that Arteaga had thought to find in the heart of Italy.

> . . . Gl'ibéri ingegni
> cattedra alzar fra noi,

[65] Ibid., p. 47.
[66] Ibid., pp. 29, 39.
[67] Ibid., pp. 75, 79. Compagnoni's article cited here is in the *Memorie enciclopediche*, no. 15 (1785), pp. 121ff.

echoed Clementino Vannetti speaking to Ippolito Pindemonte.

> . . . L'ibéro Arteaga acuto ed alto

had criticized our writers. And

> . . . chi l'opra ignora
> d'Andrés immensa?

The Spanish had dared touch historians such as Maffei and Denina, and had even denied

> . . . a Parin
> il vanto appieno d'original poeta.[68]

The dispute that Spanish ex-Jesuits aroused thus risked closing itself more and more within the bounds of the literary pretensions of both nations. But meanwhile, as we have seen, it touched sensitive points of Italian and Spanish life, bringing to light the convergence and divergence of patriotism in the two countries.

History, together with literature, thus became the preferred field of contest, contributing significantly to broadening the vision of Italian literary men toward worlds and lands earlier little known or entirely ignored. Among these above all was Spain. The Catalan Gianfrancesco Masdeu had not been wrong when addressing "the learned and honored literary men of Italy"; he spoke of the "carelessness" with which foreigners had up to that time considered the past of his country. Otherwise, as Bettinelli noted, even within Italy literary figures in Rome did not know the work of Genovesi, nor did Venetians know the work of Neapolitans.

"How surprising it is to see the history of Spaniards so forgotten in Italy."[1] Masdeu thought he would have to begin with its very earth in

---

[68] " . . . the ingenious Iberians / found a chair among us." " . . . The Iberian Arteaga acute and lofty" " . . . who does not know / the work of immense Andrés?" "to Parini / the boast of poetic originality." *Sopra il disegno e lo stile del sermone poetico italiano. Dissertazione dell'abate Giovacchino Millas di Saragozza al cavalier Clementino Vannetti in occasione d'un suo sermone* (Verona: Eredi Moroni, 1786), pp. ixff., "A S.E. il cavalier Pindemonte Clementino Vannetti. Sermone."

[1] *Storia critica di Spagna e della cultura spagnuola in ogni genere preceduta da un discorso preliminare. Opera di Gianfrancesco Masdeu barcellonese.* Tomo primo e preliminare alla storia. *Discorso filosofico sul clima di Spagna, sul genio e ingegno degli spagnuoli per l'industria e per la letteratura e sul loro carattere politico e morale* (Fuglino: Pompeo Campana, 1781), p. vii, "Prefazione generale."

making his country known. The pages he dedicated to the climate and agriculture of Spain were anything but lacking in interest. Botero and Uztáriz paved the way for him. The work of the latter, he said, was "undoubtedly a masterpiece." As for Campomanes, he referred to the "great eulogy Robertson made to him in his *History of America*."[2] These pages of the Scottish historian had in fact marked a decisive moment in the relations between Spain and Europe. He had cited the *Discourse on the encouragement of popular industry* and the *Discourse on popular education among artisans and its encouragement*, saying that "almost every point of importance with regard to interior police, taxation, agriculture, manufactures, and trade, domestic as well as foreign, is examined in the course of these works, and there are not many authors, even in the nations most eminent for commercial knowledge of those various subjects, and a more perfect freedom from vulgar and national prejudices, who have united more happily the calm researches of philosophy with the ardent zeal of a public-spirited citizen." "These books are in high estimation among the Spaniards," he added, "and it is a decisive evidence of the progress of their own ideas that they are capable of relishing an author whose sentiments are so liberal."[3] Criticizing Linguet and referring instead to Marco Foscarini and the Catalan Capmany, Masdeu arrived rapidly at a polemic with the French *Encyclopédie* (whose article on Spain was taken, he explained, from the *Siècle de Louis XIV* by Voltaire), and especially with Tuscans who had republished without correction the errors it contained about his country. "These men were very vigilant in correcting the original with notes about anything that might displease in Italy, but blind and passionate in leaving as they were all the injuries to Spain they found there." He had a great admiration for Tuscans and for Peter Leopold, "the greatest promoter of industry among currently reigning sovereigns," who was also married to a Spaniard; but such negligence and ignorance could not be forgiven by him or his subjects.[4] Even Italians, like many other peoples, had been incapable of seeing everything that Spain had offered, and offered still, as a model and incitement to reforms. "Some European countries, if they had better communication with Spain, would gain enlightenment and advantage from it, as was true in other times when there was more trade."[5] One should look, for example, at the organization of oceanic

[2] Ibid., pp. 34, 54, 93, 94n.

[3] William Robertson, *Works* (London: William Ball, 1840). *The History of America*. Notes and illustrations, n. cxciii, pp. 1078ff. See the Italian translation: *Storia di America del dottore Guglielmo Robertson, tradotta dall'originale inglese dall'abate Antonio Pillori fiorentino* (Florence: Allegrini, 1778), vol. 4, pp. 371ff., n. 51.

[4] *Storia critica di Spagna*, p. 190.

[5] Ibid., p. 80n.

commerce. "Only Spain has avoided the error of policy into which the Dutch, English, French, and Danes have fallen with the imprudent establishment of their companies."[6] The polemic against mercantilism thus became colored with recriminations and national pride. Particularly irritating for Masdeu was the deafness of Italians to the echoes and appeals of a patriotism similar to that of Spain. "Italy (I must confess), through I know not what disgrace in such a cultivated nation, so studious and wise, which in many things was the first to stir itself and rise, has remained in others asleep longer than the others." Still, something seemed to him now about to change. "Now some clear minds are awaking who for the honor of their country will quickly disperse the clouds," striking "with new rays of light the still closed eyes of others. The first honor for having undeceived and enlightened the country belonged to Saverio Bettinelli, one of the most famous writers of contemporary Italy, a truly illustrious man."[7] Whereas for Spain Masdeu looked to reformers and economists, returning continually, throughout his book, to Uztariz, Bernardo de Ulloa, Sisternes, and Campomanes, in Italy his admiring gaze turned to Bettinelli. His Jesuit and patriotic roots carried him, despite his goodwill, far from the Italian enlightenment.

Even his relationship with Giovanni Ristori, one of the most intelligent Tuscan publicists, who directed at that time the *Memorie enciclopediche* in Bologna, was destined to break on the shores of the two national sensitivities. He was to review some Spanish books, but soon became aware that he would arouse little interest by doing so. "I blush in saying it, but Italy would rather be ignorant of literary news from Spain than hear that nation spoken of with praise . . . it would rather read things it knows than ones of which it is ignorant."[8] Ristori had seemed to him an

---

[6] Ibid., p. 153.

[7] Ibid., p. 180.

[8] *Memorie enciclopediche*, no. 33, October 1781, letter to Doctor Ristori from the villa, 27 September 1781, p. 264. He had, for example, spoken of the *Historia literaria* by Raffaello and Pietro Rodríguez Mohedano, which had begun to appear in 1766, "before the publication of the history of our literature," that is, the work of Tiraboschi. Despite the success this *Historia* had in Spain, it had received "no notice in any Italian journal" (ibid., no. 3, January 1781, p. 21). He had then given news of the activity of a society of friends of the country (no. 5, February 1781, p. 38) and had polemicized with French authors about Provençal poetry (no. 6, February 1781, pp. 46ff.). The work of Conte Carlo Carasi on the *Pubbliche pitture di Piacenza* had given him occasion to correct the errors of this person with regard to the life and works of Spagnoletto, nonetheless adding: "Signor Conte Carasi in these historical errors is deserving of pardon. The history of Spanish painters is written in a language that is no longer fashionable as it once was, and our literary men have failed to obtain translations of them" (no. 8, March 1781, p. 59). He cited the life of F. Testi, published by Tiraboschi, to remind of "the high esteem that Count Fulvio Testi had among Spanish poets of his time and how much use he made of

exception to such hatred of anything new. "You yourself, who among cultivated Italians are most cultivated, with a lively spirit superior to the ordinary, you yourself have confessed to me more than once how empty you had to be of anything Spanish before establishing familiar relations with Spaniards. How surprised you were! How you exclaimed when I made you see for the first time the erudite works, the handsome editions, the fine engravings of modern Spain! How many times you yourselves lamented and repented the prejudices of your education."[9] But still, despite the familiarity thus established between the Florentine and the Barcelonian, when he published the first volume of his *Storia critica di Spagna* he read a review in the columns of the *Memorie enciclopediche* that wounded him. The optimistic picture Masdeu had presented of the economy, and particularly of Iberian agriculture, had not persuaded Ristori. There was no doubt of the depopulation of the land, and this made Spain organically inferior to France, England, and even "little Italy" with its more than twelve million inhabitants. Nor could the reviewer accept what he had read on the conquest of America. "Naked men, without iron, artillery, or discipline, with what force could they oppose warriors who frightened them with their armor and their horses, and who had ready in their hands the lightning of Jove?" And why had the importance of Italian navigators in the discovery of the New World not been fully brought to light? On one very significant point Ristori gave in to Masdeu. It was not true that the Spanish were naturally "lazy and lacking in industry." They only became so in the seventeenth century, "a period fatal for Spain, when the zeal of Philip III with a single blow deprived his kingdom of a million men by driving out the Jews and the Saracens. The need to found colonies in the New World and to maintain large armies in Italy, Flanders, and America was the reason that this flourishing kingdom fell into a state of languor and exhaustion."[10] Great difficulties lay in the way of reversing such a long-range tendency. Despite their good qualities, which Ristori fully appreciated, it was still necessary for the Spanish to open themselves above all to ideas and ways of feeling that they seemed instead to obstinately re-

the poetic compositions of that nation" (no. 9, March 1781, p. 69). He followed "Matteo Aimerich, native of Catalonia," in the effort to make known to Italians men like "the celebrated D. Gregorio Mayans" (no. 10, March 1781, p. 74). And naturally, he followed the volumes of Clavigero on the history of Mexico with particular attention (no. 16, May 1781, pp. 122ff.). The polemic of Alonso María de Azevedo and Pedro de Castro was a good opportunity for him to narrate in detail the progress of the debate in Spain on the problem of torture (no. 20, June 1781, pp. 156ff.). Volume 9 of the *Storia* by Tiraboschi brought him to a discussion of Lampillas (no. 25, August 1782, pp. 193ff.).

9 Ibid., no. 31, September 1781, letter to doctor Ristori from the villa, 20 September 1781, p. 252.

10 Ibid., no. 30, September 1781, extracts of books, Fuligno, pp. 233ff.

ject. How could Masdeu himself call Montesquieu a "superficial philosopher"? Despite the many compliments with which this review was filled, it profoundly disappointed the Spanish exile. "I thought I had done much to overcome the prejudices of your nation," he wrote to Ristori, "and I see that I have done little." The medicine he had wanted to give with his *Storia critica* had not been enough. "When you are quite cured, you will thank me for the efforts I have made for your nation more than for mine, since in the end the ignorance in Italy of Spanish matters is not a dishonor for Spaniards, but rather for Italians." It was enough to think of the small awareness of the "agrarian academies" in Spain, "called the friends of the country," as well as of the invention "in a few years of many good machines not yet known in Italy to improve cultivation and increase yield." The work carried out in the "harsh and arid mountains of Sierra Morena" (this was a reference to Olavide's work) was not appreciated sufficiently.[11] Continuing in his polemic, he was again taken up by literary disputes, by the "extravagance of imagination," the "exaggeration of speech," and the "subtleness of thoughts" usually attributed to Spaniards. But in the end he broke with such discussions, announcing with courtesy but firmness that from now on he would contribute no more to the *Memorie enciclopediche*.[12] A deep incompatibility lay hidden under the flowers of controversy.[13]

A "learned Spaniard," writing in the *Nuovo giornale enciclopedico* of Vicenza, finally explained to Masdeu that the patriotism on which he so prided himself had blinded him, depriving him of any sense of balance in his dispute with the Italians. His "exaggerations" were "incredible." "The Spanish know that Spanish ingenuity is ingenuity like that of others; if it is encouraged it becomes agile, quick, shrewd; if neglected it becomes lazy, torpid, inert, as has happened and is happening in other parts of the globe." It was enough to look at the history of Spain itself to be persuaded. "Compare the Spain of Charles III with the Spain of Charles II. Any more German government and we would still be in the torpor of the past century." Masdeu's error lay in his concept of the nation as something natural and permanent. "Spaniards know that the political and moral character of the nation is not a natural instinct that inclines people naturally to a determined mode of life or to customs conforming to a law of nature, but it is the result of government, legis-

---

[11] Ibid., no. 32, October 1781, letter to doctor Ristori from the villa, 20 September 1781, pp. 252ff.

[12] Ibid., no. 33, October 1781, letter to doctor Ristori from the villa, 27 September 1781.

[13] Compagnoni would remember this dispute in his *Colpo d'occhio sullo stato presente della letteratura italiana*, of 1788, published in *Giornali veneziani del Settecento*, ed. Marino Berengo (Milan: Fetrinelli, 1962), p. 637: "Masdeu was Hercules, while Lampillas was Atlas who took crumbling Spanish literature on his shoulders."

lation, religion." This was a lucid enlightenment conclusion. Masdeu instead, "amid the splendor spread everywhere by philosophy, adopts its name to denigrate it."[14]

In the same year that these words were published it became known that Masdeu hoped to have his *Storia critica* published by Bodoni, in Parma. A subscription was launched and the *Memorie enciclopediche* supported it by saying that "we lack such a history and flatter ourselves that Italy will receive it with applause."[15] But then nothing happened. The work, "written and published in Italian," came out, one volume after the other, in Madrid, from Antonio de Sancha, beginning in 1783. It was planned in nine volumes; the sixth was to be entitled *España restauradora de la cultura en Europa*, the seventh *España conquistadora de un nuovo mundo*, the eighth *España austriaca*, the ninth *España borbonica*. In reality, with the twenty volumes he had published in 1805, he did not succeed in arriving at the Middle Ages. Meanwhile, his hostility toward Italy and Rome increased.

What succeeded better was the effort to make known to Italians the history not of Spain, but of the Spanish empire.[16] Throughout Europe there was now a vivid interest in the past and present of the American dominions of Charles III. Raynal and Robertson were read and discussed when they wrote of these problems, "not less by politicians than by practitioners of all the sciences," the gazette of Venice reported in the summer of 1780.[17] But only in Italy fundamental books on Peru, Chile, the region of the Andes, and Mexico appeared, thanks to the presence of many ex-Jesuits coming from those parts. The most famous of these volumes, Francesco Saverio Clavigero, was also a greenhouse product, the fruit of Spanish patriotism born in a different and potentially hostile climate. He had written it, as he himself said, "to break the tedious and loathsome inaction to which I found myself condemned, and to serve my land and nation as I might."[18] He wrote it in Spanish and then translated it into Italian himself. Among his predecessors he even recalled Lorenzo Boturini Benaduci, but he did not fail to emphasize that a distance separated his own patient and erudite work from the ideas of this man who had wanted to interpret Mexican antiquities in the light of the *Scienza nuova*. "The system of history that he formed was

[14] *Nuovo giornale enciclopedico*, March 1783, pp. 117ff., "News communicated by a Learned Spaniard on the *Storia critica di Spagna*."
[15] *Notizie del mondo*, no. 39, 17 May 1783, p. 316, "Avviso," and *Memorie enciclopediche*, no. 16, May 1782, p. 128.
[16] Batllori, *La literatura hispano-italiana*, pp. 22ff., and, naturally, Gerbi, *La polemica del nuovo mondo*.
[17] *Notizie del mondo [V.]*, no. 58, 26 July 1780, p. 468, in the footer.
[18] *Storia antica del Messico*, opera dell'abate D. Francesco Saverio Clavigero (Cesena: Gregorio Biasini, 1780), vol. 1: "Prefazione," p. 1.

too magnificent and thus too fantastic."[19] The attention of Clavigero was fixed on Raynal and Robertson. The fourth and last volume was dedicated to "His Excellency Sig. Giovanni Rinaldo Count Carli, to thank him in the name of the Americans," even beyond the fidelity of the Spanish nation.[20] This element was visible also in the work of Lorenzo Hervás y Panduro, where an unlimited and unmeasured cosmopolitanism was joined with a vivid interest in the language and civilization of individual nations and a tenacious preference for anything Spanish. If much attention was given to linguistics it was because, as he said, "idioms are a vivid portrait of the human species, where one sees painted the nature of diversity in the multitude of its nations."[21]

The historical appetite of these exiles had no limit, passing from the primitive church, to developments in Spanish regions, to the *Storia, civile, ecclesiastica della repubblica di Venezia* (twelve volumes on this theme were published by the Andalusian Cristobal Tentori, but with little success), to Portugal in the age of Pombal (as we have seen when discussing Francesco Gusta).[22] With Juan de Osuna one passed on to journalism. The *Notizie politiche*, the *Notizie letterarie*, and the *Genio letterario d'Europa*, which he edited in Cesena between 1788 and 1793, are interesting for understanding the revolutionary developments of those years in the Papal States and, above all, the multifarious world of Spanish ex-Jesuits.[23]

The exile who contributed most, beyond all literary and historical

---

[19] Ibid., p. 16.

[20] His necrology is in the *Gazzetta universale*, no. 28, 7 April 1787, pp. 222ff. (Bologna, 3 April). After having praised his great learning, it concluded: "Italy was the first to have this work in its own language, with an extraordinary concurrence: the Germans, French, and English immediately made their own versions. A person of the highest taste and respectability in Spain requested in haste the Spanish original, before the Italian edition was made, perhaps so that his country would not be deprived of such a great work by one of its sons. Some intrigues then delayed the publication, but the author remained calm."

[21] *Origine, formazione, meccanismo ed armonia degli idiomi*. Opera dell'abate don Lorenzo Hervás, socio della R. Accademia delle scienze ed antichità di Dublino e dell'Etrusca di Cortona (Cesena: Gregorio Biasini, 1785), dedication to the Dublin Academy, p. 9. The previous year he published with the same bookseller a *Catalogo delle lingue conosciute e notizie delle loro affinità e diversità*. On his historiographic ideas and the discussion these provoked in Spain, see Angel Gonzalez Palencia, "Nuevas noticias bibliográficas del abate Hervás y Panduro," in *Eruditos y libreros del siglo XVIII* (Madrid: Instituto Miguel de Cervantes, 1948), pp. 193ff.

[22] *Saggio sulla storia civile, politica, ecclesiastica e sulla corografia topografica degli stati della Repubblica di Venezia ad uso della nobile e civile gioventú*, dell'abate D. Cristofo Tentori spagnuolo (Venice: Gasparo Storti, 1785). In volume 1, dedicating his work to Alessandro Almoro Tiepolo, Venetian patrician, the author spoke of himself as a "foreigner, away from my fatherland and placed by an obscure act of providence in the most unfavorable circumstances." On Gusta, see above, pp. 211ff.

[23] See Giuseppe Carlo Rossi, "La Spagna nelle 'Notizie letterarie' (Cesena, 1791–92) di Juan de Osuna," *Filologia romanza*, year 3, fasc. 1, no. 9 (1956): 90ff.

debate, to making known the economic and political problems of Spain
was Antonio Conca.[24] He was born in Onteniente (Valencia) in 1746,
entered the Company in 1760, and, like others, was expelled from Spain
in 1767. We know little or nothing about his first years. But beginning
in 1781 we have his rich, detailed, and cordial letter book, which permits
us to follow this Spaniard in his daily life as well as in his intellectual
activity.[25] For years and years he did not miss a post in writing to his
friend in Florence Giulio Perini, the noted scientist and administrator
of the Accademia dei Georgofili. Their correspondence is more sparse
in the beginning, was intense between 1784 and 1789, and then became
sporadic in the following more difficult and agitated years. His youthful
life in the Order is completely forgotten in these letters. Conca was now
well convinced that the Company was dead and buried. "That *parce se-
pulto* (spare the buried) of the gentle Virgil" seemed to him the only
thing that remained to hope for it.[26] He even reached the point of asking Perini for a pastoral letter of the Jansenist Scipione de' Ricci and
called him a "saintly bishop."[27] Not religious disputes but rather patriotism dominated his soul. Any occasion served for him to praise "patriots" and to show "zeal for the nation."[28] The surroundings in which he
had to live often aroused his anger. "The other day a Ferrarese had the
presumption to characterize Spanish nobles as proud and fanatic in my
presence. Imagine what Conca with his fire and patriotism said to
him."[29] Every year the anniversary of his departure from his native land
plunged him into sorrow. "I write to you on the anniversary of the first
day of the nineteen years of our exile from Spain. . . . Imagine my soul
immersed in this abyss of melancholy, without seeing the least glimmer
of hope."[30] His disappointment and impatience grew with his years of
exile. In the summer of 1789 he wanted to go to Livorno "to see the
Spanish squadron and my compatriots." For this he would have
"pawned even his stockings."[31] At the same time he asked Charles IV,
the new king of Spain, to be allowed finally to leave Italy along with
other ex-Jesuits. His letter book is a crescendo of "national love."[32]

　　The desire to feel close to his fatherland, to make known its best

---

[24] See Franco Venturi, "Economisti e riformatori spagnoli e italiani del '700," *R. stor. ital.*, year 74, fasc. 3 (September 1962): 539ff.

[25] Firenze, AS, *Aquisti e doni, Lettere a Giulio Perini*, mazzo 93, ins. 52.

[26] Ibid., 12 September 1785.

[27] Ibid., 11 February 1788.

[28] Ibid., 15 September 1783.

[29] Ibid., 9 May 1785.

[30] Ibid., 3 April 1786.

[31] Ibid., 24 August 1789.

[32] Ibid., 10 June 1789.

things, and to make himself valued by the authorities of his country prompted him to write a series of notices and reviews in the Florentine *Novelle letterarie*, which was edited at that time by Marco Lastri and was filled with news of works on economics, administration, technology, and law.[33] Through a series of correspondents, among whom the most frequently mentioned in his letters to Perini was Carlos Andrés, the brother of Juan, Conca received whole crates of works that he sent to Florentine bookstores and erudites, while also making them known to the readers of the *Novelle letterarie*. He then sent his "extracts" to Spain, to authors and political figures. He became the pivot of an active intellectual exchange between the two countries. Thus he made known, to give an example, the Spanish re-elaboration by the Duke of Almodóvar of Raynal's celebrated *Histoire philosophique et politique*, Cavanilles's writings on natural history, Manuel Sisternes y Feliu's *Idea de la ley agraria española*, and Sempere y Guarinos's works.[34]

In these years, the desire to do something more, that is, to provide the translation of a particularly significant Spanish work, was also born in him. "Perhaps I should translate the work of the Count of Campomanes on industry and popular education. We will discuss this," he wrote at the end of 1784.[35] He worked on it for all of 1785, sending it finally to his friend Perini to look through it at the end of the year. On 30 January 1786 he wrote that he "was consoled because he had feared it was worse than that." While still continuing to work, he contacted Campomanes, who agreed that the work be dedicated to him. "What do you think? Keep it a secret," he announced to Perini.[36] Carlo Andrés was the one to take the manuscript to Campomanes. He "was very busy . . . and thus leafed through it reading here and there, and said that it was very good, and that he had no reservations."[37] He at first planned to have it printed in Parma (but Bodoni was too slow), then in Florence, and finally in Venice. He supervised the work of composition himself on the spot. "I don't want to make a profit, but I don't want to spend either." "I hope my friends will help me distribute the copies."[38] In the summer of 1787 the book—which was a fine edition—began to circulate, and soon it began to be talked about in journals such as the *Novelle let-*

[33] See Maria Pia Paoli and Rosalba Graglia, "Marco Lastri: Aritmetica politica e statistica demografica nella Toscana del Settecento," *Annali della Fondazione Luigi Einaudi* 12 (1978): 117ff.

[34] *Novelle letterarie*, no. 53, 31 December 1784, cols. 842ff.; no. 38, 22 September 1786, cols. 605ff.; no. 12, 23 March 1787, cols. 188ff.; no. 23, 10 June 1785, cols. 363ff.

[35] *Lettere a Giulio Perini*, 20 December 1784.

[36] Ibid., 13 August 1784.

[37] Ibid., 4 September 1786.

[38] Ibid., 1 January and 14 April 1787.

terarie, the *Giornale fiorentino di agricultura, arti, commercio ed economia politica*, and the *Efemeridi letterarie* of Rome.[39] At the same time it reached Madrid, was presented to Campomanes, and was well received. The statesman said that "the preface and what he had read of the translation 'was to his taste.' "[40] It is true that Conca was obliged to wait until May of the following year to be granted a pension, which was added to what he already received.[41]

Campomanes's work, one reads in the preface of Conca, was intended above all to furnish news of the "different revolutions that had taken place in Spain in the last three centuries, that is, its period of flourishing, its decadence, and then its happy resurgence."[42] Three periods thus replaced the traditional vision of Spanish history as a flourishing followed by a decline. This could have, Conca was convinced, some significance even for understanding the situation of Italy. "It is undeniable that industry and manufacturing have also declined in Italy, where the fertile soil produces in abundance all the raw materials necessary for the arts, in the practice of which, Italians, by native disposition, are very close to the taste and delicacy of the Greeks. This is an object that deserves treatment by a citizen no less zealous than enlightened, so that Italy can be relieved of the disadvantage of a negative balance of payments in many manufactures and goods that could easily be produced in that country." "Sig. Campomanes gave this encouragement to Spain."[43] It was not that good writers on economic matters were lacking in Italy. "Abate Galiani," Campomanes himself had written, "demonstrated to France that agriculture alone is not sufficient for, or capa-

---

[39] "Languid and superficial," Conca judged the extract in the journal of Lastri (no. 28, 13 July, cols. 443ff.). (See the letter dated 30 July.) "Beautiful" instead seemed to him that of the Roman periodical (no. 40, 26 July, pp. 237ff.). (See the letter of 24 September.) The most important review was in the *Giornale fiorentino*, nos. 31 and 32, 3 and 10 August, pp. 235ff., 251ff. The work of Giovanni Fabbroni, who had read it to the Georgofili, was an open eulogy of the Spanish reformer, whose ideas he wanted to make known to Italians. "Campomanes himself and his translator give me arguments to believe that the English and Spanish are, as I always thought, the same kind of people and that a legislator could make Spain as industrious as England if he wanted." Very flattering as well was the review in the *Nuovo giornale letterario d'Italia*, no. 1 (first quarter of 1788) 10ff. "What is for us the illustrious president Verri is for Spain the Count of Campomanes. . . . Our author fights with all the energy of a philanthropist matriculation into the guilds, like their other privileges . . . the worthy translator has enriched it with admirable and appropriate annotations."

[40] *Letter of Giulio Perini*, 24 September 1787.

[41] Ibid., 9 May 1788.

[42] *Discorso sopra il fomento dell'industria popolare*, del conte di Campomanes, tradotto dallo spagnuolo da Don Antonio Conca, accademico georgofilo fiorentino (Venice: Carlo Palese, 1787), p. iv.

[43] Ibid., p. xliii.

ble of, maintaining a country."[44] But what counted was a total program, which included as much agriculture as industry, and above all could mobilize the energies of the country by reducing the number of holidays, diffusing everywhere "the use of small-scale manufacture of silk," introducing "popular industry" even "in the enclosures of convents," spreading new types of cultivation, crops, new manufactures, improving sanitary conditions and spreading inoculation, founding and developing everywhere agrarian academies.[45] A consciously artisanal and popular program was proposed for the attention of Italians that was intended to persuade them of the "risorgimento" taking place in the kingdom of Charles III.

Prevented from returning to Spain, which he much desired to do, Conca continued to seek ways to make Spain better known and to illustrate its political and economic initiative. Departing from the *Viage en España* by Antonio Ponz and taking into account what Bowles, Bourgoing, and many other English and French travelers had written about it, he compiled four thick volumes, a true portrait of Spain in the process of reforms, just before echoes of the revolution in France came to change the whole situation deeply. This time Bodoni published the work through the intervention of the Marquis of Llano, who, after having been minister in Parma, had become ambassador in Vienna. Artistic monuments, naturally, were given first place, but Conca never missed an opportunity to mention agrarian academies, writers such as Azara, Campomanes, Jovellanos, Foronda, Cavanilles, Sempere y Guarinos, and many other representatives of the most lively period of the Spanish enlightenment.[46]

The decisive moment of encounter between the Spain of Charles III and Europe, as the crisis of the old regime deepened, occurred about

---

[44] Ibid., p. 123.

[45] Ibid., pp. 8ff., 9 n. 3, 14ff., 24 n. 7, 50ff., 62ff., 151ff. The review that appeared in the *Novelle letterarie*, no. 28, 13 July 1787, cols. 443ff. (it might possibly have been the work of Conca himself), brought to light the central nucleus of this work: "The activity of the people is the true mover that can lead a province to prosperity. It is thus necessary that other groups, who are not the people, assist as much as possible. This is the aim of the book and also its greatest merit. The rebirth of the arts has already begun in Spain and has made an excellent provision for a great push of internal and external trade in the monarchy."

[46] *Descrizione odeporica della Spagna, in cui spezialmente si dà notizie delle cose spettanti alle belle arti degne dell'attenzione del curioso viaggiatore* di Don Antonio Conca, socio delle reali accademie fiorentine e de' georgofili (Parma: Stamperia reale), vol. 1, pp. 1, 13, 210; vol. 2, p. 110; vol. 4, pp. 40, 146, 351, etc.

1782. Spain at that time was confronted not as much with the criticism or indifference of Italians as with the derision and disdain of the French. And the encounter this time did not take place in a land of exile, among literary men, artists, and historians, keeping itself within the limits of academia, but involved diplomats and ministers. The Spanish reexamination of its own conscience, after having suffered for a long time the consequences of the statist and anti-Jesuitical policy of the Catholic monarchy and of his holiness Clement XIV, was thus imposed from without, from Paris. Beginning with a polarity between Spain and Italy, the dispute rapidly became cosmopolitan and European.[1]

The initial spark came from an article in the *Encyclopédie méthodique*, the colossal undertaking projected by Panckoucke, the chief French bookseller at the end of the seventies, which was launched by him finally, after long preparations, in December 1781. It was intended to be, and in fact was, the biggest book of the century; its ambition was to be the perfect and most complete encyclopedia, the complement and apotheosis of the work Diderot had imagined forty years earlier.[2] "From Voltairianism to professionalism," Robert Darnton has called the general tendency that inspired these first volumes.[3] Nicolas Masson de Morvilliers, the man responsible for the section on *Géographie moderne*, had given some proof of professional knowledge in this field by publishing, among other works, an *Abrégé élémentaire de géographie universelle de l'Espagne et du Portugal*, which appeared in 1776, but his soul was dominated chiefly by the model of Voltaire, and also by the atmosphere of more and more heated polemics aroused by Raynal. An advocate in the Parlement, he did not exercise his profession. As secretary to the Duc d'Harcourt, he had directed his vivid polemic against Fréron, Rivarol, Linguet (whom he called at this time "that reptile of the Pindus"). The preface written for the section of the *Encyclopédie méthodique* that was entrusted to him was flat. But he changed his tone when he came to speak of *Espagne*, "royaume considérable de l'Europe": "Small foreign power, poor

---

[1] See Luigi Sorrento, "Francia e Spagna nel Settecento. Battaglie e sorgenti di idee," in *Vita e pensiero* (Milan, 1928); John Dowling, "Moratin's Circle of Friends: Intellectual Ferment in Spain," in *Studies in Eighteenth-Century Culture*, ed. Ronald C. Rosbottom, vol. 5 (Madison: University of Wisconsin Press, 1976), pp. 165ff.; and above all François Lopez, *Juan Pablo Forner et la crise de la conscience espagnole au XVIIIe siècle* (Bordeaux: Institut d'études ibériques et ibéro-américaines de l'Université, 1976). A solid synthesis is in Gonzalo Anes, *El Antiguo Régimen: Los Borbones* (Madrid: Alianza Editorial Alfaguara, 1975), pp. 459ff., with a useful bibliography, pp. 506ff.

[2] The story of this publisher's undertaking has been brilliantly and solidly told by Robert Darnton, *The Business of Enlightenment: A Publishing History of the Encyclopedie, 1775–1800* (Cambridge, Mass.: Harvard University Press, 1979), pp. 395ff.

[3] Ibid., p. 447.

and weak internally, no industry or productivity, in a good climate, which is the gift of nature."[4] Citing at length "one of our greatest writers," that is, Raynal, he repeated that fortunately the Spanish did not know how to develop their empire, nor were they capable of following the example of the English colonists, but instead they left all their trade in the hands of other Europeans. The government of Spain was otherwise even unable to avoid the great famines that afflicted this country. "Spain, that now-paralyzed nation, needs a great shock to get it out of its political lethargy." Great were its "moral and physical qualities," miserable its past, rich its language. "And meanwhile this people so well born, this nation so estimable in many regards," was worthy of compassion. "The proud Spanish noble blushes to educate himself, to travel, to try something of other peoples," and rejects the sciences, economics, and commerce.[5] "This kingdom is not as populous as it could be." The "despotic administration" was the first, evident cause of the situation. "The expulsion of the Moriscos" had been "a political mistake as serious as the revocation of the Edict of Nantes." "The great numbers of monks and of the religious, the too-numerous clergy" also weighed on Spain. As for the Inquisition, in this country like everywhere else it had "restricted freedom to act and think, stifled all great and useful views, created a people made up of hypocrites and slaves, hindered progress in industry and the arts, and consequently destroyed the population." Venereal disease, excessive taxes, emigration, continuous wars, unmarried soldiers, "penal laws that stream with blood" also contributed to the depopulation of the country.[6] Charles III had taken some steps to remedy these ills, above all in religious matters. In Austria Joseph II had given an example of what it was necessary to do with his "plan that was as wisely conceived as it was firmly executed." It was now up to France to refuse finally "to exchange its gold for bulls and indulgences."[7] But in Spain the power of the Inquisition, "that barbarous tribunal," remained strong, and through its history it had committed "unheard-of excesses" and "cruelty that make one shudder," as much in Europe as in the Indies.[8] In general, priests had always been "tyrants of nations when they are not their consolation, which happens when the lassitude of government permits ecclesiastical power to cross those limits that are fixed by reason and justice."[9] Masson concluded with a portrait of the Spanish

---

[4] *Encyclopédie méthodique, Géographie moderne*, vol. 1 (Paris: Panckoucke; Liège: Plomteux, 1782), p. 555.

[5] Ibid., pp. 556ff.

[6] Ibid., pp. 559ff.

[7] Ibid., p. 560.

[8] Ibid., pp. 561ff.

[9] Ibid., p. 563.

nation, which is "perhaps the most ignorant of Europe." Foreign books were prohibited, censorship was heavy. "Today in Denmark, Sweden, Russia, and even Poland, Germany, Italy, England, and France, all these peoples, who are friends, enemies, rivals, burn with a generous rivalry to advance the progress of the sciences and arts." "But what does one owe to Spain?" To this question, which was central to his entire article, Masson responded by looking both at the past and at the present. Spain was a kind of colony of Europe; it behaved like an invalid who, "not knowing his malady, thrusts away the arm that brings him life." Thus, "even if a political crisis was necessary to break its shameful lethargy, why continue to wait?" Its economy and culture, its internal and external commerce, even its navy, showed the complete passivity and impotence of the Spanish government.[10] Daily life, even the amusements of the people (and naturally Masson considered bullfights at length), showed their pride and courage, but also their grave defects. But the author still did not end his article without indicating some, even if weak, hope for the future.

Better days for this kingdom are perhaps not far in the future; philosophy, continually repulsed, has finally penetrated the nation and has already destroyed a crowd of prejudices. The nobility affects less the vain pride that makes it ridiculous; men of merit, some of common birth, have been called to public affairs. The countryside is better cultivated, several large cities have opened manufactures . . . magnificent roads have been built for communication among different provinces; navigation and irrigation canals have been constructed; one sees on all sides paper mills, printworks, and societies devoted to the sciences and arts . . . Finally, Spain already has several famous scholars in physics and natural history. With a little more effort who knows to what heights this superb nation might rise![11]

If, in other words, there were no signs of a healthy political crisis, Masson seemed to conclude, there was no lack of symptoms of multiple reforms, which he seemed to date from the moment when a man of nonnoble origin, like Floridablanca, had reached the government.

As one sees, Masson echoed, with an emphatic tone but not without a notable adherence to the political reality of the moment, the disdain and condemnation expressed by enlightened Frenchmen from Voltaire onward toward the land of the conquistadores and the holy Inquisition. The negation of any function of Spain in modern history derived from the age-old discussion of the decadence of that land, and now, precisely in the year that ended the war, from the difficult situation in which the monarchy of Charles III found itself, as an ally of France and the

10 Ibid., p. 565.
11 Ibid., pp. 566ff.

United States, but closed in on itself to avoid suffering the ideological consequences of its alliances. It was a defensive patriotism, fearful of the possible consequences of a diffusion of enlightened ideas within the mother country, and above all in its colonies, but aware that the now evidently indispensable work of reform would provide a fatal new opening for a "continually repulsed philosophy," which now with the peace presented itself again at Spain's door. The reaction against the *Encyclopédie méthodique* and the article by Masson did not come, at least at first, from cultivated men, or even from the Inquisition (which was even unusually bending toward the work of Panckoucke), but from the government and the monarch himself. It was Charles III who sounded the note of official patriotism. Floridablanca made known to Vergennes that the sovereign had not appreciated at all what he read in Masson's article. In Paris Aranda obtained suspension of the publication of the incriminated encyclopedia. The Spanish translation of its first volumes encountered new obstacles and caused considerable commercial losses.[12] The young secretary of the French ambassador through whose hands the long negotiation passed, Jean François Bourgoing, then the chargé d'affaires, finally concluded that Spain had made a great error in transforming the dispute about Masson's article into an affair of state. "To make a show of authority in such circumstances is not to refute calumny, but to give it credit, or at least to add to its publicity."[13] The English certainly did not generally act in this way. In short, Spain did not know how to take into consideration the weight of public opinion now recognized everywhere. The first reaction of Floridablanca was to impose silence and seek to maintain reserve with regard to the problems of his land. Not that he did not know the seriousness of the situation, but he intended to reserve its resolution for the Spanish themselves. "We are more aware of our backwardness and from what it arises than . . . travelers who come to Spain to write a book." Spain could accept advice given in good faith, not ironies and irritating exhortations that increased the "antipathy of our nation toward the French."[14]

The response to Masson, written by Don Antonio José Cavanilles, a

---

[12] Defourneaux, *L'inquisition espagnole*, p. 154 n. 1. The gazette of Venice had followed these developments in a correspondence from Holland: "In a volume of the new Encyclopedia organized by subject, one should read the article "Spain," which is by Mr. Masson, and probably will bring reprobation to the author. It is known that Mr. Aranda, before leaving Paris, showed his disapproval in no uncertain terms" (*Notizie del mondo [V.]*, no. 6, 21 January 1784 [Amsterdam, 7 January]).

[13] Jean François Bourgoing, *Tableau de l'Espagne moderne*, 4th ed. (Paris: G. Dufour et Ed. d'Ocagne, n.d.), vol. 1, pp. 307ff.

[14] Letter to Ignacio de Heredia, the Spanish chargé d'affaires in Paris, 3 January 1784, published in López, *Juan Pablo Forner*, p. 355.

botanist living in Paris, had an official and academic character. He contented himself with setting forth once again the long list of Spanish glories, not failing to defend even the clergy and the Inquisition.[15] The debate began to be important only when its center shifted from scientific and literary culture to conquest and the empire, that immense political construction of which the very mass seemed to respond to Masson's impertinent question, What does one owe to Spain? The French Encyclopedists could ignore what they wanted to about Spain, but not that its men had assured "to Europe the precious future of both Americas."[16] This was an even more significant fact when compared with the results other countries had obtained with their empires. The revolt of the British colonies was barely mentioned, but the weakness of those of the Dutch and French was brought fully to light. What advantage had the native population ever derived from the English domination of Honduras? "And still these were the most industrious, powerful, and commercial nations of Europe." The cruelties of the English and French in India had been terrible and were carried out even in the age of Milton, Newton, Montesquieu, and d'Alembert. "No modern nation can reproach another with the violence and perfidity of its politics."[17]

Discussion of the Spanish conquest aroused, as one sees, a general critique of European colonization. The Spanish, who had done much to exclude their land from the ideas of the American Revolution, as well as from accusations and invectives Voltaire and Raynal inspired, thus found themselves led, by the very logic of their defense, to reconsider the problem of their transoceanic dominion. Rejecting the criticism of Masson, they undertook a defense of the oldest, most ponderous, and most backward empire then in existence, but they were obliged to open the door to increasingly pressing needs to reform its structure. Thus, for Spanish America the discussion centering around the *Encyclopédie méthodique* was a symptom of the changes that followed the end of the war. As the gazette of Lugano wrote in 1783, "Because the government wants to prevent the impression the English colonies might make in those vast regions, it thinks seriously of employing the two most effective means of keeping the Americans in duty and loyalty; the first consists of sweetening the weight of authority, and the second of garrison-

---

[15] Antonio José Cavanilles, *Observaciones sur l'article "Espagne" de la Nouvelle Encyclopédie* (Paris: A. Jombert, 1784).

[16] Words taken from an anonymous manuscript cited in D. Antonio Ponz, *Viage fuera de España* (Madrid: Joachin Ibarra, 1785), vol. 2, pp. xviiiff. This text is discussed at length in Bourgoing, *Tableau de l'Espagne moderne*, vol. 1, pp. 309ff.

[17] Bourgoing, *Tableau de l'Espagne moderne*, vol. 1, pp. 311ff., and Ponz, *Viage fuera de España*, vol. 1, pp. xlii, cruelty of the English in Asia, without any of the "defenders of justice and humanity" raising the least protest.

ing troops in those provinces where some suspect movement might be feared."[18] These measures were even more necessary because the news coming from these places was anything but reassuring. It seemed that in Peru "uprisings" continued. "It is said that in Mexico the leaders of the government have been massacred."[19] The execution of Tupac Amaru had not put an end to discontent. One of his brothers had placed himself at the head of the mutineers.[20] At the same time, during 1784, the Spanish version of Raynal's *Histoire philosophique* began to appear.[21] The translator, the Duke of Almodóvar, who had been ambassador in Russia and England, executed the task official Spain required of him with diplomatic ability, that is, by making known the European debate on conquest and empire without the risk of involving Spain in it.[22] It was a question, J. Fr. Bourgoing wrote, of "less a translation than an extract, in that he has taken care to banish from the *Histoire philosophique* anything unfavorable to despotism and superstition by rectifying the many errors that escaped Raynal with regard to the Spanish colonies."[23] Five volumes of this translation appeared up to 1790, when the

---

[18] *Nuove di diverse corti e paesi*, no. 45, 10 November 1783, p. 359 (Madrid, 14 October).

[19] *Notizie del mondo [V.]*, no. 4, 14 January 1784 (Madrid, 23 December).

[20] Ibid., no. 33, 24 April 1784 (Madrid, 6 April).

[21] *Historia política de los establecimientos ultramarinos de la naciones europeas por Eduardo Malo de Luque* (Madrid: Antonio de Sancha, 1784).

[22] "It has been no mean effort to purify it of its poisonous effusions," declared the author in ibid., vol. 1, p. v. On the author see Emilio Beladiez, *Dos españoles en Rusia. El marqués de Almodóvar (1761–1763) y don Juan Valera (1856–1857)* (Madrid: Ed. Prensa española, 1969).

[23] Bourgoing, *Tableau de l'Espagne moderne*, vol. 1, p. 305. Already in a work published by him some years earlier the Duke of Almodóvar had written that Raynal's *Histoire philosophique* was "the most seductive, the most depraved, the most curious and instructive, the most conducive to errors of all kinds, and the best and worst of what has been written in recent times." As a demonstration of this, he cited the decision taken on this book by the *Mesa Censoria* of the "famous Marquis of Pombal": "Its author is one of those extraordinary men who even in the most indifferent works of natural science and philology, innocent by their own nature, systematically diffuse the poison of their libertinage." In politics, Raynal was a "scandalous monarchomach," capable of "discrediting the most refined nations, denigrating the most illustrious ministers, and slandering the most prudent and important institutions." But still, despite all these observations, Raynal's work remained very important. "It would be useful if a skillful hand took on the task of extracting from the said work, from this heap of theories and errors, the fine wheat found within it." With regard to Spain, Ignacio de Heredia, the secretary of the embassy, who, as we have seen, intervened in the dispute on the article in the *Encyclopédie Méthodique*, sought to collaborate with Raynal with the aim of a new reprint. This was in vain, as was seen when the Genevan edition of 1780 appeared, which constrained the author to exile. There was nothing to do but proceed directly to the corrections, as the Duke of Almodóvar did some years later. *Decada epistolar sobre el estado de las lettras en Francia. Su fecha en Paris ano de 1780*, por D. Francesco Maria de Silva (Madrid: Antonio de Sancha, A beneficio de la real Sociedad

changed international situation, and the fact that South America had
begun to speak for itself, made it seem advisable to interrupt the publication.[24] The question of the Spanish empire, which bloomed for a moment in the seventies and eighties, was forcibly set aside.

The debate returned to the field of the history of culture with a discourse by Carlo Denina in response to Masson's question about what
Europe owed to Spain. This had an element of personal vindication.
The Piedmontese author, from Prussia, where he then found himself,
tried to recall that it was he who had first begun to write the universal
history of literature twenty years before Andrés's fat volumes began to
appear. He could thus present himself as a competent and an impartial
judge in a dispute that now interested everyone, from one end of Europe to the other. This was even truer because he declared he was authorized even to speak in the name of the "philosophical monarch" under whom he lived, Frederick II.[25] He had the assistance of Spanish
diplomats accredited to Berlin and Dresden.[26] This support was made
more necessary by the critical stance he assumed toward the traditions,
claims, and pretensions of France. His became the voice of those who,
for the most different and even contradictory motives, felt on the defensive toward Paris of the eighties, where the heirs of the Encyclopedists
became more and more virulent and the counterblows of adversaries of
the Enlightenment more energetic. Denina avoided the most heated
themes, saying that he would occupy himself only with Spain in the classic age without speaking of the present. He mobilized theologians, scientists, and writers of the past to defend Spanish honor, while contemporaries were completely absent (the names Campomanes, Jovellanos,
and so on, were completely missing). At the center of his argument was
not the effort to renew Spain, but the decadence this country had at its
back, the causes of which Masson, Denina emphasized, had not been
able to clarify in sufficient depth. The causes, one then read, were very
human and very banal. After so many conquests Spaniards had finally
chosen to rest. "The gold of Peru, the silver of Potosí, the delights of
Italy, the industry of Flanders, and the faithfulness of Franche Comté
had belonged to Spain. With so many advantages, how could one not

económica de Madrid, 1781), pp. 109ff. I wish to thank Aldo Garosi who, years ago, gave
me a copy of this precious book.

[24] Richard Herr, *The Eighteenth-Century Revolution in Spain* (Princeton, N.J.: Princeton
University Press, 1958), p. 71.

[25] *Réponse à la question: Que doit-on à l'Espagne? Discours lu à l'Académie de Berlin dans
l'Assemblée publique du 26 janvier l'an 1786 pour le jour anniversaire du roi par Mr. l'abbé Denina*
(Berlin: Georges Jacques Decker), "Avertissement," p. 3.

[26] Sorrento, *Francia e Spagna nel Settecento*, pp. 179ff.

rest?"[27] Then the ascendancy of the French began in Spain, barely interrupted, only for a moment, by Italians in the age of Alberoni. "Government by Italians would perhaps have been as awkward as that of the French." The fact was that the recovery of Spain was further put off.[28]

In a series of letters in the appendix of his discourse, Denina could hardly help but return to the problems with which he had started. These involved not only those historians and literary men aroused by Lampillas, Bettinelli, and Tiraboschi,[29] but also closer political ones whom he had an opportunity to discuss with Honoré de Mirabeau.[30] Spain seemed to be about to produce good histories, worthy of standing beside the "history of Naples by Giannone," that "of Tuscany by the Abate Galluzzi," or the history of Milan "by Conte Verri."[31] For the moment Mariana continued to seem to him "the best model that could be suggested." By comparison, even the famous introduction by Robertson to his history of Charles V seemed "disproportionately long."[32] A true European dialogue was thus established, which ended up by touching the most sensitive points of the culture of those years, from the tradition of Voltaire to that of the *Encyclopédie*. But the basic questions Masson raised were barely opened, especially those regarding the empire and religion. "What he says on the subject of the Inquisition," Denina wrote at the end of his discourse, "although inexact and exaggerated, has some foundation." He had added, not without reason, that the rhetorical questions at the center of Masson's article, What does one owe to Spain? After two centuries, after four, after ten, what has she done for Europe? prevented effectively deepening knowledge of fundamental aspects of Spanish history, decadence, the church, and the relationship with its subject lands.[33]

Denina's intervention was best received in Spain. His *Réponse* was republished in Madrid by "the royal printer." Floridablanca himself requested its translation into Castilian by Juan Pablo Forner, and this appeared, in 1786, from the same press. Even the letters accompanying the *Réponse* were published in Spanish.[34] Still, a decade later, in publish-

[27] *Réponse à la question: Que doit-on à l'Espagne?*, p. 34.

[28] Ibid., p. 37.

[29] Ibid., *Sur la question: Que doit-on à l'Espagne? Lettre II, à monsieur le marquis della Valle*, à Mantoue, 15 February 1786, pp. 9ff.

[30] Ibid., *Lettre III, à Monsieur le comte de Mirabeau*, 15 February 1786, pp. 17ff.

[31] Ibid., p. 25.

[32] Ibid., *Lettre V, à monsieur le comte de Mirabeau*, 25 February 1786, p. 43.

[33] *Réponse à la question: Que doit-on à l'Espagne?*, p. 34.

[34] *Cartas críticas por servir de suplemento al Discurso sobre la pregunta . . .*, traducidas por don Manuel de Urquellu, cónsul general de España en todo el círculo de la Baxa Saxonia, residente en Hamburgo (Madrid: Don Plácido Barco López, 1788).

ing a translation of Denina's *Vicende*, the editor recalled that Spaniards
should be grateful to this author "for the works he has published in
defense of our nation."[35]

Floridablanca had requested the translation from Juan Pablo Forner, a poet and pamphleteer. He also received a discourse from him,
which after some hesitation he agreed to make public and which won
the author a good monetary reward from the king.[36] The patriotic disdain, the apologies for the past, and the desire to close in on themselves
that had appeared in the previous responses to Masson found here their
point of convergence. Forner's discourse was the reactionary pole of the
discussion developing throughout Europe on the past and present of
Spain. It did not pretend to be impartial. It was important to affirm and
shout forth his exasperated patriotism. Neither the sciences nor literature was at the center of his attention, but philosophy, "useful knowledge," as he called it, the capacity of Spaniards to accept society, government, and religion as they were, without protesting, and without
rebelling. This was exactly opposite, in other words, to the French philosophes. The learned, the theologians of Spain, had never been "harmful to their country"; "they have not provoked uprisings or raised up
peoples . . . they have never preached rebellion against the powerful."
Spanish professors had never transformed peaceful university controversies into bloody battles. "In tranquil subordination they have devoted
themselves, in whatever way possible, to the study of truth."[37] Precisely
at the moment of transition to modern Spain, amid the numerous struggles of its intellectuals against any kind of "abusive power," Forner,
blind, ignorant of the future, thus defended "tranquil subordination"
against the temptation of "universal reform." "Mental superfluity" for
him was any philosophy that attempted to go beyond Juan Luís Vives
and Francis Bacon. Beginning with Descartes, Europe had done no
more than construct "vain systems" "resulting in a kind of fury."[38] "We
live in a century of prophets." Everywhere reigned "audacious and vain
verbosity." Rousseau, Voltaire, and Helvétius were the most obvious examples. Under their influence Spain was losing touch with its past, with
the age when the country had known how to operate without discord.
Distant was that "industriously inquiring antiquity" that provided the

[35] *Discurso sobre las variaciones de la literatura*, escrito en italiano por el abate Carlos
Denina, traducido por don Roque Ignacio Vico (Segovia: Imprenta de Espinosa, 1797),
unpaginated.

[36] Lopez, *Juan Pablo Forner*, p. 371.

[37] *Oración apologética por la España y su mérito literario, para que serva de exornación al
discurso leido por el abate Denina en la Academia de ciencias de Berlín, respondiendo a la question:
qué se debe a España?* por D. Juan Pablo Forner (Madrid: Imprenta real, 1786), pp. xivff.

[38] Ibid., pp. 4ff.

ideal moment of the historical vision of Forner. One should return to it in mind and soul, breaking the historical myths Voltaire had put into circulation. It was necessary to restore vigor to the "orders, laws, statutes, rites, dogmas, doctrines, uses, styles that dignity and piety made venerable."[39] To be sure, Spain had neither a Descartes nor a Newton. In recompense "we had just legislators and excellent practical philosophy."[40] Descartes and Leibniz did not differ much from Don Quixote. Spain had to effectively defend its past against the "extravagant Voltaire." Censorship in his eyes was not only necessary, but natural and beneficial. If one condemned revolutionaries, why not also eliminate those who preached rebellion? "If the rascal, the *comunero*, the man who rises against supreme authority, is condemned to the wheel, how could it be possible to leave unpunished the arrogant man of letters who spreads the seeds of rebellion and accuses of tyranny the authorities who are the depositaries of justice?"[41]

To find the deep roots of this "wisdom of Spain" Forner went back to the Arabs, bringing to light the mediating function his country had played "in those dark centuries." "The Massons, Tiraboschis, and Bettinellis" had not recognized this historical merit, but it was nonetheless effective and important.[42] Nor was it true that scholasticism was born in Spain. It had been the French, Italians, Germans, and English who put it into circulation. The traditional practical wisdom of Spain had only accepted it, late, and only partly. Vives had struggled against "barbaric Paris and dark Bologna."[43] Later, the very expression "good taste" had been born in Spain and then was diffused throughout Europe. The Italian accusations of literary corruption derived from Spain were absurd, as much when they referred to the period of Seneca and Lucan as to more recent centuries. Even in matters of law the Italians were incapable of maintaining Roman tradition, which Forner seemed to defend with particular interest, reacting again against the criticisms and hopes of what he himself called modern "enlightenment."[44]

For more than a year the Spanish press discussed the conclusions that Forner had drawn from the debate on the historical value of Spain with great animation. An editor of *El censor* wrote with bitter irony that the true sciences were, it seemed, those that produced hunger, poverty, misery, and subjection. Thus at least heaven was secured. These kinds

[39] Ibid., pp. 8ff.
[40] Ibid., p. 12.
[41] Ibid., p. 18.
[42] Ibid., p. 55.
[43] Ibid., p. 100.
[44] Ibid., pp. 128, 64.

of sciences were extraordinarily developed in Spain, more so than in any other nation of Europe, and had reached their culminating point at the end of the seventeenth century, in the age of Charles II. Unfortunately, however, with the coming of the Bourbons, agriculture and commerce had begun to develop. Fortunately, it was added, defenders and apologists in Spain for authentic traditional doctrines were not lacking.[45] Forner responded, without adding anything new. Others took up the comparison Masson already made between Spain and Africa. Denina continued to be cited by defenders and adversaries of "ilustración." The debate about Spain, after having made the rounds of Europe, became a part of the discussion of the successes and failures, and of the plans and limits, of reform in the Iberian Peninsula.

"For some years," one read in the *Courier de l'Europe* in a letter from Madrid at the end of 1782, "there has been a quiet ferment among us: our knowledge has progressed to the degree where we begin to blush at our ignorance, and the example, more than the reproaches, of Europe has made us impatient with bearing the yoke of numerous institutions that oppose cultivation of the mind and the development of talent and reason among us." The timid hopes and vague dreams of the past were no longer sufficient. It was becoming clear that something quite different was needed to "deliver us from this kind of servility." The "audacity of patriotism and the intrepidness of virtue" were now indispensable. "The great work of the regeneration of Spain can be only the fruit of the firm and enlightened will of ministers, under a dear prince, who loves the good." Thus, the announcement of projects for reform the Council of State made on 3 November 1782 was "a feast day" in Madrid. Now past decadence was left behind, and a road was taken that would restore Spain to "the rank given to her by the size and fertility of her dominions and the nature of her products."[1] At the beginning of the new year, 1783, the gazette of Venice also echoed this wave of great hopes. The "embarrassments," the "burden of enormous expenses of war" did not prevent Spain from moving toward "a more flourishing state." "It seems that the happy inclinations of our sovereign have infused even the lowest of his subjects." The patriotic societies seconded

---

[45] *El censor*, discorso 113, 12 July 1786, cited by Herr, *The Eighteenth Century Revolution in Spain*, p. 225, and Mariano and J. Luís Peset, *La universidad española (siglos XVIII y XIX. Despotismo ilustrado y revolución liberal)* (Madrid: Taurus, 1974), p. 105.

[1] *Courier de l'Europe*, no. xlvii, p. 361, 6 December 1782 (Madrid, 6 November), letter of count de la Serena.

"the aims of the ministry with care and with incredible zeal and activity." Finance and public instruction were improved. "Foreigners of all nations, and even the Jews, but these under some conditions," were to be freely admitted to Spain. "By uniting schools of the nobility with those of the lower classes a source of jealousy dividing citizens will be eliminated." The universities will be "governed through quite different norms from the present ones. The study of ancient languages will be united to that of history, geography, ethics, and arithmetic. . . . A chair of commerce will be founded."[2] Projects in religious matters were just as notable. The government would induce "Don Luigi Bertrand, the grand inquisitor," to resign and abandon his title. Benefices the Holy Office once enjoyed would in the future be paid to the academies.[3] A wind of optimism blew from Spain to Europe. "A spirit of emulation and industry advances in this realm more and more."[4] The gazette of Florence echoed the struggle launched in Madrid against the "common prejudice of ignominy and baseness" linked traditionally to certain "arts and trades." "The king has ordered that the trades of tanners and furriers, locksmiths, carpenters, tailors, shoemakers, woodcutters, and others be henceforth considered honest and honorable." Thus was uprooted a long tradition originating at the time of the "wars with the Moriscos," from the "spirit of chivalry," and from the "pride of aristocratic pretensions." Since then there had been a period when the arts, for example, that of weavers, had flourished in Seville and in other centers of Spain. But "the expulsion of the Moriscos and the extreme rigor of some tribunals entirely destroyed the active spirit of these provinces." In vain Alberoni later had attempted to reopen the current. Measures were now finally being taken to combat the "decadence in which not only arts and trades but also commerce and manufacturing generally find themselves."[5] The creation of the Bank of San Carlo was a central moment in this battle. "All the capital . . . of primogenitures, entails, the goods of confraternities, chapels, hospitals, and other pious foundations, were to be deposited in it . . . and to be considered as an integral part of the same."[6] These were initiatives that intersected news coming from Vienna about the activity of Joseph II, particularly regarding the

---

[2] On the problems of the school, see Mariano and J. Luís Peset, *La universidad española*, pp. 114ff., 218ff., 296ff. ("Economía política, ciencia difícil y peligrosa").

[3] *Notizie del mondo [V.],* no. 6, 16 January 1783 (Brussels, 3 January). On the efforts to abolish the Inquisition, which as is well known dragged out fruitlessly at the Cortes of Cadiz, see Francisco Martí Gilabert, *La abolición de la Inquisición en España* (Pamplona: Universidad de Navarra, 1975), pp. 37ff.

[4] *Notizie del mondo [V.],* no. 12, 8 February 1783 (Madrid, 21 January).

[5] *Notizie del mondo,* no. 31, 19 April 1783, p. 245 (Madrid, 1 April).

[6] *Notizie del mondo [V.],* no. 31, 16 April 1783 (Madrid, 25 March).

reform of the clergy. "In Spain," the gazette of Venice wrote, "great applause has greeted the system of His Majesty the Emperor relative to ecclesiastical discipline and the suppression of different monastic orders, and a deputation of capable subjects will be formed to put in practice a good part of this, adapted to the circumstances of the monarchy."[7] To begin with, measures were taken to put into operation a custom "that prohibits and annuls any legacy left to confessors at the moment of the death of penitents, to themselves, their churches, orders, etc., if the will was not made before the last illness."[8] The year 1783 had not ended when the news came from Madrid that "a reduction in the number of monks is finally to take place in this monarchy."[9] From Paris news came that Aranda would be put in charge of the "revolution to be imposed on the monastic hierarchy in Spain." "It is anticipated that there will be a great suppression of monasteries, and that the revenues will support a large number of young Spaniards, who will be sent to the principal cities of Europe to learn the sciences, fine arts, manufactures, and commerce."[10]

This was uplifting news that nonetheless, already in 1783, was followed with official disavowals. "The news spread in foreign journals," one read in a foreign communication from Madrid in the Venetian gazette, "of the abolition of the Tribunal of the Holy Office, is entirely without foundation, since the inquisitor general enjoys the usual protection of the court, where he goes often, particularly on days of audience and gala. Recently he published a letter of exhortation, in which he urged the people to abstain from scandalous amusements in the current carnival season."[11] As for the measures regarding monasteries, these had begun to arouse lively opposition. "In all the monasteries of Madrid anonymous writings have been found thrown in through the entrance gates." These asked for an accounting of the administration of Jesuits' property and of ecclesiastical revenues passed into the hands of the state.[12] When the rumor spread "that the king was thinking of undertaking a reform of the regular clergy, the friars became agitated and resolved to elect deputies to demand audience in the Council so as to express their fears."[13] One month later the reform effort was already

---

[7] Ibid.

[8] Ibid., no. 32, 19 April 1783 (Madrid, 1 April).

[9] Ibid., no. 103, 24 December 1783 (Madrid, 2 December).

[10] *Notizie del mondo*, no. 104, 30 December 1783, p. 839 (Paris, 9 December).

[11] *Notizie del mondo [V.]*, no. 20, 8 March 1783 (Madrid, 18 February). On Felipe Bertrán (the name of the inquisitor general, not Louis Bertrand as mentioned earlier), see Defourneaux, *L'Inquisition espagnole*, in the index.

[12] Ibid., no. 6, 21 January, continuation of the news from Madrid taken from the gazette of Clèves of 7 January.

[13] Ibid., no. 13, 14 February 1784 (Madrid, 27 January).

becoming exhausted. "For some time," one read further in the gazette of Venice, "the publication throughout the monarchy of a reform of the regular clergy has been anticipated: now one hears that since some obstacles to its execution have arisen the matter is to be deferred."[14] In September the censorship of foreign books became more severe. "The king has renewed the old edicts that prohibited the introduction and sale of all foreign books . . . that have not obtained a particular preventive permission of the Council of State. Some too-liberal works, and particularly the *Encyclopédie méthodique*, have been the occasion for the renewal of the law."[15] Change in popular traditions and customs meanwhile became as difficult as reforming monasteries and schools. In the spring of 1784 another project was formulated, which also produced little result. "The Council has decreed an absolute suppression of bullfights, barbarous spectacles that have thus far been permitted only because of the false notion that they preserved the martial habits of the people. On the contrary, it is clear that they only nourish cruelty in the spectators and that romantic notions are nourished in an effort to give merit to such ferocious bravura."[16]

In different aspects of his reform efforts Floridablanca thus seemed to follow in the footsteps of Joseph II, the energetic sovereign who in these years was showing Europe how one should relate intervention in religious affairs to economic and social concerns, creating a true and proper battle plan against the prejudices and traditions of the past. Even in Vienna resistance and revolts were not lacking, which obliged the emperor to slow down and modify his plans. In Madrid the obstacles were even more numerous, and they were truly tenacious, whereas the desire for change was weaker. In the space of not many months Floridablanca passed from an incipient program of general reform to an effort to concentrate all his attention on the economy, above all on finances. From the example of Joseph II he passed to that of Necker, the minister who hoped to save France through technical improvements, abandoning the great plans of his predecessor Turgot. Even Floridablanca was taken up by the great illusion—which led Louis XVI to ruin—of confronting the crises of the old regime not with ideas, but with techniques, not putting in question the fundamental problems, but improving administration, assistance, education, and preserving and protecting the religion inherited from the past.

The "domestic utility of the kingdom" was at the center of the policy of Floridablanca, as the Piedmontese chargé d'affaires explained on 14 June 1785. "The minister now seems to be occupied exclusively with

[14] Ibid., no. 27, 3 April 1784 (Madrid, 16 March).
[15] Ibid., no. 76, 22 September 1784 (Madrid, 31 August).
[16] Ibid., no. 25, 27 March 1784 (Madrid, 9 March).

financial arrangements," he insisted on 9 August. "It is a matter of reforming all the different categories of functionaries, of correcting
abuses that have been allowed to penetrate almost all branches of administration . . . and of increasing taxes on various items, which, naturally, causes discontent throughout the country."[17] Leaving tacitly aside
the problem of the Inquisition, monasteries, and censorship, attention
became concentrated on affairs of state. "The great expense of the recent war, for last year's expedition against Algiers, for current preparations, and above all for the ordinary needs of the fleet has produced
a scarcity of specie in the royal treasury." The "most recent convoy from
Mexico" had been "richer than usual," but it was insufficient, and recourse had to be made to loans.[18] Signs of misery were clear everywhere.
"The number of evildoers during the war has increased to the extent
that public roads, and especially houses in the countryside, are not secure."[19] For this reason Floridablanca concentrated much of his activity
on "arrangements for relief of the poor, either sick or healthy." In every
quarter of the capital was organized "a deputation composed of the
most respectable persons in habits, age, and talent, selected indiscrimi-
nately among ecclesiastics and laymen," who were charged to "visit poor
families daily and find employment for those who are able to work."
The "larger part of the provinces of Spain" had followed this example.
This was a more effective means than construction of "great works and
luxurious edifices" carried out by "many European princes," who were
not able to take into account the "great disproportion between the value
of the assistance given and the expense made."[20]

At a financial level, the decisive measures taken in an attempt to
remedy the state deficit, and the steep inflation and general rise in
prices, was the creation, on 2 June 1782, of the Bank of San Carlo. The
idea for it came from François Cabarrus, a French merchant in Ba-
yonne, who was destined to play a role of first importance in his adopted
country in the years to come. In two or three years the new institution
had been transformed into a general commercial company and the chief
force behind the mercantile and manufacturing economy of Spain,
arousing great curiosity and becoming the object of an animated international debate.[21] The gazette of Venice of August 1784 thought it

[17] Turin, AS, *Lettere ministri, Spagna*, mazzo 92, 14 June and 9 August 1785.
[18] *Notizie del mondo [V.]*, no. 43, 29 May 1784 (Madrid, 4 May).
[19] *Notizie del mondo*, no. 37, 10 May 1783, p. 293 (Madrid, 22 April).
[20] *Notizie del mondo [V.]*, no. 32, 19 April 1785 (Madrid, 29 May).
[21] J. Vicens Vives, *Historia económica de España* (Barcelona: Teide, 1959), pp. 516ff. On
Cabarrus see Antonio Elorza, *La ideología liberal en la Ilustración española* (Madrid: Tecnos,
1970), pp. 139ff. The portrait of him by Goya is significant in its vulgar expression. See
Gudiol, *Goya*, vol. 1, plate 239.

could show where it found its inspiration. "In the excellent work of Raynal ... the author had spread ideas about the trade Spain could have in the East Indies. These ideas are now realized." The new company was born with the approval of the government. "Many Spaniards believe it was the work of the banker, but it is clear that Raynal provided the chief materials."[22]

The unexpected and somewhat mysterious character of the Cabarrus company did not dissipate later, when a large bibliography of studies and works accumulated about it. "Anyone who wants to form a judgment about this bank will have much difficulty," Giambattista Vasco wrote already in 1787.[23] He had taken to examining some of the more important works that had appeared concerning it. In June 1785 Honoré de Mirabeau, with the help of Brissot de Warville and Clavière (future ministers in the years of the French Revolution), and with the support of Calonne (then the French controller general of finance), put out a defamatory work: *De la banque d'Espagne, dite de St. Charles*. It contained, as he said, his "theory of public banks."[24] Among the many replies that appeared Vasco selected the *Tableau raisonné de l'état actuel de la Banque de Saint-Charles*, which was printed in November 1786 and attributed to different publicists.[25] The intervention of Valentín de Foronda, "a zealous apologist for the bank," ended the cosmopolitan list of authors reviewed by the Piedmontese economist.[26] Confronted with Europe convulsed by speculators, government interventions, and various efforts to remedy inflation and deficits, Vasco reacted by reevoking his liberal

[22] *Notizie del mondo [V.]*, no. 64, 11 August 1784 (Madrid, 13 July), "Extract of a letter from Madrid dated 20 July."

[23] *Biblioteca oltremontana ad uso d'Italia* (1788), vol. 6, p. 242.

[24] See J. Bénétruy, *L'atelier de Mirabeau. Quatre proscrits genevois dans la tourmente révolutionnaire* (Paris: Picard, 1962), p. 105.

[25] Ibid., p. 107 n. 1, and see *Nouvelles extraordinaires de divers endroits*, no. 3, 9 January 1787 (Paris, 1 January 1787): "One sees from the first lines that it is not by Mr. Warville, and even less by Mr. le comte de Mirabeau." It was attributed to Clavière. "It is surprising that this agent, whom one sees involved in the tortuous labyrinth of finance, knows so little about the land of which he speaks. Thus, the only response being prepared in Madrid is to have it translated into Spanish and distributed to show its small value."

[26] *Biblioteca oltremontana ad uso d'Italia* (1787), vol. 6, p. 258. See *Cartas sobre el banco de San Carlos*. "La primera y última por el maestrante de Ronda D. Valentín de Foronda, de la Academia de Ciencias de Burdeos, y de la Sociedad de Valladolid; y la segunda por mr. de la Rivière." Madrid: Benito Cano, 1787. The first letter from Valentín de Foronda is from Vergara, dated 24 August 1786. That of the celebrated Le Mercier de la Rivière was a defense of Mirabeau, to which Valentín de Foronda responded in his third letter. See Venturi, "Economisti e riformatori spagnoli e italiani," pp. 552ff. To follow the evolution of Foronda from the ideas of Victor Riqueti de Mirabeau, the "delicious work of de la Rivière," and the "daring and eloquent discourse of Boulanger," to a vision distant from that of the physiocrats, see the two *Cartas sobre los asuntos más exquisitos de la economía política* (Madrid, 1789), vol. 1, pp. 213ff.

convictions. "No law can overcome public opinion."[27] The harmful effects produced by attempting to fix the price of paper money could not
be avoided or mitigated. Cabarrus, "a most ingenious speculator," perhaps not wrongly accused of having "proposed the use of paper bills in
time of war, which necessitated the creation of the bank," ably published
the accounts of the bank of San Carlo each year, which, however, when
examined closely, showed the negative aspects of its varied activity as a
privileged commercial company. "It is appropriate to observe in this respect," he concluded, "that the government of Spain truly considers the
bank to be a necessary support for its finances: something perilous from
whatever government." Neither ministers nor councilors of state were
in a position to oversee "all the gears in the complex operation of trade."
"A king who entrusts his credit to a company of merchants and considers this indispensable in preventing the ruin of his finances, must preserve this society at all costs, and consequently give in to all demands
represented as necessary for its preservation." The profits of this policy,
Cabarrus maintained, would not remain in a few hands, but would be
distributed among an "immense number" of people. Even supposing,
responded Vasco, that one gave out one share each, this would be
150,000 persons, "for whose advantage it would not be proper to sacrifice the nation." "But anyone informed of the nature of such banks
knows that shares soon accumulate in a few hands." This had also happened in Spain, where, from what was said, "the large part of them"
had "passed into the hands of foreigners." "And for the 3,000 Spaniards
who share in the benefits, can one call useful to the nation a bank that
can exercise the most extensive monopoly at will?"[28]

Confronted with the "nascent financial capitalism of Spain, personi-
fied by Cabarrus," to use the words of the historian Antonio Elorza, Valentín de Foronda not only gave his assent in practice (he owned sev-
enty-five shares of the Bank of San Carlo), he also intervened with lively
polemical writings, printed in Vergara, the seat of the most active patriotic society of Spain.[29] Vasco, on the other hand, saw the negative elements of this experiment too clearly to approve it. He saw the fatal consequence of the efforts recently being made not only in Spain, but in
the major European nations in general, as an increasing dominance of
monopolistic groups within the state. He thus reacted by reaffirming his
liberal principles.

Something similar, but in larger proportion, occurred at the same
time in Tuscany, on the occasion of a deep discussion of the *Idea de la
ley agraria española* by Manuel Sisternes y Feliu, which was published in

[27] *Biblioteca oltremontana ad uso d'italia* (1787), vol. 6, pp. 244ff.
[28] Ibid., p. 261.
[29] Elorza, *La ideología liberal*, pp. 126ff.

Valencia in 1786.[30] This was one of the numerous projects for an agrarian code that came to light in these years and found its culminating point in the *Informe sobre la ley agraria* by Jovellanos in 1795. Sisternes, a high magistrate, continued the tradition of Campomanes and Olavide. His pages were nourished by a spirit of reform and interventionism, typical of great administrators and men of state in eighteenth-century Spain.[31] In Madrid critics of his *Idea* were not lacking; it was inspired by the desire to ensure a greater liberty to proprietors, to benefit large-scale over small-scale cultivation, and to support an agrarian liberalism of the type typically inspired by physiocracy. The ex-Jesuit Antonio Conca, his relative and admirer, who at this time, as we have seen, was dedicating himself to translating into Italian Campomanes's chief work, took the opportunity to compare the ideas of Sisternes with those of members of the Florentine Accademia dei Georgofili. His review appeared in the *Novelle letterarie* of 23 March 1787. He spoke of the great inquiry Charles III proposed and of the responses that had come from intendants and other authorities. Sisternes, "in whom wisdom and patriotism go together," had wanted to give his own opinion. The state should improve "the condition of those who possess nothing, by dividing among them a part of the vacant or uncultivated lands, or those owned by the Crown and by communities." "The snares and oppression that have kept agriculture subjected and disadvantaged must be removed." "No lands must remain uncultivated, but rather some profit must be derived from all of them to support population, arts, and commerce." The execution of this "agrarian plan" was to have been entrusted to a series of linked juntas at the village, city, and provincial levels, and finally to a central junta in the capital. "We conclude: one good law favoring agriculture is worth more than a hundred writers, but these are the forerunners of the other, and thus philosophers and legislators can contribute more than others to the public good."[32]

A translation of the book was considered briefly. Sisternes wrote to Conca, who would have preferred to have it examined first by the Georgofili. During the summer, in fact, three opinions were drawn up, by Luigi Tramontani, Giuseppe Bencivenni-Pelli, and Andrea Zucchini.[33] Under the compliments, which were not few and not cold, lay the reactions of Tuscan liberal and physiocratic minds. The "idea of taking property from those who do not cultivate it within four years" seemed

[30] Venturi, "Economisti e riformatori spagnoli e italiani," pp. 546ff.

[31] On the economic discussion in Valencia and particularly on Sisternes see the important essay by Ernest Lluch, "La fisiocràcia al país Valencià: Història d'un retard," in *Mayans y la ilustración*, vol. 2, pp. 673ff.

[32] *Novelle letterarie*, no. 12, 23 March 1787, cols. 188ff.

[33] Firenze, A. dell'Accademia dei Georgofili, bl. 2, sez. 1, b. 2.

"a violation that offends the liberty of the owner." "Those who do not want to, or cannot, cultivate will sell their holdings to the cultivator." How should the state decide who was in a position and who not to cultivate land? "Leasing to the poor, and to workers with a little land, will be good if these have the means to provide some surety. . . . Cultivation requires strength, which is a kind of opulence; if this is lacking, property will pass naturally to another hand capable of cultivating it." Despite these and other similar objections, at least one of the reviewers of Sisternes's book was struck by the desire for reform it revealed. "One must agree," said Bencivenni-Pelli, "that Spain is becoming more enlightened every day, and that the society and temper of this good statesman may be capable of restoring the kingdom to its old prosperity in the course of not many years." But it was necessary to decide to abandon all the old prejudices. Not a single pasture, not a wood, should be left without a private owner. It was wrong to think of collecting a portion of taxes in kind. Even technically there was much distance still to cover. For garden cultivation Liguria's example was good. Andrea Zucchini recommended that Sisternes read "the laws and acts of this royal sovereign Peter Leopold, archduke of Austria, which have been published on the occasion of the sale of the lease of communal lands and *fattorie* and the regulations for communal authorities. . . . Because these wise laws have brought infinite advantages to the Tuscan countryside, they might also be beneficial to Spain."

The *Voto dei deputati*, which was finally compiled, represented the official opinion of the Florentine academy. The problem discussed was "grandiose and of the greatest importance for the whole of Europe." Sisternes had been right to give preference to agriculture, and thus to follow the example "of other enlightened governments that have rested public happiness on this single point." His bases were solid: "Security of property, freedom of cultivation, freedom of trade in products, equality of public obligations among owners of all classes, abolition of domains whether commons or not, . . . the elimination of legal obligations on property as much as possible." "The patriotic zeal" and "the agrarian knowledge" of the author were thus without doubt. But he was thought to be too timid and cautious on many points. "It is against public economy to assign commons lands to different members of the community." It was unacceptable to grant an advantage in the distribution of land to "shepherds, miserable artisans, and laborers." This preference would be to the "disadvantage of the nation, and finally, after notable losses from insufficient production through the years, the holdings will fall into the hands of the rich. But these are precisely those who will be able to make them yield." It was absurd to hinder bringing in foreign capital and activity. The ineffectiveness of payments in kind had been demonstrated.

The conclusion was clear. There should be complete freedom "because those who are active require it."

When Conca had the opinions in hand he could not conceal his disappointment: "To tell the truth they seemed too severe." His Tuscan critics had not taken sufficient account, he thought, of local circumstances and conditions. He was convinced that with more flexibility and less pedantry it would have been possible to give practical assistance to Sisternes in his attempt to reform. Expressed in a more acceptable way, the criticisms would have been of assistance in making a new edition of the book, where he would have been able to "weigh his judgment" with more freedom, "in the opinion of the academy, since in many things he is of the same opinion, and for political reasons he would not hazard to reveal this without first hearing the judgment of learned men." It was truly a pity that the objections of the Georgofili were not publishable. "Sisternes, although in favor of their speaking with philosophical liberty, loves his country and hates pedantry."[34]

Thus, patriotism appeared at the conclusion of this interesting discussion between Spanish and Italian reformers, accompanied by a respect, or rather love, for local traditions. The Spanish acceptance of deeply rooted elements of collectivism and agrarian egalitarianism made the discussion more difficult, and it hindered acceptance by Sisternes and Conca of the liberal model that the Tuscans proposed with much conviction. The debate between Valentín de Foronda and Giovanni Fabbroni on prizes as incentives, on monopolies, on freedom of trade in grain, and mendicancy, which developed at the beginning of the nineties in a situation then much changed, revealed a similar convergence and divergence, even if it was also an important step toward acceptance by the Spanish of ideas that were more completely liberal.[35]

Interest in the happenings and realities of Spain remained extraordinarily lively in Tuscany during the second half of the eighties. The

---

[34] Firenze, AS, *Aquisti e doni, Lettere a Giulio Perini*, mazzo 93, ins. 52, letter of 24 September, 3 and 24 March 1788.

[35] Venturi, "Economisti e riformatori spagnoli e italiani," pp. 552ff. These problems are further examined, also on the basis of new documents until recently unknown, by Renato Pasta, "Alle origini del liberalismo toscano: Il contributo di Giovanni Fabbroni (1752–1822)," in *Annali della Fondazione Luigi Einaudi*, vol. 15 (1981), pp. 179ff. Later, of notable interest, was the discussion on Spanish agrarian problems found in the *Parere della società economica di Madrid sullo stabilimento di un codice di leggi agrarie umiliato al Supremo Real Consiglio di Castiglia*, disposto da D. Gaspare Melchior de Jovellanos membro della stessa. Tradotto dall'originale spagnuolo dell'Avv. Gio. Battista Nicolosi e dal medesimo corredato di note (Palermo: Giovanni Barravecchia, 1815).

communications from Madrid in the *Gazzetta universale* were excellent.
Despite the optimistic coloring, and the accent always placed on the
good intentions of the government and ruling class, it was still easy to
guess the obstacles encountered by the reforms and the unheeding resistance in which the best projects and initiatives became entangled. The
activity of the Economic Society was followed with admiration. In no
other country of Europe did such a varied and lively effort to improve
schools and economic techniques exist. Aragon was at the center of the
picture. In Saragossa, "at the expense of the royal Aragonese society,"
four schools had been founded "for mathematics, civil economics and
commerce, design, and agriculture."[1] At the end of 1786, beside these
arose chairs "of moral philosophy and natural and public law." They
were intended to "contribute to the introduction of the most delicate
literary culture in the sciences, along with the perfection of industry and
the arts." "The school of design, which contributes most directly to advancement in the arts, is the most distinguished, as much for the number of students as for the progress they make in it." Its "protector and
founder" was Juan Martín de Goicoechea, "who with much generosity
has not ceased to support and enrich it," providing "perfect models"
from Spanish artists as well as from "engravers beyond the Alps," such
as Bartolozzi. Even beyond Aragon "patriotic societies" had become "the
cause of a thousand happy inventions and useful discoveries." Thus in
Valencia those who "have perfected the method of coloring silk cloth,
an object of great interest in that industrious city," were rewarded. A
machine "that reduces brazilwood to powder" and another machine that
"cleans hemp" were exhibited. An "ingenious mechanic" "who has distinguished himself for various useful and original inventions . . . has
been strongly recommended to Count Floridablanca," especially "his
happy invention for making all kinds of stockings from cotton or wool
thread quickly and easily." "The operation of this machine, the simplest
ever of its kind, is easy and convenient." These inventions were all the

---

[1] Here is what Pier Paolo Celesia wrote from Madrid to the Republic of Genova on 5
October 1784: "Incessant are the cares of this government in matters of national industry,
or shall we say political economy, followed by the various free societies under the name of
Friends of the Country, which are established with public satisfaction in many cities of the
realm. The one in Saragossa has just established a free public school for political economy
in which the *Lezioni* previously given from the chair in Naples and then printed by the late
abate Don Antonio Genovesi are explained, amplified, and applied to the use of the country. His book is taken as the text, with the professor adapting it to circumstances. The
spinning of linen, hemp, and cotton appears to be what is most encouraged by prizes for
the quality and quantity of work" (Genova, AS, *Archivio segreto, Lettere ministri, Spagna*, busta
2482). I owe the reference to this document to the courtesy of Doctor Giulio Gianelli,
whom I thank.

more useful because "the kingdom of Valencia has an abundance of raw materials, and cultivation of cotton has been undertaken recently, for which many lands of southern Spain are suited." This was a lively and an up-to-date picture, as one sees, of the spirit that animated the deep transformation taking place in eastern Spain.² Roads and canals were opened "for commerce with Catalonia" amid the "acclamations of the people and transports of joy from multitudes." D. Ramón Pignatelli, the initiator of the new canal, was received triumphantly, moving "very slowly because for a long time he had been the victim of tertian fevers." "When the great work is finished . . . Aragon, Catalonia, Navarre, and Biscaya directly, and for their nearness also Valencia and old Castile, will receive, one could say, a new existence proportionate to the greatness of this undertaking." The new canal was in fact greater and more important than anything the Egyptians or Persians had done in antiquity.³ Such grandiose projects were accompanied by the capillary penetration of economic societies into the smaller centers. Talavera was nothing more than a "big village." Still, even there, at the end of 1786, prizes were offered to those who increased the production of silk. In fact, its production had increased considerably there.⁴ In Seville liberation "from African chains" by Ferdinand III, the saint, was celebrated by a meeting of the Patriotic Society. Now, in the cities, there was no street where one did not find "some free school for the education of spinsters." Young boys were able to demonstrate "advancement" in their studies, "particularly in mechanics and hydraulics." The celebrations ended with the hope that "the city of Seville, animated by patriotism and its advantageous situation," would rise to the height of its ancient splendor, "making relive that age when 60 thousand silk weavers and 400,000 persons employed by them honored industry in this place and created much activity in one of the most industrious cities of the universe." But

² *Gazzetta universale*, no. 2, 6 January 1787, pp. 9ff. (Madrid, 19 December). On the Societies of Saragossa and Valencia see Demerson et al., *Las Sociedades Económicas*, pp. 389ff., 331ff. On Juan Martín de Goicoechea, see Sarrailh, *L'Espagne éclairée*, in the index. His portrait about 1788 is reproduced in Gudiol, *Goya*, vol. 1, p. 250.

³ *Gazzetta universale*, no. 6, 20 January 1787, pp. 41ff. (Madrid, 2 January). See no. 22, 15 March 1788, p. 169 (Madrid, 26 February), where there is mention of the academicians of the Society of Aragon animated by "good taste as much as by love of their country and by the noble undertaking to make their nation rise again chiefly through the infinite advantages derived from the imperial canal."

⁴ Ibid., no. 7, 23 January 1787, p. 49 (Madrid, 2 January). On the Society of Talavera see Demerson, et al., *Las Sociedades Económicas*, pp. 303ff. On other examples of economic societies founded in smaller centers, see *Gazzetta universale*, no. 33, 24 April 1787, p. 257 (Madrid, 10 April). There is a detailed and interesting program of the Society of St. James in Compostela, the center of initiative in Galicia (ibid., no. 46, 9 June 1787, p. 361 [Madrid, 22 May]).

why had Seville declined? "In the famous age of the conquest of America, about which the question of whether the acquisition was advantageous or contrary to the prosperity and greatness of our nation is still
unresolved, the city of Seville alone counted within its walls more than
16 thousand weavers of wool and silk" with whom worked "130,000 industrious hands enriching and at the same time honoring our monarchy." The problems of decadence and empire were inevitably linked to
the search for a means of revival. The question, Were schools and encouragement enough? was basic.[5] In Madrid at the beginning of 1787
the friends of the country remembered how much impetus the "book
on *Popular industry* by Campomanes" gave to the activity of economic
societies. It was now up to "zealous patriots" to give it "new vigor."[6] Incidents and difficulties were not lacking. In Talavera the large factory
of cloth of gold and silver, and lace" had been burned "to the ground."
The loss amounted "to several thousand coined pesos." This "sad misfortune is not thought to be accidental."[7] Unemployment, or as a correspondent from Madrid expressed it, "idleness arising from misery
and depravation," was an open problem everywhere. The Society of
Charity founded in Granada had made an effort: "Five hundred and
twenty-two boys and girls were clothed and sent to respective schools,
64 persons given sustenance and maintained in their offices and trades,
and 13 artisans provided with looms and all instruments necessary for
their occupations." Others, men and women, had received "opportune
and charitable assistance." But all this had been insufficient. "A list of all
the poor of the city was finally made, except criminals and vagabonds
who do not want to work to sustain the obligations of society."[8] Meanwhile, everywhere in Spain old prejudices born from the "furor of conquest" and the "enthusiasm of knighthood" began to disappear, which
had led often to "the sacrifice of useful work in favor of fantastic, ideal,
and romantic honor." "Feudal nobles, barons, and warriors who destroy
society" were no longer considered "persons of importance." Such "turbulent ignorance" had been replaced by esteem and support for those
who create new cloth factories, as had happened recently in Segovia.
The entrepreneur was ennobled, along with his progeny, on the condition that none of these should "distance himself from the healthy principles of such a worthy progenitor and renounce the effort and cares of
such an advantageous and important trade." This was "a shining example of the progress philosophy has made in the mind of our monarch."[9]

[5] Ibid., no. 8, 27 January 1787, p. 57 (Madrid, 9 January).
[6] Ibid., no. 12, 10 February 1787, p. 89 (Madrid, 23 January).
[7] Ibid., no. 24, 24 March 1787, p. 185 (Madrid, 6 March).
[8] Ibid., no. 27, 2 April 1787, p. 209 (Madrid, 13 March).
[9] Ibid., no. 31, 17 April 1787, pp. 241ff. (Madrid, 3 April). On the activity of the

These changes of mentality could also be seen in the attitudes the authorities assumed, for example, in Cordova, with regard to prisons. "These gentlemen (that is, two senators of the city), considering the misery and abandonment of poor prisoners, and above all their idleness, which is a sure source of depravation, have determined to substitute easy and profitable work." They thus procured "a great quantity of Spanish esparto and broom so as to make ropes, cord, baskets, and other things woven of different colors." "All the prisoners willingly dedicated themselves to this under the guidance of a good master of such products." Even this was an example of how Spain, "awakened from its ancient lethargy, now moves rapidly toward objects of industry and commerce."[10]

As elsewhere in Europe, in Spain as well not only the living but also the dead were touched by the will to reform. "The murderous and unreasonable practice in the centuries of ignorance of burying corpses in sanctuaries" became a symbol of a reality that was now unacceptable.[11] Already in 1783 the Academy of History had published a book on this problem.[12] In August 1787, "finally our monarch, after mature and wise deliberation, resolved . . . to establish a uniform system in all his dominions with regard to ecclesiastical burials." Within churches henceforth could repose only "royal persons, bishops, the great, the owners of church sepulchres, and those men who for their heroic virtues are universally believed in time to become objects of public veneration," that is, the supreme figures of the civil and ecclesiastical hierarchies and candidates for sainthood. For the others there were "public cemeteries, which are to be built in airy places outside of the cities."[13]

For the living as for the dead, the principal obstacles to a transformation that might go beyond charitable activity and a greater development of education continued to come from the structures of the church. At the beginning of 1787 there was much discussion in Madrid "of the trouble an imprudent Capuchin caused in the capital of Aragon to Doctor D. Lorenzo Normante, lawyer of the Royal Council." "This enlight-

---

"charitable assemblies" in Madrid, see no. 45, 5 June 1787, p. 353 (Marid, 21 May). Those assisted in the capital were 10,414 poor. Schools were opened for 683 boys and 585 girls. On an interesting discussion of local finance in the Patriotic Society of Segovia, see no. 58, 21 July 1787, p. 458 (Madrid, 29 June).

[10] Ibid., no. 36, 5 May 1787, p. 281 (Madrid, 17 April).

[11] Ibid., no. 14, 17 February 1787, p. 105 (Madrid, 30 January).

[12] *Informe dado al Consejo por la Real Academia de la historia en 10 de junio de 1783 sobre la disciplina eclésiastica antigua y moderna relativa al lugar de las sepolturas* (Madrid: Antonio de Sancha, 1786). On p. xxvii there was a discussion of the provisions in Piedmont and in Savoy, and in plate 3 the *Diseño de los cementerios de Turín, situados a orillas de los rios Po y Dora*, was reproduced.

[13] *Gazzetta universale*, no. 38, 12 May 1787, p. 297 (Madrid, 24 April).

ened man, who is above all vulgar prejudices, two years ago, with the
approval and praise of our king, had the noble disinterestedness to de-
vote himself to giving lessons of commerce and civil economy in the
schools of the Patriotic Society of Saragossa without demanding any sti-
pendium." But having held that monastic vows should not be professed
before the age of twenty-five years, and that "luxury might to a certain
extent be useful to the state, when used by the government as an instrument to encourage industry and make the arts reach perfection," he was
violently attacked by "Father Cádiz, a Capuchin . . . an enthusiastic
preacher knowledgeable in Arab philosophy, who was nourished on
metaphysics and well endowed with scholastic wares." "The vehemence
of this fanatic preacher inflamed the fantasies of the multitude, who had
been aroused before by the noise of his missions; thus, many among the
people, and several others, have begun to consider Signor Normante an
evildoer and a corrupter of Christian morality." Many were surprised
that the Archbishop of Saragossa and the Captain General of Aragon,
the two highest religious and civil authorities, did not have "the courage
to reprimand, as was their duty, the audacity of an ignorant Capuchin
who disturbed the social order and profaned sacred places destined to
teach the faithful maxims of the Gospel and the fundamental precept
of religion, which is charity." It was necessary to conclude that "the influence of friars is great and terrible in our nation."[14] An inquiry followed, "to determine the degree of rashness of the Capuchin brother
Cadiz . . . and the fundamental orthodoxy or perhaps indiscretion to
which the zealous professor was subjected." "This affair," it was said in
March, "which seems on the surface an easy decision, will not perhaps
be so in practice." "The Capuchin has on his side a powerful party . . .
the regular clergy have a powerful protagonist with unlimited and very
versatile ability to manipulate the most difficult intrigues." But Don Lorenzo Normante had "another lawyer, who was a most valorous supporter and who, besides having a particular influence in the upright
mind of our monarch, has the advantage of a good cause and of being
supported by the enlightened and worthy men of the nation."[15] Professor Lorenzo Normante had, that is, appealed to the authority and wisdom of Campomanes. Many others, even ecclesiastics, intervened on his
behalf. The Society of Saragossa became involved and sought tenaciously to defend its own position. The whole city talked of it, "from the
most miserable workman to the most distinguished citizen."[16] Local re-

[14] Ibid., no. 5, 16 January 1787, p. 33 (Madrid, 24 December).
[15] Ibid., no. 30, 14 April 1787, p. 233 (Madrid, 27 March).
[16] Report to the king on 12 December 1788, cited in Sarrailh, *L'Espagne éclairée*, p. 276.

sistance prevented a worse outcome for the professor of political economy, despite the fact that in the end he was denounced by the Holy Office.

The activity of the "sacrosanct tribunal of the Inquisition" had all but ceased. In July 1787 it was communicated from Madrid that it had "proceeded recently to carry out a trial against an unhappy lawyer of merit, tried and convicted of little faith. The criminal was conducted to the secret chamber of that terrible place and had to make there the usual auto-da-fé. This time the castigation was carried out with pity and moderation, but still the penalty was rather serious."[17]

The monasteries continued to be fortresses of traditional ideas. Often located "in deserted places" they provided hospitality for travelers and "charity to the poor and pilgrims. But since alms, not guided by a prudent policy and distributed to everyone without distinction, serve as a great field for the cultivation of idleness and inspire love for only sloth, a great number of men and women and their children, abandoning themselves to a pleasurable inertia, spend their whole lives going and coming from charitable hospices where, sure to find the necessary support, they say a happy farewell to arts or useful work." In many places, on the request of patriotic societies, the superiors had been induced to "substitute an equivalent in money to their annual alms to be employed for the founding of free public schools of industry and letters, making all vagabonds and idle persons attend them."[18] But much remained to do even in this area.

Even more difficult was the affirmation of "freedom of the press," "which began slowly to breathe in the Iberian climate," as was demonstrated also by a spirited and polemical request in verse for an increase in salary by "many officers, particularly in the cavalry." They proposed to change places with whatever priest and even "brother of whatever religion as long as he is a mendicant, not excepting the lowest grade of lay brothers."[19] The chief demonstration of the reality of the press' growth of freedom was the multiplication of journals intended "to promote literature and augment the mass of erudite and useful knowledge." In the *Gazzetta universale* of 23 October 1787 there was talk of a *Diario de Madrid* by "D. Giacomo Thevin, who lives in the Puerta del Sol." Three times a week this periodical was supposed to contain "a

This is the most complete and interesting account of the Normante affair. The texts of his lessons are listed in Demerson et al., *Las Sociedades Económicas*, pp. 395ff.

[17] *Gazzetta universale*, no. 60, 28 July 1787, p. 473 (Madrid, 10 July). The man involved was Luis Mariano Cañuelo y Heredia, one of the editors of the *Censor*.

[18] Ibid., no. 53, 3 July 1787, pp. 417ff. (Madrid, 19 July).

[19] Ibid., no. 61, 31 July 1787, p. 482 (Madrid, 17 July).

faithful extract of all the best scientific journals with which European literature is almost suffocated these days." Postal rights had been obtained. "The inhabitants of this capital will receive it in their own houses on the days indicated without any inconvenience or thought." The list of periodicals the *Diario* was to consult was long, from the *Mercure de Frances* to the *Année littéraire*, from the *Journal encyclopédique* to the *Efemeridi letterarie di Roma*. Political correspondents "from Germany, England, and other countries" would not be lacking. This was an instrument adapted to counteract the age-old influence of the Inquisition. "There can be no doubt that this periodical activity, although managed by enlightened and philosophical persons, is poorly adapted to give to national literature that greater development that it needs, since it has had over it a tribunal with much authority, but badly conceived jurisdictional limits, for more than two centuries." The conclusion was optimistic. "It is certain that Spain finds itself currently disposed to and prepared for an easy revolution, whose signs are beginning to show unequivocally in the arts as much as in the useful sciences."[20]

The "revolution" was evidently less "easy" than the correspondent of the *Gazzetta universale* from Madrid hoped. He also indicated symptoms of weariness, which were not difficult to discern when observing the Spanish reform movement. On the occasion of creating a new economic society, that of Benavente, he noted, for instance, that one did not perceive only the satisfaction "of the people involved, and enthusiasm about the foundation of so many academies." "It is sad," he added, "that the results do not correspond to the hopes, this being attributed by some to one cause and by others to another." In reality, "regulations serve for little, as do good institutions if there are not wise and learned men to sustain them."[21]

From whatever vantage point, the center of the problem was always the Enlightenment, its energy and diffusion. The birth of new and significant periodicals was reported with special care. Thus, at the beginning of 1788, a sheet appeared, "which, however capricious its title, can be of all the more pleasure to the public if it is published as announced. The authors of this encyclopedic journal have called it the *Duende de Madrid* (The Elf of Madrid), and it proposes to criticize literary and scientific productions with philosophic liberty."[22] Another, "containing the

---

[20] Ibid., no. 85, 23 October 1787, p. 673 (Madrid, 2 October). On the *Diario* and on Santiago Thévin (or Thébin) see Luís Miguel Enciso Recio, *Nipho y el periodismo español del siglo XVIII* (Valladolid: Universidad, 1956), pp. 16off., and Paul-Jacques Guinard, *La presse espagnole de 1737 à 1791. Formation et signification d'un genre* (Paris: Centre de recherches hispaniques, 1973), p. 226 and n. 38.

[21] Ibid., no. 84, 20 October 1787, pp. 665ff. (Madrid, 2 October).

[22] Ibid., no. 1, 1 January 1788, p. 1 (Madrid, 11 December).

essence of the principal journals of all Europe," circulated three times a
week. A third was published every Monday, "with the name *El Observador*," and was occupied "not only with arts and sciences, but also with
government and legislation." "Thus, in a few months three encyclopedic
sheets have appeared in this city, which, directed by philosophical persons and by unprejudiced men, can contribute much to the development of prejudices [*sic*], to the perfection of arts, culture, and science,
and to the advancement of industry and commerce."[23] The year 1787
was significant in the development of Spanish journalism.

The reforms, however, marched in place. At the beginning of 1788
the *Gazzetta universale* made a comparison between the progress of the
idea of toleration in France and the useless efforts in this direction beyond the Pyrenees. "While the Parlement of France has succeeded in
supporting the good intentions of that sovereign with regard to the
Protestants," one reads in the sheet of 23 February, "it is disappointing
to see come to nothing all the efforts made by our ministry not only for
the toleration of the Jews and other individuals who are not Catholic,
but also for a reform of the religious orders, and a better system for the
clergy." The difficulties appeared precisely in the deputation "designated for this great purpose." It was agreed that the clergy should be
subjected to "annual contributions," "to be distributed for public needs,"
but this avoided touching the center of the problem, that is, "the widespread celibacy" and the excessive numbers of clergy.[24] As to their qualities, criticism was not lacking even by the authorities. "Assemblies of
respectable men held privately in Madrid" called attention to the "low
morality, disapproved and contrary to the Gospels and other sacred
writers, as well as to the spirit of the church" that was professed by ecclesiastics who continued to conceal "fraud, contraband, and disobedi-
ence to the civil laws, . . . all kinds of homicides, resistance, violence,
robbery, and assault as much on the public roads as in cities, continual
opposition to officials of justice, their ministers, and the military, despite
the vigilance of magistrates and penalties decreed by the courts." Laxity,
in other words, masked disorders of the clergy and impeded a thorough
struggle against brigandage and above all against internal smuggling.
These were serious words, which Floridablanca translated into a series

[23] Ibid., no. 9, 29 January 1788, p. 65 (Madrid, 8 January). On the *Duende de Madrid*,
the *Espíritu de los mejores diarios que se publican en Europa*, and *El observador*, see Guinard, *La
presse espagnole*, pp. 339ff., 265ff., 343ff. The first was soon condemned by the Holy Office
and survived for only six or seven issues. The second had as a collaborator Valentín de
Foronda and became one of the most important periodicals of the end of the eighteenth
century. It was sequestered only once and had the protection of Floridablanca (ibid., p.
272 n. 130). *El observador* had a short life and was also condemned by the Holy Office.
[24] *Gazzetta universale*, no. 16, 23 February 1788, p. 121 (Madrid, 5 February).

of "propositions," somewhere between a decalogue and a list of points of law.[25]

Meanwhile in Madrid, "assemblies summoned by our monarch, always with the greatest secrecy," continued. "It is believed that ecclesiastical matters, and the reform of the regular orders, is their chief concern."[26] No concrete reform emerged in the spring of 1788. Instead, there was an outbreak of devoutness at the court as well as among the people. It all started in an atmosphere of obstinate official silence. The deputies from Barcelona had promised not to speak of a surprising discovery made in their city. But it became known nonetheless that the body of San Pedro Nolasco had been found with all his writings, "deposited in his room and sealed with his own hand, by the wise and exemplary Jesuit of Barcelona P. Giacomo Pedralbes, resident in the College of Bethlehem, in 1764," that is, three years before the expulsion of the Jesuits from Spanish territory. Pedralbes was then exiled and died in Ferrara "with great sanctity on 8 March 1786." "High" was the "impression" this discovery made in the mind of Charles III, and in "all classes of the people." The "pious excavation" of the body of San Pedro Nolasco was carried out with solemnity. The circumstances surrounding it had "much that was strange and admirable and showed clear signs of divine origin." Even from a point of view "not less Christian than philosophic and impartial," it did not seem "likely that divine providence would have made disappear from the memory of men for five centuries and a half a French saint who honored our nation, his century, and humanity, to make him reappear for the veneration of the people without some high and evident purpose."[27] The reasoning was perfect, but the fact on which it was based remained uncertain: by whom and when were the bones of the founder of the Fathers of Charity found? Another silence followed while papal authorization was awaited to organize "a feast proper to our nation, dedicated to moving the sacred body and to making this mysterious event luminous and memorable, which brings much honor to Spain and considerable glory to the reign of Charles III."[28] Little was known about the saint who had been found, but for-

[25] Ibid., no. 21, 11 March 1788, pp. 161ff. (Madrid, 19 February). On the campaign against contraband, with the religious and political implications it involved, see no. 23, 18 March 1788, p. 177 (Madrid, 26 February). On the war of the state against the "practitioners of contraband," see no. 27, 1 April 1789, p. 209 (Madrid, 18 March). In no. 33, 22 April 1788, p. 258 (Madrid, 8 April), one reads that "the new legislation against contraband has sent to the prisons many obstinate persons in this ingrained business." The polemic continued for the whole year.

[26] Ibid., no. 30, 12 April 1788, p. 234 (Madrid, 25 March).

[27] Ibid., no. 47, 10 June 1788, p. 369 (Madrid, 27 May).

[28] Ibid., no. 53, 1 July 1788, p. 417 (Madrid, 17 June).

tunately Pedralbes, the Jesuit exiled to Italy, had taken care to write a life of him. In Barcelona the "greatest secrecy" was maintained throughout the summer. "When they are in a situation where they are able to speak freely," the deputies said, "they would reveal surprising things." The excavations continued, and the place of discovery was veiled from "public curiosity." There were even "ill-intentioned souls who tried to reduce the memory of the illustrious prophet to ridicule and did not hesitate to give him the reputation of a fanatic and a visionary." "But we hope the happy outcome of the miraculous discovery will soon put an end to the impudence and small faith of these."[29] Still, in October it was not yet time to "let the public feast on the religious pride of venerating the body of San Pedro Nolasco." No one had ever seen the body. The bishop of Barcelona had to make known that, "after the most lively and zealous search, it was not possible to enjoy the consolation of recovering the sacred body." There remained only to guess how such equivocation had come about. "Meanwhile, the barriers were taken down, the roads were repaired, and the excavated dirt from the grave site was taken to a nearby cemetery."[30]

San Pedro Nolasco thus seemed to become the saint, or at least the symbol, of the failure of religious reform in Spain. In reality the true candidate for this negative sainthood had already existed for decades, and he accompanied Charles III through his long life. We are assured by the *Gazzetta universale* that "amid the grave cares of the exercise of sovereignty our most pious monarch has not neglected to turn his beneficent gaze from time to time toward the great goal of the Palafox beatification." With admirable tenacity he had attempted to wrest from Rome the beatification of Juan de Palafox y Mendoza, a Mexican bishop who disliked the Jesuits and was their enemy. Decades passed. The Company of Jesus was expelled by the king himself. "Philosophy and severe morality" had prevailed in Spain. Other orders that at first opposed the bishop of the Puebla de los Angeles in the end recognized in him "the defender of effective grace, the conciliator of a pious Dutch church treated harshly by Rome, the persecutor of philosophical Pelagians and semi-Pelagians, and the best example of a saintly bishop." Under the pontificate of Clement XIV began "to sound sweetly in the pious ears of the good faithful the sweet name of the venerable one." It was hoped that under Pius VI the "hoped-for end" would finally be reached. But Palafox never became a saint. Neither the severe incense of Jansenism nor the support of Charles III could do so much. And neither could "money, one of the most indispensable requirements for overcoming

[29] Ibid., no. 74, 13 September 1788, p. 585 (Madrid 26 August).
[30] Ibid., no. 84, 18 October 1788, pp. 665ff. (Madrid, 30 October).

obstacles," or "the piety of so many faithful in our realm," among Americans, that is.[31] He remained a failed saint, whose image seemed to contain all that Charles III had not succeeded in accomplishing during the
thirty years of his reign.

    As one progressed through the eighties, the political repercussions
at the top from the difficulties multiplying in the way of Floridablanca
became more and more serious. The apparent harmony the old sovereign created was visibly crumbling; polemics took on tones that were
more and more bitter. Censorship, much liked and praised by Forner,
when applied to a society where the most pressing problems were already clear but where it was impossible to discuss them openly, turned
to satire and insult what could otherwise have been the beginnings of a
debate.[1] Thus the *Diario de Madrid* of 4 August 1788 published a poem
entitled "El raposo" (The fox). It had a polemical style that had something baroque about it, and it was intended to discredit Floridablanca in
the eyes of the king. Accused of being a vizier, of acting with pride,
astuteness, and so on, he was accused above all of committing an inex-
piable sin, that of thinking everyone equal.

> Todos los animales,
> grandes, pequeños, mansos y furiosos,
> eran para el iguales:
> con rigor los trataba y aspereza,
> y despreciaba fuerzas y grandeza.[2]

For this, all the animals finally united, ending up by inflicting on him a
slow and cruel death. The most diverse forces tended, in fact, to build a
coalition against him. One can see this in a plot by Italians "indicted as
criminals for having published certain anonymous papers, satires, de-
famers and calumniators of Your Excellency," among whom we find the
adventurous Giovanni Del Turco, whom we met in an earlier volume of
this work as the collaborator with Count Aleksej Orlov in the Russian

---

[31] Ibid., no. 1, 3 January 1789, p. 2 (Madrid, 16 December). See Venturi, *Settecento
riformatore* 2, in the index.

[1] Numerous and interesting documents on this situation are collected in *Obras originales del conde de Floridablanca y escritos referentes á su persona*, ed. D. Antonio Ferrer del Río
(Madrid: Biblioteca de autores españoles, 1899), vol. 59, pp. 273ff.

[2] "All the animals / great, small, tame, and wild, / were equal for him: / he treated
them with rigor and harshness, / and disregarded their strength and greatness" (Ferrer
del Río, *Historia del reinado de Carlos III en España*, vol. 4, pp. 230ff., 235 n. 1).

expedition to the Mediterranean in 1770 and the following years.[3] The fact that all the accused were foreigners gave the defense of Floridablanca a desired patriotic and even xenophobic character against "the many foreigners who come to Spain for pretended or indefinite reasons, without the state gaining anything from their presence."[4] The group of Italians was accused of wanting to "discredit and defame our government." Particularly offensive was the judgment they had made of Charles III, called "a passive, stupid, inert, and insensitive man." "What are we to say of the more than republican spirit that everyone breathes or the main clauses of the libel?" With their criticisms they had attempted to provoke "a general commotion of souls and a very dangerous fermentation of future revolutions."[5]

When these pages were written, in 1792, Charles III had already been resting in the grave for some years (he died on 14 December 1788). A new epoch had begun in Europe. In Spain, the conflict between Aranda and Floridablanca (in which the group of Italians was involved) became increasingly acute. The slow decline of Floridablanca became more rapid. In 1792 the new king, Charles IV, had him arrested and imprisoned in a fortress. The years of goodwill, patriotism, and hope for an "easy revolution" had ended.

Another reflection in Italy of the age of Charles III can be gleaned from the many funeral orations that accompanied his demise. From Spain itself came (it was soon translated into Italian) a posthumous portrait intended to present him as an exemplary monarch, free from any temptation to despotism. "Charles thought of himself not as a despot, nor as superior to the natural rights of property and the law, but as the legitimate administrator of the patrimony of the kingdom." He was an administrator more than a statesman; nevertheless, he was capable of collecting the fruits of reform when they were ripe. His policy toward the American colonies was presented as a masterpiece of calm acceptance of changes that were now unavoidable. He had found the transoceanic trade concentrated in Cádiz and carried out "by one fleet and one convoy, almost as is generally done in the East and in barbarian nations with caravans," and he left it free of any "tyranny of monopoly"

---

[3] "Defensa legal por el excelentísimo señor conde de Floridablanca," in *Obras originales*, pp. 359ff. See Venturi, *The End of the Old Regime, 1768–1776*, pp. 74ff. On the impression on Del Turco of Spanish culture, see ibid., pp. 87ff.

[4] "Defensa legal," p. 365.

[5] Ibid., p. 367.

and profitable "to all his provinces."[1] Having arrived in Spain from Naples, he found "a court that had within it all kinds of scandalous filth." He "transformed it into the most proper and clean court of Europe." The palaces he had inherited were "constructed through the dictates of ancient despotism." Now modern architecture had triumphed in the capital. Many "vestiges of the barbarous system" from before the arrival of Philip Bourbon still remained in the body of Spain, despite "barely healed scars." The work of Charles III had been devoted to removing them.[2]

The point of rupture—Monsignor Onorato Caetani, the author of another eulogy, admitted—had undoubtedly been the expulsion of the Jesuits. "This expulsion can be considered a Spanish matins, fatal for the Jesuits, which will remain as memorable to the world as the Sicilian vespers."[3] From that point onward Spain entered a phase of intense transformation. "All of Catalonia was filled with manufactures. Communications with the capital began to be opened, and magnificent roads were planted with useful trees. Irrigation or navigable canals were built. . . . Excellent manufactures for paper, print shops in the best taste, societies devoted to the fine arts and sciences would sooner or later reduce prejudice and ignorance."[4] The colonization of the Sierra Morena transformed "this inhospitable land, full of woods and wastelands, the haunt of evildoers, . . . into one of the most delightful spectacles offered by nature and regulated by the arts and industry." Pablo Olavide had made rise there "the new city called Carolina . . . one of the most gracious that one can encounter in Europe with regard to beauty, novelty, and symmetry." Colonel Vincenzo Imperiali, captain of the Italian guards in Madrid, praised it in writing to the Duke of Belforte, on 10 March 1776, in a letter that Monsignor Caetani was pleased to report in full. He was certainly not unaware of what had happened shortly after, in November 1776, with the imprisonment of Olavide by the Inquisition. But of that the ironic and tormented Monsignor Caetani did not speak at all, seeming content to show the reformer of Sierra Morena at the height of his glory.[5] His preference clearly was for those who, like "Raimondo Pi-

---

[1] *Orazione funebre in morte di Carlo terzo monarca della Spagne ecc. ecc. ecc.*, tradotta dallo spagnuolo nell'idioma italiano (n.p., n.d.), pp. 9ff. This was the work of José Nicolas de Azara. The translator was Giuseppe Maria Pagnini. It was printed by Bodoni in Parma.

[2] Ibid., pp. 13, 17ff.

[3] Onorato Gaetani [*sic*], *Elogio storico di Carlo III re delle Spagne* (Naples: Stamperia reale, 1789), p. 97. On the author, see Luigi Fiorani, "Onorato Caetani. Un erudito romano del Settecento," *R. Stor. Ital.*, year 84, fasc. 1 (March 1972): 238ff.

[4] Gaetani, *Elogio*, p. 78.

[5] Ibid., pp. 121ff. He did not fail to note, as he did for many other persons named in his *Elogio*, that Vincenzo Imperiali was his relative, and he added that this official had

gnatelli, Count of Fuentes, canon of the cathedral of Saragossa," belonged to the number of ecclesiastics "who in all times are well thought of by the state."[6] Varied and liberal was the culture of Monsignor Caetani. He continually cited Linguet and Raynal, Büsching, Adams, De Felice. His political horizon was dominated by the recent formation of "a strong republic in the thirteen United States," which was nonetheless menaced in his opinion by the corruption that would result even there from growing wealth. This was all the more so because the Americans had made that "great political error," to say it with Machiavelli, of not establishing a dominant religion. Disorder and confusion would fatally follow, and the question of a monarchy would arise again. "Would it be possible," Caetani asked, "to create a monarchy with the advantages of that of England or Poland, without having the disadvantages?"[7] Only in this way would one be able to eliminate the vice that remained at the root of the American constitution, "founded on the social contract of Jean Jacques, a writer who without knowing either man or the system of natural laws has wanted to be the legislator of families and political bodies." To make the people the only sovereign was "the same as leading the nation to ruin." "Were they perhaps unaware in Philadelphia of the ferocious excesses such a power had produced in Athens and Rome?" The history of Italy also taught what it meant to give all power to the people. It was, as Dante said in *De monarchia*, like crying: "Long live our ruin; death to our happiness."[8] Washington and Franklin were names that "would be perpetuated in universal history." But the recent death of Charles III reminded one how open the problems of the new republic beyond the ocean were, and how pressing was the need for a monarchy like that which for long years had ruled Spain.

A comparison between the religious policy of Charles III and the ideas of Rousseau returned often in these official farewells. Cesare Brancadoro, archpriest of the archdiocese of Fermo, addressing Pope Pius VI, underlined the danger of the "model of a 'civil religion' behind the new dogmas of the philosophe of Geneva, which it was desirable to substitute for the one professed by our fathers." The formula of a *Contrat social* was no other than "a monstrous joining" of two incompatible terms. Charles III had fully understood this. Even his "beneficence" did not derive from "a pagan and natural philosophy, but from a purified

been educated in Rome, "in the same place as Count Algarotti, Count Pietro Verri, and Father della Torre."

[6] Ibid., p. 123n. The portrait painted of Ramón de Pignatelli by Goya is in Gudiol, *Goya*, vol. 1, p. 277.

[7] Ibid., pp. 217ff.

[8] Ibid., pp. 218ff.

and immaculate philosophy of religion described by an apostle."[9] Similarly, in the oration delivered in the name of the city of Naples, there was a violent attack against "those modern libertine philosophers who abuse the names of enlightened minds and great thinkers and are in truth no other than an unhappy society of carnal men who do not know God, and who, with distorted judgments, altered views, and different estimations, call good evil and evil good." Against such souls it was necessary to contrast the "unity of politics and religion," never forgetting that the philosophes were "implacable enemies of all sovereignty." Otherwise one must entrust oneself to the "great guiding name of S. Gennaro."[10] Even orators less hostile to the Enlightenment insisted on the defensive measures Charles III took during his reign against the forces that seemed to menace religion. Father Castriota recalled how in 1751 he had prohibited, "with grave penalties, the group known as Freemasons."[11]

Reforms, as much in Naples as in Madrid, were emphasized by Pietro Napoli Signorelli, who painted in black the subjugation of "Sicily to the abject situation of a province," before the arrival of the young Bourbon king. "Our disordered countryside saw the armed wisdom of the laws become more and more timid, uncertain, and precarious before the powers and excesses of feudalism . . . the fields were depopulated of workers, and the woods and mountains filled with desperate brigands." After the tenacious work of improvement undertaken in Italy, Charles III had acted in Spain with the aim of "banishing idleness and populating the cities." "Perhaps it was not known that to him were owed so many societies, so many 'Friends of the country,' so many academies for cultivation and economics."[12] Canon Tataranni instead emphasized the work of reform of conscience in civil life. In the religion of Charles III the impulse to respect "the empire of conscience" in individuals seemed

[9] *Meditazione su l'urna reale di Carlo III di Borbone re delle Spagne* di monsignor Cesare de conti Brancadoro . . . arciprete della metropolitana di Fermo, dal medesimo umiliata alla santità di nostro signore Pio VI felicemente regnante (Parma, 1789), pp. 11, 22. On the author see the article by Giuseppe Pignatelli in the DBI, vol. 13, pp. 801ff.

[10] *Ne' solenni funerali di Carlo III Borbone monarca delle Spagne celebrati dall'eccellentissima città di Napoli*. Orazione del P. D. Raffaele Marmile C.R. (Naples: Gennaro Migliano, 1789), pp. 19, 23.

[11] *Pe' solenni funerali di Carlo III Borbone monarca delle Spagne*. Orazione di Pier Luigi Castriota delle Scuole pie . . . recitata nella chiesa del suo real convento di S. Pasquale de' PP. Alcantarini della provincia di Lecce nel borgo di Chiaia di questa città di Napoli (Naples: Vincenzo Flauto, 1789).

[12] *Ne' funerali in morte del cattolico monarca Carlo III*, celebrati nella R. Chiesa de' Santi Giovanni e Teresa, regio patronato di S. M. Cattolica. Orazione di Pietro Napoli Signorelli, segretario perpetuo della R. Accademia di scienze e belle lettere di Napoli (Naples: Filippo Raimondi, 1789), pp. 4ff., 20.

to have triumphed. "Since the day-to-day freedom of manners and the refinement of polite society resemble the almost imperceptible gradations between good and evil, vice and decency, lies and the truth, it is important today more than ever to counterpose an interior authority to this obscure depravation, one that will see through the mysterious subterfuges of dissimulation and pretense that are so active and organized." "A just and pious monarch" had "shamed the audacity and pride of the cardinal who wanted to introduce into this illustrious metropolis the tremendous and horrible tribunal of the Inquisition," just as he had opened the way to the policy continued by his son Ferdinand IV which prevented the people from falling victims to the court of Rome. He had thus put an end to "those multiple acts of intolerance that have dirtied the pages of history" and to "those scenes of seditions, wars, and terrors that the controversies of scholastic theology have raised in the great theater of the world."[13] This "evangelical doctrine" had led Charles III to give new vigor to the army, and to magistrates, and to remove from "feudal nobles . . . the power of their tyranny," as well as "their pride and rashness in making war with sovereigns." "He thus was the first to begin to humiliate that ferocious monster of human cruelty."[14] When he arrived in Spain obstacles increased in his path. "He viewed the tribunal of the Inquisition with dislike, he viewed with indignation the celibacy of priests and friars, which had produced such a void of population. He saw an immense continent almost deserted and abandoned. . . . He saw the mechanical arts in the hands of foreigners, and that natives thus rotted in idleness and laziness."[15] He did not become discouraged. "Aware of the close relationship between Christian morality and politics, he prepared himself for the prosperity of his kingdoms."[16] Campomanes had been "the creator" of his agrarian policy. "This great man saved from idleness and indigence infinite numbers of beggars; he instructed them in the trades of the countryside, in industry, and the mechanical arts; to some he gave rural implements, to others those of artisans; some he sent to places of education; he offered them prizes to make their best interests into a hope; he made them competitive, citizens, and sons of the state."[17] Great also was the effort of the sovereign regarding the transoceanic and internal trade of Spain. Tataranni's con-

---

[13] *Ragionamento sul carattere religioso di Carlo III*, umiliato a Ferdinando IV re delle due Sicilie dal fedelissimo e ossequiosissimo suddito il canonico Onofrio Tataranni (Naples: Donato Campo, 1789), pp. xivff.

[14] Ibid., pp. xviff.

[15] Ibid., p. xxiv.

[16] Ibid., p. xxvi.

[17] Ibid., p. xxviii.

clusions were optimistic as well because he intended to present the work
of the father as an incitement and model for his son, the king of Naples.

From Palermo came a first effort to view the work of Charles III in
the light of the great currents of European culture, from the "celebrated and renowned Englishman William Robertson" to the "erudite
and renowned, although too liberal, French author the Abbé Raynal."
These had now taught how mistaken the traditional policy of Spain was
with regard to the American territories. "An ancient policy lacking in
philosophy had kept those great colonies almost entirely separate from
their common mother Spain." The "advantageous results" Charles III
obtained in changing this policy "have proceeded and continue with a
rapid progress unprecedented in the history of nations," the Scottish
historian had written.[18]

In Parma the disappearance of Charles III was seen instead against
the background of uncertainty and disquiet that became heavier in Europe as a whole at the beginning of 1789. Charles III, beyond all the
reforms and improvements he made, had the great merit of showing
how to keep a people quiet. His great secret rested in the confidence he
had in religion. "What miracle makes all of Spain so faithful to its king
and peaceful in his shadow, so singular within itself, while such a great
part of the world is miserably shaken by turbulent events? Give me a
monarchy faithful to God, and it will also be faithful to its king. Charles
III had submissive and obedient subjects because first, with virtuous
zeal, he made them submissive and obedient to God." His "spirit of
Christianity" had impressed on him and his people the marks of "peaceful habit." His "firm attachment to holy church," his "great esteem for
all things holy and for holy persons," had produced in Spain an ideal
but rare situation of political and social peace.[19]

The official celebration held in Turin added little or nothing.[20] The
one organized in Rome by order of Charles IV, instead, is particularly
significant. The neoclassical interpretation of the will to renewal that
had grown in Spain in recent decades found in the ceremonies, pictures,
and architecture put together by Nicolas de Azara on this occasion its

---

[18] *Orazione in morte del re cattolico Carlo Terzo recitata nella chiesa cattedrale di Palermo dal
P.D. Saverio Granata C.R. a di' XXIX aprile 1789*, pp. 6, 10.

[19] *Orazione funebre in lode di don Carlo III re delle Spagne e delle Indie*, recitata nella chiesa
de' rr. pp. cappuccini il dí VIII di gennaio 1789 in occasione delle solenni esequie fatte
celebrare dal real infante di Spagna don Ferdinando I, duca di Parma, Piacenza, Guastalla
ecc. ecc. ecc. dall'abate Bernardo Botteri, proposto dall'insigne colleggiata del Battistero
di Parma (Parma: Real Stamperia, 1789), pp. 25, 29ff.

[20] *Nei funerali di Carlo III re delle Spagne*. Orazione detta nella metropolitana di Torino
da Carlo Luigi Buronzo del Signore, vescovo d'Acqui e conte principe del S.R. impero
addí XVII febbraio 1789 (Turin: Reale Stamperia, 1789).

most typical and energetic expression. Ugly, deformed, "almost barbaric" in his eyes was the church of San Giacomo degli Spagnuoli, where the funerary observance was to be held. He covered up its decorations and unacceptable features, which reminded one of the Dark Ages and were unworthy "of such a magnificent nation as Spain." At the center of it he had a cenotaph constructed, "a temple of the purest architecture," taking as a model "what the Athenians under the direction of Cimon erected to Theseus in the century of Pericles, the happiest century for the fine arts. Its order is Doric and it is of such noble simplicity that it enchants." At the top of this temple one saw "religion embracing a medallion in the form of a cameo containing the portrait in low relief of the hero of the function." At the center was an "urn of porphyry formed exactly like the one of Marcus Agrippa that was for many centuries in the Pantheon and is now in San Giovanni Laterano." Along the nave were pictures, "in the form of low reliefs with some of the most famous acts of Charles III," the work of followers and imitators of Mengs. The symbols, the costumes, the gestures, all tended to transform the life of the king of Spain into a classical representation, an eternal classicism, timeless. Even the medallions that accompanied the pictures tended to enhance this transformation. The work of Olavide in Andalusia, purified now of all the effort and pain it had cost, became a kind of apotheosis of the sovereign "*completatoris orbis terrarum*" (fulfiller of the terrestrial sphere). The "king in a toga," as Azara himself wrote, was represented in the act of holding "a plow pulled by two oxen guided by a fist, as in the ancient ritual of founding colonies, alluding to the one founded by His Majesty in Sierra Morena."[21]

The neoclassical forms thus reevoked the work of Charles III in its original intentions, in the great hopes these had raised, letting fall aside as useless chaff the difficulties, obstacles, rejections, and rebellions that Spain expressed along its route. In the churches, the memories, and the archaeology of Rome, the taste for Mengs, in the hand of Azara, tended to eternalize, immobilize, and crystallize the passions and impulses of the generation of Goya and Jovellanos.

In the same days that Azara organized the funeral rite in the church of San Giacomo, Jovellanos, also remembering the dead sovereign, spoke of a "happy revolution" that had taken place during the thirty

---

[21] *Descrizione dell'apparato funebre per le esequie celebrate dalla nazione spagnuola nella sua chiesa di San giacomo di Roma alla memoria di Carlo III per ordine di Carlo IV di lui figlio, re di Spagna, essendo suo ministro plenipotenziario presso la Santa Sede D. Giuseppe Niccola de Azara* (Rome: Presso Marco Pagliarini, stampatore di S.M. Cattolica, 1789), pp. vff., viii, xii, and xx.

years of Charles III.[22] The death of the sovereign seemed to have come
to fix for an instant the course of Spanish history, in its growing mo-
mentum and effort to carry out a "general reform," and in its "kind of
regeneration."[23] Soon echoes of the French Revolution arrived. But already at the beginning of 1789, before these crossed the Pyrenees, the
nation seemed to have stopped at the highest point of its effort at renewal and attempt to reform. Of this standstill the death of Charles III
seemed both a symbol and a sign.

[22] Gaspar Melchor di Jovellanos, *Elogio de Carlos III*, Leído a la Real sociedad de Madrid en la Junta plena del sábado 8 de noviembre de 1788, in id., *Obras en prosa*, a cura di
José Caso González (Madrid: Clásicos Castalia, 1969), p. 192.
[23] Ibid., pp. 189, 185.

IV

The France of Necker

THE FALL OF TURGOT, ON 12 MAY 1776, WAS SEEN NOT ONLY TO BE the failure of a policy of reform that in the immediately preceding years had enlarged and deepened from freedom of the grain trade to feudal rights, from the suppression of corvées to that of the guilds. The crisis was also perceived as a true change of course, the outright abandonment of a politics of principles. The age of the *Encyclopédie* was at an end. France turned its back on Voltaire, on the physiocrats, and on the now dispersed group of philosophes and turned toward a future with uncertain and misty contours, vague and attractive, but without those certainties indicated by the Enlightenment, which Turgot seemed to have reanimated.

Foreign policy did much to bring about the fall: the great economist knew well that reforms and a policy of intervention in America were incompatible. Apparently Louis XVI and his ministers selected the most traditional course: rivalry with England, a struggle against it on all the continents, and a revenge for the defeats suffered in 1763, at the end of the Seven Years' War. It was, in short, the policy of Choiseul, perfected and systematized by Vergennes, a typical example of a version of *raison d'état* distilled through the experience of the eighteenth century, and without any broader vision. This was a sufficiently candid policy to lead, out of hatred for London, to a rapprochement between Versailles and Philadelphia, that led, if only after two years of uncertainty and tergiversation, to a true alliance between the French monarchy and the nascent union of English colonies in America.[1] No one missed the paradoxical and irregular character of this convergence. Diplomatic, military, and financial affairs were, in fact, entrusted to men outside of the normal picture of French politics, to schemers, upstarts, and adventur-

---

[1] See Samuel Flagg Beamis, *The Diplomacy of the American Revolution* (Bloomington: Indiana University Press, 1957).

ers. It was not that France had disdained in the past making use of such
instruments. It happened especially when republics were involved. This
was the case in 1746 when it became necessary to reach some agreement
with Genova in the struggle against the Empire. There had been no
hesitation at that time in making use of a generally propagandistic image of France as a beneficent protector of republics.[2] But a comparison
between 1746 and 1776 shows how much things had changed in thirty
years. In between had been the crises of Poland, Switzerland, and England. Now, in 1776, it was impossible for the French government not
to be aware of the fact that to be tied to the America of the Declaration
of Independence involved a considerable risk. This peril was evident
when it became a question of involving the Spain of Charles III and of
defying the clear danger that the example of North America might be
reflected more or less immediately in the colonies of Central and South
America. Even the French colonies St. Dominique and Martinique were
all but solidly faithful to Versailles.[3] In France the enthusiasm the new
alliance and war aroused rapidly took on the role of a substitute, a recompense, for the lack or delay of reforms, and for the fall of the hopes
aroused by the beginning of the new reign. Franklin in Paris in some
sense restored a center of diffusion to the Enlightenment that it seemed
to have lost after the disaggregation of the group of the *Encyclopédie*.
And despite all the prudence, ability, and care of this American patriarch, it was impossible not to recognize that the center of the policy he
represented was not the military duel with England, but the revolt of
the Americans, not the interests of this or that country, but the political
liberty of a new nation, not the diplomacy of monarchical absolutism,
but nascent American republicanism. This policy of ideals and principles flowered and affirmed itself precisely when Turgot was obliged to
abandon his contested affirmation, within France, of the idea of liberty
and economic progress. He had tried to prevent France from taking the
route of active support for the colonies beyond the ocean precisely because he knew such an obligation would divert too much energy, too
many economic and political resources, from the necessary priority of
carrying out projected reforms without delay. Now, after his fall, the
desire to resume the struggle with England was tied more closely to the
American mirage. The France of Louis XVI assumed more and more
openly the function of a protector for the new liberty arising in the west.
Hard political and strategic reasons had prevented Louis XV from be-

[2] See Franco Venturi, "Genova a metà del Settecento," *R. stor. ital.*, year 79, fasc. 3
(September 1967): 777ff. and fig. 13.

[3] Charles-André Julien, *Les Français en Amérique de 1713 à 1784* (Paris: Centre de documentation universitaire, 1977).

coming the paladin of the Polish republic a few years earlier. There were efforts then as well through agents and volunteers, but in 1772 the paradoxical alliance of the Polish confederates with the absolutistic and despotic government of the old French monarch had failed before the agreement between Vienna, Berlin, and St. Petersburg.[4] Now a new great hope was arising, that is, that France might put itself on the side of those who proclaimed, through the mouth of Jefferson, that men had the right to change any government that had become insupportable to them. The hope was even livelier since behind the French was the smarting reminder of their inability to exercise such a right themselves. In this sense, one can truly speak of an American "mirage" in France.[5]

It was precisely this detachment, this imbalance between principles and reality, between realpolitik and great aspirations, that made possible and in some sense necessary the experience of Necker, that is, the long dominance of the Genevan banker at the head of the French finances. The paradoxical nature of his government has been emphasized often: he was a Protestant in a land where his coreligionists were persecuted, a bourgeois in a monarchy where a resurgence of nobles made itself felt in different ways; he had in his hands the key ministry of finance and was charged with finding money for a war that risked becoming a world war, but he had no possibility of influencing fundamental decisions, those regarding the course of the conflict itself. Undoubtedly some aspects of the historical paradox that carries the name of Necker have seemed more incomprehensible because they were viewed through modern and nationalist eyes rather than through the cosmopolitan eyes of the eighteenth century, the only ones that can lead us to an understanding of him. Thus, the Genevan origin of the banker was in reality only an episode and aspect of that complex relationship between monarchy and republics at the end of the old regime which we have observed in previous decades with regard to Genova and Poland and will see again with regard to Geneva and Holland: a kind of symbiosis that ensured the survival and continuity of both forms of government (and they fell together in the period of the French Revolution and the Napoleonic empire). The function Necker exercised at the heart of the French finances was otherwise only an example of the weight, in all states of the old regime, of that complex network of families and professional groups that crossed all frontiers, from Russia to Spain. Banks, armies, letters, and arts were the most evident examples of this cosmopolitanism, which was not only a fashion or tendency of the eighteenth

[4] Franco Venturi, *The End of the Old Regime, 1768–1776*, pp. 172ff.

[5] Durand Echeverria, *Mirage in the West: A History of the French Image of American Society to 1815* (Princeton, N.J.: Princeton University Press, 1957).

century, but a fact anchored deeply in the multiform political and social reality of Europe as a whole. One of the great merits of Herbert Lüthy has been to give us a detailed and precise picture of one of the most significant aspects of this cosmopolitan reality, the ramifications everywhere (including Italy, and above all Genova and Tuscany) of families of Protestant financiers.[6] Lüthy's book is thus the best introduction to a study of Necker's work precisely because it places him against the background of his coreligionists and compatriots.

But for the Genevan banker Jacques Necker to become the minister of finance of Louis XVI required a quite exceptional atmosphere, that of France during the seventies. Neither the history of social groups nor that of international organizations, and even less that of court intrigues, can explain a phenomenon such as this, so surprising in the eyes of contemporaries. Only the history of ideas and principles, and the debate that ignited around the physiocrats, preparing, accompanying, and following the experience of Turgot, can give us the key to understanding Necker's success and the limits of his policy. The merit of the most important recent work on him, Henri Grange's *Les idées de Necker*, consists in having put the problem into this perspective, even if, as we will see, not all of his conclusions seem acceptable.[7] Certainly this work is a step ahead of the otherwise admirable book by J. F. Bosher, which concentrates on the technical and administrative aspects of Necker's work, seeking, in the instruments created and used by him, the force and originality that were missing in his more general economic and political perspective.[8] Bosher's pages are acute, intelligent, and nurtured by deep research. But still, the important function of Necker in the second crisis of the old regime of the seventies and the eighties went beyond administration. "From business to bureaucracy" is a trend corresponding to a general evolution of the state, and not only in France. But this was still a stage, a technique, not an outcome or a solution. To improve, as Necker effectively did, the instruments for collecting taxes and administering the finances in general would not have been a final end in itself. What use would these improvements be? More general problems reemerged every day through confrontations with the thousand difficulties Necker attempted to overcome, as we can see in the chronicle of his activities narrated by Jean Egret.[9] However, such a traditionally con-

---

[6] Herbert Lüthy, *La banque protestante en France de la révocation de l'édit de Nantes à la révoluton* (Paris: SEVPEN, 1959).

[7] Henri Grange, *Les idées de Necker* (Paris: C. Klincksieck, 1974).

[8] John Francis Bosher, *French Finances, 1770–1795: From Business to Bureaucracy* (Cambridge: Cambridge University Press, 1970).

[9] Jean Egret, *Necker ministre de Louis XVI* (Paris: Champion, 1975).

ceived political narrative also soon seems insufficient. We are overtaken by the flow of events and are not able to pause over the developments and nodal points that emerged in the rapid changes of these years. There is a further, animated reconstruction in the recent book by Robert D. Harris.[10] Building on the discussions of Lüthy, Grange, Bosher, Egret, and others who have occupied themselves with the Genevan, Harris has tended to write a defense, even a rehabilitation of Necker, with the risk of treating him as a man rather than treating the problems and arguments with which he had to deal.

The chief cause for the continual alternation, which has now lasted two centuries, between a generic apologetic vision of Necker and a minute technical valuation of his actions has its roots in the writings of the Genevan banker himself. These do not have, or pretend to, a true scientific value; they remain plans and memoranda without authentic economic or historical reflection. They are precious and indispensable documents, but they need to be considered in the broadest perspective of his age. We are no longer in a period, like that, for example, of his great predecessor Machault in the middle of the century, when the minister of finance could content himself with writing decrees, leaving to writers like Voltaire to explain and support his policy. The great discussion of the age of the *Encyclopédie* had not occurred in vain. Necker had to explain and justify himself in relation to cultivated public opinion. The age of the philosophes was in crisis, and even declining, but the problems they had raised could not be forgotten, not even for a moment. A banking technician like Necker had to explain continually what his position was with regard to the great questions of power and justice. His program could not help but touch on the great problems of economic and political freedom. "Religion and government" were at the heart of his writings, as they had been of those of the young Diderot. To be sure, these problems were perceived with less intensity and lucidity, and with different conclusions, but they were still alive and unavoidable. Precisely by accepting this Enlightenment platform Necker was able to win supporters among Parisian intellectuals, whereas his rivals and followers, like Calonne and even the leaders of the parlementary party, were less successful. The ability and intelligence of Necker's wife had a part in this undoubted success. But the chief merit belonged to Necker himself, who did not hesitate to throw himself into the turbulent waters of the Parisian debate between the reigns of Louis XV and Louis XVI.

Let us open his *Eloge de Jean-Baptiste Colbert*, which appeared in 1773. Already on the title page we see his choice of position. He could not

---

[10] Robert D. Harris, *Necker: Reform Statesman of the Ancien Régime* (Berkeley: University of California Press, 1979).

have adopted a more characteristic motto: *Est modus in rebus, sunt certi denique fines, quos ultra citraque nequit consistere rectum* (There is an order in things, certain limits beyond which right procedure cannot stand). Forbonnois had already used it in 1767 in his *Principes et observations oeconomiques*. Moderation, the *ne quid nimis*, became the chief word of the day against physiocrats and liberals at the beginning of the seventies. They were accused of being abstract, theoretical, rigid, exaggerated, always incapable of adapting to the reality of things.[11] In other words, moderation was counterposed to principles. What should predominate was not ideas but a strong political personality capable of operating with firmness and rigidity to "defend ceaselessly public interests against private ones, society against the individual, and the future against the present."[12] Thus Colbert had acted, and Necker intended to do the same. He presented himself to his readers as a kind of reincarnation of the famous minister of Louis XIV. This man had shown that he was able to act to change France. Then the theoreticians intervened. "The writers came later; they reduced what he had shown by his actions to a system." To understand him it was necessary to return, beyond all theorizing, to the reality of his work: "Let us proceed in the light of his actions; let their light guide us, and if possible, we will approach his thought."[13] It was not at all true that Colbert had "displaced agriculture in favor of manufactures."[14] He had built canals and roads and struggled against usury to facilitate agricultural credit. In the fundamental question of the export of grain he was guided by circumstances. He did not trust the "power of freedom of trade." He had not forgotten that competition established an equilibrium, but in ways that were anything but immediate or pacific. The passage from one equilibrium to another occurred over a period of time, which is bearable when goods of luxury or convenience are involved, but is a "terrible interval when it is a question of a product that one cannot stand to be deprived of for a single day, where doubt itself is a danger, where the disquiet of a moment can disturb a whole province, weaken the sources of confidence, and produce even worse evils."[15] France, already in the age of Colbert, and even more so a century later, was not a land that could be governed by mediocre administrators convinced that they possessed "the secret of the universe." The size and strength of the nation made any drastic simplifica-

---

[11] See Franco Venturi, "Galiani tra enciclopedisti e fisiocrati," *R. stor. ital.*, year 82, fasc. 1 (March 1960): 48ff.

[12] J. Necker, *Eloge de Jean-Baptiste Colbert. Discours qui a remporté le prix de l'Académie françoise en 1773* (Paris: J. B. Brunet, 1773), p. 23.

[13] Ibid., p. 27.

[14] Ibid., p. 30.

[15] Ibid., p. 41.

tion impossible. The comparison with Geneva, his homeland, was always present before Necker's eyes. Small republics "exist only for the pleasures of equality." "But in a monarchical land, where rank and birth accustom one to distinctions early, those of wealth do not offend; on the contrary, they provide a consolation by giving talents a means of ascent." The poor, condemned by proprietors "to seeking only what is necessary," were accustomed to look to the rich "as beings of a different species and to their magnificence as an attribute of their grandeur. It is not that the poor are made unhappy by this spectacle: like the rays of a great day the show dazzles their eyes and distracts them from the pain of envy."[16] Parisians need not fear: the Genevan banker would know how to remain in his place as a great technician of a society that was quite different from the Republic of Geneva. He had taken the side of the moderates, those who knew how to make the proper distinctions not only between Paris and Geneva, but also between France and "emerging nations," such as the American colonies. In "poor countries" it could be advantageous for "landed property to be much divided."[17] The story was different in rich nations like France. For France, Necker began to sketch out a program of improvement and change in his *Eloge*, which was important, to be sure, but did not touch the roots of the economic and social realities of the nation.

When, with the death of Louis XV, "M. Turgot suddenly undertook to substitute the straight lines of theory for the innumerable twistings of tradition," as "Baron de Staël," Necker's nephew, wrote half a century later, this last published, in 1775, right in the midst of the *guerre des farines*, an attack on the government that sought to strike at the most delicate point of its policy, the freedom of trade in grain.[18] Necker's book *Sur la législation et le commerce des grains* was a great success, even beyond the frontiers of France.[19] In Italy, a version edited by Giambattista Graziosi Dragolovich was published in Naples in 1780 by the Società letteraria e tipografica, the publishing house organized and directed by Giuseppe Galanti. It was like returning to the polemic that had found its most brilliant expression ten years earlier in the famous *Dialogues sur le commerce des bleds*, by the Abate Galiani. This book had been much admired by Madame Necker, as well as by her husband. "These

---

[16] Ibid., p. 53.

[17] Ibid., pp. 94ff.

[18] *Oeuvres complètes de M. Necker publiées par M. le baron de Stael son petit-fils* (Paris: Treuttel et Würst, 1820), vol. 1, "Notice sur M. Necker," p. lv.

[19] For Catalonia, for example, see the interesting study by Ernest Lluch, "El mercantilismo industrialista (Capmany y Caresmar) entre el capitalismo comercial y los gremios catalanes," *Anales de economía*, no. 10 (April–June 1971): 19ff.

are all new ideas," he wrote when it appeared.[20] Five years later, in 1775, the lightning intuitions of the Neapolitan Abate, his paradoxical comparison between southern Italy struck by ruinous famines and France seeking to set priorities among agriculture, manufacturing, and commerce, had settled into the mind of Necker. The restless experimentation and skeptical empiricism of Galiani solidified into a firm refusal to put French society to the too risky test either of physiocratic ideas or of any other experiment that did not take sufficiently into account the heavy, complex, and solid structure of the nation. The economic and demographic development it hypothetically could hope to achieve in the future did not justify in his eyes the hunger, death, and suffering that any too drastic reform risked inflicting on contemporaries. How could one compare, morally and sentimentally, "a thousand citizens who perish" today with a "thousand one hundred whose births were hoped for? The man who exists now is the one who knows happiness and suffering: he is alive and obliged to give up his life; he is my fellow creature, and I have made a pact with him; for him the laws are made, and these do not oblige men to multiply on Earth, but they prescribe death for those who give it to others. I cannot consent to this cold mental compassion for future generations, which would close our hearts to the cries of the ten thousand unfortunates who surround us."[21] Nor did he intend to close his eyes to the practical consequences of fluctuations in the market, which economists insisted on observing only from the point of view of statistics and mathematics. To be sure, the high price of bread was an incentive to agriculture. After the liberalization in 1764 many new fields were brought under cultivation. Nevertheless, this was the worst possible incentive, "which depends on the cost of subsistence for the multitude and general tranquillity. In the last analysis this encouragement is like an immense and rigorous head tax, imposed suddenly on all laboring men to benefit all men of property."[22] "When proprietors raise the price of foodstuffs and fail to raise the wages of labor for industrious men, it creates between these two classes of society a kind of dark but terrible struggle, . . . in which the strong oppose the weak under the law; property with its weight oppresses the prerogatives of the man who lives by the work of his hands."[23]

[20] Ferdinando Galiani, *Dialogues sur le commerce des bleds*, giusta l' "editio princeps" del 1770 e con appendici illustrative di Fausto Nicolini (Milan and Naples: R. Ricciardi, 1959), p. 377. On the debate about grain in general see above all Steven L. Kaplan, *Bread, Politics and Political Economy in the Reign of Louis XV* (The Hague: Martinus Nijhoff, 1976).

[21] *Della legislazione e 'l commercio de' grani*, opera di M. Neker. Traduzione di Giambattista Graziosi Dragolovich giureconsulto ed avvocato napoletano, presso la Società letteraria e tipografica (Naples, 1788), vol. 1, ch. 13, p. 50.

[22] Ibid., ch. 16, pp. 6off.

[23] Ibid., p. 61.

These assertions led Necker to a single and precise political conclusion: the state must intervene directly; it cannot, and should not, trust the market. Thus the incentive of high prices should be replaced with fiscal easements favoring proprietors. "The end of all the concerns of a true statesman" must be "general harmony" among "the different classes of society."[24] The people do not foresee their future much beyond tomorrow. "The bread that nourishes them and the religion that consoles them" are their only true preoccupations.[25] This was a static situation, which still should not be put too much to the test. "Amid pain and indigence they peacefully endure the spectacle of the idleness, abundance, and apparent happiness of the rich; they flatter themselves to regard these as being of a different nature—whose pomp and grandeur are a kind of evoked magic—but when a well- or badly founded fear of . . . subsistence takes hold of them, this fear strikes their deepest sentiments, all their energy awakens, and that infant people, which allowed itself to be led with reins through the inequality of property and a thousand objects of privation and envy, becomes a lion that roars when it fears not to have what it needs."[26] It was thus useless to attempt to persuade those who did not understand reason "with force" (we are in the days of the *guerre des farines* and its repression). Then what should one do? Give in before the "prejudices of the people"? The answer, at least on one essential point, the one of bread, could be only positive. Economic reasonings must give way before the passions of the people, before their will to see their own subsistence guaranteed.[27] While the evidence evoked by the physiocrats might succeed in creating agreement among "men who think and argue . . . it will never succeed with the people, because their coarseness, blindness, and ignorance are attached to social laws that will never change."[28] Or rather, to put it better, Necker concluded in a semi-ironic, semifatalistic tone that the people would change only if proprietors decided to feed their laborers "without exacting the sacrifice of their whole workday." "Give them also books and teachers, so that these people can reason about their public prosperity, and understand, perhaps through the study of economic calculus, that the more bread costs the more they should be happy." Meanwhile it was necessary to admit that the ignorance of the people was one's own fault: "In this matter we must treat them with prudence and not irritate them when it chances that the only sentiments the people can have, and the only ones we have let them have, offend our rela-

[24] Ibid., ch. 20, p. 81.
[25] Ibid., ch. 24, p. 104.
[26] Ibid., p. 105.
[27] Ibid., p. 106.
[28] Ibid., p. 107.

tions." "On the other hand," Necker added, "if the blindness of the people could be dissipated with evidence, through the actions of modern
science, would one be sure that this increase in enlightenment would be
an advantage to the proprietors? If the people became capable of understanding abstract truths, would they not also acquire the faculty of
meditating on the origins of social rank, on the origins of property, and
on all institutions they might oppose? Finally, was it certain that an inequality of conditions was not necessary to preserve all the social inequalities born from it?" This was a fundamental doubt, which Necker
nonetheless hastened to dismiss and set aside. "All these inequalities,"
he concluded, "will never end, and the people will be the same in all
ages; they do not understand the reasoning behind the high price of
bread and never will." England was proof of this. There, "through the
nature of government and the higher level of wages, the people are less
degraded and participate more in the general enlightenment." Through
the election of deputies they also have a way of defending themselves,
contrary to the situation in France. "The people of France are inevitably
poor because they are numerous and lack the means to make themselves
heard, or to defend themselves against the control of the proprietors."
"The English people, therefore, have many kinds of interests in society;
the French have none, because they are indifferent to everything except
the price of bread." "When they are sometimes seen to unite tumultu-
ously in public events, this is not because they understand, because they
take part, as we often try to persuade ourselves so as to give more proof
to our feelings, but rather because they always carry within them the
sense of their own misery. They take any opportunity to express this
and to blame their misfortune on someone, because they do not know
what an abstract reason might be and never will." In Great Britain the
people were "much closer to sovereignty, and whole groups of artisans
can bring their suffering to the base of the throne to complain of the
high price of bread or the scarcity of work. In France the slightest gathering is prevented, and none is permitted by law. Thus misery, death,
and sickness destroy many families before the people dare complain."[29]

As we see, the English experience of the late sixties and early seventies had an effect. The deep movement that agitated the countryside
and the ports of Great Britain confirmed Necker's admiration for the
political and social constitution of England.[30] Now, in 1775, the disorders that responded to the liberalization Turgot wanted in the Ile de
France persuaded him that the French situation was quite different:

[29] Ibid., pp. 108ff.
[30] See Walter James Shelton, *English Hunger and Industrial Disorders: A Study of Social
Conflict during the First Decade of George III's Reign* (London: Macmillan, 1973).

what could be obtained with freedom beyond the English Channel had to be achieved by concession in France, as a benevolent act made by the sovereign. Precisely because they were caught in a dilemma between oppression and violence the French people had the right to ask the state for that support, those guarantees, which they could not achieve with their own hands. "A sovereign should regard the misfortunes of his people in proportion to the importance of their grievances and the ease with which these might be remedied." How could one maintain—as the Parlement of Toulouse had done—that "the king does not owe support to his people"? This was not something that could be left to the "caprice of liberty." It would be a "fatal error," the equivalent of abandoning the people to the proprietors.[31] The everlasting misery of the people found its origins precisely in the aim and ability of proprietors to pay them the "smallest wages possible, providing the barest necessity."[32] "The people are condemned by the effects of the laws of property never to obtain more than necessary in exchange for their work." This situation could be changed in theory by overthrowing the laws and proceeding to a "division of the land." But this remedy would be equally "unjust" in that it was impossible to realize. A single way remained open: "Sovereign and legislative power cannot exercise its benevolence for the people if it does not ensure them at least the necessity to which they are reduced and liberates them from anxiety through the prevention of the variations in price that disturb the set relationship between their work and subsistence: this care and precaution depend uniquely on the wisdom of the grain laws."[33]

Comparison with lands besides England, that is, Holland and Poland, only made clearer the unique situation of France and its provisioning laws. This was a nation of "twenty-four million people, the majority of whom live by bread alone," with difficulties in internal transportation, a circulation of specie equal to half of that of Europe as a whole, a population whose temperament was quick and heated, entirely concentrated on the present, and with a "vivacity of spirit that leads to exaggeration." France was hardly a nation where one could or should further stimulate the desire for luxury, commercial avidity, speculative appetite, or remove from the rich and powerful the restraint arising from "public disdain" and fear of "popular movements." This was a monarchy where, contrary to republics, there was no legal possibility of making one's voice and rights heard, but nonetheless public opinion vigorously affirmed itself "stronger and clearer than the law." One should

[31] *Della legislazione*, ch. 24, pp. 111ff.
[32] Ibid., ch. 25, p. 114.
[33] Ibid., pp. 116ff.

count on this, utilizing, for example, popular hatred against hoarders and monopolists to create a provisioning policy inspired by "sensitive apprehension" and a spirit of justice, which would by no means prevail if matters were abandoned to the laws of the market.[34] "Oh you who govern, never forget that the larger number of men were not meant to make laws. Condemned to continuous labor, they do not participate in the growth of knowledge, and their weakness and quiet continually implore your protection. Those who participate in the goods of the earth ['ceux qui ont une part aux biens de la terre,' reads the original] ask of you no more than liberty and justice." Instead, "those who have nothing need your humanity, your compassion, and finally laws that moderate the force of property against them."[35]

With his crude social realism Necker thus presented himself as the man who better than anyone else knew and denounced the perils of the situation in which France had come to find itself, without an escape route, without safety valves, with an immense populace instinctively drawn up against proprietors and the government. But he was also the man who refuted, out of weakness and political passivity, the only means of escape that existed, the one that a generation of philosophes and physiocrats had just indicated: a diffusion of culture, an enlargement of political interests, and a deepening of public opinion. After all, the remedy he had ironically suggested to French proprietors—that is, to create schools and teach their own peasants how to read and write— had begun to be realized by Maria Theresa in her Imperial domains, and soon her son Joseph gave strong support to a similar initiative. In France, the followers of Quesnay insisted more and more on the same direction.[36] It was they as well, beginning with Victor Riqueti de Mirabeau, who indicated another possible remedy: create autonomous and capable centers of local administration that would forge a whole network of new relationships between central authority and the needs of the provinces. Turgot had insisted on this theme, well knowing that it was an essential instrument for opening the situation in France. Rejecting the plea of physiocrats and Encyclopedists, Necker limited himself to a narrowly paternalistic policy. What he asked, however, was cautious prudence more than an energetic capacity to confront the explosive problems whose dangers he knew well. His social fatalism was merely a confession of an inability to confront the situation. As in Poland, where those who described peasant serfdom in the darkest colors were also

---

[34] Ibid., vol. 1, pt. 2, ch. 5, pp. 150ff.

[35] Ibid., vol. 2, ch. 11, pp. 115ff.

[36] Manuela Albertone, *Fisiocrati, istruzione e culture* (Turin: Fondazione Luigi Einaudi, 1979).

those who were less inclined to find a means for constitutional reform, in the France of Louis XVI as well the extraordinary lucidity with which Necker indicated the deep roots of the growing conflict had the effect of immobilizing the king and his ministers.

The grave delusions that accompanied the fall of Turgot explain the favor with which the ideas of Necker were received toward the end of 1776. Galiani took this as a triumph of his own: "I thank the skies now for an event that completes the glory of the king, and yours (dare I say?), and mine, and that of our age," he hastened to write to him from Naples.[37] "The public has viewed the rise of M. Necker with the greatest satisfaction," wrote Diderot to Grimm a day later. And the philosophe added: "M. Necker has enlightened views, justice, firmness, high-mindedness, and I hope, like all honest people, for the long life of his administration." He did not fail to add to his congratulations, however, a certain deluded detachment: "I hope that the impossibility of doing good does not discourage him from the simple task of preventing evil." And he ended up by saying that he was glad to have succeeded in "marching straight ahead," in not breaking, that is, with Turgot, while continuing to appreciate Necker, and vice versa.[38] His support of the Genevan banker had in reality deeper roots than such seemingly opportunistic conduct suggests. A conviction tied him to Necker: the society in which they lived and operated was oppressive and unjust. Neither juridical nor economic reforms could change such a hard and massive reality. Already ten years before, Diderot had explained to Beccaria that abolition of the death penalty and torture would not resolve the problem of punishment, injustice, oppression, and social disaggregation. Then came the collaboration of Diderot with Galiani in the publication, diffusion, and defense of the *Dialogues*. The name Machiavelli came spontaneously to their lips to symbolize the emerging will to reveal naked effective reality beyond all programs, intentions, dreams, or hopes. Even the followers of Quesnay, the physiocrats, forced themselves to provide a realistic and objective vision of society, without letting themselves be influenced by vain hopes or pious intentions. The pictures provided by one side and the other were not very different, based as they were no longer on juridical and historical categories, on privileges and ranks, but on proprietors on one hand and all other classes on the other. Necker was even cruder in his elimination of such distinctions than the physiocrats were. The substantial difference between the two points of view, between Necker and the economists, lay elsewhere: the followers of

---

[37] *Opere di Ferdinando Galiani*, p. 1134, Naples, 16 November 1776.

[38] Denis Diderot, *Correspondance*. Publiée par Georges Roth et Jean Varloot (Paris: Les éditions de minuit, 1970), vol. 15, pp. 16ff.

Quesnay saw society in movement, in the process of organic internal transformation, and they sought to indicate the stages of its future development. The vision of Galiani and Necker was much more static. Necker's phrases sound like an everlasting condemnation of laborers to a minimum wage, ignorance, and resignation, relieved only by useless outbreaks of rage. But Necker's conclusions, in their elementary nature, indicate the knot hidden behind all these discussions. Society was unchangeable; was it thus vain and even dangerous to think of reforms? Or rather, reforms would not succeed, unleashing tumults and even greater opposition; was society thus impossible to change? Was disappointment with failed reforms what created such a static and conservative vision of society? Or, after much vain and abstract talk about reform, had one finally reached that moderate wisdom which alone could provide the hope of having escaped from a period of storms and revolutions?

The political outcomes of such alternatives are revealing. Both the physiocrats and their adversaries thought a strong central authority was needed, but for the first this was a matter of "*despotisme legal*," that is, of a juridical guarantee for the free functioning of economic laws. For the others authority was a defense against disorder, an intervention intended to provide bread for all. For the first, authority needed to be guided by reason, science, and evidence. For the others, the sovereign needed to be guided by prudence, and above all by compassion or, as Necker said it, by "*sentiment social*."[39]

Morellet, one of the sharpest critics of Necker's book, indicated accurately the uncertainties and contradictions hidden within it, which made it incoherent from the point of view of theory and ineffective from a practical point of view. The general principles with which he began did not correspond to the policy he proposed. Like Galiani, Necker was also an enemy of the "system of free trade," even if at the same time he refused to adopt those coercive measures that alone could make a system of regulation function.[40] The Genevan banker was not capable of the coherence of Linguet, who was an open defender of direct intervention by the sovereign "to assist his people," and always willing to enter into conflict with, according to him, those monsters of exploitative proprietors.[41] Necker, on the other hand, after having painted

[39] "Sur la législation et le commerce des grains," in *Oeuvres complètes de M. Necker*, vol. 1, pt. 1, ch. 26, p. 144.

[40] *Analyse de l'ouvrage intitulé De la législation et du commerce des grains* (Amsterdam and Paris: Pissot, 1775), p. 7.

[41] Ibid., p. 43.

in dark colors the aims of those providing work, contented himself with a few palliatives.

It is clear that the principles of M. N. *** would have led him to much stronger consequences than he announced. If property is an inevitable and constant cause of low wages and unhappiness of the people, if proprietors are despots, predatory animals, lions who defend their rights like crocodiles, if the effects of proprietors' reducing wages cannot be checked before these became even more serious in times of calamity, except through momentary acts of the sovereign power in defense of the people (because M. N. *** excludes any other means, and chiefly a new division of the land, which he rightly considers impractical), he must necessarily consider all the limitations on property in the old statutes legitimate in detail.[42]

The traditional system of controls could and should be replaced with full economic freedom, not sugared or weakened by a politics of compromise. But precisely the intermediary way taken by Necker ensured him support. Strong and deep was the resistance of old rules and old ideas. "It is difficult to abandon a widespread opinion, and particularly a popular opinion that ensures one the support of the multitude." This is precisely what had induced Necker to seek to connect "incompatible things: a general theory and diametrically opposed practical maxims." Against such a compromise Morellet continued his battle as a good philosophe, convinced that logic itself would suffice to demonstrate the weakness of the position of his adversary. "An intelligent man" would soon persuade himself that the means he suggested fatally involved "terrible consequences."[43]

Behind the "benevolent arguments" of Necker "for respecting the eternal prejudices of the people," even Condorcet, in his *Réflections sur le commerce des blés*, "discovered the plutocratic conviction that it was in the interest of the rich to keep the poor under the sway of prejudice and ignorance." A fear of disorder and popular revolts—the philosophe was convinced—was at the bottom of the thought of the Genevan banker.[44]

Even the echo that resounded in Italy of the publication of Necker's book on the grain trade was symptomatic of the intensity with which these problems were felt everywhere in Europe. Let us open the *Gazzetta letteraria*, the mouthpiece of one of the most important publishing houses on the peninsula, that of Giuseppe Galeazzi in Milan, a periodical that for some years, since 1772, had been directed by Giambattista Vasco, the best Piedmontese economist of the eighteenth century. The

[42] Ibid., p. 42.
[43] Ibid., pp. 56ff.
[44] Baker, *Condorcet*.

first impression of the reviewer on reading Necker's book was clearly
negative: "Precepts dictated with the tone of a legislator, reasonings
enunciated with an air of persuasion, images, pathetic descriptions, pre-
sumptuous declamations, are the merits that will give momentary fame
to this work." His polemic against the physiocrats was erroneous:
"Sometimes he states false principles, sometimes he seeks support from
facts poorly verified, and sometimes he infers from true principles consequences the opposite of what would naturally seem to derive from
them." His vision of France as a kind of "closed system" was wrong. The
monarchy of Louis XVI was not "a state surrounded by hungry lands";
in reality it was in close contact with the "general market of nations,"
where prices tended to adjust themselves better and more rapidly than
in countries where the intervention of the "authority of the government" was continuous and insistent. A limited and controlled freedom
might favor the "ill-gotten gains of a few," but "unlimited liberty" would
increase "the riches of the nation" and "multiply the products of agriculture, keeping them at a more moderate price," while "wages and the
labor force would by themselves reach a just and lasting balance." This
was thus a defense of the principles of the economists, which the Italian
reviewer enjoyed echoing but added some words that revealed the deep
uncertainties these debates aroused: "If we must express our own opinion, we would tend to favor free trade, but in a way adapted to the circumstances of time and place. Above all, before permitting this freedom, it would be good to warn the nation well in advance. Peoples are
like children: sovereigns support them; if they are abandoned without
warning, they fall, but, if they are forewarned, they pick themselves up
easily and learn better to direct their steps."[45] There was a paternalistic
attitude in the Lombardy of Maria Theresa as well, a new absolutism
born spontaneously of problems created by the push toward liberalization. This was the easiest, and the most obvious, response to the doubts
that a clearer knowledge of social reality aroused in the minds of all.

Necker's effort to bring to reality the ideas he had expressed so
broadly in the years before his ascent to power was intense during the
winter of 1776–1777. In order for the state to exercise the functions he
intended to give it, it was necessary first of all to proceed with its transformation and reconstruction.

[45] *Gazzetta letteraria*, no. 25, 21 June 1775, pp. 197ff. The author explains that he took
his criticisms from a "confutazione del libro di Necker," and that is from one of the numerous writings of Condorcet, Morellet, or the Abbé Roubaud that repeated the point of
view of the economists and of Turgot.

Again watching Necker struggle with tax farmers and bankers, courtiers and bureaucrats, a conclusion imposes itself. France is revealed as backward and antiquated not only in penal and civil law, but also in administrative unity, in the diffusion of schools, in a thousand other problems, as the Encyclopedists never tired of repeating, and in the very basic structures of the financial life of the state. Reforms also did not succeed because there were no instruments for carrying them out. Turgot had confronted the essential problems and had fallen from power. Necker attempted to escape the vicious circle by attacking the old regime at a particularly sensitive point, the relationship between private and public finance. When one remembers that a conspicuous part of the funds utilized by the state did not come directly from tax collection, and not even from contracts with the tax farmers, but from loans that the tax farmers and a myriad of significant officials granted to the treasury at high interest, it becomes clear why the public debt continually increased and why French finances were in peril. The symbiosis of private business and public finance was so strong that it not only impoverished the state, but also made reforms that had been accomplished elsewhere impossible. In Milan the tax farm was replaced with direct administration in 1771, above all through the work of Pietro Verri. A national bank, intended to give public and no longer private guarantees to the state, had appeared in Holland in 1609, in Sweden in 1656, in England in 1694, in Denmark in 1736, in Prussia in 1765, and in Russia in 1770. In France one has to wait until 1800. As J. F. Bosher, the scholar who understands these problems better than any other, explains, "under the *ancien régime*, the Royal Treasury was only one among many *caisses* (an independent account or fund for collecting and disbursing money) which received and paid out royal revenues." The absence of centralization was such that "the receiving *caisses* often fed the paying *caisses*, and paid the interest on government bonds and annuities, without the money passing through the Treasury at all. . . . Most of the time vast sums lay frozen in the various *caisses* beyond even the knowledge of the Treasury." With a decree of 18 October 1778 Necker began to establish in principle that all *caisses* were extensions of the royal treasury. "Then, in a great series of laws, he abolished the posts of an army of Treasurers in all government services . . . finally, he ordered the replacement of the forty-eight Receivers General by a twelve-man commission. These reforms were expensive, for the price of each suppressed post had to be repaid to the incumbent."[1]

---

[1] John Francis Bosher, "French Administration and Public Finance in Their European Setting," in *The New Cambridge Modern History* (Cambridge University Press, 1965), vol. 8, pp. 586ff. By the same author see *French Finances*, pp. 62ff. (a general evaluation of the

In Italy, and above all in Tuscany, Necker's work was followed with great interest from its first steps. The Florentine gazette *Notizie del mondo* presented him to its readers on 16 November 1776. To be sure he was a Protestant, but it was necessary to remember that "the greatest minister of the treasury that France ever had was Protestant." Still it was not of Sully, but rather of Colbert that Necker had written a eulogy. "Last year he published a little book, *Legislation and trade in grain*, which, although strongly criticized and quite disapproved of by the economists, still showed that it was written by a more than common man."[2] The sympathies of the Florentine editor continued to be with the physiocrats, with the "celebrated economists Roubaud and Baudeau." Necker had the good taste, as soon as he reached the government, of liberating the latter from the exile imposed on him as a follower and supporter of Turgot. The gesture was all the more real in that Baudeau had "already criticized and fully disapproved the antieconomic works" of Necker.[3] It was necessary to recognize that this was a "generous minister."[4] In the spring of 1777 the Abbé Baudeau experienced "a prosperous change of fortune." "He has obtained a pension of 4 thousand livres from one abbey, permission to continue publishing his works, and even his famous journal entitled *Ephémérides du citoyen*."[5] The *Gazzetta universale* also announced, in November 1776, that France had a worthy finance minister.

As soon as it was known by the public that the king had entrusted the general direction of the royal finances to M. Necker, royal bonds, which had fallen in value in recent months, rose considerably. Shares in the Compagnie des Indes, valued at 1,750 to 1,780, soon rose to 1,900. In fact, the greatest advantages are anticipated . . . from the certain wisdom of the said M. Necker. . . . He has made his superior abilities known through several works of truly sublime talent, lacking in partiality, and filled with vast and excellent information about the finances. His work on the grain laws, although against the system of the economists, was published during the administration of M. Turgot and at a time when that minister had established the most extensive freedom of that trade. He developed and defended the system of Colbert in a eulogy that won the prize of the French Academy two years ago.

politics of Necker), 92ff. (on the importance of private enterprise in public finance), 146–47 (general scheme of the *caisses* before and after the reform of Necker in 1781).

    [2] *Notizie del mondo*, no. 92, 16 November 1776, p. 709 (Paris, 30 October).

    [3] Ibid., no. 99, 10 December 1776, p. 766 (Paris, 25 November).

    [4] Ibid., no. 100, 14 December 1776, p. 773 (Paris 26 November). On the exile of the physiocrats, see also the *Gazzetta universale*, no. 72, 7 September 1776, p. 569 (Paris, 20 August).

    [5] *Notizie del mondo*, no. 42, 27 May 1777, p. 331 (Paris, 12 May). On these developments see Georges Weulersse, *La physiocratie sous les ministères de Turgot et de Necker (1774–1781)* (Paris: Presses Universitaires de France, 1950), p. 235.

There was thus general satisfaction, clouded only by the clerical polemics due to Necker's Protestantism.[6] "One of the favorite principles of the great Colbert," one read in September 1777, "was that taxes, to be lucrative, must be simple and easy to perceive, and collected by a small number of persons. M. Necker has developed these principles in a sublime manner, which has merited him the approval of the Academy and the applause of the public; currently he is putting them into practice."[7]

Increasingly insistent rumors of war spread everywhere. The support that France intended to give to the American colonies was a theme appearing more and more frequently in the columns of gazettes throughout Italy. The figure of Necker remained the central point of these diverse and contrasting problems. "Amid the problems of providing for public revenue raised by the current crisis M. Necker, the director general of finance, does not leave untried every means of improving the administration of that department or of introducing into it order and light," one read in the *Notizie del mondo* in November 1778.[8] Two months later, at the moment of war with England, "the confidence that all the present ministers have inspired in the nation" proved to be a fundamental element in arousing "the zeal that is evident throughout the realm" and the "love of the nation for a just and beneficent king."[9] Problems still existed. In the spring it seemed for a moment that Necker would be obliged to hand in his resignation. "The whole nation would receive with ill will the loss of that enlightened minister, whose economic views are directed uniquely to support the state."[10] The "second Sully of France," even if supported by a "second Henry IV," was obliged to consider the problem of an increase in taxes, while continuing to hope to do without it.[11] Particularly eulogizing was the tone of the gazette of Venice: "One can never sufficiently admire the wisdom of a minister who, while limiting himself to simplifying operations and introducing order and clarity, has procured great advantages for the state."[12] "We have ascertained," we read some issues later, "that one of the projects of M. Necker is to lower the entrance tolls on goods of prime necessity for the people of the capital and at the same time to enlarge the barriers of the city so that there will not be so many houses in the suburbs that are

---

[6] *Gazzetta universale*, no. 92, 16 November 1776, p. 729 (Paris, 29 October).

[7] *Nuove di diverse corti e paesi*, no. 38, 22 September 1777, p. 293 (Paris, 8 September).

[8] *Notizie del mondo*, no. 91, 14 November 1778, p. 725 (Paris, 27 October).

[9] Ibid., no. 1, 2 January 1779, p. 1 (Paris, 19 December 1778).

[10] *Nuove di diverse corti e paesi*, no. 14, 5 April 1779, p. 108 (Paris, 22 March).

[11] *Notizie del mondo*, no. 100, 14 December 1779, p. 815 (Paris, 30 November).

[12] *Notizie del mondo [V.]*, no. 95, 20 November–1 December 1779, p. 788 (Paris, 12 November).

exempt from tolls."¹³ At the end of February Venetians could read in
six tightly packed columns of their gazette the complete text of the decree of 9 January 1780 on the general tax farm.¹⁴ His enemies were still
quite active, the gazette of Florence warned, but Necker continued to
pay no attention to them, "having the protection of his sovereign." "The
whole nation is more and more involved in supporting the current
war."¹⁵ Even beyond the borders of France the propaganda assumed
dithyrambic tones. It was reported in Amsterdam: "Here we consider
M. Necker to be the god of finance. France has never had such a wise
administration."¹⁶

With the spring of 1780 the political horizon seemed to enlarge rapidly. The difficult but fruitful convergence of the benevolent French
monarchy with the republican ideals of the United States of America
led naturally to a reopening of problems that went beyond the efficiency
of armies or of finance. All of Europe was changing in the year that saw
Joseph II become sole emperor after the death of his mother, Maria
Theresa. For Necker, actively assisted by his wife, it was time to return
to that "*sentiment social*" which he had been obliged to set temporarily
aside, but which alone could respond adequately—he was convinced—
to the deep tensions in the body of the French monarchy.¹⁷ The *Notizie
del mondo* spoke of his new "plans regarding hospitals" and of the "hospice of charity" that Madame Necker had founded a year before "in the
parish of St. Sulpice."¹⁸ "M. Necker continues to occupy himself with
plans for making the prisons of this capital less unhealthy," one read
some issues later. "He, together with his wife, went . . . to visit, console,
and assist the unfortunates inhabiting them; Madame Necker also has
been to the general hospital, where she met at length with the superior,
with whom she discussed the smallest details of that place, having already examined the beds, the bedding, and the food given to the sick."¹⁹
The *Gazzetta universale* reported in full the "plan regarding the property
of hospitals," underlining "the deep necessity dictating such a needed

¹³ Ibid., no. 6, 26 January 1780, p. 43 (Paris, 7 January).
¹⁴ Ibid., no. 14, 23 February 1780, p. 129 (Paris, 11 February).
¹⁵ *Notizie del mondo*, no. 17, 26 February 1780, p. 129 (Paris, 11 February).
¹⁶ *Lettres hollandaises, ou Correspondance politique sur l'état présent de l'Europe, notamment de
la République des Sept Provinces Unies*, vol. 2, August 1779, p. 114.
¹⁷ See Egret, *Necker*, pp. 140ff., "Les 'idées de bienfaisance.'"
¹⁸ *Notizie del mondo*, no. 19, 4 March 1780, p. 147 (Paris, 18 February).
¹⁹ Ibid., no. 25, 25 March 1780, p. 194 (Paris, 10 March). See *Notizie del mondo [V.]*,
no. 20, 15 March 1780, p. 157, "Continuation of the News from Paris of 22 February":
"M. Necker, director of the finances, the first to do good without impunity, is loved and
honored by the nation. They continue to visit the hospitals and prisons, and it is confirmed
that they have had built at their expense a hospice for poor invalids."

change, which is expressed with clarity and energy, gifts that reveal a man of genius."²⁰ Out of "gratitude" the farmers general "plan to provide 24 million livres yearly . . . to assist the hospitals and pious foundations established by his wife."²¹ At the same time a sensational piece of news spread: "Among the different reform proposals the government has projected there is even one for closing the so-called Bastille."²²

The massive judicial apparatus posed anew a large obstacle to the general need for improvement. "It is desirable," read the same gazette, "that the spirit of reform, which under the present reign has become inexorable in matters of finance, extend to much that concerns the courts." Some initiative came from the provinces. "Several seigneurs have begun to establish tribunals of conciliation . . . made up of gentlemen, parish priests, and others, who deal with matters without the help of counsel."²³ In June *La gazzetta di Milano* listed "a quantity of projects" waiting "on the carpet of M. Necker" from the "sale of royal property" to the "reestablishment of the Jewish merchant company" to provisions for "the poor in hospitals."²⁴ In September, after much deaf resistance on the part of the justices, a first and still very partial concession to the spirit of humanitarianism finally arrived: "On his feast day (25 August) our monarch abolished the torture of the so-called preliminary question with which, through a barbarous custom derived from centuries of ignorance, accused criminals were tormented a few moments before being executed."²⁵ The Venetian gazette, reporting this edict in full, said it constituted "certainly a memorable epoch in the laws of humanity."²⁶ In September, while still in the midst of the "disturbance of the war," Louis XVI did not lose sight of the "establishment of new prisons" and the suppression of those "underground."²⁷ Other sparse and often inadequate judicial reforms followed. "Since the number of suicides increases in proportion to the reversals of the interests of particulars, the Parlement has ordered that the bodies of those who have killed themselves

---

²⁰ *Gazzetta universale*, no. 19, 4 May 1780, p. 146 (Paris, 16 February).

²¹ Ibid., no. 35, 29 April 1780, p. 273 (Paris, 11 April).

²² *Nuove di diverse corti e paesi*, no. 17, 24 April 1780, p. 131 (Paris, 14 April). In the *Notizie del mondo [V.]*, no. 33, April 1780, p. 261 (Paris, 10 April), there was talk of selling "the Gothic edifice of the Bastille (for three millions) with the right to build on the lot a design that was to be specified."

²³ *Nuove di diverse corti e paesi*, no. 18, 1 May 1780, p. 139 (Paris, 17 April).

²⁴ *La gazzetta di Milano*, no. 24, 14 June 1780 (Paris, 26 May).

²⁵ *Nuove di diversi corti e paesi*, no. 38, 18 September 1780, p. 300 (Paris, 5 September).

²⁶ *Notizie del mondo [V.]*, no. 78, 4 October 1780, p. 620 (Versailles, 19 September).

²⁷ *Nuove di diverse corti e paesi*, no. 38, 18 September 1780, p. 307 (Paris, 5 September). In the spring of 1781 Madame Necker intervened in favor of a prisoner incarcerated for twenty-two years in a fortress in Picardy. They gave him "an airier and more commodious room" (*Notizie del mondo [V.]*, no. 34, 28 April 1781, p. 265 [Paris, 13 April]).

be taken from the sight of the public, because through the indulgence
practiced for some time with regard to their families suicides have become much more common." The justices were otherwise convinced that
"gambling was the cause of the ruin of many persons." They thus intended to prepare a "regulation" about this.[28] Reading these notices, it
seems that one hears the last tired exchanges of the dialogue that Diderot had begun with Beccaria with much paradoxical vigor in 1766.
The ills of society were so great and so numerous that the best intentions of the legislator ended up seeming ridiculously impotent.

In February 1781 Necker made the most important gesture of his
first ministry. By publishing his *Compte rendu au roi* he intended to provide both "a balance sheet and a program."[29] He turned to public opinion not only to seek indispensable support at a difficult moment, but
also to ensure that it had the right, even if not legally, certainly morally
and politically, to know the situation of the finances and the state administration. It was enough to look at England—which was also experiencing moments of extreme difficulty—to be aware of what lay at the
root of the "immense credit" it was able to count on. It was not only a
matter of the "nature of its government," but also of the publicity that
surrounded its economic life and the "public notoriety to which it sub-
mits the state of its finances." "Each year a report is presented to Parliament; it is then printed, and all the lenders, knowing regularly in this
way the balance established between revenue and expenditures, are not
troubled by doubts, suspicions, and chimerical fears, the inevitable companions of obscurity." The political and economic fate of the nation
would depend, even in France, on "public confidence."[30]

He thus attempted to make a compromise between the mentality
and methods of banking and the desire for beneficence and efficiency
of monarchical absolutism. With great ability and discretion he listed the
useless expenses, the abusive pensions and harmful privileges he forced
himself to abolish. He explained clearly which financial mechanisms he
had put into operation. His goodwill seemed capable of bending and
liquefying any obstacle. He dealt with the farmers general, he said,
"with the greatest ease." These were no longer the rapacious financiers
of long ago. Prudent and cultivated, they had "honestly embraced views
of wisdom and moderation."[31] When this atmosphere of confidence and
goodwill was reinforced one could again take up reforms, like the abolition of the corvées, which Turgot had sought to impose (but Necker,

[28] *Notizie del mondo*, no. 20, 10 March 1781, p. 158 (Paris, 23 February).

[29] Grange, *Les idées de Necker*, p. 35. On the circumstances of its publication, on 19
February, and on its extraordinary success, see Egret, *Necker*, pp. 169ff.

[30] "Compte rendu au roi," in *Oeuvres complètes de M. Necker*, vol. 2, pp. 2ff.

[31] Ibid., pp. 53ff.

to be sure, took care not to carry this comparison with his predecessor further).[32] The problem of the grain trade, which had been much discussed, was hardly touched on, almost as much as to say how useless too-general theories were. It was necessary to avoid "giving oneself over to extremes" and to take care not to "subject this trade to a fixed and general law."[33] The *Compte rendu* concluded with a chapter on "hospitals and prisons."[34] He requested the approval of the sovereign, not without appealing proudly, as he said, to public opinion, "which evildoers will seek in vain to stop or tear down, but despite their efforts, justice and truth will prevail."[35]

The echoes resounded widely.[36] The gazette of Venice told how in Paris "the crowd was immense in the place where this interesting work was distributed, and that 12 thousand copies were handed out to the public. Many persons remained without and were obliged to write to bookstores where every day there is further distribution. One only needs to read this interesting work to persuade oneself that it merits the greatest praise and is a work in which clarity and nobility of style correspond to the importance of the subject."[37] The beginning of the work was published in the same gazette, and some days later it was said to be so important that the journal would "publish it as soon as free space is available."[38] In Florence one reads that "many thousands of copies of the work entitled *Accounting made to the king by M. Necker* were insufficient to meet the demands of a public much taken by the curious details and grand views found in this luminous document."[39] The effects Necker desired seemed to be realized promptly. "The new loan in rentes has been taken up with a rapidity that would seem extraordinary if it had not been supported by the confidence that the *Accounting made to the king by M. Necker* has given to the administration of the finances. Notes have already risen by two percent."[40]

All parts of Europe resounded with echoes of the *Compte rendu* in the spring of 1781. This was not without some comment about precedents. "The *Compte rendu* of M. Necker has been translated in Berlin with notes in which the author attempts to demonstrate with facts that the greater part of the regulations and improvements proposed by M. Necker have been in effect in the Prussian states for a long time. On

---

[32] Ibid., p. 93.
[33] Ibid., p. 130.
[34] Ibid., p. 133.
[35] Ibid., p. 139.
[36] Grange, *Les idées de Necker*, pp. 35ff.
[37] *Notizie del mondo [V.]*, no. 21, 14 March 1781, p. 163 (Paris, 27 February).
[38] Ibid., no. 23, 21 March 1781, p. 175 (Paris, 6 March).
[39] *Notizie del mondo*, no. 22, 17 March 1781, p. 171 (Paris, 11 March).
[40] Ibid., no. 25, 27 March 1781, p. 194 (Paris, 13 March).

this occasion it was made known that M. Necker is of Prussian origin and that his grandfather was born in Custrin."[41] In April the gazette of Lugano wrote that the *Compte rendu au roi* had "received the most admirable reception among the cultivated nations of Europe. In London, besides being reprinted in French, it was soon translated and published in English. In Amsterdam, Hamburg, and Basel there have been copious reprints, and in The Hague it has even come out in Dutch. The brothers Van Duren in Frankfurt am Main have printed a translation in German. . . . The exemplary merit of this work has been spoken of in all the periodicals, even in Italy."[42] In Tuscany, in May, it was reviewed in the *Novelle letterarie di Firenze*.[43] In June two booksellers of the city offered it for sale.[44] A version was published in Milan.[45] Another soon appeared in Venice,[46] and a third in Naples.[47]

The *Compte rendu* marked the highest point of Necker as minister. His decline followed. Already in 1780 the campaign of criticism and attacks against all his actions intensified. The most virulent libelles appeared in the name of Turgot. They did not at all correspond to the ideas of the great economist but reflected instead in an acrid and petty form the hostility of many courtiers and above all tax farmers and bank-

[41] *Notizie del mondo [V.]*, no. 33, 25 April 1781, p. 263 (Cleves, 14 April).

[42] *Nuove di diverse corti e paesi*, no. 16, 16 April 1781, p. 128, "Avviso."

[43] *Notizie letterarie di Firenze*, vol. 12, no. 21, 25 May 1781, cols. 333ff. "It has raised a great clamor in Europe . . . presents a good picture of the political spirit of this century. The previous minister was banished. In fact the obscurity and error in which it was once thought to keep the people favors only arbitrariness on one side and diffidence on the other."

[44] *Notizie del mondo*, no. 44, 2 June 1781, p. 352, in the footer.

[45] *Conto presentato al re di Francia dal sig. Necker, direttore generale delle finanze nel mese di gennaio 1781. Stampato in Parigi per ordine di Sua Maestà nella Tipografia reale*. Traduzione dal francese di G. C., Eredi di Antonio Agnelli (Milan, 1781). See *Nuove di diverse corti e paesi*, no. 16, 16 April 1781, p. 128, "Avviso." After having talked of the "remarkable applause" that had greeted this work in France, "where more than sixty thousand copies have already been sold," it announced the Italian translation, "by Giuseppe Coltellini, secretary of the Royal Ducal communal government of Milan."

[46] *Conto reso al re dal sig. Necker direttore generale delle finanze sul mese di gennaro 1781, stampato a Parigi per ordine di Sua Maestà e tradutto con alcune spiegazioni* (Venice: Carlo Palese, 1781). On pp. 122ff. one finds a "Spiegazione di alcuni termini," an interesting glossary of the science of finance.

[47] *Conto presentato al re di Francia dal sig. Necker direttore generale delle finanze nel mese di gennaro 1781, stampato in Parigi per ordine di Sua Maestà nella tipografia reale*, traduzione dal francese di G.C. (that is, Giuseppe Coltellini, the author of the version that appeared in Milan) (Naples: Michele Stasi, 1781). It was dedicated to the "Illustrissimo D. Vincenzo Pecorato, administrator of the royal customs of Naples." "No one more than you, Sir, can judge matters of finance, a science learned by you in the position that you have occupied for so many years with the satisfaction of the prince and the nation" (p. viii). On pp. 226ff. was added the "Lettera scritta dal sig. presidente de Vaux facendo le veci di primo presidente del parlamento di Grenoble a Mr. Necker, direttore generale delle finanze."

ers whose interests and pocketbooks were affected.[48] After the publication of the *Compte rendu* "jealousy" had no further restraint. The *Notizie del mondo* reported that such an attack was "worthy of the scorn of those who love truth and esteem virtue."[49] Nonetheless, one month later it stated that "every day works directed against the *Compte rendu au roi* of M. Necker" appear. These were sold "clandestinely." "No one has yet distributed publicly anything against the work."[50]

A large number of these writings were soon collected in a syllabus that pretended to be impartial but in reality was animated by a will to damage Necker.[51] Amid a thousand bits of gossip there was an effort to attack and end the accord between the financial needs of the monarchy and the methods put into operation by the Genevan banker, which were considered too republican and cosmopolitan. "Born a republican, you cannot love monarchy, you are a banker, you are tied to all bankers." He was accused of continually offending the great: "In a monarchy one must take into account the distinctions among rank and the respect due to persons." [52] "A republican and a republican banker does not ordinarily have a strong taste for monarchy," warned another libelle.[53] It was wrong and dangerous to try to make economic problems the center of French policy, when everything should be subordinated to the needs of war and victory. Necker's policy had already cost a lot of money. "It will yet cost torrents of blood to continue the war; let us hope it will not cost America its independence!" "God be praised!" it concluded, "you are not the one who weighs the destiny of the French empire."[54] The king, and the practiced courtier Maurepas, would know how to put an end to the dangerous experiments of the Genevan banker. A wind of monarchical reaction and aristocratic rebellion breathed out from these pages.

The worst blow awaiting in the shadows, however, was not an nth libelle against Necker, but the publication in April—clandestine this time as well—of a private memorandum by him to the king on local administration. Already in the *Compte rendu* Necker had touched on this problem generally, in a chapter entitled "Administrations provinciales." "Only an imbecile would not see the poison hidden in it," remarked the annotator of the *Collection complette*.[55] Now, in the *Mémoire donné au roi*

---

[48] Egret, *Necker*, pp. 162ff.

[49] *Notizie del mondo*, no. 25, 27 March 1781, p. 193 (Paris, 13 March).

[50] Ibid., no. 34, 28 April 1781, p. 269 (Paris, 13 April).

[51] *Collection complette de tous les ouvrages pour et contre M. Necker, avec des notes critiques, politiques et secrètes* (Utrecht, 1782), 3 vols.

[52] "Lettre de M. Turgot à M. Necker," in *Collection complette*, vol. 1, pt. 1, pp. 2ff.

[53] "Réponse à la lettre de M. Turgot a M. N. ***," ibid., vol. 1, pt. 2, p. 3 n. c. (Each work is numbered separately.)

[54] Ibid., p. 53.

[55] *Collection complette*, vol. 2, p. 64 n. 1.

par M. Necker en 1778, made public in 1781, the intentions of the minister became quite clear. It was an attack on the existing system of taxes.
Intendants and delegates had been "timid before the powerful and arrogant toward the weak." It was difficult to obtain justice from them,
and even more difficult to obtain encouragement. "From this perhaps
comes the general indifference for the good of the state which increases
daily."[56] When injustices become excessive, then finally the local Parlement "stirs itself and places itself between the king and his people."[57]
The Parlements would not do anything but protest, without ensuring
any effective control. Neither representatives of the central authority
nor local magistrates had been able to create an efficient administration
in the provinces. To be sure, it was necessary to leave police powers to
the intendants. But only local elective commissions, made up of proprietors, should have in hand the financial functions currently filled by the
intendants. By taking this route "one would perhaps gradually deliver
the people of the countryside from the yoke under which they live."[58]
This was to reopen the problems already foreseen by the physiocrats,
from Turgot to Malesherbes.[59]

There were nonetheless some elements that differentiated the project of Necker from those inspired by physiocracy, as there were in the
parallel reforms carried out in previous years in the lands of Maria Theresa, in Lombardy, for example. Instead of amalgamating more and
more the different categories of proprietors in the projected local assemblies, Necker intended to base these on representation by estates,
with delegates from the nobility, clergy, and the Third Estate, establish-

---

[56] "Mémoire donné au roi par M. Necker en 1778," ibid., vol. 3, p. 5.

[57] Ibid., p. 7.

[58] Ibid., p. 8.

[59] See Egret, *Necker*, pp. 126ff.; and Harris, *Necker*, pp. 176ff. But one should consult
above all the interesting work edited by Pierre-Samuel Dupont de Nemours, *Oeuvres pos-
thumes de M. Turgot, ou Mémoire de M. Turgot sur les administrations provinciales, mis en parallèle
avec celui de M. Necker, suivi d'une Lettre sur ce plan et des Observations d'un républicain sur ces
Mémoires et en général sur le bien qu'on peut attendre de ces administrations dans les monarchies*
(Lausanne, 1787). Turgot's *Mémoire* started with the following statement: "The cause of
evil, Sire, comes from the fact that your nation has no constitution." *Observations d'un républicain,* by Brissot de Warville, was an attack on Necker, accused of having "forgotten
the principles of republican government, even though he was born in one of them" (p.
119). The proposal to abolish the intendants was absurd in a monarchical regime. It was
asking the king to condemn himself. "The evil his intendant does in his province, the king
does in his kingdom" (p. 117). Nor did he have the sense to attempt slow and measured
reforms. "I hold that in order to be complete a revolution must be accomplished suddenly" (p. 121). Otherwise menacing interests would join together against the reformer.
In a republic, where discussion was free, it was necessary to proceed differently. "Demonstrate good before doing it, but in a monarchy, do good before demonstrating it" (p.
122). Turgot had operated in the latter manner and one should proceed in that way in
the future.

ing "a wise equilibrium among the three orders."[60] He did not choose this option out of sympathy for nobles, and his criticisms of parts of France where these had the financial administration in their own hands were harsh. He was even less partial to the privileges of ecclesiastics. What counted for him was to create "a wise constitution and an equilibrium among the different orders."[61] Precisely for this reason he proposed doubling the vote of the Third Estate. That is, his effort was concentrated on an attempt to give a constitutional value to the traditional orders of French society. Only in this way did he think it was possible to remove the provinces from the despotism of intendants, as well as from the arbitrary actions of local magistrates. The Parlements should return to their judicial functions, without having the shortcomings of local authorities pushing them continually to transform themselves into mouthpieces for public opinion.

These intentions made a strong impression on contemporaries. We, at a distance of more than two centuries, can see how Necker had taken a dead-end route. His effort in 1789 to give a constitutional value to the relationship between First, Second, and Third estates would shipwreck the old regime. The proposal of the physiocrats to entrust local administration to proprietors, whatever their rank, might seem more coherent to us. But for many in 1781 who read these choice revelations of the private intentions of Necker there was a violent revulsion. Did the government truly intend to attack the power of the parlements? One remembered that "their authority is legal and constitutional: it comes uniquely from the assembled nation," one of the polemicists wrote. "Thus to despoil the parlements, Sire, I can legally propose to you nothing but the Estates General." To act otherwise would be to fall into a "frightful despotism."[62] Necker was meddling with the "ancient national forms" of the "French constitution." What would he have said if a Frenchman tried to establish himself in Geneva for the purpose of sowing discontent and "prepare a revolution"? Would not the "Council of Two Hundred" have the right to condemn him to death? In ancient republics the tyrannicide was considered the most virtuous of citizens. "The most mild and civilized of Frenchmen are no less deeply aware of attacks against their rights and their liberty."[63]

The situation became so tense in the spring of 1781 that it gave rise to a rumor of Necker's dismissal a bit everywhere. It was spoken of in

---

[60] "Mémoire donné au roi," p. 10.

[61] Ibid., p. 20.

[62] "Lettre d'un bon François," in *Collection complette*, vol. 3, p. 33. On the conservative French constitutionalism of the second half of the eighteenth century see the interesting research of Dieter Gembicki, *Histoire et politique à la fin de l'Ancien Régime. Jacob-Nicolas Moreau (1717–1803)* (Paris: Nizet, 1979), with a rich bibliography.

[63] "Lettre d'un bon François," in *Collection complette*, vol. 3, p. 41.

Geneva, with the addendum that the king still would not permit it.[64] "There was great surprise" in Milan when "his dismissal from office" was known.[65] The "blustering news" had already appeared in the Florentine *Notizie del mondo*.[66] "The loss of this great man is deeply mourned," it was communicated from Paris a few days later.[67] On 7 July the same journal explained the consequences of his demise. "Commerce continues to experience the effects of the fall in the price of bonds in anticipation of the dismissal of this minister. There is no money at the Bourse and consequently business is at a standstill."[68] In Venice the fall of Necker, announced on 6 June, was interpreted three days later as the result of an encounter between the Genevan banker and the parlements. It was in fact "generally attributed to the *Memoir on provincial administration*, which his enemies had published one month earlier . . . and which turned all the judiciary against M. Necker."[69] In July, "Gasparo Storti, Venetian bookseller," sold, "for 15 soldi, a little book in 4to with 16 pages, printed on good paper with new type, and the title: *Elogio del sig. Necker, direttore generale della Finanza del re di Francia*."[70] In the autumn no more than regret remained for the failed reforms of recent years: "The innovations introduced by M. Turgot and Necker were received with acclamations by most of the nation, but these two great men could not sustain themselves in such a delicate position; all the good they had planned, although in different ways, fell with them."[71]

At the moment of Necker's dismissal a brochure dated 1 May 1781, which J. Egret calls "witty and well informed," circulated in Paris entitled *Lettre de M. le marquis de Caraccioli à M. d'Alembert*. It appears that the author was Philippe-Henri de Grimoard.[72] Certainly it was not the Neapolitan ex-ambassador to London and to France who left Paris in those days for Sicily, where he had been named viceroy. In Naples he encountered Galiani, in a "bad mood" because of the fall of Necker, and begged him to get a copy of the work that carried his name, whose news he had just heard.[73] Necker appeared in this little work as a kind

[64] *Notizie del mondo*, no. 38, 12 May 1781, p. 302 (Geneva, 30 April).

[65] *La gazzetta di Milano*, no. 23, 6 June 1781 (Paris, 21 May). Still on 23 May this sheet, referring to rumors circulating in Geneva on the coming dismissal of Necker, added that it was generally thought "the king would not permit it" (ibid., no. 21, 23 May 1781 [Geneva, 2 May]).

[66] *Notizie del mondo*, no. 4, 5 June 1781, p. 358 (Milan, 30 May).

[67] Ibid., no. 46, 9 June 1781, p. 362 (Paris, 25 May).

[68] Ibid., no. 54, 7 July 1781, p. 426 (Paris, 22 June).

[69] *Notizie del mondo [V.]*, no. 45, 6 June 1781, p. 351 (Paris, 21 May), and no. 46, 9 June 1781, p. 362, "Extract of a letter from Paris of 29 May."

[70] Ibid., no. 53, 4 July 1781, p. 428, in the footer.

[71] Ibid., no. 90, 10 November 1781, p. 718 (Paris, 29 October).

[72] Egret, *Necker*, p. 60 n. 53.

[73] *Opere di Ferdinando Galiani*, pp. 1154ff., Naples, 9 June 1781, to Madame d'Epinay.

of magician of politics and finance, capable of "mystifying the whole French nation": "È molto maraviglioso" was added in Italian.[74] But still, what had he done in reality? "Suppressions without reimbursements, reforms without profit, loans without limit or measure. . . ." He had unleashed the power of money over France, carrying with him an incredible number of enthusiastic followers. Now this whole fantasy was at an end. The publication of the memorandum on provincial administration had been "a thunderbolt for its author."[75] It was seen that his policy led "to the subversion of all constitutional forms," to the "overthrow of the monarchy." To d'Alembert was attributed the judgment that this was "the crime of a foreigner, convicted by his own writings to having appeared before the throne as the calumniator of the whole judiciary and the fomenter of murmurs against those entrusted with authority among the people."[76] The danger was all the worse in that he had a large following, described by the anonymous author as an immense procession led by the "gilded banners of the bank," followed by the clergy and Protestants, "united for the first time behind the same banner, half sacred, half profane." There followed "the friends at court" and a "great troop of dupes, sottish admirers, enlighteners and provincials, all with gaping mouths and eyes fixed on the tables of the *Compte rendu*, which serves as their standard." There one read "the great words of beneficence, reform, assistance, and liberty." A "noisy music" accompanied this cortège, "composed by men of letters who set the tone, as they pretend to everywhere these days, journalists and economists holding the trumpet of the Abbé Raynal and serving as kettledrummers, and a crowd of hacks on wages doubled by those whom they serve to echo."[77]

Even the bitterest enemies of Necker could not deny—one could see it even in the variegated procession they imagined of his followers—that the Genevan banker, in the brief years of his government, had stirred up a vast and complex movement in public opinion.[78]

[74] "Lettere di M. le marquis di Caraccioli a M. d'Alembert," in *Collection complette*, vol. 3, p. 44.

[75] Ibid., p. 49.

[76] Ibid., p. 50.

[77] Ibid., pp. 57ff. The "Lettre de M. le marquis de Caraccioli" was soon translated into Italian. See *Gazzetta universale*, no. 26, 30 March 1782, p. 208, "Avviso," where one reads: "From the presses of Ranieri del Vivo has come out an interesting letter written by Marchese Caraccioli to M. d'Alembert about M. Necker, which is sold at the price of a half paolo by the same and by Pagani."

[78] Already in the summer of 1781 the *Courier de l'Europes*, no. 7, 24 July 1781, p. 51 (Paris, 15 July), noted that "the statements distributed for or against the administration of M. Necker have become very rare: their collection will be a precious thing in a few years."

V

From Diderot to Mirabeau

IN 1778 VOLTAIRE AND ROUSSEAU DIED. AN EPOCH ENDED IN France.[1] The demise of the two enemy philosophes was also echoed quickly in Italy, where, as everywhere else, attention was concentrated more on the final apotheosis of Voltaire than on the desolate and solitary end of the Genevan philosophe. In the spring news of the arrival in Paris of the "Nestor of the French Parnassus" came to Florence, together with news of imminent war between France and England.[2] It was nearly thirty years "that he had been absent from Paris."[3] "This whole capital is immersed in a strange enthusiasm for having M. Voltaire at its breast again." Innumerable persons went to pay him homage. "One of the visits most dear to him was certainly that of Dr. Franklin, who came with his nephew." When asked what he thought of the "new legislation of the American confederation," he said he thought it was "so good that if it had been made forty years earlier even I would have gone to establish myself in your free country." To the nephew he said, "never forget God and liberty."[4] In the theatrical triumph accorded him during a performance of his *Irene* applause burst out particularly when a passage was recited "that was immediately applied to the Americans, who defend and vindicate their liberty against the despotism (as is thought) of their fellow citizens and against the violence of mercenary seasoned troops who are forced in vain to subject and exterminate them."[5] The enthusiasm was all the more significant because he returned to Paris as an exile and was thus still, as he said jokingly, "contraband" in the reign of Louis

---

[1] A thick, special issue of the journal *Dix-huitième siècle*, no. 2 (1979), has been dedicated to *L'anneé 1778*.

[2] *Notizie del mondo*, no. 19, 7 March 1778, p. 150 (Paris, 17 February).

[3] *Gazzetta universale*, no. 18, 3 March 1776, p. 138 (Paris, 17 February).

[4] *Notizie del mondo*, no. 22, 17 March 1778, p. 173 (Paris, 2 March).

[5] Ibid., no. 29, 11 April 1778, p. 229 (Paris, 25 March).

XVI.[6] Every word from him, every gesture, replayed the gap between ecclesiastical authority and his more and more numerous admirers. It was said that the archbishop had put the king on guard against the presence of the philosophe in France. The partisans of Voltaire, on the other hand, "eager to take advantage of every circumstance they thought might serve his triumph, regarded with great importance the commission to have his bust sculpted by M. Pigal at the king's expense."[7] Again Louis XVI stood ambiguous and uncertain before the world surrounding him. He tolerated Voltaire more than he accepted him. In the theaters and academies, meanwhile, Voltaire finally enjoyed "the triumph that . . . all of France had long since awarded him."[8] The Masonic ceremony was no less enthusiastic. "M. Voltaire was received on the 7th with much solemnity into the Masonic lodge of the Nine Sisters, which meets in the former novitiate of the Jesuits. M. de la Lande, the famous astronomer, presided over the ceremony." They told Voltaire that "the Nine Sisters needed an Apollo." He said "he was unworthy; . . . because of his age and celebrity he was exempted from the ceremonial generally required of candidates." "Happiness and pleasant conversation continued throughout the dinner." Dixmérie made a compliment that contained a kernel of truth about the relationship between the whole movement of the Enlightenment and Freemasonry:

> Au seul nom de l'illustre frère
> Tout maçon triomphe aujourd'hui.
> S'il reçoit de nous la lumière,
> Le monde la reçoit de lui.[9]

Giovanni Fabbroni, a young Tuscan and a witness to this ceremony along with the celebrated scientist Felice Fontana, wrote, in a letter to his friend Clementino Vannetti, about the reverence with which Voltaire was received into the lodge of the Nine Sisters. "At the end, amid cheers, he was crowned with laurels, dressed with the regalia of the great Helvétius, and put in the place that great philosophe once occupied, to which he first bowed, kissing it several times, and then rising to

---

[6] Ibid., no. 24, 24 March 1778, p. 190 (Paris, n.d.).

[7] Ibid., no. 26, 31 March 1778, p. 205 (Paris, 16 March).

[8] Ibid., no. 32, 21 April 1778, p. 253 (Paris, 6 April).

[9] "In the very name of the illustrious brother / All Masons triumph today. / If he receives light from us, / The world receives it from him" (ibid., no. 36, 5 May 1778, p. 285 [Paris, 21 April]). See *Gazzetta universale*, no. 36, 5 May 1778, p. 282 (Paris, 21 April). See also no. 103, 26 December 1778, p. 831 (Paris, 5 December). The *Nouvelles extraordinaires de divers endroits*, no. 32, 21 April 1778 (Paris, 13 April), called the place where the ceremony occurred "the Freemasonic Lodge of the Jesuits, which meets in the former novitiate of the Jesuits."

his feet said to us laconically: 'Sirs, the honor you bestow in admitting me among you makes me, for the first time, experience pride, and, even more, feel thankfulness.' "[10]

The death of the eighty-five-year-old Voltaire, on 30 May, provided hasty and passionate opportunities for taking stock and interpreting his extraordinarily rich and varied personality. "Aristippus in the morning and Diogenes at night, he took pleasure in greatness and disliked the great. . . . He loved the court and was bored by it . . . , upright of mind and unjust at heart . . . a libertine without temperament," wrote the gazette of Florence.[11] One point, however, remained firm: "He died as he always lived, with scorn for religion and its ministers." He had great satisfactions in his life. "The illustrious defender of Calas . . . had the pleasure to hear the sentence of the parlement revoked." "A philosopher king always honored him with his correspondence and friendship."[12] In Paris his disappearance long continued to be "the subject of almost all conversation." "But now that the lion is dead, many have come up to pluck at his beard; and thus various gross and indecent satires are given out to the public against the life of this unequaled man."[13] He was not yet dead when his agitated afterlife began.

By contrast, the disappearance of Jean Jacques seemed almost a flight. But his profound appeal never ceased to resound in the minds of contemporaries. "Man and republican," he had to the last asked to remain worthy "of these two supreme qualities" and to honor their "sacred dignity" by dying "poor, if necessary," and living "free and independent."[14] Just as the funeral orations in tribute to Voltaire were being talked about, the rumor spread of the "unexpected death of Jean Jacques Rousseau."[15] He did not leave behind him a *Political Testament* like

[10] Carlo Teodoro Postinger, "L'amicizia di Clementino Vannetti col fiorentino Giovanni Fabbroni," *Atti della R. Accademia di scienze, lettere ed arti degli Agiati in Rovereto*, 3d ser. vol. 10 (July–December 1904): 240ff.

[11] *Notizie del mondo*, no. 59, 25 July 1778, p. 469 (Paris, 8 July).

[12] Ibid., no. 50, 23 June 1778, p. 397 (Paris, n.d.).

[13] Ibid., No 54, 7 July 1778, p. 429 (Paris, 22 June 1778). See *Gazzetta universale*, no. 59, 25 July 1778, p. 472, "Avvisi"; "A little book with the title *Aneddoti sugli estremi della vita e morte del sig. di Voltaire* . . . published by Antonio Giuseppe Pagani has been seen in print." The conclusions of Alfieri are well known; he spoke of the "humiliating confrontation of seeing Voltaire in his last days in Paris applauded, followed, acclaimed, and in triumph much more than any prince ever was. And there will come a time when one will not even remember the number of the Louis reigning then, except that a Voltaire triumphed in Paris in his time" ("Del principe e delle lettere," in *Scritti politici e morali*, vol. 1, ed. Pietro Cazzani [Asti: Casa d'Alfieri, 1951], p. 135).

[14] *Gazzetta universale*, no. 10, 3 February 1778, p. 80 (Paris, n.d.). The words cited are taken from a letter dated 2 December 1777, "on misanthrophy and liberty."

[15] *Notizie del mondo*, no. 51, 27 June 1778, p. 405 (Paris, 9 June).

the one Parisian booksellers hastened in those days to attribute to Voltaire. Nor did he inspire a *Eulogy* like the one Palissot wrote to try once again to separate Voltaire from the other Encyclopedists, a *Eulogy* that Zacchiroli immediately translated "egregiously."[16] Rousseau left "some very spicy memoirs of his life that were intended to appear after his death."[17] The figure of Jean Jacques always remained enigmatic. "He was a misanthrope and a cynic, but still rightly more esteemed than Voltaire for the greater depth of his mind and for his less surprising and perhaps more masculine eloquence, although it was sometimes used to uphold paradoxes, and finally for his great disinterestedness, a rare thing to find among men." Had he not renounced a large pension granted him by the king of Prussia, his "admirer and friend," preferring the "poor occupation" of copying music? "Always ready to remain alone, like a savage even in the most populous cities, he had finally retired to Ermenonville to enjoy more liberty, which was his idol."[18]

With the loss of Voltaire and Rousseau, many from the world of the *Encyclopédie* still remained, but few could now call themselves truly active. The activity of Holbach had culminated between the sixties and the seventies, at the moment of the first crisis of the old regime. His last important work, *La morale universelle*, much admired by Diderot, appeared in 1776. D'Alembert, more and more enclosed in the academic and scientific world, was now distant from the lucid political vision that had led him to write, twenty-five years earlier, his *Essai sur la société des gens de lettres et des grands*. Helvétius had died in 1771, and his posthumous work *De l'homme* was published in 1773.

Alive and active, certainly, was Diderot, the first of the Encyclopedists, but even for him, the final period of his existence reveals, when viewed closely, the side effects and delays that characterized the Enlightenment in its concluding age.[1] The seventies and beginning of the eight-

---

[16] Ibid., no. 10 2 February 1779, p. 80, in the footer, and no. 17, 27 February 1779, p. 136, "Avvisi."

[17] *Notizie del mondo [V.]*, no. 51, 27 June 1778, p. 405 (Paris, 9 June). The *Gazzetta universale*, no. 73, 12 September 1778, p. 584 (Paris, n.d.), records among the works left by Rousseau "the legislation of Poland" and the "memoirs of his times." It then translated the first page of the *Confessions*.

[18] *Notizie del mondo*, no. 59, 25 July 1778, p. 469 (Paris, 8 July).

[1] See Anthony Strugnell, *Diderot's Politics: A Study of the Evolution of Diderot's Political Thought After the Encyclopédie* (The Hague: Martinus Nijhoff, 1973), and *Diderot. Les dernières années (1770–84). Colloque du bicentenaire*. Textes réunis et presentés par P. France et A. Strugnell (Edinburgh, 1985). On all these problems and personalities consult the chap-

ies (he died on 19 February 1784) saw many of his most vivid and important works appear from his pen, *Jacques le fataliste*, the *Supplément au voyage de Bougainville, Est-il bon, est-il méchant?* and also his passionate philosophical, political, and economic considerations, the *Apologie de l'abbé Raynal*, the *Réfutation d'Helvétius*, the *Observations sur le Nakaz*, the *Politique des souverains*, to cite only his most famous works. Yet not a page of this treasury could be read by contemporaries, and it had to wait tens and even hundreds of years before it was published. He wrote for himself and for a most restricted elite of sovereigns and privileged people of Europe, who were capable sometimes, like Catherine II, of appreciating his value, but certainly not of drawing inspiration from it for their own politics. He carried to the extreme the paradox of the philosopher and literary man free from all ties and prejudices, detached and distant from the world, who at the same time never gave up talking of the two things that truly interested him, religion and government, that is, ideas and human society. His was not a renunciation; it was rather a desire to restate his ideas in a situation that he sensed increasingly to be without any outlet. It was an effort to move toward a free and happy world emerging more and more vigorously within a society that he felt to be in decline, in decadence.

Even if his words reached contemporaries only in a mutilated and muffled form, his actions and attitudes could not help but call attention to the center of his paradox, stimulating discussion of the value and function of philosophie in the age of the despotism of Catherine II, the American Revolution, and the uncertain policy of the French monarchy. He too was persuaded, like many other writers and thinkers of those years, that liberty was increasingly menaced in Europe, that republics were in decline, while the power of tyrannies continued to grow. His hostility toward Frederick II became less and less veiled. More and more clear became his sympathy for free England, and above all for men like Wilkes, who tended to give new vigor to the British constitution. He admired the first battles of the American rebellion. Such doubts and considerations were saddened, after 1770, by a comparison with what was happening in France, where old institutions were unable to hold, while nothing seemed able to replace them. He also put his trust in Turgot for a moment and placed his confidence in the ability and humanity of Necker, but such hopes and confidences were satisfying only on a practical, a daily, and an immediate level. In the depths of his soul he convinced himself more and more that France was corrupt, that

ter entitled "La svolta degli anni settanta-ottanta," in the fundamental work by Furio Diaz, *Dal movimento dei lumi al movimento dei popoli. L'Europa tra illuminismo e rivoluzione* (Bologna: Il Mulino, 1986), pp. 467ff.

it had now entered a road of irreversible decline. "There is a high mountain with a steep slope on one side and a deep precipice on the other; between the slope and the precipice there is a plain of moderate dimensions. The emerging nation climbs the steep slope. The formed nation walks along the plain. The declining nation proceeds along the edge of the precipice, and at great speed: there we are."[2] There were many causes for such an inexorable decline: the reversal of Choiseul's policy, the crushing of the parlements, restrictions of liberty. But beyond such contingent elements was something else, which Diderot tried to define and describe, but which always ended by presenting itself before his eyes as a massive, opaque reality that reason and the desire for reform did not succeed in laying bare, or even touching. In France "an unbelievable inequality of fortune among citizens" existed. "There is a center of true opulence; around this center exists an immense and vast misery." Merit, education, "enlightenment," and virtue no longer counted for anything. "Gold opens the door to everything. It has become the god of the nation. There is only one vice, which is poverty. There is only one virtue, which is wealth. One must be rich or despised."[3] There was a deep penetration of gold into all the receptacles of the nation, the nobility, intellectuals. It was a deep and limitless corruption. But still, the structure of France was solid. Neither foreign invasion, of which Helvétius had spoken, nor the corruption of gold would have its effect. "This kingdom of France is a dreadful machine; it will take much time to take it apart."[4] Considering the rhythm of daily events one could still count on this resistance. Diderot did this, following the highs and lows of the seventies. But a basic pessimism prevailed in the end, canceling out all illusions. "In the moral as well as the physical world it is easier to descend than to rise. A descending body follows its natural penchant; it is against its nature, through some accidental or violent shock, to rise again for a moment."[5] More and more France appeared to him as a land "affected by an old and almost incurable disease."[6]

This was a bitter thought that contributed to turning Diderot's eyes toward other horizons, above all toward Russia. Not personal vanity, not practical necessity, and not even the hope of being able to put his own imprint on a new nation engaged in a decisive moment of its history

---

[2] Denis Diderot, *Mémoires pour Catherine II*, ed. P. Vernière (Paris: Garnier, 1966), p. 21.

[3] Ibid., pp. 145ff.

[4] Ibid., p. 149.

[5] Id., *Oeuvres politiques*, ed. P. Vernière (Paris: Garnier, 1963), "Observations sur le Nakaz," p. 401.

[6] Ibid., p. 365.

carried Diderot to St. Petersburg in the winter of 1773–1774 (even if undoubtedly some element of such aims was not lacking in the complex motivation that pushed him to such an unusual undertaking). When one closely examines the memoranda he wrote for the empress at that time, to discuss them with her in long interviews—and, above all, when one considers the *Observations on the Nakaz*, which he wrote in Holland in the spring of 1774 on his return—a conclusion imposes itself: Diderot was moved by a vigorous and an incorrigible faith in the regenerative and transforming force of liberty. He had no illusions about Russian society, as he did not about French society, even if, as was natural, he had a much more superficial knowledge of Russia than of his own country. He tried every means to inform himself about Catherine's empire, but the obstacles he encountered were not few and often insurmountable. He did not close his eyes to the political despotism that surrounded him or to the peasant serfdom he did not see but felt everywhere, before the imbalance that the efforts of Peter and his successors had impressed on the life and very physiognomy of the country, or before the new capital, so peripheral, abnormal, constructed and inhabited by foreigners. But still, from his first interview with the empress, when he wrote for her an *Essai historique sur la police* and narrated a rather fanciful history of the political institutions of France, he emphasized the central point of his argument: better an illusion of liberty than no liberty. What was needed above all was to place oneself in the way of developing an effective legal order, thus preventing the central peril of any monarchical government, the tendency, that is, to become despotic. This was "the ruin of a nation."[7] The recent history of France since the expulsion of the Jesuits demonstrated it. Arbitrary government is always bad, even when in the hands "of a good, firm, just, and enlightened master." The teaching of Montesquieu and the example of England demonstrated that only political liberty could guarantee just and effective government. "The right of opposition seems to me a natural, an inalienable, and a sacred right in the society of men. . . . One of the greatest evils that can afflict a free nation is two or three consecutive reigns of a just and an enlightened despotism. . . . Woe to subjects whose monarch transmits to their children this infallible but terrible policy! Woe to the people in whom remains no shadow of liberty, even a distorted one! Such a nation falls into a sweet sleep, but it is a sleep of death."[8] To avoid such a destiny Russia should have transformed the legislative commission that the empress had convened in 1767 into a true and proper permanent national assembly, limiting its field of action carefully, but ensuring it with

[7] *Mémoires pour Catherine*, p. 33.
[8] Ibid., pp. 117ff.

a permanent weight and dignity that no other Russian institution possessed (certainly not the senate, which counted for nothing).[9] This would be a seed of political liberty, which Diderot thought could grow rapidly and securely in Russian soil, parallel to the development that he held to be natural for a true and proper Third Estate. Contrary to what had happened to the French parlements, a legislative commission developed and reinforced in this way would not limit itself to registering the legislative will of the sovereign. While even "this body," he concluded, "would be in time only a ghost of liberty, it would still have an influence on the national spirit, because a people needs to be either free, or better still, believe that it is so; this belief always has most valuable effects."[10]

This seed would not be able to develop if its soil were not prepared with an intense political effort, through education and the suppression of privileges. Describing this work, Diderot spoke for France as well as Russia. The two were made parallel by the great effort to transform themselves into nations where culture, merit, and free customs would replace the distinctions and contrasts of the past. Just as in his youth he had seen in the group of philosophes the nucleus of a transformation of France as a whole, so now, for Russia, he thought of colonies of freemen, "very free ones, like the Swiss, for example," as a leavening for the change he hoped to contribute to bringing into being.[11]

His experience in St. Petersburg was bracing but hard. On his return through free Holland, Diderot took Catherine's *Nakaz* into his hands again, intending to start a dialogue with her no longer made up of suggestions, incitements, and winks, but based on incontrovertible principles. "The only true sovereign is the nation; the only true legislator is the people," he began.[12] Seen from this point of view, Russian government was undoubtedly despotic. The only real problem the empress was called to resolve was whether she intended "to preserve despotism and transmit it to her subjects or abjure it."[13] This was a basic decision, on which depended the possibility of activating the "plan for civilization" that Russia needed.[14] It was necessary to choose. "Why is Russia less well governed than France? It is because the natural freedom of the individual is reduced to nothing and sovereign authority is unlimited. Why is France less well governed than England? It is because sovereign author-

---

[9] "Observations sur le Nakaz," p. 364: "The Senate is nothing, *vox clamantis in deserto*."
[10] *Mémoires pour Catherine*, p. 127.
[11] "Observations sur le Nakaz," p. 351 n. 1.
[12] Ibid., p. 343.
[13] Ibid., p. 345.
[14] Ibid., p. 350.

ity is still too great there and natural liberty is too restricted."[15] Backward tendencies were not lacking even in Great Britain, as elsewhere.
The government of George III attempted to imitate that of France. Yes,
Louis XV had tried to "set up an Asiatic government."[16] To oppose such
tendencies it was insufficient to have a national law code, the action of
public opinion, or even the diffusion of education, even if these were
factors of great importance. Political institutions were indispensable; "a
witness to this is the English Parliament, which seems to me a great
counterbalance to the power of the king."[17] In France the same direction could have been taken through "periodic meetings of the Estates
General." Catherine instead left the chief element uncertain, that is,
what power was to be reserved for those "intermediary bodies" about
which she had nonetheless spoken.[18] "From the destruction of our parliament and the corruption of that of England," he concluded, Catherine had to draw the inspiration to create "something better than both
of them."[19]

A free legislative power would direct its efforts to clear away the ruins of the past (more easily done, Diderot was convinced, in a place like
Russia than in France), and to remedy the fundamental injustice of the
empire of Catherine II, that is, the serfdom of peasants, but above all to
create the basis of a society not egalitarian, not uniform, but free, cultivated, and happy, forever transforming itself and progressing, capable
of self-regulation without continual controls and juridical regulations.[20]
He returned in thought to his discussions with Rousseau and the physiocrats. No. Human society, he was increasingly convinced, should not
be impeded in its development by moralistic condemnations of luxury
and the arts, or even by purely utilitarian considerations. Beyond both
of these was a creative force that should be given free play. "I do not
want to stop progress." "Arrange two or three important points and

---

[15] Ibid., pp. 355ff.
[16] Ibid., p. 356.
[17] Ibid., p. 359.
[18] Ibid., p. 360.
[19] Ibid., p. 363.
[20] Ibid., p. 365 ("In France, one must commit an incredible number of injustices when
abolishing privileges. . . . There is a big difference between a people that is policed and a
people to police; the condition of the first seemed to me worse than the condition of the
second"), p. 386 ("The empress has said nothing about the freeing of the serfs. But it is
still a very important point. Does she want her nation to remain in slavery? Is she unaware
that there is no true police, or laws, or population, or agriculture, or commerce, or wealth,
or science, or taste, or art where there is no liberty?"), and p. 406 ("To avoid the abuses
of servitude, and prevent its dangers, there is but one means, that is, to abolish servitude
and govern only free men").

leave the rest to the interest and taste of individuals."[21] There could be only one conclusion: "Don't kick the beehive; let the bees work in peace."[22]

When he wrote these words Diderot was now far, and not only physically, from Catherine II and the atmosphere of St. Petersburg. His *Observations* still continued to have its own autonomous but contested existence. The empress, although repeatedly asked, refused to receive or read them. The Russian ambassador at The Hague took them from Diderot surreptitiously, by theft. Only after the death of the author did a copy reach Russia. It was judged harshly by Catherine II, who—it seems certain—ordered it burned. The *Observations* did not come to light until 1920, concluding, after a century and a half of delay, the paradox that remained at the root of the discussion between the philosophe and the empress of all Russia.

The problem, one could even say the incubus, of despotism continued to dominate the last years of Diderot. In 1781, when Samuel Romilly came to find him in Paris, the philosophe "talked very eagerly on politics and inveighed with great warmth against the tyranny of the French government." The France of Louis XVI and Vergennes was then at the culmination of its glory as an ally of America, but the thought of Diderot did not detach itself from the perils that everywhere, and above all in monarchical nations, continued to menace liberty. "He told me that he had long meditated a work upon the death of Charles the First, that he had studied the trial of that prince and that his intention was to try him over again, and to have sent him to the scaffold if he had found him guilty, but that he had relinquished the design. In England he would have executed it, but he had not the courage to do so in France."[23]

The tormented political thought of Diderot—almost an underground torrent—found at the end a unique and clear outlet in the *Essai sur la vie de Sénèque le philosophe, sur ses écrits et sur les règnes de Claude et de Néron*. A first edition appeared in 1779, to be then revised and enlarged in 1782, when it appeared with a slightly different title.[24] Even

---

[21] Ibid., pp. 445ff.

[22] Ibid., p. 449.

[23] *Memoirs of the life of Sir Samuel Romilly, written by himself, with a selection from his correspondence*, edited by his son in three volumes (London: John Murray, 1840), vol. 1, p. 63. He added that "d'Alembert was more cautious." See now Gianluigi Goggi, "L'ultimo Diderot e la prima rivoluzione inglese," *Studi settecenteschi*, fasc. 7–8 (1987): 349ff.

[24] See Paolo Casini, "Diderot apologiste de Sénèque," *Dix-huitième siècle*, no. 2 (1979): 235ff. For the text I have used the edition edited by Hisayasu Nakagawa published in Tokyo by Takeuchi in 1968 in two volumes, a critical edition that permits rapid assessment

though it was filled with autobiographical elements, the *Essai* is not a confession. It was born rather of the profound revulsion Diderot felt when confronted with the decision of his brother-enemy Rousseau to pour out to posterity all that he had not been able, or had not wanted, to say in life. Diderot's was not a confession, but a justification, an apologia. It did not open directly to readers, but was intended to explain the significance of his actions to them. It was a history of himself that had to be guessed at through the classical model Diderot chose as the object of his essay. It was an image, almost a statue, of the philosophe in the robes and behind the mask of Seneca. As the Roman philosopher had accepted to the end, to suicide, the task of living in a difficult, tragic, horrible epoch, thus also the French philosophe defended his own merit of never having renounced the affirmation of enlightenment and virtue, without having allowed himself to be discouraged, not even by the awareness of his own limits, his own defects and weaknesses. "One must preach to others everything that is good and praiseworthy, whether one is capable or incapable of it."[25] Seneca had not rejected the life of his own times; he had acted in the forum and at the court. He had not been "a hypocritical Stoic."[26] Diderot, for his part, had never been tempted to follow Jansenists or Jesuits.[27] Moralism had dominated the existence of Rousseau, a great writer and an exceptional personality; he had been not a philosopher but rather a demagogue. The political crime of Jean Jacques, that of having contributed to divide and weaken the party of the philosophes, had been unforgivable. All had been pardoned him by the enemies of enlightenment, who were grateful for the part he had taken in the struggle against the Encyclopedists. "The people of the world" had even forgotten his "treatise on the inequality of conditions," remembering only that he had come over to their side against those who preferred "talents and virtue to opulence and honors." Rousseau had, in short, sinned in the area that had counted the most for Diderot, that of "political religion."[28]

It was necessary to return to Seneca to understand the difficulties, the torments of a philosopher whose lot was to live in an age when "the powerless Senate was without authority, the Pretorian guard without discipline, and the people without energy," as he said with words that, once again, derived from ancient Rome but echoed the passions of

of the differences between the 1779 version and that of 1782 and preserves the pagination of the originals (henceforth: *Essai sur Sénèque*).

[25] *Essai sur Sénèque*, vol. 1, p. 59.

[26] Ibid., p. 71.

[27] Ibid.

[28] Ibid., p. 90.

France, Russia, and modern Europe.[29] Despotism was an insidious peril, present everywhere, always renewed. "The strictures of despotic governments limit the mind without one's being aware of it; there is an automatic prohibition of a certain kind of strong ideas, as if one were avoiding a wounding obstruction, and when one is accustomed to this small-minded and circumspect procedure it is difficult to return to a more frank and an audacious one."[30] From this came the importance of the experience of the past, of classical examples. From this above all came the exceptional value of a new fact that had come to lighten the horizon of the world "after centuries of general oppression." "The revolution that has begun beyond the seas," the American Revolution, finally contained a promise of freedom. Everything would now depend on the capacity of the "brave Americans" to give life to a society in which liberty could maintain and develop itself. "Can these brave Americans . . . prevent the enormous growth and unequal distribution of riches, luxury, the corruption of manners and power, in maintaining their liberty and preserving their government?" Before them, like all other peoples in history, was a peril they had in all ways to force themselves to prevent, "the abuse of prosperity." The example of England, of that great power, "mistress of land and sea," from which they had freed themselves, should always remain alive in them, to avoid taking the way of British corruption. "They should believe that it is not through gold, or through growth of manpower, that states sustain themselves, but through morals." Like many others at the time, even Diderot feared for the life of the young plant that had sprouted beyond the ocean. Thus, even he took refuge, however open he was to praising modern progress, in the ancient models of republican moderation and virtue.[31]

The Life of Seneca guides us through the contrasts, turns, and agonies of the last years of Diderot. His increasingly active participation in the *Histoire philosophique* of the Abbé Raynal shows him in his final effort to resume the activity of organizer and animator that had led him to create and complete the *Encyclopédie*. His method in both enterprises might be defined as guided collaboration. Without plans, letting himself be guided by inspiration, without pretense of limiting his own work or that

---

[29] Ibid., p. 108.

[30] Ibid., vol. 2, p. 24.

[31] Ibid., pp. 134ff. See the Italian version, by Secondo Carpanetto and Luciano Guerci, with a note by Luciano Canfora, *Saggio sui regni di Claudio e Nerone e sui costumi e gli scritti di Seneca* (Palermo: Sellerio, 1987).

of others, he took part in a collective undertaking, without destroying its varied and disparate character, inserting a word where it seemed indispensable, coloring with wise pen strokes the picture as a whole, reviewing and retouching it continually to make it more vivid and responsive to the exigencies of the moment.

It would be praiseworthy, certainly, in knowing his work, to find these pen strokes, to establish exactly where the prose of Diderot ended and where that of the other collaborators began. That is what some of the best and most accurate modern scholars of Diderot have sought to do, on the basis chiefly of the *fonds* Vandeul, recently placed at the disposition of scholars.[1] There is an obvious risk, in doing this, of diminishing the historical effect of these interventions of the philosophe. These are significant, to be sure, for reconstructing his more or less secret life as a writer and thinker, but they are important above all because they reached readers bound up in a volume as a whole, in continual internal dialogue with the other collaborators. We must return to the text of the *Histoire philosophique* and read it as contemporaries read it, that is, as a work by the Abbé Raynal, even if many were not ignorant of the fact that this prolific publicist was not alone in his work, that many assisted him, including Diderot. It was a collective work, in which anonymity contributed to creating a common atmosphere, and it was effective often precisely because it left one to guess, or suggest, a considerable variety of tones and opinions. Let us leave to Diderot the function that circumstance led him to take in the *Histoire philosophique*, that of a hidden inspirer, and go back to looking at this work for what it effectively was, a mirror of the world of the seventies, the encyclopedia of dreams

---

[1] Herbert Dieckmann, *Inventaire du Fonds Vandeul et inédits de Diderot* (Geneva: Droz, 1951); id., "Les contributions de Diderot à la *Correspondance littéraire* et à l'*Histoire des deux Indes*," *Revue d'histoire littéraire de la France*, year 51, no. 4 (October–December 1951): 414ff.; Hans Wolpe, *Raynal et sa machine de guerre. L' "Histoire des deux Indes" et ses perfectionnements* (Paris: M.-T. Genin, 1957); Michele Duchet, "Diderot collaborateur de Raynal: À propos des 'fragments imprimés' du Fonds Vandeul," *Revue d'histoire littéraire de la France*, year 60, no. 4 (October–December 1960): 531ff.; id., *Anthropologie et histoire au siècle des lumières* (Paris: Librairie François Maspero, 1971) (It. tr. *Le origini dell'antropologia* [Bari: Laterza, 1976–77], 4 vols.). The research by Gianluigi Goggi is fundamental, *Studi sull'illuminismo. Collana diretta da E. De Angelis*, nos. 1 and 2; Denis Diderot, *Pensées détachées. Contribution à l'Histoire des deux Indes* (Siena, 1976) (henceforth Goggi 1); id., *Mélanges et morceaux divers. Contribution à l'Histoire des deux Indes* (Siena, 1977) (henceforth Goggi 2); and id., "Diderot et Médée dépeçant le viel Eson," in *Colloque international Diderot (1713–1784)*. Actes réunis et préparés par A.-M. Chouillet (Paris, 1985). See also Edoardo Tortarolo, "La réception de l'Histoire des deux Indes aux Etats-Unis," soon to be published in the Acts of the conference "Réception et lectures de l'Histoire des deux Index au dix-huitième siècle," Wolfenbüttel, 1–3 May 1987.

and passions, victories and defeats, of the Enlightenment in the age that extended from Choiseul to Necker.

This does not always make for pleasant and easy reading. A heavy pall of eloquence and rhetoric covers these pages, an indication of unresolved passions, incapable of dissolving themselves in limpid reason or in a precise will to action. The heavy volutes of Raynal's prose nonetheless remain significant, and in the end they lead us to the central nodes of enlightened thought in the years of crises of the old regime.

The success of the *Histoire* was immense and it grew from the first edition, which appeared in 1772, to the second in 1774, and above all to the third in 1780, the one in which Diderot massively intervened. There were about twenty reprintings authorized by the author, to which one has to add forty or more pirated editions. And this was a work of many volumes, often with illustrations, indexes, and an atlas in the appendix. With rapid avidity the *Histoire*, like Diderot's great dictionary, was absorbed, modified, and diffused on a grandiose scale by the growing publishing industry of the last decades of the century.[2]

The thousand criticisms directed at the *Encyclopédie* had even included its alphabetical organization. A new version, the *Encyclopédie méthodique*, had adopted a compromise, combining systematic treatments with the arrangement of articles in alphabetical order. Raynal

[2] See Anatole Feugere, *Bibliographie critique de l'abbé Raynal* (Angoulême: Imprimerie ouvrière, 1922; Geneva: Slatkine Reprints, 1970). Another edition adds to the many listed here (Goggi 1, p. xl).

I have used the sumptuous third edition: Guillaume-Thomas Raynal, *Histoire philosophique et politique des établissements et du commerce des Européens dans les deux Indes* (Geneva: Jean-Léonard Pellet, imprimeur de la ville de de l'Académie, 1780), 4 vols., and an atlas (henceforth: *Histoire*, with volume number). It begins with a proud portrait of the author, drawn by Ch. N. Cochin, in which Raynal is caught writing his work. In the background one glimpses the great works of the century: the *Histoire naturelle* by Buffon, the *Encyclopédie*, and so on. Below is the dedication "To the defender of humanity, virtue, liberty," where one sees indeed virtue and liberty break and abandon the symbols of oppression and corruption from crutches to crowns, to take up the republican cap and embrace the classical shield of the ancients. The dedication is signed by Eliza Draper, the friend of Sterne, who in dying had invoked history, fame, and the phoenix, "symbol of that genius that never dies," and had exhorted Raynal "to show himself as the defender of humanity, truth, and liberty," receiving from him the oath "to write no line in which your soul might not be found" (that is, Sterne's). (See *Histoire* 1, p. 320.) It is said that these words should be attributed to Diderot (Goggi 2, p. 396). They are in any case a true emblem of the inspiration that united Raynal and Diderot in these pages. The engravings that accompany these volumes were the work of J.-M. Moreau le Jeune and illustrate well the general inspiration of the work, striving to unite refinement and protest, minute description and political symbolism, anecdote and denunciation (see above all the engraving that accompanies the frontispiece of volume 3: "An Englishman from Barbados sells his mistress," a graphic manifesto against slavery finicky in form and dramatic in content).

made a jump, attempting to arrange the immense amount of material his readers expected from him historically, which extended from natural history to the most burning political problems, passing through economics, ethics, religion, and so on. This was definitely philosophical history, that is, not descriptive in the manner of natural history, and it stopped at every point of its course to ask the origins of the phenomena considered and their moral and political legitimacy. It was thus a narrative, interrupted by sudden breaks before continually recurring questions of why and what to do. The uneven movement was accentuated by the interventions of Diderot, who was determined not to abandon a problem before having gutted it but still insisted on the conception of the *Histoire philosophique* itself, that is, the effort to join information and research of reasons and causes. The fusion of history and philosophy sometimes emerges as entirely extrinsic, editorial, and journalistic, but often the relationship between facts and problems is made energetically, with a will to tear down the veils and an enlightened enthusiasm for guessing and mapping out the future. This was universal history, but quite different from what had appeared in the past, as for example in the *Universal History*, which a group of British writers had published some decades earlier and that, in translation, became diffused through all of Europe.[3] Not chronological arrangement, but the continual emergence of the most diverse problems determined the rhythm of the work of Raynal. The central thread was provided not by the succession of peoples and civilizations, but by the economic links that connected them through the centuries. "What united, clothed, and civilized peoples?" "The voice of enlightened men . . . answered: it was commerce."[4] This was thus not economic, but commercial history. It is not that Raynal did not pause on the relationship between trade and agriculture and industry. But commerce alone seemed to furnish him with the keys to understand the development of human civilization. This judgment was significant at the moment the *Histoire* was written and published. The English empire seemed to be coming apart precisely because of trade and financial problems. In Great Britain, as in France and Holland, the center of all debates was the India companies. Witness everywhere a revival of conflicts about customs dues, commercial wars, and state intervention after the shipwreck of the great physiocratic plan for universal free trade. In 1776 Adam Smith made his classic definition of mercantilism and the new economic liberalism. Raynal was historically before Smith. His economic history presents itself as a mercantile adventure. It was

---

[3] See Giuseppe Ricuperati, "Universal History: Storia di un progetto europeo. Impostori, storici ed editori nella Ancient past," *Studi settecenteschi*, year 1, fasc. 2 (1981): 7.

[4] *Histoire*, 1, p. 3.

not intended only as a picture of "moeurs," customs, and civilization, following the model indicated by Voltaire, but a history of civilization, of the intervention of merchants and sovereigns, from the Phoenicians to the wars being fought in the years when the book was written. It was not a description of the contemporary world, but an imaginative reevocation of how this was formed through discoveries, conquests, revolts, and submissions. Colonization is an essential element in this picture, but still it was inserted into a broader discussion of the value of "civilization" through the centuries, in the double sense of civility and of becoming civilized. It was a history that was both *philosophique* and *politique*, one reads in the title, arranged to examine the very principles of human society as well as the means, the instruments, that had served to transform it, and the prospects that now opened before it.

A preliminary question opened the *Histoire* and then returned continually at each of its essential turns: was it worth the trouble to leave nature behind, the woods and primitive life, to enter the tormented, bloody, complicated process of "civilization" with which almost all peoples, in different ways, were finally sooner or later taken up? "Everything has changed and will change again. But have past and future revolutions been, and will they be, useful to humanity? . . . Will life be better, or will it only change?"[5] Raynal knew well that in every man of his age there was, more or less hidden, the dream of a return to natural simplicity. "What man is so attached to the advantages of our societies, so distant from our sufferings, not to return sometimes in thought to the depths of the forest, or envy the happiness, innocence, and repose of patriarchal life?"[6] Not even the consoling vision of general progress made it possible to set aside this need. Raynal believed too firmly in the "perfection" of the classical world; he was too aware of the decline during medieval centuries, and the return of humanity to slavery, to the "stupidity and inertia that long remained the initial state of man." In his excursions through the world he had observed too many "isolated nations," the Egyptians, Spartans, Japanese, to have confidence in a more or less linear progress.[7] The most diverse and varied forms of civilization did not succeed in obliterating the initial wrench out of nature or bury grief for the lost primitive world. When he saw the Europeans reach Africa, a cry arose from his pages: "Flee, unhappy Hottentots, flee: bury yourselves in your forests." The whites were "ferocious beasts." "Take up your hatchets, raise your bows. . . ."[8] The arms of the

[5] Ibid., p. 2.
[6] Ibid., p. 204 (see Goggi 1, p. 133).
[7] Ibid., pp. 6, 8, 171.
[8] Ibid., p. 205 (see Goggi, 1, p. 135).

conquerors were cunningness and concealment. The Siamese were right, when confronted with tyranny, to hide in the forests, "where they led a savage life, a hundred times preferable to that of societies corrupted by despotism."[9] The whole history of commerce and colonization explained why modern man could not rid himself of a nostalgia for the primitive world. Observing the natives of Brazil, Raynal could not stop convincing himself that "a singing and dancing savage is always happy." How could he not be, deprived as he was of thoughts of the afterlife? And if primitive men were sometimes corrupted by their "soothsayers," who had "misused their credulity," the remedy was not difficult to find. "From time to time impostors are slaughtered, which discourages a spirit of deception." Without government, the primitives did not even suspect that a man might have command over his fellow men. They were not dominated by "love of country . . . an artificial sentiment born in society, but unknown in the state of nature." The very rhythm of their life was diametrically opposed to that of civilized men. "These enjoy the benefits of nature only in their infancy. In proportion as their appetites and reason develop, they lose sight of the present and occupy themselves entirely with the future. Thus the age of passions and pleasures, the sacred time that nature intends for enjoyment, is passed in speculation and bitterness." The savage instead "feels that the source of his pleasure is within himself and that his country is everywhere."[10]

But even for Raynal, as for many others of his generation, nostalgia for nature, although a continually recurrent theme, neither impeded nor stopped the passionate discovery of civilization, the admiration for that human cosmos which, although by means of a thousand horrors, had ultimately arisen from the arrangements of international trade that now linked the whole world. Colonization, bitterly resisted and condemned on all continents, reappears in these pages as a form of peaceful civilization, when for example France is urged to intervene in Madagascar "to extricate an unhappy people from the horrors of barbarism, give them honest customs, exact government, wise laws, a beneficial religion, useful and agreeable arts," thus raising that people "to the level of educated and civilized nations."[11] Or again, when Raynal, comparing the different efforts at civilization in South America, finally in some way justified the efforts of the Jesuits in Paraguay to "make the savages change from a nomadic life to the state of society" by uniting religious and civil authority in the hands of the Company of Jesus, reuniting in this way the two powers that had remained divided in Europe from the

[9] Ibid., p. 439.
[10] Ibid. 2, pp. 366ff. (see Goggi 1, p. 137).
[11] Ibid. 1, p. 418.

time of the fall of the Roman Empire.[12] With the suppression of the Jesuits "the most beautiful edifice erected in the New World was pulled down."[13] His condemnation of the system of colonization of the Spanish in Mexico and Peru was decisive, like that of the Portuguese in Brazil and the English in the north. Diderot raised his voice high in eulogy of Las Casas, the apostle of the Indians. "You were greater for your humanity than all your compatriots together for their conquests."[14] He harshly censured the degeneration, the "metamorphosis," of Europeans in their dominions beyond the sea. Without pausing the *Histoire* returned to the problem of the right of conquest itself, which was acceptable only when uninhabited or abandoned lands were involved.

From these affirmations of principles and general questions there was a continual departure in order to consider specific and concrete problems raised by the history and politics of the colonizing countries. Raynal's work was intended to be a universal history, but it ended up naturally becoming a picture of Europe at the end of the eighteenth century, and it was passionately tied to problems that dominated the passage from the seventies to the eighties. After having traced a true and proper economic, and above all financial, history of France, Diderot turned directly to the young sovereign Louis XVI to show the brilliant lights and deep shadows of the situation in which the country found itself. "You reign over the most lovely empire in the universe. Despite the decadence in which it is fallen, there is no place on earth where the arts and sciences affirm themselves with such splendor." His subjects were patient, faithful, affectionate. From France "had not Europe as a whole received that social spirit that so happily distinguishes our age from the centuries that have preceded it?" But still, evils had multiplied at home and abroad. "Gold has become the god of the nation." In Paris rich and poor made up "two classes of citizens." The provinces were collapsing under the weight of taxes. The peasants were "condemned to die in misery." A series of suggestions, too various and disparate to be effective in reality, followed these considerations. What counted most in his eyes was firmness, the will to act, without fearing the accusation of having taken the way of innovation. "The meeting of the estates of a great nation, the return to primitive liberty, the respectable exercise of the first acts of natural justice, would these be innovations?"[15] It was the first time that a philosopher of the importance of Diderot had made the same demand as the Parlements, from the convocation of the Estates

---

[12] Ibid. 2, pp. 285ff.
[13] Ibid., p. 290.
[14] Ibid. 2, p. 298.
[15] Ibid. 1, p. 475 (see Goggi 2, pp. 5ff.).

General to the reestablishment of legality. Incisive also was Diderot's criticism of French colonization in India, on the American islands, and in Canada. Trampling down the "violent tendency" of people "to govern themselves," crushing conquered lands under "exhaustive privileges" of "exclusive companies," even the French like all European peoples had ended by creating a greater and greater separation between the metropolis and the colonies.[16] Social relations were as unjust as those that existed between city and countryside in France. "We are mad in the way we act with our colonies, and inhuman and mad in our conduct toward our peasants." The system of the corvées was as harmful in the mother country as in the colonies. Thus these last, if they did not succeed in obtaining justice, would have to break their ties with the metropolis.[17] The concrete measures Diderot suggested were still, even in this case, more moderate than the indignation that produced them. The contrast between general principles and local realities was not easy. Large estates were even necessary in the Caribbean Islands. The problem of slavery did not seem to be resolvable without some compromise. What counted most was that the philosophes not surrender in principle, and that they be in a condition to be able to discuss freely and autonomously. In the long run "that spirit of enlightenment which supports and guides us when morality collapses on its ruinous foundations will guide the court of Versailles toward those good principles that we ourselves have so often placed before its eyes."[18] It was always difficult to convince the government. It would refuse to listen or, at most, "the most important speculations" would be "sent to an office and submitted to the decision of a committee."[19] The bureaucracy would bury any good idea. But the only thing to do was to continue to write and polemicize, without ever losing sight of the fact that the only truly solid thing in France was precisely the philosophy of enlightenment. To be sure, one could follow with interest the efforts to reform this or that of the country's ills and, for example, as Diderot did, support the work of Necker and his wife. "While her husband works on a larger scale to diminish the number of unfortunates, she occupies herself with details that could assist those who exist."[20] This was not adulation, but sincere esteem. In reality, with this attitude Diderot only emphasized what he had said in polemic with Beccaria. He placed his confidence not in juridical reforms, but in the reaffirmation of principles and the daily effort to alleviate the ills of

[16] *Histoire* 3, pp. 232, 334, 336, 437.
[17] Ibid., pp. 438, 464, 465.
[18] Ibid., p. 493.
[19] Ibid., p. 494.
[20] Ibid., p. 265.

a society that was corrupt and in decline. The impossibility of tearing down and redoing the whole structure of the state and of French society ended by leading to a similar conclusion. "To the extent that we have opened our eyes to the absurdity of our institutions, we have occupied ourselves with correcting them, but without ever daring to redo the edifice entirely. We have remedied abuses with new abuses, and in an effort to patch up, reform, and palliate we have put into our customs more contradictions than are in those of the most barbarian peoples."[21]

When the volume in which these words were inserted was published, the English colonies in America had already proclaimed the right of the people to rebel against a government that did not have their consent and to institute another one, founded "on such principles, and organizing its powers in such form, as to them shall seem most likely to effect their safety and happiness."[22] The *Histoire* accepted this point of view. With the decisive assistance of Diderot, Raynal inserted the American Revolution at the heart of his *Histoire*, thus giving a value in principle to that alliance between the insurgent colonists and French foreign policy which had raised many hopes and preoccupations in the world of writers, diplomats, and the court. He made a model of the incipient American Revolution, an example for all colonies, a prophecy of a deep change in the very relationship between the continents.[23] "If some happy revolution occurs in the world, it will be through the actions of America. After having been devastated, this New World will flourish in its turn and perhaps command the old one. It will be the asylum of our peoples trampled by politics or hunted out by war. The savage inhabitants will make the laws and the oppressed foreigners will become free."[24] As the physiocrat the Abbé Roubaud wrote, in a now difficult effort to defend the status quo, "deceived by his kind heart, the Abbé Raynal has, undoubtedly without noticing it, sacrificed to the American insurgents the national happiness of all civil societies of the universe by submitting their preservation or dissolution to the arbitrary passions of humanity . . . he has shaken the foundations of all the empires of the world in subjecting their constitutions to the revision and arbitrary sentence of their subjects."[25]

In the background of this great and incipient world transformation was England. The evident sympathy of the *Histoire* for the American

[21] Ibid. 1, p. 6.

[22] See the contemporaneous version of the Declaration of Independence cited in Franco Venturi, *The End of the Old Regime, 1768–1776*, pp. 436–37.

[23] Carlo Borghero, "Raynal, Paine e la rivoluzione americana," in *La politica della ragione*, ed. P. Casini (Bologna: Il Mulino, 1978), pp. 349ff.

[24] *Histoire* 3, p. 231.

[25] *Courier de l'Europe*, no. 30, 12 October 1781, p. 239 (London, 12 October).

insurgents did not cancel out an old, deeply rooted admiration for this model of free nations, even if it now found itself, incautiously, in conflict with its colonies. No one could deny its political, economic, and philosophical experience. The American Revolution should not make one forget the previous revolutions on the British Isles. "England is, in modern history, the country of great political phemonena. It is there that liberty has been seen to struggle most violently with despotism . . . liberty in the end triumphed . . . even over religious fanaticism, everyone has agreed on its triumph . . . amid civil discords and in moments of calm the exact and deep sciences have been seen to be carried furthest there." The English constitution remained the only one, "since man has lived in society," in which "the laws have ensured him his dignity, his personal liberty, his freedom of thought, where they have made him, in a word, a citizen, that is to say, a constituent and an integral part of the state and the nation."[26] Great Britain had in short opened a way, and it was now the turn of the colonies and of the Europeans to take it to its logical end, keeping in mind the difficulties that the experience of England had brought to light. The constitution of Great Britain, like that of the colonies, was no more than "a reform of that feudal government that had oppressed all of Europe," preserving "many customs," for example, the rights and privileges of nobles.[27] It was now up to the insurgents and their partisans to pass from reforms to integral reconstruction.

France and England were thus the two poles of the *Histoire*. The other countries of Europe were pictured often in a fading and not rarely deceptive light. Only the pages dedicated by Diderot to Russia shone, where he brought to the public the conclusions of what he had tried to say in private to Catherine II. Although with some denigration, the intellectual, economic, and administrative recovery of Spain was followed with interest, but the pages dedicated to Sweden after the revolution of Gustavus III are unrevealing; and even less penetrating are those dedicated to Denmark, which was still viewed as an example of despotism, although it had given proof of having emerged from the absolutistic crisis of the late seventeenth century. Informative, but without much flavor were the thousand bits of information about Holland. Equally conventional was the treatment of the German empire, admired for its constitution without the most recent developments of German culture being much revealed. What one read about Austria was out of date in its information and deprived of any authentic curiosity, which, just as the volumes of Raynal were being printed, passed into the hands

[26] *Histoire*, p. 509 (see Goggi 1, pp. 287ff.).
[27] Ibid. 4, pp. 370.

of Joseph II. Vigorous and balanced instead was the continuation—and conclusion—of Diderot's long polemic against Frederick II. Italy was hardly mentioned, except naturally to remember the glories of the Renaissance and of its art. What Diderot wrote about Venice was a caricature, alluding to the debates there "six years ago" on the plans to abolish the Council of Ten.[28] Ignoring completely the temperament of the Venetian enlightenment, Diderot did not find more to offer than a melodramatic scene of horror and despotism, the reflection of a period now past.

The limits of the *Histoire* are clear if one looks in it for a picture of Europe in the seventies. It was not by chance that Alexandre Deleyre was charged with writing an indispensable completion. His *Tableau de l'Europe*, with numerous additions and modifications, then accompanied the later editions of Raynal's work.[29] Despite the great interest of these pages, the gaps are evident. The *Histoire* did not have enough energy to dominate the reality of Europe in the years of the opening of the last crisis of the old regime. The faith shown in the American Revolution and the increasingly acute polemic against despotism nonetheless pointed the way to the future. From reading these thick volumes one receives a certainty that the ambiguities of the present could not be avoided without an appeal to the "general will." "To act without consulting the general will, without collecting, so to speak, the plurality of votes in public opinion, is to alienate hearts and minds, to discredit all, even goodness and honesty."[30]

There was a large response in Italy to the "illustrious work of the Abbé Raynal," "one of the few who truly honor the eighteenth century."[31] We have seen what a rush there was in Siena to translate it, and how in Venice it became the chief source of information for what was happening beyond the ocean.[32] The travels of Raynal as well as his writings were followed with great attention in Italian gazettes, almost as if he were a sovereign. "There arrived on the 25th the celebrated author of the *Philosophical and Political History of the Two Indies*, the Abbé Raynal," one read in the Florentine gazette on 9 August 1777, "and it is said that he has the idea of visiting the Seven Provinces one after another. He receives the greatest demonstrations of esteem and respect, as has been the case in England and everywhere."[33] When Joseph II was

---

[28] *Histoire* 4, p. 537.

[29] Venturi, "Un encyclopédiste: Alexandre Deleyre," pp. 76ff.

[30] *Histoire* 4, p. 537.

[31] *Notizie del mondo*, no. 18, 4 March 1775, p. 139 (The Hague, 7 February).

[32] See chapter 1, above.

[33] *Notizie del mondo*, no. 64, 12 August 1777, p. 508 (The Hague, 27 July).

in Paris in 1777 and attended a meeting of the Académie where d'Alembert, with delicate consideration, since he was traveling incognito, chose to speak on the two synonyms "simplicity and modesty," the absence of two persons struck the emperor. He had not seen "on the list he had been given the names of M. Diderot and of M. l'Abbé Raynal." "He expressed his astonishment to M. d'Alembert." "The academician, who must have been surprised by the question, responded that these gentlemen had not attended."[34] It was not just an excuse. In fact, Diderot and Raynal remained voluntarily outside of the Parisian academic world. Independent philosophes, they remained, one might say, at the margin between the writers and scientists of the Académie and the journalists and writers of libelles who were increasing in number and had begun to find a typical niche in the *Courier de l'Europe*, where this incident is reported. Distant and detached was the great figure of Diderot, enclosed within his passionate secret activity. Instead Raynal attracted more and more attention and was considered everywhere as the chief and freest publicist of Europe.

There were echoes of this even in Italy before the end of the seventies. Giuseppe Galanti, when reviewing a Dutch edition of the *Histoire*, in seven volumes, reported that it had encountered "much success" and that the author possessed a "truly brilliant fantasy." But was it legitimate to write a book of history "with the gestures of a poem"? Could one, for instance, imagine Constantine freeing the slaves when he converted to Christianity?[35] These objections and reservations were put aside when it became known, in June 1781, that Raynal, after the new edition of the previous year, had "to suffer the inconvenience of leaving Paris," as one read in the Venetian gazette. "Informed by his friends that his *Histoire* and perhaps his person were to be denounced to the Parlement on the 21st," he had resolved to escape.[36] Instead of removing the "philosophical observations," which in the first editions had not "matched the spirit of administrators or clergy," he had taken advantage of the new edition to add "some even stronger paragraphs." "Especially the manner in which the author speaks of the current war was not approved." "Many would like to see him leave for America." And when he was put on guard against the "persecutions" that he risked arousing, he responded: "I will never betray the cause of liberty."[37] Even in Florence, as one sees, there was obvious value in the new edition of the *Histoire*, the one in which Diderot had intervened with greater vigor. What was not noticed

34 *Courier de l'Europe*, no. 2, 6 June 1777, p. 9 (Paris, 29 May).
35 *Giornale fiorentino*, September 1788, p. 356, and see November 1788, p. 442.
36 *Notizie del mondo [V.]*, 9 June 1781, p. 362, "Extract of a letter from Paris of 29 May."
37 *Notizie del mondo*, no. 48, 16 June 1781, p. 378 (Paris, 1 June).

at a distance was the coincidence between the fall of Necker and the necessity for Raynal to leave France.[38] The condemnations of the Parisian Parlement and the Sorbonne soon threw new fuel on the fire. Even the Tuscan *Annali ecclesiastici* openly defended Raynal.[39] In his exile at Spa he was "the delight of the various nations gathered there." "He has received the most flattering distinctions from His Majesty the Emperor and from Prince Henry of Prussia, and has not at all changed his manner, his dress, or his conduct. Just as he was not embittered by persecution, so also he does not let himself be moved by favor."[40] Berlin appeared for a moment to become the center of activity for the Abbé Raynal. On his installation the Academy of Berlin opened a discussion on the chief problems of the art of history: "What are the duties of a historian and what are the qualities he should possess? Which historians among the ancients and moderns have fulfilled their duties? Did modern historians have to overcome greater obstacles than the ancients?" The replies could be in "French, Latin, German, English, or Italian."[41] At the same time he gave himself over to a showy philanthropy. "The famous Abbé Raynal," one read in the gazette of Venice in May of that year, "who joins in himself the not common virtue of elevating humanity through its own merits, and the glory of illuminating it through his superior writings, has recently consigned to the consistory of the French church of this capital [Berlin] the sum of one hundred ecus to provide dowries for the most virtuous and industrious young girls of the community."[42] Was it not said that he was engaged in "a work about the revocation of the Edict of Nantes in 1685"?[43] Meanwhile in Italy there were echoes of the polemic that Paine and Cerisier had unleashed against his interpretation of events in America. Many were the errors that "Raynal had put forward about the origins and causes of the uprising of the Northern Provinces of America," said Thomas Paine. "It remains to be seen," read the *Corrispondenza universale*, "whether someone else will criticize the rest of the work and show the fanatical adorers of Raynal how many blunders . . . are in it."[44] The events of his exile were mingled with the misfortunes of the most famous work of Sébastien Mercier, the *Tableau de Paris*, which had appeared at the same time as

[38] Denis Diderot, *Oeuvres philosophiques*, ed. P. Vernière (Paris: Garnier, 1961), p. 637 n. 1.

[39] *Annali ecclesiastici*, 1782, no. 5, "La Sorbona contro Raynal. Dialogo comico pantomimico."

[40] *Notizie del mondo*, no. 75, 21 September 1781, p. 598 (Spa, 26 August).

[41] Ibid., no. 35, 3 May 1783, p. 282 (Berlin, 15 April).

[42] *Notizie del mondo [V.]*, no. 42, 24 May 1783 (Berlin, 3 May).

[43] Ibid., no. 82, 12 October 1782, p. 653 (Frankfurt, 30 September).

[44] *Corrispondenza universale*, 1783, Libri nuovi, fasc. 9, p. 100.

the last edition of the *Histoire* and was considered a "foolhardy and spicy work."[45] The chapter about the Bastille risked having the author shut up there and sent the publisher to prison.[46] Raynal and Mercier, it was said, both took refuge in Neuchâtel. There the first, "now very elderly, took a wife" while M. Mercier, author of the *Tableau de Paris*, "died in the arms of the historian of the establishments of commerce in the Indies."[47] Both reports were false: Mercier did not cease to write his books, which were characteristic of the atmosphere of the eighties, and Raynal continued to live out his glorious exile throughout Europe.[48] Nor certainly did the renewed prohibition of his *Histoire philosophique et politique* by the Church of Rome do any damage to him.[49]

By that date, the beginning of 1785, Diderot had disappeared. The condemnation of Raynal and his flight from France had affected him profoundly. He responded by stopping his procrastination and publishing his *Essai sur Sénèque*—and it is probable that Raynal himself contributed, during his passage through Bouillon, to editing this work.[50] He continued to defend Raynal obstinately, even when the attacker was Grimm, his friend from youth. In his *Lettre apologétique* of 25 March 1781 he reaffirmed the rationale of his life as a writer, consecrated entirely to liberty, against prudence, compromises, and the talents of those who had changed themselves into both instruments and victims of those in power. "You forget, my friend, how men of genius, courageous men, virtuous men, in contempt of those grand idols before which so many idiots do the honor of prostrating themselves, you forget how they wrote their books." It was imprudence or insensitivity that moved Raynal, but the desire to break with the followers of the maxim that it was better to live than to philosophize. And if Grimm dared to laugh at such courage, it only remained for Diderot to state, sadly, that the soul of his old friend had "suffered in St. Petersburg, in Potsdam, at the 'oeil-de-boeuf' and in the antechambers of the great."[51] Raynal had done no more in publishing his *Histoire* than to continue the battle

---

[45] *Notizie del mondo [V]*, no. 51, 27 June 1781, p. 401 (Paris, 11 June).

[46] *Notizie del mondo*, no. 51, 26 June 1781, p. 406 (Cleves, 12 June), and no. 51, 7 July 1781, p. 426 (Paris, 22 June).

[47] *Notizie del mondo [V.]*, no. 21, 13 March 1784 (Brussels, 21 February), and *Notizie del mondo*, no. 22, 16 March 1784, p. 203 (Paris, 28 February).

[48] One sees, for example, in the *Notizie del mondo [V.]*, no. 68, 25 August 1784 (Paris, 6 August): "Passing through Lausanne Prince Henry of Prussia ate dinner at the house of the famous Abbé Raynal with a Prince of Brunswick and with M. and Madame Necker."

[49] *Notizie del mondo [V.]*, 8 January 1785 (Rome, 1 January), "Libri proibiti": "Already prohibited by the Sacred Congregation of the Index with the decree of 10 February 1784."

[50] Diderot, *Correspondance*, vol. 15, p. 241 n. 21.

[51] Ibid., pp. 212ff.

fought by them as youths, in the years of the *Encyclopédie*. In these pages lived again "reason, enlightenment, force, delicacy, and an unlimited love of mankind."[52] How could one reprove the author for not being a historian comparable with the great models of the classical and modern world? "Oh well, Raynal is a historian such as there has never been before; so much the better for him and the worse for history." What counted was the charged polemic that emerged from these pages. "The book I love, which kings and their courtiers detest, is a book that makes Brutuses be born, whatever one calls it."[53]

If Diderot looked for his ideal to a writer capable of making "Brutuses born"—and in this mirror his own image becomes confused with that of Raynal—there appeared for a moment, in the agitated pages of this *Lettre apologétique*, the figure of one who seemed born instead to exalt despots and give life to slaves. Linguet, at the opposite pole from his libertarian exaltations, was for Diderot an incarnation of the false and artificial. It was not a matter of this or that idea, but of a complete absence of authenticity. With Rousseau he had and continued to have violent polemics, but how could one not recognize the fundamental sincerity of what this man had written? "Why is Jean Jacques eloquent? Why is Linguet only a declaimer? It is, on principle, that I feel the first speaks truly, even when he is false, and the other, without principle, is false even when he speaks true. Rousseau lies only initially; Linguet lies from beginning to end."[1] Diderot did not pause to provide proofs for his judgment. But the very harshness of his condemnation revealed the importance of the case: in effect Linguet was one of the chief publicists of Europe, who had taken a growing number of readers from Raynal on the opposite side. Without the one, as without the other, the crisis of the Enlightenment in the seventies and eighties would be incomprehensible.

One should not be misled by the most superficial and obvious aspects of Linguet's personality. One is certainly struck by his advocacy, by his continual return to the same themes, by his demonstrated incapacity to deepen and develop his own ideas, which when examined closely were few and always the same. But, however rigid and repetitive, his ideas were not, it must be admitted, without historical significance. Rousseau and Mably had placed at the roots of human society the idea and desire

[52] Ibid., pp. 221ff.
[53] Ibid., p. 223.
[1] Ibid., p. 215.

for equality. Linguet substituted security, the guarantee of not dying of hunger, the certainty of being fed and looked after. Certainly Diderot was right; this was not a principle, like equality. It was no more than the statement of an undeniable need of human nature. It was a fact, not an idea. But still, it was a statement that could not help but be striking in an age of rapid change, insecurity, migration to cities, spreading mendicity, and even brigandage. Linguet, unlike the Encyclopedists and physiocrats, did not inquire into the reasons for these ills of society, he did not indicate the remedies, and he even showed a scorn for all those who took on the route of liberal reforms. In some matters he was closer instead—if only in a distorted way—to Rousseau or Mably. In his vision of history security was substituted for equality, and difficult for him as well, even impossible, was a return to the beginning. For Rousseau and Mably, original equality is lost. For Linguet, at the back of humanity lies the best possible social state that humanity can know, that is, slavery, when the lord had every interest in maintaining life and in guaranteeing the existence and reproduction of his human property. With the end of slavery (the principal blow responsible for this break was attributed by Linguet to the barbarian invasions and feudalism) began an epoch of risks, hunger, uncertainty, which modern society had made only worse, as much for peasants as for artisans and workers. Distant, on the horizon, there were Oriental despots, who still maintained something of the benevolent nature of ancient slavery. Thus Linguet never tired of praising the Ottoman Empire.

Born as a ponderous revolt against modern progress, the center of Linguet's thought always remained an immobile paradox. His slavery was a myth; it was not a model. Equality, even when present as a lost paradise, continued to ferment in the minds of eighteenth-century reformers. The slavery of Linguet did not even serve to deepen what was still a central problem for the whole of Europe in the second half of the eighteenth century: the abolition or transformation of peasant servitude. Nor was Linguet a precursor of the numerous writers of the eighteenth and nineteenth centuries who were apologists for serfdom, the good rural seigneur, and the patriarchal village and who condemned wage work, the development of manufactures, and so on.[2] Linguet in fact distinguished accurately between slavery and serfdom, reserving his praises only for the first of the two forms, while the second was included in his repeated condemnations of everything that was feudal. Nor could

---

[2] See Elias Bickerman, "Pouchkine, Marx et l'internationale esclavagiste," *La nouvelle Clio*, no. 8 (September 1750): 146ff., and Peter Kolchin, "In Defense of Servitude: American Proslavery and Russian Proserfdom Arguments (1760–1860)," *American Historical Review* 85, no. 4 (October 1980): 809ff.

ancient slavery be compared, according to him, with the modern slavery of blacks in America. It was, in short, a distant, umbilical incarnation of the need for security found, according to him, at the beginning of time. Although we can find in his work occasional interest for a rural reality that was changing, he never missed emphasizing that in the modern world only central political authority was able to work effectively to ensure bread for all, to prevent "scarcity" from turning into "famine." Turning his gaze to the past, he confessed he was convinced of the beauty of villages where peasants were paid in kind: "It was wheat harvested with their own hands. It was their subsistence for many months."[3] But now, in the modern world, there was no other means than the rigid control of the price of foodstuffs by state authorities.

Translated into political terms, this view of the history of humanity—from ancient slavery to modern insecurity through the collapse of feudalism—led to an open polemic against any division of power, against any balance of constituted bodies, in short, against any organization of freedom. Montesquieu was his preferred target. The French parlements were the most frequent object of his polemics. His judgment of the British constitution was generally negative. He thought that an improvement in the living conditions of anyone who was not rich or privileged was impossible, except through a concentration of power, without any controls or counterweights, capable of operating without obstacles, always active in eliminating the barriers that centuries of uncertainty and weakness had finally put in the way of all states. There stirred here as well the distant myth of Oriental despotism, but when confronted with the ideas and reality of the modern world it took diverse forms, from an exaltation of absolute monarchy to eulogies addressed to Cromwell and his ability to reassemble power after the revolution. It broke out finally in a positive assessment of the cautious and empirical policy of Necker and in an apologia for Catherine II, Joseph II, Gustavus III, Peter Leopold, even Pope Pius VII, in short, for the various forms of what we call enlightened despotism, which Linguet admired as much for the reforms it accomplished as for the power it knew how to assemble and maintain. Departing from a radical critique of the seeds of constitutionalism he found in Montesquieu, and passing through the multiple delusions produced by attempts at reform in the sixties and seventies, which colored his skeptical and realistic vision more and more, Linguet ended by seeking a form of power capable of ensuring daily life and tranquillity for the masses in the modern world. He went, in short, from despotism to dictatorship.

---

[3] *Annales politiques, civiles et littéraires du dix-huitième siècle* (Lausanne: Société typographique, November 1779), vol. 7, p. 215.

The principal obstacle he encountered along his way, and against which he struggled with the greatest rage, was *philosophie*. Perhaps the king of France would be persuaded finally to exercise his full power. Perhaps the sovereigns of his time would finally recognize that the advice he gave was right. In fact Louis XVI never rejected him entirely, and Joseph II made use of his journalistic talents for a while. The Catholic Church, after the difficult experience of the last decades, from Pombal and the suppression of the Company of Jesus, should be induced—Linguet was convinced–to act with greater energy for its own salvation and that of states threatened by different types of disaggregative tendencies. One obstacle seemed irreducible to his realistic logic, and that was the two-headed monster with the name *Encyclopédie* and physiocracy. This was the exact opposite of the deep aspiration toward security, of which he intended to be the interpreter. This was the true enemy, the source of all the doubts and uncertainties he wanted to combat. From this was born the destructive idea according to which the sovereign should give himself over to the merchant, to economic development, without intervening to control prices—above all, for indispensable commodities, and first of all bread, which could not and should not be considered a commodity, so essential was it for all those born neither proprietors nor rich. Nor was it true that high prices of grain favored the development of agriculture. It was above all false that wages would adjust by themselves automatically to variations in the price of grain. Until governments ensured this adjustment (Linguet proposed a kind of sliding scale, without ever indicating the practical means for realizing it), the only solution would be a systematic provisioning of grain guaranteed by the state. But in order to effect this, authority was necessary, which was undermined in a thousand ways by the philosophes, whom he described as always ready to ask for subsidies, privileges, pensions, but never inclined to provide solid political support for those acting to confront problems in the economy, finance, war, peace, the disorder of the parlements, and the greed of the privileged orders.

The picture Linguet presents of the party of the philosophes after the defeat of Turgot is certainly crude and unjust, petty and grudging, but it nevertheless touched real wounds. He says relatively little about Diderot, who in his eyes had at least the merit of not being an academic and whose difficulties in his relations with Catherine II he emphasized. He directed the larger part of his attacks against d'Alembert, whom he accused of being the head of an academic sect, incapable of establishing a new, lively, and fruitful relationship among sciences, literature, and arts, but content to continue to use the forms of refined civility in order to keep alive the contrasts and polemics of the past, thus being, as Linguet said, "the executor of the testament of the *Encyclopédie*."[4] These attacks prevented him from seeing the new forces appearing from the tradition represented by d'Alembert, that is, from the more moderate wing of the *Encyclopédie*, which continued to develop in these years: it is enough to think of Condorcet, for example. Linguet, in short, blinded as he was by hatred, did not perceive the long process that would lead from late Encyclopedism to the "*idéologues*." After the defeat of Turgot, after the deaths of Voltaire and Rousseau, Linguet thought the spirit that had sustained the philosophes was exhausted, both among the more moderate and among the more enthusiastic and utopian. He was also convinced of the definitive defeat of the physiocrats, whose development continued until the initial phase of the French Revolution. At the end of the seventies, he believed, in short, that he could liquidate the entire Enlightenment movement, from its philosophical roots to its political and economic conceptions, from Montesquieu onward.

The innumerable books and other works published by Linguet in the sixties—above all the *Théorie des loix civiles, ou Principes fondamentaux de la société*, which appeared in 1767—aroused curiosity and polemics. But his name began to have weight only on the day when he put his hand to a periodical edited entirely by himself and that revealed his vast ambition from its very title: *Annales politiques, civiles et littéraires du dix-huitième siècle*. It began to be published in London on 30 March 1777, and its success was immense. Suddenly the *Annales* affirmed itself as the chief publishing enterprise of the time. Reeditions, some authorized but most unauthorized, multiplied. Polemics thickened. The nearing and then the outbreak of the war between France and England made Linguet's position more difficult, and he ended up by taking refuge in Belgium. His subscribers nonetheless continued to increase, and the flock of booksellers who attempted to profit from his initiative grew.

The echo of the *Annales* was soon heard in Italy. The Literary and Typographic Society of Yverdon hastened to notify Italians, through the gazette of Lugano, that it would be able to get subscriptions.[5] The Florentine bookseller Filippo Stecchi soon convinced himself that it would be advantageous to publish one version. A translator was found, ready to assume this not small undertaking: Luigi Semplici, a curious, adventuresome person in the ecclesiastical and journalistic world of Tuscany, a collaborator in the *Gazzetta di Firenze*, the *Notizie del mondo*, and the *Gazzetta universale*.[6] A first obstacle had to be overcome, the

---

[4] *Annali politici, civili e letterari del secolo decimottavo*, vol. 5 (1779), p. 43.

[5] *Nuove di diverse corti e paesi*, no. 43, 27 October 1777, p. 336, "Avviso."

[6] Maria Augusta Timpanaro Morelli, "Persone e momenti del giornalismo politico a Firenze dal 1766 al 1799 in alcuni documenti dell'Archivio di Stato di Firenze," *Rassegna*

clearly unfavorable opinion of the censor, Francesco Seratti. "I have found in this work, in fact," the censor wrote, "passages that are very bold, harmful, and injurious to sovereign law, to sovereigns in general, and to some sovereigns in particular." The *Annales* would not be permitted if such affirmations were not modified. It would be no use employing the well-known expedient of indicating a distant or imaginary place of publication: for periodicals it was necessary to know where one was to send one's subscription. "It is probable," Francesco Seratti concluded, "that this refusal of permission could be appealed to His Royal Highness, who will resolve things as he likes."[7] As far as one can tell Peter Leopold finally gave a favorable opinion. The fact is that Linguet's *Annales* began to appear in Tuscan clothing at the beginning of 1778.[8]

From the first issues ideas appeared that could not help but strike Florentine readers, if for no other reason than the breadth of the political panorama into which they were inserted. They invited reconsideration of the situation of Europe as a whole. In the seventy or more tight pages of the "Preliminary Reflections" that began his periodical Linguet summarized his fundamental ideas on the "Current Political Situation of the Globe" and on the "Current State of Legislation in Europe," considering the "military" situation, "finances," "commerce," the "culture of the spirit," the "arts," the "sciences," and "customs," ending with a vision of "society in general and the singular revolution that threatens Europe."[9] Everywhere Linguet noted signs of decadence and decay. The only remaining hope was in the absolute will of monarchs. They alone could defeat republican and free traditions, the heralds of further weaknesses and ruin. France was "humiliated by disasters and losses suffered without, tormented within by the kind of exhaustion felt after some great movement, . . . oppressed by a prodigious national debt,

degli archivi di stato, year 31, no. 2 (May–August 1971): 467ff. In Milan, B. Ambrosiana, T. 137 sup., ff. 23–24, are six letters by L. Semplici to I. Bianchi, dated 1779 and 1780, from Florence where there is talk of Bianchi's contribution to the *Gazzetta universale* (I owe this reference to the courtesy of R. Pasta).

    7 Florence, AS, *Reggenza*, filza 626, fasc. 13, n.d. I owe this reference, like others that follow, to the courtesy and skill of Maria Augusta Timpanaro Morelli, whom I wish to thank again.

    8 *Notizie del mondo*, no. 5, 17 January 1779, p. 40, in the footer: "There has come to light the first issue of the Italian translation of the *Annali politici, civili e letterari del secolo XVIII*, the periodical of M. Linguet, which was printed originally in French in London and The Hague. Subscription . . . one zecchino per year. . . . It will be distributed in monthly issues."

    9 *Annali politici, civili e letterari del secolo decimottavo*. Opera periodica del Sig. Linguet ora tradotta per la prima volta in idioma italiano da L.S.A.F. (that is, Luigi Semplici, Abate Fiorentino), vol. 1, *Uno avulso non deficit alter* (The Hague, 1778). At the expense of Filippo Stecchi, pp. 1ff., "Riflessioni preliminari."

which, increasing from one day to the next, presents an obstacle to the
satisfaction an able minister might still flatter himself on finding in that
kingdom." Fortunately, France had "a precious treasure in its youth and
the good intentions of the king." England, "oppressed by grandeur and
conquests," was experiencing "the horrors of civil war . . . , reduced,
whatever the outcome of the American war may be, to see only rabid
enemies or formidable slaves in its children." Italy was "reduced to nothing, or rather to the enjoyment of a fine climate under a peaceful and
mild government, an existence decorated by the relics of ancient glory."
Spain offered only "a great name and a shadow of its former power."
Its empire would let itself "be seduced soon by the brightness of liberty,
if this remains to the Americans." Finally, Germany awaited "the moment when feudalism, which still enervates it, will expire before monarchy." Sweden had finally broken "the yoke of a humiliating and despotic aristocracy, as are all aristocracies, and seeks asylum in the
absolute authority of one alone against the disadvantages of limited and
divided power." Like other peoples before it, Sweden had created "a
sovereign so as not to tremble any longer under a thousand tyrants."
Poland awaited only "a hereditary king to rise marvelously." Prussia and
Russia, "born and growing in strength like Hercules in the cradle, are
no longer in their infancy and have to fear only their premature vigor
which has opened eyes to their growth too soon."[10] Everywhere Linguet
criticized republican tradition, in England, Poland, Holland, emphasizing that such states had the worst and most cruel penal laws (was not in
his eyes "torture an invention of republican despotism"?).[11] He found
the reforming efforts of states like Prussia, Sardinia, and Russia praiseworthy.[12] In this area France had encountered the worst of obstacles, a
"league of tyrannical men of letters and oppressive philosophers." From
this had been born a new fatalism, "more dangerous under the cloak of
philosophy than under that of religion." Only by this means had that
"singularity unique in history" appeared of a "society formed to compile
an alphabet of sciences that transformed itself into a powerful party." It
had formed itself into a "little philosophic aristocracy," which threatened to change the very nature of the nation's politics: "We have been
on the eve of effecting an absolute change in the constitution of a great
kingdom, a total subversion of its government."[13] This was a failed revolution that concealed the "singular revolution" menacing not only
France but all of Europe. How could one close one's eyes to a fact much

[10] Ibid., pp. 2ff.
[11] Ibid., p. 11.
[12] Ibid., p. 10.
[13] Ibid., pp. 43ff.

more important than the disputes of philosophers and economists, that is, the increasing social disequilibrium brought on by economic liberty? Ever greater, on one side, grew luxury and well-being, and on the other, "never were privations more universal and murderous to the class condemned to them." "Never perhaps in its apparent prosperity had Europe been so close to total subversion, all the more terrible in that desperation would be its cause. . . . We have arrived, by a diametrically opposite route, precisely where Italy found itself when slave wars drenched it with blood and brought fire and the sword to the door of the queen of the world." This was a "cruel event" produced when "a philosophy more subject to prejudice than error itself" had "the foolhardiness to advocate freeing the serfs."[14] Certainly "the terrible imbalance in wealth" established in Europe tended, despite all palliatives, to "hasten the moment of the great revolution I have predicted." "The principles that imperceptibly lead to it are preparing themselves everywhere. We have seen peasants rise up with arms in their hands to change their situation in Bohemia and Italy and become intolerable; we have seen, at a moment when all seemed to forecast calm in France, a spark set off a great fire and carry embers of sedition as far as the throne."

In short, as we see, what aroused such catastrophic prophesies in Linguet was the first crisis of the old regime in the sixties and seventies. Even Italy was included by him imaginatively in the drama of peasant revolts, from Bohemia to the *guerre des farines* that led to Turgot's fall. It is characteristic that Linguet passed completely in silence over the revolt of Pugačev, which better than any other might seem to correspond to the slave revolt he prophesied. One might say that he did not want to cast shadows on the image of Catherine II. His violent rejection of enlightened ideas, as well, prevented him from seeing any positive outcome of these warning movements, or from giving them any liberating value or significance. They remained slave revolts in his eyes and could lead only to more and more ferocious and cruel repressions, or to "some new Spartacus, made audacious by desperation, illuminated by necessity," able to call "to liberty the companions of his misfortune, destroying the murderous and false laws" by which they were oppressed, obtaining "for some a full portion of the goods of nature, and for others the restitution of that sweet security that assures slaves of repose in spirit in exchange for the wealth left to their lords, and a peaceful life in exchange for domination, whose yoke they accept and love."[15]

This "revolution" always remained in the background of the agitated

[14] Ibid., p. 58.
[15] Ibid., pp. 70ff.

political landscape presented by Linguet to his readers in the *Annales*. In the foreground stood his bitter polemic against the French parlements, and above all, his vision of Eastern Europe, where more and more serious threats of war and destruction seemed to arise. Russia and Turkey, more similar than is generally believed, would be able to seize Europe in pincers, "the most dangerous it has had to fear since the barbarian invasions." But the problem of the Crimea, and above all of Poland, had saved Europe, for the moment, "from the peril to which their union might expose it."[16] Linguet paid particular attention to Poland, which he saw as a nation in some way regenerated, a nation in which "the excess of misfortune has produced a kind of new birth."[17] At the other end of Europe, in Portugal, the fall of Pombal seemed to reopen the question of the Jesuits.

The variety of problems treated, and the peremptory tone with which Linguet stated his conclusions, aroused a vivid curiosity in Tuscany, mixed with some revulsion. Already in April 1778 one read in the gazette *Notizie del mondo* that an issue of the *Giornale fiorentino* had recently appeared, "calling to account M. Linguet and his *Annales*."[18] A periodical with this title, from the bookseller Gaetano Cambiagi, had in fact begun to appear at the beginning of 1778, with a vast program of reviews "of what appears from the most important presses of Europe."[19] It was compiled by Francesco Xaverio Catani, one of the most enterprising and sensitive Tuscan journalists in those years.[20] In the first issue there was an attack on Linguet, a "political adventurer" who pretends "from his cabinet to give legislation to all of Europe." He shows great disdain for all governments. For him "princes live in idleness and act like tyrants." The certificate for political nullity that Linguet had given to Italy also struck Catani, who felt there should be some manner of response. "It was a great shame for Italy, 'although reduced to nothing,' to leave certain spirits at liberty who enrapture the minds of the weak with artificial language." How could Linguet have said that Italy contained nothing other "than pieces of statues, broken columns and such, only of interest to antiquaries"? The greatest powers of Europe had competed for Italy, and it still contained "cities, kingdoms, and republics, one of which is a miracle of nature." "Dear M. Linguet, leave your cabinet, come to Italy to observe it better and your enthusiasm will make

---

[16] Ibid., vol. 1, p. 92.

[17] Ibid., p. 98.

[18] *Notizie del mondo*, no. 29, 11 April 1778, p. 236, in the footer.

[19] Ibid., no. 2, 6 January 1778, p. 16, in the footer.

[20] Capra, *Giovanni Ristori*, pp. 23ff., and the entry "Catani, Francesco Maria Xaverio" of the DBI, by A. M. Timpanaro Morelli, vol. 22, pp. 302ff.

you blush."[21] In successive issues the *Giornale fiorentino* made an effort
to contrast its own political reflections with those of the *Annales*. It
showed all possible admiration for the English people, "at the same time
warriors, philosophers, and merchants," guided by a government
"partly monarchical, aristocratic, and democratic." As for Italy, while
"the pope, after the suppression of the Jesuits, no longer interests courts
or politicians" and while Genova had "lost Corsica but enjoyed the small
pleasure of not seeing that island independent," the young monarch of
Naples had succeeded in capturing "the affection of his subjects who do
not know, like some others in Italy, how to hide their sentiments."[22] The
uprising of the Americans attracted more and more attention in the
Giornale fiorentino. Its origins were sought in the incapacity of the English to preserve all the liberty they had enjoyed in the past. "Today they
are not so attentive in electing those to whom they confide the assumption of maintaining it. ... What would become of wise constitutions
when those who should maintain them find their interest in overthrowing them?" Nor was this involution limited only to political forms.
"Meanwhile the people see themselves diminish, needed workmen disappear from the fields, commerce imperceptibly loses its ancient luster,
without the hope perhaps of being able to recover quickly."[23]

Similar attacks on Linguet, accompanied by attempts to imitate his
journalistic style, elicited a vivid reply from the pen of Zacchiroli, which
was published by Filippo Stecchi, the editor of the *Annales*.[24] Catani and
his collaborators were treated like "sons who ill-treat their fathers."
"The idea, Sirs, of your new journal seems to me taken entirely from
the journal of M. Linguet. In its first sheets it begins by giving a general
idea of the actual political situation of Europe: you in your first number
did or tried to do the same. It is written freely, and you write with a
tone you call courageous, but that wise moderation gives a less honorable, but perhaps more characteristic, name. ... You are true sons of
M. Linguet."[25] "This man has long enjoyed the most luminous reputation. Do you know that Europe admires him as a profound writer? The

[21] *Giornale fiorentino istorico-politico-letterario*, January 1778, p. 2. On the participation
of Catani in the discussion about Pombal, see chapter 3, above.
   [22] Ibid., pp. 35ff., 43ff.
   [23] Ibid., February 1778, pp. 82ff.
   [24] *Riflessioni sul primo numero del 'Giornale fiorentino' per l'anno 1778 fatte dalle Dama S
. . . , alla quale trovasi indirizzata la lettera sulla ipocondria iserita in quel primo numero di quel
giornale alla p.* 22 (London: Filippo Stecchi, 1778) (a copy of this work, together with other
documents on the polemic of Zacchiroli, is found in the Biblioteca Nazionale di Firenze,
with the call number 2 B 26). It is mentioned in the *Gazzetta universale*, no. 31, 18 April
1778, p. 247, "Avviso."
   [25] Ibid., pp. 5ff.

republic of letters counts him among the few principal writers who honor our century." As for what he had written about Italy, Zacchiroli had to note: "I would rather Linguet had been wrong."[26] Catani still did not stop his attacks on Linguet. "Asking this author what 'true politics' is, is like asking a porter the physical cause of the gravity of bodies." All his merit consisted in the "decisive tone" he had assumed.[27] Responding to Zacchiroli, he refused to be put on the same level as Linguet. Certainly both wrote "freely." "But Linguet is without prudence or reason," while the *Giornale fiorentino* was "without interest or passion."[28] In May, Catani confessed his hope "that some day the magic incantation might disappear by which some are stricken when reading these *Annales*."[29]

This polemic only reveals the fascination Linguet's prose aroused in Italy.[30] In the "Avviso" with which the bookseller Filippo Stecchi announced the one-volume collection of materials constituting the third volume of the *Annales*, he did not refrain from calling Linguet "the Tacitus of our century." "We think we have made a precious gift to Italy by bringing to light the most beautiful work of this worthy writer." "All men of good sense call him the true historian of the century, the most exact journalist, the most reflective, the most truthful, and at times the most religious." Linguet in fact showed that he abhorred the thought "of seductive literary men who ridicule the most sacred things" and even "persecuted them with zeal and flagellated them bitterly." [31] As one sees, Linguet's violent campaign against *philosophie* was received favorably by the editor, who made use of it to cover up and render acceptable the political and social criticisms the *Annales* disbursed left and right. Otherwise Linguet was by no means hostile to practical, judicious reforms, which were valuable according to him precisely because they were born of immediate needs and not of the general theories of the philosophes. On this terrain Tuscany could appear to his eyes "like Russia," "the example of a well-thought-out and wise legislation as distant from license

---

[26] Ibid., p. 8.

[27] *Giornale fiorentino*, March 1778, pp. 97ff.

[28] Ibid., April 1778, p. 159.

[29] Ibid., May 1778, p. 202.

[30] The editors of the *Supplément au Journal Universel de littérature*, 1778, p. 57, showed much surprise for what was happening in Florence: "From their first steps the editors of the *Giornale* exercise themselves in striking, one might say, the breast of their wet nurse, because it was the *Annales politiques* of M. Linguet, which very sensibly gave them the idea of the plan of this work, and it was precisely M. Linguet whom they are against." They accused him of "having represented Italy very poorly as a small marquisate, where monuments and statues are collected for the curiosity of some antiquarians. . . . The compilers of the journal of Florence have a lot to do; they will never succeed in reasonably paralleling modern Italy with Italy at the time of Augustus or Trajan."

[31] *Annali*, vol. 3 (1779), p. 375, "Avviso."

as from tyranny." The grand duke had shown the way to "get rid of the
Gothic rust that still covers and erodes all our establishments, and the
servile subjection to certain defective institutions adopted from the Romans."[32] Thus the new Tuscan laws on hunting rights seemed wise to
Linguet, and even more so if one took into account the fact that "the
hunting laws of all of Europe are in a terrible state."[33] Praiseworthy also
was the abolition of "banishment," judicial exile, as well as "branding,"
the mark of infamy. Certainly the example of Geneva, "miniature republic, an extract, if one can say so, of a government, an atom of a
state," was not what should be followed with regard to the first of these
two problems. "There it is the most common punishment," but, "because of the smallness of its territory, a sentence of exile is ridiculous."
As for the mark of infamy, Linguet wrote, "The man thus degraded—
carrying always the proof of a conviction on his body and its shame in
his heart, or rather a desire more for revenge than remorse—would feel
excluded from the possibility of returning to the path of virtue." How
could one not praise Tuscany, which had thought "of suppressing this
absurdity and peril?" "Criminals declared sufficiently guilty to justify a
penalty short of death will be imprisoned or employed in useful labor
by which they will expiate the voluntary evil they have committed
through the forced good they do for society."[34] But then, after expressing his agreement with the spirit of reform, when Linguet found himself before the work of Beccaria, he reacted as he always did in the presence of the philosophes. Here, in volume 5, is his attack on *Dei delitti e
delle pene* and the whole group of Milanese intellectuals.[35] For Linguet it
served directly as a pretext to continue his campaign against the Encyclopedists. For Italians his theme stood at the center of their whole reform activity. The accusation of plagiarism directed against Beccaria
could not help but offend them.[36] From Rome Monsignor Onorato Caetani wrote to Beccaria himself "with the tone of a man filled with truth
and Italian honor against Linguet."[37] Pietro Verri did not even want to
read Linguet's prose. He was unhappy that he had not been attacked,
"along with England, M. d'Alembert, and civil liberty," the usual targets

[32] Ibid., vol. 4 (1779), p. 111.

[33] Ibid., p. 112.

[34] Ibid., pp. 117ff.

[35] Ibid., vol. 5 (1779), pp. 271ff., "Aneddoti singolarissimi sopra il libro intitolato Trattato dei delitti e delle pene." In the French edition this is found in vol. 5, pp. 401ff.

[36] Cesare Beccaria, *Dei delitti e delle pene. Con una raccolta di lettere e documenti relativi alla
nascita dell'opere e alla sua fortuna nell'Europa del Settecento*, ed. F. Venturi (Turin: Einaudi,
1965), p. 454. On pp. 458ff. is the reply of Gorani to Linguet.

[37] *Carteggio di Pietro e di Alessandro Verri*, vol. 10, p. 365, Milan, 1 September 1779.

of the French writer, that is.[38] Great, nonetheless, was the interest aroused in Lombardy, so much so that "many manuscript copies of the satire against Beccaria" were made.[39]

The interest raised among Italians by Linguet's *Annales* came above all from the considerations he scattered throughout his periodical about international developments and the world situation during the first years of the war for American independence. He could not close his eyes to the fact that French volunteers were flocking to assist the insurgents "inebriated by the words *liberty* and *rights of man*, with which passing enthusiasm adorned the standards of America, and which cast on our shores a false and bewildering light." This was a war—he was obliged to admit—that seemed to promise "the most brilliant palms, honors, if one can say so, greater than in all other wars."[40] But even when confronted with the emerging United States Linguet had great difficulty escaping from sad reflection on the vanity of any effort to truly change things on one side of the ocean or the other. The growing value of the American Revolution ultimately imposed itself on him as well. He had difficulty repeating that the liberty of the colonies beyond the Atlantic left Europeans indifferent: the facts themselves, month after month, led him to conclude that the American example would have deep consequences. "Where does the interest that all of Europe takes in these insurgents come from? It is not founded on the justice of their cause. The invasion of Poland was much more unjust than the measures taken by the English against their colonists, and no one is moved by that. It is not the liberty with which Massachusetts Bay flatters itself that arouses our enthusiasm for its inhabitants. . . . The Iroquois, Hurons, Arapahos, etc., are incontestably free as well, and we have for them neither friendship nor admiration." It was necessary to admit that Europeans regarded the Americans as a mirror of their own fate. If one admired the insurgents, "it is only to defend their personal interests; it is in fact our own cause that they plead: in making their case against the English Crown they attack the abuses of all monarchies. They discuss rights dear and precious to all men. In our European prisons, through the bars that affirm our slavery, we are enraptured to see troops armed against servitude in the far distance. . . . The American Revolution is seen as a simple chastisement of English pride: one can discern in it a terrible lesson given to all powers." After such words, it was difficult for him to return to saying he preferred "peaceful servitude" to "tempestuous independence." He had difficulty repeating that there had always

---

[38] Ibid., p. 310, Milan, 3 July 1779.
[39] Ibid., p. 319, Milan, 14 July 1779.
[40] *Annali*, vol. 4 (1779), pp. 51ff.

been and always would be "the great who luxuriate" and "the small who are deprived."[41] The American Revolution had stolen his battle cry, which extended beyond his ponderous, unchanging vision of human society almost to spite him.

A similar judgment to Linguet's of the American Revolution as mirror and accuser of the ills of Europe was strong in Gaetano Filangieri, who was setting the foundations of his *Scienza della legislazione* in the years when the volumes of the *Annales* began to appear. His critique of the English constitution and of the interpretation Montesquieu gave to it took shape while he was reading the pages of the French publicist. He drew from Linguet what he wrote of importance on the reigns of Henry VIII, Charles I, and William of Orange in the political evolution of Great Britain. Even a central element in his evaluation of Cromwell is taken literally from Linguet (but not from reading the Florentine version).[42] From this came Filangieri's uniting of the English concept of felony and the mode of operation of Nero and Tiberius.[43] His observation of the power of the king to corrupt and influence Parliament came from the same source.[44] Despite these and other similarities, the conclusions of Filangieri and Linguet diverged, the first tending to give more power to Parliament, and the second radically condemning the very idea of a separation of powers. The thought of Filangieri converged in the end with that of English radicals, while Linguet again moved in the direction of dictatorship.[45]

Despite the echoes the *Annales* aroused in Milan and Naples, its basic center of diffusion was Florence. The issues of the Tuscan version continued to appear one after another, even if more slowly than had been promised. In a kind of advertisement appearing at the end of the third volume, the bookseller Stecchi appeared very satisfied with the approval that had "increased every day" for the work of Linguet. "In the three volumes that have already appeared anyone can see how much weight his writings have, and how the host of other journals that appear daily loses value beside Linguet's *Annales*."[46] At the beginning of 1780 Filippo

[41] Ibid., vol. 3 (15 February 1778), pp. 308ff.

[42] *La scienza della legislazione*, vol. 1, pp. 160ff., 166, and *Annales*, vol. 1, "Réponse à un souscripteur impatient," pp. 295ff.

[43] *La scienza della legislazione*, vol. 1, p. 162, and *Annales*, p. 297.

[44] *La scienza della legislazione*, vol. 1, p. 166, and *Annales*, p. 303.

[45] See chapter 1, above. I owe these comparisons to the courtesy of Furio Diaz and Luciano Guerci. For other reflections of Linguet in southern Italy see *Illuministi italiani*, vol. 5, *Riformatori napoletani*, ed. F. Venturi (Milan and Naples: Ricciardi, 1962), p. 340 (with regard to Francesco Longano), p. 1066 n. 1 (with regard to Giuseppe Maria Galanti), and p. 1093 (with regard to Giuseppe Palmieri).

[46] *Annali*, vol. 3 (1779), p. 375.

Stecchi made an association with Raineri Del Vivo, whose name appears on the cover of the fourth volume. But the delay persisted. It was the fault of the translator, Abate Luigi Semplici, the booksellers held. Semplici blamed the editors instead and finally decided to take the whole undertaking into his own hands, associating himself with Vincenzo Piombi, another active journalist. On 1 January 1780 a *Manifesto* appeared which promised to satisfy the requirement for punctuality to readers. "The universally warm welcome encountered by the Italian version of the *Annales* of the incomparable modern historian M. Linguet," it read, "has fully confirmed the merit of this illustrious work even in Italy. Italy, however, is displeased to find that this edition is so late, postponed almost a year after the original by its author. The associates have hoped to bring it out for some time, but the editor has not cooperated." Linguet was now publishing volume 7. It was best to leave the back issues as they were and provide the current volume, "which begins with the last three months of 1779 and continues for the current year 1780. . . . Thus the public will be fully content to have a recent journal that is unique." When this was done the remaining gaps would be closed, filling "imperceptibly the missing preceding volumes to complete the work." The price would remain one zecchino a year. Naturally, Filippo Stecchi and Raineri Del Vivo protested against this project of the "priests Semplici and Piombi." The authorities had to intervene to try to get booksellers and translators to agree. Francesco Seratti proposed that Stecchi and Semplici form a society and divide the profits equally. Whether this or another solution was arrived at for the new edition (they even considered giving Semplici five soldi a page for his version), it is certain that Linguet's journal continued to be published more or less regularly in Florence in Italian translation.[47] And so much interest was raised that Stecchi and Del Vivo considered starting a similar undertaking on their own, a "literary magazine," with the hope of giving life to a "larger project than publishing and literature together have thus far imagined." It was a matter of providing the public with "everything new that appears in a year in Italy, France, England, etc." They would begin with a kind of chronicle of the reign of Maria Theresa, who had just died, and continue with the works of Machiavelli, with those of Rousseau, "gallantly adorned in good Italian," and especially with "the General History of M. Voltaire." Besides these classics there would be

[47] Florence, *AS, Segreteria di Stato*, anno 1780, prot. 2, no. 41 B, *Serie affari*. See *Notizie del mondo*, no. 6, 18 January 1780, p. 40, in the footer, where Stecchi and Del Vivo offer some of the still missing issues of the *Annali*, promising to accelerate their work. Even the *Gazzetta universale*, no. 5, 15 January 1780, p. 40, "Avvisi," began to carry announcements of issues of the *Annali* and continued to carry similar notices in the successive numbers.

news taken from all the gazettes, or extracts from "foreign journals." "Our Florentine historical, political, and literary journal" would be absorbed in this immense miscellany. Francesco Seratti called this undertaking a true "hodgepodge."[48] The planned "literary magazine" never appeared. Stecchi and Del Vivo forced themselves to publish at least some of the great works they had planned. At the end of volume 4 of Linguet's *Annales* they advised subscribers that they had been obliged to cease "printing two works by Voltaire . . . the *Questions encyclopédiques* . . . and the *Histoire générale*." But they promised that they would "publish shortly another prospectus to collect subscriptions for the *Histoire générale* alone." If this project also ended in failure, two works by Linguet would replace Voltaire's work: the *Histoire des révolutions de la république romaine*, and also the *Empire romain*, would appear from the presses of Stecchi and Del Vivo.

Meanwhile, in the spring of 1780, the situation became more and more disquieting for the French original of the *Annales*. "It is said that orders have been given that this can no longer be imported into the kingdom [that is, France]; the prohibition will be quite serious since there are, it is said, 5,000 subscribers at two louis a year."[1] But the success was such that there continued, even in Italy, to be efforts to take subscriptions for French reeditions of the famous periodical launched by Linguet "to give asylum to truth in politics and literature." "Nothing is excluded except satire and adulation. It contains all that characterizes the present century and honors the human spirit, or restores what is badly understood by it, or furthers its progress; all the principal events of our epoch are represented with general views and reflections." "The faithful record and verified history of revolutions in politics and legislation, in jurisprudence, letters, and customs," were the basis of this periodical, where "one is never permitted to attack divinity or morals."[2]

[48] Florence, AS, *Reggenza*, filza 626, fasc. 105.

[1] *Notizie del mondo*, no. 39, 13 May 1780, p. 307 (Paris, 28 April). The notice was taken up in the Venetian gazette *Notizie del mondo [V.]*, no. 39, 20 May 1780, p. 310 (Paris, 28 April).

[2] *Notizie del mondo [V.]*, no. 70, 6 September 1780, p. 564, in the footer, and no. 74, 20 September 1780, p. 596, where a whole page is dedicated to an advertisement of this reprinting done by the Dutch bookseller Frederick Gosse. In the same journal, no. 80, 11 October 1780, p. 644, in the footer, there is a long list of Italian booksellers, from Ancona to Bergamo, from Bologna to Treviso, etc. where it was possible to subscribe. On the political and editorial vicissitudes of the *Annales* in this period see the study by Darlene

But the news that arrived from beyond the Alps at the end of the summer of 1780 was anything but joyous. Having gone to Paris to pass a few days, one read in the gazette of Lugano, "he was arrested on 27 September, just as he was about to leave for the country, and has been taken to the Bastille. It has since been learned that on 3 October his house in Brussels was sealed."[3] The most varied rumors circulated. Some held that Linguet's situation was not tragic. "His friends hold that his detention will not last long. In fact, the government, which laughs at the sarcasms of this lively writer, treats him with indulgence, having allowed him to read and write in prison." It was said that his imprisonment was due "to a too-spirited letter he had written to Marshal Duras."[4] Certainly the matter caused much fracas. "There is talk of nothing else at present," it was reported in Venice in a communication from Paris, "than of the celebrated M. Linguet. We cannot console ourselves with seeing, at a moment when important political developments are about to be determined, such an enlightened observer closed up in the Bastille. It is talked of in a thousand ways. Some deify this illustrious prisoner, others display an equally shameful passion for tearing him down. On such occasions hatred is most vivid, and friendship lags. . . . But it is sad to see the world taste and savor the pleasure of hearing the estimable and celebrated author of the *Annales* enclosed within four walls and deprived of any human commerce . . . as for the reasons for his arrest there are so many. . . ."[5] His voice continued to sound even when he was in prison. And it was, as always, a voice of protest. "A letter of M. Linguet," it was communicated from Paris, "has been circulated in the city," . . . sent from the Bastille on 7 October, which has made much clatter. It serves to demonstrate the actual sentiments of such a great man, who is required as so many others have been to expiate his excess of freedom of the pen in the anguished confines of a horrid prison."[6] Even *La gazzetta di Milano* echoed the anxiety the situation of Linguet aroused everywhere.[7] At the beginning of 1781 a rumor spread that he had died mad. "Writers weep the misfortunes of this famous writer," read the Florentine gazette.[8] Again hypotheses heaped up about the reasons for his imprisonment, and now about his tragic end. He had

Gay Levy, *The Ideas and Career of Simon Nicolas Henri Linguet: A Study in Eighteenth-Century French Politics* (Urbana: University of Illinois Press, 1980), pp. 186ff.

[3] *Nuove di diverse corti e paesi*, no. 43, 23 October 1780, p. 344 (Leiden, 9 October).

[4] Ibid., no. 44, 30 October 1780, p. 347 (Paris, 20 October).

[5] *Notizie del mondo [V.]*, no. 86, 1 November 1780, p. 681, "Continuation of the news from Paris of 17 October."

[6] *Gazzetta universale*, no. 92, 14 November 1780, p. 725 (Paris, 31 October).

[7] *La gazzetta di Milano*, no. 1, 3 January 1781 (Paris, 15 December).

[8] *Gazzetta universale*, no. 1, 2 January 1781, p. 1 (Paris, 19 December).

advised Holland, it was said, in a policy of hesitation against French interests. It seemed that he had actually invited the emperor to annex
Lorraine.⁹ The same sheet that carried these rumors denied, some days
later, that Linguet had been hanged in prison.¹⁰ In truth he was neither
mad nor dead. But his imprisonment extended beyond any prediction.
La gazzetta di Milano reported in the summer of 1781, "from a public
sheet in Germany," that Linguet's friends hoped in vain to see broken
"the sad chains with which his oppressors have bound him . . . his prison
is also an ignominious grave. . . . We are as little informed now of the
prison that holds him as we were six months ago."¹¹ Only on 11 June
1782 could the *Notizie del mondo* announce that "on the morning of Pen-
tecost the celebrated writer M. Linguet left the Bastille."¹² The gazette
of Lugano added that "the lieutenant general of police himself went to
the Bastille to give him the happy news."¹³ It seemed that he would even
be able to resume publication of his *Annales*. "But one does not know,"
wrote the *Notizie del mondo*, "if they will be so avidly read as before, since
it is said that he will be obliged to submit them to the censorship before
making them public through the press."¹⁴

During the period of Linguet's imprisonment, after September
1780, the *Annales* continued to be published in its Italian version in Florence, taking advantage of the silence of the author to catch up on the
backlog that was accumulating, as we have seen. The translator was no
longer the same. Luigi Semplici had to leave Florence at the beginning
of October 1780 after a conflict with the government about ecclesiastical
politics.¹⁵ Beginning with volume 9 of the *Annales*, the mark "LSAF" was
replaced with small dots. In February 1781 it was announced that the
year 1780 was completed, and that "next March, despite uncertainty
about the death of the author, the association will be formed anew.
. . ."¹⁶

The success of the *Annales* had been too great for there not to be a
temptation to fill in for Linguet when he was immobilized in the Bastille.
This, in fact, is what the Genevan journalist Jacques Mallat Du Pan did,

⁹ *Notizie del mondo*, no. 3, 9 January 1781, p. 17 (Paris, 26 December).
¹⁰ Ibid., no. 7, 23 January 1781, p. 49 (Paris, 9 January).
¹¹ *La gazzetta di Milano*, no. 35, 29 August 1781 (Cleves, 3 August).
¹² *Notizie del mondo*, no. 47, 11 June 1782, p. 369 (Paris, 28 May).
¹³ *Nuove di diverse corti e paesi*, no. 23, 10 June 1782, p. 179 (Paris, 31 May).
¹⁴ *Notizie del mondo*, no. 47, 11 June 1782, p. 369 (Paris, 28 May).
¹⁵ Morelli, "Persone e momenti," p. 468. I owe the verification of the date to Renato
Pasta.
¹⁶ *Notizie del mondo*, no. 15, 20 February 1781, p. 120, in the footer. The *Gazzetta universale*, no. 103, 23 December 1780, p. 820, in the footer, had already announced that "in
volume 9 begins the other translation."

beginning in January 1781. He had already collaborated with Linguet for some time as much in the editing as, above all, in the distribution of the journal.[17] Thus appeared in Geneva the *Annales politiques, civiles et littéraires du dix-huitième siècle; ouvrage périodique, pour servir de suite aux Annales de M. Linguet*, which continued into 1783, changing its title in March of that year to *Mémoires historiques, politiques et littéraires sur l'état présent de l'Europe*. In all six volumes came out. Mallet du Pan accentuated the reformist elements ("if there is a happy people, wisely governed, good, simple, and peaceful it is in Tuscany"),[18] eliminated polemical elements typical of Linguet, and continued to provide an intelligent and a colorful picture of Europe and the world, letting his attention dwell particularly on the republican tradition (Venice, Holland, and above all Geneva, his homeland) and on conflicts between the young Emperor Joseph II and the Roman Curia. He knew well, above all after the Genevan revolution of 1782, that the European political sky forecast a storm ("a wind of revolution and revolt seems to blow from all points of the horizon"),[19] and he sought to counteract this with a moderation taken partly from Voltaire and partly from the sensitivity of patricians of his native city, who were inclined to and even desired being supported and protected by the French monarchy, but anxious not to be absorbed or dominated by it.[20] He always preserved the panoramic and cosmopolitan vision he had cultivated and developed in the period of his agitated but fruitful collaboration with Linguet. This contributed not little to ensuring a notable success for his *Annales*, which is indicated, as happened frequently in those years, by the number of pirated and illegal editions of his work. He finally declared publicly that he did not recognize any other editions besides the one he edited himself and "the Italian translation done in Florence."[21] In fact, beginning with volume 10, which carries the date 1781, the *Annales* by Mallet Du Pan was placed beside the earlier one of Linguet in the edition of Stecchi and Del Vivo. Volume 12 carried his essay "Recent Revolution in Geneva" and his "General Reflections on This Event and Its Consequences," which were fundamental to the debate on republics in the eighties.[22] What he wrote on the "ministerial revolution" that had occurred in England was also of

---

[17] Francis Acomb, *Mallet Du Pan (1749–1800): A career in Political Journalism* (Durham, N.C.: Duke University Press, 1973), pp. 106ff., and on the decision of Mallet Du Pan to publish his own periodical, p. 129. This study has completely renewed our knowledge of these editorial affairs.

[18] *Annales* (by Mallet Du Pan), year 2 (1781), p. 161.

[19] Ibid., vol. 4 (1782), p. 173.

[20] See vol. 2, chapter 6.

[21] *Annales* (of Mallet Du Pan), vol. 4, p. 3, "Avis aux souscripteurs."

[22] *Annali*, vol. 12 (1782), pp. 235ff.

notable interest.[23] The events of the war remained at the center of his
attention, even if he said he would soon return to occupying himself
with economic problems. Above all, in France "the plans of M. Turgot
and those of M. Necker have vanished like the shadows of magicians:
the fashion for speaking and speculating like a financier has departed
with them: wars have distracted attention, but soon it will return."[24] This
was all the more so because the problem of poverty was becoming more
serious. "An indigent man, according to the policy of Europe, is a being
worse off than a stray dog and counts for nothing in the human species," above all "in capitals where the human species shows itself in the
lowest degree of abjection." The volumes of the *Annales* edited by Mallat
Du Pan concluded with a decisive moment in the history of these years,
"the signing of the peace," which put an end to the war for American
independence.[25]

The vacuum left by the arrest of Linguet in Tuscan journalism does
not seem to have been completely filled even by the publication of the
Annales of Mallet Du Pan. Three Florentine booksellers, Antonio Buonaiuti, Antonio Benucci, and Luigi Carlieri distributed a *Prospectus* toward the end of 1782 in which they promised an Italian version, with
cuts and additions, of a journal they said had begun to appear in France
on 1 July of that year.[26] "Periodicals have multiplied to such an extent
for some time now that presenting novelties to the curiosity of the public
seems a foolhardy enterprise," one reads. But still, there was space for
a sheet of observations, and not only of news. "Not that the authors of
good gazettes, and of our accredited journals, are not provided with a
spirit of observation," he added, "but obliged as they are to observe the
form of their work, they have to give in either to the torrent of news
they announce or to the books of which they give notice." Beyond the
Alps some suggestive examples of a transformation in journalistic activity were not lacking: it was enough to open the *Courier de l'Europe* to be
persuaded of this. The very grandiosity and singularity of what was taking place in the world suggested new reflections and meditations. "This
century is one of extraordinary events. . . . Are the causes that have pre-

[23] Ibid., pp. 138ff.
[24] Ibid., vol. 13, p. 121.
[25] Ibid., p. 155.
[26] *L'Osservatore. Opera periodica da servire di continuazione agli "Annali politici, civili e letterari del secolo del sig. Linguet." Tradotto dal francese con aggiunte per uso degli italiani.* It carried the place of Lausanne and promised "a volume of 96 pages in 8ᵛᵒ every month" at
the price "of one lire of Florence per volume." On pp. 3ff. was printed the "Prospetto." A
copy of the three volumes of this periodical is found in Florence, Biblioteca nazionale,
with the call number 12.8.83. It was announced in the *Gazzetta universale*, no. 100, 14
December 1782, p. 808, "Avvisi."

pared and brought to maturity these so surprising events well known? Can one calculate fairly and precisely the energy and influence of men on constitutions? Here is a large subject on which most interesting observations could be made." To be sure, the philosophes had tried to answer such questions. One lived in the "century of philosophy and light." "But was this light, although diffused so widely, quite clear? Had not opposition, and a spirit of party and system, perhaps obscured it?" Had not "political liberty" led perhaps to "tumults," its "inevitable companions," and thus did this not risk "bringing on the misfortunes of peoples sooner or later"? The very nature of human society evoked profound doubts.

In all lands and under whatever constitution, property, the sacred bond of society, has certainly produced great problems. It is unfortunately true that of the two classes of the human species, one possesses everything, and the other is in need of everything; it is unfortunately true that the class of proprietors, although much less numerous, remains enclosed within itself and makes the innumerable crowd of unfortunates who are obliged to live from the daily work of their hands tremble under the most absolute dependence. But was this state of affairs truly a necessary and an inevitable consequence of property? Did not the way in which governments were formed, the intersection of events and circumstances, the reciprocal relationships among nations, and their different internal and external mechanisms enter into the picture and play a part? And then, when after one had analyzed everything that can give rise to property, could not some other internal relationships make all the problems disappear more easily than one might think through certain simple but wise laws?

The increasingly central position economics assumed in the life of nations raised the hope for a solution of problems arising from a society divided into two opposing classes. "Ancient legislators required good habits and bodily strength of their people. Our politicians want real and relative wealth." In general, the most diverse problems required reexamination. "There are infinite observations to make, prejudices to destroy, errors to combat, and truths to develop." Otherwise it was necessary to make the most of the favorable moment in which one found oneself: "One should profit from these precious moments of liberty that can increase and perfect the light of the century and contribute infinitely to the happiness of nations."

Thus the journalists of the *Osservatore*, with daring steps, set themselves to provide, in the first issue of their sheet, a "Reasoned Prospect of the Present Situation of the World." They were optimistic about France. They admired the resilience of England, which "in the midst of a civil war keeps its head always high."[27] "To the proud Englishman,

[27] *L'Osservatore*, vol. 1, no. 1, p. 6.

jealous of the shadow of liberty that remains to him, victim of the ambition of his ministers, the price would never seem too great of buying
the pleasure, for him inexpressible, of saying to his king, through a representative, that a revolution had put the crown on his head, and that
another, similar one could knock it off."[28] Even Spain provided a good
example of courage. "We do not know of a worse-ordered monarchy,"
or one so weakened, but "still it rises from decadence to advantage."
"The war in which it is currently engaged will finally restore it to its old
vigor."[29] Germany had enriched itself, becoming "as flourishing as Italy
was in the sixteenth century."[30] Poland had finally put itself on the road
to reform.[31] As for Russia, a reexamination of the work of Peter the
Great provoked a discussion between the French author and the Italian
translator. The first held that "instead of the quickness of the Eastern
forms of Asiatic justice" the emperor had introduced "the delay of republican forms," still allowing "Eastern customs and laws to remain in
full force." "He did no more than add new torments to those already
employed in his states." As for serfdom, far from abolishing it he reinforced it, through "the greatest despotism."[32] How could one create "a
new people" without changing "their inclinations and tastes"? To this
the Italian editor objected, in a long note, that Peter to be sure had done
what he could. If he did not succeed in his intent, it was necessary to
"blame [not] his genius, but rather the immensity of ills and calamities
of his times, the serious opposition, and his lack of education."[33] In the
following issues America was placed at the center of a broad panorama
of the world situation. Raynal was criticized for his "vain declamations,"
which were useless for understanding the "great revolution" taking
place there.[34] It was affirmed emphatically that, on 4 July 1776, "the
United States imposed on themselves a constitution that added the external force of monarchies to the internal advantages of republican government."[35] The third issue of the *Osservatore* was in some sense a special
number devoted to the "recent Genevan revolution."[36] In the second
number of volume 2 its end was announced, suffocated by the intervention of France, Sardinia, and Berne.[37] The editors of this small but lively

[28] Ibid., p. 7.
[29] Ibid., pp. 10, 16.
[30] Ibid., p. 31.
[31] Ibid., p. 36.
[32] Ibid., pp. 46ff.
[33] Ibid., pp. 49ff. n. 1.
[34] Ibid., vol. 1, no. 2, p. 157.
[35] Ibid., p. 168.
[36] See below, vol. 2, chapter 6.
[37] *L'Osservatore*, vol. 2, no. 2, pp. 49ff.

periodical concentrated more and more on problems of juridical and economic reform. Thus they offered readers one of the most typical and significant products of Tuscan thought. Under the title "Legislation: On the Imprisonment of Debtors" were published the pages of Cosimo Amidei on this question.[38] The edict of Peter Leopold in this matter naturally was not lacking.[39] The efforts of men like Targioni Tozzetti to know better and improve the situation of Tuscany were remembered with warmth.[40] But the larger number of pages were employed in attempting to give an idea of the political and economic problems of the United Provinces, Great Britain, Ireland, Spain, Portugal, Russia, France, Switzerland, and Greece.[41] Echoes of polemics more or less directly inspired by Linguet against the Parisian philosophes were not lacking. La Harpe was bitterly attacked. Anticlerical ideas were put in a bad light by showing with what altruism and generosity the clergy of Bourgogne had acted in a recent period of scarcity. "After these tender examples of humanity and beneficence, to which I could add an infinite number of other cases, I think of the injustice, or better the atrocious and dogged hatred, of our philosophers in calumniating the clergy and accusing them for the spirit of sedition introduced in a part of the nation."[42] Even the *Osservatore* ended its short career with the peace, "one of the major achievements of the eighteenth century."[43] "To impartial eyes it seems that in this treaty France deserves honor, Spain has received damages, there is good fortune for America, and I would suggest shame for England if it had carried out hostilities with less glory."[44] The periodical thus ended with the names of the Americans who had signed the peace preliminaries: "Riccardo Osvald, Giovanni Adams, Beniamino Franklin, Giovanni Jay, Arrigo Laurens."

A comedy, or more properly a scenic representation of the questions and interest that the fate of Linguet had aroused in Tuscany, was pub-

[38] Ibid. It is printed in Cosimo Amidei, *Opere*. Introduzione, testo e nota critica a cura di Antonio Rotondò (Turin: Giappichelli, 1980), pp. 299ff. In *L'Osservatore*, vol. 2, no. 2, pp. 146ff., we read: "Not having printed this discourse has given the public the pleasure of obtaining from the author many desired additions to the same, to which the author himself, in a new edition to be made, has promised a preface for which this is the content." See this preface, pp. 257ff.

[39] *L'Osservatore*, vol. 2, no. 2, pp. 87ff.

[40] Ibid., vol. 3, no. 1, pp. 21ff.

[41] On this last place of particular interest is the "Riflessioni critiche ad un'opera intitolata Lettera sopra i greci antichi e moderni con un parallelo dei loro costumi," by Sig. Guys, in *L'Osservatore*, vol. 2, no. 2, pp. 170ff.

[42] Ibid., p. 145.

[43] Ibid., p. 195.

[44] Ibid., pp. 196ff.

lished in Florence in the spring of 1783.[45] A modern reader—that is, one who has read the work of Robert Darnton, *The Business of Enlightenment*—will find himself on familiar ground. As in the well-known book of the American scholar, so also in this little Florentine work the central subject is the printing industry in the period after the completion of Diderot's *Encyclopédie*. Money and organization, underhanded blows, and imbroglios follow one another in both. The government is dragged into the current and it has but one response, the lettre de cachet and the Bastille. The Tuscan author was extraordinarily well informed about these intrigues and this political weakness and violence. His scenes are placed with agility in the Paris of 1780. The imaginary characters interact effectively with real-life ones. Italian curiosity and interests are linked intelligently with French problems. At the center was Linguet. The basic problem in these pages could have been formulated with the famous words of Diderot: "Est-il bon? est-il méchant?" And the Italian author left the answer uncertain. The surroundings in which Linguet moved were to be sure the worst. But he himself, who was he? what did he really want?

The first act unfolds in a "study with two side doors." "The room reveals all the simplicity and disorder of a man of letters." On the ground, among other papers, are writings of d'Alembert thrown down in disgust by Linguet. Panckoucke enters, the most enterprising of the Parisian booksellers, the great remaker of the *Encyclopédie*, for some time the enemy of Linguet, from whom he had taken over the management of a periodical, thus obliging Linguet to take refuge abroad in order to publish the *Annales*. Neither one nor the other has forgotten his past grievance, but Panckoucke, having heard of the return of Linguet from Brussels, has come to propose a resumption of relations between them. The secretary of Linguet, Saint Péravi (this seems to be an

---

[45] *Notizie del mondo*, no. 42, 27 May 1783, p. 340, in the footer, where is announced "a book written in the form of a comedy, entitled" *La prigionia del signor Linguet annalista del secolo decimo-ottavo*. Commedia in tre atti in prosa del signor X (London, 1783). A copy can be found in Florence, B. Marucelliana, with the call number 7.C.IV.17.6. In the *Notizie del mondo* of Venice, no. 67, 20 August 1783, in the footer, one reads: "Leonardo e Gio. Maria fratelli Bassaglia have published a new comedy in three acts with the title *La prigionia del sig. Linguet* in 8ᵛᵒ and it is in effect a theatrical representation of the most true circumstances leading to that memorable event which constitutes an epoch in the literary history of the celebrated French annalist." The work, as much in the Florentine as in the Venetian edition, is anonymous. That it was by Francesco Saverio Catani, a lively journalist whom we have seen intervene in the polemic about Pombal and in the discussions of the Giornale fiorentino, and whom we encounter often in the debates of the eighties, is suggested by a "Lettera a stampa con aggiunte a penna da Firenze 27 aprile 1784" that can be found in Savignano sul Rubicone, R.A.F., B. Amaduzzi, Miscellanea di vari giornali, vol. 1, p. 36, where a list of his writings is provided, among which is "Prigionia del sig. Linguet."

imaginary character, but a journalist who was active in those years did actually have the name Jean-Nicolas-Marcelin Guérineau de Saint Pér-avy), recalls that Linguet "is obstinate in good as well as evil, and often prefers a useless show of obstinacy on a position he has taken to his real advantage." The situation was all the more cause for concern because "the government has looked askance at him for some time." He would have done better not to have returned to Paris at all. "A man of letters without prudence is like a theater with a comedian without rouge." "Orders of arrest" (that is, lettres de cachet) "are no longer as fashionable as in the previous reign," but they are always to be feared. Protectors would be needed to ward them off, "but the ambition and independent spirit of Linguet has not permitted him to lower himself to that extent." The king respects him, but his ministers? It was more and more difficult to move in a world of publishing where "booksellers don't trouble themselves to know if a book is good or bad, only if it has a market."[46] Imbroglios of all kinds multiplied. Linguet himself had to return to Paris— he says so himself on arriving at his study—to collect a sum owed to him by his correspondent Le Quesne, who in actuality was plotting a trap for him with the police. He feels the earth sinking beneath his feet and bursts out particularly against the booksellers, "that rabble"; to liberate himself from them he had created his journal. He felt "his civil existence," the very freedom to express himself, menaced. For this reason, "unfortunately," he would continue to live outside of France. "Without a wise liberty of thought there would be no more writers, and consequently no longer sciences or arts: their relationship is clear. Here, as in many other lands, a man of letters does not know how to take up his pen without necessarily offending someone. Too many men have an interest in the prolongation of certain abuses, too many transgressed rights, too many old and deeply rooted errors, too many forms of prejudice, too many cruel enemies who hate you for your whole life if they cannot persecute you." He felt more and more alone in this defense of his own liberty. "The philosopher sometimes feels obliged to sacrifice himself to the whims and customs of society." Linguet insisted instead on his desire "to keep away from the common road." "What evil, basically, do men of letters do? If they sometimes address the great with a firm and an austere tone, they never raise a murderous or rebellious hand against them." Writers know that "errors cannot be cured if they are not fought publicly and without hesitation." He himself would never seek protection from those who dispense fame and riches. "I have always hated the name patron. . . . I know such persons too well: their

[46] *La prigionia del Signor Linguet*, pp. 5ff.

aspect irritates and disgusts me. On the other hand I pity the man of letters who lacks the courage to hide his misery and flee an outrage."

Reading correspondence that has just arrived confirms again that he is both "extraordinarily famous" ("from the most miserable carpenter's assistant to the first courtier of the king, all know M. Linguet") and particularly exposed to all kinds of threats and perils. As his secretary, Saint Péravi, concludes, "It seems that in this century it is almost a disgrace to be known and admired as a man of letters."

The arrival of the "Marchese of Castel Bianco, an Italian nobleman," contrasts the uncertain and disturbing situation of Linguet with the more traditional and imitative culture of a maker of verses and a tragedy, now in Paris to meet French literary men. "If I returned to my country without having seen Linguet, I would pass for an ignoramus and a dolt." He could already list a large number of writers he had encountered, from d'Alembert to Diderot, from Dorat to La Harpe, from Ducis to Marmontel, and "so many other poets, poetasters, literati, and journalists who have escaped my memory. I absolutely must see this one as well." Meanwhile, he chats with other persons also awaiting Linguet, among whom is a member of the Academy of Sciences, who attacks the *Annales* violently for the defense of absolutism that so often appears there. "Linguet pretends that the king of France can capriciously remove offices from magistrates, deprive the nation of its courts, impose arbitrary impositions without any legal form, only according to his will." But still, the French government, far from appreciating the support of Linguet, had persecuted him in every way. His temperament was indeed too imperious and independent. "Linguet entertains all paradoxes that pass through his head, he embraces all bad causes, and one is not allowed to contradict him." Despite the great fame the *Annales* had won him, "the greater part of his readers are disgusted with his egotism. At first sight he appears moderate: the object of his modesty is always to keep the public in suspense by talking about himself." His mind is taken over by wickedness, by "such an inexhaustible depth of wickedness that, denied unlimited freedom in France, he went elsewhere to express himself with greater vehemence and got many readers."[47] The conversation between the Italian marquis and the French academician, inspired by the principle that "those who cultivate letters are fellow citizens and brothers," culminates, when Linguet arrives, in a scene of adulation and vanity on the part of the two who had disputed up to then the most obscure aspects of his mind. But while the double language of the Frenchman is nothing other than a part of the net stretched to capture Linguet, the convictions of the Italian reaffirm the value and efficacy of

[47] Ibid., pp. 22ff.

philosophie: "Despite some remnants of barbarity, a salutary light supports and surrounds us. The two great scourges of humanity, superstition and ignorance, are by no means destroyed, but they are at least brought down, and when they raise their voices, they appear odious and ridiculous. Philosophy is like a star circulating above the earth: it illuminates successively all points of the globe: now its rays are perpendicular, now oblique, but sooner or later. . . ."[48]

The second act sees Linguet together with the Marquise de Germancé, "a spirited woman, his lover," who, abandoned by him in Brussels and having arrived in Paris, is decided to murder him with a pistol and obtain immediate restitution from him of the huge loan she gave him to launch the *Annales*. "This feminine devil," comments Saint Péravi, seems to have "the head of Elizabeth and the heart of Attila." Linguet feels more and more isolated: "My straightforward conduct and my unrestrained opinions have won me malicious rivals and rabid enemies." In his antechamber the examination of his prose and personality by those who are there ostensibly to admire them continues more and more harshly. The Italian marquis assures his interlocutor of the "great name" Linguet enjoys in his country. "All read his writings and are enchanted." But others object that "the *Annales* is full of great words and small views," that the colors the author uses are elementary and contrived, and that often he uses the pens of others; Le Quesne ends up calling him "the Harlequin of modern journalism." The Italian visitor says he is convinced that the vanity of Linguet is "the worst of his defects," but his critics, with their violence and envy, seem more disgusting to him. "I would not have believed Linguet had so many enemies here," he concludes. "How different from the reputation he enjoys in England, Germany, and Italy is the view of him held in his own country!"[49]

A monologue by Linguet opens the third act. He has finished writing an article on the ambition of the great, which he rereads: "This truth could cause me some distress . . . but all the distress in the world is not equal to the pleasure of having the truth for oneself. . . . I want to write with frankness." He truly did not intend to imitate the prose of d'Alembert in any way. "In reading it my mind is distracted despite myself. I forget I am reading. An unexpected lethargy takes hold of my spirits. I take off the chaff and throw the man of excellent taste into a corner. To wake myself up, I take up a volume of the *Nouvelle Heloïse* . . . in an instant I am attentive, my spirits warm; I feel agitated by a thousand different movements. I read a volume in a moment, and when I see there are six more my heart beats with joy and pleasure; I would like to

---

[48] Ibid., p. 36.
[49] Ibid., pp. 41ff.

prolong forever this delicious reading." When Saint Péravi interrupts him trying to persuade him to leave Paris immediately, he refuses and returns to his solitary meditation. "Perhaps I have not yet suffered enough. . . . With apparent serenity the disgusting secrets surrounding me reveal themselves, and my sadness, veiled at times with a forced smile, becomes more bitter in my heart." An officer and soldiers enter to take him to the Bastille. "I am going to be buried perhaps forever in a horrible prison. . . . Vile souls, you will be infinitely content, you will no longer have to fear my reproaches, or my laments, and will launch your perfidious blows against me with impunity. . . . Ah! If I were only the last victim that iniquity, prepotency, and intrigue could throw into an eternal prison." The Marquise de Germancé, turning to Saint Péravi, weeps for literature and for a talent that finds no other reward than prison. "I advise you to remain idle. The pen and the tongue are equally dangerous. Now there will be no more imprudent speaking or writing. Try, if possible, to reach the temple of virtue without saying a word."[50] With these words the day of 27 September 1780 ends, the day of the arrest of Linguet.

A brief but energetic review of this theatrical piece appeared in the *Memorie enciclopediche* of Bologna, which can possibly be attributed to Ristori. "The whole world cries out against journalists. They are called hirelings, venal, ignorant, indiscreet, superficial. But if among them rises by chance a name of genius distinguished by his talents, who disdains prejudice and fights heatedly for the truth, what recompense awaits him? The miserable Linguet dying at the bottom of a tower is a frightening picture that inspires loathing, saps assurance, and would make the pen fall from the hand of any writer. Ah! It is always better to be an erudite pedant, a stupid compiler of texts, a ridiculous annotator. One's life is the price paid for not being pedantic or stupid."[51]

While in Florence and Venice copies of this comedy were being distributed, Linguet made his voice heard again, through an exceptional journalistic coup. Already in the first days of 1783 the Venetian gazette *Notizie del mondo* reported that his *Mémoires sur la Bastille* had certainly "attracted universal attention to himself."[52] In Florence, in March, the echo of the extraordinary success of this work arrived. "He is Dante who describes the Inferno and its most cruel torments. The impression born

[50] Ibid., pp. 61ff.

[51] *Memorie enciclopediche*, no. 28, September 1783, p. 220, *La prigionia del Signor Linguet*.

[52] *Notizie del mondo [V.]*, no. 3, 8 January 1783 (n.d.). In no. 8, 23 January 1783, London, 3 January, Linguet's letter to a friend was published, where one reads: "I am busy with printing some *Memorie sopra la Bastiglia*. . . . The picture is terrible, but I have not changed the colors. I have every respect for the person of the king." In no. 26, 29 March 1783, Paris, 14 March, two and a half pages of the *Memorie* were reproduced.

from reading this work is so strong that it cannot be imagined except from a pen as expressive and lively as that of the author."[53] The curiosity was such as to induce some of the most reputable booksellers, Ranieri Del Vivo, Giuseppe Molini, Vincenzo Landi, and Antonio Benucci, to undertake the distribution of this work as soon as parts of it arrived, "at the price of two paoli each."[54] A few months later the Tuscan version appeared.[55]

The work carried the motto *Surrexit e mortuis* (He rose from the dead) and opened with a curious engraving. The idea was taken—as Linguet indicated—from the *Courier du Bas-Rhin*, "that is to say, the most esteemed periodical by honest and enlightened men, and by true philosophers." Even in the symbols he chose Linguet was thus aligned with the gazette directed by Jean Manzon, who more clearly than anyone upheld the principles of enlightened despotism, of a Prussian type. The image was an invitation to Louis XVI to fulfill, in the very heart of France, his duty as an energetic and reforming sovereign. One saw a statue of the king, with all the attributes of royalty, rising "amid the debris of a half-ruined chateau, supposed to represent the Bastille. This prince holds out his hands benevolently toward the prisoners he has just rescued, whose attitudes express their gratitude. . . ." Lightning bolts from heaven strike the very symbol of despotism, the clock located inside the Bastille with two low reliefs representing a man and a woman in chains. Below is a caption taken from Voltaire's *Alzire*: "Soyez libres: vivez."[56] After having narrated with great agitation his encounters with Vergennes, with Marshal Duras, and with the most varied French authorities, Linguet showed how all the different roads he had at one time or another thought of taking in order to find a country where he would feel free and independent had closed before him (there even was a project "to go to Italy and try to forget in the study of monuments of past centuries what I have suffered in this one").[57] Like a trap opportunely baited, the Bastille had closed on him. "What is signified in France by the bizarre name lettres de cachet is a particular malady native to that kingdom, like the plagues of Egypt, smallpox in Arabia, and the showers of burning cinders near volcanoes." They corresponded to acts of Roman despotism and to manifestations of *raison d'état* in Sparta. Even

---

[53] *Notizie del mondo*, no. 22, 18 March 1783, p. 174 (Paris, 4 March).

[54] Ibid., no. 25, 29 March 1783, p. 204, in the footer. The second issue was announced (no. 29, 12 April 1783, p. 236, in the footer).

[55] *Memorie della Bastiglia* (London, 1783). This was announced in the *Notizie del mondo*, no. 47, 14 June 1783, p. 380, in the footer.

[56] "Mémoires sur la Bastille et la détention de l'auteur dans ce château royal, depuis le 27 septembre 1780 jusqu'au 19 mai 1782," in *Annales*, vol. 10 (1783) pp. iiiff.

[57] Ibid., p. 13.

in England the Tower of London served as a prison for prisoners of state. What distinguished France was the way in which this power was exercised. Life in the Bastille was "horrible." "It is like nothing ever practiced or that is practiced today in the world."[58] Without books, without paper, completely isolated, without knowing of what one was accused, the prisoner in the Bastille is a victim of "that perpetual agony that eternalizes the pains of death."[59] His minute and insistent description of the smallest details of life in prison, continuing for pages on end, had the effect of closing the reader in the immobility, the silence that reigned in the Bastille. Linguet was right: never before had there been such a precise picture of the life of someone struck down by a lettre de cachet. All the acts that led to this horrible isolation were carried out in the name of the king. "By signing an order of imprisonment, you think you are only carrying out a legitimate act of your authority," he concluded addressing the sovereign. The king did not even trouble himself to know what happened in the Bastille. This was the same prince who had recently abolished torture and the "question" for those already condemned. "You are far from suspecting that in your kingdom, in your capital, under your very eyes, exists a place devoted particularly to exercising over innocence a question a thousand times more cruel than all the preliminary questions you have forbidden, since they broke only the body, while that of the Bastille tears at the body only to penetrate more effectively into the soul." Now, after the publication of the *Mémoires*, it would no longer be possible to close one's eyes to such an "infernal regime." "You will no longer ignore it. The veil is torn. . . . Give to Europe and the world the spectacle of a miracle that you are worthy of working. Speak: at your voice we will see the walls of this modern Jericho fall down, a thousand times more worthily than for the ancients with lightning from heaven anathema to men."[60]

With this appeal Linguet contributed much to making the Bastille the symbol of absolutism. He asked Louis XVI, by tearing it down, to demonstrate the capacity of the monarchy to return to the route of reforms. It was a decisive moment. France had emerged victorious from the war of American liberty. Would it be capable of eliminating, at the very heart of Paris, the most visible instrument of an archaic judicial and political tyranny? The silence that answered Linguet's appeal was the equivalent of a confession of impotence. The destruction of the Bastille would later coincide with the fall of the old regime. Diderot in his writings had wanted to resurrect Brutus. Linguet, after the most strange

[58] Ibid., pp. 50ff.
[59] Ibid., p. 55.
[60] Ibid., pp. 103ff.

circumlocutions, and taking the most unexpected route, ended up supporting the takers of the Bastille.

In the spring of 1783 publication of the *Annales* resumed. "In a notice to subscribers this celebrated author offers to the public," one read in the gazette of Venice, "some observations on the resumption of his work, and also on the distribution of the same." His mind, he said, had not changed. But now he held different political opinions, particularly about liberty. "The Bastille is an excellent telescope for admiring England and its laws." The British constitution was "incontestably the most perfect," precisely because it guaranteed "personal liberty." "I had been too struck by some defects that seemed to me to obscure it. But I have tested by experience that there is nothing comparable to a secret letter" (that is, a lettre de cachet). [61] As much the engraving as the text of Linguet's *Mémoires* struck the editor of the journal of the Venetian bookseller Graziosi, who returned to it twice in March, while remaining an alert distributor of the *Annales*.[62] On the first page, under the heading of the issue of 12 April, was a large advertisement for this periodical, to which one could subscribe "for two gigliati a year" for twenty-four numbers, "each of four pages." There followed a long list of subscribing booksellers in Milan, Pavia, Lodi, Cremonza, Piacenza, Mantova, Florence (Buonaiuti), Venice (Graziosi himself), Bergamo, Vicenza, Padova, Palma, Udine, Treviso, Salò, Modena, Trento, Roveredo, Rome, Bologna, Ferrara. One could receive the *Annales* not from booksellers, but through the post, in Trieste, Naples, Turin, Genova, Ravenna, Ancona, Rimini, Pesaro, "and in some other places in Italy and beyond. . . ."[63] This was a capillary penetration, as one sees, with Venice at its heart.

In Florence, meanwhile, the publication of the Italian version resumed; it attempted to keep abreast of the original.[64] The most diverse problems accumulated in the pages of these two last volumes of the *Annales*, numbers 14 and 15. At the center was the worsening of the crisis in Holland, hard pressed by the war with England, menaced by the intervention of Joseph II, and insufficiently supported by France. In 1782 Geneva provided the example of an unfortunate attempt at internal renewal of republican forms and principles. Now the United Provinces

---

[61] *Notizie del mondo [V.]*, no. 13, 12 February 1783 (London, 24 January).

[62] Ibid., no. 25, 26 March 1783 (Paris, 12 March), and no. 26, 29 March (Paris, 14 March).

[63] Ibid., no. 31, 12 April 1783, and no. 38, 10 May 1783, in the footer.

[64] *Notizie del mondo*, no. 15, 22 February 1783, p. 120, in the footer; no. 33, 26 April 1783, p. 268, in the footer; no. 40, 20 May 1783, p. 324, "Avvisi" (Ranieri Del Vivo had finished vol. 13 and was now publishing what came from London), and no. 81, 11 October 1783, p. 652, in the footer ("the delay does not depend on the editor, but on the author, from whom is awaited the continuation so as to put the missing sheets in order").

started out on the road that carried it also, in 1787, to the collapse of its own effort at revolutionary regeneration. Linguet did not have much new to offer on these subjects, partly because he was closely tied, at least for a certain period, to the policy of Joseph II.[65] But his vision, which was broad and panoramic, as well as agitated and stormy, continued, even if to a lesser degree than earlier, to attract the attention of many during the years that followed his imprisonment.

The fall of Necker, the exile of Raynal, and the imprisonment of Linguet opened the years of the eighties and set the tone for an age that presented itself to men of open minds as anxious and difficult. It was an age punctuated by the deaths of those who had created the age of light: on 2 August 1780 Condillac died; on 20 March 1781 Turgot; on 18 July 1782 the Abbé Coyer; on 29 October 1783 d'Alembert; on 31 July 1784 Diderot; on 23 April 1785 Mably; on 15 April 1789 Buffon; on 21 January 1789 d'Holbach; while the death of Victor Riqueti de Mirabeau, one of the two who, with Quesnay, had lighted the great tower of physiocracy, was announced in Paris the day of the taking of the Bastille, on 14 July 1789. These death knells made even deeper the solitude left by the deaths of Voltaire and Rousseau in 1778. Already on 15 June 1781 one read in the *Courier de l'Europe*: "Voltaire, Rousseau, and the Abbé de Condillac being dead, our literature has begun its decline." Some of the reforms being carried out at that time, like the abolition of the "preliminary question," showed that the impulse promoted by these writers had not ceased. This statement still did not fail to arouse bitter thoughts. The new decrees "seemed to be the fruit of the writings of philosophers who have demanded such laws for forty years." But how could one not add: "They were insulted while living, there was an attempt to silence them, and their advice was followed after their deaths."[1] Some years later an anonymous article in a Paris daily made such sorrowful considerations into a kind of apologia. "Four lamps," it read on 27 April 1788, "suspended in the Temple of Genius, in the bosom of France, enlightened the universe." With Montesquieu men began to distinguish "the false spirit of legislation from its true spirit." After him, they could still live amid "bad institutions," but they were no longer deceived. With his death this lamp was extinguished. Then arose "a brilliant and consoling day, pouring out all gradations of light like

---

[65] His views made the round of the chanceries. Thus we find the "Réflexions du sieur Linguet touchant la Hollande," in Turin, AS, *Materie politiche in genere*, mazzo 62, 1779.

[1] *Courier de l'Europe*, no. 48, 15 June 1788, p. 379.

the sun, penetrating all objects and making them more beautiful," giving man "a deep feeling of humanity." "With Voltaire this lamp was extinguished." Rousseau then carried "the sacred enthusiasm for virtue," capable of destroying "the barbarous prejudices that make slaves and tyrants." With him even this lamp was extinguished. Buffon, "like God, who collected in the small space of the arc all the works of his creation," had collected "on the temperate banks of the Seine animals, vegetables, and minerals . . . in all forms, all colors, all qualities." Now "nature in mourning laments in silence. With Buffon, the last lamp was extinguished." "What remains to us?" he concluded. "The feeling of our losses, and despair of recovering them."[2]

The new fires lighted during the eighties lacked the humanity, enthusiasm, and universality of Montesquieu, Voltaire, Rousseau, and Buffon. Disquieting was often the light they diffused, troubled the reflection they met in French society. We have seen this in the case of Linguet, but we must say the same and worse for the new generation of writers who were taking the place of the philosophes while these disappeared. In speaking of them, it is difficult to resist the temptation not to use terms that would be coined by other, later, revolutions: "enragés," "nihilists." (One of them, for that matter, Mercier, invented the closest precedent to this last term: "rieniste.") The violence of polemics was substituted for the will to reform, as the Florentine *Gazzetta universale* noted when it reviewed one of the first and most typical products of these young men, *The Chains of Slavery* (the work of an anonymous author), which we know was a product of the pen of Marat. "It is a political declamation against government or rather against those who control it . . . a book full of grand views, but perhaps developing them—rather than seeking the happiness that is sought in all societies—would only reawaken dissension."[3] The *Essai sur le despotisme*, one of the first works by Honoré-Gabriel de Mirabeau, is a particularly inflated and rhetorical work, where it is not easy to discern the vigorous political passion that was nonetheless developing in the mind of the author. When France found itself on the side of the American insurgents, liberal views and diplomatic necessities sought an uncomfortable compromise. We have seen this in speaking of Raynal, who also had Diderot as a collaborator. Other efforts, which were also of notable importance in the diffusion throughout Europe of new debates that emerged from the revolution of the United States, ended up at a lower level. Nothing could be more

---

[2] *Journal de Paris*, no. 118, 27 April 1788, p. 522.

[3] *Gazzetta universale*, no. 69, 27 August 1774, "Notizie letterarie," p. 551. See Luciano Guerci, "Marat prima della rivoluzione: Le catene della schiavitù," *R. stor. ital.*, year 91, fasc. 2–3 (August 1979): 434ff.

equivocal than the *Courier de l'Europe*, edited in French in London, which counted chiefly on circulation in the kingdom of Louis XVI. The old regime permitted a degree of latitude that is not easy to imagine in our century. The war between France and England interrupted neither commercial traffic nor intellectual relations between the two countries. The temptation to transform the *Courier de l'Europe* into a center of espionage was too great for the French government to disallow the journal. On the other hand the possibility of making news that was little pleasing to Versailles known beyond the Channel was too obvious for it not to be utilized by the English. The result was a chaotic system of permissions and prohibitions, a broad distribution in Holland and other places, and more important, a true mirror of free British politics offered, more or less directly, to anyone who wanted to know about it. Friends and enemies of England could know, better than before, what a free country was. But, above all at the beginning of the war, there was little in this sheet that could help to understand the nexus at the bottom of the alliance created between the French monarchy and the American republic. Typical was a long poem of Gudin de la Brenellerie, dedicated to his friend "M. de Beaumarchais." As long as it was a question of denouncing the tyranny that the English had extended over all seas and all continents, and of showing France in the role of a liberator ("The world awaits deliverance from her alone"), the letter proceeded in a straightforward way. But the historical precedents evoked were less obvious:

> Quand jadis de Nassau l'audace politique
> brisa le joug du pape et le joug monarchique,
> il invoqua nos rois, il en fut ecouté
> la Hollande à la France a du sa liberté.

Nor did the historical function of France limit itself to breaking monarchical yokes; it also broke aristocratic oppression, creating liberty everywhere.

> Craignant ses propres chefs et la race autrichienne
> Gênes plus d'une fois, Gênes nous dut la sienne.

This policy led to strange consequences:

> La France est le soutien des peuples opprimés
> et souvent sert d'asyle aux rois détronés.[4]

---

[4] "When once the audacious politics of Nassau / broke the papal and monarchical yoke, / it invoked our kings, it was heard / Holland owed its liberty to France." "Fearing its own leaders and the Austrian race / Genova more than once, Genova owed its [liberty] to us." "France is the support of oppressed peoples / and often provides asylum for de-

These contradictions were not to be resolved by singing a hymn to the tune of "God Save the King" and invoking

> Louis
> le gardien de la liberté.[5]

Thus not from Paris, but rather from Geneva and Holland, came the most passionate responses to the tensions concealed within French politics.[6] The best-considered words came, when peace was near, from England itself, and from the mouth of one of the chief experts on economic and political problems of these years, Josiah Tucker. When one of the numerous and lively Florentine periodicals of the time, the *Novelle letterarie*, received the book he had written on this subject it judged it "full of intelligence and true, reasonable, and deep politics." And it was right. Tucker took up again the line of Turgot, which in polemic with Necker had not wanted war, and at the same time put France on guard against ideas that came from America.[7] "I will not speak as an Englishman, but as a citizen of the world."[8] The victory of the Americans brought revolutionary ideas to the top. "Do you really want the destructive principles leading men to equality to serve as a rule for the politics of France?" Republican political forms had triumphed. "A mania for republics is now the style."[9] Everywhere there was a passage from a need for reforms to demands for rights. There was nothing worse than "giving men lessons in revolution and then punishing them if they revolt. . . . Statesmen should recollect that there are critical crises, even in the most despotic countries, when the government has to give in to the cries of a furious populace."[10]

Turgot, with whom Tucker had been in contact while he was in power, had rightly attempted essential reforms. "It was a beautiful dream, an unreal phantom, as he himself said later in a letter. And as a reward for having wanted to do such eminent service to his country, he

---

throned kings" (*Courier de l'Europe*, no. 33, 23 October 1778, Mélanges, p. 263, "Épître à mon ami M. de Beaumarchais").

[5] "Louis / the guardian of liberty" (*Courier de Bas-Rhin*, no. 23, 18 September 1778, p. 182).

[6] *Novelle letterarie*, 13 March 1783, p. 207, London. On Tucker see chap. 2.

[7] *Cui bono? ou Examen des avantages que les plus grandes victoires, ou les succès les plus complets, dans la guerre actuelle, pourroient procurer aux Anglois, aux Américains, aux François, aux Espagnols ou aux Hollandois, en forme de lettre à monsieur Necker, ci-devant directeur général des finances de France*, par J. Tucker, doyen de Glocester (Rotterdam: Bennet et Hacke, 1782), p. 18.

[8] Ibid., p. 1.

[9] Ibid., pp. 16ff.

[10] Ibid., p. 19.

was scuttled."[11] Now France found itself confronted with what Price and the same Turgot had called "the first example of a great people with neither king nor nobility."[12] The Americans were accomplishing their revolutionary experience (in danger, he said "of the tyranny of a hundred vultures"). But the great hope they had lighted, that of "being governed in the mode of Locke," in a "republic based on equality and liberty," would not go out.[13] "Cui bono?" Who would it benefit?

The author of a *Histoire de la guerre d'Amérique* sought to understand the deeper causes of this mirage. The work, it seems, was never published, but the *Courier de l'Europe* spoke of it at length. What was happening beyond the ocean seemed important to the author first because it corresponded to a transformation taking place everywhere: political problems were giving way to economic ones. America was, above all, an "emerging nation," but it was not savage or primitive. Its historians were not poets; at its roots was "an enlightened age, when the arts and sciences were cultivated before the land was cleared, where spirits are elevated without morals being corrupted, where bodies are hardened without hearts becoming vicious . . . , a people such as Lycurgus would have wanted to see in Sparta." By striving to act and fight the Americans had spontaneously stated that "the time of their minority had passed."[14] These were important observations: the primitivism that accompanied the first crisis of the old regime and had made one look with new eyes at the Corsicans, at the Danes of the Edda, at the Scots of Ossian, and at the Greeks of Maina had now passed. At the height of civilization, at the culmination of the development of sciences and arts, a "new nation" had now appeared. The tutelage of the past and of authority was collapsing. It was precisely at this moment that Kant defined *enlightenment* as the departure of humanity from adolescence.

But this did not happen in Paris, which, at the beginning of 1783, received the great news of the end of the war and the definitive independence of the Americans. Concern and anxiety rather than a sense of liberation were foremost in all minds. In America itself, as we have seen, difficulties of all kinds heaped up before the young republic. In France there was a resumption of partial, insufficient, and retarded attempts at

[11] Ibid., p. 42.
[12] Ibid., p. 76.
[13] Ibid., p. 78.
[14] *Courier de l'Europe*, no. 34, 26 April 1782, p. 272, "Prospectus de l'Histoire de la guerre d'Amérique."

reform, made more necessary by the debts the long war left. A diffused sense of political impotence, accompanied, as happens, by a growing lack of confidence in politics itself, was at the center of the climate of these years. But the rage, the protests that resulted from this and increased, did not strike directly at laws, institutions, or the basic structure of the old regime. The American Revolution was admired, but there was no serious attempt to imitate it. It seemed too far away, and even too beautiful and pure, for a country oppressed by a sense of its own corruption. What was attacked was the culture inherited from the generation that was disappearing, that enlightenment which had become entrenched in the academies, in the publishing houses, in the lodges, clubs, and journals and which now seemed weak and fragile because it lived on its own, without being protected by the government, which continued to mistrust the heirs of the Encyclopedists, or by the parlements, traditional enemies of light, or, naturally, by the Church. The philosophes continued to be isolated, even if they seemed to have many instruments of affirmation and propaganda in their own hands, even if kings and emperors placed themselves in contact with them and even asked, as Joseph II had done, why the most famous among them were not academicians. The intrigue of talent among the powers of the old regime still continued after a half century, since the time when it had permitted the young Diderot to go ahead with the *Encyclopédie*. This was an extraordinarily complicated game, which often took the form of intrigue and maneuver precisely because there was no autonomous institution capable of effectively defending intellectuals and scientists. The modern university was not yet born. Museums, hospitals, observatories, and libraries were important centers (how could one think of Buffon without remembering the Jardin des Plantes?), but these were continually evolving and were open not only to new ideas, but also to the most varied political and social influences (the work of Necker and his wife is only one example, even if a very significant one). This was but an apparent fragility (the Enlightenment, despite concern, was far from being extinguished), which suggested the line of attack of Linguet and induced many others to follow in his footsteps to state that physics, chemistry, and medicine were controlled by an intellectual establishment.[1]

It was not in the area of political ideas that the confrontation at the beginning of the eighties occurred, but rather in the academic, techni-

---

[1] The broadest, richest picture is found in Charles Coulson Gillispie, *Science and Polity in France at the End of the Old Regime* (Princeton, N.J.: Princeton University Press, 1980). A long discussion of these problems is in *The Ferment of Knowledge: Studies in the Historiography of Eighteenth-Century Science*, ed. George Sebastian Rousseau and Roy Porter (Cambridge: Cambridge University Press, 1980).

cal, and scientific one. Famous was the case of the German healer Mesmer, the inventor of animal magnetism and creator of the Société de l'harmonie universelle. The gist of his propaganda—which had a large echo in all of Europe—can be summarized as follows: get men like Franklin or Lafayette and many other important persons to discuss, defend, or combat the virtues of a universal fluid that simply did not exist. It did not lead, as Robert Darnton, the recent researcher of this curious phenomenon has said, to the "end of the Enlightenment" (which would have taken more than this), but it certainly revealed how much effort and time not a few true scientists had to waste defending themselves from inventors of theories as vague as they were insubstantial, and how such fantasies succeeded in persuading, or at least impressing, men whose rational defenses we might have thought much more solid (the example of Lafayette is particularly characteristic in this regard).[2] Lesser disasters were produced by other "philosophe-prophets," such as Jean Luis Carra and Jean Paul Marat.[3] The presentation, in the *Courier de l'Europe*, of the *Nouveau principes de physique* by Carra, reveals the extent to which a hearing was given to such "absurdities" and "dreams of an imbecile," according to the denomination they were ultimately given in the columns of this gazette by the noted scholar "De La Lande, of the Academie des Sciences."[4] Even Carra pretended to have discovered the "universal agent to which God had given the property of changing matter in any way and producing all the marvels of nature." After having thus explained the whole universe Carra ended up with a "history of man in his moral development."[5] The eulogies of this work some months later in the same journal became dithyrambic. "It is one of the works of genius of the age that make known in an instant the sphere of our knowledge." It was "a work adapted to effect a marked revolution in physics and astronomy . . . the style is very pure and correct."[6] And for some time still one heard talk of Carra's experiments with "electrical magnetism."[7]

These scientific fantasies were accompanied and followed by political and philosophical prophecies. It seems that already in 1773 Carra had published in London a work entitled *Système de la raison ou le prophète philosophe*, which, however, I have not been able to find. He republished

[2] See Robert Darnton, *Mesmerism and the End of the Enlightenment in France* (Cambridge, Mass.: Harvard University Press, 1968).

[3] The term "prophète philosophe" was used by the first; it appears already in 1773. See n. 8.

[4] *Courier de l'Europe*, no. 11, 7 February 1783, p. 87 (Paris, 17 January 1783).

[5] Ibid., no. 31, 16 October 1781, p. 242.

[6] Ibid., no. 29, 9 April 1782, p. 228.

[7] *Journal de Paris*, no. 132, 11 May 1784, p. 572.

it at the beginning of the eighties in Bouillon and a decade later, in 1791, in Paris, to demonstrate how much he was "ready and prepared for the revolution of 1789."[8] In a certain sense he was right: through strange fantasies his passionate will to transform enlightenment into a force, a political reality, emerged in these pages. At the end of his work he found a symbol for his unstoppable energy. Like many other writers of the age he let himself be seduced by the fashion for studies in physiognomy and threw himself into constructing a whole theory about the significance of the forehead in the interpretation of man. "I have always examined men's foreheads, I have judged the form of that part of the body in relation to status and education, and I am never deceived either as to capacity or to virtue." The most beautiful foreheads he had ever seen were those of the "three or four chief philosophers of this century." One of them had seemed to him worthy of wearing "the crown of the four continents, if reason and equity weighed into the scales of society." "The one with the most beautiful forehead, if he accepted the scepter of nations, would keep it only long enough to make sensible laws, to establish a good social order, to confound fools and evildoers, and finally to establish on earth the reign of peace, truth, and goodness. The name of this great man is Diderot."[9] In this philosophe, sovereign of the world, Carra saw the incarnation of an aspiration that he knew he could never entirely satisfy. It was a deep-seated imbalance that expressed itself sometimes as a provocation directed against the great and powerful because they were persecuting and crushing him. More than once he demonstrated that he was organically unable to accept reason and philosophy. "I throw this bone at the most tyrannical of tyrants; let him pick at it or complain, let him send out spies, let him send out hangmen, I am ready . . . posterity will know both of us."[10] Around him, even the best writers, such as the author of the "fine book" the *Théorie des loix civiles*, Linguet himself, had bent to write "the most impudent paradoxes favorable to despotism," thus demonstrating that they were "well paid and well sold."[11] This was the general rule. "Once ensconced in their sophisms, the shameful and proud latch on, one might say, to fashions, words, and the civil laws." Misery, oppression, awareness of injustice, led slowly and obliquely to revolt. Still, this philosophe-prophet looked to men of the future: "They have arms: let them use them to cultivate a piece of their own land; let them use them to purge that same land of

---

[8] *Système de la raison ou le prophète philosophe*. Par M. Carra. Imprimé a Londres pour la première foix en 1773. Troisième edition (Paris: Buisson, 1791), "Avis de l'éditeur," n.p.

[9] Ibid., p. 65 n. 32.

[10] Ibid., "A mon livre," p. xvi.

[11] Ibid., pp. 76ff. n. 40.

the monsters that devour it. What do they risk? Death. Ah well! it is better to die than to serve as trophies for men stupefied by pride and steeped in vice, who make a game of the lives of their fellow men and want absolutely to destroy the seeds of right reason, the only real good of man, the only way he can become wise and contented."[12] Even here, as one sees, academic confrontations, scientific fantasy, and political revolt created a strange and suggestive mixture. We encounter Carra a few years later in eastern Europe, observing the problems of the Ottoman Empire, and then will see him, as is known, in the events of the French Revolution.

This was a trajectory not dissimilar to that of Marat. Even here one is struck above all by the echo that responded to his activity: "Already so celebrated in learned Europe," we read in 1781, "he flies from discovery to discovery with an astonishing rapidity." His discoveries in optics had made a "strong impression," it is said, on physicists who had remained faithful "with a too blind faith to the prophecies of Newton." Marat had attacked "this idol of the day" and had defied "those who are most committed to his cult."[13] The next year it was written that "M. Marat, to whom physics already has such numerous and great obligations, has just changed the face of electricity, as he changed the face of optics."[14] The *Nuovo giornale enciclopedico* of Vicenza, to cite an Italian example, spoke in 1782 of the "learned applications" of Marat in electricity. "Ordering all known phenomena under a restricted number of causes, he brings the science of electricity to the level of even the least learned readers."[15] Even in Marat the desire to vulgarize science found its outlet in a universal law, capable of revealing the whole universe.[16]

His social vision was equally rigid. His *Plan de législation criminelle*, prepared for a competition advertised by the Academy of Berne but published later in the *Bibliothèque philosophique du législateur* by Brissot, strongly reflects the discussion of penal legislation begun by Beccaria and then intensely pursued throughout Europe; but at the bottom of his reasoning was a conception that was particularly his own. Marat was convinced that he lived in a society without social mobility, where the poor were condemned to be so, where there were no escape routes, and even less hope for change. Marat felt this social fixity was a moral evil, like a sin, like an incitement, a compulsion to corruption and degradation. The laws are no other than the reflection of a society where "a part

---

[12] Ibid., pp. 8off.
[13] *Courier de l'Europe*, no. 33, 23 October 1781, p. 259.
[14] Ibid., no. 22, 15 March 1782, p. 170.
[15] *Nuovo giornale enciclopedico*, November 1782, p. 30.
[16] See Gillispie, *Science and Polity*, pp. 290ff.

of the nation counts for nothing."[17] Obeying them is a matter more of prudence than of duty. The "social order" in reality is a relationship between slaves and masters. "Cast your eyes on the different peoples of the earth; what do you see besides vile slaves and imperious masters?"[18] "We are born masters or slaves, in opulence or in misery, in elevation or in obscurity. Despite the changeability of human affairs, only a very small number of individuals ever leave the rank they were placed in by birth, and they never leave it except through intrigue, baseness, cunning, or happy accident."[19] If we think of the life of Marat—like that of Carra, Brissot, and many others—and take these words as a confession, we feel how much the society in which they lived pressed down on their shoulders. Men had renounced, he said, "the primitive community of goods of the earth to make their fatherland their property." The result was the misery of the masses. Society had abandoned them, making them fall back into the state of nature and thus authorizing them "to reconquer, with arms in their hands, the rights that they could not have alienated except to ensure for themselves better advantages. All authority set up against them is tyrannical, and the judge who condemns them to death is a miserable assassin."[20] As one sees, Marat made rigid, violent, and general ideas that had fermented in Rousseau and in Beccaria. But yet again there was no escape from the gloomy society in which he lived. He declared that he did not want to justify theft or "open the door to anarchy."[21] Revolt was just as impossible as reform. Brissot, commenting on these pages, spoke of Marat's "penchant for republican ideas."[22] There was undoubtedly British influence in his work, but behind all the incitements to a freer life he was dominated by an inexorable sense of oppression, a longing for justice that could not find articulate expression.

The confrontation between the tradition of the *Encyclopédie* and contenders like Marat and Carra occurred at first on a scientific and technical level. For political ideas, the trial by fire came after 1789. The contrast between their physical and chemical fantasies, and the firm and decisive steps being taken in science precisely at this time, could not help

---

[17] "Plan de législation en matière criminelle," in *Bibliothèque philosophique du législateur*, vol. 5, p. 121. On the *Bibliothèque* see below, pp. 431ff.

[18] Ibid., p. 118.

[19] Ibid., p. 120.

[20] Ibid., pp. 123ff.

[21] Ibid., p. 149.

[22] Ibid., p. 167 n. 1.

but strike contemporaries. It is enough to think of the experiments of
Lavoisier, "that truly transcendent genius," as the Florentine *Notizie del
mondo* called him. "He is the first to appear in the sanctuary of the Academy with a scale in hand to weigh phlogiston"; he who, perfecting the
system of the English Priestley, began again to "find an inflammable gas
better than the one of vitriolic acid mixed with iron filings. . . . The
progress of his work is slow, but there are certain results: this valiant
man gives to science a new glory and utility."[1] From the discoveries of
Lavoisier there was in fact no turning back. Apparently more uncertain,
but certainly even more impressive, was the parallel conquest of the air.
How this came to Montgolfier has been told magisterially by Charles C.
Gillispie, who has let us follow step by step how the traditional paper
industry of the Montgolfier and Johannot families, one Catholic and the
other Protestant, in a small provincial town of France, Annonay,
through technical improvements, comparisons with Holland, bitter
struggles with the corporative mentality of the guilds, access to capital,
and an effort to attract the support of the estates of Languedoc, succeeded—a bit from publicity but more from irresistible scientific curiosity—in imagining, constructing, and launching the first balloons. The
history of their invention is almost an apologia for a successful reform
in the sunset of the old regime, because of the obstacles they encountered, but above all because of the enlightened will through which they
won their energetic and elegant victory. Science and technology, desire
for success and affirmation of virtue, met in this history, which was tied
at every step to individuals and problems deeply immersed in a reality
that was not at all imaginary or fanciful.[2] "Here there is talk of nothing
other than globes and flying spheres," the gazette of Lugano reported
from Paris on 29 September 1783. The government had thought it
proper to inform the public officially of the experiments, "so as to avoid
the surprise and terror they might create in the people."[3] In November,
just when one learned that d'Alembert was "at the last moment of life,"
confirmation arrived in Florence that the machine of Montgolfier and
Rozier "raises and lowers itself at will and without any risk to the people

[1] *Notizie del mondo*, no. 44, 2 June 1784 (Paris, 14 May). On Lavoisier, see Gillispie,
Science and Polity, in the index, and writings by Henry Guerlac, listed in Gillispie, p. 564.
[2] Gillispie, *Science and Polity*, p. 444, now taken up and completed in id., *The Montgolfier
Brothers and the Invention of Aviation, 1783–1784* (Princeton, NJ: Princeton University Press,
1983). On Italians who participated in international aeronautic life at its beginnings, see
the bibliography in the article "Andreani, Paolo," by Letizia Vergnano, DBI, vol. 2, p. 128.
There is an interesting letter of this individual to P. Frisi from Paris, 3 July 1784, in which
there is talk of Condorcet, and so on. Milan, B. Ambrosiana, Mss Y 153 Sup., f. 119.
[3] *Nuove di diverse corti e paesi*, no. 39, 29 September 1783, p. 301 (Paris, 19 September),
and no. 37, 15 September 1783, p. 283 (Paris, 5 September).

in it."[4] The minds of Parisians were nonetheless assaulted by still another novelty. "To the mania for flying spheres has been added a mania
for animal magnetism . . . , all run now . . . to see M. Mesmer, who with
a wave of the hand cures without the trouble of medicine, diet, blisters.
. . . There is no precedent for such a rapid and immense fortune as that
of M. Mesmer. . . . He, who knows the volatility of Parisian minds, is
already preparing to depart to bring health to other European cities."[5]
Of the two modes, that of Montgolfier soon prevailed. In October the
gazette of Florence announced that "the common feeling that aerostatic
balloons would endanger the system of Mesmer has been realized. Not
only has magnetism given way to balloon mania, not only has the sensible public left M. Mesmer in perfect repose, or rather oblivion," but
without further followers he was the object of public ridicule.[6] The
Montgolfiers continued their conquest not only of the heavens ("electric
clouds of a particular beauty, which are impossible to describe," found
by Blanchard over Holland in July 1785), but also of certain corners of
Europe that could be discovered only by approaching them from above
(descriptions of the welcome of certain peasants make one think of the
stories of contemporary navigators in the South Seas).[7] The balloons
constituted, as a recent scholar has written, a revealing element in the
formation of a new consciousness.[8]

The element common to Mesmer, Carra, Marat, and other similar
"philosophe-prophets," besides their opposition to academic knowledge,
which was destined to fall naturally without leaving a trace given the
fragility of their arguments, consisted, as we have seen, in a kind of
global vision of the universe and a pretense to have found the formula
that explained all phenomena. It was, in short, a religion of scientific

---

[4] *Notizie del mondo*, no. 91, 15 November 1783, p. 726 (Paris, 18 October).

[5] Ibid., no. 37, 8 May 1784, p. 323 (Paris, 20 April). See no. 39, 15 May 1784, p. 340
(Paris, 27 April): "Here is the discovery of the secret of animal magnetism . . . it is in
substance only an electric shock."

[6] Ibid., no. 84, 19 October 1784, p. 707 (Paris, 5 October). For Venice, see *Notizie del
mondo [V.]*, no. 36, 5 May 1784 (Paris, 23 April). There is another long piece on Mesmer
in no. 1, January 1785 (Paris, 17 December). A good picture of the intellectual atmosphere
in the last months of 1784 is in the letters of Paolo Frisi to Luigi Castiglioni (Milan,
B. Ambrosiana, Mss Y 153 Sup., f. 105 (Paris, 30 July 1784): "M. Mesmer, who here was
always regarded by men of letters as a charlatan, is now losing his reputation even among
his partisans" (f. 115, Paris, 23 September 1784 [animal magnetism and balloons] and f.
117, London, 28 October 1784, "Lunardi air voyager. . . . He earns a great deal").

[7] *Notizie del mondo*, no. 66, 16 August 1785, p. 525 (Ysselstein, 31 July), and *Journal de
Paris*, no. 209, 27 July 1784, pp. 891ff.

[8] Maurice Quinlan, "Balloons and the Awareness of the New Age," *Studies in Burke and
His Time* 14, no. 47 (Spring 1973): 221ff. (He takes into account the international atmosphere and mentions on pp. 224 and 227 the Italians Lunardi, Zambeccari, etc.)

appearance and mystifying content, capable of revealing the point of arrival to those who believed: the end of the long, difficult, and perilous terrain, which science instead had set out to cross step by step. It was an enlightened religion, which for its impatience, incapacity, and blindness rejected the very methodological core of the Enlightenment: the value of the search, which was always preferable, as Fontanelle had once said, to truth already found.

The effects of another religion, parallel to the scientific one, were more durable and important. It was born of the contemplation of the human experience as a whole, from the primitive world to the modern one, to use the terms of Court de Gébelin, the chief interpreter of it and in some sense its chief priest. The common element of the two religions, scientific and historical, was revealed symbolically on the day when, in June 1784, a notice in a journal announced that "M. Court de Gébelin, author of the *Monde primitif*, director of the museum in Rue Dauphine, and an ardent apologist for animal magnetism, died in the night of the 12th and 13th in the arms of the magnetizing doctor at the very moment when he intended to cure him through magnetization."[9] He was at that time considered almost a new Rousseau: the Comte d'Albon requested that a mausoleum be constructed for him "as Marquis Girardin did to the memory of Jean Jacques." To this Louis XVI responded that he should rather pay the debts of this man of letters who had died in the arms of Mesmer.[10] In the lodge of the Nine Sisters, under the presidency of Lalande, "M. the Marquis de Marnésia" read a "eulogy in prose" dedicated to him in March 1785, and the "Chevalier de Cubières" presented one in verse.[11] Volume 8 of his work indicated, from the title, the amplitude of problems he had wished to embrace: *Monde primitif, analysé et comparé avec le monde moderne, considéré dans divers objets concernant l'histoire, le blason, les monnoies, les jeux, les voyages des Phéniciens autour du monde, les langues américaines etc.* Despite the extraordinary scope of his research, the nucleus of his thought, without being solid, was nevertheless simple and clear. At the origins of humanity had been not a state of nature similar to that of barbarous and savage populations, but a primitive state where man was in direct contact with nature through words, images, and agricultural labor. At that time "words were indistinct from reason"; common to all was "the basic grammar that governs all languages"; symbols and allegories revealed the "sacred reposi-

9 *Notizie del mondo*, no. 45, 5 June 1784, p. 388 (Paris, 18 May). The gazette of Venice, *Notizie del mondo [V.]*, no. 44, 2 June 1784 (Paris, 14 May), called Court de Gébelin a "heated apologist for animal magnetism."

10 *Notizie del mondo [V]*, no. 52, 30 June 1784 (Paris, 18 June).

11 *Journal de Paris*, no. 71, 12 March 1785, p. 292.

tory of the spirit and wisdom of the first men."[12] An "eternal unchange-able religion" coincided with an order that was both eternal and unchangeable, "which united the sky with the moon, body and soul, metaphysics and moral life, men and societies, empires, generations."[13]

History is thus "the torch of nations"; however, the point was not to seek out its vicissitudes, or to study its events, but "to compare these events with an eternal and unchangeable law."[14] The study of words, of etymologies, of grammatical structures, was substituted for the study of facts. The history of humanity, not that of men, was his ideal: "The annals of the universe rather than those of isolated nations. This will not be the history of a certain people or a certain century, which is of little account and only an amusement in idleness; it will be the history of all peoples, of all centuries, because one will return to the principles of history itself."[15]

The political consequences of such a vision were clear as well. Court de Gébelin wanted a return to a primitive world charged with emotions, but without any social content. He did not appeal to the egalitarianism of Rousseau and Mably, and not even to the security of Linguet. His search for origins was allegorical, poetic, religious; at most he evoked the harmony of the rural world, the patriarchal relations of humanity at its origins. His restoration of primitive order ended in Masonic cere-monies, in neoclassical taste, in a promise of palingenesis, not in reform-ing action. The essay we have cited to this point, the "Vue générale du monde primitif," concluded in fact with a kind of prophecy: "The time is not long, already one sees the dawn break, already the friends of or-der make their voices heard, already Europe begins to set aside carnage, quarrels, disputes. . . ."[16]

These ideas were taken up again and developed by his chief pupil, Rabaut de Saint-Etienne, one of the most intelligent interpreters of re-ligious needs in the eighties, as he later became one of the most lucid and courageous defenders of liberty in the years of the revolution, to the point of paying with his life for his opposition to the Jacobins. Prot-estant like Court de Gébelin, he was also educated in close contact with the world of Switzerland and northern Europe. He felt, like his master, a stranger in a land deprived of toleration and also decided to recon-

---

[12] *Monde primitif analysé et comparé avec le monde moderne . . . par M. Court de Gébelin* (Paris: Chez l'auteur, 1773–1782), vol. 8, pp. xiii, xv.

[13] Ibid., pp. xviiiff.

[14] Ibid., p. xvi.

[15] Ibid., p. lviii.

[16] Ibid., p. lxix. An analysis of the diffusion of the *Monde primitif* is in Daniel Roche, *Le siècle des lumières en province. Académies et académiciens provinciaux, 1680–1789* (Paris and The Hague: Mouton, 1978), vol. 1, pp. 293, 318.

quer a fatherland by writing and preaching.[17] He found in Court de Gébelin "the Oedipus who gives us the word for all of antiquity," but he attempted to verify with a "philosophical spirit" and to deepen historically what he had read in the *Monde primitif* about fables, language, and society of the "first ages."[18] Origins exercised a great fascination on him as well, as on all of these philosophers of history at the end of the eighteenth century (it is enough to think of Herder), but he remained firm in his departure point, anchored in that "century of philosophy" which had demonstrated itself capable of rediscovering, of reliving, even the most distant and diverse human realities.[19] Noteworthy was his effort to understand "primitive men" and their nature as "robust infants," interesting was his appeal to Bacon against Rousseau, and not without significance was his desire to return to the facts, expressed sometimes in curious metaphors of a positivistic tone, like the one that defined chronology as "the thermometer of history."[20] With agriculture these reevocations and visions touched ground even for him: "What civilized humans was the beneficent soil."[21]

In this affirmation physiocracy and the religion of the primitive world seemed to come together. Frequent in fact were the points of contact between the idea of a natural order in both, above all in the years following the death of Quesnay. Turgot, Dupont, and others continued to speak of economics. But, close to them, above all among the followers and admirers of Victor Riqueti de Mirabeau, was born a kind of religion of the social order, which had numerous points of contact with other parallel contemporary scientific and historical currents. It is enough to read the eulogy of Quesnay by Romance de Mesnon, published in 1775, to see physiocratic ideas coalesce into a totally comprehensive vision, ca-

[17] "Fatherland that did not know me, where I was always a stranger, where I had at least many excellent friends, could you, sensitive to the word of order, continue forever, and filled with glory, truth, light, serve as a model to the whole universe and create only creatures who are happy," Court de Gébelin had written (*Monde primitif*, vol. 8, p. lxviii). It is difficult to find a more typical modern example of the messianism that is born from exclusion and marginalization. Rabaut wrote *Le vieux cévénol, ou anecdotes de la vie d'Ambroise Borely, mort à Londres âgé de 103 ans 7 mois et 4 jours*, to describe what it was like to be deprived of all rights, like Protestants in France.

[18] "Lettre sur la vie et les écrits de M. Court de Gébelin adresseée au Musée de Paris," in *Oeuvres de Rabaut-Saint Etienne*, précédées d'une notice de sa vie par M. Collin de Plancy (Paris: Laisné, 1826), vol. 2, pp. 384, 365.

[19] Jean Paul Rabaut de Saint-Etienne, *Lettres à monsieur Bailly sur l'histoire primitive de la Grèce* (Paris: Laisné, 1787), p. 301. Here is also the page where he describes the "interior emotion" of "he who, in the vast deserts of Siberia and far from all human habitation, sees the traces of cities and proof of an ancient population."

[20] Ibid., pp. 58, 68.

[21] Ibid., p. 341.

pable of furnishing a certainty that went beyond any demonstration or proof. Quesnay, even more than formulating economic laws, had "enunciated the true laws of nature buried under the heap of human systems and contradictions."[22] Rightly Heraclitus had said: "There is a common and divine universal law, from which all the others have proceeded." "The science of economics is the development of this truth. . . ."[23] Property is not only an indispensable instrument of associative life, it is "the *reason* for all positive laws and the *cause* of all the groupings of men."[24] A new Socrates, Quesnay had revealed "its shape exactly."[25]

As for Riqueti de Mirabeau, "the friend of men, could he not have had some liking for the author of the *Monde primitif?*" It was Court de Gébelin himself who posed this rhetorical question.[26] Nor could he not appreciate one of the last works of Mirabeau, *Les devoirs*, which was published in 1780 in Milan and edited by the Abate Longo. In fact, he inserted a long summary of it into one of his volumes.[27] This "analysis" was anything but lacking in interest, if only from a terminological point of view, rich as it was in words that were then beginning to seek out a political and social meaning destined to increase in the following decades ("notable," "notabilité," "juste-milieu"). But it is above all the religious turn of these pages that makes them historically significant. The religion of proprietors: "Those of the productive class above all, who have great holdings on the earth and under the sky, suspended always between fear and hope, have absolute need of a master and a belief that provides them support from on high. If one takes from them their form of religion, that religion which counsels modesty to success and consoles adversity, they would soon fall back on worse or better principles; the lazy would follow their passions, the philosophers their metaphysics." As for the traditional cult, "it is the only fraternal act remaining among the members of a developed and rich society, distinguished by its ranks and fortunes."[28] These pages can be put beside those of Necker on the importance of religious opinions. Men of the seventies and the eighties, as we see, were not deluded about the gravity of the problems and traditions that tended to block their hope of renewal. And, varying with

---

[22] Romance de Mesnon, *Eloge de François Quesnay* (London and Paris: Didot, 1775), p. 43.

[23] Ibid., p. 49.

[24] Ibid., p. 63.

[25] Ibid., p. 91.

[26] *Monde primitif*, vol. 8, p. ix.

[27] Ibid., p. 569.

[28] Ibid., pp. 578ff. On the late works of Mirabeau, in particular *Les devoirs*, see Georges Weulersse, *La physiocratie sous les ministères de Turgot et de Necker*, pp. 310ff.

situations and persons, they fell back on an enlightened conservatism or launched themselves toward palingenetic dreams and hopes.

Two men, among a crowd of many others, lived out the rebellions and aspirations of the eighties with particular intensity: Brissot and Mirabeau. For both of them *philosophie* tended increasingly to become force and political action. From a young lawyer and journalist, provincial and backward, the first became one of the most influential publicists of Europe, and the second, from a libertine and rebel, became a tribune of the people.[1] The cost of their transformation was high for both. Humiliations and defeats were not spared them; nor were compromises and blows. Filled with obstacles, exhausting, was their path among journals and editors, authorities, and the police, in a France that seemed immured in an impossible conservatism and in an England that had hardly emerged from the crisis of 1780, in an America that was victorious, but far away and different, and in a Europe where reform movements were taking new and unexpected forms. Nevertheless, for neither one nor the other was the initial impulse that moved them lost. In their many pages was a revolutionary reply to the aspirations and contradictions of the last crisis of the old regime.

Brissot himself said, in a kind of self-portrait, that he was "made to be more a philosopher than a politician." But how could one be a philosopher amid so many contradictions? "He wanted to liberate philosophy from the yoke of despotism, he sought the means, and he thought he would find them in politics and became a politician." "If only liberty establishes itself, Phedor [the name of the personage he selected] will return to be what he should be, a philosopher."[2] This was a moment that never arrived: new obstacles continually came between him and philosophy; his whole life was a vain search for a sufficiently solid liberty for him to return to himself.[3] He was taken up with the life of a journalist: he wrote in haste hoping one day to find a more appropriate and lasting form for his thought. When Diderot died in 1784, the *Journal de Paris* noted that this had also been the fate of the great Encyclopedist.[4] Brissot ended up by persuading himself that he had taken the right

---

[1] See Guy Chaussinand-Nogaret, *Mirabeau* (Paris: Seuil, 1982).

[2] *Mémoires de Brissot . . . publiés par son fils* (Brussels: Louis Hauman, 1830), vol. 1, p. 49.

[3] The study by Eloise Ellery is still useful: *Brissot de Warville: A Study in the History of the French Revolution* (New York: Burt Franklin, 1970; reprinted from the original, which appeared in 1915).

[4] *Journal de Paris*, no. 237, 24 August 1784, p. 1008.

road, and he fought against the prejudice "that makes the useful and important profession of gazetteer mistrusted." "They are the best friends of a free people, its first teachers." In the end he considered himself one of those "*gazetiers philosophes*" made to be "priests, mission-aries, angels sent from heaven for the happiness of men."[5] This was a mission to which modern historians have not given credence. George Lefebvre spoke of his "wandering life as a paid newsman" (as if the jour-nalist, and for that matter even the professor of the Sorbonne, did not of course receive a wage).[6] For Robert Darnton, among the many sins of Brissot, those committed through his contact with London journal-ism, which was still the freest in Europe, have not been forgotten.[7] But still, it is difficult to deny that Brissot tried truly to be a "*gazetier philo-sophe*" and to bring the ideas, torments, and doubts of the late Enlight-enment to European journalism. The transition to political activity passed, even for him, through the task of editing journals.[8]

With a kind of open ingenuousness, in which we recognize his whole self, he wanted to begin his work by confronting the most general prob-lems, addressing the question of truth itself. "I sought to see whether anything true, certain, perfect, existed in this century where all ap-peared to be true, positive, perfect."[9] He proposed to his readers not a general system, but "meditations founded entirely on analysis."[10] The results of his analysis ended with a general statement of the illusions of the century. The shadows and errors had not disappeared, the truth remained veiled, and it was not true that one now lived "in the midst of light." Many facts previously unknown had been accumulated, but causes remained unknown. "Man is always the plaything of errors; they rock him from leading strings until his hair turns white."[11] Schools

---

[5] *Mémoires*, vol. 1, p. 260.

[6] George Lefebvre, *La révolution française* (Paris: PUF, 1951), p. 226.

[7] Robert Darnton, "The Grub Street Style of Revolution: J.-P. Brissot, Police Spy," *Journal of Modern History* 40, no. 3 (September 1968): 301ff. The very use of the term "Grub Street" to indicate the Parisian literary proletariat in the eighties seems inappro-priate; there was a notable difference between French and English publicists in these years. See the article, in many ways penetrating and acute, by the same Darnton, "The High Enlightenment and the Low-Life of Literature in Pre-Revolutionary France," in *Studies in Eighteenth Century Culture*, vol. 3, ed. Harold E. Pagliaro (Cleveland: The Press of Case Western Reserve University, 1973), pp. 83ff.

[8] Brissot himself has given us a picture of London journalistic life as he saw and judged it in his *Journal du Licée de Londres ou Tableau de l'état présent des sciences et des arts en Angleterre* 1, no. 1 (January 1784): 3ff.

[9] *Mémoires*, vol. 2, p. 72.

[10] *Courier de l'Europe*, no. 11, 7 February 1783, p. 87.

[11] *De la vérité ou Méditations sur les moyens de parvenir à la vérité dans toutes les connoissances*

served only to twist brains. Academies and scientists aroused secret envy
more than incitements to follow the ways they indicated. Youths abandoned their senses to encyclopedic and disordered reading. They were
motivated by a desire for glory and riches. It was time for them, as for
the author, to return to themselves and to self-dedication, "to the well-
being of my fellow men," Brissot concluded, "in which I believed little,
but enough to continue in my work." In the general uncertainty a single
point remained firm: "The good of humanity: that is the unique sign
with which to distinguish true from false science; that is the mark of the
divine author. Scholars who do not work for this are in my eyes only
infants."[12] It was thus necessary to throw oneself "into the study of morality and politics."[13] The problem of "criminal legislation" was central,
a meeting point between the desire for truth and the decision to dedi-
cate oneself to the good of humanity.[14] How could one not react to seeing "a despot crush his subjects, prisons overflow with the unfortunate
. . . , fields deserted, scaffolds"? There was a spontaneous desire to imitate the old man of the mountain, to form "young disciples, to familiar-
ize them with the idea of death, to send them through the earth like
avenging angels to strike down the guilty and ensure the triumph of the
just." "Sometimes I would like to be the divinity himself, or his representative," so as to put to torment "bad kings, the intolerant, proud magistrates." But in reality "I have only my voice and my pen, I speak and
write against abuses and against oppression."[15] The temptation to put
himself at the head of the judiciary was strong, as was the dream of
being politically omnipotent. But what remained of these visions was a
pen, the daily work of a journalist.

A little before these philosophical confessions, the first juridical work
of Brissot, his *Théorie des loix criminelles*, appeared. The motto was taken
from an English poet, Thompson, and was an appeal to patience and
wisdom:

> O great design! if executed well
> with patient care and wisdom temper'd zeal.

But the passions of Brissot continued to boil even in this effort to "apply
philosophy to jurisprudence."[16] He had to walk a long and tortuous

---

humaines, par J. P. Brissot de Warville (Neuchâtel: Société typographique; Paris: Desauges
et Belin; Lyon: Grabit et Rosset, 1782), pp. 4ff.

[12] Ibid., p. 7.

[13] Ibid., p. 8.

[14] Ibid., p. 9.

[15] Ibid., p. 19.

[16] *Théorie des loix criminelles*, par J. P. Brissot de Warville (Neuchâtel and Paris: Desauges, 1781), vol. 1, p. 1. As Robert Darnton, the best scholar of the book trade in eigh-

road to reach his conclusions. From the circles of young lawyers, to which he belonged and where he encountered many friends and enemies, among them Robespierre, he arrived at his more or less open rebellion against the world of the courts. It was difficult for him to get off his back the weight of his social origin, son as he was of an innkeeper in a small town of the provinces. Later he could say with pride that he came from the "class in society" from which came Theophrastus, Horace, Virgil, Massillon, Diderot, Franklin, and the two Rousseaus. But meanwhile he had to enclose himself, once he reached Paris, within the small sclerotic world of the law, the center of the bastion that for decades had impeded all reform in France. Escaping from it meant fatally, he discovered, falling into the torpid world of editorial and journalistic undertakings. What drew him out of this uncertainty was the light he was discovering in Voltaire, Rousseau, d'Alembert, but it was above all the example of a man, a famous lawyer, rebellious and persecuted, who alone was capable of breaking through the satisfied complacency of legal tradition. He looked to this man when he found himself, about 1777, alone, isolated in his ardent passion for truth, "an implacable enemy of despotism, but unhappy, seeking support, a friend, assistance." As a "young neophyte" of enlightenment, he saw in this man an example of successful rebellion.[17] "M. Linguet was at the highest point of his glory when I gave myself over to the study of criminal legislation. His example inflamed me . . . I resolved to imitate him." To express openly "the philosophic fever, the burst of independence, that turns all thinking heads at the age of twenty" he learned from Linguet not to pause before great names and models of past generations, but to express his own revolt and open a passage through the stagnant world in which he felt he was suffocating.[18] The limits, the defects of Linguet, were evident. "He was a man of letters without being a man of science." Although he was a "lawyer superior to others," that "sublime philosophy" without which

teenth-century France, writes, Desauges was "a Parisian book dealer who specialized in prohibited works." Robert Darnton, "Trade in Taboo: The Life of a Clandestine Book Dealer in Prerevolutionary France," in *The Widening Circle: Essays on the Circulation of Literature in Eighteenth-Century Europe*, ed. Paul J. Korshin (Philadelphia: University of Pennsylvania Press, 1976), p. 41.

[17] *Mémoires*, vol. 1, pp. 63, 216, 218.

[18] J.-P. Brissot de Warville, "De la Décadence du barreau françois, des inconvéniens de l'ordre des avocats, de la manière de les rendre utiles au public, surtout dans les matières criminelles," in *Bibliothèque philosophique du législateur, du politique, du jurisconsulte ou Choix des meilleurs discours, dissertations, essais, fragmens, composéssur la législation criminelle par les plus celèbres écrivains, en françois, anglois, italien, allemand, espagnol etc. pour parvenir à la réforme des loix pénales dans tous les pays, traduits et accompagnés de notes et d'observations historiques, par J. P. Brissot de Warville, auteur de la Théorie des loix criminelles* (Berlin and Paris: Desauge, 1782), vol. 6, pp. 344ff.

it was impossible to "animate, enliven, or immortalize works about legislation" was lacking in him.[19] Brissot debated such contradictions at
length, forcing himself to be realistic but then abandoning himself again
to his dream of being a reformer. When Linguet fought so energetically
against judges and lawyers that he was driven out of the profession, he
saw a model in him: "His radiance, when devoted to liberty, saved his
reputation and talent . . . from that moment he returned to himself, he
was himself." He admired, in the *Annales*, the "fine audacity" Linguet
showed in revealing abuses in the laws.[20] Like many others, Brissot as
well, after the arrest of Linguet, was convinced that he would never
leave the Bastille: "I had no doubt that his death sentence was pronounced irrevocably." How could he not continue in his admiration? "I
was young, I liked the double career he had followed gloriously from
the time I knew him." Only after his resurrection did he allow himself
to criticize him, even for some statements in the famous *Mémoires sur la
Bastille*.[21] Many years passed before Brissot arrived at a balanced judgment about a person as fleeting as Linguet: "One cannot deny the
warmth of his style, his brilliant images, his talent for sarcasm. He
served liberty without knowing it by attacking the tyranny of magistrates
and academicians in an opinionated way. . . . But he has to be criticized
for prostituting his talent to panegyrics of despotism, for defending the
most iniquitous causes and revolting paradoxes, for his satire of respectable writers. Linguet wanted to erect altars and make them from the
ruins of statues of great men who were worth more than he."[22]

Brissot was too enthusiastic, and too provincial and ingenuous, to
follow Linguet and other critics of the Encyclopedists and physiocrats
along the road of iconoclasm against the great men of the Enlightenment. "I would, to be sure, like to submit to criticism some of the unworthy supporters of that cause; I would like to chaff at their egoism
and arrogance and denounce their despotism, . . . but I would regret
attacking the philosophes as a group whatever might be the errors of
many of them; I would blush particularly at allying myself with an enemy of Jean Jacques Rousseau."[23]

Arriving in Paris when France was in mourning for Louis XV, and
leaving it to go to London when the whole capital was celebrating the
return of Voltaire, Brissot received as a precious talisman a note of en-

---

[19] Ibid., pp. 370, 374.
[20] "Fragmens sur les loix criminelles tirés des Annales politiques et civiles de M. Linguet," in *Bibliothèque philosophique*, vol. 9, pp. 75ff.
[21] Ibid., pp. 70ff.
[22] *Mémoires*, vol. 3, p. 16ff.
[23] Ibid., vol. 1, p. 162.

couragement that the philosophe wrote to him urging him to struggle for reform in penal legislation. A thin but strong thread tied him to the period before 1778. He looked to Franklin, who was also in those days the center of Parisians' attention. "He had broad and deep knowledge, but he wanted it to be useful above all to the people." The aim of this "true philosopher" was to diffuse culture and lower the price of books.[24]

Even in the varied and tempestuous life that awaited him in London (for instance, as collaborator in that *Courier de l'Europe* "that one finds from Paris to St. Petersburg"),[25] Brissot continued to collect the most diverse threads of thought, knotting them around the great theme of crimes and punishments. He wanted nothing to be lost from the task of the century. He emphasized not contradictions and internal differences but the trend, the general movement, that put side by side men and ideas different in everything except a common will to reform. Boulanger, whom he much admired, thus came to find himself next to Court de Gébelin. Helvétius, Rousseau, and Raynal were there to show that the truth was revealed not by academies, but by individual energy and thought.[26] When he confronted the problem of penal law, he made use of everything, expanding his view to France, England, Italy, Spain, and other European nations. He retraced themes of physiocracy in speaking of Le Trosne, referred to Servan and La Chalotais, young parlementaires of the seventies, and reopened discussion with Montesquieu. But soon his *Théorie des loix criminelles* no longer seemed to him a sufficiently big picture. He planned a history of penal jurisprudence, and beginning in 1782 brought out in ten volumes a *Bibliothèque philosophique* to collect and annotate the texts that most struck him. It was a journalistic inquiry, with many gaps and much ignorance, that is often revealing of the obstacles that impeded the circulation of ideas in a Europe that was theoretically cosmopolitan, but still often bounded by limits of experience, situation, and local language. He moved, like many of his contemporaries, from the delusion of the failed reforms of the seventies, from an awareness that Turgot had not succeeded even when he asked for partial and limited changes, such as the abolition of the corvées or the revision of the laws against smuggling. Avoiding instinctively the compromises of the years of Necker, Brissot still said he was convinced that there was no other response to the defeats of the recent past than a return to the sources of the will to reform, to Montesquieu, Helvétius, Linguet, Blackstone, Beccaria, in his tentative list. The encouragement to resume the task did not come from France, but from what was hap-

[24] Ibid., p. 252.
[25] Ibid., vol. 2, p. 27.
[26] *De la vérité*, p. 178. On Boulanger see p. 216.

pening "in several great states of Europe," through the work of a
"young sovereign," Joseph II, as well as in Russia, Prussia, Sweden, and
Tuscany, where a "revolution in all the codes of law" was being accomplished.[27] In these lands the impetus *philosophie* gave had revived. "To
what does one owe this happy initiation of reforms? To improved
knowledge of political morality, that sublime science without which
there is no true philosophy, no enlightened lawgiver, no equitable magistrate."[28] This was a deep faith in enlightenment that contrasted with
the skepticism of the passing generation. "Perhaps the present generation will not believe me, will not read me, but the generation growing
up in silence that will replace it, youth, that precious part of humanity,"
would welcome and adopt "some of my ideas" and "realize them one
day."[29]

This reformist tendency was all the more meritorious given the profoundly pessimistic vision Brissot had of the society in which he expected to act. The "human species" seemed to him prone to "complete
degradation."[30] "The "social burden" weighed "entirely on the poor."
Not the rich, but rather the poor paid taxes, suffered the severity of the
laws, were called to defend their country in militias. "The rich have
made themselves exempt and the poor are forced to give their families,
of which they are the sole support, over to misery. They go far off to
fight people they do not know, who have never offended them." The
hunting rights of lords prevented the poor even from scavenging in the
wild. If prices rose, the poor were the victims, since "the rich did not
increase wages."[31] Everything seemed to demonstrate that society and
its laws were nothing but a "conspiracy of the strongest against the
weakest, of the rich against the poor, of authority against humanity."[32]
Should one thus reverse all the different forms of oppression? Should
one cut the central knot, the very idea of property? The temptation was
strong, all the more so because one was dealing with a right that had its
basis in the needs of all beings, animals, plants, and men. The only le-
gitimation of property in the state of nature was use.[33] Should one thus
follow the example of Lycurgus? The only way to "pull up the roots of
crime," he had said, was to abolish property itself. Thus, to "prevent

[27] *Théorie des loix criminelles*, vol. 1, pp. viff. "Everyone seems to announce a coming
revolution in the criminal legislation of all of Europe" (ibid., p. 6 n. 4).

[28] Ibid., p. xiii.

[29] Ibid., p. xvii.

[30] Ibid., p. vii.

[31] Ibid., p. xivn.

[32] Ibid., p. 3.

[33] *Recherches philosophiques sur le droit de propriété considéré dans la nature, pour servir de
premier chapitre à la Théorie des loix de M. Linguet, par un jeune philosophe* (n.p., 1780).

adultery he put all wives in common, to make Spartans heroes he enslaved them to his harsh legislation, finally, to put an end to the sad effects of the passions, he permitted only those for the public good."[34] This was a dialectic of reversal about which Brissot reflected at length. The conclusion, however, was negative: it was impossible to follow the example of Lycurgus. Equality could exist only among hunting or agricultural peoples, not in commercial lands. Sparta itself ended in corruption, showing the instability in its system. Not institutions, but customs could and should be changed. But a deep uncertainty remained at the bottom of this emerging desire for radical reforms, a continuing regret at not having cut the social knot earlier, a doubt about the utility of the difficult task of remaking laws when one was unsure that one could repair the total degeneration of society in this way.

The writings of Brissot are a singularly clear mirror of these doubts and uncertainties. Is it truly possible, he asked himself, to improve customs? He answered in the affirmative, asking, to begin with, that "the good customs of the virtuous beings inhabiting the countryside" not be corrupted. The people of the provinces and countryside must be preserved from any contact with the modern world of cities. Nor did this doubt seem to fade when, while in this mode of tepid conservatism, he ended up by concluding: "Good peasants, get drunk, but never drink coffee," or when he suggested the institution of "pesthouses where the inhabitants of the cities are forced to purify themselves before going into the countryside." Far from that "abyss of horrors" of the capital, the peasants would be able to maintain their vigor by celebrating their "simple festivals." Sumptuary laws, useless in cities, would be "excellent in the countryside."[35]

At the opposite pole of this exasperated Rousseauism was Brissot's growing admiration for the English world in which he came to find himself. There he found those republican seeds that developed in the following years. He could admire Joseph II and Peter Leopold, but at the center of his political experience always remained the liberty he found beyond the English Channel. He followed the London riots against Catholics in 1780 with passion and was surprised at this violent denial of harmonious and enlightened progress, evidence of the "crisis" in which Great Britain found itself. But his faith in England was not basically shaken, and he continued to emphasize the merits of British legislation even where it did not much merit his praise, especially penal legislation.[36] America was not central to his attention, even if he published

---

[34] *Théorie des loix criminelles*, p. 44.
[35] Ibid., pp. 50, 52ff.
[36] Ibid., p. 292.

the constitution of Pennsylvania in his *Bibliothèque philosophique* and promised, without later doing so, to make known those of the other United States. His interest in the New World came later, in the second half of the eighties. At first Brissot presented himself as a defender of the state and society of England, breaking on this fundamental point with Linguet, tying himself to Bentham, admiring the great inquiry on prisons of Howard, and observing their administration closely.³⁷ His interests, in this as in other similar areas, were always more social than political: even in England he looked at penal legislation above all as a means through which to penetrate the most obscure recesses of the social world, like an instrument that made "an exact anatomy of the most hidden parts of society."³⁸

Italy, as we have seen, came immediately after France and England in the list of countries indicated by Brissot in the frontispiece of his *Bibliothèque philosophique*. Beccaria, to whom the volume that initiated this collection was dedicated, had opened to him not only a new way of looking at society, but a nation, with all its diversity and promise. As for others among his contemporaries, it was a great surprise to see a book like *Dei delitti e delle pene* come from a place like Italy, a land that naturally evoked an image of political and religious oppression. In the text of Beccaria he seemed to find traces of the surroundings in which he was born. "One might desire more order in the plan of this work, more clarity in certain chapters, more daring in others. It seems that the author, by enveloping himself within an algebraic calculus, has wanted to disarm the criticisms of his too-clairvoyant enemies, or to speak only to sages."³⁹ Slowly and reluctantly Brissot rejected the malevolent legend Linguet invented to explain the presence of a work like Beccaria's in the world of Italy.⁴⁰ He had to give in to the evidence: the philosophical spirit of Voltaire and Montesquieu had penetrated Italy and had given life to "such a daring and luminous work that one is surprised to see it emerge from a land where the Inquisition still reigns."⁴¹ This was all the

---

³⁷ Ibid., vol. 2, pp. 166, 182 n. 87, 183, 190. See also *The Correspondence of Jeremy Bentham*, vol. 3 (January 1781–October 1788), ed. Ian R. Christie (London: Athlone Press, 1971), in the index.

³⁸ *Bibliothèque philosophique*, vol. 1, p. xi.

³⁹ *Théorie des loix civiles*, vol. 1, p. 9.

⁴⁰ "This anecdote has no support besides the weak testimony of an informer so vile that he will not tell his name" (*Bibliothèque philosophique*, vol. 1, p. 5 n. 1).

⁴¹ Ibid., p. xiii. A little later he wrote that Beccaria had been "the first to open eyes to the abuse of penal laws" (ibid., p. 12), and he added that "M. Beccaria is too modest; I know of no country where one had dared to write earlier than he in defense of men exposed to false principles and the atrocity of the courts." In England nothing of the kind had been written, even though the practice of the courts in that country was better (ibid., p. 63 n. 1). He ended by saying: "I am distressed that one copies Beccaria so frequently

more so because it was not difficult to see that in Italy Beccaria had a large following, arousing discussions and polemics that Brissot utilized and resumed. Through Beccaria names like those of Paolo Risi (whom he obstinately called Rizzi), Gherardo d'Arco, Filippo Maria Renazzi, Tommaso Natale di Monte Rosato (whom he always called simply Monterosate), Francesco Albergati Capacelli (whom he called Caparelli), Francescantonio Pescatore, Massimiliano Murena, Giacinto Dragonetti (although with many errors in reporting the titles of his books), and Paolo Vergani are not only cited by him but discussed. Almost like a meeting of two excavators in the same field was his discovery of Carlantonio Pilati, about whom he knew little, but whom he much admired for his criticisms of Roman law and for what he found written in his *Traité des loix civiles*.[42] Against French legists such as Muyart, Brissot took up a rigorous defense of Beccaria, whom he accepted in all his central points, from what he said about torture and the death penalty to his affirmation of asylum and confiscation. Nor, Brissot knew well, were these only theoretical discussions: these ideas had planted solid roots at least in some parts of Italy. Tuscany especially appeared to him as a model, to which he did not cease to return. In the *Théorie des loix criminelles* he proclaimed that Peter Leopold "had given commerce its liberty, industry its rights; he suppressed monopolies and dangerous controls, reestablished, as much as possible, equality among citizens, turned his attention to public education . . . his firmness restrained the excesses of underlings." He forced himself always "to remove the source of crimes rather than to punish them." This resulted in a reduction in the number of crimes, "and perhaps they will disappear entirely when the body of the state is purified." It was an example for everyone. "Doubtless, the same operation carried out everywhere would produce the same revolution. Let government thus take up the philosophic spirit that has raised Tuscany from its ruins."[43] The grand duchy became the reformist pole of a political vision that did not exclude a complete transformation of society and the laws, but he knew this was very difficult. To those preferring "a more imperceptible reform" Brissot answered: "I also would prefer an imperceptible reform, but to tell the truth, a radical and thoroughgoing policy is more assured in its effects and perhaps also

without giving him credit. It is a consolation to philosophy that some write for the good of being cited" (ibid., vol. 3, p. 105 n. ii).

[42] See *Bibliothèque philosophique*, vol. 10 (1785), in the index. For Pilati see also vol. 8, pp. 50ff., where his *Voyages* is cited without Brissot's knowing he was the author.

[43] *Théorie des loix criminelles*, vol. 1, p. 97. See also vol. 2, p. 244 n. 261. Significant in vol. 1, p. 83 n. 32, is the citation in the *Gazzetta fiorentina* of 5 June 1779 of a theft that had occurred in Grappoli. On the abolition of imprisonment for debt, see *Bibliothèque philosophique*, vol. 9, p. 204.

more practical." One could still content oneself with an envious glance at lands where this seemed immediately possible: "A thousand times happy America, where that reform could be executed from the bottom, and in all its parts!"[44] In Europe, the stimulus continued to come from Tuscany, from the Empire (when Joseph II replaced Maria Theresa), from Russia (despite the criticism that Brissot directed, as we will see, at the *Nakaz* of the empress), from the Prussia of Frederick II (seen by him, at first, with singular indulgence), from the Sweden of Gustavus III, and so on.

This was a European vision in which Brissot, along with Italy, tried to include even Spain. Through a Castilian version of the *Courier de l'Europe* he hoped to contribute to remedying the "deep ignorance about the English situation" that he knew prevailed on the Iberian Peninsula.[45] Spain and Portugal were "even less advanced than Italy," even if they seemed to be taking some steps forward, beginning with an "awareness of their ills."[46] Spain, he said at the end of 1782, "is an exhausted country; one cannot cultivate it without mixing in more fertile soil, foreign soil." He thus proposed opening the peninsula to modern ideas, spreading there theses from the logic of Condillac and urging it to participate in the great debates of modern science: on electricity, for example, counterposing "to Nollet, Franklin; to Franklin, Marat; to Marat, Priestley or Volta."[47] The lack of close communication of Spain with more enlightened lands seemed to him to explain the reaction apparent beyond the Pyrenees. "The persecution of the unhappy Olavides, and his unjust and ridiculous condemnation, demonstrates that the Spanish are falling back into the thick darkness from which their commerce with France might have drawn them out. Spain not only regards Hume and Voltaire with horror, it solemnly burns them, and the hand, the fatal hand of the inquisitors, dares to raise itself against the altar dedicated to genius."[48] When confronted with apologies for torture that arrived from Spain, like the one of Pedro de Castro, he could only exclaim: "Should Spain not blush in producing Castros when Italy, which is said to be buried in superstititon, has produced Beccaria and Rizzi?"[49] Some hope was rekindled in his soul on reading the *Correo literario de la Europa* of January 1782 and the proposals for reform it contained.[50] But, on

---

[44] *Bibliothèque philosophique*, vol. 3, p. 23. He spoke of a "general reform" that was indispensable and possible in America (p. 240).

[45] *Mémoires*, vol. 2, p. 43.

[46] *Bibliothèque philosophique*, vol. 8, p. 52.

[47] *Courier de l'Europe*, no. 48, 13 December 1782, p. 382.

[48] *Théorie des loix criminelles*, vol. 1, p. 70.

[49] *Bibliothèque philosophique*, vol. 4, p. 182.

[50] Ibid., vol. 9, p. 302.

the whole, Spain remained for Brissot above all an example of the difficulties and obstacles that the Enlightenment continued to encounter everywhere.

The Genevan revolt of 1782 brought him, as we will see, new hopes and new delusions. It prompted him to reflect on the very value of republican tradition, on the organization and activity of the people, on the spirit of sacrifice. It put him in contact with Genevan exiles, inducing him to question the moderation of Mallet Du Pan, who was guilty of having taken up again and developed the "despotic" elements in the thought of Linguet. The ultimate conclusions he drew from this experience were apparently paradoxical and in reality voluntaristic: if Geneva had been defeated it was because of writers who had not been able to defend it with sufficient energy and vigor. "Who lost Geneva? Its writers. Except for one or two, none of them bears reading; no one has read them. Who made Geneva interesting? Rousseau, through the magic of his style."[51] In the difficult battle of enlightenment, everything could be done with words and the forms through which they were propagated. Intellectuals had the highest responsibility.

In the last period of the *Courier de l'Europe*, Brissot expected to start a journal, published first in Neuchâtel and then in London by the same bookseller Cox who published the gazette in which he was also a collaborator in Hamburg. It was called at first *Correspondance universelle, ou ce qui intéresse le bonheur de l'homme et de la société*. The second issue lost the adjective "universal," which it resumed in the third. Twelve issues, it seems, came out between December 1782 and November 1783, which were collected in two volumes with the dateline London and Neuchâtel, 1783. Its importation into France was immediately prohibited, there was little circulation, and the affair ended with a debt of 10,000 livres.[52] He had written in his *Théorie des loix criminelles* that the great difference between the modern age and the centuries of Alexander, Augustus, and the Medici consisted in the fact that these had not known how to be cosmopolitan, while now "what part of Europe does not participate in the general blessing of enlightenment"? "Philosophy makes its voice heard as far as the deserts of Siberia," while polar lands had seen "men of letters" amid their ice.[53] Now his *Correspondance* was to be a "table of the principal political and civil reforms accomplished in Europe," carrying "secret anecdotes on the administration of European states." It

[51] Ibid., vol. 10, p. 225.

[52] J.-P. Brissot, *Correspondance et papiers*, publiés par Claude Perroud (Paris: Alphonse Picard, 1912), pp. xxv, xxix. I have been able to see only the three issues preserved in Paris in the B. Nationale, with the call number Lc².91.

[53] *Théorie des loix criminelles*, vol. 1, p. 61.

would occupy itself with new novels that had appeared, like *Les liaisons dangereuses*, and with a "witch condemned to the pillory." It would have spoken of Bentham, Raynal, Galiani, the great reforms of Joseph II, and England awaiting peace at the beginning of 1783. This was a lively chronicle in which Beccaria again made his appearance, as a model writer on reform. "Beccaria made himself read. . . . He spoke all at once of reason, humanity, algebra, in a matter where hangmen alone seemed to have set down the law."[54]

The relative lack of success of the *Correspondance universelle* contributed to persuading Brissot how important a more solid and broad organization was than the network of booksellers and distributors to which he had entrusted himself. In London there was an immense number of associations for the most diverse purposes and "for all ranks, under the name of *clubs, meetings*, and *associations*." "This liberty of association is perhaps the best rampart of the constitution; it is also the source of a multitude of works of hidden beneficence." In Paris as well had begun a ferment of assemblies composed generally of "men of letters" who had felt a need to organize themselves to "perfect the sciences." The "museum" created by Court de Gébelin, which Brissot naturally remembered, was a model, but it was enough to open the *Journal de Paris* to be aware that this was far from the only one. Even popular courses in sciences, in more or less improvised poetry, in languages (instruction in Italian was the most sought after, followed by English), multiplied.[55] Reading societies, which have been much discussed in recent decades, were only one aspect of this varied flourishing of cultural associations.

The Lyceum Brissot created in London would have had a cosmopolitan character.

In a salon devoted to this object and noted in the public papers, it is proposed to unite foreign scientists once a week with English men of letters and all artists

---

[54] *Correspondance universelle*, no. 3, vol. 1, pp. 138, 140.

[55] On the teaching of languages see, for example, the announcement of "M. Stella, professor of the Italian and Spanish language, encouraged by the applause he has received in the Salon de la Correspondance and the Musée de M. Pilatre de Rozier." "At the end of his presentation he will improvise in the Italian language on an air of Figaro and will read fifty octaves in Italian on an event in the recent war" (*Journal de Paris*, no. 127, 7 May 1785, p. 517). Other courses by the same Stella were announced in no. 133, 13 May 1785, p. 540. In the same daily was a report of a meeting of the Masonic lodge of the Nine Sisters (no. 71, 12 March 1785, p. 292); the announcement of a course in English and German (no. 197, 16 July 1785, p. 815); the news that Condorcet had accepted the post of professor of mathematics and would make the inaugural discourse of the lyceum (no. 51, 20 February 1786, p. 205). There was further talk about the Lyceum in no. 75, 16 March 1786, p. 301, and it was added: "In this moment when the taste for clubs is so general in Paris, there is a society composed only of distinguished foreigners, known by the name of Société des Adelphes. . . . All subjects, except for the sad fact of politics, are under our jurisdiction."

or amateurs who have an interest in the progress of the sciences and arts. This will be a club, a kind of literary stock exchange. New products of the arts will ornament its interior and conversation; the reading of foreign journals, declamations, an interesting speech, the reading of a new poem, a new experiment, will appear in the meetings from time to time. Perhaps lessons will be given there when arrangements are complete. Perhaps the example of the Paris Museum will be followed by having a public assembly each month, where one will be able to see foreign artists.

A periodical would reflect this multiple activity. "What the assembly will be for men of letters in England, the *Correspondance* will be for men of letters from foreign countries. They will be brought closer to one another."[56] This time the printing was done in France, "with *approbation et privilège du roi,*" and as points of distribution there was talk of London, Versailles, Boulogne-sur-mer, Calais, Hamburg, Mästricht, and Ostend. This was the Nordic world, with strong political passions and where interest in the multicolored nature of British society tended naturally to transform itself into a caricature, a "charade." Journalism showed itself in all its effectiveness, far from all academicism and even from any historical partiality. "Robertson and Gibbon would be incapable of editing a gazette."[57] England provided an example of what politics could mean in its spontaneous force and energy, and also in its limitations and restrictions. In politics, the English "do not hear enough about humanity in general; they limit themselves to their empire. . . . English politics is only the science of national egotism." In France a series of books on natural and human law, on "social law," and so on, was being published, but in England one saw nothing of its kind. It was enough to compare Locke and Rousseau to understand the difference. "Rousseau embraced all of humanity in his point of view. Locke saw only the English people." But how much heat concrete political discussions generated in Britain! "The American Revolution, which ended this year, has hatched an innumerable swarm of pamphlets and volumes." Brissot appealed as proof of the ever renewed vivacity of British political life to the tempestuous current of radical writers in England who accompanied the birth of the United States of America, Tom Paine, among others. "The virtue of mixed or republican governments," he concluded, "is in the conflict of passions, their force is in the struggle of parties, the state flourishes

[56] *Licée de Londres ou Assemblée et Correspondance établies à Londres pour la réunion et la communication des gens de lettres de tous les pays, avec le Journal, ou Tableau périodique de l'état actuel des sciences et des arts en Angleterre, dirigé par J. P. Brissot de Warville* (Paris: Valleyre, 1784), vol. 1, no. 1, pp. 4ff.

[57] *Journal du Licée de Londres ou Tableau de l'état présent des sciences et des arts en Angleterre,* par J. P. Brissot de Warville (Paris: Perisse; London: Walter and Elmsley), vol. 1, no. 1, January 1784, p. 9.

when they are in balance."[58] As he wrote in the prospectus of his journal, England owed its force to the "excellence of its constitution. The trunk is still firm, even if some branches are rotten. If political men are corrupted and degraded, civil men are still there; their title in the original contract of society is not torn out. In a word, the Englishman has a fatherland; he knows and feels it. That is what he has of grandeur and energy, what makes him intrepid in war, and what raises him in the sciences."[59]

In the brief months of publication of his journal Brissot dug, with extraordinary capacity, into English reality, without at all hiding its contradictions and perils, but always aware of the exceptional possibilities of development that were contained within it. But how can one explain the obstinate conservatism that accompanied much research and discussion in London? The London police were abysmal and there was no hope of improving them. In Parliament motions to reform civil and criminal legislation were defeated. The English continued to be convinced that it was "dangerous to innovate." The electoral laws remained what they were, reinforced by the doubt "Are we worth more than our fathers?" It was an argument born of ignorance, but irreversible. Palliatives and compromises remained without effect. It would be necessary to proceed more radically. The Duke of Richmond was right in his proposal of universal suffrage. "Each individual is an elector. This equality makes society closer to its primitive, natural state. His enemies think this is philosophic folly. They torture their souls with this word."[60] Radicalism had been defeated precisely through the growing deviation of ideas from social reality. It was stupefying to see how parliamentary debates were "at the same time full of politics and not very philosophical." Interest was rapidly turning from internal to external problems. Fox now spoke above all of India. But "had one examined to see if this bill would further or not the well-being of peoples submitted to English domination?" The political struggle absorbed all attention, to the detriment even of the scientific and technical curiosity that was much diffused throughout Europe. "In France all dream of balloons, in London all are occupied with India and the ministry. The Montgolfiers "in London are the Foxes and Pitts," and no less is written there about India and the ministry than in France about balloons."[61] It was still necessary to recognize that the discussion of political and civil liberty was not only lively

---

[58] *Tableau de l'état des sciences en Angleterre en 1783. Politique.* Ibid., pp. 23ff.

[59] *Licée de Londres ou Assemblée et Correspondance*, p. 1.

[60] *Tableau de l'état présent des sciences et des arts en Angleterre*, vol. 1, no. 4, April 1784, pp. 233ff.

[61] *Journal du Licée de Londres*, vol. 1, no. 2, February 1784, p. 99.

and important in London, but closely tied to daily political life. After Montesquieu and De Lolme, it was the turn of the English to restate fundamental questions. Priestley, who in France was known only for his studies of physics, had taken an important step, even if it was insufficient, in examining the relationship between civil society and government. David Williams then intervened, sustaining that "civil liberty ties the hands of citizens, prohibiting harm of citizens. Political liberty ties the hands of government, prohibiting harm of society." But while writers were thus moving in the direction of a liberal conception in which the state intervened less and less, and always negatively, the British government seemed to derive from similar ideas a greater and an uncontested liberty of political action. The internal crisis that had accompanied the American Revolution had been very serious, and now, assured of peace, every chance and hope of reform were liquidated. "The nation lampoons its ministers; it ridicules them in its caricatures, but no longer sends them to the scaffold. Behold the fate of the man who lost America. He quietly descended from the ministry and has risen to it again in triumph. Talk of ministerial responsibility after that! It is no more than a word with which to quiet big children." It made one think that Jean Jacques had been right in his critique of English liberty. English writers, even radicals like David Williams, still did not think that this evil was without hope of remedy. "He believes that by remembering ancient Saxon government one would be able to root out a part of the abuses that stain parliamentary elections."[62] The shadow of the gallows and myth of the Saxons at the root of the tradition of English republicanism appeared momentarily in the report of Brissot. The book by John Andrews, *An Essay on Republican Principles*, which was published in a second edition by Richardson in London in 1784, offered him a good opportunity to take up this historical and political comparison again. "It is to combat the spirit of republicanism that Mr. A. devotes himself to this work: he traces its origins and finds them in the reign of Charles I." These times were now too distant: the cruel evils brought on by the revolution had little by little been forgotten. Now "the republican system" was again developing, despite the fact that the government of George III could hardly be called despotic. "The American war has resurrected all the arguments that were supported in the time of the republican Parliament at the point of the sword, and it must be confessed that the government has given them free reign." During the same conflict, "there was a crowd of English on the side of America who had big hopes for its triumph and success." Thus there was a moment when "philosophy rose above patriotism and love of humanity above personal inter-

[62] Ibid., vol. 1, no. 5, May 1784, pp. 320ff.

est," Brissot commented. With the victory of the American Revolution "the hopes of these English philosophers were fulfilled." Now, after the victory, they did not have enough strength for an internal battle. It was indispensable, as Andrews had done, to return to the origins, asking himself what had prevented the Long Parliament and men like Hampden, Pym, and Prynne from winning. The republican system had not been responsible, but rather the situation in which they found themselves, born as they were "too early for their century, a century that did not follow their giant steps: they had to deal with fanatics, and such an astonishing revolution should be the work of calm and reflection, and the broadest enlightenment." Precisely for this reason the debate in England about that period of English history was disquieting. The republican Mrs. Macaulay naturally received his sympathies, while he criticized what Hume had written. But new circumstances had arisen in the discussion. The work of John Andrews had to be considered "by those who occupy themselves with this important subject; they will find new considerations on ancient and modern republics that merit discussion."[63] Ferguson and Gibbon also could not help but attract his attention.[64] The discussion of the origins and history of Christianity seemed to him particularly important. "Everything focuses today," he wrote in February 1784, "on the theological quarrels of Dr. Priestley and his adversaries. All respected men, all men of letters, know its smallest details." The distance between England and France, even in this area, remained great. The polemic on the "corruption of Christianity" by Priestley was a typical example. The English remained within the Christian world, truly sustained by ideas of Socinianism, Unitarianism, and so on. Gibbon, "the celebrated historian," was considered "one of the most dangerous unbelievers . . . for having tried to explain the miracle of the establishment of Christianity." But, with all the admiration one might have for him, if he was thought of as a disbeliever how could he be compared with Helvétius, Fréret, and Voltaire?[65] Otherwise the strangest modern superstitions also flourished in England, between Rosicrucians, Martinists, and the followers of Swedenborg. The only pos-

[63] Ibid., vol. 2, no. 3, September 1784, pp. 145ff. On Catherine Macaulay see also vol. 1, no. 1, January 1784, p. 32, and vol. 1, no. 5, p. 335 (departure of Mrs. Macaulay for Boston: "It is to be desired that the hand that traced the history of the Long Parliament and the promises of Cromwell might trace that of the astonishing revolution in America").

[64] Ibid., vol. 1, no. 1, January 1784, pp. 35ff.

[65] Ibid., no. 11, February 1784, pp. 71ff. Like Hume as well, Brissot would add later, even Gibbon showed himself tied to the crown. "A member of the last Parliament, he always voted for the ministry" (ibid., vol. 2, no. 3, September 1784, p. 161). It is curious to note that Brissot gave notice in vol. 2, no. 3, September 1784, pp. 187ff., of the Pisan translation of Gibbon and the criticism of Nicola Spedalieri, who took Gibbon to task ironically for the religious scruples of "ultramontanes."

sible remedy was to return to Condillac and learn from him "to believe nothing without evidence and without clear and coherent ideas."[66] It was necessary to remove all religious content from metaphysics, making it purely and simply "the science of ideas." Brissot, as one sees, in his discussion with the English, and not without reference to Berkeley, had thus arrived at the margin of what would soon be the thought of the *idéologues.*[67]

He concluded his comparison between France and England, writing: "Europe owes to France the light that brightens it." "In the politics of humanity the French have produced excellent works that have no rivals in England, works true for man in all countries, good for all meridians, consoling for all individuals, for the slave as for the free man. . . . The English have written for themselves alone. The French have written for the universe."[68] But it was enough to "glance at the political state of England from the month of January 1784 to the month of May" to feel oneself taken up again by the flux of British politics. The Irish rebellion was taking a turn reminiscent of the American Revolution. Even a bishop, of Derry, had put himself on the side of the volunteers. "A bishop at the head of a party preaching liberty. This is a new apparition!" In India the situation became more and more difficult. Great Britain, "too powerful, too rich, is gnawed by corruption: overgrown, her base will collapse." But even in this apparent ruin it was able to save itself. "More compact, she will dominate with her virtues." "Yes, as long as liberty reigns in her bosom, London will astonish the earth; her strength is not in her walls, her vessels, her arms, her colonies; it is in the liberty that makes her citizens so proud, which in its perfection attracts so many strangers to her breast, in the liberty that makes all spill their blood to defend it. Liberty, there, is the sole base on which one can sit to build the structure of an empire with solidity."[69]

At the height of all this enthusiasm Brissot met his own ruin. "At present there are many prisoners in the Bastille," we read in the gazette of Venice on 14 August 1784. "Their number has recently been increased by the author of an outspoken journal entitled the *Licée de Londres.*"[70] A Florentine sheet called it "a licentious journal."[71] The sale of this periodical had been forbidden in France, the publishing house

---

[66] Ibid., vol. 1, no. 2, February 1784, pp. 70ff.

[67] Ibid., p. 67. For his polemic against mystifying doctrines, see the violent attack against the book *Des erreurs et de la vérité*, which had claimed to "explain all the sciences with the most disagreeable and tedious nonsense." "Never has an orator been so unreasonable" (ibid., vol. 2, no. 2, August 1784, p. 70).

[68] Ibid., vol. 1, no. 6, June 1784, p. 358.

[69] Ibid., pp. 372ff.

[70] *Notizie del mondo [V.]*, no. 65, 14 August 1784 (Paris, 26 July).

[71] *Notizie del mondo*, no. 66, 17 August 1784, p. 55 (Paris, 3 August).

in Neuchâtel had not succeeded in selling it either for commercial reasons or because of censorship, and it was not able to sell the *Bibliothèque
philosophique* or the *Théorie des loix criminelles* either. Buried in debt, imprisoned for two months in the Bastille, Brissot collapsed under the
weight of his misfortunes. He seemed for a moment to give up the
dream that had sustained him for all these years, that is, to give political
power to *philosophie*. Did he agree to serve the Parisian police in some
way? This is possible, although not certain. From the beginning of his
career he had nurtured fewer illusions as to the possibility of remaining
unscathed in the world of the courts and of Parisian and London journals than the historian who has best and most deeply investigated these
crises in the life of Brissot, Robert Darnton.[72] He knew from nearby the
thousand compromises through which he had to operate in order to
survive and work. He succeeded, despite all, in expressing original and
significant ideas. It is on this that we must fix our attention to understand the reason, the link, tying the Brissot of the eighties to the protagonist of the revolutionary era. Even Darnton, like most other scholars,
including G. Lefebvre, has looked at the London years of Brissot as a
precedent, a prefiguring of his actions among the Girondists. For Marat,
as for Mirabeau, even Condorcet, and for Brissot the long years of publication before the revolution are generally seen only as a preparation
for the great drama that followed 1789. Following closely what Brissot
wrote shows how this preparation was particularly important precisely
in the world of ideas, in the passage between *philosophie* and *idéologie*, in
the contrasts between cosmopolitanism (especially French) and patriotism (especially English), between a propagandistic will and a scarcity of
instruments and means. Sometimes events in 1792 are prefigured. But
these can be understood better if the symptoms of crisis, from the Enlightenment to the fall of the old regime, are observed with their own
internal logic, forms of expression, and dramas. These can seem small
when set beside the ones that ended with the guillotine, but they certainly help us to understand better even those, provided that we follow
them step by step in their slow and intricate development.

The echo that responded in Italy to Brissot's ideas and writings helps
us to see their significance. It was a larger and more favorable echo than
one might expect. A periodical with the significant title *Lo spirito
dell'Europa letteraria e politica* reported the following at that time:
"Among the events that raise the sensitivity of virtuous souls one can

---

[72] Darnton, "The Grub Street Style of Revolution."

well count the arrest of M. Bris . . . de War . . . in the Bastille." "That
estimable citizen, whose crime is unknown," was clearly a victim of despotism.[1] The journals left by him were looked upon with great interest.
The most important Venetian journal of that time, the *Giornale letterario*,
which generally carried the title *Progressi dello spirito umano* and was published by the editor Graziosi, provided in the 16 December 1782 issue a
"Progetto" to begin a "Corrispondenza universale per benefizio universale dell'uomo e della società" in the following year. This would involve
"political rights" and "civil rights," beginning with the principle that "the
happiest nation is the one where all rights are arranged so as not to
impede the happiness of anyone." Locke, Montesquieu, and Rousseau
would be the guide and inspiration of the editors, who had the intention
of "spreading and propagating enlightenment throughout Europe." In
a note it was added: "One is assured that a similar communication has
already been attempted in Germany by an order that behind certain
ceremonies reveals a reputable aim, an order to which several princes,
and even sovereigns, have not disdained to subscribe. If the double object of their institution is beneficence and instruction, its members
should favor our project. This hope is all the more important because
another order in France, with some similarity to the first one, has taken
on the task of mitigating the misfortunes of the wrongly accused, and
other not less interesting works." As one sees, the *Corrispondenza universale* thus intended to insert itself into the Europe-wide movement of
Freemasons and Illuminati. The first number of the new periodical was
to come out in London in January 1783, and to ensure its greatest possible diffusion it would be written "in French, Italian, and English."
"The first and second issues in Italian will appear in April next." Subscriptions could be paid to "M. de Lunel, in Ruga due pozzi S. Sofia in
Venice, or to the Typographic Society in Neuchâtel." Vincenzo Formaleoni, who became a noted publicist in the following years, was associated with the project of the *Corrispondenza universale* in some way. The
periodical intended to be, as one reads in the "Avvertimento" of the first
issue, "a picture of the present century, which will also serve as history
for the future. When it was barely published beyond the Alps it had the
most rapid and happy success, and this example has encouraged us to
present it decently clothed in our language, to make of it a gift perhaps
not unwelcome to all of Italy." The hand of the translator would remain
anonymous, and "the address of the authors and even the place of publication of the work itself would be unknown." "But as long as they remain courageous and enlightened, impartial and exact in their periodi-

---

[1] *Lo spirito dell'Europa letteraria e politica*, 3 March 1785, p. 40, Paris, "Aneddoti."

cal publication, what need is there to know more?" Like its prototype, "written in good French and published beyond the mountains," the *Corrispondenza universale*, "printed in intelligible Italian," would come out twice a month and cost twenty paoli. "At the end of each article will be found the initial letter of a name. This letter, it seems, was not put there by chance. The authors, following the example of the Encyclopedists, have wanted partly to veil themselves. The style, the subject, and above all that letter will serve as a light to the more curious to guess the author. We have proofs and unequivocal light to unmask all, but scrupulously copying the original of a work, we do not want to alter it, especially out of fear of displeasing the authors."[2] This was truly a charade, as one sees, which the following issue did not help to resolve. In the footer of number 2 readers were invited to turn "in Milan to Sig. Giuseppe Galeazzi, in Turin to the brothers Reycends and Sig. Gaetano Balbino, in Florence to Sig. Giuseppe Molini, and in Venice to Sig. Simone Occhi" (that is, to the most important booksellers in Italy).[3] In the gazette of Lugano of 17 March 1783 one read: "A society of men of letters has resolved together, it seems, to strike down all the writers in European journals. Concealing their names and addresses, they have begun, without any warning, to publish the first issues of a periodical that will soon be known throughout Europe with the title *Corrispondenza universale d'ogni genere di letteratura*, and since this lacks information to satisfy every kind of person, it will be augmented with announcements of universal literature, thus corresponding even more closely to the title of the enterprise."[4] That the model and initiative came from the Société typographique and the group around Brissot is also indicated by a French correspondent, Lunel, resident at that time in Venice, who wrote to Neuchâtel complaining of the difficulty he encountered in distributing the periodical. The public was indifferent, he said. "Anything that resembles a romance is in vogue in that country; serious things are not so well received. They are Sybarites and feed themselves only with bonbons."[5] This Lunel can be identified as Sala Delunel, "a Spaniard full of wit and knowledge, who writes as well in Italian as in Spanish," who was considered for a moment, as Brissot tells us in his memoirs, for the pro-

---

[2] *Corrispendenza universale in ogni genere di letteratura. Opera periodica scritta da una società di letterati oltramontani*, vol. 1, for the year 1783, London, A spese dello stampatore, fasc. 1, pp. 3ff., "Avvertimento."

[3] Ibid., no. 2, p. 64, "Avviso."

[4] *Nuove di diverse corti e paesi*, no. 11, 17 March 1783, p. 88, "Avviso."

[5] Neuchâtel, B. publique de la ville, Fonds de la Société typographique, Venice, 24 May 1783, and *Mémoires de Brissot*, vol. 2, p. 43. On the effort, unsuccessful because of the opposition of Charles III, to obtain permission for a Castilian version of the *Courier de l'Europe*, see Guinard, *La presse espagnole*, p. 30.

jected Castilian version of the *Courier de l'Europe*. But where was this *Corrispondenza universale* published? There were in fact two editions. The typeface used and other typographical details of the first make one think of Milan. The second was undoubtedly Tuscan.

The polemics of Brissot raised, from the first pages of this periodical, protests from Italians against any kind of traditional and empty academicism. A "precious and pedantic style" had already sufficiently abused the "patience of reasonable readers." "Now is the time to vindicate justice, truth, and reason so shamefully offended in so many puerile and erroneous collections that are distributed carelessly throughout Europe. Our century is in this way stained, letters are abased, language is distorted and in need of support and correction." An Italian had given the example and had opened the way. Beccaria had written against torture. Monarchs had heard him and abolished this mode of "absolving the robust skeleton and condemning the weak and innocent." Now was the time for a general reform. "It is time to take courage and defend with firm voices the interests of nations before the tribunal of philosophy. The courageous truth never tires of destroying fantasy, superstition, and ignorance. All eyes are now open to see, all tongues are ready to speak, only pens to write are lacking. It is up to them to accomplish little by little a total demolition of the old temple consecrated to prejudice and error. The way is already open, although choked with briars." It was thus promised to address monarchs "with firm and secure tones," while keeping "always at heart their own interests as well as those of the people." "Let us seek," they concluded, "to unmask cabals and intrigues, to improve customs, to occupy ourselves, in short, with seeking public happiness. Finally, when we cannot succeed, we will be content with dedicating our hopes."[6]

We have already seen how the American Revolution raised a deep echo among the editors of this journal.[7] "The revolution occurring in Germany in the regular orders," that is, the religious reforms of Joseph II, steadily attracted the attention of the editor who signed himself with the letter *R*.[8] Another *L* (Lunel?), in his "Quadro della guerra attuale che si vuol finire," proclaimed his right to judge current developments from "the high tribunal that reason has erected on the most solid foundations." "Public opinion, which becomes more and more enlightened, and which nothing stops or intimidates, has its eyes opened to nations

---

[6] *Corrispendenza universale*, no. 1, pp. 5ff.

[7] See chapter 1, above.

[8] *Corrispondenza universale*, no. 1, pp. 13ff. On tolerance, of interest is the unsigned article in no. 19, "Supplizio," pp. 478ff. and the one, also unsigned, in no. 23, "Dalla tolleranza secondo Salviano e S. Agostino," p. 551.

and courts. It penetrates the cabinets where politics is enclosed. There
it judges the holders of power, their passions and their weakness, and
with the empire of its genius it rises everywhere, above ministers of
lesser monarchs, to correct and contain them. Unhappy those who disdain and despise it! . . . Unhappy those who do not have the strength to
support its gaze! These pass judgment on themselves and take up a burden too heavy for their weak hands. They will thus cease compromising
both themselves and the state."[9] In short, public opinion, when confronted with the results of the long war, now asked, and even required,
the dismissal of the entire European ruling class. Deep were the contrasts among the same allies in a conflict that "from one angle was in
many respects no more than the work of a king and ministers, but from
another was a truly national war involving the greatest interests of England."[10] Dark was the horizon on all sides with the likelihood of new
civil and general wars. Contributor "M" also returned to the value of
public opinion: "In the space of thirty years alone there has been an
important and a sudden revolution in our ideas. Public opinion in Europe is now a preponderant force, which cannot be resisted."[11] Ancient
great problems, like that of one's fatherland, emerged changed by the
great international conflict that was concluding.[12] Along with peace returned, even in the *Corrispondenza universale*, local questions, and individual technical and economic reforms. But the lessons of past years had
not been in vain. Age-old questions were being confronted with new
vigor. In some "Riflessioni sulla spopolazione e sterilità delle campagne
di Roma" the property of "princes, monasteries, and mortmain," which
monopolized whole regions, was attacked. "No private citizen possesses
even a handful of land."[13] This situation had to be reversed. "Estates
from now on will be required to have true proprietors, pass freely from
father to son, be alienable, and we will see instantly reborn the old industry of the Romans of cultivating the land." From antiquity came
good examples of "laws against the inequality of fortunes." At that time
"all were citizens because all were proprietors, because property makes
citizens; land is the bond that attaches people to their fatherland." Then
later "to restore peace in Italy the only possible means was to reduce the
pride of feudal lords and impoverish rich masters." Even outside of Europe evils resulted from the sequestration of property. "The continual

---

[9] Ibid., p. 35.

[10] Ibid., no. 2, p. 47.

[11] Ibid., "Apologia della letteratura e dei letterati," p. 63.

[12] Ibid., no. 3, pp. 69ff., "Abbozzi di pensieri sull'Amore di patria in uno stato mon-
archico." Unsigned.

[13] Ibid., no. 9, pp. 220ff.

uprisings that take place in the states of the Ottoman Empire, the Persians, etc., have no other origin than the great inequality that reigns among subjects. When someone appears capable of maintaining a thousand persons for some time, he rises up against the legitimate prince." The case of Latium was therefore no more than a particular example of a general question. "Let us therefore conclude our reflections on the depopulation and sterility of the Roman Campagna in such a way as to make the remedy applicable to all states. Divide ownership of land among citizens in equal or at least not too disproportionate parts."[14]

In the issue from which these words are taken the publication of the fundamental text by Cosimo Amidei, *La chiesa e la repubblica entro i loro limiti*, began.[15] Among miscellaneous articles, economic and social problems were put more and more in the forefront. The contributor signing himself "M" spoke in the name of malcontents and, turning himself to landowners, said: "If the philosopher had to borrow his language from the farmer he would exclaim: 'We are all born equal. We must thus all participate equally in the same joys and misfortunes. If there is to be some useful distinction, it should be given to those who work to support others. . . . A few among the rich, only aware of their own interest, think they make up the whole nation and conclude from their own well-being that we are happy.' " The right of inheritance did not justify this situation in any way. "It was never in the power of the great in past ages to take over a right that all acquire at the moment of their birth, that belongs to them as a patrimony given by nature. . . . Give back to us, illegal possessors, those lands that you usurped and are unable to cultivate. You will see us, more than you know, full of zeal for the nation that we now hate as the theater of our degradation." The internal struggles of Sparta found their root in the existence of Helots. Nor did "farmers in the greater part of Europe" differ from these except in their "apparent liberty." One should proceed at least to divide the "vast terrains in each village, which because held in common remain uncultivated and liable to the usurpations of the powerful."[16] Grave also was the responsibility of the rich for producing the misery of other types of people. "Coral fishers have barely enough to live on. To avoid the greed of our bankers, they are obliged to get money from Venetian merchants and Livornese Jews," who keep their pay low so as to make "abundant profits." Why not "form a society or company among us to provide our fishermen with money at lower interest?" "The fishing industry would be-

---

[14] Ibid., pp. 223ff.
[15] Ibid., pp. 224ff. See Amidei, *Opere*, pp. 151ff.
[16] *Corrispondenza universale*, no. 18, "Invenzione delle arti," pp. 454ff.

come an inexhaustible resource for our nation."[17] In general, the relationship between rich and poor was paradoxical. "It is an axiom of the anatomy of animals that their strength and speed are in inverse proportion: the stronger they are, the slower, and the quicker, the weaker. Similarly, the richer a man is, the less he seems to work, and the poorer he is, the more physical and political attention his work requires. The money that stagnates in the strongboxes of individuals and does not circulate in the hands of the nation, which are its natural channel, is robbed from public utility." Even when nations were rich in the past, one now saw signs of misery. "Since the Venetian nobility no longer engages in the traffic of the sea as it once did, many senatorial families are in extreme poverty. A numerous body of nobles presides over the government of that republic. The people are nothing with regard to government. Opulence once enjoyed makes us experience the needs and aspirations of the rich; the anxiety and desperation of actual misery makes us ready to defend ourselves."[18] From the *Correspondance universelle* of Brissot the Italian editors had not only taken the rigorous egalitarian aims that animated their pages. Strong also was their effort at a cosmopolitan breadth of view, which was reflected above all in a kind of appendix on "New books" attached to each issue, with a discussion of what was published in Germany, France, and England. Condorcet's views on the Montgolfiers were reported.[19] *La scienza del buon governo* by Sonnenfels, in the Milanese edition of 1784, was reviewed most favorably.[20] It was noted that the *Traité des loix politiques des Romains* by Carlantonio Pilati inserted itself into the discussion started by Montesquieu, Condillac, and Mably. "Sig. Pilati has supported his arguments with such authority and such great weight that one must admit he is right."[21] The *History of Scotland* by Robertson, published by Occhi at Venice in 1784, was compared with the version that had appeared earlier in Tuscany. "The Florentines, as good Catholics, having translated this *History* for the book trade, leave out the monuments of the historian's strength, which can be considered the cure used by a confessor, who to remedy the incontinence of a penitent makes him a eunuch. But Abbate Antoniutti gives us a faithful translation, adding notes from time to time where a less perceptive reader could be seduced by the prejudices of the author."[22] The reviews of Italian writers were lively,

[17] Ibid., no. 18, p. 464.
[18] Ibid., pp. 465ff.
[19] "Libri nuovi," special page, following p. 280.
[20] *Corrispondenza universale* (1784), no. 22, p. 297.
[21] Ibid., p. 304.
[22] Ibid., no. 23, pp. 309ff. On Pietro Antoniutti, see del Negro, *Il mito americano*, pp. 159ff.

for example, of a collection of works by Pietro Verri and his *Storia di Milano*: "He has impartially portrayed greatness and depression, obscurity and glory, vice and virtue, as they have presented themselves in the succession of time. One of the greatest merits of this history is that it was written by a philosopher; the political views and praiseworthy sentiments of humanity make its reading of the greatest interest."[23] Distant was now, as one sees, the model Brissot provided. The *Corrispondenza universale* inserted itself more and more into the Italian world, above all into that of Tuscany and Lombardy.

From the provinces of Venice, probably from Treviso, came in 1785 a singular testimony to the interest—partly hidden, but not less felt— that the ideas of Brissot aroused in Italy: a translation of the *Theorie des loix criminelles*.[24] It was dedicated to "S. Eccellenza il N. A. Francesco Pesaro K., procuratore di S. Marco," a patrician of great importance who, in the sixties and seventies, had opened himself to economic problems and collaborated with Andrea Memmo in the effort to abolish the guilds. He then continued in the direction of cautious reforms, hostile to the anticlericism of Andrea Tron but not closed to guidance that came from beyond the Alps. The singular destiny of being the first patrician to administer Venice in 1798 when it passed into the hands of the Empire awaited him.[25] The "Discorso preliminare del traduttore" was in reality a kind of synthesis of the polemic between Beccaria and Brissot: "The foundations on which our penal laws are erected are examined and they are seen to be composed of confused materials heaped together, which are not very concordant because repugnant and contrary." "A prince who reigned in Constantinople, dominated by an imperious woman," had a code compiled "by a miserly and venal man." Montesquieu was the first to unveil such enormities, and Voltaire then followed along the way opened by him. "These two great men of letters animated the genius of the nation to consider that science with a philosophical eye, reveal its errors, and indicate reforms. In France among these was distinguished Linguet, whose works contain excellent considerations on legal reform," as well as Servan, Dupaty, Le Trosne, and many others. "Italy, not less than France, saw friends of humanity raise their voices against legal abuses, cry out against the atrocities of the laws, declaim against the tyranny of judges, and arouse the attention of sov-

---

[23] Ibid. (1783), fasc. 12 and 13, pp. 219ff., 225ff. See also fasc. 15, pp. 243ff., September 1783, a discussion of Gianrinaldo Carli in the *Giornale di Vicenza*.

[24] *Teoria delle leggi criminali di G. P. Brissot de Warville* (Neuchâtel: A spese di Giulio Treno, 1785).

[25] Giovanni Tabacco, *Andrea Tron e la crisi dell'aristocrazia senatoriale a Venezia*, 2d ed. (Trieste: Del Bianco, 1980), pp. 70ff., 180ff.; and Gaetano Cozzi, *Repubblica veneta e stati italiani. Politica e giustizia dal secolo XVII al secolo XVIII* (Turin: Einaudi, 1982), pp. 363ff.

ereigns to reform their codes." "To thee, Oh human Beccaria, my Italy owes that salubrious revolution that so honors its tribunals. Your ardent and luminous work considerably sweetens the barbarous forms of procedure and teaches judges to better respect the rights of man." Other writers followed, whom the editor listed according to the selection, and even the spelling, Brissot had used in his work: Renazzi, Monterosato, Paolo Rizzi, Simoni, Pescatore, D'Arco, to which he added Filangieri, whom the French author had not known or recorded. Brissot was followed even in his predilection for British legislation, where reforms had been less necessary, this being "more in conformity with the principles of the social contract." "Humanity and the civil liberty of the individual being more respected there than elsewhere, the English nation has less need than the Italian and French to devise criminal laws. Bacon, Locke, Cumberland, authors of excellent treatises on universal justice, are held in great veneration among them." Among the most recent works he recorded that of the "celebrated Fielding, *An Inquiry into the Causes of the Late Increase of Robbers*, and two other works, which have the titles *Principles of Penal Law* and *Considerations on Criminal Law*."[26]

"M. de Warville was the first and only one who with this *Theorie des loix criminelles* has undertaken to organize these as a system. He has succeeded perfectly." The translator of the work had been deeply moved. In these pages he had discovered, he said, the inspiration "to exercise, if not with praise at least without blame, the profession to which I was destined." The young lawyer from the provinces had found, it seems, his reason for life in Brissot. He saw in him the heir and continuer of Voltaire. "When this genius was buried in the tomb that was honored by so many literary men, society despaired of finding his true defender, but the guiding star of France last year gave back its adornment to the nation, its support to the sciences, and its friend to society." Brissot was freed from prison; "that tempest had now been overcome." His words found a particularly favorable echo in Italy, the country where "perhaps more than in any other nation of Europe there is interest in a rectification of laws." "We have recent examples in the grand duchy of Tuscany and the kingdom of Naples. Equally intent on the welfare of its citizens, the august republic of Venice by sovereign decree has in the last year required compilation of a reformed code of criminal law and created an honorable commission of senators and jurists for this sublime task." Nu-

---

[26] That is, *Principles of Penal Law*, by William Eden, and the *Considerations on Criminal Law*, by Henry Dagge, which Brissot cited in the *Discours préliminaire* of his *Bibliotèque philosophique*, vol. 1, p. xv. On these writers see Leon Radzinowicz, *A History of the English Criminal Law and Its Administration from 1750* (London: Stevens, 1948), vol. 1, *The Movement of Reform*, in the index.

merous indications, throughout the world, augured general reform. "The great Catherine and the king of Sweden have already shown the road to be taken. Pennsylvania provides a perfect model. Everything announces a happy change in Europe."[27]

The provincial reflection and optimism were in difficult contrast with the climate of Paris in the summer of 1785, when Brissot was released from the Bastille. The strangest rumors circulated in that world of clubs, lodges, and lyceums that had been proliferating in recent times, distorted and disquieting reflections that the gazettes did not know how to assess. "A gallant rumor is now the object of conversation at all gatherings," one reads in a Florentine sheet. "This is the discovery of a society of wealthy and distinguished persons, about twenty men and women, who have rented the castle of Ermenonville, where the famous Jean Jacques Rousseau died, and have founded in the same an assembly with the title *Illuminati*. They live in a grand manner with a party of hunters under the specious pretext of occupying themselves with research in physics and the study of chemistry and alchemy. This society has been discovered, however, to follow nothing other than the system of the Albigensians, Templars, and Adamites; in fact, when the government was informed, it had their 'eternal father' arrested, who is said to be a certain Chevalier Duplaine, a Portuguese, and he was taken to the Bastille. Still, this whole affair is so obscure and delicate that it is talked about with much caution."[1] We are far, as one can see, from the drama of the Bavarian Illuminati, from that unfortunate but important effort to create a semiautonomous political instrument to guide and force the hand of reforming princes. In France, among memories of Rousseau, worldly refinements, and medieval memories, everything seemed to end in smoke. A little later the personage whose name is still the symbol of such refined deceptions appeared. "The celebrated doctor Count Cagliostro," one reads in the same gazette in the middle of August, "is the object that fixes the attention of the government and conversation. The first occupies itself continually in guessing how a person who does not seem to have any known fortune, and takes nothing for his cures, might have a house furnished as if he enjoyed 80 thousand livres of revenue; the gossips laugh continually at this imaginary count who resembles the subject of a Chinese novel."[2] At the end of the year the gazette of Lu-

[27] *Teoria delle leggi criminali*, "Discorso preliminare del traduttore," pp. ixff.

[1] *Notizie del mondo*, no. 44, 31 May 1785, p. 345 (Paris, 17 May).

[2] Ibid., no. 65, 13 August 1785, p. 514 (Paris, 25 July).

gano called him a "vile alchemist, initiated in all the slight of hand of
Egyptian and charlatan magic."[3] A year later, now far from Paris, he
said he would return there "when the Bastille had become a public walk-
way."[4] What the club of the Adelphi had called a "sad politics" meanwhile gained the upper hand. There was the affair of the diamond
necklace, while economic and political problems became more and more
encumbering. The crisis of the Enlightenment became one with the crisis of France.

Conte Honoré de Mirabeau was the energetic voice of both one and
the other. We have seen him as the champion of equality against the
Cincinnati of the American Revolution and as a vigorous defender of
British liberty. We will see him in contact with Genevan exiles and a
violent partisan of Dutch patriots, and then involved in the most intricate affairs of the European old regime, from Spain to Prussia. His echo
in Italy was less clear and defined than that of Brissot, and it was mixed
with the rising cries that came from beyond the Alps in the eighties.
Only with the beginning of the French Revolution did his figure rise up
against the horizon with all its massive presence. There we will find him
again.

Thirty years earlier, Diderot had given out the password that dominated the second half of the eighteenth century. "Let us hasten to make
philosophy popular," he had written in his *Pensées sur l'interprétation de la
nature*. These were suggestive words that everyone had interpreted in
their own way. Already in the year that the book of Diderot appeared,
in 1754, the German philosopher J. A. Ernesti took from it that *Popu-
larphilosophie* that dominated so much of the German *Aufklärung*: to
make philosophy popular it was necessary to simplify it, vulgarize it, diffuse it. Morality would be the guide, Socrates the symbol, to whom for
no one *"in philosophia fuit popularius"* (was [this] popular in philosophy),
as the same Ernesti said.[1] In England, France, and America politics, "sad
politics," emerged in all its varied forms, beautiful and ugly, exalting
and depressing. Making philosophy popular had meant taking the de-

---

[3] *Nuove di diverse corti e paesi*, no. 50, 12 December 1785, p. 296 (Paris, 2 December).

[4] *Notizie del mondo*, no. 69, 29 August 1786 (Paris, 25 August).

[1] Johannes August Ernesti, *De philosophia populari prolusio* (Leipzig, 1754), p. iii. See
Benno Böhm, *Socrates im achtzehnten Jahrhundert: Studien zum werdegange des modernen Per-
sonalichkeit Bewusstsein* (Neumünster: Karl Wachholtz Verlag, 1966; reprint from 1928), p.
119 n. 1; and Roland Mortier, "Diderot, Ernesti et la 'philosophie populaire,'" in *Essays on
Diderot and the Enlightenment in Honor of Otis Fellows*, ed. John Pappas (Geneva: Droz, 1974),
pp. 207 ff., where the text of Ernesti is republished, translated, and commented on.

sire for liberty, equality, protest, and independence to the people and among the people. Diderot's sense of urgency, his appeal to haste in making philosophy live, resounded through reforms and revolutions, and through the two waves of European crises between the sixties and the eighties. At the time of his death the Americans, English, Poles, Genevans, Dutch, and soon other peoples were responding, each in their own way, to the question of what it meant to make philosophy popular, and they were collecting the first fruits, acid, tasty, or already spoiled, of the Enlightenment's penetration into the political and social reality of the European world.